NmL/sc

BIRDS
BRITANNICA

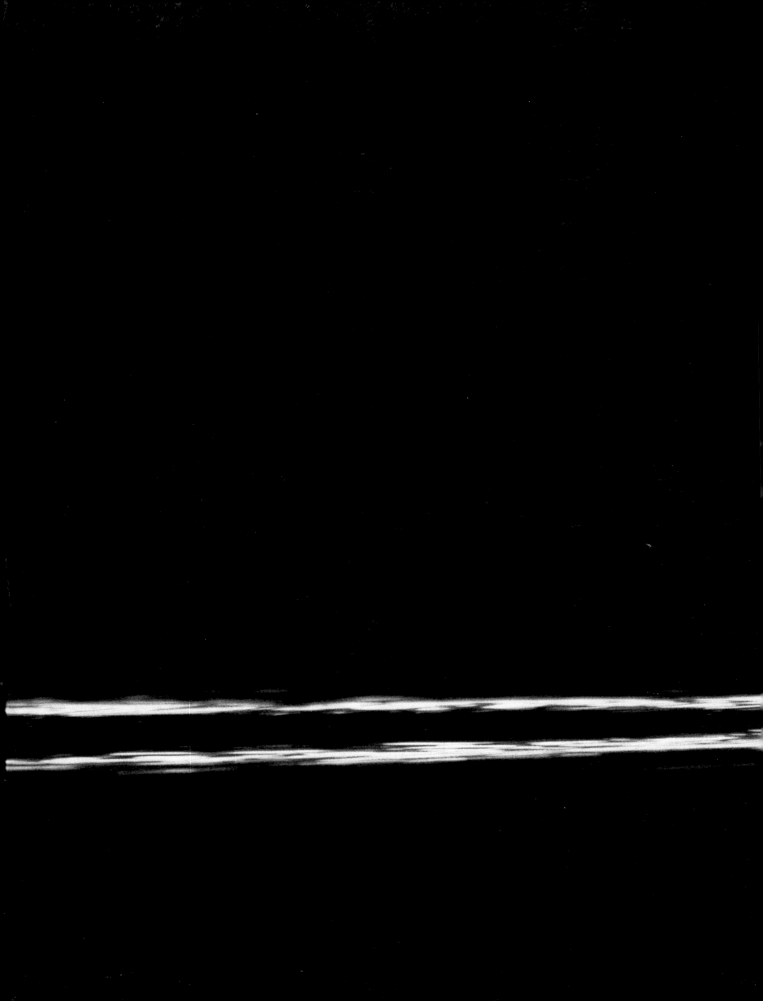

BIRDS
BRITANNICA

MARK COCKER

AND

RICHARD MABEY

With photographs and picture research by Chris Gomersall
and specialist text research by Jonathan Elphick

Chatto & Windus
LONDON

Published by Chatto & Windus 2005

2 4 6 8 10 9 7 5 3 1

Copyright © Mark Cocker 2005

Mark Cocker has asserted his right under the
Copyright, Designs and Patents Act 1988
to be identified as the author of this work

First published in Great Britain in 2005 by
Chatto & Windus
Random House, 20 Vauxhall Bridge Road,
London SW1V 2SA

Random House Australia (Pty) Limited
20 Alfred Street, Milsons Point, Sydney,
New South Wales 2061, Australia

Random House New Zealand Limited
18 Poland Road, Glenfield,
Auckland 10, New Zealand

Random House (Pty) Limited
Endulini, 5A Jubilee Road, Parktown 2193,
South Africa

The Random House Group Limited Reg.
No. 954009
www.randomhouse.co.uk

A CIP catalogue record for this book is
available from the British Library

ISBN 0 701 16907 9

Papers used by Random House are natural,
recyclable products made from wood grown
in sustainable forests. The manufacturing
processes conform to the environmental
regulations of the country of origin.

Typeset by SX DTP, Essex
Printed and bound in China by
C & C Offset Printing Co., Ltd

Design: Peter Ward

For
Derek Goodwin and Ian Wallace

and to the memory of

David Bannerman
James Fisher
Desmond Nethersole-Thompson
Max Nicholson

All among the household gods
of British ornithology

CONTENTS

INTRODUCTION

Birds Britannica is a companion volume to *Flora Britannica* (1996) and, although the two books stand independently, Richard Mabey developed the idea for this one from his work on the previous project. Sadly a period of poor health, which Richard himself has explored in his own book, *Nature Cure* (2005), prevented him from playing a major role in *Birds Britannica* for several years.

While it might not be usual for a writer to acknowledge a debt to a co-author, I wish to mark my enormous sense of gratitude to Richard Mabey, who could not have been more generous or gracious in allowing me to assume responsibility for a book which, in many ways, perfectly encapsulated my main interests as an author. The opportunity to write *Birds Britannica* has been a great privilege.

However the book has never become mine alone, partly because it is a compilation of public responses to birds, of which I was merely editor. Richard also read the text on its completion and suggested a number of refinements, while perhaps an even greater contribution was his authorship of *Flora Britannica,* which has been a daunting model for this second volume, supplying both inspiration and example.

Like its predecessor, *Birds Britannica* is not an identification guide, nor is it a behavioural study, although both these subjects enter its field. Rather it is an attempt to describe the points of intersection between the lives of the humans and the birds inhabiting these same small islands. It is about our shared ecological history, for better and for worse. The very presence, in Britain and Ireland, of rooks, lapwings and skylarks, for example, is directly attributable to our own activities: without agriculture such birds of open country would not be here at all. The lapwing tumbling and wheeling in its unforgettable sky-dance while the farmer ploughs the fields below is a perfect expression of that link.

And *Birds Britannica* is about many other ways in which we interact with birds. An observer standing at the edge of the same ploughed fields, simply enjoying the lapwing as it performs its joyous display, has a relationship as significant as the man in the tractor. Without these indefinable feelings of fellowship, mankind might not feel anxious about whether certain birds survive or not. There would be no conservation measures, when lapwing populations, as now, fall in the face of agricultural change.

Birds touch us in many different ways: as beautiful subjects for study or contemplation; as simple companions; as inspiration for art, literature or music; as markers in the seasonal round, key inhabitants in our sense of place; as symbols of joy or love; perhaps also as objects of frustration and sometimes of bitter controversy. Species like magpie, carrion crow and cormorant arouse enmity and admiration in almost equal measure. Others such as mute swan, common swift and nightingale are frequently invoked to convey some of our most cherished ideas about beauty, freedom and even life itself.

In compiling *Birds Britannica* I have been, in many ways, as interested in what is *untrue* about birds as I have in that which is firmly known. Although the book is not an attempt to restate the enormous body of bird folklore, which was mainly assembled at the start of the twentieth century and was archaic even then, I have included myths and stories about birds especially where they retain

Detail from the Holkham Bible of the early fourteenth century. The bird on the right is clearly identifiable as a goldfinch, but the 'pelican' in the centre looks more like a hawk.

modern resonances. With some species humans have enjoyed a far deeper and longer intimacy, occasionally stretching back hundreds – if not thousands – of years, and where those historical relations illuminate the present or contrast sharply with modern times, I have attempted to capture the evolving pattern.

One way in which birds used to enter our lives more fully was as a source of food. Although today we might all be aware of grouse- and pheasant-shooting or the wildfowler's more varied bag, how many of us any longer think of black-tailed godwit, ruff or dotterel as table delicacies? While we might assume that the eating of these lesser-known roasts was a product of rustic poverty and consigned to a distant past, it is closer, sometimes uncomfortably so, than we may imagine.

Following the model established by *Flora Britannica*, we invited members of the public to send in their stories of birds and bird lore. One of the great values of this has been to give *Birds Britannica* access to aspects of our social life that might be neglected by more formal literature. People have offered remarkable and intriguing stories of sparrow or blackbird pie and moorhen stew, which were eaten well within living memory. Although we may not now have the stomach for some of these dishes, we should not flinch from recording them. In many respects our grandparents, and certainly their grandparents, exploited the multifarious natural resources of these islands in much the same way that the Yanomami people utilise the products of the South American rainforest. We extol one as a model of sustainability and harmonious balance with nature. We should not condemn the other as a form of barbarism simply because it lacks a distant exotic setting.

While this kind of exploitation is now at the margins of our relationship with birds, the sense of engagement with them has not diminished at all. If anything it has increased. The Royal Society for the Protection of Birds has over one million members, making it the largest wildlife non-governmental organisation in Europe. More than any other type of animal, birds seem to have a capacity to inspire our admiration and affection.

Often they play the role of ambassadors in our wider relationship to the world of nature. They move freely across boundaries between the domestic and the wild, between our sense of what is familiar and what is unknown. To watch a fulmar gliding effortlessly through the dark inhuman space of an Atlantic storm is, as Peter Matthiessen observes, 'to risk unnameable intuitions of mortal solitude and transience, one's own swift passage toward the void'. To listen to tawny-owl song on a cold, clear January night captures both the beauty and mystery of that one habitat still forbidden to a day-loving primate like ourselves – the darkness.

Repeatedly public contributions sent to us expressed how birds enrich people's lives on a daily basis. The same deep urge to celebrate was a core reason for initiating *Birds Britannica* eight years ago, and it is also now at the very heart of the completed book.

The British Ornithologists' Union official checklist of British birds (third edition, 2000) lists 575 species. We considered all of them for inclusion in *Birds Britannica*, and covered more than 350 of them in the main text. The remaining species, which are not treated, are listed in Appendix 1. Most of them are extremely rare and all were deemed to have very little or no cultural profile.

The English and scientific nomenclature and the order of species in *Birds Britannica* follow the British Ornithologists' Union checklist with a minimum of exceptions.

Hundreds of contributions were sent in by members of the public. A full list of contributors is given in the Acknowledgements. Many of the submissions were handwritten. Every effort has been made to transcribe both the authors' names and the contents accurately, but I apologise if there are any errors or omissions. These can be corrected in any future editions.

Vernacular names of birds (indicated by VN) are given at the beginning of each species account and are spelt as we received them. I have listed only those vernacular names for which there is strong evidence for their continued use and existence, usually in the form of contributions from the public. I have also attempted to indicate the geographical range of popular names, and the full variation of spellings.

The Notes list all the sources of information for *Birds Britannica* and are arranged under the same family headings as the Contents list for text. All of the first-hand contributions used in *Birds Britannica* are identified in these notes by the name of their author, his or her town or village and county. In a very small number of cases, where no other details are available, I have listed an item simply with the author's name and noted it as an email contribution.

Book references are listed in the Notes in two ways. For the most important literary sources I have cited only author, title and page number, with the full bibliographic details listed in the Select Bibliography. When a book was used for one or two details only, then the full reference appears solely in the Notes. About a dozen books and two journal series were used extensively and are listed in abbreviated form. The abbreviations are explained in the opening paragraphs of the Notes.

Mark Cocker,
Claxton, Norfolk,
2005

BIRDS
BRITANNICA

'Loon', a word referring to its eerie, moaning calls, is an old name for the red-throated diver and is still used in Orkney.

Diver family *Gaviidae*

Four species of diver occur in Britain and Ireland, but one of them, the **Yellow-** or **White-billed Diver**, *Gavia adamsii*, is a vagrant (from Arctic Canada, Russia and northernmost Scandinavia) which has appeared in these islands on fewer than 200 occasions, with 90 per cent of records occurring since 1958.

Red-throated Diver *Gavia stellata*. VN: Loon, Rain Goose (Orkney and Shetland). This is the commonest species of diver in Britain, and a widespread winter visitor to almost the entire British coastline. Occasionally there are huge concentrations on the east coast. In the Moray Firth in October 1982 there was a build-up of 1500 birds, while the winter of 1999/2000 saw a remarkable gathering of about 2000 birds off Suffolk, one of the largest ever recorded in north-western Europe. This assembly was thought to be triggered by concentrations of sprats in the southern North Sea, and it is interesting to note that old East Anglian and East Lothian names for divers are respectively 'sprat borer' and 'spratoon'.

As a breeding species the red-throat is more restricted in range, with a 1994 population estimate of just 934 pairs.[1] More than half of these are in Shetland, a further 10 per cent breeds in Orkney, while in Scotland itself red-throats nest mainly north and west of a line between Glasgow and Moray.

The larger, more beautiful and even rarer **Black-throated Diver**, *Gavia arctica*, shares a similar mainland distribution, but is an inhabitant of large freshwater and sea lochs. It is absent from Shetland and Orkney, its own strongholds being in the Outer Hebrides and the coastal areas of Wester Ross between Lochs Gairloch and Broom. Both red- and black-throats have achieved a steady reclamation of their old Scottish breeding haunts after heavy persecution in the nineteenth and early twentieth centuries by an alliance of egg collectors, taxidermists and fishermen. The recent confiscation of 27 clutches of black-throated diver eggs – part of 21 illegal egg collections – suggests that at least one of these factors plays some role in keeping the British total at just 150 summering pairs.[2]

Despite their scarcity and limited distribution, divers have had a strong impact, mainly on account of their voices. During spring and summer, males and females of both red- and black-throated species produce a wide range of calls, including a magically atmospheric and eerily beautiful yodelling sound that has some similarities to the human voice, as well as evoking a wide range of other animals: 'Wailing-call . . . accompanied by strong harmonics that impart characteristic tonal quality, rather resembling meowing of cat'[3]; 'a most mournful and eerie, long-drawn, mewing wail or shriek, like cry of a person in extreme pain'[4] (red-throated diver). 'A more drawn-out note which may acquire the rhythm of a hen's cackling . . . a hoarse "kowk" compared to croak of

Black-throated divers nest by the remote lochs of north-westernmost Scotland.

Raven . . . a remarkable and far-carrying goose-like clamour . . . the loud and wild cries of assemblies in May, sounding in distance like noise of a crowd of people shouting and laughing'[5] (black-throated diver).

Ironically, the diver species whose calls are probably most familiar to a British audience is seldom heard in the wild in this country. In the last half-century there has been just one confirmed breeding record of the **Great Northern Diver**, *Gavia immer* (VN: Immer/Ember Goose; Orkney and Shetland), in northern Scotland in 1997. Otherwise it is a winter visitor to British and Irish coastlines from Iceland and elsewhere in the north-western Atlantic. Yet it is a widespread resident in North America, and its repertoire includes the most striking and far-carrying cries: 'Often strident or screaming, gives impression of uncontrolled idiotic laughter.'[6]

It is these resonant calls that have become a standard background sound-effect in numerous films and television dramas where the creators wish to evoke an atmosphere of mystery, suspense and northern wilderness, although often the recordings are used without any regard for their true seasonality or the bird's genuine distribution. The call has also been commemorated in popular song, such as, 'Old Devil Moon' ('Wanna cry, wanna croon/Wanna laugh like a loon'), a jazz standard performed by artists such as Frank Sinatra and Ella Fitzgerald.

'Loon' is the family name used in North America and draws on the divers' powerful vocalisations. It is a corruption of the old Norse *lómr*, meaning 'moaning bird'. While in Britain 'diver' eventually assumed primacy in ornithological nomenclature, 'loon' survives as the vernacular alternative for the red-throated diver in Orkney and Shetland. The name is also enshrined in a place name on several of the islands: ' "*Looma Chun*" can be found on Rousay, on Hoy and in both the West and East Mainland, and means "lochan of the divers"; all of the sites still have breeding divers today.' On Shetland 'Loomi Shun' (Divers' Tarn) is quite widespread.[7]

The two other Scottish names still in currency are 'immer goose' (great northern diver) and 'rain goose' (red-throated diver).[8] The first of these comes from Norn, the old lost Orcadian language, and finds its echo in the bird's scientific name (*Gavia immer*) and in the current Icelandic name for the bird, *him-brimi*, meaning literally 'the surf roarer'.

The folklore scholar Edward Armstrong argued that the second of the Scottish names, rain goose, is the final British vestige of a large body of diver mythology that once 'extended around the crown of the world'. For widely dispersed communities such as the Buriats in Siberia and Native American tribes like the Delaware, the diver was a revered creature, a key player in their creation stories and a winged helper in the shaman's journey to the spirit world. The rain goose's power to foretell the coming of storms was part of its ancient status as a bird of omen – a belief that was just on the edge of its range in northernmost Britain.[9]

Divers were certainly familiar to the region's neolithic inhabitants and their remains have been found at Pictish middens just to the south of Kirkwall in Orkney. As well as featuring in the Scottish diet until at least the eighteenth century, the birds were used as a form of medicine. The Scottish traveller and author, Martin Martin, records that in the Hebrides the great northern diver was valued because 'there is about an inch deep of fat upon the skin of it, which the natives apply to the hip bone, and by experience find it a successful remedy for removing sciatica'.[10]

To the Hebrideans it was known by the beautiful Gaelic construction, *Bun a' Bhuachaille*, 'herdsman of the tide races', which reflects perfectly all the British divers' consummate adaptation to an aquatic lifestyle. The bill is long and dagger-like, the head and long neck are smoothly arched, while the body lies low in the water so that in profile divers can assume an almost reptilian sinuosity. They are at home in the roughest of sea swells and are famous for the depth and duration of their dives. One great northern was recorded as having remained submerged for three minutes,[11] but the claim of a bird caught in a net set at a depth of 180 feet (54m) is unsubstantiated,[12] while a dive supposedly lasting 15 minutes sounds like pure fantasy.[13]

Grebe family *Podicipedidae*

Pied-billed Grebe, *Podilymbus podiceps*, is by far the rarest of the six species of grebes occurring in Britain: a straggler from North and South America that has been recorded in the country about 30 times. It is a small brown compact species, similar in size to the little grebe but with a deep and, in summer, black-banded bill. Some of the transatlantic crossings of pied-billed grebes may have been partly or wholly ship-assisted. Certainly the second individual ever to reach these shores, in July 1965, came aboard a Shell tanker, *Ondina*, two or three days out of Venezuela and survived until Liverpool, where it was taken into captivity and subsequently died.[1] Yet the bird can adapt well to a European setting. The first ever to be seen – the first, in fact, for the whole of the Western Palearctic – may well have survived in Somerset from 1963 until 1968.[2]

Little Grebe, *Tachybaptus ruficollis*. VN: Dabchick (widespread). Eric Ennion, the bird artist, wrote that 'Grebes are like Queen Anne furniture, splendid in front but not so fine behind. Nature spent her ingenuity on their ruffs and tippits – she had none left to provide them with proper tails.'[3] The little grebe has lost out on both counts. It has no ruff or crests and no grebe is more without a tail than this species, which can look almost ball-like in shape.

Yet it is engagingly diminutive and characterful, with

The little grebe is a bird of confined watery habitats – ponds, open drains and even dykes – as well as large lakes and reservoirs.

a lovely chestnut and dark-brown breeding plumage and a remarkably loud trilling call that is one of the classic sounds of the British riverbank in summer. The quality that has captured our attention most is its uncanny gift for sub-aquatic escapology. At the least disturbance these nervous birds make an instant, ripple-less exit and once they vanish underwater little grebes invariably head for the nearest vegetation, where they remain invisible with only their bills above the surface.

Many of the old regional names – 'divedapper', 'divedop', 'doucker' and 'divy duck', to list just a few – celebrate the bird's sudden, noiseless plop beneath the surface. For some observers the instantaneous character of its disappearance had an almost sinister quality. One archaic Scottish name, 'mother o' the mawkins' (mawkin: a female demon), hinted at supernatural powers. All the names have now disappeared from the vernacular leaving just the single survivor, 'dabchick', as an alternative to the far less suggestive but officially favoured 'little grebe'.

The commonest of our grebes is a widespread and apparently increasing resident on most forms of British wetland habitat, including large lakes, coastal estuaries, small ponds and slow-moving rivers. Like all grebes, it has disproportionately large lobed feet and the legs are set right back on the body to aid propulsion through the water. This particular adaptation gives it an awkward front-heavy posture on its rare visits to dry land and accounts, incidentally, for the extraordinary names 'foot in arse' and 'little footy arse', which are on, or only just below, the horizon of memory in Lancashire and Orkney respectively.[4] Exactly the same idea is enshrined in the grebes' family name, *Podicipedidae*, a conjunction of the Latin *podex* (rump) and *pes* (foot), which was once more pithily rendered as 'arsefoot'.

While their occasional weak flutters across the surface of the water give an impression of poor flight, little grebes are capable of longer journeys. Ringing recoveries suggests that they routinely cross the North Sea, and in 1986 one was found exhausted on a gas platform 55 miles (91km) north-east of Great Yarmouth, Norfolk, from where it made the short journey to dry land by helicopter.[5] Most of these flights are nocturnal and the birds are routinely attracted to offshore light-vessels and lighthouses: 'During a night-time mist-net session at [Bardsey] lighthouse . . . a bird fell to the ground nearby. Because it was so dark I had no idea what it was. It squirmed and wriggled like an animal and its legs seemed to be in the wrong place. Not until the torch arrived could we see what it was.'[6]

Although many of these disoriented individuals are fatally injured in such collisions, not all are so unfortunate. One bird, downed by a torrential rainstorm, was discovered in the middle of a Devonshire road 'one wild February evening in the late 1960s':

> I returned home to wife and family who were somewhere between homework and bed having largely demolished a plate of whitebait for supper. Children hopefully proffered remaining scraps of raw fish to the refugee, by now established in a box by the Rayburn. Total rejection. No response. On reflection, we filled the sink with water. Common sense was prevailing. When introduced, our visitor plunged to the bottom, swam round and re-emerged, bobbed enthusiastically beneath the running tap only to dive again to retrieve fragments of fish tossed into the water.
>
> Not content, after a few minutes our now-hero finally surfaced and marched, no swaggered, up the draining-board to clear all vestiges of my intended supper still on the worktop. At last satisfied, then came a triumphant return to the sink, much joyful water-play beneath the running tap to our general delight and, finally, several submerged laps of victory. Much later the weather had subsided, near midnight I walked across a field in pallid moonlight to slip our small guest, refugee no longer, into the reeds at the edge of the lake. It would not be too long before dawn.[7]

Great Crested Grebe, *Podiceps cristatus*. VN: Great Crest (widespread); Great Cressy (Yorkshire). It is undoubtedly the most familiar and popular member of the family. To birdwatchers it is often known as the 'great crest', while to many (like fishing and boating enthusiasts) who have no special bird interest but are familiar with its aquatic habitat, it is often simply called 'the grebe', as if it were the only member of the family.

This is not solely on account of numerical abundance, although it is the second-commonest of the four resident species, with a population of more than 12,000 breeding adults. Two major factors in its popularity are the striking summer plumage, most notably the corolla of elongated black and chestnut plumes on the head and neck of both sexes, and the elaborate rituals that great crests perform each breeding season. The grebes' dance, when a pair faces each other through a lengthy sequence of neck-swaying, head-shaking or bill-touching actions – all performed in elegant symmetry and often mirrored in the surface of the water – is one of the most affecting and beautiful scenes in British nature.

The display mainly consists of four highly ritualised ceremonies, the most dramatic of which is the ghostly penguin display, when a bird dives and then rises slowly from the water with neck stretched, head bowed forward towards its partner and its underbody exposed like a

Milliners once used great crested grebe head plumes and the dense body plumage, known as 'grebe fur', in the adornment of hats and as trim for other garments.

slender silvery-white vessel. Equally famous is the weed ceremony, a classic pas-de-deux when two birds rise up off the surface and tread water, with necks craned, breasts pressed together and their beaks draped with weed.

Sir Julian Huxley was the first to recognise the significance of these displays in 1912, when he spent several weeks watching grebes on the Tring reservoirs in Hertfordshire. His pioneering insights into how the mutual displays established the emotional synchrony necessary for successful mating and were highly ritualised forms of more functional behaviour (in the case of the weed ceremony, Huxley argued that it had evolved from actions relating to nest-building) were described in a ground-breaking paper read to the Zoological Society of London in April 1914. Huxley's work was seminal in the establishment of ethology – the study of comparative behaviour – as an important branch of biological science.

While their displays now give a sense of occasion to grebe sightings, for many years any kind of contact with the bird was touched by an aura of specialness. That response was a lingering echo from the time when it had been one of Britain's rarest breeding species. In the second half of the nineteenth century it was persecuted to the brink of extinction. The grisly character of the slaughter, and then the grebe's stirring recovery at the end of the century, form an extraordinary story in their own

The elaborate breeding 'dance' performed by great crested grebes is one of the most beautiful scenes in British nature.

right, but they are also a chapter in the wider narrative of nature conservation in Britain.

Until the Victorian era the bird was widespread if less common than it is today. The flesh was considered poor eating, but the eggs were prized both as food and for sale to collectors. In areas like Norfolk grebe nests were routinely robbed. Richard Lubbock noted in 1845 that: 'The eggs are always taken when found; I have known thirty or forty collected from one broad.' At Hickling in 1863 one dealer received six dozen eggs for barter and in the spring of 1867 a Great Yarmouth dealer sent seven dozen eggs of little and great crested grebes to London for sale to collectors.[8]

The main reason for the massive slump in numbers was the popular use of grebe feathers in women's fashion accessories. The summer plumes on the head and neck were considered an ideal source of ostentatious adornment. Just as important was the fine, soft, but extremely dense feathering on the bird's body known as 'grebe fur'. To the living creature it is important for its insulatory and waterproofing properties; for the fashion-oriented costumier it became a perfect fabric for hats, muffs, boas, shoulder capes and other trimmings.

Until the mid-nineteenth century the British market had been supplied from southern continental Europe. In 1768 Thomas Pennant reported that a single grebe skin taken from Lake Geneva could fetch as much as fourteen shillings.[9] All this changed with a chance letter from one Richard Strangwayes to *The Zoologist* journal in 1851.[10] In the correspondence he commented on the ease with which he had obtained 29 grebes in Norfolk and noted that the bird's breast feathers were a 'fashionable and beautiful substitute for furs'. Strangwayes' letter is credited with encouraging a switch from the European

source to a harvest of native stock and by 1860 a rough count indicated just 42 pairs in the whole of Britain.

Fortunately the decline coincided with the passing of five successive laws, between 1870 and 1880, to safeguard waterbird populations from hunting, and the grebe's dramatic collapse was prominent in the authors' minds as they framed the legislation. The last of the measures, the Wild Birds' Protection Act, imposed a close season from March to July that aided recovery, but also pushed the price of grebe fur up to £1 for a single skin. Determined collectors and milliners continued to deal more or less with impunity, and in February 1881 six grebes were openly displayed for sale in Great Yarmouth market. The demand did not completely die out until 1907[11] and even by the date of the first major census of the species in 1931, they were still being shot for taxidermists and because of their presumed damage to fishing interests.

The 1931 census, known as the 'Great Crested Grebe Enquiry', was itself a remarkable event and a measure of the bird's widespread popularity. At that time it was one of the earliest, largest and most successful population studies for a single species ever conducted. It attracted publicity from specialist wildlife publications and national newspapers, with *The Times* running a major feature on the project. The BBC also broadcast a general appeal as a prelude to the news. It received help from 1300 volunteers and included coverage of 1000 British lakes.[12] At its conclusion it revealed a breeding population in England, Scotland and Wales of 1234–1241 pairs.[13]

Apart from protective legislation, there were other social changes during the middle years of the twentieth century that were extremely favourable to the great crest's recovery. The most unlikely benefits came from what are usually considered the classic forms of habitat destruction – road building and house construction. Yet there is a fascinating correlation between these forms of development and the grebe's doubling of its numbers by 1975 (6800 adults).

The rise in car ownership to 7.5 million by 1959, and a virtual trebling of road freight in the 20 years from 1954 were paralleled by an inevitable growth in the road network, most notably the creation of 3000 miles (5000km) of motorway.[14] Coupled with a major increase in house building, this led to massive requirements for building materials. In the second half of the twentieth century it was a rule of thumb that each house, with its associated infrastructure – roads, pavements, and so on – required 100 ton(ne)s of gravel.[15]

The increased excavation at alluvial deposits led to the formation of many new flooded pits, especially across lowland England. Among the chief beneficiaries of all this inadvertent habitat creation was the great crested grebe. The species seems to adapt easily to the gravel pit's deep water and steep-sided banks. It appears tolerant of the fishermen and sailors who take up residence just as readily as the bird. A pair in full breeding regalia is the perfect natural adornment to any new lake, while the presence of its chalky oval eggs in their heaped platform of floating vegetation still serves as a classic measure of how quickly nature reclaims this man-made environment for its own.

Red-necked Grebe, *Podiceps grisigena*. This is the only one of the five European grebes that still does not breed in Britain, although small numbers now summer routinely. Nesting attempts have been made since 1983, especially in southern Scotland, but so far without proven success. The species is better known as a scarce winter visitor mainly on the British east and south coasts and much more rarely on the east coast of Ireland. Occasionally numbers increase as a result of severe weather in northern Europe and such influxes have occurred six times since 1865, with the last in 1979, which involved an estimated 481 birds.[16]

Slavonian Grebe, *Podiceps auritus*. VN: Slav (birders). Despite a recent decline in its fortunes, a tiny population of just 40–70 pairs of this beautiful small grebe has held its own in the Scottish Highlands since it was first proved to breed in 1910. It is better known as a winter visitor to the British coast, when about 400 birds are present, mainly in sheltered coastal waters.

Black-necked Grebe, *Podiceps nigricollis*. Several ornithologists have commented on the seemingly incompatible blend of beauty and peculiarity in the bird's facial appearance. 'The steep forehead and the slender tip-tilt bill gave them an expression which was almost comical – that blend of imp and cherubim met sometimes in a small and freckled boy. But the most amazing feature was the eye, a brilliant ruby-red impossible to capture in a sketch-book. Small wonder the old authors called them "The Firey Eye."'[17]

It is a routine winter visitor to British coastlines in small numbers and a relatively recent colonist as a nesting species. Along with its continued rarity, it is highly unpredictable in its choice of breeding location and can take up residence almost anywhere. In 1971 a pair brought a transient air of distinction to a small pond formed by water pumped from a coal mine. The first ever British breeding record involved five pairs found at a site in Wales in 1904, while the first English nesting birds were discovered at the Tring reservoirs, Hertfordshire in 1918.

However the most remarkable breeding record relates to the discovery of a large breeding colony in central Ireland, in the 1920s. Two brothers, J. Ffolliott Darling and T. S. Darling, first reported the presence of nesting birds and donated a pair in breeding plumage with three downy young to the Dublin Museum in 1918. However both men died without disclosing the exact whereabouts of their discovery and, to make matters more complicated, the site was in a region rich in small secluded loughs. Ffolliott Darling's diary account gave slight clues to its location, but more tantalising was its obvious importance for such a rare species: 'In one patch of sedge, 15 × 20 yds [14 × 18m] I saw nests of 10 B.n Grebe; 4 G.C. Grebe; 5 Little Grebe, and 6 Black-headed Gulls' nests, eh what! They must have been fighting like blazes, lots of nests were spoiled. I found many Black-necked Grebes dead, but none of the others. I took a G.C. Grebe's egg from a B.n Grebe's nest. I sent a series of young and old to Dublin Museum.'[18]

After eight years of detective work, two ornithologists, C. V. Stoney and G. R. Humphreys, finally identified the mystery site as Lough Funshinagh in southern County Roscommon. It turned out to be much more significant than they could have anticipated. 'The astonishingly large size of the colony . . . makes this one of the most important discoveries of recent years.'[19] In 1930 they estimated 250 pairs mainly concentrated in a large reedbed. Sadly, Funshinagh, like many turloughs in central Ireland, was subject to periodic drying out and the Shannon hydro-electric scheme built in 1934 possibly accelerated the process. Thereafter the colony dwindled rapidly and, while a few pairs nested intermittently until the 1950s, they had vanished completely by 1960. At the grand old age of 92, G. R. Humphreys wrote an account of Funshinagh's ornithological heyday 49 years after he had rediscovered the site. Today several small isolated populations of black-necked grebe breed widely across England and Scotland and sustain a fluctuating national total of 40–80 pairs.

The red eyes of a breeding black-necked grebe have an almost supernatural intensity. Small wonder that old naturalists called it the 'Firey Eye'.

Albatross family *Diomedeidae*

Many of the world's albatrosses are entirely confined to the far southern hemisphere and historically they were encountered only by the most long-distance travellers, such as whalers and merchant sailors to distant British colonies.

However, our cultural associations with the albatross have largely been shaped by a Briton who never actually saw the living bird, Samuel Taylor Coleridge. Since the publication of his 'Rime of the Ancient Mariner' in 1798 the albatross has become indelibly fixed in the language as a metaphor for any insupportable burden or source of penance, although in the poem itself Coleridge employed the bird as a symbol of a fundamental life force, against which the mariner transgresses when he raises a crossbow to kill the ship's guardian spirit.

In real life, no ill omen attached to killing albatrosses. Instead, early British sailors, in the absence of fresher fare, routinely caught them with hook and line for the table. Typically, during Captain Cook's second voyage on the *Resolution*, the ship's botanist, Joseph Banks, noted that they ate 'part of the Albatrosses shot on the 3rd [February] which were so good that every body commended and Eat heartily of them tho there was fresh pork upon the table'. Albatrosses were apparently eaten on all three of Cook's voyages.[1]

If sailors felt that there was no strict taboo on killing albatrosses, there was at least a countervailing super-stition among them that some albatrosses, like many other kinds of ocean-going bird, were the reincarnated souls of lost seamen. The British zoologist Leo Harrison Matthews recorded one old sea salt's extraordinary response to a passing albatross:

Hermann watched him gliding alongside the weather leach of the main lower topsail just above the main yard-arm, and looking down over the bulging belly of the course. 'See what he's doing?' he said. 'He's having a look at the blunt-line and clew-line lizards to see they're all clear for running and won't foul if we have to clew up in a hurry for the next squall; they always do that. I wonder how long ago he went overboard.'[2]

Albatross feathers were also collected and then found their way into the millinery trade as the raw material for boas and decoration in women's fashionable headgear. In 1909 F. J. Stubbs even found an albatross 'hanging among the Christmas turkeys … in a game-dealer's shop in Leadenhall Market. When he saw it "the bird appeared quite fresh, and bright red blood was dripping from its beak".'[3] Mariners also made rugs or foot warmers from the plumage, tobacco pouches out of the large webbed feet, and used the bones to make needles and pipes.

A tobacco pipe made from an 'albatross' tibia was part of a long-undetected hoax inflicted by that indefatigable prankster, Colonel Richard Meinertzhagen, on the Linnean Society. It was gifted to the organisation in 1958 as 'Darwin's Pipe' and is exhibited to this day in a collection of society treasures at the foot of the staircase in Burlington House. It was said to have been made from the thigh bone of a waved albatross from the Galapagos. For 40 years none of the society's distinguished scientific membership noted that the length of the bone implied 'an albatross that once stood two metres high (on rather spindly legs!)'. Closer inspection also revealed that 'the silver marks on the stem of the bowl indicate manufacture in Birmingham in 1928'.[4]

Black-browed Albatross, *Diomedea melanophris*. VN: Mollymawk (used mainly by sailors and other naval personnel). It routinely occurs north of the Equator and has now been recorded about 70 times in Britain and Ireland, while many other sightings of unidentified albatrosses probably involve this bird. It is one of a medium-sized group of species sometimes referred to generically as the mollymawks in ornithological literature. Black above and white below, it has a large, pure-white softly domed head, whose benign appearance is contradicted by a dark 'brow' curving up in two crescents, which give it a 'serious almost disapproving, facial expression'.[5]

It has a body length of about about 3 feet (95cm), while its wings can reach almost 8½ feet (2.5m) across, at least one-third longer than our largest resident seabird, the northern gannet. The impressive wingspans of albatrosses explain their capacity for long-distance vagrancy and their status as the ultimate avian symbol of ocean-going grace and freedom.

Most British and Irish records have naturally involved birds passing at sea, with the island of Cape Clear off south-westernmost Ireland claiming more than any other location. Yet there have also been three land records: one exhausted individual picked up near Linton, in Cambridgeshire, in July 1897 and a second at Staveley, Derbyshire, on 21 August 1952. Despite colliding with telegraph wires the bird was uninjured and after being photographed by the *Derbyshire Times*, was sent by train to a release point in Skegness.[6]

By far the most celebrated British albatross was a long-staying singleton eventually known as 'Albert

The DIY sign guiding birders to Albert's usual resting spot on the cliffs at Hermaness.

One of the lighthouse keepers on the Bass Rock stands just a couple of metres from the black-browed albatross during its stay in the summer of 1967.

Ross' or, more simply, as 'Albert', which was recorded intermittently at gannetries in Scotland over three decades. Its discovery on 18 May 1967 on the Bass Rock in the Firth of Forth was an occasion of monumental good fortune. Professor W. H. Thorpe, a student of gannet vocalisations, 'had just photographed a group of nesting Gannets and, on looking up from his camera, was astonished to find a Black-browed Albatross standing only ten yards away. Realising he had taken its photograph with the Gannets, he quickly took another before it flew off and disappeared. When [they] were developed, he was relieved to find that he had not been suffering from hallucinations.'[7]

Once news of the bird was circulated it became an instant celebrity in the Scottish media and during its residence over three successive years on the Bass Rock it drew observers from across Britain. It was caught in its first summer by one of the lighthouse keepers, who dazzled it with a torch one night and picked it up to remove a piece of Courlene (polythene twine) net tangled around one of its feet. Sadly, the opportunity to ring the bird was not taken and there will never be incontrovertible proof that the albatross which later appeared at a gannetry at Hermaness, Unst, in 1972 was this same individual. However there is virtually unanimous agreement that the Bass Rock albatross and 'Albert Ross' were one and the same.

It returned again in 1974 to the Hermaness cliff, at the northernmost extremity in the Shetland archipelago, after which it was seen annually – sometimes appearing as early as February, in some years displaying to nearby gannets and, from 1976 onwards, even constructing a nest. However from July 1987 there followed a prolonged absence until March 1990, when it resumed its spring visits until a final sighting on 7 July 1995:

The bird's rediscovery prompted a second wave of birders to make a pilgrimage to see Albert in his lonely vigil. Forced out of his normal ledge by gannets, he sat in a slightly different and more inaccessible position. Some birders took it upon themselves to construct a sign out of stones and rocks – an arrow on the clifftop with the word 'Albert' beside it to guide subsequent visitors. Even several years after Albert's final appearance, 'is the albatross still here?' was one of the commonest questions asked of the Hermaness warden. This prompted the Scottish Natural Heritage to write an obituary for Albert, which is displayed in the interpretative centre.[8]

While it was christened Albert, the bird's sex was never truly established, although the absence of infertile eggs in 'his' nests suggests that it was male in more than name. Towards the end of its long but isolated existence, it was known that other albatrosses had been seen within a couple of hundred miles of its station at Hermaness, but Albert never discovered a mate. In 1991 there was a wry note in the journal *British Birds*, 'The loneliness of the long-staying albatross continues; the only worse possibility for it would be the sudden appearance of another of the same sex.'[9]

If one accepts that the black-browed albatross seen with gannets in the Westmann Islands, south of Iceland, in 1966, then at the Bass Rock in 1967–9 and later at Hermaness from 1972 to 1995 all referred to the same gannet-fixated individual, then it endured at least 30 years of solitude in the wrong hemisphere. Yet Albert fell short of the record set by the longest-staying albatross, a bird seen at a gannet colony on Myggenaes Holm in Faroe from 1860, until it was shot by a latterday ancient mariner in 1894. It was nicknamed the 'King of the Gannets', although when it was finally killed it was found to be a queen.[10]

It is a striking irony that while Albert is the only albatross many birdwatchers have seen, and was probably the most photographed and watched individual bird ever in these islands, the British as a nation have responsibility for three out of every four black-browed albatrosses on the planet. Some 380,000 pairs breed in the Falklands, most notably at Steeple Jason (157,000 pairs) and Beauchene Islands (103,000 pairs).

The Falkland albatrosses were early beneficiaries of the region's whale and sealing industries and were notable attendants at the flensing and rendering factories for the vast quantities of offal produced. However, the relationship between the bird and regional fisheries has now reversed completely. The Falkland black-browed albatrosses have been severely affected by longlining trawlers operating off South America's southern Atlantic coastline. The albatrosses catch the baited hooks as they are discharged from the boat and are then dragged under and drown. Steeple Jason colony has lost more than 41,000 pairs since 1995, and the overall decline in the Falkland albatross population has been put as high as 30 per cent over the last 20 years.

Fulmar, Petrel and Shearwater family *Procellariidae*

Northern Fulmar, *Fulmarus glacialis*. VN: Mallimack, Mallie (Orkney); Maalie (Shetland). It is essentially an inhabitant of high Arctic circumpolar waters and one of the most ocean-going of all Britain's common breeding birds. The classic sighting is of a distant grey cruciform banking effortlessly through the peaks and troughs of a storm-driven sea. Yet in late spring fulmars can create a less dramatic impression. On still mornings it is not uncommon to encounter a pair planing in leisurely fashion, sometimes at barely more than head height, over the low-lying coasts of southern England as they prospect for new nest sites.

In some ways the second is the more exciting vision, since it represents the vanguard of a remarkable ongoing expansion that has carried the fulmar from a single ancient breeding station on the island of St Kilda to sites along almost the entire British coastline. Only areas around the Humber, Wash, Solent and Bristol Channel have so far resisted the bird's advances.

The history of the fulmar in Britain is virtually inseparable from the man who first set out to chart it, and even among a community as obsessional as ornithologists, James Fisher's devotion to the species seems positively monomaniacal. His monograph, *The Fulmar* (1952), running to 496 pages and based on 15 years' research, is one of the masterpieces of British ornithological writing. The bibliography alone ran to 2378 references and was so long it had to be published separately from the book.

Fisher meticulously recorded the species' nineteenth-century expansion site by site, beginning in Shetland in 1878, on the sheer red sandstone formation known as the Kame of Foula, the second-highest cliffs in Britain. The new colony was apparently occasioned 'by the stranding of a dead whale, which was accompanied by a small flock of these birds, who remained to breed'.[1] Throughout the 1890s fulmars consolidated their Shetland bridgehead, then moved steadily southwards through the British archipelago, arriving to breed in Orkney (Hoy, 1896), the Outer Hebrides (North Rona, 1887), Caithness (Dunnet Head, 1900) and then Sutherland (Strathy Point, 1905).

By 1907 they were in Donegal and by 1930 they were on the Stack Rocks in Pembrokeshire. Six years later they were proved to breed on the slate cliffs at the Calf of

Man, and in June 1944, while British troops were storming the Normandy assault beaches, the fulmar extended its own benign invasion to Cornwall, where the county's first-known egg was found near Padstow.[2] Although coastal counties like Norfolk have few suitable sites for a cliff-nesting bird, fulmars were encouraged to breed on the low boulder-clay 'cliffs' at Weybourne in 1947, after ornithologist and schoolmaster Dick Bagnall-Oakeley drafted Gresham's schoolboys into digging artificial ledges.[3]

The expansion has continued with a general infilling of sites between the various pioneer colonies, although there have also been fresh territorial gains, such as Jersey and Guernsey in the 1960s, and Suffolk and Sussex in the 1970s. More recently fulmars have taken to breeding on inland quarries and crags up to 12 miles (20km) from the sea, often at sites no less inaccessible than the coastal locations:

During the late 1970s I was walking along a path at Prestatyn Mountain, in north Wales, when I was surprised to see a couple of fulmars gliding round a limestone cliff, with steep surrounding slopes. Hoping to discover an unusual inland nesting site, I scrambled up an increasingly steep slope. Soon, I was nearly level with the suspected breeding ledge when I grabbed the branch of a handy stunted shrub, but it came away in my hand and I was soon on my way down heading for a modest but potentially fatal drop over the edge of another small cliff. When I landed in a large gorse bush I could hear the fulmars high above cackling as if in mockery. I found out that they had indeed started nesting at the site, and later colonised one a good deal further inland, at the old limestone quarry in Dyserth, about 4 miles from the coast.[4]

Further adaptations in their nesting behaviour include the substitution of castle ramparts and other high-walled coastal structures for the original sea cliff. Now the birds are such habituées of these often imposing locations that they have become an integral part of their wind-swept character:

Fulmars have bred on the mighty rock and castle at Bamburgh in Northumberland since 1934. Early on a

A fulmar in flight is the epitome of effortless grace.

13

The St Kildans survey their fulmar catch in August 1884.

morning in May 1961 I took up my position with recording gear at the foot of the cliff. At twenty past five they began to appear, flying and gliding on pearly-grey pinions with consummate ease and uttering their quiet, little-known grunts. The light from the rising sun illuminated the castle's towers and caught the undersides of the outstretched fulmars' wings with a golden glow. They now began to fly to the rock ledges, either to hover for a few seconds and drop away, or pitch rather inelegantly on a shelf. With my parabolic microphone focused on a high narrow ledge I captured the characteristic chuckling and cackling now beginning to echo around the castle. I have also listened to fulmars on Tantallon and Dunrobin Castles, as well as buildings in Stonehaven and Banff, old ruins and inland quarries 3.5km from the sea.'[5]

The name 'fulmar' was first transmitted into common usage during the early eighteenth century by Martin Martin, the Scottish writer and traveller. Prior to his description the bird had no widespread English vernacular name, although it was known in Scotland (probably mainly by sailors and fishermen) by a word of Dutch origin, 'mallemuck' – literally *malle* (foolish) and

mok (gull), in reference to the ease with which it was once captured. A version of this, mollymawk, is still used as an alternative title for seven species of albatross, and variations of 'mallemuck' survive as a name for the fulmar in Orkney and Shetland.

Martin Martin first encountered both the Norse name and the bird itself in 1697, when he was land steward to the MacLeods, lairds of St Kilda. For the tiny Gaelic-speaking community on these remote Atlantic islands, fulmars had been at the heart of their culture for at least 1000 years, as a source of food, fertiliser, fuel and even medicine. Writing of the oil, Martin suggested that 'It is good against rheumatic pains and aches in the bones; the inhabitants of the adjacent isles value it as a catholicon for diseases; some take it for a vomit, others for a purge. It has been successfully used against rheumatic pains in Edinburgh and London; in the latter it has been lately used to assuage the swelling of a sprained foot, a cheek swelled with the toothache, and for discussing a hard boil; and proved successful in all three cases.'[6]

Whenever strangers arrived on the islands, the isolated, largely germ-free locals caught a cough that quickly passed even to breast-feeding infants. 'The most sovereign remedy against this disease, is their great and beloved

The old 'cleits', where the St Kildans once stored their harvest of fulmars and other seabirds, still cover the hillsides on Hirta.

catholicon, the *giben*, i.e. the fat of their fowls, with which they stuff the stomach of a Solan goose [a gannet], in fashion of a pudding; this they put in the infusion of oatmeal, which in their language they call *brochan*.'[7]

Although they utilised almost all seabird species breeding on the islands (including, in Martin's day, the now-extinct great auk), the St Kildans' staple food was fulmar meat. Right up until a few months before they abandoned the island for good in 1930 they were living off its salted flesh.[8] The main harvest coincided with the period when the single downy chick is at its plumpest – between 12 and 26 August. This was a time of intense activity in which the entire community participated, and when the St Kildan men put to the test their awesome mountaineering skills.

One of the challenges posed by this form of fowling was the young fulmar's ability to regurgitate a stream of strong-smelling oil. In fact it was from this habit that the bird derived its Norse name: *fulmar* means literally 'foul gull'. The St Kildan men countered this potential unpleasantness by seizing the bird from behind and 'by taking hold of its bill, which they tie with a thread, and upon their return home they untie it with a dish under to receive the oil'.[9] Neil MacKenzie, minister to the St

Kildans between 1829 and 1843, suggested that if the men could seize the bird before it could raise its wings, it would be unable to vomit on its assailant:

Caught in the right way its neck is speedily twisted and broken and the head passed under the girdle. When the man has got strung about him as many as he can conveniently carry, they are passed up to the women who are waiting above. At once they are divided into as many shares as there are men in the group, when the womenkind and children seize upon their shares and begin to drain out the oil into receptacles, which are generally made of the blown-out and dried stomachs of the Gannet. This they do by the very simple means of holding the bird bill downwards and gently pressing, when about a gill of oil [according to Fisher, about ½ pint/0.3l] flows out by the bill.[10]

In addition to the flesh and oil, the feathers were also a valuable resource until the 1890s and were the islanders' main means of meeting their rent payments. In 1847 each family's rent was about seven St Kildan stone (168 pounds/76kg) of feathers of fulmars, gannets and puffins.

Fulmars normally have a rather 'serene' air, but they are capable of noisy gull-like squabbling, especially when they gather around fishing boats as the trawlermen gut the catch.

About 80 fulmars produced a stone of feathers (which represented nearly 5 ounces/142gm for each bird and 20 per cent of its body weight).[11]

The palatability of fulmar meat has been a source of dispute. To the unaccustomed palate it was forbidding fare: 'It smells of the oil got from the fat of fish'; 'a strong rancid smell . . . can cling for many years to the feathers'. Fisher himself found adult fulmar 'unpalatable and musty', while friend and co-author Ronald Lockley described it as 'like paper, or worse'. Opinions converged on the notion that the adults were best in spring, the young were better than their parents, and the eggs were the tastiest of all. A scientific study of the palatability of eggs placed the fulmar's above that of the turkey and not far behind that of the chicken.[12] The St Kildans themselves were unanimous. Martin wrote, 'the inhabitants prefer [fulmar], whether young or old, to all other; the old is of a delicate taste, being a mixture of fat and lean; the flesh white, no blood is to be found but only in its head and neck; the young is all fat'.[13]

Fisher calculated that on average, until the community's final exodus, 'over 100 fulmars found their way each year into each man, woman, and child. Tinned food, regular steamships, increased numbers of tourists, private and public charity, made no difference to fulmar-taking; all were irrelevant; none could affect the St. Kildans' desire for fulmar-oil, fulmar-flesh in his porridge, or fulmar-feathers to pay his rent.'[14]

As the human population dwindled, so the annual offtake of young and adult fulmars itself declined from around 12,000 to 4000 birds. Even so, the fulmar's breeding population remained remarkably constant and did not dramatically increase after St Kilda's abandonment in 1930. That stability introduces an interesting irony. While St Kilda was the only breeding location at least from medieval times until 1878, it was not the source of the fulmar's great invasion. The Foula birds and all of the other spreading colonies were thought to derive from Faroe and, ultimately, from Iceland, where the number of colonies increased from one in 1640 to 155 by 1949.[15]

There is supportive evidence for a more northerly origin in behavioural differences between the two populations. While the St Kildan birds are primarily cliff-nesting and have not occupied the island's numerous man-made stone structures, fulmars in Shetland and Orkney show a marked attraction for old crofts and byres. It is one of the more unnerving facets of Orcadian life to pass an old croft, only to be confronted by a vision, just above eye-level, of a scrawny-necked Muppet-like creature swaying snake-like on the low flagstone roof in readiness to fire its jet of oil.

Although the St Kildans were expert at avoiding this projectile vomit, MacKenzie records that during the August harvest their clothes were soaked in oil. Even today the same fate routinely befalls researchers attempting to ring cliff-nesting fulmars:

The main prerequisite for fulmar ringing is a strong stomach, as the warm, yellow, greasy, foul, fish-smelling vomit has the consistency and colour of melted butter and occasionally it contains fine strips of a reddish substance which looks like cooked tomato peel. Avoiding the full facial vomit experience is not too difficult for experienced handlers when they know the bird's whereabouts. The problems arise mainly with unknown birds whilst climbing. Suddenly sticking your head over a ledge and coming face to face with a vomiting fulmar chick is an unpleasant experience. The other major problem is being hit by multiple rounds, which you cannot avoid, for while ringing one chick, other adults and youngsters may be showering you from all sides and from above.[16]

One of the problems faced by ornithologists is the fact that the young fulmar's stomach often contains more than a single 'round'. 'Many is the novice who has avoided the first moist, musty mouthful only to suffer the second. There is much head shaking before the third gobbet comes; but come it often does.' Fisher's personal record was the seabird equivalent of a six-shooter, while more than 3 yards (2.7m) was the all-comers' record for distance on level ground, although – with the help of altitude and gravity on the cliffs of St Kilda – the range can increase to ¼ mile (0.4km).[17]

The following anecdote makes plain the remarkable persistence of the stench:

After leaving Fair Isle I travelled by fishing boat to help out at Falsterbo Bird Observatory in Sweden and amongst my clothing was a well-washed jumper I had worn while ringing fulmars on a couple of occasions (my regular jumper had become so foul that I had disposed of it). Months later while hitching back to the UK my luggage was stolen. I gave the police all the information and a couple of months after returning

home they were pleased to inform me that some of my old property had been recovered. A large parcel eventually arrived and even before I opened it the familiar smell of fulmar oil invaded my nostrils. It was the dreaded ringing jumper along with a few other items, now also well impregnated with the awful smell.[18]

Fulmar oil has a far more effective deterrent than simply its odour. Proof of this came in July 1968 when four young white-tailed eagles were released on Fair Isle in an attempt to re-establish the species as a breeding bird in Britain. By the following summer three had either died or left the island and the last bird, a male, was found in a cave, his plumage heavily soiled with vomit from fulmars.[19]

As long ago as 1927 the oil was analysed and found to be as rich in vitamin A as cod-liver oil and chemically very similar to the wax found in the head cavity of sperm whales. The red colouring is an indicator that the fulmar has been feeding on planktonic crustaceans or cephalopods (squid) that have themselves fed on crustaceans. With a diet more or less identical to several types of whale, it is not surprising that the two krill-eating predators are often found in association. It was a relationship that whalers noted and exploited from the earliest times.

If whalers used fulmars to find their quarry, then the birds quickly learnt to reciprocate. From the seventeenth century onwards fulmars were noted as routine attendants of whaling vessels for the offal thrown overboard: 'scarcely a whale has died or been flensed in the open in the North Atlantic without attracting fulmars,' wrote Fisher.[20] Once they had acquired the habit, fulmars adapted to whichever human operation was in progress in their feeding area. Ronald Lockley described how gutting operations on a cod trawler near Rockall were an equally powerful draw:

The crew swiftly gutted the catch during the next hour. The 'dirt' (entrails, small and unsaleable fish and squid) was hosed through the scupper. Some three thousand fulmars fought to get the best portions – the liver and guts – leaving the squid and spiny fish to the more timid great and sooty shearwaters. For a few minutes the dense mass of the white and grey bodies of the fulmars quite obliterated the sea close to the trawler. With a home-made fowling net [we] were able to scoop up as many fulmars as we wished during these gutting periods. Some we marked on the heads with dabs of red paint, so that we could identify them later at a distance. When placed on deck the fulmars waddled along helplessly, unable to take wing, but

The low chalk cliffs at Hunstanton, Norfolk, are typical of the fulmars' more recent nesting sites in southern England.

once released they were all grace and beauty as they glided with few wing-beats about the ship. In the next few days 'them red-headed mollies' were reported over the radio by astonished skippers of trawlers working in the Rockall Bank when they talked together at frequent intervals throughout the next twenty-four hours.[21]

Fisher pointed to the fulmar's exploitation of a relatively new, highly concentrated food source to explain its meteoric increase in the last two centuries. However a rival theory proposed by Professor Wynne-Edwards suggested that a new genotype developed in Iceland, which was better adapted to lower latitudes and to breeding successfully in small scattered groups, as opposed to the densely packed sea-cliff colonies around the Arctic rim. Whichever is true, it is certainly the case that fulmars are now routine scavengers. In more recent years this has led to them eating some of the less appetising forms of human waste being dumped at sea:

Among the more unnatural items I have recorded are rubber contraceptives ... probably picked up by adults in mistake for polychaets (Nereidae) or squids (Cephalopoda), and sheet polythene from what looks like carrier bags. Bubbles of expanded polystyrene are frequently ingested, in quantities which almost fill the stomach ... Adult and nestling Fulmars, while being ringed, have also disgorged numbers of plastic beads, about 5mm in diameter, used industrially in bulk injection moulding and the like; they are composed of polyethylene resin which solidifies on contact with water during manufacture, and they float. The beads find their way into the marine environment when malfunctions in the filtration process occur, sometimes resulting in millions being discharged.[22]

Soft-plumaged Petrel, *Pterodroma mollis* (**Fea's Petrel**, *P. feae*/**Zino's Petrel**, *P. madeira*). This is a gadfly petrel, so named for its highly erratic flight pattern. It is a widespread seabird of the southern Atlantic Ocean and similar in size to a Manx shearwater. Recent developments in an understanding of its taxonomy have led to the recognition of two distinct forms in the northern hemisphere. Zino's petrel (or freira) breeds only on Madeira and numbers just 20–30 breeding pairs, making it one of the rarest seabirds in the world.

The very closely allied Fea's petrel (also known as the Cape Verde petrel and, more pithily, as gon-gon) is almost identical in appearance but enjoys a less parlous conservation status, with an estimated world breeding population of about 1000 pairs on the Cape Verdes and a further 150–200 pairs on Bugio, the southernmost of the Deserta Islands. It is probably this endangered species that accounts for most (if not all) of the approximately 40 records that have occurred in Britain and Ireland since the first ever in August 1974 (Cape Clear, County Cork). These have been reported from well-known seawatching locations as widely spread as Norfolk, Northumberland and Pembrokeshire.

Capped Petrel, *Pterodroma hasitata*. This Caribbean seabird, known to breed only on Haiti, appears on the British list by virtue of a bird picked up at Southacre, Swaffham Heath, Norfolk, in the spring of 1850. A young boy found it fluttering from one gorse bush to another and, although it was clearly disoriented and exhausted, it had enough strength to bite its captor violently on the hand. The young boy then killed the bird, only to have his prize taken from him by the local landowner, who happened to be out hawking at the time.[23] The only other record derives from a two-week-old corpse found on the tideline at Barmston, Humberside, on 16 December 1984.

Bulwer's Petrel, *Bulweria bulwerii*, is an all dark-brown seabird found across middle latitudes of the Atlantic and Pacific Oceans and breeding as close as the Canary Islands. It has only been recorded in British and Irish waters on four occasions. The most recent was a bird off South Walney, Cumbria, on 17 April 1990.

It was first discovered by a Norfolk-born clergyman, James Bulwer (1794–1879), who gave his name not only to the species, but also to the genus. More unusual is the fact that he is commemorated in its Dutch, French, German and Spanish names. Bulwer probably found his petrel in 1825 on the largest of the Deserta Islands just south-west of Madeira, and noted the bird's bizarre calls – 'a singular noise, like that of children crying'.[24] Elsewhere it has been described as a 'Low barking chuff, often repeated ... resembling steam engine pulling away'.[25]

The bizarre character of the bird's vocalisations is well illustrated by an anecdote recounted in the diaries of Colonel Richard Meinertzhagen. In April 1924 he visited the Deserta Islands to collect birds with his assistant, whom he referred to simply as 'old Thorpe'. While they worked in the spring twilight, Meinertzhagen heard a mysterious cry and thought it had been emitted by his employee. Old Thorpe was apparently not the sort of person to indulge in this kind of levity, so beyond a quiet chuckle to himself the Colonel let it pass. However when the noise was instantly repeated Meinertzhagen, who described it in his diary as a curious 'Punch and Judy' sound, dissolved into laughter and accused his assistant of being a ventriloquist. Not only was the charge strenuously denied, but Thorpe suggested the noise had originated with the Colonel himself.

Both then stared hard at each other as a third party announced '*Ough, ough, aah*' in high squealing tones, followed by a voice that seemed to declare purposefully to them, '*Was yer, was yer, would yer, was yer, was yer.*' The two men stepped out into the evening shadows and realised the calls were coming from the nightjar-like birds swooping around their tent. They were Bulwer's petrels.

They kept up their entertaining barrage for much of the night, but the final showdown came when one bird landed on the rock next to the Colonel's bed. Its initial *Ough, ough, aah*, was answered with more tears of hysterical laughter, then a military boot flung in the bird's direction. The Bulwer's petrel vanished into the darkness but not before one last immortal complaint: '*Was yer, would yer, would yer, was yer, was yer.*'[26]

Cory's Shearwater, *Calonectris diomedea*. This graceful seabird, sometimes referred to as a 'mini albatross', is an inhabitant of eastern Atlantic and Mediterranean waters. It is the largest of the 'tubenoses' (see page 25) to breed in Europe, with a wingspan only marginally less than that of a lesser black-backed gull. Smoky grey-brown above and immaculately white below, it is an inveterate oceanic wanderer and routinely moves to the eastern seaboard of the USA and Canada during the autumn before turning south to winter off southernmost Africa. The flight action suits its free-ranging habits and at times is 'suggestive of an albatross ... rather than of the more laborious flight of other shearwaters'.[27]

It breeds widely on offshore islands in the Mediterranean and on several eastern Atlantic archipelagos, such as the Berlengas off Portugal and the Salvages (Selvagens) to the south of Madeira. On the latter islands many thousands of birds were annually harvested by

Great shearwaters have learned to attend fishing boats for their promise of easy pickings.

Portuguese fishermen for over a century: 'their flesh is salted for selling in Madeira, while their down is used for making eiderdowns and their oil for the upkeep of brass fittings on boats'.[28] Although the cull has reduced in recent decades, it has had a long-term negative impact on breeding numbers.

The Atlantic birds are the main source of occasionally large-scale movements of Cory's shearwaters off British and Irish coastlines in late summer and autumn, where they have been best observed from Atlantic promontories in Cornwall (St Ives and Porthgwarra) or County Cork (Cape Clear). The most extraordinary Cory's event occurred in July and August 1980, when an unprecedented and unrepeated passage of 10,939 birds moved off Cape Clear (16 August), with counts of 2735 (19 July) and 1202 (13 August) off Porthgwarra. That year there were estimated to be 17,230 in British and Irish waters, ten times the total ever recorded until that date.

Great Shearwater, *Puffinus gravis*. 'Great' on account of its large size compared with most other shearwaters, this is actually slightly smaller than the Cory's shearwater. However, it has one of the most effortless flights of all British seabirds. Glides of ½ mile (0.8km) are

routine and there is a record of an unbroken glide spanning 1½ miles (2.4km).

It is dark ash-grey or black above, with white underparts, and its identification in Britain involves careful separation from Cory's shearwater. This is particularly the case because both birds are routinely driven here by the same Atlantic weather systems and are observed at the same locations. These coincidental factors have often led to them being considered 'sister' species, but the two are, in fact, from separate genera and breed in completely different parts of the Atlantic.

While great shearwaters nest no nearer to Britain and Ireland than the 37° S meridian, more than 6000 miles (10,000km) away, they are in some ways more 'British' than almost any other bird. Virtually the entire world population breeds on Nightingale and Inaccessible Islands, in the Tristan da Cunha group, and on Gough Island, about 230 miles (370km) to the south-east, all three of which are part of the British Crown Colony of St Helena. The total for Nightingale alone is put at four million birds.

If British by birth, great shearwaters are cosmopolitan by nature and perform a staggering clockwise migration that embraces much of the Atlantic Ocean. In April the adults leave the nest colonies and head north-west towards the eastern coast of North America, appearing in huge numbers off the Grand Banks in Newfoundland and as far north as Greenland. In late summer they begin a southerly movement partly through the eastern Atlantic, which brings them within range of British and Irish shores. They are annual in moderate numbers although occasionally passage can involve thousands of birds. One of the most notable of these occurrences came on 14–15 September 1965, when 9295 passed Cape Clear in southernmost Ireland.[29]

Sooty Shearwater, *Puffinus griseus*. VN: Sooty/ies (birders). With its characteristic looping flight and the bright silvery 'flash' on its underwing linings, this otherwise all-dark, medium-sized shearwater can be seen off almost any British and Irish coastline in autumn. The encounter carries a particular kind of satisfaction because it implies an heroic odyssey of about 10,000 miles (16,660km) performed by every bird seen in our waters. Sooties breed at the other end of the earth, mainly on offshore islands in the southernmost Atlantic and Pacific Oceans.

Although the 'wintering' birds seen in our hemisphere are usually silent, their nesting grounds in locations like the Falkland Islands are known for the bird's bizarre nocturnal vocalisations: 'an eerie howling call . . . repeated rhythmically and sometimes sustained for half a minute'; 'the most ghastly sounds . . . like choking cats . . . grating and choking with noise like gurgling intake of breath'.[30] Once the chick is fully developed, the adults abandon it and begin their post-breeding movement out of the southern Atlantic in the late austral summer (our early spring), then move up North America's east coast, before heading into British waters during late summer and autumn.

Manx Shearwater, *Puffinus puffinus*. VN: Cockersudie, Cockersootie (Shetland). It sounds like one of those British names – Sandwich tern and Kentish plover are two classic examples – that reflect the parochialism of early British ornithologists. However, in this instance there is some justification since 90 per cent of the planet's Manx shearwaters, some 250,000–300,000 pairs, nest in Britain and Ireland. Remarkably, most of these birds are thought to occur at just three sites: on the islands of Skokholm and Skomer off the Pembrokeshire coast and on the Scottish island of Rhum, where they will breed on mountainsides up to a height of 2000 feet (606m). There is a sprinkling of other colonies mainly on the west coasts of Ireland, Wales and Scotland, with small outlying populations in Orkney and Shetland.

Although a tireless wanderer at sea, like all its family members, the Manx shearwater is an ungainly creature when it comes ashore. It usually shuffles along the

Manx shearwaters produce a nocturnal sound so bizarre it once had the power to terrorise a Viking war party.

ground on 'all fours', wings beating or fluttering while the bird supports itself on bent tarsi, or occasionally makes short distances running on its toes. To compensate for this obvious vulnerability, it nests in an underground chamber at the end of a burrow or in a crevice among rocks. Another protective strategy is to come ashore after dark, a pattern of behaviour that accounts for one of the great spectacles associated with the species:

> The time to watch Manx shearwaters at sea off the Pembrokeshire coast is when an evening high tide surges through Jack Sound into St Bride's Bay to be met by strong westerly winds. The birds gather in huge flocks offshore prior to visiting the nest colonies on Skomer, its satellite Middleholm and Skokholm to the south. They sweep downwind, before turning to glide westwards almost as effortlessly over the swell. Others sit in huge flocks, or rafts, riding the rollers, from time to time rising up to join in the endless procession.[31]

In some ways it seems ill-equipped for a nocturnal existence: 'The eye of the shearwater is surprisingly small: a little chocolate disk no larger than the head of a blue-bottle, or the head of Britannica on a penny.'[32] They compensate for any lack of visual contact both with each other and with the topography of their nest chambers by

Manx shearwaters sometimes gather in huge rafts involving thousands of birds.

a constant barrage of calls – vocalisations that are as impressive and atmospheric as the dusk gatherings that precede them:

We didn't see our first Manx shearwaters until we became wardens of the newly established Skomer Island National Nature Reserve in mid-March 1960. Inspired by our friend and former resident on neighbouring Skokholm, Ronald Lockley, we hurriedly constructed nest boxes inside the cellar. The birds wishing to use them gained access through appropriately sized holes at the foot of the supporting walls. One particularly noisy pair adopted a box directly beneath the bathroom and to be serenaded by Manx shearwaters during one's ablutions is an experience not easily forgotten.

The darker the night – one without moonlight and with a gentle drizzle or mist is the ideal – the louder and more persistent the calls, which they produce on the wing as they flight in, or as they emerge from the burrows, or even while underground. How does one describe the indescribable? Ronald Lockley called it 'a bedlam of weird screaming . . . a wild howling' or 'the crying of insane spirits'. Yet listening to their chuckles and screams is also a truly magical experience like no other.[33]

The one notable irony deriving from the name is that Manx shearwaters actually nesting on the Isle of Man now number fewer than 20. Yet there was once a colony at the Calf reputed to be among the largest ever known. It was also an ancient site, having been occupied by at least the early eleventh century, judging from references to it in the Icelandic *Njal's Saga*. Prior to an assault upon Ireland, a Viking war party anchored beneath the Calf in 1014. There the anonymous chroniclers heard and reported the eerie nocturnal clamour of the Manx shearwater colony but, unaware of the sound's genuine origins, turned the shearwaters into hostile night ravens. With this new identity the birds served as a powerful ill omen for the coming expedition and were even said to have attacked the Viking fleet and inflicted fatal casualties.[34]

Until its demise at the beginning of the nineteenth century, probably because of predation by rats, the Manx colony was a focus for a widespread trade in cured shearwater meat. The species had been a food item since prehistoric times and young birds were especially valued partly because they were easy to catch: 'the holes are commonly of that width and depth, that a man's hand and arm can reach the birds'. More important still was the fact that the adults feed their single chick on a partly digested fish soup extremely rich in fat: 'One of them may weigh nearly a pound weight, and is so fat, that one half of it will run to an oil. Some reckon it the most delicious morsel in the world, and others the most detestable.'[35]

The seventeenth-century ornithologist Francis Willughby recorded that as soon as the Calf of Man chicks were full-sized, 'they who are intrusted by the Lord of the Island draw them out of the Cony-holes, and that they may the more readily know and keep account of the numbers they take, they cut off one foot and reserve it . . . They usually sell them for about nine pence the dozen, a very cheap rate . . . Notwithstanding they are sold so cheap, yet some years there is thirty pounds made of the young Puffins taken in the Calf of Man.'[36]

Willughby's upper figure for the harvest suggests a maximum annual offtake of just under 10,000 young shearwaters. In his day 'puffin' or 'puffing' was the original name for a young Manx and simply meant a 'fatling', on account of the bird's pot-bellied appearance. Eventually it came to be used as a trade name for any rotund seabird of economic value, a generic use that was all the more likely, given that puffins and Manx shearwaters were both collected and eaten and, being burrow-nesting species, sometimes share the same rabbit-warrened coastal slopes. While the Latinised version, *Puffinus*, survives as the scientific name for the Manx, a word of Norfolk origin, 'shearwater', eventually took precedence as its English name in the eighteenth century. 'Puffin', on the other hand, came to be associated solely with the small black-and-white auk of comic manner and parrot bill.

The harvest of Manx shearwaters also occurred in Ireland and Scotland, and on the island of Mingulay the crofters used to pay their rent in barrels of salted shearwaters. In St Kilda there was such a demand from dealers for Manx eggs that the birds there almost declined to the point of extinction.[37] They were also collected and eaten in Shetland and Orkney, where there existed a parallel name for Manx shearwater, spelt 'lyre', 'lyrie' or 'liri', which, like 'puffin', also meant 'fat'. While it has probably passed from current usage because of the species' virtual extinction on the islands, this version is enshrined in several Shetland place names that mark the location of old Manx colonies, like Lyra Skerry on Papa Stour and Leera Stack on Unst.[38]

If the young shearwater's excess of fat was a valuable economic resource to our ancestors, its true ecological function is to give the immature a healthy surplus when it is finally deserted by the adults. Their own input to raise the single offspring spans almost four months, but the young bird remains alone in its burrow for a further eight to nine days, before making its maiden flight entirely unaccompanied. Even during the chick's initial two months after hatching, only a single parent remains with it in the nest chamber. The other parent goes out to sea to feed, returning after one or two days with a full crop of partly digested small fish or squid. There is evidence from ringed birds that some of the Welsh Manx population travel to feed on heavy concentrations of sardines in the Bay of Biscay, a round journey of about 1200 miles (2000km).

One of the most mysterious aspects is their uncanny ability to navigate to the nest burrow in the dark from such remote feeding locations. Among the first to study it was Ronald Lockley, who organised the ringing of more than 40,000 Manx shearwaters between 1927 and 1951, mainly on the island of Skokholm, where he lived for more than 20 years. Another line of investigation was to take captive birds and release them at distant locations.

The first attempt was coordinated with the ornithologist David Lack, a master at Dartington School, Devon, who happened to be visiting Skokholm with the children of Bertrand Russell and the architect and environmental campaigner, Clough Williams-Ellis. Lack's party took a Manx with them and released it from Start Point in Devon at 2 p.m. on 18 June 1936. The bird called Caroline was back in her nest on Skokholm, 225 miles (375km) away, at 11 p.m. that same evening.[39]

A year later the experiment was repeated, this time from Venice, and the bird took 14 days, five hours and ten minutes to complete the 930-mile (1550-km) journey overland, although Lockley believed that the bird undertook a far longer sea route of 3700 miles (6166km). By far the most impressive example of shearwater navigation by a bird released at an entirely unfamiliar location involved a Manx shearwater taken to the USA in an aeroplane. 'After release at Boston airport, Massachusetts, this individual returned to its burrow at Skokholm . . . in 12½ days. The distance is just over 3000 land miles, and this performance meant an average daily passage of 244 miles; but allowing for normal deviation in flight, resting and feeding periods, the speed of return must have been much greater.'[40]

For sheer cumulative distance, however, no individual shearwater is more impressive than a bird caught on Bardsey island off the north Welsh coast in 1957. It was thought to have been five years old then, but was subsequently caught and ringed on four other occasions – 1961, 1978, 2002 and in April 2003. This last retrapping confirms it as one of the oldest recorded birds in the world, but during its half-century of annual journeys to and from wintering areas off the South American coastline the bird is estimated to have flown 5,000,000 miles (8,045,000km) – more than ten times to the Moon and back.

Balearic Shearwater, *Puffinus mauretanicus/* **Yelkouan Shearwater** *P. yelkouan.* While the usual pattern of a British Manx shearwater rising and falling beneath the waves is a crisp vision in black and white, matters become more complicated as soon as you arrive at the Straits of Gibraltar. In the Mediterranean the shearwaters' upperparts assume different tones of brown and the underparts are sullied with a variable dirty grey wash.

The taxonomy is even more knotted. Various authorities argue over recognition of one or two separate shearwater species, the Balearic *P. mauretanicus* in the western Mediterranean and the Yelkouan *P. yelkouan* in the eastern Mediterranean. While the first has long been recognised as a regular autumn migrant off British and Irish shores, the appearance of the second is still a matter of dispute.

Little Shearwater, *Puffinus assimilis.* A bird mainly of the southern oceans, it is a rare visitor to British and Irish waters and is characterised by small size, short wings and an almost auk-like fluttery flight that lacks the looping ascents and wave-riding glides of other family members. There have been just over 100 records, mainly in the autumn and concentrated at the usual seawatching hotspots like Cape Clear, County Cork. Occasionally a disoriented individual has appeared inland, such as the sickly bird that was caught before it expired at Rostherne Mere, Cheshire, in June 1977.

The other striking land record was an individual male on Skomer Island, Dyfed, which was first detected by an oystercatcher-like call coming from beneath the ground. Eventually it was caught, ringed and released by its 'nest' burrow, to which it returned for a number of nights during July 1981. Remarkably it was found again in the summer of 1982 at the same spot, while a female may have been heard in May of the following year. These occurrences raised the tantalising hope of a long-distance colonisation from the little shearwater's nearest strongholds in Madeira and the Canary Islands. However, to date that promise remains unfulfilled.[41]

Storm-petrel family
Hydrobatidae

Wilson's Storm-petrel, *Oceanites oceanicus.* One of the great scholars of British ornithology, James Fisher, lent his weight to the contention that Wilson's petrel was the commonest bird on the planet and the theory held sway in ornithological mythology for many years. In truth its numbers fall far short of Africa's super-abundant avian locust, the red-billed quelea, *Quelea quelea*, but Wilson's petrel is nevertheless the world's most abundant seabird.

The species, which is named after the Scottish-American ornithologist, Alexander Wilson (1766–1813), is not much bigger than and barely more than twice as heavy as a house martin, yet it is an extraordinarily rugged wanderer across the world's most hostile oceans. It breeds around the Antarctic and on many of the archipelagos beyond the 40° S meridian, but it also makes long migrations into the northern Atlantic during the austral winter. This large-scale exodus from the southern hemisphere brings small numbers within range of British and Irish waters, but most sightings are well away from mainland shores.

Despite the petrel's remarkable long-distance migration, its flight pattern when feeding is surprisingly erratic and almost feeble-looking: 'Often walks on water in characteristic attitude with wings stretched level or slightly raised like a butterfly's and tail fanned, planing along in a series of hops with feet dangling side by side.'[1]

In recent years a portion of the Sole sea area about 50 miles (80km) south-south-west of Scilly has proved the most reliable 'spot' for the species. Birdwatchers have joined shark-fishing expeditions or have chartered their own special seawatching boats to reach this sector of the Western Approaches, which is increasingly known as 'Wilson's Triangle'. To date the British and Irish records number just 40 individuals and most have been in the 1990s since the discovery of 'Wilson's Triangle'.

European Storm-petrel, *Hydrobates pelagicus.* VN: Alamotti, Mootie (Orkney); Ala Mootie (Shetland); Stormy (Stormies), birders. Of the commoner birds breeding in Britain and Ireland, this is also one of the least known, least-observed species, yielding only in mystery to its even more enigmatic cousin, the Leach's petrel. The last population estimate of 160,000 pairs was highly speculative, largely because the whereabouts of nesting colonies are incompletely understood, the known sites are mainly on small offshore islands and often inaccessible, while the breeding birds themselves are nocturnal and notoriously difficult to count.

European storm-petrels come ashore only under cover of darkness and fly around their nest burrows looking like strange bats and making a noise that resembles 'a fairy being sick'.

They nest in underground cavities, in natural rocky crevices, in holes among dry-stone walls and in rabbit, shearwater and puffin burrows, some of which may still be occupied by the original tenant. In these, stormies excavate a small side-tunnnel, although shared holes carry great risks for the 1-ounce (28-gm) squatters. 'Battered corpses were found . . . in both shearwater and Puffin holes. There have also been cases of Puffin . . . and shearwater . . . entering and destroying nests in my study burrows. For the most part, however, the entrances are too small to allow the entry of the larger birds. Some of my burrows have entrances barely two inches in diameter.'[2] Recent census workers have resorted to endoscopes to inspect these tiny mouse holes, or tape recordings of their vocalisations in order to count responses from sitting birds.

The storm-petrel's underground song is a harsh, loud purring punctuated by an abrupt '*chikka*' note that was described by Charles Oldham as 'like a fairy being sick'. The song can be of extraordinary duration and, following a study of the bird, Peter Davis wrote: 'I have not attempted to beat Oldham's record of an unbroken run of churring with 983 "chikkas", though I have no doubt

that this could be done, for the sound will issue from the burrow for literally hours at a stretch.'[3]

There are a few places close to the breeding colonies, especially in north-western Scotland and western Ireland, where stormies are easy to find. During high summer and in calm conditions the tiny birds can be seen way offshore fluttering above the sea like a marine version of the house martin. The one habit that has brought them most closely into association with humans is their practice of following ships.

Like all this group of seabirds, storm-petrels have long prominent nostrils that account for their common name, 'tubenoses'. The birds also have a remarkably acute sense of smell, enabling them to pinpoint oils and other fatty substances floating at the surface in otherwise empty stretches of ocean. Important sources of food in both historical and modern times have been the offal jettisoned by fishing and whaling vessels.

Once food has been located, storm-petrels hover just above the sea surface with legs dangling, so that it looks as if they are actually walking on the water. The family name 'petrel' is itself connected with the behaviour and has long been thought to indicate an association with St

25

Peter. However, according to that wonderfully dry, wonderfully erudite scholar of British bird nomenclature, W. B. Lockwood, petrel is a corruption of 'pitteral', itself an echo of the pitter-patter of its feet upon the sea surface. The association with St Peter was simply a later invention.[4]

Another curious archaic name, 'Mother Cary's chicken', has been a matter of even greater debate. One explanation suggested it had been attributed to the species by a particular nineteenth-century crew, after some especially evil old woman or witch of the same name (curiously, the word 'witch' is itself another old name for the bird). Otherwise it was claimed to be a corruption of *Mater cara*, 'Dear Mother', a name for the blessed Virgin, to whose care sailors' lives were entrusted. But Lockwood rejects both notions in favour of a theory that there was an old unrecorded name for the bird, 'Mother Mary's chicken'. Sailors, fearful of its status as an ill omen, deliberately modified this to Mother Cary's chicken.[5]

All these ideas reflect the deep superstitions that once surrounded the bird. Because they are genuinely associated with rough sea conditions, storm-petrels came to be viewed as signs of coming bad weather, or more widely as bringers of general misfortune. Another variation on the theme held that the birds were the souls of lost sailors, or the embodiment of wicked sea captains doomed to rove the wild oceans for ever. It is this pattern of lore that explains why 'stormy petrel' has passed into the language as a figure of speech for one – as the *Oxford English Dictionary* puts it – 'who delights in strife or whose appearance on the scene is a harbinger of coming trouble'.

Leach's Storm-petrel, *Oceanodroma leucorhoa*. This is our most enigmatic breeding bird. It is a summer visitor to the north-westernmost parts of Scotland and to a single Irish breeding station on the Stags of Broadhaven in County Mayo. The other nest colonies read like a list of the wildest and most romantic spots in all Britain: Sula Sgeir, North Rona, the Flannan Isles, St Kilda, Foula, Ramna Stack in Shetland and Sule Skerry. Locations are selected partly for their remoteness and partly for the absence of mammalian predators such as rats and cats.

Apart from time spent by each parent incubating the single white egg, Leach's petrels pass the hours of daylight way out in the Atlantic beyond the edge of the continental shelf. They breed in subterranean burrows and visit the nest only during the hours of Celtic twilight, making an accurate population census almost impossible. The most recent estimate for Britain and Ireland is just educated guesswork (10,000–100,000 pairs).

When the adults come ashore at night, they call to each other in order to aid location of their individual underground chambers and in so doing create one of the most

Far out to sea by day and strictly nocturnal on land, the Leach's petrel is without cavil our most mysterious breeding bird.

eerie and atmospheric sounds in British ornithology. The main calls have been described as 'demoniacal laughter' and 'a staccato musical laugh', while 'a goblin on acid' has a strongly contemporary ring.[6]

Just as enigmatic is a 'special sound during coition, a warm rhythmic trilling series of similar notes like "mmmmm, mmmmmm-mm, mmmmmm-mm", heard only on one night during whole season from any given burrow'. Eric Simms, the ornithologist and sound recordist, analysed tapes made by Ian Wallace on St Kilda and found that the long drawn-out crooning passages can last for more than a minute and contain more than 800 notes in 60 seconds.[7]

The bird's avoidance of land means that it is seldom observed from mainland Britain. (Typically, it took me a quarter of a century to see one.) Yet Leach's are not difficult to identify, partly because of a unique flight style: 'fluttering along close to the ocean, now down into the trough of the wave, anon skimming over the crest to half-fly, half-run, with patting feet, down the smooth surface of the next';[8] 'very buoyant and erratic, springing and bounding through the air with abrupt changes of direction, now gliding like miniature shearwater, now

The best chance to see Leach's petrels is when they are blown into coastal waters by autumn gales.

beating on buoyant wings like a nightjar, or turning with incredible swiftness'.[9]

Erratic they may seem but Leach's petrels are remarkable for their powers of endurance and navigation. In a reversal of the experiments used to investigate the ability of Manx shearwaters to orient themselves during migration (see page 23), two Leach's petrels were caught on their breeding grounds at Kent Island in New Brunswick, Canada, and transported to England, where they were released in Sussex. The birds were back at their Canadian nest burrows in under a fortnight, having covered almost 3000 miles (4800km).[10]

When British birds make their normal autumn migration to tropical latitudes in the Atlantic, Leach's petrels can be seen occasionally at a handful of mainland sites, probably the most unlikely of which is the Mersey estuary in Liverpool. As the breeding population sets off in a south-westerly direction towards the wintering area, a deep depression occasionally tracks across the Atlantic towards northern Scotland and catches them in strong north-westerly winds. This forces them through the narrow sea passage between County Antrim and the Mull of Kintyre and the weather conditions bring about 'a never-to-be-forgotten ornithological experience', when Leach's petrel can literally be seen at an observer's feet:

> If north-westerlies continue to blow, the birds may be pushed into the relative shelter of the Mersey Estuary, between Liverpool and the Wirral peninsula. The geography of the estuary is that of a curved funnel . . . The petrels shelter there during the worst of the storm, but as the depression moves east over Scotland . . . they begin to reorient themselves towards the open ocean. As they fly through the narrow mouth of the estuary, they pass by on the opposite side of the river

from Seaforth, giving excellent views to birdwatchers at New Brighton.[11]

Known as 'wrecks', these storm-driven displacements can also occasionally push the birds way inland:

> I'll never forget one blustery December day in the Severn valley north of Bewdley in Worcestershire when I . . . glimpsed what appeared to be a small black wader with a striking white rump struggling against the gusts. To my complete confusion, as the bird flew into a clear patch of sky, it had a forked tail and dangling legs . . . a Leach's Petrel! There were a few seconds in which to identify it, before a gust of wind swept it down the valley, over the treetops and out of sight towards whatever fate awaited it. It remains the only bird on my local patch for which I've felt such a sense of disbelief, exhilaration and apprehension as to its future.[12]

There have been several major wreck events in recent times, most notably in 1952 and 1978. The first was by far the most serious to be recorded last century. Birds were scattered across almost every part of the British Isles and all but three Irish counties, while casualties exceeded at least 6700, with 2400 of these at Bridgwater, Somerset. Living birds were seen over inland reservoirs, gravel pits, sewage works and were even caught in car headlights as they flew above a Norfolk road. Two of the more unusual records include a corpse retrieved in London's Regent's Park and a bird living with hens for several days in Christchurch, Hampshire.[13]

Swinhoe's Storm-petrel, *Oceanodroma monorhis*. The first British records of this all-dark seabird from the north-west Pacific, where it breeds on islands off the

The capture of our first-ever Swinhoe's storm-petrel at Tynemouth in July 1989 was hailed as one of the most unlikely developments in recent British ornithology.

Korean and Japanese coasts, were heralded as 'one of the more astonishing developments in Western Palearctic ornithology of recent decades'.[14]

On 23 July 1989 some bird ringers were tape-luring European storm-petrels to their nets at the base of Tynemouth's north pier, when they caught a larger unfamiliar species. A detailed description was taken after the mystery bird had been ringed, photographed and measured, although it took three years and analysis of its cyctochrome-b mitochondrial DNA sequences to establish its identity as a Swinhoe's storm-petrel and a new bird for Britain. Remarkably, three days after the first was caught, the same group of birdwatchers trapped a second. Incredibly, they then captured a third in the following July, and proceeded to retrap this same individual on eight occasions in five consecutive years. Only the nineteenth-century story of Britain's first ever capped petrel, discovered by a child on a gorse bush near Swaffham, Norfolk, has the same element of nigh-impossible serendipity.

Gannet family *Sulidae*

Northern Gannet, *Morus bassanus*. VN: Crockak (Unst); Solan, Soland or Soland Goose (northern Scotland, Orkney and Shetland); Sula, Guga, primarily for young birds (Outer Hebrides). For much of its history the gannet was known by the older and now exclusively northern names listed above. These were in turn derived from an Old Norse word, *Sula*, whose literal meaning is 'cleft stick, in reference to the crossed wing-tips, black in contrast to the pure white of the rest of the plumage, and so conspicuous when the birds are sitting or standing'.[1] This original word is to be found in the name of the unoccupied islet near North Rona, called Sula Sgeir, which still supports an ancient gannetry.

The species is not only our largest and most impressive seabird, but has generated a rich cultural history that spans hundreds – if not thousands – of years. This enhances its status as one of Britain and Ireland's great environmental treasures, but it is founded most securely on the fact that more than two-thirds of the world's population (186,500 pairs) are concentrated in these islands at just a couple of dozen gannetries.

Many of the larger nesting sites are found at remote offshore locations. Yet the bird is both widespread and easily seen from most of our shores, and this is especially true in autumn when gannets journey southwards to wintering sea areas off Iberia or West Africa. They often linger en route to feed in shallow coastal stretches and even venture well into the deeper estuaries such as the Firth of Forth, Humber and Wash.

Their large size, 6-foot (1.8-m) wingspan, and gleaming white plumage, broken only by black tips to the wings and a subtle yellow-buff tone to the crown, make adults unmistakable. By contrast, the gugas (the recently fledged birds), which take four years to achieve full adult dress, are a uniform smoky grey-brown and can be mistaken for immature gulls. But gannets between these age groups present a bewildering array of piebald intermediates that can be even more confusing to unwary observers. Fortunately at all stages the bird has a strongly cruciform shape, a powerful majestic flight and a long dagger-like bill.

It is perhaps not surprising, given the gannet's easy grace and power as it planes through high winds just above a sea swell, that it has inspired a number of British aircraft manufacturers to take its name for their prototypes. 'Gloster developed a wooden-framed bi-plane during the 1920s called the "Gannet" and although this was a fairly short-lived model, in the 1940s Fairey also made a "Gannet", a high-performance anti-submarine aircraft, that was much more highly regarded':

A previous Fairey aircraft, the Fleet Air Arm's first carrier-based fighter with the same firepower as the Hurricane and Spitfire, also had a seabird's name – the Fulmar. But a bit more curious is the De Havilland Albatross, given the bird's linguistic association with an unwanted burden. They built it for Imperial Airways as a long-range passenger plane and at the time its cruising speed of 210 mph was amongst the highest in the world. However the fact that it was made of wood led critics to suggest that it was in fact an albatross around the neck of Imperial Airways. It could not compete with all-metal designs such as the DC-3 and the outbreak of World War II effectively denied it any chance to really prove itself.[2]

When gannets are feeding their aerial progress is often punctuated by a sudden drawing in of the wings and a dramatic arrow-like descent into the water below – a plunge-diving technique which is the bird's trademark and which makes the species a consummate catcher of fish. Gannets seldom penetrate more than 15 feet (4.5m) beneath the surface and remain submerged for only a few

Diving gannets can hit the water at more than 100kph. There is a spongy bone plate at the base of their bills to reduce the impact.

Breeding gannets at their colony on Bass Rock.

seconds, but the impact is extraordinary and the birds have specially developed neck muscles, a protective layer of air-filled sacs under the skin of the head and neck, a spongy bone plate at the base of the bill, special membranes to guard the eyes and a peculiar nostril configuration to keep out the water:

> The gannet's dive, like the peregrine's stoop, is a marvel of co-ordination that automatically induces naturalists to reach for the purple ink . . . Starting from the normal height of about 9m (c30ft) they tip steeply, or gradually, into a gravity plunge. Sometimes they will accelerate with power-strokes. They may fall into a long, straight plunge at a constant angle, sometimes vertical; or, more spectacularly, manoeuvre on the way down, angling, adjusting, half-turning, even cork-screwing or angling beyond the vertical before striking the water . . . A gannet may be travelling at more than 100 km/h (60 mph) when it hits the water, often with a leaden thump that resounds for hundreds of metres on a calm day . . . Its passage through the water churns up a milky wake through which the bird is seen as a pale green blob fizzing into the depths.[3]

Gannets often feed in concert, pouring down from the sky in rapid succession like so many projectiles. Sometimes the flocks can be 1000-strong, which, on top of the dive's requirements for strength, accuracy and speed, demonstrates the birds' remarkable gift for mutual avoidance. A mass attack is triggered by the presence of large shoals of classic fish prey such as herring or mackerel (an old Norfolk name was 'herring gant', while in Yorkshire it was 'mackerel gant'). On these occasions the gannet's white plumage acts as a marker that draws in other birds and alerts them to the presence of the food concentration.

It is also believed that gannets enjoy some form of symbiotic feeding relationship with fish-eating cetaceans. One of my most memorable visions involved a panorama of surfacing common dolphins churning the sea from below, while hundreds of white missiles rained down on the same stretch of north Atlantic from above.

At other times singletons or small parties of gannets will follow in the wake of large ships – they are regularly in attendance behind cross-Channel ferries, for instance – or will circle high above the vessel as if in search of edible flotsam. While many seabirds adapted very quickly to scavenging offal and other items discarded from boats, the gannet was a relative latecomer to this human-created harvest. July 1947 may have been the first occasion that the species was ever recorded to take advantage of the easy pickings, when the ornithologist Kenneth Williamson saw a bird off Orkney taking bread scraps thrown to the gulls.[4]

Since that date it has become a routine feature of gannet behaviour and has been proposed as a contributory factor in the bird's fourfold increase during the twentieth century. The voracious squabbling during attendance at ship scraps also partly explains the bird's unfortunate reputation for greed and the use of 'gannet' as an avian equivalent for 'pig':

> I will never forget in the Royal Navy in WW2, when one saw another rating tucking into a rather large meal we would place a fist on our hip and, whilst moving the resultant arm 'triangle' to and fro, would all make 'eurr, eurr, eurr' noises very like the sound gannets made as they swooped down on the 'gash' (waste food) being emptied over the side. The sailors' name for a person gorging himself was, as you'll gather, a 'Gannet'.[5]

The bizarre records of a dead gannet found with a 17-inch (43-cm) splinter of fishbox stuck in its crop and another with a brass rod of similar length, which it had presumably mistaken for a fish, supports the idea of a bird with highly experimental tastes.[6]

Gannets also famously scavenge human-manufactured objects to adorn their nests. As long ago as the seventeenth century Martin Martin reported gannet nests on St Kilda containing 'a red coat, a brass sundial, an arrow and some Molucca beans'.[7] In recent times lengths of nylon rope and sections of discarded fishing net are regularly used like a seaweed substitute to line the nest perimeter. These indestructible fibres can be a serious hazard to the birds, and it is possible to find gannets hanging dead from their own nests after they have become entangled in a fluorescent orange or electric-blue nylon noose. Others get the lengths wrapped around their heads and beaks and starve to death, although I have seen one apparently healthy adult flying above a ship with a length of blue nylon dangling out of its bill.

While an individual gannet is always an impressive bird, it is in aggregate at their communal breeding sites that they become one of the great spectacles in British nature. Gannetries assault all the senses, making their most immediate impression on the nose. As you move

The gannets' white plumage acts as a marker when they are feeding and helps to draw in other birds.

towards one, even before any birds are visible, a powerful stink of ammonia balloons out to envelop you. The Bass Rock in the Firth of Forth is one of Britain's largest and historically most famous gannetries. Its proximity can be detected long before the great guano-covered dome of volcanic rock comes into view. 'In a small boat on the Firth of Forth it is surprising how far land smells can travel, especially in a thick east-coast haar. The smell from the Bass gannetry is so strong and carries so far offshore that it can well be used as an aid to navigation and is far superior to a foghorn.'[8]

The bird's scientific name, *Morus bassanus*, commemorates the species' long association with the Bass, a link confirmed by documentary evidence as far back as the mid-fifteenth century.[9] However, the great seabird scholar and polymath James Fisher believed that there was a reference to it in the Anglo-Saxon poem of the seventh century, 'The Seafarer'. Fisher's own translation of the relevant passage ran:

> There heard I naught but seething sea,
> Ice-cold wave, awhile a song of swan.
> There came to charm me gannets' pother
> And whimbrels trills for the laughter of men,
> Kittiwake singing instead of mead.[10]

Fisher not only located it in East Lothian but surmised, from the variety of birds seen, that it described some moment between 20 and 27 April.

Although ornithologists visited the Bass Rock from the time of Willughby and Ray in the late seventeenth century, the principal contact with the gannetry was by those who went to collect the birds as food. Historical records confirm that from at least 1510, and thereafter for more than three and a half centuries, there was a continuous annual harvest, mainly of the youngsters. The cull averaged about 1500 birds until the final decades of the nineteenth century, when it finally ceased in 1885.[11]

Opinions on the palatability of gannet flesh have been strongly polarised and the adverse judgements have tended to increase in line with the decline of any harvest and trade. However gannets were shot in Shetland and sold to London restaurants during the more austere conditions of the Second World War, when their flesh was marketed as 'Highland goose'.[12] The reactions of wartime diners were not recorded, but modern gannet authority Bryan Nelson, who lived on the Bass Rock for three years, felt that 'to my coarse palate, they can be so delicately fishy that only the after-taste discloses it; some mute swans I ate tasted far fishier'. However, he also suggested that one gannet recipe – in which the birds were pickled, dried and eaten raw – 'would rival cowhide'.[13] Daniel Defoe, who tried the meat during a visit to Edinburgh, was of much the same opinion: 'As they live on fish, so they eat like fish, which, together with their being exceedingly fat, makes them, in my opinion, a very coarse dish, rank, and ill relish'd, and soon gorging the stomach.'[14]

Nelson records that they were baked by the hundred in brick ovens just opposite the Bass and eaten by Irish labourers, who preferred the flavour to their usual potatoes. Even in 1876 as many as 800 were being taken off the rock and, after being wrapped in rhubarb leaves and partly cooked, were sent to the markets of industrial northern England, such as Sheffield, Manchester and Newcastle.[15] Yet gannet had by no means always been a food for the poor. It had a long pedigree as an item at Scottish royal banquets and maintained a high price (of about 20d. a piece) in the poultry markets in Edinburgh until at least the middle of the eighteenth century.[16]

Gannets were also culled on the small island of Ailsa Crag off the Strathclyde coast, but the harvest on St Kilda, which was maintained for hundreds of years and finally ceased in 1910, was by far the most celebrated. This was partly on account of the dramatic setting of the gannetry, which is also the largest in the world, and partly on account of the death-defying rock-climbing feats of the men who collected them.

The islanders had to scale virtually sheer rock faces to reach the birds nesting on the tops of Stac Lee (544 feet/165m) and Stac an Armin (627 feet/190m), the two highest sea stacks in Britain. Adults were taken early in the spring, when they were reputed to be at their most tasty. The eggs, which could be preserved for up to eight months in beds of peat ash, were also highly prized by the islanders and even eaten raw, although Martin noted that they had 'an astringent and windy quality to strangers'![17] The St Kildans also used the breastbone as

At 33,000 pairs the gannet colony on Boreray in St Kilda is the largest in the world, as well as one of the most spectacular.

part of their oil lamps, while the fat was employed as a medicine and the gannet's cured stomach functioned as a bag to store all kinds of products.

The harvest of the gugas, which occurred in August when the birds were just about to fly, was a moment of great communal activity. Teams would climb to the top of the stacks, where they had built stone shelters to accommodate them in case of poor weather. On the agreed night the catchers would work through the hours of darkness, sometimes clubbing 1100 birds in a six-hour period, an average of one every three minutes for a team of 10.

Once they had been killed, the gannets were flung down to colleagues waiting below. The prospect of being hit by a bunch of 8-pound (3.6-kg) birds falling from a

Above: The men of Ness load their guga harvest from the Hebridean island of Sula Sgeir.
Below: Nylon fishing net is a handy alternative to seaweed when it comes to nest building, but it can sometimes end up as the gannet's noose.

height of 500 feet (150m) was not to be taken lightly and usually they were aimed to the side of the boat, where the men could paddle to retrieve them. Even so, the dangerous swells and strong winds around St Kilda meant that a significant number were lost.

Remarkably there is a surviving vestige of Scotland's traditonal guga harvest, which occurs in the northernmost part of the Outer Hebridean island of Lewis. The local men from Ness take part in an annual cull of birds from the gannetry on Sula Sgeir, a tiny archipelago about 40 miles (68km) north-north-east of the Butt of Lewis. The hunt is deeply embedded in Lewis culture and its local importance is enhanced by the speaking of Gaelic by the participants, the friendly rivalry between neighbouring villages and the sense of an ancient tradition maintained.

The quota, usually of about 2000 birds, is fixed by the Scottish Executive, on the basis of advice from Scottish Natural Heritage, and is set to ensure the continued viability of the colony. Over the period of the hunt 10 men live on the island, where they also gut and prepare the skins. Birds are cleaned and then singed on an open peat fire that is fuelled by the bird's own oily offal. The sooty residue is cleaned off the skin and any remaining feathers burnt away with a blow-torch.

At the end of the hunt the filleted skins, encrusted with salt and looking rather like large brownish-yellow kippers, are stacked ready for loading on to the boat. Around 4 to 6 ton(ne)s of gannet flesh are then transferred to the vessel and when the team finally arrives back in Stornoway it is welcomed by a large party of well-wishers. Each of the 10 guga hunters receives about 200 birds, many of which are given away to members of the Ness community, although they can sell for anything up to £10 a brace and are considered of the same elevated status as 'caviar to a Russian'.[18]

Cormorant family
Phalacrocoracidae

Great Cormorant, *Phalacrocorax carbo*. VN: Hiblin, Palmer, Skarf, Skarfie (Orkney); Scarf/ie (Shetland); Black Diver, Billy Diver (western Ireland, particularly Cork), Scart (Northern Ireland); Cormie (anglers). We often make our first childhood acquaintance with this large, dark, sometimes ungainly, but also curiously beautiful and powerfully heraldic waterbird through the well-known nonsense poem:

The common cormorant (or shag)
Lays eggs inside a paper bag,
You follow the idea, no doubt?
It's to keep the lightning out.

But what these unobservant birds
Have never thought of, is that herds
Of wandering bears might come with buns
And steal the bags to hold the crumbs.

Swimming cormorants are a curious blend of serpentine grace and clown's feet.

Individual family traditions have given rise to an array of subtle variations on the original wording, but the poem retains a capacity to evoke childhood memories, in one case 'of walking endless miles with my father on the Cornish coast and these equally beautiful and wonderful birds'.[1]

Yet not everyone has such positive views of cormorants, which have a capacity to excite strongly opposed opinion. Negative attitudes may still draw partly on the bird's ancient status as a creature of ill omen.

A habit of holding out their drying wings like an openly draped black cloak gives a judicial or clerical air to cormorants, and accounts for several archaic names such as 'parson' (Sussex, Hampshire) or 'Mochrum elders' (Wigtown), a reference to the forbidding Presbyterian leaders of the kirk session. The posture can also have a sinister Gothic character, especially when combined with the cormorant's liking for high, exposed perches.

Individuals occupying prominent public spaces were the cause of deep suspicion. In 1766 a cormorant that took up residence on Carlisle Cathedral was brought down after being shot at more than 20 times; and a bird perched on Boston steeple in 1860 was finally downed by the church caretaker. Even earlier, Milton invoked the widespread anxiety about cormorants in his description of Satan in *Paradise Lost*:

Thence up he flew, and on the Tree of Life,
The middle tree and highest there that grew,
Sat like a cormorant; yet not true life
Thereby regained, but sat devising death.

The species' contemporary portrayal by some communities as a 'Black Plague' or 'Black Death' sounds like an echo of this satanic imagery, but is, in fact, a reflection of the bird's modern population increase and its prowess as a catcher of fish.

Despite their fat-bodied, big-footed appearance and clumsy gait on dry land, cormorants have a serpentine grace in water and are highly efficient predators. They have been recorded to take 86 species of fish, from tiny fry to 2½-foot (76-cm) conger eels. An elastic throat pouch and a specially hinged beak means that, unlike grey herons, they can also cope with large flat fish, which look like small plates bulging in the distended gorge once the birds have finally shovelled them down. However, for sheer dietary eccentricity, little beats the record of a

Much to the annoyance of many anglers the cormorant's beak can unhinge at the base, allowing it to swallow the largest or flattest of fish.

cormorant eating a waste-filled plastic bag or the individual found with an 11-inch (28-cm) kitten in its stomach.[2]

For centuries fishermen tried to control cormorant numbers because of the competition they were thought to represent, but since 1967 the species has enjoyed legal protection. In recent decades the impact of cormorants on freshwater fish stocks and the illegal persecution of the species have become important environmental issues.

Cormorant numbers have risen since the 1970s to around 13,000 pairs in Britain and Ireland, and the increase has coincided with the expansion of the continental subspecies, *sinensis*. Both these European birds and the British race *carbo* adapt well to freshwater locations and at inland sites can form tree-nesting colonies, such as the large one at Abberton Reservoir, Essex. They have also shown a recent liking for tall electricity pylons as a tree substitute for both roosting and nesting purposes. Four pairs successfully bred on one of these tall manmade structures at Willington gravel pits in Derbyshire in 1998.[3]

In winter the cormorant population is boosted by a further seasonal influx so that the total on British inland waters could be as high as 6000–10,000 birds. These are inevitably drawn to gravel pits and reservoirs stocked with high densities of coarse fish, and fishermen become especially incensed when they see 'their' quarry being gulped down by the large black birds.

The widespread perception among anglers that cormorants seriously damage fish stocks accounts for the bird's recent 'Black Plague' image. This achieved its emotional climax in the *Angling Times* issue of 4 December 1996, when the front cover featured the photograph of a masked gunman with four dead cormorants above the words, 'These birds must be killed'. The editor was taken to court on a charge of incitement to kill a protected species under the Wildlife and Countryside Act, but the case was subsequently dismissed by the Peterborough magistrates.

The language and tone of the anglers' 'great cormorant crusade' has been highly charged: 'this eating machine destroys fisheries. If this means we shoot them, then so be it'; 'unless something is done there is no future for fishing clubs – they must employ full-time cormorant killers'; 'these birds must be stopped before they destroy our sport'; 'associations countrywide must face up to the fact that the "Black Death" are devastating waters indiscriminately'. However, accompanying claims that cormorants will 'endanger the future of at least 14 different native British coarse fish' or that they can eat their body weight in fish a day – roughly 6 pounds

(2.75kg) – and that they can dive to 120 feet (36m) are little more than fishermen's tales. Cormorants and native fish have coexisted since the last ice age, while the true figures for their daily fish requirement is 12–31 ounces (330–880gm) and for the maximum depth of their dive about 31 feet (9.5m).

Fishermen have even taken to cyberspace in order to broadcast anti-cormorant views. Cormorantbusters.co.uk is a website devoted to a campaign to reduce the bird's British population. The site features a number of articles that blend genuine outrage and accurate natural history with pure fantasy: 'I totally believe that the *sinensis* cormorants were deliberately and illegally introduced into the UK by extremist birdwatchers. This was a criminal and reckless act.' A more subtle, and in some ways more fascinating, form of denigration is expressed in the use of an archaic vernacular name for cormorant – 'sea crow' – which invites association with the bird family most widely vilified in Britain.

In circumstances where birds can be proved to have a serious impact on fish numbers, licences to shoot are granted. In the 1996/7 winter, 79 licences were issued in England and Scotland leading to the slaughter of 424 birds. By 2000 the number legally shot rose to 820. The angling press also reported the widespread illegal killing of cormorants: 'I have spoken to people over the last 12 months who claim to have eliminated in excess of 1,500 cormorants'; 'I know that more than 600 birds have been killed – I've shot 200 myself'. In the now notorious *Angling Times* issue of 4 December 1996, under a section entitled, 'How To Tackle The Problem', contributors discussed poisoning them with 10 paracetamols crushed inside a dead fish and catching them with hook and line in order to drown them.[4]

The issue is by no means straightforward to investigate, nor would it be easily resolved even if the birds were guilty. Culling one set of cormorants often only creates a vacuum and the artifically maintained stocks of fish simply draw in replacements. 'It is relatively easy to show that in some instances birds eat insufficient fish of commercial interest to present any serious problem to a fishery, but very difficult to demonstrate damage in places where they *are* eating large quantities of such fish':

This is because releasing fish from predation does not necessarily lead to higher catches at the end of the day. Such fish could be lost through other causes – to other predators, or by suffering poor growth or higher mortality associated with high fish density. The difficulties involved put fisheries' managers and anglers at a disadvantage. They may see large numbers of fish-eating birds congregating at their fishery to consume large amounts of valuable fish, but have to prove serious damage is occurring before they are allowed to kill birds. Currently, a large sum . . . of money is being spent on fish-eating bird research . . . The outcome is eagerly anticipated – by fisheries' interests, bird protectionists and ecologists alike.[5]

British fishermen have long resented the cormorant's fishing prowess, but in modern times have failed to utilise it, as the Chinese have done since the fourth century BC, when they started to employ domesticated birds to catch fish for them. One Briton who briefly explored the practice was James I. He maintained an aviary of cormorants (along with ospreys and otters) on the Thames at Westminster and also appointed a 'Keeper of the Royal Cormorants', who was dispatched as far away as Italy with birds from the king's collection. James devoted large sums of money to the hobby, including £286 for his Westminster cormorant house and the construction of nine ponds. The office eventually lapsed with Charles I, but remarkably one of James I's original keepers survived into the reign of Charles II and, aged 95, petitioned the new king to restore the position.[6]

Cormorants are often creatures of ingrained habit. At Castle Loch, for example, in the parish of Mochrum, near Wigtown, they have utilised the same rocky islands for their nest colony since the mid-seventeenth century, and the fact that a local place name – Scar Island – is derived from the Gaelic for cormorant, *scarf* or *scart*, hints at even greater antiquity.[7] The birds' faithfulness to a particular location and their routine patterns of behaviour, especially their constant movement in lines or arrow-shaped formations to and from the roost or nest site, have often made them a distinctive and reliable feature marking the daily and seasonal round.

At places like Holkham Hall in Norfolk, where there was a traditional roost for much of the second half of the twentieth century, 'the first cormorants arrive in the late evening and nervously circle their spot, a small wooded island in the lake surrounded by parkland':

These first birds eventually pluck up courage to land on their favourite tree, a large dead sycamore. The perched birds then become quite vocal, producing loud guttural croaks and churrs. Frequently these individuals are displaced by fresh arrivals. Sometimes the new birds get their landing wrong, miss their perch, and crash down through the branches and plummet on to the water with a loud splash.

Occasionally groups of twenty or thirty arrive at considerable altitude. To lose height rapidly they employ an erratic twisting and tumbling flight, each

When cormorants perch they can strike impressive sculptural poses, like these birds on Morecambe promenade.

cormorant taking its own path and with the large webbed feet fully spread to further break the airflow. This spectacular feat is called whiffling and the excitement is greatly enhanced by the antics and loud calls of the perched birds. As darkness falls many birds begin to sleep, each one tucking their long bills between their mantle and scapular feathers. When they are fully assembled the light has almost gone, but there is just enough to illuminate the magnificent and beautiful structure of a dead sycamore with its canopy covered by a multitude of cormorants silhouetted against the western sky. At this moment I quietly slip away through the dark woodland.[8]

The cormorant's enduring site loyalty can itself be the source of another problematic issue. Their droppings eventually build up and can kill the trees in which they spend the night. At Holkham Hall the bird's fouling of the area was presented as one more justification by anglers for the colony's eventual extirpation. The roost trees were felled in 1997.

Their guano also eventually fouls the nest colony and this may play some role in a periodic shifting of location. 'The stink and mess of a large cormorantry is indescribable and revolting to our noses . . . It takes more than one winter's rain to wash a cormorantry clean. Naturally we cannot impute a notion of cleanliness and sweetness to the cormorants, but I think this constant change of site is a hygienic measure nevertheless.'[9]

Cormorants appear to show a regard for cleanliness in other contexts. The birds often have loafing sites, like the gravel island on the North Scrape at Cley Marshes, Norfolk, where they rest for hours between bouts of offshore fishing. Individuals frequently waddle to one side to conduct their toilet, which involves planting the feet with the solemn ritual of a sumo wrestler and raising the tail, to fire out the great jet of white guano.

Although cormorants look all-black at range, they are in fact much more subtly coloured, depending on age. The young birds have variable amounts of white or oily brown on the underparts, but adults in breeding plumage have a strong bronze-brown sheen to the back and wings, while the black feathers are variously glossed bottle-green, blue and even purplish in some lights. With their erect crests, bright yellow-orange facial skin, white lozenges on the flanks and frosty throat plumes, they can be remarkably handsome birds.

The powerfully heraldic creature that sits atop the Liver Building in Liverpool city centre resembles a cormorant drying its wings after a good fish meal.

One location in which cormorants stand a higher chance of being regarded for their beauty is Liverpool, where it is the city emblem. The original Liver bird featured in the medieval civic crest was the Eagle of St John, in honour of King John who had granted the city its original charter of liberties in the thirteenth century. This seal was lost during the civil war and, when a replacement was designed in 1655, the artist depicted a bird closely resembling a cormorant. With wings outstretched in typical drying posture and with a spray of seaweed in its bill, the cormorant appears on the city library's book plate. A more ambiguous Liver bird appears on all council correspondence, on the city hall and other municipal buildings, civic vehicles, the city flag and, most famously, in two 18-foot (5.5-m) copper statues on top of the Royal Liver Building on Pier Head.

An obvious cormorant features in the badge for Liverpool Football Club and it is interesting to reflect that some of those taking to the Kop on a Saturday afternoon will unwittingly accord the bird hallowed status as the insignia of their football team, but may well condemn it the following morning as the 'Black Plague' that ruins their Sunday fishing.

European Shag, *Phalacrocorax aristotelis*. VN: Scarf, Scarfie, Tappo (Orkney, Shetland); Green Cormorant (West Cork). The fact that in Orkney and Shetland the local names are used interchangeably for great cormorant and European shag is indicative of the identification problems posed by the two species. They are very similar in appearance and habit, although shags are much more birds of rocky coastline. Shags are also smaller, more finely built, thinner-necked and even more sinuous and graceful when fishing. Their dive is often prefaced by a forward thrust that can lift the bird clear of the water before it plunges under.

The respective populations of shag and cormorant are strongly at odds with public perception. People are usually more familiar with cormorants, particularly because of their widespread presence on inland waters and even over major cities like London. However, the shag is three and half times more numerous, with a British and Irish population of almost 46,000 pairs (in turn, its present population in these islands is approximately half the world total).

In recent years the shag has undergone a remarkable increase in Britain: 'in the early years of the 1900s there were 10 pairs breeding between the Rivers Tay and Humber, in 1963 there were 1,900 there, in 1985–87 about 4,000 – an average increase of about 10% per annum for almost a century'.[10] They are most numerous on Scotland's north-western coasts and in the outer isles, where their crowded colonies on steep cliff faces can present a

The European shag is a bird of 'gloriously green eyes' and smutty innuendoes.

powerful spectacle: 'Disturbed birds lean forward, cackle loudly and writhe their snaky necks in an impressive threat display, a cold gleam in their gloriously green eyes.'[11]

The change of fortunes probably reflects a reduction in human persecution. Like its larger relative, the shag has long been viewed as a competitor for fish stocks but until the Second World War it was also shot for sport. The Summer Isles (to the north-west of Ullapool) 'endures each year the deplorable spectacle of visitors to hotels and boarding-houses – yea, and even shooting-lodges as well – coming out in launches and shooting at these frightened birds as they fly from the cliffs. The carcasses are left where they drop.'[12]

The shag has a long Scottish pedigree as a table item. Middens in East Fife and at an early medieval Pictish broch in Orkney have yielded up the bird's bones.[13] As late as the nineteenth century a brace was deemed the equal 'of a good plump hare',[14] although Thomas Bewick was sceptical of this verdict. He noted their 'strong and offensive smell', and wrote that 'before they are cooked, they must undergo a certain sweetening process, part of which consists in their first being skinned and drawn, and then wrapped up in a clean cloth, and buried for some time in the earth'.[15] One can only guess at the flavour possessed by this half-rotten fishy bundle.

Shags are coastal birds and are rarely found in freshwater habitats, but occasionally may be 'wrecked' by strong northerly and north-easterly gales, which drive the disoriented birds far inland. A documented wreck occurred in stormy weather in January 1958. This scattered birds across southern England and on the evening of 24 January, 20–30 shags were found north of Luton. The surreal vision presented by these reptilian birds as they perched in an array of Gothic postures on the church at Shillington and on tombstones in the graveyard was described as 'one of the most remarkable sightings in the annals of Bedfordshire ornithology'.[16]

The establishment of 'shag' as standard slang for sexual intercourse has led to a burdening of the bird's name with an unfortunate level of innuendo. However, in the winter of 2002 the Shetland Youth Information Service took advantage of the double entendre and nicely blended old and new names in the creation of 'Scarfie the Safe Shag', a 7-foot (2.1-m) tall model of the seabird, complete with hard hat and steel-toecapped boots. While a similarly sized condom was banned from the town streets by Shetland's elders, Scarfie was deemed not to undermine public morality and was allowed to walk around Lerwick pressing home the message of safe sex.[17]

Pelican family *Pelecanidae*

Great White Pelican, *Pelecanus onocratalus*. This huge, distinctive waterbird has an uncertain status as a member of the British avifauna. There were 16 records in the twentieth century, although the possibility that all were escapees from captive stock (including the famous pelican collection in St James's Park) has muddied the waters for ornithologists. Purists' anxieties have only been confirmed by the antics of birds like the one at Chew Valley Lake, Avon, in 1975, which landed on the roof of a parked car.

Escapes are not new. In 1662 the Russian ambassador supplied Charles II with his first pelicans for the royal wildfowl collection in St James's Park. The following year the disappearance of one of these birds coincided with the arrival of a pelican at Horsey Broad, Norfolk. The bird was shot and stuffed and ended up in the possession of Sir Thomas Browne.[1]

The original birds in the St James's Park collection were not, as they are now, white pelicans. They were the larger and now much rarer Dalmatian pelican *P. crispus*, a species that was once indisputably a British bird. Fossil remains have been found in Somerset and Cambridgeshire dating from as recently as the Iron Age. Some authorities have posited its survival in the Fens into historic times, but there is no concrete evidence and one of the only recent records, a bird that first appeared in Essex in the autumn of 1967 before making a stately progress through wetlands in Kent, Sussex, Hampshire, Dorset, Cornwall and finally the Isles of Scilly, was eventually deemed to be another escapee.[2]

Bittern and Heron family *Ardeidae*

'Butter bump', 'battle bump', 'bottle bump', 'bitter bump', 'boomer', 'mire drumble', 'bog bumper', 'bog drum', 'bull o' the bog', 'bittour', 'buttal' and 'bog blutter' – this wonderful catalogue of alliterative invention is just a sample of vernacular names once used for the **Great Bittern**, *Botaurus stellaris*. The variety is testimony to its complex social history in Britain, yet on first acquaintance with its physical appearance, the bittern looks a dull brown bird without any of the colour, crest and elegant plumes of its relative, the grey heron.

Evil omen, Sunday roast and icon of wetland conservation – the great bittern has played many parts in Britain.

To those familiar with it, the plainness of its plumage belies an extraordinary gift for self-transformation:

The neck of the bittern is deceptive as is the shape of the whole bird, which can seemingly metamorphose according to situation. On one occasion when I released a nearly fledged young bird into the reedbed I was amazed by the snake-like way it moved so effortlessly through the dense reed. Yet when cornered a bird will flatten itself with wings stretched out slightly so that it looks like the top of an open umbrella with only the bill pointing out and the yellow eyes fixed on its 'assailant'.[1]

The bittern's other characteristic posture is a fear display, when the bird thrusts head and neck vertically, with the bill pointing skywards, and freezes. It can hold the pose motionless for up to 45 minutes and has even

specialised feathers on raised pads on its body, and is worked into the plumage during preening. It helps the birds keep free of fish and eel slime but it also alters their appearance. 'Its colour depends on when it last powdered itself: it may look as if it had just been dusting in a flour bin, it may be Eton blue, Oxford blue or purple. It gets nearest to a stuffed Bittern in pouring rain, which washes the powder off.'[4]

In 2001 there were just 28 booming bitterns in Britain, mainly concentrated at large reedbed sites in East Anglia and at the RSPB's Leighton Moss reserve in Lancashire. Even this figure represents a 25 per cent increase on the previous year. With the exception of the corn crake, which has a similarly unmistakable and unbird-like call-note, the bittern has enjoyed a higher environmental profile than almost any other British bird. It has assumed a flagship status, not just for its own individual reedbed habitats, but for almost all lowland wetlands.

This has been achieved despite serious disadvantage – no bird, again with the exception of the corn crake, is more shy. Most birdwatchers regard any sighting as touched with a sense of occasion, while for the ordinary person the bittern's invisibility means it exists more as an idea than as a living reality. Yet this has hardly been a barrier to widespread concern. In recent times the decline in numbers of bittern has been raised in the House of Commons on several occasions.[5] A typical expression of the bird's new prominence was the re-designation of the railway between Sheringham and Norwich as the 'Bittern Line'. The choice of name reflected not simply its passage close to the bird's old haunts in the Broads, but the railway's shared vulnerability to extinction. The culmination of political and media concern was the allocation in 1997 of £1.5 million from the European Union to restore bittern habitat and reverse its decline to a target level of 100 'pairs' by 2020. The fact that this works out at £15,000 a brace is a measure of how high a priority bittern conservation has become.

One of the most fascinating aspects of its current status as environmental icon is the radical 'personality' transformation that this represents. There was a time when bitterns were seen in a much more utilitarian light – as a quarry for wildfowlers and a welcome addition to the dinner table. They were also maligned as creatures of ill omen, a negative attitude that was enshrined in the Old Testament.[6] The bittern's cultural journey from these old stereotypes and its imago-like emergence as wildlife celebrity is the main topic for consideration here.

It was almost certainly hunted from neolithic times and remained a dietary item until at least the nineteenth century. It is noteworthy, however, that Mrs Beeton offers no recipe for the bird. Nor can any recent gourmet

been recorded to adopt it while swimming: 'The bird took the posture horizontally . . . and at once looked like an old stick drifting in the water, pushed by the wind.'[2]

A few years ago there were six bitterns wintering regularly at Wintersett Reservoir, the birds ranging widely during the day but always returning to roost in a tiny reedbed. They usually roosted at the top of the reeds with bills pointing skywards. One day a severe storm hit the area and flattened the reedbed. I went along that evening expecting the birds to have found somewhere else to roost. To my amazement all six appeared on the now flat reedbed. They then proceeded to lie on the ground with bills outstretched horizontally. It was as if the urge to blend in by aligning their plumage with vertical reeds persisted when the reeds were flat.[3]

The other change in the bittern's appearance is brought about by a substance known as powder down. The fine blue dust is derived from the breakdown of

Catching bitterns for the pot was often achieved at the cost of a bloody knuckle and sometimes worse.

(or ornithologist) comment on its flavour. Yet the powderdown pads apparently 'have a repulsive acrid taste' and a cook needs proper knowledge of how to treat these, otherwise, noted the French naturalist George-Louis Buffon, they communicated a strong stink of the bog to the whole carcass.[7] By Mrs Beeton's day, ignorance of how to prepare bitterns for the table may have been significant in their decline as a dietary item.

It is known that bittern was a popular dish in the Middle Ages. In the London poultry markets the authorities issued tables of rates to regulate prices, and these inform us that between the thirteenth and seventeenth centuries the official price for bittern showed a 500 per cent increase, rising from sixpence to two shillings and sixpence. Throughout the period a bittern remained roughly pegged at one-third the cost of a swan, the most expensive table bird. Yet in 1328 some bitterns cost the royal household three shillings and sixpence each. By modern standards this was exorbitantly expensive: a skilled labourer, like a mason, would have had to work for 21 days to earn the money necessary for a brace.[8] Even by 1802 a bittern could still fetch half-a-guinea, the average weekly wage of an agricultural labourer.[9]

It is not surprising that for centuries they were very much a feature of the high table. They were served at the coronation banquet for Henry IV, while at a royal meal in 1387 Richard II treated his guests to a prodigious feast that included 120 sheep, 140 pigs, 14 salted oxen and 1200 pigeons. Just five bitterns (or possibly herons; the two are not clearly distinguished) appeared on the menu.[10] For sheer volume consumed, however, nothing compares with the banquet for the Chancellor of England, George Neville, when he was invested as Archbishop of York in 1465. This extraordinary meal outstripped even monarchical extravagance and included 400 swans, 2000 geese, 1000 capons and 204 bitterns.[11]

Although it was clearly an expensive table item, bittern was not an aristocratic preserve, in the way that peacock and, at one time, pheasant had been. It was almost always listed in dietaries from the late Middle Ages and is mentioned in many ceremonial dinners attended by provincial worthies. In the fourteenth and fifteenth centuries, for instance, it was eaten at corporation dinners held in King's Lynn[12] and there is also a record from 1567, when a Mr Balam of Norfolk sent eight brace of bitterns, five herons and nine cranes,

together with a host of other local wildfowl, to grace his friend's table on the occasion of a daughter's wedding.[13]

Despite its legendary shyness, the bittern was not considered an especially difficult quarry. In the sixteenth century William Turner observed that it was 'sluggish and most stupid, so that it can very easily be driven into nets by the use of a stalking horse'.[14] Willy Percy, one of the bird's most eccentric students, noted that when a bittern was absorbed in producing its resonant boom, it was possible to 'dash across the intervening space to find Botaurus half-defiant, half-cringing at your feet . . . you may pick him up, for in such circumstances his physical or emotional condition seems to rob him of the power . . . for sudden flight'.[15] During the 1920s and 1930s it was apparently a common trick performed by the keepers at Hickling Broad to stalk and catch booming bitterns.

Percy observed that such a stunt was sometimes at 'the cost of a blood-stained knuckle from a stab from his bill', and Thomas Bewick noted earlier that, when wounded by a sportsman, the bittern 'eyes him with a keen and undaunted look, and when driven to extremity, will attack him with the utmost vigour, wounding his legs, or aiming at his eyes with its sharp and piercing bill'.[16] These lines resonate with contemporary bittern researchers, who have to approach nests during their work:

Visits are timed to coincide with the female bittern being away from the nest so there is usually little chance of disturbing an adult. The nests are surprisingly small and the chicks, endearing little balls of ginger down with big green legs, make a lovely trilling call similar to little grebe. Once they are 2–3 weeks old they make a determined effort to escape and may repeatedly stab with their bills at your face. This we are relatively pleased to see since it is a sign of a fighting spirit. When handling adults it is recommended that goggles are worn because the aim and weapon are much more ferocious.[17]

While hunting was undoubtedly a pressure there were also counter-measures to protect bitterns. At a fourteenth-century baronial court of the Bishop of Ely, fines were imposed for collecting their eggs, and later Henry VIII issued legislation protecting 'euery egge of euery Bittour'. In their traditional strongholds the population remained stable until the nineteenth century, and the Norfolk ornithologist Richard Lubbock recalled that prior to 1843 'a party of fen shooters would kill 20 to 30 Bitterns in one morning when they were plentyful in Feltwell and Hockwold Fens'.[18] But the pincer pressure of hunting and habitat loss formed the background to the bittern's steady disappearance, and rarity eventually conferred on it a fatal lustre with egg collectors and other trophy hunters.

Yet the bittern's demise as a breeder was not unwelcome to some people – a response shaped by an ancient notion that a bittern's distinctive booming note in spring was an omen of disaster. The seventeenth-century cleric Bishop Hall wrote of one acquaintance that 'If a Bittourn fly over his head by night, he makes his will.'[19] Such ideas may even have led to a degree of persecution. In the late eighteenth century bitterns that nested on an island in Bruntwood Loch, Galston, in Ayrshire were driven away 'owing to superstition'.[20] The poet Oliver Goldsmith commented on 'the detestation' shown towards the bird by local people and added:

> I remember in the place where I was a boy, with what terror the bird's note affected the whole village; they considered it as the presage of some sad event; and generally found, or made one to succeed it. If any person in the neighbourhood died, they supposed it could not be otherwise, for the [bittern] had foretold it; but if nobody happened to die, the death of a cow or a sheep gave completion to the prophesy.[21]

The power of prophecy was one of a number of curious notions surrounding the bittern's boom. Even its production was little understood and several false beliefs were widely held. *The Canterbury Tales* articulated a widespread theory that the bird plunged its beak into the water and blew: 'And as a bitore bombleth in the myre, She leyde hir mouth unto the water doun,' explains Chaucer's Wife of Bath.[22] As late as the eighteenth century Daniel Defoe showed faith in a rival theory: 'here [in the Fens] we had the uncouth musick of the bittern, a bird . . . who, as fame tells us, (but as I believe no body knows) thrusts its bill into a reed, and then gives the dull, heavy groan or sound, like a sigh'.[23]

Modern eye-witness accounts eventually established that the genuine facts are in some ways no less extraordinary. After a preliminary series of clicks and coughs, with its whole body quivering, the booming bittern draws in air with its head thrust forward and then produces the loud, resonant and rather mournful note in a great exhalation. While the voice organ of most birds is the syrinx, the male bittern is exceptional in generating its call by physical expulsion of air from the oesophagus. At the approach of the breeding season the walls of the food pipe strengthen, allowing it to be inflated and to act as a resonating chamber. The increased musculature around the oesphagus can sometimes account for up to one-fifth of a male bittern's entire body weight.

The sound, issued in repeated sequences of usually three to four evenly spaced notes, is reminiscent of someone blowing into the top of an empty bottle and has the lowest frequency of any call by a British bird. It is also uncannily ventriloquial and can be extremely far-carrying. On occasions it has been heard to travel more than 3 miles (5km) and in parts of Suffolk foghorns on local ships were once known as 'sea bitterns'.[24] The sound of the bird is echoed in almost all the old vernacular names listed at the beginning of the account. Yet today possibly only one has been salvaged for posterity: the RSPB has a bittern news circular called the *Butterbump*.

In many ways the bird's disappearance from Britain for almost half a century brought an end to the old pattern of public attitudes. Its going may have been unmourned by the superstitious, but its return was heralded as a cause for celebration. The first nest was found by Emma Turner and Jim Vincent at Sutton, near Hickling Broad in Norfolk, in 1911. Turner's first-hand account of that 'never-to-be-forgotten 8th July' is filled with an extraordinary sense of drama:

> As there was no sign of any Bittern we both plunged into the reed-bed, determined to make a thorough search before dark. The water was above our knees, and the reeds were so dense that neither of us could see the other . . . At last came a joyful shout, 'I've got one youngster; come, quick' – and I pressed forward headlong in the direction of his voice. How we gloated over our prize as he stood there, transformed into the semblance of a bunch of reeds! . . . It was now 8.30 and the sun was setting. What was to be done with the young Bittern now we had found him? I insisted on some third person seeing our captive lest the unbelieving world should scoff, so I carried the wild, beautiful thing to dry land. This was no easy task: to begin with, I was too excited to hold him, and he could not be tucked under my arm because of sundry fierce thrusts upwards which he made with his bill. We had for the moment lost 'our sense of direction', but . . . soon hit our trail and emerged triumphant.[25]

The BBC helped set the new tone towards the bird when Jim Vincent gave a broadcast on its return entitled, 'The Romance of the Bittern'.

After the species re-established itself as a localised breeding bird, extraordinary efforts were made to uncover something of the secretly screened life within the reedbed. Lord Willy Percy, uncle to the author Gavin Maxwell, was one of the bird's most dedicated enthusiasts. Throughout the 1930s Lord Percy spent a remarkable 132 days keeping vigil at bittern nests in the Norfolk Broads. Eighty-seven days were in succession at

Young bitterns are endearing balls of ginger down with over-sized green feet. This one is being radio-tagged by RSPB researchers.

a single site between April and July 1934. His book *Three Studies in Bird Character* is full of original research and includes many important photographs, including a sequence of a bird devouring a 28-inch (70-cm) eel.

Another aristocrat captivated by the bird's 'mystique' was Lord Buxton, creator of the Anglia TV series *Survival*, who originally offered £1000 in the 1950s to anyone obtaining film footage of a bittern booming. Buxton claimed it was a vision he had 'yearned to see for decades'. Later, however, on achieving his wish with a captive bird, he could not avoid a sense of comic anticlimax: 'Quite honestly I was a bit embarrassed at first, because the bittern looked as if it was blowing off through its backside. This seemed a rather tawdry climax to the greatest discovery on earth and I wondered in what language I was going to announce it to the world.'[26]

Focus on bitterns acquired a new intensity when they suffered a second population slump during the last years of the twentieth century. The 1997 nadir of just 11 booming males at seven sites triggered a redoubling of political and scientific efforts led by English Nature and the RSPB. Ironically the fruits of their initiatives have made a mysterious and little-observed creature into one of the most studied birds of modern times.

Field research has involved fitting bitterns with radio transmitters. While the leather straps attaching the five- and two-inch (13- and 5-cm) aerials to the leg eventually wear through and fall off, the detailed monitoring these have allowed has brought major discoveries about an individual bird's use of reedbed habitats, survival rates and nest productivity. The possibilities for females to raise two broods in a season or to reach breeding maturity in their second calendar year are among the most important revelations. About 70 birds, including three-quarters of all bittern chicks hatched since 1997, have now been radio-

tagged. Detailed recording analyses of the bittern's boom have also shown that individual males can be audially 'fingerprinted', allowing their movements and survival to be monitored from year to year. Some of the most closely studied birds at the RSPB's Minsmere reserve have acquired distinct personalities:

In 1997 there were two regularly booming males and five breeding females, so polygyny must have occurred. It is assumed that one male, nicknamed 'Alfie' (after the philandering film character), mated with them all. Both males were radio-tagged in May and an examination showed that while both had blue bases to their bills, Alfie's was a much more intense shade, giving him a distinctive 'macho' appearance. The territories of both males were plotted using radio-tracking. Nest-finding revealed that all five nests were on the periphery of Alfie's territory, well away from the other male.[27]

The less successful male eventually became known as Sanjay, after the *EastEnders* character famous for his inability to have children.

The research has been matched by recent habitat works, partly funded by an EU grant of £1.5 million. Thirteen of the main English and Welsh sites for bittern have been enhanced, although the headline project involves the creation of major reedbeds in the heart of the species' old fenland stronghold. The 500-acre (200-ha) RSPB reserve, Lakenheath Fen, in Suffolk has been flooded and planted, and it is hoped that these former carrot fields will soon resound with booming bitterns. Even more noteworthy is the Needingworth Quarry/ Ouse Fen project near the village of Needingworth, Cambridgeshire. The site is currently worked and owned by Hanson Aggregates, but the plans for the next 25 years involve its progressive conversion to a wetland reserve. On completion this will cover 1750 acres (708ha) and will include a reedbed of 1150 acres (465ha), the largest of its kind in Britain, with sufficient habitat to support more bitterns than the entire current UK population.

The **American Bittern**, *Botaurus lentiginosus*, has been recorded about 60 times in Britain and Ireland. Two-thirds of the records come from before 1914, reflecting the transatlantic bird's parallel decline in population to our species during the twentieth century. Slightly smaller and with much plainer tawny upper-parts, the American bittern is also less dependent on dense cover and thus easier to see. In 1946 the author and naturalist Ronald Lockley 'almost stepped on an American Bittern ... which he surprised as it stood among boulders on the shingle of Abermawr beach on the west side of Ramsey Island, Pembrokeshire'.[28] Several vagrant individuals have been sufficiently confident to enable hundreds (if not thousands) of observers to get better views than most have ever enjoyed of the native bittern. One of these stayed at Magor, Gwent, from 29 October 1981 until 3 January 1982. Another at Martin Mere, Lancashire, remained from 24 January until at least 12 May 1991.

The **Little Bittern**, *Ixobrychus minutus,* has all the shape-shifting plasticity and secretive manner of its close relatives, but on a miniature scale. It is the smallest species of heron in Europe and its light weight – no more than a small orange (5½ ounces/157gm) – enables it to move through dense reed with supreme agility. It can easily clamber to the top of large reed stems, where it will occasionally sit hunched and compressed like a huge, bizarre warbler.

While it is a summer visitor to wetland habitats along the Channel coasts of France, Belgium and the Netherlands, it is usually recorded in Britain and Ireland only when migrants overshoot these continental destinations. There have been more than 350 records, and singles and pairs have regularly been seen in suitable habitat during the breeding season. In the nineteenth century nesting was suspected at Norfolk (South Walsham Broad), the county with the greatest number of Little Bittern records. Last century summering birds were present in Kent (1947), Surrey (1956), Huntingdonshire (1958), West Glamorgan (1976) and Somerset (1970). Yet there was seldom stronger evidence of breeding than the male's curious spring call – a short repeated croak that sounds halfway between a loud frog and a hoarse dog. However, 1984 brought the first ever confirmed breeding record when three young were reared at Potterick Carr in South Yorkshire.[29]

Black-crowned Night Heron, *Nycticorax nycticorax.* Usually known more simply as the night heron, this is a strikingly attractive species with white underparts and completely pearl-grey upper wings, offset by patches of glossy black on the back and crown. The bird is nocturnal and rather secretive in habits, roosting in thick bushy cover by day and emerging to feed with the onset of dusk. In poor light its compact shape and short rounded wings may give the impression of a large owl in flight, while the brown-coloured juvenile is more reminiscent of a bittern than a heron.

It has a wide, if fragmented, distribution across Europe and breeds as far north as the Netherlands. There have been more than 500 occurrences in Britain, but purists consider many records in these islands to be tainted by the presence of free-flying feral colonies at a number of well-known sites. Ornithological guilt was the background to the first attempt at introduction. In July 1868 Lord Lilford accidentally shot a bird on the River Nene and, 'in the hope of atoning in some measure for my offence, I turned out two young Night Herons at Lilford in the summer of 1887'.[30] These efforts came to nothing, but in 1936 a more enduring colony was established in the gardens of the Royal Zoological Society of Scotland, at Corstophine, Edinburgh. The original stock involved three pairs of the American race *hoactli*, and these slowly increased until the mid-1970s when they were estimated to number 40–50:

> The birds flight regularly in the evening from the park to feed in burns, pools, and marshes around Edinburgh . . . returning to the zoo in the early morning. At least eight nesting sites are known to exist inside the zoo; at one time these were confined to three separate areas; the tall trees in the garden to the south of the Fellows' House; near the gate leading to the vegetable garden at the eastern end of the crane enclosure; and in the trees and bushes around the sea-lion pool.[31]

Since that time the Edinburgh colony has become less prone to wandering, breeds entirely within the zoo and is 'apparently wholly dependent upon captive conditions and artificial feeding'.[32] However a similar free-flying colony of about 30 birds at Great Witchingham Park, Norfolk, stills casts an uncertain shadow over some night herons seen in eastern England. Most of the accepted records refer to birds found in spring, but in 1996 two birds stayed for much of the spring and summer at Dungeness, Kent. In 1997 five were present for a similar period in Holkham Park, Norfolk, and two at Shapwick Heath, Somerset, the birds raising hopes of the species' imminent colonisation.

The **Green Heron**, *Butorides virescens,* is a tiny green-backed species roughly the same length as a coot but only about a quarter of its weight (6 ounces/170gm). It has a wide range across four continents, mainly in the southern hemisphere, the nearest breeding colony to Britain being on Egypt's Red Sea coast.

Yet the four British records are thought to have been birds of the American race, *virescens*, which some regard as a separate species from those occurring in the Old World (the African and Asian populations are known variously as green-backed, striated or mangrove heron, *B. striatus*). The first ever to appear in Europe was found near St Austell, Cornwall, in October 1889, when it was shot by a gamekeeper after the exhausted bird was almost caught by his spaniel. It was then sent to a Bristol taxidermist where it was spotted by chance by a west

Cattle egret by name but not always by nature. The birds will follow in the wake of most types of livestock or wild game after the insects flushed by trampling hooves.

country birdwatcher, M. A. Mathew, who sent it to the British Museum.[33]

It took more than 80 years before the possibility of an escapee was finally discounted and the green heron was accepted on to the British list. It took more than 90 years, however, for the species to recur, when a second bird turned up at Stone Creek, Humberside, in November 1982. On this occasion it shared the same drainage ditch with a great egret, *Egretta alba*, a species breeding no nearer than the Netherlands, and of which there had been just 23 previous records.[34]

Squacco Heron, *Ardeola ralloides*. This is a rather inelegant name for one of the most beautiful herons in Europe and is thought to derive from a local Italian word imitating the bird's harsh voice. It is a small, compact and rather solitary species, but in summer the adults are distinguished by ochreous or golden buff lacy plumes all down their back, and long, narrow dark-edged crown feathers, which form a sumptuous head-dress. At the height of the breeding season the normally greenish legs also become bright pink or coral-red, and the basal half of the bill turns from green to steel-blue. Even more dramatic than this seasonal transformation is the bird's metamorphosis once it flies, when an essentially light-brown creature suddenly seems to turn almost pure white.

It has appeared in Britain and Ireland on a little over 100 occasions, normally when birds migrating out of Africa overshoot their breeding grounds in southern Europe. Many of the British birds occurred in the nineteenth century and there was a marked reduction in records after the first quarter of the twentieth century, when the species' continental population suffered severe persecution for the plume trade (see Little Egret, page 48). More recently the bird has been strongly affected by loss of wetland habitat and has declined throughout much of Europe.

Cattle Egret, *Bubulcus ibis*. Although there have been barely more than 100 records of this small, short-legged, stubby-billed egret, it has a truly global range embracing six continents and is a contender as the world's most cosmopolitan bird. Its meteoric expansion is also considered 'one of the great avian success stories'.[35] It colonised South America from Africa in the 1930s, then pressed northwards deep into Mesoamerica and the USA, while achieving a parallel invasion of Australia and New Zealand during the 1960s.

It was once known as the buff-backed heron because of long hair-like ginger-coloured plumes extending down its back during the breeding season. But this is something of a misnomer and for most of the year it simply looks white. The current name derives from its habit of feeding on invertebrates disturbed by grazing animals. 'When the particular cow that a Cattle Egret is feeding by moves quickly to another part of the pasture the bird will often trot after it with a comical-looking shambling gait . . . When it has seen potential prey the Cattle Egret stalks it, takes aim with an odd little waggle of its head that always reminds me of a golfer addressing the ball, and then catches it . . . with a quick lunge.'[36]

In South Africa the species had a reputation as a tick-bird and was believed to clean cattle of their parasites; it was even introduced into parts of Australia because of its presumed favour to livestock farmers. Cattle egrets do occasionally pick off flies and ticks, but these are not a major part of their diet. However, the distinguished ornithologist, Derek Goodwin, 'once saw a Cattle Egret behave in a remarkable way':

It was in Egypt (during the Second World War) and a rather miserable-looking water buffalo was lying down on the bare, sun-baked earth outside its owner's mud-walled house. A Cattle Egret was standing by its head and . . . eating flies that clustered thickly at the corners of the buffalo's eyes. It caught the flies in the usual way except that, instead of stabbing fiercely forward to seize them, it picked them very gently, obviously not causing the least discomfort to the buffalo.[37]

The bird's association with livestock partly explains its recent success, the egret spreading with the expansion of ranching in the southern hemisphere. But cattle are not the only herbivores with which the birds associate. In Africa they will just as readily feed beneath the trampling feet of most wild game species, but especially wild buffalo and hippopotamus. In Europe they will piggy-back the merino sheep of Extremadura or ride through the marshes of the Camargue on its famous white horses.

They are also an increasingly common sight in the middle of Mediterranean and subtropical cities, feeding on traffic islands or waste ground and rubbish dumps, where their normally immaculate plumage becomes sullied with urban grime. At dusk large flocks of cattle egrets moving to their traditional roost sites can be an impressive natural addition to the usual scenes of rush-hour traffic. In some places they are actually a part of the daily human exodus. In Morocco and Abu Dhabi it has been shown that cattle egrets use roads as a navigational aid, flying above the man-made route and following it through all its arbitrary twists and turns until they reach the roost.[38]

Almost nine-tenths of all the British records have occurred in the last 30 years, reflecting the species' more leisurely colonisation of central Europe, which has now advanced as far as northern France. Prior to 1970 there had been just 14 birds, and some of the pre-war records were complicated by the release during the 1930s of cattle egrets of the Asiatic race *coromanda*, by both the Zoological Society at Whipsnade Zoo and Mr A. Ezra of Cobham, Surrey. 'These birds have wandered in all directions and have been reported . . . as far apart as Devon, Somerset, Monmouth, Wiltshire, Leicester, Notts, Merioneth, Kent, Essex, Cambridge, Norfolk, Lincs, Perth, and even Iceland.' Eventually the feral egrets could be recognised by rings on their legs bearing the legend 'Zoo, London'.[39]

Little Egret, *Egretta garzetta*. This medium-sized all-white heron, with its distinctive yellow feet and black legs, is one of the most successful colonists of Britain in recent times and a possible beneficiary of global warming. Prior to 1957 there had been just 23 little-egret records ever in Britain, and even by 1990 there were barely more than 600. Yet since that date there have been as many as 1000 birds on the British and Irish coasts at any one time, although precise numbers are difficult to assess because of their high mobility between sites.

The British population is part of a much wider European expansion that started in the 1950s. Some little egrets began increasingly to spend their winters on the Atlantic coasts of first Spain and then France, until finally establishing a breeding outpost in Brittany in 1960. This was consolidated for 20 years and formed the launch pad for the bird's eventual crossing of the English Channel.

The first ever breeding record in Britain came in 1996 at Brownsea Island Nature Reserve, near Poole in Dorset, followed a year later by the first Irish record. The birds breeding at an undisclosed location in County Cork now form an incipient colony of up to 12 pairs, while the egrets at Brownsea have increased to five pairs. In 1997 another pair successfully bred at an undisclosed location in Hampshire.[40] The species is still most common as an autumn and winter visitor to sites in south-west England, like the Exe and Tamar estuaries. Here the birds stand out so clearly against the sombre wetland landscape that they are easily picked out from passing trains.

Feeding little egrets seem to have two distinct personae. Much of the time they stand silent, almost somnolent, at the water's edge with the long neck and bill withdrawn into the breast to give them a hunched, sunken-shouldered appearance. On other occasions they break into a frenzy of fishing activity, sploshing through the shallows in an almost balletic feeding dance, with the wings half-opening and shutting as the bird adjusts its balance, until it comes within range of scattering fish fry, when it stabs down with great precision.

The little egret helped shape the course of international bird conservation.

Dressed to kill – this old sense of style caused the deaths of many tens of millions of egrets and other birds.

In the breeding season little egrets acquire an even greater elegance with the assumption of lacy plumes on the back of the crown, breast and mantle. These are strikingly beautiful and, while it would be hyperbole to say that they changed the world, it would not be exaggerating to suggest that these feathers helped shape the course of British and international bird conservation.

For centuries egret plumes had been used in human costume, especially hats. As early as the seventeenth century Willughby had written of 'their use in caps and head pieces for ornament, and which are sold very dear in the cities subject to the Turk'.[41] In the nineteenth century the craze for colourful or decorative bird feathers hit the three traditional centres of high fashion – London, Paris and New York – to such an extent that the ornithologist Frank Chapman, walking the streets of the American city, noted 40 species of bird in 700 women's hats.[42] The resulting trade was on a global scale and involved birds right across the spectrum from ostriches to humming-birds.

However, the highly elaborate plumes found in the breeding plumage of many herons were especially favoured. Their spring scapulars can have a delicate gauze-like structure and in a species like the great egret they can reach almost 20 inches (50cm) long. Feathers used in the millinery trade were known rather oddly as 'osprey' through a false association with 'spray', which presumably described their overall shape and effect.

To some, the entire business was a source of fabulous wealth. In 1914 in India 1 ounce (28gm) of feathers was trading at 10–28 times the value of an equivalent weight in silver; when smuggled into Europe they were fetching as much as £15 an ounce, which represents about £875 at today's values. One response to the booming enterprise was the development of egret farms, where breeding birds were held in pens of up to 60 pairs. When the eggs hatched, the brood was removed and hand-reared, allowing the egrets to re-lay. Sometimes a pair was raising four to five broods a season. The adults were then plucked four times a year without being killed, each bird producing a little over ⅓ ounce (9gm) of feathers.[43]

However, the principal means of obtaining egret

Proto-environmentalists publicised the grotesque slaughter involved in Edwardian fashions in July 1911.

plumes – because wild birds were thought to produce the most pristine sprays – was through snaring and shooting the breeding colonies. The exact scale of the slaughter has never been decisively established, with estimates ranging widely between five million and 200 million birds annually. It is known, however, that in the first quarter of 1885 a total of 750,000 egret skins were sold on the London market, that in 1887 a single dealer handled two million skins, and that in an 11-month period of 1906 the feathers sold in London showrooms weighed 37,000 ounces (1050kg).[44] While the great nineteenth-century ornithologist Alfred Newton calculated that a kilogram represented 150 herons, other authorities have suggested that it could have taken as many as 300 great egrets or 1000 little egrets to produce that weight of feathers.

In Britain one of the responses to this carnage was the foundation in 1889 at Didsbury, Manchester, of the Society for the Protection of Birds by a group of pioneering female conservationists. One of their goals was 'inducing a considerable number of women of all ranks and ages to unite in discouraging the enormous destruction of bird life exacted by milliners and others for purely decorative purposes'.[45] The one indulgence these high-minded ladies allowed themselves was the use of farmed ostrich feathers. Fifteen years later their pioneer organisation received a royal warrant and became known as the Royal Society for the Protection of Birds, which has eventually blossomed into the largest wildlife NGO in Europe, with more than a million members.

The legal suppression of the plume trade did not come into full effect in Britain until 1920, and even this outright ban was widely circumvented by illegal trappers and dealers. Fortunately one of the striking aspects of its aftermath was the remarkable recuperative power of egret populations. The little-egret expansion into central Europe as well as Britain and Ireland represents the vanguard of that ongoing recovery.

Great Egret, *Egretta alba*. Apart from the three species of swan, this is the largest all-white bird occurring in Britain and Ireland and, except for a completely albino grey heron or a distant little egret, it is unmistakable. The only source of confusion is its name, which at various

The grey heron is the most widespread large predatory bird in Britain and Ireland.

times and in various parts of its near-global range, has been 'large egret', 'great egret', 'greater egret', 'great white egret', 'great white heron' and, across the Atlantic, 'American egret'. Great egret seems now to have gained a final dominance. A recent range extension and a substantial increase in the breeding populations of eastern Europe have mirrored the greater frequency of British records, which now stand at about 115. More than 85 per cent of these have occurred since 1978.

Grey Heron, *Ardea cinerea*. VN: Frank (mainly northern England); Harnser, Old Frank (East Anglia); Johnny Crane (Lancashire); Hegri, Haigrie (Shetland); Heronshaw (Bedfordshire, Cambridgeshire); Norry-the-bogs [its Gaelic equivalent is *Síle na bportaigh*] (County Kerry); Julie-the-bogs [*Nóra na bportaigh*] (Cork). If the great bittern has captured our imagination by its rarity and shyness, then the grey heron has achieved a similar prominence by sheer adaptability and success. Almost the size of a golden eagle, it is the most widespread large predatory bird in Britain and Ireland and is as familiar a sight over the city centre as it is above the wildest Scottish loch. The bird's slate-grey plumage, its slow and rather laboured flight on broad wings,

together with that characteristic aerial profile – the long trailing legs and dagger-like bill extending beyond the forward thrust of its bulging neck – make it unmistakable even to the most untrained eye.

Herons have flourished particularly in the era of increased environmental awareness and while there is some illegal persecution by fishing interests, heron numbers have risen by one-third in the last 30 years. With 6000–6300 nests in England alone, the population is probably higher than at any time since records began and the total for all four countries is estimated at about 13,650 pairs. It breeds across the entire archipelago with the only significant gaps in the central Scottish Highlands north of the Great Glen, the Cairngorm region and parts of central Ireland. Usually requiring tall trees as a nest site, grey herons are sufficiently flexible in breeding habit to have representative populations in the virtually treeless Shetland and Orkney.

Owing to their habit of nesting communally in early spring, when their big stick-built platforms stand out in the leafless canopy, breeding grey herons have been easy to find and count. Largely as a consequence, the British Trust for Ornithology (BTO) has organised virtually

The heronry in London's Regent's Park was established in 1968 and has expanded in line with the bird's national increase.

annual sample studies of the heron population for more than 70 years. These have been punctuated by full countrywide surveys in 1928, 1954, 1964 and 1985. Together they represent one of the most complete sets of population data for any bird in Britain and the 'longest-running single-species survey in the world'.[46]

Tall mature trees are the most common nesting location, although grey herons have been recorded to use a variety of other situations: amid small pools on a beach, on islands in the middle of lochs and lakes, on the ground beneath a conifer plantation, on low bushes and on hillsides amid heather and bracken. Sea cliffs are a regular location for northern heronries, and at one time accounted for 7 per cent of all Scottish colonies. One impressive example, about 80 feet (25m) from the base of a cliff near the Point of Ardnamurchan, once included hundreds of birds, but was finally abandoned in the 1930s after decades of use.[47]

While heron colonies can be short-lived associations, some can be both centuries old and can involve hundreds of birds. In the late eighteenth century Thomas Pennant saw a well-known heronry at Cressy Hall, near Spalding, Lincolnshire, which he claimed was so crowded that he counted an improbable 80 nests in a single oak tree.[48] Twenty-five nests is the highest documented total in a

single tree. A more trustworthy record refers to a heronry in the small triangle formed by the Sussex towns or villages of Beckley, Udimore and Rye, for which there is documentary evidence dating back to 1297. In 1840 it was said to comprise 400 nests, one of the largest heronries ever recorded in Britain. Yet the fortunes of heronries can fluctuate wildly and without apparent cause. Typically by 1896 the colony had dwindled to just 15 pairs, only to recover again to 119 nests by 1930, followed by another dip to 38 by 1993.[49]

The current largest British colony is now at Northward Hill RSPB reserve in north Kent, where there were 156 pairs in 2001, an impressive number, although representing a decline from the peak count of 234 pairs in 1983. The nests are spread across a north-facing ancient oak wood in trees of about 65 feet (20m) height and, although the heronry is closed to the public to prevent disturbance, occasional visits are made by the warden, Alan Parker, and his staff to count the birds:

Entry is gained by pushing through dense brambles into the edge of the oakwoods. Since the great hurricane of 1987 the formerly bare ground has been colonised by dense bramble and elder. This impedes progress, but also ensures that we are smeared with generous amounts of fishy heron droppings which coat the bushes, and occasionally fall from above. The smell is impressive. Noise is everywhere, the constant *ekk ekk ekk* calls of begging youngsters, rising to a deafening crescendo when food arrives, and the various calls of the adults mask the song of nearby nightingales. As we move quietly through the woods, calling herons leave and circle above us, while those birds already disturbed return to their nests, or stand grumpily in a group outside the wood. Nests become denser – up to 10 in a tree – and the risk of an unpleasant reminder of the heron's diet increases.

Herons often void their stomach contents when disturbed at the nest, and to be hit on the head by a half-digested eel, the head end melted away by the bird's strong stomach acids, is not unknown! Heron pellets also splatter down. These large versions of the familiar owl pellets are wet when fresh and often break up, but many intact examples lie around and are quickly gathered up for later inspection. Under the trees we see further evidence of a range of prey, dropped during the youngsters' tussles when adults arrive with food. Mostly these are eels or fish (could that be a goldfish?) but the grey, furry pellets, and the skulls inside, show the herons' preference for water voles. The skulls of rats and the horny wing cases of water beetles also regularly survive the digestive process, but fish remain only as a smell. While counting we also see sad reminders of the fate of any young which fall from the nests, dried-up corpses hung up in the branches.

Anxious not to retrace our steps and disturb the birds again, we force our way out into the bright light through dense bracken, and return to the office for a thorough wash, a change of clothes and a tense period of comparing notes and adding up, although we have to wait for a repeat visit later in the season to be sure of the final total.[50]

The species' preference for tall mature trees has ensured that many heronries are in old parkland and on long-established estates, where they were historically welcomed as a valuable resource. From the early medieval period until at least the nineteenth century, the grey heron, like the bittern, was an important and relatively expensive table item. In 1517 a wood belonging to an abbot in Somerset yielded a seasonal return of about 100 young herons. At the officially decreed rate for the period, the herons were worth as much as £8 8s., a small fortune in the early sixteenth century.[51]

The heron's fish diet suggests that eating its flesh required a strong stomach. Brian Vesey-Fitzgerald wrote,

Grey herons nest communally and some heronries have been in continuous use for hundreds of years.

'I have eaten heron and found it a loathsome experience', while W. H. Hudson reported that it 'was tough and had a NASTY TASTE'.[52] Yet earlier palates were completely unfazed. A sixteenth-century commentator thought bittern 'not so hard of digestion as is a Heron', but also noted that 'A young Heron is lighter of digestion than a Crane'.[53] Known as 'branchers', the young birds were widely viewed as the most flavoursome and tender, and were captured off the nest or nearby with a long pole and hook. They were then held in a fattening aviary or 'stew'.

Roast heron was especially relished at state banquets and ceremonial occasions. In 1465 at Lord Neville's celebrations for his appointment as Archbishop of York, 400 herons were listed on the menu. It remained a highly popular dish in the sixteenth and seventeenth centuries, and even in 1812 'the executors of Thomas Sutton, founder of the London Charterhouse, gave a feast . . . when amongst the joints and game roasts were included six herons'.[54] Max Nicholson pointed out that 'as lately as the [1830s] Lord Carnarvon's friends at Pixton – now Allers Wood (Somerset) – ate them skinned, stuffed and roasted like hare, with strawberries and cream to follow, and up to at least 1896 the young were largely shot for eating on Romney Marsh'.[55]

Pond owners occasionally put out plastic herons to deter the real thing from coming to eat their fish. Unfortunately the sight of one 'heron' can actually act as a lure to its neighbours.

While this form of harvest was widespread, for hundreds of years the favourite method of catching herons was undoubtedly with hawk or peregrine. The grey heron was among the most cherished quarry species in the sport of falconry. The soul of the contest in what appeared a well-matched encounter was the struggle by the larger heron to fly higher than its opponent: 'Now if the hawk getteth the upper place he overthroweth and vanquisheth the heron with marvellous earnest flight.' In return it was believed that the heron could spear its assailant with its dagger-like bill. In fact, this was highly improbable and just as unlikely was the belief that the heron 'routs Eagles and Hawks, if they attack it suddenly, by very liquid mutings of the belly', which were thought to rot the raptor's feathers.[56]

Although the sport inflicted continuous losses on heron numbers, falconry was especially popular among the nobility and, from the king downwards, there was a self-interested concern to protect the bird from other forms of exploitation. In the fifteenth century there were stringent statutes outlawing the collection of heron eggs and the use of firearms within 600 yards (550m) of a heronry. A law in the late sixteenth century imposed a heavy fine for killing birds with gun or bow. A second offence was punishable with the loss of the right hand, and a third offence could incur a death sentence. Protective legislation enacted by James I remained on the statute books until the nineteenth century.

In many ways the fortunes of British grey herons have been a perfect barometer of shifting social and cultural patterns in the countryside. The popularity of falconry had conferred almost 500 years of legislative protection, but by the nineteenth century the pastime had virtually disappeared. The development of angling as a major sport, especially for trout and salmon, converted the heron from the falconer's cherished quarry into the fisherman's main competitor.

With their long legs and neck, as well as the predator's classic blend of intense concentration and inexhaustible patience, herons are supreme finders and catchers of fish. One of my strongest childhood memories involves a bird flushed from the banks of a tiny Derbyshire stream below our garden. Unusually, the heron was caught unawares and it had to run from beneath overhanging trees before rising into its steady rhythmic beat. In some ways more captivating than the heron were the two medium-sized trout at the water's edge, which it had regurgitated in response to danger. Most extraordinary of all, however, was the fact that they lay by a stream in which I had never once before seen a fish.

A patient stalk through the shallows is the standard *modus operandi*, but herons have also been known to land on the back of cormorants and rob them of their fish, to steal food from a bittern, to wade into the water and swim like a duck, to dive into a deep dyke like a grebe and surface with a 2-pound (900-gm) pike. At Abberton Reservoir, Essex, up to seven herons were recorded plunge-diving from the air, while another heron was seen 'fishing near a crowd of gulls and divers a quarter of a mile out to sea from Aberystwyth; after trying once to get a fish it rose easily from the water and returned to the rocks'.[57]

Their adaptability also extends to fishing by electric lamp:

while travelling along the M4 in Greater London, I passed Queen Mother Reservoir. It was quite dark, but the nearest edge of water was illuminated by lights from the motorway. In this small crescent of light there were five to seven Grey Herons ... standing within 2–3m of each other in characteristic hunting stance. They were presumably able to fish in the artificial light, which, in view of the number of herons in such a small area, may well have been also attracting fish.[58]

Bleak, carp, chub, eel, flounder, grayling, gudgeon, lamprey, miller's thumb, minnow, perch, pike, roach, rudd, salmon, stickleback, sturgeon, trout and stale kippers have all been recorded in the diet.[59] But many dubious fishing tales have accreted to the heron's genuine prowess. The account in the *Irish Times* of a bird taking a 4-pound (1.8-kg) salmon grilse probably lies in the realm of fantasy. Despite its ecclesiastical credentials, so too does the statement of Bishop Stanley that a dead bird in Scotland contained 39 trout. Barely more credible is the word of a Scottish keeper and the head watcher of the Loch Lomond Angling Association, who estimated the weight of a sea-trout taken from a heron's stomach at 3 pounds (1.35kg).[60]

Fish skeletons found beneath nest trees are far stronger evidence. Near a nest site in Montgomeryshire was a 'perfect chub skeleton measuring twelve inches' (30cm), and specimens up to 14 inches (33.6cm) long have occurred. It was apparently 'fright which caused a brood of young herons in Dam Wood to throw up two eighteen-inch-long eels and a water-vole'.[61]

Although fish form the main diet, herons readily adjust their hunting techniques to other prey. For dietary eccentricity little compares with the stories of semi-tame herons that seized and swallowed a Persian kitten, lumps of beef, or ripe plums stones and all.[62] However, moles, water voles, mice and rats are more routine dietary supplements. In Berwickshire a heron was once recorded hunting for rats in a sheep-yard, and T. A. Coward saw one eat five rats in succession. 'Twenty-four herons walking line abreast over a newly-cut oat-field were probably rodent hunting.' Stoat and weasel have both been recorded as prey, while the list of birds is long and varied: little grebe, the young of moorhen and mallard, the chicks of lesser black-backed gull, adult water rail, redshank, hoopoe, blackbird (grabbed off a birdtable), robin, starling (caught in mid-air) and sparrow.[63]

In the summer of 1987 we were visiting the bird reserve at Holme, in Norfolk. As we watched a heron flapped languidly to a point on the edge of the lagoon just a few yards from a female shoveler and a single almost fully grown duckling. It flew slowly over them, landed and in a flash struck down with its bill at the duckling, grabbed the bird and continued in flight a few yards further on to the bank. The adult shoveler seemed to experience a few moments of confusion but seconds later started feeding once again as if nothing

Two grey herons are clearly visible in the stained-glass window in Selborne Church, Hampshire.

had happened. We sat in stunned silence and were amazed by the speed of the whole affair – the incident lasting just a few seconds – the agility of the heron as it snatched the duckling, the large size of the prey and the ferocity with which the attack was completed.[64]

Awed and envious of the heron's capabilities at catching fish, humans have sought various explanations for the success. These include the notion that the heron's powder down is luminous, allowing it to fish by night; or that the bird exudes a fish-attracting oil; or that hairs on the heron's legs play in the water and entice the fish; or that they shake their body scales on to the surface to act as bait, or wriggle their toes to simulate worms. Some thought they could harness the heron's gifts by utilising its body parts. In *The Compleat Angler* Izaak Walton suggested that 'any bait anointed with the marrow of the thigh-bone of a heron, is a great temptation to any fish'.[65] Unfortunately for Walton's theory there is no marrow in a heron's thigh-bone.

In the eighteenth century John Williamson recommended to fellow anglers the following preparation: 'Heron's bowels cut in pieces, and put into a phial and buried in horse-dung, will turn to oil in fifteen days; an ounce of asafoetida is then mixed, when it will be the consistency of honey.'[66] Smeared on the fishing line, this apparently worked wonders in the west of Ireland. For the modern fisherman, however, simple deference seems to suffice: 'It is customary in the Scottish Borders to raise one's hat on seeing a heron and wish it "Good Morning". Not to do so would bring bad luck.'[67] The fisherman's envy also led to outright persecution during the nineteenth and early twentieth centuries. Even by 1928, the date of the first national census of British herons, its coordinator, Max Nicholson, found:

> the counties in which Herons are shown to be killed on a large scale are Derby, Devon (parts), Gloucester, Hampshire, Hereford, Leicester, Lincoln (part), Northumberland (?), Nottingham, Westmorland, Wiltshire, Yorkshire (parts), Anglesey and Caernarvonshire. In some of these areas the campaign is so well organised and financed that the Heron as a breeding species is unable, or practically unable, to survive, and those areas appear to act as a drain on the Heron population as a whole . . . in a county north of the border . . . on every Thursday regularly the keepers turn out over the whole length of a certain river and shoot all Herons, Cormorants, Dippers, and birds considered destructive to fish.[68]

Although the grey heron has enjoyed full legal protection for decades, the wish to neutralise its fishing prowess has not diminished. However a government-authorised licence is now required to shoot individual birds and this is only granted where serious economic loss can be proven, a condition that disqualifies all except fish farms and similar establishments. However, the artificially high concentration of the heron's usual prey creates its own self-defeating syndrome and the elimination of one bird usually just creates space for its replacement.

The more usual method of tackling heron depredations involves some form of deterrent, which is especially popular with keepers of garden ponds. There are apocryphal tales of single birds cleaning out thousands of pounds' worth of ornamental fish, and a whole range of scaring techniques have been employed. The most effective are a complete net covering of the water surface and a barrier cordon around the pond, since herons dislike stepping over objects to reach water. Although a series of intersecting wires alone does not always work: 'A fish farmer near Selkirk reported that herons were back in numbers and feeding under the lines. Myself and a colleague borrowed a night vision scope and were amazed to see that the birds were gliding down, "feeling" for the fishing lines and then dropping through into the pond when a gap was found.'[69]

More high-tech methods marketed by one company include a ghetto blaster wired up to a photocell, which triggers a loop tape of the grey heron's alarm call, prefaced by a recording of dustbin lids being clashed together. A less successful technique is the deployment of life-size model herons, based on the notion that herons are territorial and will be discouraged by a rival. In practice, herons are often communal feeders and the presence of a plastic lookalike only serves to alert another bird to a potential food source.

The **Purple Heron**, *Ardea purpurea*, is something of a curiosity. It is an annual visitor in very small numbers to Britain and Ireland, mainly in spring and summer. But a quarter of a century ago it seemed to hold out the promise of colonisation as a breeding species. By the 1970s the bird had expanded its range in central Europe and had increased substantially in the Netherlands, only then to suffer a reversal of fortunes throughout much of Europe. While it still nests in northern France and the formerly thriving Dutch colonies are only 200 miles (320km) from the East Anglian coast, breeding birds have never surmounted the Channel.

The purple heron is more silent, more secretive, more beautiful and, paradoxically, less attractive than the resident grey. The inelegance derives from the big feet, a longer, finer bayonet-like bill and an even longer neck. When airborne, that pipe-like extension bulges in a pronounced inverted S. On the ground it often gives the bird a distinctly primitive, reptilian appearance. When the purple heron freezes in alarm, the bird's upperparts can resemble an inanimate object: 'when fully stretched out, it can easily be passed off as a stick or branch growing amongst the reeds'.[70]

The purple heron's counter-claim to beauty is founded on its rich blend of colours, which is most striking on a breeding adult: the chestnut-and-cream neck broken by narrow vertical lines of black, the slate upperparts glossed with purple, the rich dark vinous underwings and the lanceolate plumes of cinnamon chestnut on the lower mantle.

Stork family *Ciconiidae*

Black Stork, *Ciconia nigra*. Unlike the bold, gregarious, farmland-dwelling white stork, this handsome relative is shy, solitary and an inhabitant of woodland and forest swamp. It is also far less common in Europe than its better-known cousin and has none of the latter's fertility symbolism. There are an estimated 10,000 pairs in Europe compared with 125,000 white storks, but while the latter is widely declining, the black stork is expanding its range, increasing in number and enjoys a far wider Asian and African distribution. In Britain and Ireland, however, it remains no more than a rare vagrant with under 150 records.

White Stork, *Ciconia ciconia*. The remarkable tolerance which these charismatic birds show towards human beings, their adoption of man-made structures as a nest site (including anything from medieval cathedrals to satellite installations), and feeding habits that are highly beneficial to the farmer are all at work in the white storks' status as one of the world's most familiar and beloved birds. The appearance of huge north-bound flocks migrating out of Africa at the onset of the growing season has also helped cement their place as a Europe-wide emblem of spring and fertility for thousands of years. This explains the guise in which this bird is more frequently encountered in literature and other media – as the bearer of human babies.

Yet the British and Irish have made little contribution to the vast body of lore surrounding Europe's great avian symbol. The only known breeding record is of a pair that nested on St Giles Church in the middle of Edinburgh in 1416. Otherwise it is no more than an irregular visitor in small numbers to these islands, with a maximum of about 50 in any calendar year. Stork records have come from the whole of Britain and Ireland, but with greatest frequency in the south and east.

In the seventeenth century Sir Thomas Browne was well aware of the stork's occasional appearance in the Norfolk Broads. Unfortunately many of the birds appearing in these earlier centuries were shot and killed, suggesting that the species' reputation as a general good-luck charm had little significance for British fowlers. In more recent times visiting storks have met with new attitudes – and new hazards.

In April 1967 there was a notable influx of at least 13 individuals on the east coast of England, two of which took up residence on Halvergate Marshes, Norfolk. The birds remained for eight months and roosted each evening on

White storks have been regular if rare visitors to Britain and Ireland for hundreds of years.

one of two derelict drainage mills, 'sleeping side by side on the sails'. They were even seen to perform short evening courtship displays as they alighted on the structure:

By the first week of October, however, both storks were feeding close to the A47 Yarmouth to Acle trunk road. Reports of the birds quickly reached the local press and from then onwards they were spotted daily ... As winter progressed, the storks began accepting food from road workmen and by Christmas this had become a regular habit. One December afternoon, a police motor cyclist found them both on the actual roadway!

High winds on December 27th brought disaster when one stork apparently collided with overhead power cables. It was quickly picked up and placed in a cowshed where the body shortly disappeared. The surviving stork remained close to the New Road until early April 1968 despite fears for its survival. At the height of the frosty weather it was fed daily by more

The white stork is the classic symbol of fertility throughout Europe. Sadly there have been just two nesting attempts in Britain – in Edinburgh in 1416 and in West Yorkshire during 2004.

than one Yarmouth naturalist and funds were made available by the RSPCA.[1]

Occasionally it has been possible to chart the exact movements and point of origin of the storks passing through Britain, as in the case of three sibling birds seen in south-west England in 1971. They first appeared on 9 September at Combe Down, near Bath. On the same day one of the storks fell down a large school chimney and was taken into captivity, while the other two moved on to Cornwall. They remained there for over a week and were last sighted flying high over St Mary's in the Scilly Isles on 18 September. Three days later one of the two birds was found 'in a bad condition' 1200 miles (2000km) away on Madeira. Both birds bore rings on their right legs and, from the serial numbers on these, it was possible to establish that they had fledged at Frøstrup, north Jutland, in Denmark, leaving the nest at 11.00 hours on 6

September. The lone bird in Madeira had thus covered the entire journey in just 15 days.[2]

In some ways, just as remarkable as the odyssey performed by the fledglings was the life history of their parents. The mother had flown into a telephone wire 11 years earlier and, when taken into care by a local farmer, had lost the use of her right wing. However her new custodian kept the bird in his garden and placed her in an outhouse during the winter. He also sited a cartwheel on a post 6½ feet (2m) off the ground as a nest platform, complete with a ladder for the flightless bird to climb up. In the spring of 1968 a male arrived and the pair mated, rearing a brood of four young. Although the male migrated south in the first autumn, thereafter he stayed with his invalid mate every winter. The pair were fed mainly with pails of fish-heads provided free of charge by a local fishmonger, and every year people came from all over Denmark and from abroad to visit this celebrated bird family.[3]

Ibis and Spoonbill family
Threskiornithidae

Glossy Ibis, *Plegadis falcinellus.* Superficially like a long-legged, all-dark curlew, the glossy ibis is an extremely beautiful bird, particularly in spring when the whole of the upper body is a deep rich burgundy and the wings and scapulars are glossed with iridescent green and purple. It has a wide transcontinental range, although in Europe it is confined largely to southern Mediterranean and Balkan wetlands and even in these areas numbers have been severely reduced by habitat loss.

Its presence in Britain and Ireland relies on long-distance wanderers, with a flock of about 20 in Orkney in 1907 representing the largest single group. Records declined steeply during the twentieth century in line with the bird's reduction elsewhere, and since 1957 it has appeared on fewer than 80 occasions, mainly in coastal counties, with only a handful of records from Ireland.

The birds are mainly brief autumn or winter visitors, with the notable exception of an ibis that appeared at Stodmarsh, Kent, on 14 December 1975. The bird recurred for four years until it was joined by a second on 28 October 1979. This ibis 'pair' ('one was smaller than the other with a relatively shorter bill and subtly different proportions') were Stodmarsh regulars until 1985 and maintained an extraordinarily precise routine:

At the time I was an RSPB Group Leader and regularly took parties round Stodmarsh in winter. I used to delight in demonstrating my apparent omniscience by positioning the group directly under the birds' flightline into roost and then announcing that they'd be along in so many minutes. Such was the regularity of their habits I'd scan eastwards at the appropriate time, pick them up as they flew in and they'd sail over our heads at the appointed moment! As long as you made sure your timing was okay by a few earlier visits it wasn't hard to do, but a great trick which always astonished my companions.[1]

The birds also wandered to other Kent wetlands and sometimes into neighbouring counties, but their lack of a genuine migratory instinct raised the possibility that they were escapees from captivity. Such misgivings hardly diminished the pleasure given to thousands of observers over their combined 17-year residence.

Eurasian Spoonbill, *Platalea leucorodia.* With spoonbills there seem to be no half-measures. Either they

When a pair of spoonbills bred successfully in eastern England in 1998 it was thought to be the first occasion for 330 years.

are asleep and immobile for hours on end, perched on one leg with the head and that long captivating 'spoon' invisible among their back and wing feathers, or they are engaged in intensive feeding activity. On these occasions the feet paddle vigorously, stirring up bottom sediments, while the bill is held fractionally open and scythes constantly back and forth through the shallows, creating a wake that regularly washes into the eyes. Suddenly a larger morsel necessitates an upward jerk of the head that flicks the prey to the back of the mouth, and then on the bird strides to resume its military semi-circular sweep.

Spoonbills are mainly scarce spring visitors to Britain and Ireland, with occasional wintering birds on estuaries in south-west England, County Cork and around Dublin. However a fivefold increase in the Dutch population to around 700 pairs by the late 1990s led to increased numbers summering on the east coast of England. In 1996 a flock of 19 at the RSPB's Minsmere reserve in Suffolk was the largest gathering for decades and raised the tantalising prospect of a recolonisation. This hope was fulfilled two years later, when a couple of fledged young at an undisclosed location finally ended a 330-year breeding absence.

Throughout the Middle Ages spoonbills had nested widely in southern England and parts of Wales. The long list of old names for the bird, such as 'shoveler' (later transferred to the duck, see page 97), 'shovelard', 'shoulard', 'pauper' and 'popelar' (with alternative spellings like 'popel', 'poppel', 'popler', 'popeler', 'popelere' and 'popard') suggests a long vernacular tradition and hints at the bird's familiarity as a table item. This is confirmed by sixteenth-century statutes protecting spoonbills from egg collectors and disturbance. In the year books of Henry VIII there is the report of a case of trespass brought by the Bishop of London against a defendant who had taken a lease on church land in Fulham. While the defendant had been grazing the ground with his livestock, he had also helped himself to the prelate's breeding colony of herons and spoonbills.[2]

As with the grey heron, spoonbills were considered most tender as nestlings, when they were known as 'branchers'. These were gathered from their breeding colony just as they were preparing to fledge. It was almost certainly such succulent youngsters that were served to Thomas Wolsey when he visited King's Lynn in the August of 1521 (the cardinal's table also groaned with other dishes including three bitterns, 10 cygnets, 12 capons, 13 plovers, eight pike and three tench).[3]

Adults were also apparently netted on the coast and then, according to one sixteenth-century account, 'fed in confinement on fish and the insides of fowls, and other offal from the kitchen'. In the eyes of Dr Thomas Moffet, once they had been 'taken home and dieted with new garbage and good meat, they are nothing inferior to fatted gulls'; strong praise indeed, given that gull meat was highly regarded.[4]

East Anglia was almost certainly the bird's British stronghold and there are records dating back to 1300 of a breeding colony in my home village of Claxton, Norfolk. More than 300 years later Sir Thomas Browne recorded a colony 'breeding upon topps of high trees' just across the Yare valley at Cantley and Reedham. However, by Browne's day habitat loss was already squeezing spoonbills out of their old English haunts.[5]

The drainage of the Fens under the direction of the Dutch engineer Cornelius Vermuyden in the mid-seventeenth century almost certainly eliminated an important breeding area. By the time Vermuyden's works were completed in 1651, the spoonbill was close to extinction. Yet there are one or two vestiges of its presence in what are now the great agricultural flat lands spread between Norfolk, Cambridge and Lincolnshire. On the eastern edge of the old Fens, near Feltwell and to the south-east of Wisbech, are two Poppylot Farms, celebrating an archaic name for the bird, which probably signified the proximity of old spoonbill colonies.[6]

Swan, Goose and Duck family *Anatidae*

Mute Swan, *Cygnus olor*. With their pure-white plumage and the slow, serene grace of all their movements upon the water, mute swans are the epitome of avian beauty. The species is also one of the largest flying birds in the world and its powerful wing strokes and the male's occasional territorial threat-display leave us in no doubt of its wild condition. But more usually there is an unparalleled aura of gentleness about mute swans. They are often the cherished recipients of the child's bag of bread scraps, and a tiny palmful of crumbs outstretched towards that long elegant head and neck is a classic scene in any city or town park.

Perhaps it is an image that gives us a clue to the swan's enduring appeal. The deep contrast between the benign manner and the sheer potential in a creature weighing anything up to 33 pounds (15kg) – and some of the largest have been almost 39 pounds (17.6kg) – reinforces a perception that this bird 'trusts' us, and vice versa. While the statistics seem to bear out the notion of mutual regard – the 45,000 adults in Britain and Ireland are roughly half the European total – there is a core irony attaching to the mute swan's 'friendly' character, because it is the product of an enormously long, essentially exploitative relationship between the British and one of their favourite birds.

Unlike any other wild species, mute swans were once considered to be the property of the crown, which granted rights of ownership to local dignitaries throughout the country. To ease their capture and prevent them straying too far, the birds had their wing tips cut off on one side, leaving them unable to fly. The characteristic and hugely impressive rhythmic throb of an airborne swan, which W. B. Yeats called the 'bell-beat of their wings', was virtually unknown in Britain for at least 500 years. This control of the population, and the ownership marks cut into the beaks of each individual bird, were geared towards serving the dining tables of the nation's first estate with one of their most prestigious dishes: roasted swan.

Historically it was the most expensive table item furnished by our wild avifauna. A large individual can

When mute swans arch their secondaries over their backs like this they look the very picture of avian grace, but it is, in fact, a threat display known as 'busking'.

yield a roast of anything up to 20 pounds (9kg), and sheer size seemed to cement its status as the most elevated of dishes. It was a classic feature of the banqueting table and there are records of Henry III issuing requests from York around the Christmas of 1251 for swans from across much of northern England. The total placed on the royal board that holiday season was 351 birds (about 3 ton(ne)s of swan flesh), giving an indication of the scale and sophistication of the English harvest.[1]

The whole business of managing and catching mute swans eventually came to be governed by a system of rules called the 'swan laws', the earliest known form of which dates from 1482. However these statutes almost certainly formalised customs that were centuries old, and even in 966 there are references to the Saxon King Edgar granting rights over local swans to the abbots of Croyland in Lincolnshire.[2] The central principle of the legislation was the bird's unique status as crown property, although ownership could be conferred on the king's subjects if their name was entered on to an official list of owners, known as the swan roll. This enormously prestigious right was reserved for substantial landowners

and, while it could be bought or bequeathed, it was always jealously guarded as an important status symbol.

Many of the affairs arising from the swan laws were overseen by a crown official called the Royal Swan Master, a title that has now been modified to Swan Marker. With his network of regional deputies, he ensured that most of the British population was caught each summer. The birds were seized using a long pole known as a swan-hook, enabling the ownership of adults to be established through examination of the pattern of cuts, notches or brands that each individual bore on its upper mandible, and sometimes in conjunction with other identifying marks on the webbed feet and the side on which the pinioning had been done. These swan marks are thought to have been a direct extension of the primitive brands first used on cattle and other stock, and the earliest known example was that for the prior of Coxford in Norfolk dating from 1230. Yet by the reign of Elizabeth I there were at least 900 registered marks in Britain.[3]

The capture of breeding adults also allowed swan officers to allocate the new generation of cygnets to their owners. Where mating had occurred between birds

A remarkable image of mutual trust that gives the lie to the old school-yard adage: 'beware of swans because they can break your arm with a single flap of their wings'.

bearing different marks, then the resulting brood was divided according to strict regulation. Any adult birds that were unmarked were automatically the property of the crown.

The foremost scholar on the mute swan's part in British cultural history was the eminent ornithologist Norman Ticehurst, who used local records of bird numbers from the sixteenth century to give an indication of the total swan population during Tudor times. He found that in 1587 there were 41 broods on the River Lea between Tottenham and Bishop's Stortford and, extrapolating from these figures, he calculated that the whole of the Lea and its tributaries held 700 birds. Based on similar sets of data, Ticehurst conservatively estimated that the Fens alone held a swan population of 24,000 birds, almost as many as the total in the last census for the whole of Britain.[4] Not only do the statistics demonstrate how the bird flourished despite heavy exploitation, but they conjure up an image of the Fens in their heyday as a wetland of extraordinary natural riches.

Although social prestige and the desire to keep up age-old rituals were integrally involved in these customs, the real engine driving the whole process was the English love of swan meat. In *The Canterbury Tales* Chaucer's epicurean monk selected it as his favourite roast, and no doubt the swan's presence on the feasting table was esteemed as much for its visual impact as for its piquant reputation. Birds were sometimes skinned unplucked, then roasted and reassembled in all their finery, 'with the added glory of gilded beak and feathers'.[5]

Even at the medieval peak of swan consumption, the cygnets were preferred before adults, although later palates found even these tender youngsters unappetising. The most frequently repeated adverse judgement is that of the seventeenth-century ornithologist Francis Willughby, who felt that: 'As the bird itself is far bigger than a goose so is its flesh blacker, harder and tougher having grosser Fibres hard of Digestion of a bad and melancholic Juice yet for its rarity serves as a dish to adorn great men's tables at feasts and entertainments being else in my opinion no desirable dainty.' Charles Darwin was less condemnatory, suggesting that the swan was neither fish nor fowl, 'but something halfway like Venison with Wild duck'.[6] Two contemporary opinions shadow the idea of swan meat's indeterminate quality ('like fishy mutton') or simply its resemblance to fish, with one noted ornithologist deeming it to be more fishy than gannet flesh.[7]

However, it was not loss of appetite that brought an end to the eating of swans. It was simple economics. Medieval swan keeping was big business only because swan itself was exorbitantly expensive. A single bird in the late fourteenth century cost between three and four shillings, about a month's wage for a labourer. Anyone caught stealing one was forced to pay a substantial fine in grain, which had to be sufficient to bury the carcass when suspended by the beak with its feet just touching the ground.[8] Like the year's imprisonment meted out to those caught stealing a swan's egg, the penalties were an attempt by the landed classes to protect an important financial resource. But with competition from the cheaper and more easily domesticated turkey, which was introduced in the mid-sixteenth century, and given the intensive labour and high costs of catching and marking swans, the traditional system of ownership began to decline, until by the mid-nineteenth century it had vanished almost completely.

Yet several important remnants of our great swan culture still survive in England. Perhaps the best known is the annual swan-upping, held each July on a stretch of the mid-Thames. The Dyers and the Vintners are two of London's oldest livery companies and are direct descendants of the medieval trade guilds. Both companies, together with the Crown, retain their ancient rights of

Every year the Queen's Swan Marker and the swan uppers of the Vintners and Dyers livery companies make a five-day journey up the Thames. They catch and mark all the birds they encounter, thereby maintaining a vestige of the swan husbandry that dates back more than 1000 years.

ownership of swans and every year they set out sporting traditional striped jerseys and with a swan feather crowning their naval caps. The Queen's Swan Marker leads the party as they make their way steadily upstream towards Abingdon in Oxfordshire. Dr Chris Perrins, who has accompanied the expedition many times, writes:

For years it was done for little more than tradition, but it has since become a useful conservation tool. The Swan-Uppers were the first to notice the marked decline in numbers that started in the 1960s and were the only people with data to back it up. In earlier times, the Uppers used to set off from Tower Bridge, but the progressive concreting over of the City end of the river has meant that swans have long since ceased to nest over most of the lower stretch of the Thames and so Upping has had to move upstream; nowadays it starts at Sunbury in Surrey. It takes five full days to cover all 77 miles of this course, which in 2001 held some 60 pairs of swans with about 185 cygnets. The Upping team consists of six long rowing-boats (two for each organisation); each of these boats has 2–3 rowers (all with excellent track records in rowing races) plus the skipper (in three of the boats, this is the Crown's, Dyers' or Vintners' Swan-Marker).

The aim is to locate all the broods and catch them: this involves the boats going upstream line-astern, until level with the family and then moving in so as to pin them against the bank with a semi-circle of boats. Once this is done, the boats draw in closer and closer until the birds are enclosed in a very small space and can be lifted into the vessel. It sounds easy, and often looks easy, but that is only because of skilled boatmanship and long practice; and, it doesn't always work!

Since the parent birds are flightless at this stage, they are usually caught too (historically, this was important for establishing ownership). The large cobs are wont to object to being handled and this can make the event considerably more exciting. Once caught, the cygnets' health is checked, any fishing tackle or hooks are removed, the two Companies mark (nowadays they use rings, but they used to mark them with nicks in the beaks) their share of the birds (they get a quarter each) and the families are then released, the adults somewhat indignant, but otherwise none the worse for their ordeal.[9]

On completion of the upping, the Dyers' swan team writes up its figures in beautiful leather-bound volumes and later in the year both companies crown the successful activities with an annual swan feast. The Worshipful Company of Dyers commissioned Sir Peter Scott to paint a series of large pictures of mute swans for their hall, where the paintings still hang. However, the venue is too small for the banquet, which is held in October and attended by anything up to 180 guests, and so they use the premises of one of the other livery companies. It is interesting to note that the modern sensitivity and aversion to eating swan has affected even this last bastion of traditional ownership. While one of the menu items is labelled as 'Dyer's cygnet', it is in fact goose.[10]

Abbotsbury on the Fleet in Dorset is the other major location where the ancient traditions of swan keeping are still maintained. The original monastic order established a swan colony here at least 700 years ago. In natural conditions mute-swan pairs are highly territorial, so it is suggested that the monks selectively chose males lacking in the bird's instinctual aggression in order to develop a

The Swan Inn at Clare in Suffolk has the oldest carved inn sign in Britain.

population that would nest at 'barely two neck lengths from each other'.[11] When Henry VIII dissolved the abbey, the property and its swannery passed to the Earls of Ilchester, and even today the Abbotsbury swan mark, nicked from the bird's webbed feet, is known as the 'hive of Ilchester'.[12]

Although birds are no longer harvested for the table, the swannery continues as a visitor attraction. Swans are still provided with winter feed and nest material and some of the young are managed in a unique manner. The first five pairs to hatch are put with their broods in separate rearing pens, and to their natural offspring are added other cygnets until each 'extended family' can include up to 20 young. Although at one time these would have been the birds fattened and kept for the table, today they are fed until September and then simply released.[13]

In modern Britain swans have left another and more pervasive legacy in our cultural life – the number of places, streets, hotels and inns named after the bird. London in particular has many swan references, which reflects a time when the birds themselves were present in conspicuously high numbers. In the late fifteenth century

the secretary to the Venetian ambassador at Henry VII's court wrote that 'it is a truly beautiful thing to behold one or two thousand tame Swans upon the river Thames . . . which are eaten by the English like ducks and geese'.[14] Old Swan Wharf and Swan Lane are next to London Bridge, while Swan Mead, Swan Pass and Black Swan Yard are less than ½ mile (1km) from Tower Bridge, and at least eight of the 17 current London swan pubs lie a similar distance from the river.

In the sixteenth century there was also a Swan Theatre just south of the Thames in Southwark, and while this was eventually destroyed, its name was revived in Stratford-upon-Avon for the building erected in 1986, on the site of the old Shakespeare Memorial Theatre. The Swan title carries a double association with the Bard, both through reference to its Southwark predecessor, where Shakespeare's plays were performed, and because the playwright himself was famously described as 'the Swan of Avon' by fellow poet Ben Jonson.

Across Britain the large number of pubs named after the bird probably reflects not just the social significance of the swans themselves, but also their regular occurrence as a motif in local heraldry. The Sheffield ornithologist Steve Shaw has assembled a list of more than 770 pubs with swan titles and estimates that they represent nearly a quarter of all those named after birds, with variations including the Swan's Nest, the Swan & Cygnets, Swan & Peacock, Swan & Railway, Swan & Pyramids, Ye Olde Swan and the oddly named Weeping Swan in Mistley, Essex (see Appendix 3, page 473). Once a place acquires a swan establishment, it seems to trigger a self-perpetuating tradition. The pubs in York are typical. Forty years ago it had a Swan, a White Swan, an Old White Swan, a Black Swan and a Cygnet. Today it has acquired three more Black Swans and two other White Swans.[15]

Another notable Swan pub is in the village of Clare, Suffolk, which features a wonderful early fifteenth-century wooden image of the bird. This 10-foot- (3-m)-long carving, originally a corbel to an oriel window in the nearby manor house, represents the oldest carved inn sign in Britain.[16] A number of other similarly aged establishments acquired swan names in apparent reference to Anne of Cleves, Henry VIII's fourth wife. The Cleves house was one of several European dynasties that claimed descent from a mythic swan-knight. However, legend also has it that Anne's association with the most graceful of birds was an ironic reference to her physical charms which inspired Henry to his own malicious nickname, 'the Flanders Mare'.

Perhaps the most interesting and contentious pub title is the Swan with Two Necks. There are examples in Hardley, Worcestershire, in Pendleton-in-Ribblesdale, Lancashire, in Todmorden, Calderdale, and in Watford, Hertfordshire, with two in Cheshire, at Macclesfield and Nantwich (there is also a Swan with Two Nicks nearby in Little Bollington).[17] While a bizarre two-headed creature is invariably depicted on the modern pub sign, such a monstrosity has, of course, never occurred. One theory, apparently first proposed by Sir Joseph Banks, is that it represents a linguistic modification of the 'Swan with Two Nicks'.[18] This is a reference to the ancient mark once used by the Vintners' company to identify their birds. Others dispute the idea, partly on the grounds that none of the pubs so called occurs near the Thames, where the Vintners' swans reside. Alternative explanations suggest that its origins lie with an heraldic symbol depicting two swan heads encircled by a coronet, or that it was a simplified representation, used on the inn sign, of two swans swimming side by side.[19]

The old practice of catching swans and cutting the wing bone to render them incapable of flight, not to mention the identification scars made on the beaks and feet, would probably be seen today as indefensible cruelty towards one of our most stately birds. But the historical management of swans was actually a positive factor in their survival. In fact, without the swan laws, it is conceivable that the bird would have become extinct in Britain – a fate that befell populations on the Continent where there were no checks on hunting. Ironically it was the steep decline in swan ownership in the eighteenth century that led to a large decrease in numbers. Once any strict protection was lifted, swans became a target for anyone intent on securing a sizeable bird for the pot.

A general recovery did not begin until the early twentieth century and although the trend continued into the post-war period, swans suffered another significant decline in the 1960s. There are a number of new hazards in modern Britain for a bird of this size, including the serried ranks of electricity pylons that march across the countryside with their interconnecting cables. Swans seem to have poor forward vision and flying birds have been known to crash into much larger obstacles, such as bridges, buildings and even the cliffs of Dover. However, power lines are especially dangerous for them and in the 1960s in Kent 21 birds, one-third of the local population, were killed in two months on one ¼-mile (½-km) stretch of line that lay between their roost and feeding areas.[20] Today in places with high swan concentrations, including Slimbridge in Gloucestershire and the Ouse Washes and Welney reserves in the Fens, the lines are fitted with large, solid, colourful balls to help reduce accidents.

But by far the most serious threat to mute swans came from lead poisoning caused by the ingestion of weights used by anglers. The development of cheap non-degradable nylon lines and split lead-shot led fishermen to abandon snagged lines much more often than was previously the case. The small lead weights were also easily lost and in some popular spots up to 1961 weights were found in an area of just 144 square yards (120sq m). Other systematic searches done at Woodstock pools in south Wales found 1451 weights in one section of water and calculated that the total for the whole pool was 27,000 pieces.[21]

The lead gets into the bird's system because of the swan's habit of eating grit to aid the gizzard in the break-down of its tough vegetable diet. The toxic metal is released into the bloodstream, where it seriously affects the neuromuscular system and can eventually cause the bird to starve to death. A swan with a 'kinky neck', with the lower section collapsed on to the bird's upper back, is the classic sign of poisoning.

In the 1980s lead poisoning was thought to be killing at least 3370 birds in England a year and led first to a voluntary curb on lead weights and then to an outright ban in 1987. Since this took effect, swan numbers have undergone a remarkable recovery. Chris Perrins of

Oxford University, who did much of the research on the effects of lead on swans, and who was appointed a Lieutenant of the Royal Victoria Order for his services to the royal bird, comments:

> Recent sample surveys strongly suggest that they have almost exactly doubled, while on the Thames the situation is even better. In 1978 they were down to only 9 pairs with 30 cygnets between Sunbury and Henley, but in 2001 the figures were 37 and 110. Nevertheless, there are still a number of lead-poisoned swans. Even if many of these are not as sick as those in the 1980s, a high proportion of the birds have elevated blood lead levels. It is not wholly clear where all this lead is coming from: some may be i) long-lost leads picked up by the birds in their search for grit, ii) illegal lead weights; in a recent survey of tackle removed from swans 34 of 249 (13.7%) sets of tackle which included weights contained 96 illegal leads, iii) the (legal) tiny lead dust shot, still used by many anglers.[22]

It is an extraordinary fact, given the bird's universal popularity, that it has long been a victim of purposeless harassment and violence, especially from teenage boys. A watercolour by Thomas Heaphy (1775–1835) entitled 'Two servant boys taunting swans' shows that the problem of disturbance, which is currently estimated to cause the loss of a high percentage of swan eggs, is by no means only a modern issue.[23] Given the consistency of the attacks over the centuries, one wonders whether there may be a latent erotic motive to these adolescent violations of an elegantly curved, virginally white bird. In the 1960s a bird was found with an aluminium arrow right through its neck (despite the horrible projectile it apparently managed to live a fairly normal life).[24] More recently up to 100 mute swans on the River Lea in the London boroughs of Haringey and Enfield have been killed by poachers, many of them decapitated with swords.[25]

Fortunately the mute swan is not without its own defence. Just the loud hiss of this wonderfully misnamed bird can be disturbing. If hissing fails then it is capable of delivering a blow with its large bill. But most intimidating of all is the myth that dates back hundreds of years and is still known to every British school child: 'beware of swans because they can break your arm with a single flap of their wings'.[26]

If the mute swan is known for its gentleness then the other two swan species found in Britain and Ireland – **Bewick's Swan**, *Cygnus columbianus*, and **Whooper Swan**, *C. cygnus* – are equally well known as free-roaming symbols of northern wilderness. In fact they are often referred to as 'wild swans' to distinguish them from

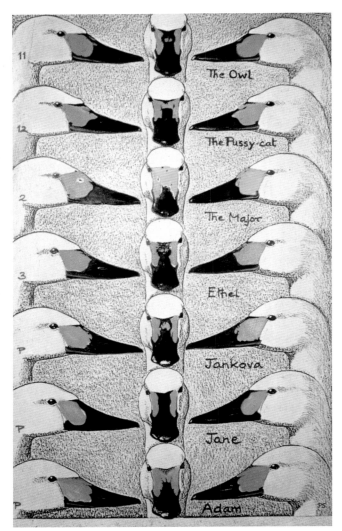

The late Sir Peter Scott was the first person to appreciate how each Bewick's swan has a unique pattern of yellow and black on its bill that enables individual recognition.

their semi-tame siblings. Both come to us in winter from the far north, in the case of the Bewick's from high Arctic Russia and Scandinavia, and wild swans are sometimes thought to herald icy conditions: 'At Elterwater, on the Lancashire–Westmoreland border, their [whoopers'] presence is regarded as a sign of cold weather.'[27]

Yet it is typical of the many contradictions in folklore that wild swans were also viewed historically as good omens. Even today their arrival in northern Scotland or the outer isles evokes a sense of reassurance in autumn, and of loss with their going in spring: 'We always miss the swans when they leave. The constant presence of so many large and heavy birds so near the house makes winter more interesting . . . The strong beat of their wings is a familiar sound as they fly over the roofs, and their haunting call is the accompaniment to every day

Every year 3,000-5,000 Bewick's swans fly to Britain from the tundra of Arctic Russia.

from November till February or March. It seems lonely and silent without them.'[28]

There was once a Celtic taboo against shooting the birds, which certainly lingered as late as the 1930s, and prompted one *Shooting Times* correspondent to write in the following irritated vein:

> In your last issue I notice remarks on prejudice against the shooting of wild swans in the Highlands. Perhaps he has overlooked the fact that all this nonsense . . . had its origins in the superstitions of our imaginative race . . . Swans were popularly supposed to be akin to angels, and to shoot one was to bring disaster on the shooter. This nonsense is responsible for any past feeling on the subject, and in the interests of sport it is best to dispel it once and for all. One word of advice to the swan shooter may not come amiss.
>
> You want a big game bag.
>
> H. E. B. MACPHERSON, Kingussie [29]

Both wintering swans have powerful and characteristic bugling calls, although they lack the far-carrying 'creaking throb' of the mute swan's flight feathers. Bewick's swans' calls are high-pitched, musical and, in concert, can suggest the 'baying of hounds'; I often also hear the hunt horn mingled with the pack. Whooper swans have a note routinely transcribed as '*ahng-ha*' or '*whoop-a*', from which the name originally derives. It sounds more honking and goose-like, although it can resemble a trumpet or even a child's musical bicycle horn. Whooper swans are bigger birds, the calls correspondingly deeper and stronger, while the long trachea

required to produce it may be the source of the famous myth of the swansong. Apparently a dying bird makes a prolonged 'final expiration of air from the convoluted wind-pipe, producing a wailing flute-like sound given out quite slowly'.[30]

While mutes have mainly orange beaks, whooper and Bewick's have black bills with diagnostic patterns of yellow: 'Head on, the yellow of Bewick's forms a letter B, and the yellow of Whooper is a W.'[31] Remarkably, the mix of colours on the Bewick's bill is different in every single bird. (It may well also be true in whooper swans, although they have been less well studied.) The consistency of the feature was first noted in 1964 by the artist and conservationist Peter Scott, when Bewick's appeared at the famous 'Swan Lake' in front of his studio window at Slimbridge, Gloucestershire (now headquarters for the Wildfowl & Wetlands Trust). The bill-colour 'fingerprint' allowed each bird to be named and recognised and formed the basis of a long-term study by WWT staff:

> Each bird has a dossier containing a drawing of its bill pattern, its family connections, its yearly arrival and departure dates and, for most of them, a series of portrait photographs . . . Seven people have so far been involved in the study and have had to learn the names and face patterns of many swans . . .
>
> The names of most single swans are descriptive like Lemon, Splodge, Y-front, Primrose. Puns are frequent and mates are often given names which go logically together, for instance, Kon and Tiki, Swan and Vesta, Antony and Cleopatra, Stars and Stripes.[32]

The whooper swans at Welney, Norfolk, are part of the largest wintering swan population in Europe.

The other key development in long-term swan studies was the use of rings 'made of coloured laminated PVC called "darvic" with individual letter and number codes engraved on them so that it is possible to recognise individual birds in the field . . . in 1967, Malcolm Ogilvie obtained some darvic direct from ICI and experimented at Slimbridge with making rings of the material . . . the breakthrough came when he learnt to shape the plastic into circles after softening it in boiling water. A few tame Mute Swans were ringed during the summer of 1967 and the first wild Bewick's in November of that year.'[33] The innovation has yielded some extraordinary insights into swan behaviour:

One Bewick's Swan family left Slimbridge in January on a mild south-westerly wind and rapidly reached the Elbe estuary in Germany. Then the temperature suddenly dropped and snow began falling. The disillusioned swan family reappeared at Welney; then, even more surprisingly, at Slimbridge the next day. It was calculated that they would need to stay three weeks at Slimbridge to regain weight lost on the abortive first leg of their migration. And this was just what they did![34]

Slimbridge has another important link with the history of the Bewick's swan in Britain, in the form of an old telescope mounted at the reserve and used to watch the birds on the lake. Originally this ancient eyepiece, bearing a date of 1798, was the property of the celebrated artist and ornithologist Thomas Bewick, after whom William Yarrell originally named the swan in 1830.[35]

While Bewick's swans will venture as far south as the Cornish coast in winter, they never stay to breed in Britain. Whoopers, by contrast, are much more likely to linger in the spring and sometimes nest. In the eighteenth century there was a small regular breeding colony on Orkney, although this was finally extinguished by egg collectors and other disturbance. On the mainland two injured birds managed to breed every year in Sutherland from 1912 to 1918, until soldiers returning from the war took up arms against the flightless swans and killed them both. In recent decades two to five scattered pairs, some of them probably feral birds, have managed to breed every summer with varying degrees of success.

Most of the whooper swans wintering in Britain are from Iceland and make the journey each autumn in a single 600–800-mile (1000–1330-km) flight. During one set of exceptional weather conditions some Icelandic birds were detected on radar heading for Ireland at an altitude of more than 26,000 feet (8000m), where the birds seemed able to cope with the desperately thin air and the icy temperatures, which can be as low as –50°C.[36] However 'recent radio-tracking indicates that they normally fly only just above the sea, and occasionally rest on it'.[37]

On arrival, whoopers generally stay north of a line between the Wash in eastern England and the Shannon estuary in the west, with most remaining in southern Scotland and Ireland. The major exception is the large concentration in the Fens, at the RSPB's Ouse Washes reserve and the WWT's Welney. Together these sites, a combined 3500 acres (1400ha) in area, help support the single largest wild-swan population anywhere in Europe with up to 5000 Bewick's and 1900 whoopers.

When the WWT first acquired Welney in 1968, it was established as an area for Bewick's swans, but there was then no tradition of wintering whoopers. Even as recently as the winter of 1979/80 the flock of whoopers there consisted only of 100 birds. Numbers of both species have steadily increased over the last few decades, partly because the swans have adapted to feeding on stubbles and sugar-beet tops in the surrounding farmland. They are also attracted by the secure winter roosts provided by the two reserves where the WWT supplies birds with additional food.

The presence of so many huge birds has not been without its hazards, both for the swans and the local residents. At one time swan collisions with electricity cables were almost weekly events, and in one foggy period 50 Bewick's swans were killed in a single night. In 1996 the National Grid marked the large power cables with orange balls along a 5½-mile (9-km) stretch on either side of the Ouse Washes, at a cost of £400,000. This has reduced swan fatalities, but birds continue to hit the smaller domestic cables and even now short power blackouts are an occasional feature of winter life in Welney.[38]

Yet the arrival and winter presence of the birds is embedded in local tradition. A Bewick's swan has recently replaced a Canada goose on Welney's village sign, and each year the WWT holds a swan festival to celebrate the area's national and international reputation for the birds. Most dramatic of all, however, is the dawn and dusk movement of birds to and from the arable areas and their roosting locations. It is one of the great ornithological spectacles in the English winter, and at Welney it reaches a climax with the use of floodlights as night falls, when up to 2000 swans and ducks gather around the warden and his wheelbarrow of food.

Bean Goose, *Anser fabalis*. This large grey-brown goose was apparently much commoner in the nineteenth century, especially in southern Scotland. The name indicates it was once an agricultural pest; an archaic alternative was 'corn goose'. 'The French name is *Oie de moissons* or Harvest Goose; in Germany and Scandinavia it is *Saatgans* and *Sadgas* which means Seed Goose; while in parts of Russia it is *Gumennik*, the thresher goose. It was the first British species to capitalise on farm crops in a big way.'[39]

However problems with identification of grey geese cloud the pronouncements of early ornithologists, and bean goose was not even separated from pink-footed goose until 1833. There is still uncertainty over the taxonomic status of the two forms occurring in Britain: *fabalis*, the 'taiga' bean goose of Scandinavia and Russia west of the Urals, and *rossicus*, the shorter-necked, heavier-billed 'tundra' bean goose that occurs further north and east in Arctic Russia.

Fabalis is the only race to visit Britain in any number. There are now just two regular wintering flocks, one near Slammanan to the south of Falkirk in Stirlingshire, which averages about 140 birds. The larger, longer-established population occurs in the Yare valley close to the Norfolk village of Cantley, where the winter landscape is dominated by a monumental sugar-beet factory. Sightings of the Cantley flock invariably include the factory's towering chimney with its long wind-slewed plume of vapour as part of the backdrop.

The Yare beans were first found in 1924 and have returned almost annually and increased gradually to a 1991 maximum of 485. They are among the few birds in Britain whose migration route, complete with stopover sites en route, is known with great precision. The birds nest in central Sweden towards the very south-western edge of the species' range. At the end of the breeding season in mid-September they move to north-west Jutland, Denmark, where they feed mainly inside a 10,000-acre (4000-ha) private reserve. In mid-November about a third of the Jutland population then continues the journey south-west to Norfolk.

Part of the reason for this detailed knowledge was the capture and marking of 36 beans in 1987 with numbered blue plastic neckbands, which have enabled the monitoring of individual birds. Of these, 22 eventually turned up among the Cantley flock. The other reason for our present understanding is the detailed work undertaken by Mariko Parslow-Otsu. She has watched the birds for many years, even tracking their movements with great precision across the North Sea and enlisting family help in her research:

At dawn on 14th February 1992 my husband [John Parslow] watched as the last 65 Bean Geese of the winter flew off NE from their roost in the Yare Valley; 7 hours 22 minutes later, 650km away on the coast of Jutland, they came in from the North Sea, passing 50 metres over my head. They landed a short way inland,

In recent winters the sugarbeet fields of north Norfolk have held as many as 112,000 pink-footed geese, which is about 40 per cent of the world's entire population.

joining the other Bean Geese which had wintered with them in Norfolk and which had migrated, as several units, over the previous two weeks. By late April they would be on their way north again to breeding grounds in central Sweden.[40]

Parslow-Otsu has discovered that, in defiance of their name, bean geese are now highly dependent upon winter grass for food. The over-grazing of the Yare marshes by sheep, together with human disturbance, particularly from birdwatchers and light aeroplanes, has had an adverse effect on the Norfolk flock. But probably the most important reason for a recent decline in numbers to a 30-year low of just 149 in 2000 is the mildness of our winters, which reduces the need for birds ever to leave Denmark.

Pink-footed Goose, *Anser brachyrhynchus*. VN: Pinks (birdwatchers and wildfowlers). It has the smallest breeding range of any of our grey geese, occurring only in central Iceland, eastern Greenland and western Svalbard. Yet it is also our commonest wintering goose by a wide margin, with almost a quarter of a million birds. They form conspicuous flocks, and few people living in pinkfoot areas fail to notice their spectacular aerial manoeuvres. A V-formation of birds across an ice-blue sky is an archetypal image of winter and has a sense of purpose and implicit hierarchy that has intrigued us for centuries:

Wildfowlers have frequently written on this aspect, claiming that it is always an old gander who takes on this role. This is quite likely, but . . . certainly not an invariable rule . . . Adult birds are more likely to lead the young than the other way around, although there is little evidence for the male doing more leading than the female . . . [and] it is easily observed that the lead in a flying flock changes frequently, different birds forging ahead or coming to the front when there is a slight change of direction. A flock of flying geese has a corporate purpose and direction shared among its component individuals, not directed by a single leader.[41]

The function of the V is assumed to be an aerodynamic advantage to each member of the formation, even the lead bird. 'The downbeat of the wing produces a corresponding swirl of rising air behind it which, if the next bird can beat into it at precisely the right point, will give it additional lift, thus reducing the effort needed to maintain height and forward speed.'[42] In fact, pinkfeet seldom achieve this theoretical pattern. The birds often rise and fall in relation to one another, while

Sir Peter Scott's dramatic oil paintings of geese flying in echelon against a winter sunset or dawn are among the most famous images of British wildlife.

the V formation regularly mutates into simple strings, diagonal and even J-shaped lines, or just shapeless mobs all heading in the same general direction.

Whatever the exact purpose, the movements of grey geese spread across the heavens in constantly shifting patterns, and accompanied by what W. H. Hudson described as their 'wild exhilarating clangour', is indubitably one of the most inspiring scenes in British and Irish ornithology.[43] In places like Dumfriesshire, the west Lancashire 'Mosses' and the coastal plain of Aberdeenshire they are an important part of regional identity. 'A skein of geese coming from the sea, calling excitedly, is such a wonderful sight, a sign of autumn, and they express wildness like few other birds. You can be sitting in an office in Aberdeen and suddenly the elevated cries of a mass of pinkfeet moving south, high in the sky, reminds you that there is a real world out there that makes yours seem irrelevant.'[44]

Wildlife artists such as Sir Peter Scott and, more

recently, James McCallum, have returned to the subject again and again. The endless space of the icy blue skies and the slow wheeling movements of the flocks help create a reassuring impression that geese are part of the timeless ritual of our winter landscapes. Ironically, where pinkfeet are concerned, any sense of permanence or stability is largely illusory.

The last 50 years have witnessed massive changes both in the character and location of pinkfoot flocks. The most important underlying development has been a huge increase from a 1951 census of just 30,000 to an estimated 230,000 before the end of the millennium. There are five historical pinkfoot areas: in Grampian, in Tayside and the Lothians around the Firths of Tay and Forth, in Dumfriesshire, Lancashire and Norfolk. The history of the East Anglian pinkfeet is a perfect measure of the species' rapidly shifting fortunes, because as recently as 1975 the area did not hold any at all. In the 1930s the development of an aircraft firing range at a traditional

In places like the Lancashire 'Mosses' and the coastal plain of Aberdeenshire, wintering goose flocks are a dramatic part of the regional identity.

roost site and the wartime ploughing of feeding areas drove the geese away for 35 years. Now, however, north Norfolk holds the single largest concentration with up to 70,000 in some winters, representing about a quarter of the entire world population.

A factor behind the national increase has been a ban on the sale of geese in the 1970s. While it is still perfectly legal to hunt them, there is no commercial market for birds surplus to wildfowlers' personal requirements. Since the 1960s pinkfeet have also benefited from a marked shift in feeding habits from pasture or saltmarsh to arable land, such as winter stubbles and old potato fields. However, the most important arable crop to be exploited by pinkfeet is a product of our own very human sweet tooth.

The grubbing out of hedges and the high chemical inputs associated with growing sugar beet means that it is usually stigmatised as an environmental disaster, but for pinkfeet it has been a positive development. After the harvesting of the crop, the birds move in to feed on the waste leaves, stalks, root crowns and any weeds. Even the accompanying increase in field size, which has resulted in the classic beet-and-barley prairie in many arable counties, has been a boon to ultra-wary birds requiring all-round vision for their security.

In Norfolk pinkfeet were first recorded on sugar beet in 1966, since when beet has become a mainstay of their winter diet. On occasions very large numbers build up on relatively tiny areas, as at Flitcham in west Norfolk:

We measure the time geese spend at Abbey Farm in 'goose days'. A goose day is equivalent of one goose spending 8 hours on a field. For instance, 1000 geese present for 2 hours equals 250 goose days. In 1993–94 a total of about 308,000 goose days were spent at Abbey Farm. Over 97% of these were on beet fields. Most of these were on 110 acres of beet land with light grazing of another 40 acres. Field shape, size and position seem to be important factors in deciding where geese feed. They seem to prefer fields which give good all-round visibility . . . They also tolerate traffic, provided vehicles don't stop.[45]

The British birds have been the focus of a remarkable long-term ringing study initiated in the 1950s by Peter Scott. He put out stuffed decoys to lure in pinkfeet and fired specially designed rocket nets over them using 25-pound (11-kg) artillery shells. On one occasion in October 1951 the BBC sound recordist Eric Simms accompanied him on a cannon-netting expedition:

In the afternoon a single juvenile Pink-foot appeared, circled, made off and came back for another look. We held our breath. Then we saw the characteristic backward beating of the wings, and the bird was down. Small parties came over and bigger numbers arrived ... Ten seconds later there was a tremendous 'whoosh' as the rockets leaped forwards with the net. Underneath were 64 Pink-footed Geese safe and unharmed. These were all removed, examined, ringed, marked with dye for easier identification later. The most thrilling aspect of the operation was the recovery of two marked birds. Both had been given identity tags as nestlings on the breeding grounds in Iceland in the summer of the same year when Peter Scott and James Fisher had gone north for geese.[46]

A single firing of the rockets has caught as many as 500 birds, and throughout the 1950s just short of 14,000 were ringed. Pinkfoot studies were resumed in the 1980s, but this time using plastic numbered collars or leg rings that can be read in field conditions. Many of the new birds were captured at the Wildfowl & Wetlands Trust reserve at Martin Mere, Lancashire, where they are lured using waste potatoes and carrots.

The two projects have confirmed a picture of remarkable flexibility and movement between the various British sub-populations. Individual groups will move steadily southwards after landfall in Grampian in the early autumn, calling at all the intervening pinkfoot areas until they arrive in Norfolk in late winter. It has even been suggested that birds will commute between Lancashire and Norfolk in a single day. Among this great variation some birds also show exceptional site fidelity. Marked geese have 'been recorded feeding in the same few fields in Aberdeen on the same dates in successive springs, yet having spent the winter months near King's Lynn. Two well-known individuals (CAP and CAZ – the lettering of their leg rings) have returned to the same [Norfolk] field five successive winters.'[47]

Pinkfoot movements are often triggered by bad weather and a cold snap or snow can lead to abandonment of a traditional roost site for the entire winter. Sometimes neither the pinkfeet's powerful flight nor the cohesion of the V formation can avoid disaster. In January 1978 a violent hailstorm killed 140 geese, when they were probably 'overtaken by a tornado or funnel cloud and forcibly sucked upwards to a considerable altitude like toy balloons. Death or unconsciousness quickly followed. Their involuntary return to earth ... occurred along a 50km path extending from near Castle Acre to just south of Norwich.'[48]

White-fronted Goose, *Anser albifrons*. The grey goose with a high yelping call, dramatic white blaze on its forecrown and variable slashes of burnt brown across the

The lesser white-fronted goose played a small but intriguing role in shaping the British Broadcasting Corporation.

breast comes to Britain and Ireland from two widely separate breeding grounds. The small number of birds largely wintering in southern England arrive from Arctic Russia and are concentrated at the Swale estuary, Kent, and by the Severn, adjacent to the Wildfowl & Wetlands Trust headquarters at Slimbridge, Gloucestershire. Its founder, Peter Scott, partly selected the location because of its proximity to these traditional wintering grounds (see Lesser White-fronted Goose below).

Scott was also the first (with Christopher Dalgety) to recognise that the white-fronts coming from western Greenland to winter in Scotland and Ireland are of a separate race, *flavirostris*, and are distinguishable by their larger size and a long orange (not pink) bill.[49] The two main congregations of this subspecies gather on the Wexford Slobs in Ireland and on Islay in the Inner Hebrides, also long famous for its exquisite single-malt whiskies and for a large flock of wintering barnacle geese.

In the 1980s Islay's two key attractions were at the heart of a major conflict: a distillery selected an area known as Duich Moss as a source of peat for its whisky, but the place was already the largest roost site for Greenland white-fronts in Britain. Eventually all parties were reconciled: Duich Moss was saved by a high-profile campaign and became a National Nature Reserve, while the distillery obtained peat from another suitable source.

Islay's farmers have also long complained about the agricultural damage inflicted by rising populations of barnacles and Greenland white-fronts (in the mid-1990s they numbered 30,000 and 15,000 respectively). They too have now been largely mollified by management payments from Scottish Natural Heritage.

Lesser White-fronted Goose, *Anser erythropus*. The smallest member of the genus has a reputation for physical elegance: 'perhaps the most beautiful of all the world's grey geese';[50] 'almost immaculate appearance of plumage striking'.[51] By a large margin it is also the rarest grey goose and enjoys the unalluring celebrity of a Red Data Book species, which is considered threatened with extinction throughout its global range. There have been only about 130 records in Britain and Ireland, the first in 1886, a bird shot on the Northumbrian coast by Alfred Chapman, brother of the celebrated hunter and author, Abel Chapman.

Yet for sheer impact the first was undoubtedly eclipsed by the second – or third – record, identified by Peter Scott. (Scott considered the second to be a bird seen by his friend, Will Tinsley, in Lincolnshire, but it was never accepted in the official records.) Acting on a hunch that lesser white-fronts might just occasionally visit Britain in the company of wintering flocks of greater white-fronted geese, Scott paid a visit to the grazing marshes on the Severn estuary, Gloucestershire. The area still supports England's largest population of the commoner species and while sifting through 2000 birds in December 1945, Scott's friend, Howard Davis, 'said quietly, "There's a bird here which interests me. Would you have a look at it?"' In his autobiography, *The Eye of the Wind*, Scott wrote:

> In a few moments he had directed me to the goose in question among the tight mass of geese in front of us, and the instant my binoculars lit upon it I realised that it was a Lesser Whitefront. My spine tingled. Here almost too easily was proof of my far-fetched theory. It was, no doubt, a small discovery but for me it was a moment of unforgettable triumph, a turning point; or is it only in looking back on it that I have invested it with so much significance because it changed the course of my life?
>
> . . . as we walked back . . . I came to the conclusion that this was the place in which anyone who loved wild geese must live. Here were two empty cottages which might become the headquarters of the research organisation which had been taking shape in my mind over the war years . . . I looked at my surroundings with a new eye, an eye to the future, for this was the beginning of the Wildfowl Trust.[52]

As he intended, Scott founded the Wildfowl Trust (now the Wildfowl & Wetlands Trust) at Slimbridge near where he saw his lesser white-fronted goose and the place has since accounted for more than 50 records of the species.

Yet that sighting had a bearing not only on the choice of headquarters for one of Britain's foremost conservation organisations. It was Scott's pioneering television work, especially his award-winning series *Look*, that helped to establish the BBC's Natural History Unit in 1957. In turn its location in Bristol was 'largely determined by the fact that Peter Scott had chosen Slimbridge as his home'.[53] Some will no doubt find a peculiar kind of satisfaction in the idea that a part of the British Broadcasting Corporation was shaped by a small rare goose with a pink bill and golden eye-ring, breeding no nearer this country than the wooded tundra of Fennoscandia, beyond the Arctic Circle.

Greylag Goose, *Anser anser*. The rather odd name is a conflation of the bird's dominant colour and *lag*, an old term for goose, apparently arising from a traditional farmyard cry when driving the birds, '*lag-lag-lag*'. But W. B. Lockwood suggests, 'It is highly probable that this simple name is in fact of great antiquity. It can hardly be a coincidence that a comparable syllable *lak* lies behind Gaelic *lacha* duck, a name which can be shown philologically to have been in existence for at least a millennium and a half.'[54]

Given the comic waddle of the domesticated bird and a general reputation for lack of intelligence (e.g. 'silly goose'), it may be surprising to learn that the wild species was once an object of reverence. Throughout much of its massive Eurasian range the greylag was the focus of a complex religious mythology. More than 5000 years ago among the city-states of the Tigris–Euphrates delta, geese were associated with Gula, a fertility deity and precursor of the better-known Sumerian goddess Ishtar. For the Egyptians, geese were a symbol of Ra, the sun god, while in ancient Greece and Rome they were birds sacred to Aphrodite and were treated as an erotic motif, with goose fat being considered an aphrodisiac.[55] It was, incidentally, their religious importance in Rome that explains the presence of geese on the Capitoline Hill in 390 BC, when the birds gave their famous alarm that allowed the invading Gauls to be repulsed.

It is perhaps even more surprising to learn that in modern Britain there are one or two surviving fragments of the greylag's ancient role as fertility symbol. The well-known children's nursery rhyme 'Goosey goosey, gander' contains a clear undercurrent of sexual innuendo:

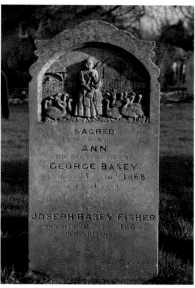

Above: Greylag geese were reared partly for their plumage, which supplied the instruments of both war and peace: feathers to fletch arrows and quills to make pens. Right: This headstone in Ashby St Mary churchyard, Norfolk, reflects the long tradition of goose husbandry in East Anglia.

Goosey goosey, gander,
Whither shall I wander?
Upstairs and downstairs,
And in my lady's chamber
There I met an old man
Who wouldn't say his prayers;
I took him by the left leg,
And threw him down the stairs.

The word 'goose' itself has explicit modern connotations, and in Elizabethan times it was slang for a prostitute, while in the nineteenth century 'gooser' and 'goose's neck' were terms for the penis.[56]

The other intriguing relic of greylag mythology is the widespread custom of drying and pulling the 'wishbone' from the Christmas turkey and other festive roasts. In earlier times the bird was always a goose, eaten at the traditional feast of Michaelmas, and the lucky piece of anatomy was a breastbone known as the 'Merry Thought'. Changes in fashion have led to a gradual mutation of the ritual, but at its root was a magico-religious attachment to geese and a genuine belief in their powers of prognostication. The goose bone was taken as a particularly strong indicator of coming winter weather, but it was also a more general oracle and was said to have guided the campaign during the First Crusade in 1096.[57]

The wildfowl specialist Janet Kear speculates that it was the eastern race of the greylag goose, *rubirostris*, which was originally tamed by humans. This is borne out by some of the earliest images of domesticated birds, painted about

3360 years ago in ancient Egypt, where the British race does not occur. The theory gets further support from the physical characteristics of our common modern breeds, which share the grey cast to the feathers and pinkish bill of *rubirostris* (British wild birds have an orange bill). However Kear also believes that once domesticated geese reached Britain they interbred with local wild populations; 'it is said that it was this "outbreeding" that kept the old English Grey Goose unimproved for so long'.[58]

Wild birds would almost certainly have been incorporated into the huge domesticated flocks kept in a swathe of eastern England between Lincolnshire and Suffolk. They were reared both for their flesh and their feathers, which had a whole variety of uses. The word 'pen' derives from *penna*, the Latin for feather, and goose quills were used for writing until the invention of the steel nib in the nineteenth century. The primaries from the left wing were especially prized, 'because their curvature bent away from the eyes of right-handed writers'.[59] The old proverb 'A goose-quill is more dangerous than a lion's claw' was a predecessor of the better-known version comparing the power of pen and sword.[60] Even the name of the well-known ink brand, Quink, was said to derive from an old name for a goose (possibly Brent goose) whose quills were used for writing.[61]

Goose feathers were not just instruments of the peaceful arts, but also those of the battlefield, where they were once important as the material for fletching arrows. The stiff flight feathers anchored in the shaft controlled the arrow's passage through the air, and it was once said that

75

England was saved by 'the crooked stick [the bow] and the grey goose wing'.[62]

It was an enduring autumn ritual to drive the goose flocks from all over eastern England to the poultry markets in London's Cheapside. The birds sometimes had their feet covered in tar and sand to protect them and were walked at an average daily rate of 8–9 miles (13–15km). According to Thomas Bewick they started at three in the morning and continued late into the evening. Until the nineteenth century flocks of several thousand were a common sight on the main East Anglian roads to the capital.

Our own long-standing contact with farmyard geese – the heavy waddling gait, coarse honking calls and ship-like grace of their movements on water – gives most of us a sense of familiarity with the greylag, even though truly wild birds breed only in northern and western Scotland. There are about a thousand pairs in this traditional stronghold but in winter these are joined by more than 80,000 migratory greylags, originating mainly from Iceland.

The bird has also become more familiar to us because of a widespread recolonisation of Britain and Ireland involving free-flying but non-migratory feral birds. These are particularly numerous in eastern England, Shropshire, the Lake District, Anglesey, south-west Scotland and in Ireland around Strangford Lough and in County Wexford. The spread into town parks and popular walking spots is leading to a degree of public resentment, on account of the bird's general noisiness, its occasional aggression, super-abundant droppings and sheer success (greylags are increasing at about 5 per cent a year).

Snow Goose, *Anser caerulescens*. This beautiful all-white goose with black wingtips is well known to us through Paul Gallico's children's story of the same name. Set in wartime Britain, it was actually based on the 1930s lifestyle of the nation's most famous 'goose man', Sir Peter Scott, who at one time lived in a lighthouse near Sutton Bridge in Lincolnshire. Gallico was apparently inspired by the story of a real-life wild pink-footed goose, Annabel, which joined tame pinkfeets in Scott's own growing wildfowl collection. Annabel stayed with the pinioned birds throughout the winter of 1936 and only departed for Iceland on 15 May 1937, a date long after the normal return period.

Although Scott never expected to see Annabel again, 'on 9 October 1937 he heard a cry from a speck in the sky, and down she came without hesitation to settle a dozen yards away from Peter, and his bucket of corn – a "plump little round person . . . I was overwhelmed," he wrote, "with joy and relief and wonder."' The following May Annabel was summoned by instinct to return north once

more and while Scott looked for her the following October, it was in vain.[63]

Annabel returned no more in real life, but was reincarnated as a snow goose in Gallico's bestselling book, while Scott himself was reinvented 'as an outcast hunchback painter living in a lighthouse'.[64] When the American edition appeared, the actor James Robertson Justice sent his artist friend a copy 'with a note saying "this should be actionable"':

[Scott] had earlier told Gallico of his boat and lighthouse and felt that, at the beginning of the story he was only thinly disguised; however, he did not think that a claim that he had been injured by the tale would be recognised by any court. A more agreeable proposition was the invitation to illustrate the next edition and Gallico's request that Fritha [the book's young heroine] should be painted to resemble Mrs Scott [the novelist Elizabeth Jane Howard].

The various editions of *The Snow Goose* have sold in millions and, when the inevitable film version was being prepared, the staff of the Wildfowl Trust were asked 'to hand-rear a goose to take the title role . . . Although used in the flight shots, he had to be understudied by a Hollywood-trained bird after he bit the human star, Jenny Agutter.' The bird was known as 'Snoose' and lived at Slimbridge for 20 years, 'nipping a few ankles, but . . . fully part of the Snow Goose flock and father of some of its goslings'.[65]

Truly wild snow geese breed in high Arctic Alaska, Canada and Siberia and are widespread in North America during winter months. Occasionally they turn up in Britain and Ireland as vagrants, although they are also widely kept in ornamental collections. As well as the Slimbridge flock, there are long-established free-flying feral populations on the Inner Hebridean islands of Mull and Coll and at the royal Sandringham Park in Norfolk. The birds with the strongest likelihood of genuine transatlantic origins are those arriving with Greenland white-fronted geese in Ireland and western Britain. But the difficulty of sifting the genuine wild grain from the domesticated chaff is fully demonstrated by the full-winged captive birds at Slimbridge, which have been known to 'migrate' to France in cold weather.

Canada Goose, *Branta canadensis*. The populations of this handsome North American goose exhibit the greatest variation in size of any bird. The smallest races can be half the length and just one-seventh the weight of their biggest relatives.[66]

It was the large nominate *canadensis* from America's Atlantic seaboard that was first brought to Britain in the

Canada geese are handsome but not always welcome additions to the town-park lake.

late seventeenth century, when King Charles II acquired some for his wildfowl collection in St James's Park. With their striking black-and-white plumage and musical honking calls, Canadas were then quickly taken up as a fashion statement on many country estates. However it took almost two centuries for the transatlantic 'alien' to gain acceptance as a British bird.

Today it is probably the one goose with which most people are familiar. Ironically its widespread residence in town parks, reservoirs, gravel pits and other public spaces is partly a product of early attempts at population control. By the 1950s some Canada flocks had built up to the point where they had become a localised agricultural pest. The problem was tackled by rounding some of them up during the moult period, when they become flightless, and relocating them to unoccupied areas. At the time council-run parks were a common release site.

However it was not appreciated that Canada geese are highly sedentary. While this contributes to the build-up of numbers in certain areas, the crowded conditions also limit breeding success, by preventing some birds from finding unoccupied nest sites. Once they were released into virgin territory, the constraint was lifted and their numbers mushroomed for several decades at a rate of 8 per cent a year. Current estimates suggest a British and

Irish total of almost 61,000 birds, with the vast majority in England.

The bird's hard-nosed success has ensured that it has undergone an image change during the last 40 years, from parkland ornament to public nuisance:

> In the nearby Priory Gardens, Orpington, they throng so closely around that it is difficult to feed other birds and, to call one's attention to their needs and I think in irritation when not fed, some ganders grab, pull and bite hard. My friend is nearly 80 and not too good on his legs, and nearly fell down once, when one unexpectedly seized the end of his windcheater and gave it a strong jerk. On our next visit, when my eyes were on birds further away, one grabbed me by the flesh of my thigh and for some seconds pulled and bit hard. It hurt even through thick trousers. Clearly (like tame Mute Swans) such birds might do serious harm to a small child.[67]

They are also prodigious grazers of grass and, at times, of arable crops, with three geese estimated to be the equal of one sheep. Their digestive system also seems to process the vegetation at an alarming rate, with the squidgy green cigar-shaped droppings apparently

Barnacle geese were long thought to originate from marine crustaceans, partly because the mystery of their Arctic breeding grounds was not fully unravelled until the twentieth century.

appearing every four minutes (about 28 ounces/800gm per day).[68] Not only do they foul the water, the lakeside and the surrounding lawns, but droppings 'collected in parks, to which the public had access, were screened for a range of bacteria, including some that are well-known causes of illness in man':

> These bacteria . . . were shown to survive and multiply in the droppings for up to one month after their deposition by geese. Canada geese ranged further from water than other waterfowl species and thus distributed their droppings over a larger area of parkland grass . . . lead[ing] Canada geese to pose a greater health risk than other wildfowl studied here.[69]

A hope that wildfowlers might take out excess birds and stem the Canada's population rise has never been fulfilled, partly because the bird's low-flying habits and general complacency towards humankind make them very poor sport. In some places, such as London parks, council officials employ various methods to keep their numbers down. The moulting adults are rounded up and shot, and the eggs are sometimes pricked or coated with liquid paraffin or removed and replaced with egg substitutes. However, the measures are controversial. The adults' bright colour and 'honking brashness' – not to mention the yellow-downed fluffiness of the youngsters – have endeared them to many.

More serious still than their park-fouling antics is the significant threat they are believed to pose to aeroplanes, and the world's aviation fleet is 'currently being redesigned to allow for the collision risk they pose'. The Civil Aviation Authority also funded the BTO's Naturalised Goose Survey in 2000. The good news is that the large annual increases have slowed and populations have reached a maximum in many areas.[70]

Barnacle Goose, *Branta leucopsis*. VN: Rood Goose (south-west Scotland); Barny, Grollog (birders). It was Giraldus Cambrensis who first gave prominence to the story that lies behind the bird's odd name (and the equally unusual name for the cirrhopod, the goose barnacle *Lepas fascicularis*). In his *Topographica Hibernica* of 1186, the Welsh-born cleric and chronicler gave an account of a fowl he claimed to have seen during an expedition to Ireland:

The brent goose had an ambiguous reputation as a roast. One wildfowler's recipe suggested boiling with an old boot: after three days 'throw away the goose and eat the boot'.

There are . . . many birds which are called Bernacae . . . They are produced from fir timber tossed along the sea and are at first like gum. Afterwards they hang down by their beaks as if they were seaweed attached to the timber . . . Having thus . . . been clothed with a strong coat of feathers, they either fall into the water or fly freely away . . . I have frequently seen, with my own eyes, more than a thousand of these small birds, hanging down on the sea-shore from one piece of timber.[71]

Thus arose the myth of the goose born of a seashell, which endured for 500 years and breathed its last only in the early twentieth century. Today the bird's name is one of the few surviving traces (the association recurs in the Welsh language, where *gwyrain* serves as a secondary name for both animals),[72] but as Edward Armstrong wrote in *The Folklore of Birds*, the story of the myth still fascinates 'for the light it sheds on the credulity and mendacity of scholars'.[73]

Among the savants taken in by Geraldus' original version was the man often deemed Britain's first ornithologist, William Turner. His equal in the field of

botany, John Gerard, compounded credulity with deceit by claiming to have witnessed himself the birds emerging from their barnacle shells. 'What our eies have seene and hands have touched,' declared the tale-spinning Gerard, 'we shall declare.'[74] However it is worth noting that the Hohenstaufen emperor, Frederick II, heard the legend and disbelieved it three centuries before either Turner or Gerard ever turned the matter over. He even dispatched envoys north from his Sicilian palace to gain first-hand material – a thoroughness which supports the argument that '*Stupor Mundi*', the 'Wonder of the World', was Europe's first true ornithologist.[75]

While most people had dismissed the story by the early nineteenth century, there were still occasional cranks claiming the discovery of a goose-bearing tree or insisting on the original myth. Even last century the local people of Kerry were said to cling to the ancient traditions, although it probably represented a canny triumph of expediency over belief, because the bird's fishy origins allowed Kerry folk to eat fresh goose meat during Lent when flesh was otherwise forbidden.[76] The locals extracted additional advantage by referring to the other common black goose of the Irish seashore in winter, the brent goose, as a barnacle. They were thus able to kill (and eat) two birds with one name.

In some sense one can understand the original mistakes. The real story behind the goose flocks that arrive each autumn was in many ways as remarkable as the tale of a bird-bearing seashell. Barnacle geese come from three distinct and, by medieval standards, fabulously remote areas – Novaya Zemlya in Arctic Russia, Svalbard and Greenland. The barnacles from the last two regions winter exclusively in Britain and Ireland, while the Svalbard population of 27,000 birds is almost entirely dependent upon just a single estuary – the Solway.

The locals have long celebrated the relationship between these beautiful birds and the landscapes of south-west Scotland. Dumfries has a traditional holiday in the first week of October called the Rood Fair, which shares its name with the 'Rood goose' that arrives at much the same time. Just down the road from Dumfries lies the most important site for barnacle geese on Solway, the Wildlife & Wetlands Trust reserve of Caerlaverock, where one can see as much as one-third of Svalbard's entire population in just a couple of fields.

The air is full of their barks, yelps and humming sound. The flock suddenly opens up like the fur of a cat parted by wind. A roe deer has emerged from the nearby hedge; she reaches a high wire fence and clears it in a standing bound. The living carpet of barnacle geese reforms and still the day resounds with their yapping calls. As the sun begins to sink across the Solway in mid-winter, the geese become unsettled in preparation for their evening flight. A minute or so after half past four a flock rises a quarter of a mile away. Like a pack of barking dogs they approach. The noise grows louder until they pass overhead. Soon more and more geese are on the wing, sharp against the clear sky. A torrent of calls grows in intensity – the sound of Christmas-time in this wilderness of saltmarsh, sandbank, rough grazing, wind and tide.[77]

Brent Goose, *Branta bernicla*. The smallest and darkest of our geese is a common sight, particularly on Irish coasts and along English south-east and eastern shores. These birds are strongly associated with the intertidal area of coastal estuaries, where their daily movements are often completed in wavering black lines strung out across vast expanses of mudflat and ice-blue winter sky. Even in strong winds and at a considerable distance, brent flocks can be picked up by their low-pitched babble of guttural calls, which can build at short range to an almost deafening clamour – to nineteenth-century ears 'like a pack of hounds in full cry'.[78] Close encounters are more common now that they have lost much of their suspicion of human figures in the coastal landscape.

Yet at one time it was the classic punt-gunner's bird. William Yarrell wrote, 'The London markets are abundantly supplied with these Geese ... a few may be seen in almost every poulterer's shop in winter.'[79] In his *Bird-Life of the Borders*, Abel Chapman celebrated the brent as 'right royal sport'. Chapman stressed the bird's extreme wariness and the challenge of getting close, but on occasions they could offer easy pickings – 'a mark like a barn door' – and there are claims of single shots bringing down 27 birds (as well as eight shelduck and 120 knot).[80]

Parallel contradictions recur in matters of flavour. While it was considered excellent eating by an earlier age, a recent opinion is hardly fulsome: 'In Norfolk and Essex I've heard that the only way to get a good meal from a brent is to boil it in a pot for three days with an old boot then throw away the goose and eat the boot.'[81]

Over-hunting was only a secondary factor when brent-goose numbers tumbled to an all-time low in the early twentieth century. During winter the species is highly dependent upon a plant of the intertidal zone called eelgrass, *Zostera marina*, and when this was severely affected by a parasitic disease, the brent goose declined in similar fashion. In the 1950s the wintering flocks in Britain numbered just 14,800 birds, and this was nearly half of the entire western European total. Fortunately enhanced protection and the recovery of eelgrass stocks were the background to the bird's own return to earlier abundance. In the late 1990s there were more than 90,000 in Britain and Ireland.

While each country supports populations of wintering brent geese, the birds are of separate subspecies and arrive from completely different parts of the circumpolar tundra. The brents in southern England fly mainly from the high Arctic areas of eastern Russia and well over two-thirds are concentrated in four main wetland areas: the Wash, the north Norfolk coast, the Thames and Blackwater estuaries. The Irish birds, known as 'pale-bellied brents' for their grey-white lower breast and flanks, breed in the eastern Canadian Arctic and perform the longest migration of any goose – 4735 miles (7000km). It is thought to involve non-stop journeys of more than 1800 miles (3000km), including an heroic crossing of the 10,000-foot-high (3000-m) Greenland icecap.[82]

In May 2002 six brents – 'Austin', 'Arnthor', 'Hugh', 'Kerry', 'Oscar' and 'Major Ruttledge' (named after senior Irish, British, Canadian and Icelandic ornithol-

The distinctive wavering lines of brent geese in flight are a regular spectacle along the winter coasts of Ireland and south-east England.

ogists) – were caught in Iceland during their return journey to Arctic Canada and were satellite-tagged by the Wildfowl & Wetlands Trust. Part of the plan was to let the public follow the sextet's progress on a dedicated website, but matters did not work out exactly as the Trust had hoped. Two birds ('Austin' and 'Arnthor') soon ceased to transmit a signal and were 'lost in action'. 'Oscar' and 'Hugh' were eaten by Arctic foxes in Iceland, while 'Kerry's signal was tracked to his final resting place – the larder in an Inuit hunter's cottage on Bathurst Island. His tragic end was subsequently immortalised in a Dave Gaskill cartoon in the *Sun* newspaper.

Eight months after the project was launched only a single goose was still going strong. Mike Daw of WWT suggested, 'The researchers' money was always on "Major Ruttledge".' Given that he was named after Robert Ruttledge, one of the great figures of Irish ornithology who lived to be 102, one can understand their hopes for his namesake's longevity. Mike Daw adds, 'It isn't exactly what we had planned for the project but it does clearly tell the story of the great dangers faced by pale-bellied brent geese on their epic migration.'[83]

Red-breasted Goose, *Branta ruficollis*. With its rich chestnut-red breast and cheek spot, framed by a crisp latticework in black and white, this exquisite little goose must rank as one of the world's most attractive wildfowl. On its breeding grounds in Arctic Siberia the species has an intriguing symbiotic relationship with nesting rough-legged buzzards or peregrines, around whose eyrie as many as ten goose pairs can be sitting on eggs. The uncomfortable bargain lasts until the goslings hatch, the peregrine gaining an early warning system against intruders while the geese enjoy protection from ground predators like Arctic fox.

Very occasionally red-breasted geese become 'entangled' on the Arctic breeding grounds with migrating flocks of brent geese and then arrive at the wrong winter destination. This probably accounts for most of the species' 60 records in Britain and Ireland.

Egyptian Goose, *Alopochen aegyptiacus*. It is typical of our churlish attitude towards introduced species that Egyptian geese have had to wait nearly 300 years before finally being accepted as true British birds and included on our official list. Despite its conspicuous appearance and localised distribution, the species was more or less ignored until the 1970s, when even basic information about its population size was absent. Today its behaviour and ecology in Britain are still largely neglected, except for the birds of Holkham Park, Norfolk, which have been the subject of a detailed long-term study by ecologist Bryan Sage.[84]

Even the bird's most devoted champion would

The Egyptian goose is, in fact, neither a goose nor exclusively Egyptian and has the unusual habit of nesting in trees.

probably accept that 'gypos' can look very strange in the English landscape. They are not true geese, but are more closely related to the shelduck and share its hole-nesting habit. They also take readily to trees and will place their down-filled nest in a hollow stump as much as 80 feet (24m) off the ground. While the female sits tight, the male stands guard, perched on an upper bough and, in the absence of a tree hole, they have also been known to make do with old buzzards' or crows' nests.

To the unwary birdwatcher who stumbles upon a pair in woodland or in the middle of an empty field well away from water, they can be highly confusing. On the ground the dark eye patch gives them an odd, almost piratical look; once airborne, a pair of these mainly brownish birds are suddenly transformed by a great blaze of white on the forewing.

It was probably the exotic colours that first attracted British landowners to adorn their estates with the birds. The first introduction was into the king's own collection in St James's Park in 1678, where Willughby and Ray saw and referred to them as the 'gambo-goose' or 'spur wing'd goose'. Although the species still occurs on the lower Nile and was even domesticated and revered by ancient Egyptians, its range spreads right across sub-Saharan Africa and most of those brought back to Britain in the eighteenth century originated from the Cape.

Their numbers slowly built up at several estates, such as Bicton and Crediton near Exeter in Devon, Gosford in East Lothian and the Duke of Bedford's Woburn Abbey, but almost half of the British population can be found in Norfolk. They particularly thrive in the grounds to a number of large halls such as Holkham, Gunton and Blickling, where the combination of old woodland and extensive water meets the birds' unusual requirements.[85]

While we think of parkland as the quintessential English landscape, Dr Bill Sutherland has suggested that

Egyptian geese, like the human occupants of these country estates, are responding to the strong African resonances in this kind of habitat:

> Evolutionary biologists have suggested that, as a result of humans evolving in the African savanna, their innate ideal of landscape beauty is a lush savanna . . . [T]his is why, when given an opportunity . . . humans create a habitat of scattered large trees, short grass and water, of which the parkland linked to stately homes is the most extreme example. It seems entirely appropriate that these recreated savannas should also be occupied by Egyptian Geese.[86]

Those who have become highly familiar with this British 'exotic' can experience reverse feelings of disorientation when they encounter them on their nativecontinent. The bird has a harsh, almost donkey-like braying call, which is now a classic background sound of winter at sites like Holkham. The very same vocalisation can then seem weirdly out of place when heard at an African wetland, where it often accompanies the trumpeting of elephants, the snorts of hippos or the roar of male lions.

Common Shelduck, *Tadorna tadorna*. VN: Links Goose, Sly Goose, Ringer Goose, Skeldro (Orkney); Links Gjus (Shetland). They are the classic ducks of intertidal flats and coastal estuaries, and are often to be seen shovelling steadily with plasticine-red bills across a vast expanse of mud. On a hot summer's day the heat-haze and distance reduce them to little more than shimmering blurs way off at the tide edge.

Confusion with drake shoveler is a regular identification pitfall for unwary observers, but on a good view there is no mistaking this large goose-like bird, when the gloriously iridescent green head and chestnut breast-band stand out against the gleaming white body. The first part of the name is of Dutch origin meaning 'variegated' or 'piebald' and was originally written as a separate word – sheld duck – while variations such as 'shell duck', 'shield duck', 'sheldrake' and 'skelduck' were once all in use. The Orcadian 'skeldro' carries an echo of the last of these lost names. (See also Oystercatcher, page 189.)

The species is found widely across Britain and Ireland and in more recent decades has increased its population (to about 12,000 pairs) and spread into new breeding areas, colonising (or possibly recolonising) inland waters, especially across a swathe of the Midlands between Cambridge and Huntingdonshire, then north-west into Cheshire. However there is a definite coastal bias in the distribution, arising partly from the bird's requirement for an underground nest chamber.

Rabbit holes in sandbanks and dunes are the standard

Shelduck are highly distinctive inhabitants of many British and Irish coastal estuaries.

choice, although shelduck will at times adapt to cavities in hayricks, tree holes as much as 20 feet (6m) off the ground, clefts between boulders, in walls, tombs and even on open fields or saltmarsh, while another common variation is between the foundation timbers of coastal buildings or inside an abandoned structure. A shepherd's hut on a stretch of Kent coast once held four pairs for several years.

A covered chamber offers obvious concealment to the conspicuously coloured female with the actual nest being as much as 10 feet (3m) from the entrance. The birds acquire additional protection by choosing holes in the middle of bramble or gorse patches – hence the Welsh name, *Hwyaden yr Eithin*, 'furze duck'. But the preference for rabbit burrows once led to a degree of persecution. During the nineteenth century in places where rabbits were an important economic resource, such as on the Breckland warrens of Norfolk and Suffolk, the ducks were eradicated because of their alleged disturbance to the warrens' intended occupants.

The shelduck's habit of nesting in a ready-made burrow or hole means that breeding pairs will investigate all sorts of odd places, such as hayricks, derelict buildings and heaps of old rubble.

In the past, they were also shot more widely for the pot, although modern wildfowlers dislike them because of their wariness and poor eating: 'There are few more exasperating things that befall a wildfowler than when, after hours of patient watching in cold and discomfort, his only reward is a Sheld duck, shot in the dusk under the mistaken idea that it is a goose or some other worthy fowl.'[87] Brian Vesey-Fitzgerald, one-time editor of *The Field*, noted enigmatically that 'The flesh to my taste resembles childhood memories of a box of cheap paints.'[88]

An anecdote illustrative of its meagre reputation was told by a warden at Blakeney Point, Norfolk:

one visitor connected with the Press was questioning me about cooking and asked me the best way to cook Shellduck [*sic*]. I thought he was 'pulling my leg' so I told him to place a brick with the Duck in the oven, and when he could get a fork into the brick, the bird would be done. To my amusement I found the recipe was reproduced in a current publication which I now prize in my souvenir collection.[89]

One of the most striking scenes presented by shelduck is that of a family leaving the burrow for the nearest water, which may be as much as 6 miles (10km) away. Until recently in Lancashire it was erroneously thought that the adults carried them to the sea on their backs.[90] It is certainly possible to find parents marshalling up to 20 newly hatched chicks in a pioneer tramp across dry land, while clutches of 32 eggs have been recorded.

The huge clutches are a product of dump-nesting by other females that have no burrow of their own. While it is a form of brood parasitism akin to that of the cuckoo, in the case of the shelduck there is no deliberate damage to the original eggs, nor is the duped parent necessarily an unwilling host for another bird's offspring. Later in the breeding cycle, parents often augment their own natural brood with the young of other pairs. These enlarged crèches of youngsters are known as 'packs' and can involve as many as 100 birds. The single or pair of adults guarding them is often highly territorial towards other shelduck families, sometimes fighting in defence of their pack or in an effort to further enlarge it.[91]

Fortuitously the extra-parental duties of a few

Shelduck often try to adopt the ducklings of other pairs and some of the resulting crèches can involve as many as 100 birds.

individuals allow the rest of the off-duty adult population to complete another important summer ritual – the shelducks' July moult migration. Several thousand British and Irish birds gather in large flocks on the Wash and at Bridgwater Bay on the Severn estuary, but the vast majority fly to the Heligoland Bight off the coast of north-west Germany. Up to 180,000 shelduck, almost the entire north-west European population, build up on the area's massive expanses of shallow tidal flats, which give the birds relative safety during their vulnerable period of flightlessness.

In the past such huge concentrations of largely defenceless birds were an obvious target for wildfowlers, the shelduck being clubbed to death for their meat. Otherwise the skins were sold for a mark apiece to local furriers, who stitched four together to make them into muffs.[92] In the mid-twentieth century the British were also an unlikely cause of high mortality when the Knechtsand area of Heligoland was used as a training area for RAF bombers. Between 21 August and 17 September 1954, bombs killed 12,384 duck, most of them having their lungs ruptured by the intense air pressure caused by the explosions.

The following year the Air Ministry recognised the extent of the devastation and agreed not to use live ammunition during the shelduck's critical moult period from July to September. Today the one possible threat to such a high concentration of a species' entire population comes from pollution in one of Germany's most industrialised areas.[93]

Mandarin Duck, *Aix galericulata*. Along with another import from the Far East, golden pheasant (see page 173), the male mandarin is a strong candidate as Britain's most beautiful bird. With its tall orange 'sails' ('due to the enormously enlarged inner web of the innermost secondary of each wing'), the chestnut 'side-whiskers' and the thickly layered ruff of emerald, copper and white crown feathers, the plumage has about it an element of artifice, even improbability.[94] In fact when one of the first Europeans to visit Japan, Engelbrecht Kaempfer, saw them in their native home he wrote: 'One kind [of duck] particularly I cannot forebear mentioning, because of the surprising beauty of its male, call'd "Kinmodsui" which is so great, that being shewed its picture in colours, I could hardly believe my own eyes, till I saw the Bird itself.'[95]

It was first brought back to Britain in the mid-

The ancestors of Britain's mandarin duck population originally escaped from ornamental wildfowl collections.

eighteenth century, but it was 1834 before a pair at London Zoo bred successfully, and almost a further century before the mandarin gained a toehold as a feral bird. This was largely thanks to the efforts of aviculturists like Alfred Ezra – the man who attempted the establishment of cattle egrets in Britain (see page 48) and who owned the last surviving example of the enigmatic, now extinct pink-headed duck, *Rhodonessa caryophyllacea*.

Six pairs of mandarins were given to Ezra in the late

1920s by the celebrated French ornithologist Jean Delacour, after the latter had found them in a Paris market still in their bamboo cages and in a sorry state, with many birds dying or already dead. The survivors settled in Ezra's magnificent wildfowl collection at Foxwarren Park near Cobham, Surrey, and once they started to breed they soon spread into the surrounding countryside. However, Ezra's encouragement of mandarins did not always meet with success. In 1930 he also helped set free 99 birds in London parks and the grounds of Buckingham Palace and Hampton Court, but these all quickly vanished from the release sites.

Another famous wildfowl collection where mandarins had a prominent place was at Fallodon, the Northumberland home of Lord Edward Grey. Although the Liberal statesman never established a self-sustaining feral population, he was highly successful in encouraging an otherwise rather shy species. Some birds would even come to feed while perched on his shoulder. The Scottish ornithologist Seton Gordon went to visit Grey in the hope of photographing the mandarin's extraordinary tameness. The two men were sitting on a bench by Fallodon's lake when a male mandarin flew towards him and 'made a beautiful landing on Lord Grey's head. Standing on this remarkable perch the Mandarin actually began to display . . . In quick succession two more Mandarin drakes flew up and alighted on the back of the white seat – one on either side of Edward Grey and at an equal distance from him.' An extraordinary and now famous series of photographs resulted.[96]

The stronghold of free-flying 'wild' birds has always been the Home Counties, particularly around Virginia Water in Surrey and the neighbouring Windsor Great Park in Berkshire, where the abundant naturalised rhododendron provides them with the dense cover they relish. Yet the current population of about 7000 birds is still expanding and there are good numbers in Hampshire, Dorset and around the Severn estuary, with healthy outposts as far away as Perthshire and County Down in Northern Ireland.

Although the males are brightly coloured, mandarin ducks can be surprisingly difficult to see because of a preference for streams and pools with densely vegetated banks. The birds have a high ratio of wing area to weight and this gives them great manoeuvrability in the highly restricted air space of woodland habitats. They are able 'to plunge gannet-like with half-closed wing' before pulling up just before landing on the water's surface.[97] Aerial agility, together with the adults' extremely sharp claws, also equip them for an unusual choice of nest site – holes in trees sometimes 10 feet (3m) deep inside the trunk. The thick fluffy down and light weight of the

Seton Gordon's photograph of Lord Grey depicts the great Liberal statesman on his Northumberland estate with a mandarin duck perched on his head.

ducklings mean that they in turn can survive a maiden leap of sometimes up to 50 feet (15m).

At Fallodon, Lord Grey's mandarins found an alternative to the tree hole in the hall's many chimneys. 'Once Lord Grey was awakened very early by a noise in the bedroom chimney, which resembled a sweep's brush. Gradually the noise worked its way down the chimney till, as he had anticipated, a Mandarin duck appeared in the empty grate.'[98] Thereafter the chimney pots were netted each spring.

While the scarcity of natural tree sites may well limit the bird's further spread (jackdaws and squirrels are major competitors), mandarins have occupied a largely vacant ecological niche in southern England, and take readily to nest boxes. Also, their remarkable appearance means that they are widely welcomed as a newcomer to the British avifauna. Until recently their supporters could also claim that, given the bird's severe decline in the Far East, the British population could play an important part in the species' survival. However the recent 'discovery' of a previously unknown population of 60,000 birds in China has largely neutralised the argument, and further releases of captive stock have been made illegal.

The male mandarin's sumptuous plumage has earnt the bird a treasured place in Japanese and Chinese art and literature. For more than 2500 years they have been regarded as symbols of beauty and of fidelity and marital contentment because of the lifelong bond presumed to exist between male and female. So far little of the complex oriental mythology has reseeded itself in the Home Counties, but it has made its mark indirectly in one particular British environment. The birds are regularly depicted – often with great artistic licence – in the furnishings, wall-hangings and paintings that adorn the nation's thousands of Chinese restaurants.

Some sense of the bird's fabled constancy, albeit in a rather misplaced form, also surfaced in the following anecdote:

> A few years ago a pair of mandarin ducks landed on our pool. The female disappeared, but the male bird remained and he became the surrogate father to a family of ducks. The mallard drake drifted away and the mandarin replaced him, keeping in constant close contact with the female duck and her brood of ducklings. He looked so proud of them all and stayed until the young were fully grown and flew away.[99]

Eurasian Wigeon, *Anas penelope*. Its fast, twisting flight and tightly bunched flocks make this handsome duck a favourite with wildfowlers. It was especially popular among the old punt-gunners and on the Ouse Washes as many as 39 could be downed by a single shot from their great-barrelled fowling pieces.[100] It is known as a 'half-bird' by the poulterers on account of its relatively small size, while the flavour of the meat varies according to the birds' diet. Those grazing grass or arable crops make good eating, but wigeon feeding on one of their preferred maritime plants such as eelgrass can be salty and 'fishy'.[101] Irrespective of the taint given to the meat, the attractiveness of eelgrass to wigeon encouraged Frodsham wildfowlers to try to introduce it to the Mersey, hoping to lure in their favoured sport duck.[102]

Wildfowlers, like birdwatchers, undoubtedly enjoy wigeon simply for the sheer pleasure of the male's calls which, unlike the tuneless quacks of most ducks, is a resonant, far-carrying whistle: 'What a grand noise they make as they come tearing down, one, two, three hundred feet in a few seconds, to rock and sideslip as they near the surface of the water and churn it to a lather with their thousands of outstretched feet.'[103] The bird's name (occasionally still spelt 'widgeon') is partly imitative of the sound, and a large gathering in full voice is one of the classic sounds of the British winter and must rank among the most evocative vocalisations by any of our birds.

Only about 400 pairs breed in this country (and just a handful in Ireland) and most of these are in Scotland north of the Tay. However, it is one of the commonest wintering wildfowl, sometimes with almost half the European population (as many as 380,000 birds) arriving in peak winters. Several British wetlands hold huge concentrations such as those on the Ribble estuary in Lancashire (86,000 birds) and the Ouse Washes (30,000).

The **American Wigeon**, *Anas americana*, the New

The chorus of high whistling calls from a wigeon flock is a wonderfully atmospheric sound filled with a wider sense of cold air, winter skies and flat, contour-free landscapes.

World counterpart of our own species, is a duck of comparable beauty and has occurred in Britain and Ireland on more than 400 occasions. Some of these records have involved flocks of up to 13 birds.

Quiet, unobtrusive and easily overlooked, the **Gadwall**, *Anas strepera*, has achieved a steady expansion in the last century of both its breeding range and wintering population, possibly because of northern Europe's ameliorating climate. The British winter total now stands at more than 15,000 birds, with particularly important gatherings at Rutland Water in Leicestershire, Wraysbury Gravel Pits in Berkshire and the Ouse Washes in Cambridgeshire.

The increase in breeding numbers to around 1000 pairs is just as impressive, given that in 1850 there was just one in the whole country. Two wild gadwall were caught at Dersingham Decoy in east Norfolk and given to the Reverend John Fountaine, who pinioned and then released them at a nearby lake called Narford (now Narborough), where they have bred ever since. Within 25 years there were about 70 free-flying birds and these began a slow advance across the Breckland meres, arriving in Suffolk before the end of the century and reaching the Norfolk Broads in 1916. Since then further releases of captive stock have helped to establish breeding gadwall mainly south-east of a line between the Humber and Severn estuaries, with an important Scottish colony of completely wild birds at Loch Leven, Tayside.

The origin of the gadwall's odd-sounding name is rather puzzling. John Ray first used it in the seventeenth century, and W. B. Lockwood concludes that it is onoma-topoeic, reflecting what he calls an 'incessantly chattering species'.[104] He is supported in this by the *strepera* part of the scientific name, which derives from a Latin verb meaning 'to rattle' or 'make a noise'. The male does produce a harsh grunting, while the female has a quieter, drier version of the mallard's 'quack'. But many authorities agree that this is a remarkably silent duck befitting its shy manner; the vocabulary of the female is not even fully described. In short, while the name may echo its calls, these are hardly the bird's most notable feature.

To suggest that the gadwalls' most arresting characteristic is their beauty may sound like deliberate provocation, because at any distance males look simply grey and black, females all-brown. Yet on close inspection the 'plain' areas on the male's flanks and breast are made up of grey-and-cream vermiculations of the most exquisite subtlety.

Eurasian Teal, *Anas crecca*. The artist Eric Ennion perfectly captured the pert charms of the region's smallest duck:

The collective name a 'spring' of teal probably arises from a flock's near-vertical take-off and its wild jinking movements in flight.

The drake teal is one of our most attractive resident wildfowl.

At a distance [the males] just look dark unless they happen to veer round and get caught foursquare in sunlight. Then, suddenly, the rich chestnut head with its emerald slash across the cheek flares out. The buff lines light up on the face, the black-rimmed yellow wedge appears below the tail. Even the pencilling of the body plumage and the flecks on the tawny breast stand out sharply for a moment. And then the vision fades.[105]

Like wigeon, teal was known as a 'half-bird' or 'half-duck' by poulterers and wildfowlers, although in truth it is often as little as one-third or quarter the weight of a good-sized mallard. Nonetheless it is highly prized by some gourmets 'as the tenderest morsel of all the Duck family' and was at one time imported in large quantities from the Continent.[106]

It has also long been a favourite for the table. We know that at George Neville's banquet in 1465, 4000 teal and mallard were served to the guests. The proportion of each species in this total is unknown, but judging from the recipe below, even teal would have represented a substantial dish:

This duck is a treat, the meat is gamey, a little like venison but fine-textured. Most quail recipes adapt well for teal – just increase the cooking time by five or so minutes – but one teal per person should satisfy all but the largest appetites. Dredge the birds in seasoned flour and fry in butter for 2–3 minutes – turning as they colour. Remove from pan and fry chopped onion, leeks and raisins or red cabbage and apple; add half pint of liquid (part port and part stock), replace birds on top of the vegetables, cover and braise for twenty minutes.[107]

Male teal have a gentle, pleasant piping call, which they utter in flight to help maintain the cohesion of the flock. Together with the sound of the wings, the calls allow wildfowlers to identify them even in pitch darkness and their tight formations mean that a single accurate shot can often bring down several at once.

Yet they are generally reputed to be a difficult target. The collective name, a 'spring' of teal, nicely conveys their ability for almost vertical take-off and once airborne they 'immediately start swerving and corkscrewing in a most bewildering fashion'.[108] With their small size and slender-winged appearance, they often look more like medium-sized waders than wildfowl. The wheeling and jinking movements also give a strong impression of high speed; 'I have even heard a great authority mention 150 m.p.h. as the normal speed of teal. Personally I should doubt very much if it attains

A female mallard followed by her downy flotilla is a classic scene of most village ponds, town parks and city-centre gardens.

50 m.p.h. . . . and I am quite sure that the mallard is a good deal the faster bird.'[109]

The name, 'teal', probably imitative of the male's call, is of great age and dates back at least to the thirteenth century. Although a host of alternative spellings have been used in the intervening 800 years, the bird is unique for never having been known by any other name.

Three other teal species have been recorded as vagrants in Britain. There have been 13 British and Irish records of the beautiful **Baikal Teal**, *Anas formosa*, from far eastern Russia and China. Unfortunately all are clouded by the possibility of escapes from ornamental wildfowl collections, in which it is a favourite (despite the species' reluctance to breed in captivity). The wild population now has the unenviable status of a Red Data Species and has been subjected to intense hunting pressure in its winter range, where in 1947 three Japanese wildfowlers were said to have caught about 50,000 birds in under three weeks.

The **Green-winged Teal**, *Anas carolinensis*, is the North American counterpart of our own teal species and is remarkably similar in appearance, yet it has been recognised more than 420 times in the last 45 years with a high percentage of the records in Devon, Cornwall and the Scilly Isles. The more markedly distinct **Blue-winged Teal**, *Anas discors*, is another regular transatlantic visitor to Britain and Ireland.

Mallard, *Anas platyrhynchos*. VN: Stock Duck, Stockie, Stocker (Orkney and Shetland). Just as the great crested grebe is often known simply as *the* grebe, so this is the species most people think of when they talk of ducks. In fact to the Victorians it was known simply as the 'wild duck', the current name being reserved exclusively for the green-headed male. It is our commonest, most widespread, large waterbird. It counts as home most types of wetland, from temporary ponds to the vast intertidal flats in the Wash, while the opportunity to get its feet wet is almost the only habitat requirement.

The female's unmistakable decrescendo quacking – the male has a quieter note usually described as '*rab*' – is part of the soundtrack, imagined or real, in almost every watery landscape. But the classic location where most of us hear and see mallard is at the village pond or in the town park, where they vie with the pigeons and swans as the birds we most love to feed.

The wild birds have been the original source for at least 20 officially recognised domesticated breeds developed since the fourteenth century, including the all-white Aylesbury and the oddly built, front-heavy Khaki Campbell. Some of these cultivated strains are regularly lured back to the mallard's ancestral state and any wild flock includes a few of these escaped 'sports', which mingle and interbreed freely with their pure-bred

Originally the species was called simply the 'wild duck', and only a drake was known as a mallard.

relatives. The motley assortment of hybrid plumages and the highly confiding manner of most town-park gatherings can lead to an assumption that the species has a relationship with humans not far from that of domestic fowl.

But mallard sometimes remind us of their authentic character. Stumble on a sitting female in early spring and she will instantly flush off the nest in a state of great alarm. Rather than flying away, she thrashes at the ground with her wings as if mortally wounded. The whole performance is a distraction display intended to lure predators from the nest, but the duck looks genuinely helpless and terrified. There is no sense now of a bird willing to feed from the hand. If you uncover the nest itself – a warm sphere of duck-down encircling a trove of smooth, waxy, buff-green eggs – the vision compounds the impression of a secretive and untame creature.

A childhood memory confirming the mallard's wild instincts was the sight of a drake in a Buxton park eating a good-sized crayfish. Despite the heavy armour and pincers, the alien-looking crustacean was helplessly clamped in the duck's beak. The experience was all the more striking given that most books list mallard as the classic surface-feeding dabbler. In truth they readily submerge. They have been observed on a number of occasions systematically diving for 'fallen acorns in 2–3 ft of water'.[110] Mallard also delve for shellfish, crabs, shrimps, beetles, leeches, frogs, tadpoles, even eels, as well as eating vegetable matter of all kinds, from aquatic plants to potatoes. The mallards of London's St James's Park seem to have a particular taste for flesh and have been noted eating dead birds as large as wood pigeons, but they are also known to snatch up sparrows that drop their guard in the lakeside mêlée for bread scraps.[111]

Part of the bird's huge success is a catholic taste not only in diet, but also in choice of breeding site. They live for most of the year near water, but in spring females happily fly off to nest on open heather moors or deep in woodland. The more typical situation is among tall marshy vegetation or rough grassland, but other locations include hollow trees, old crows' nests, the crowns of pollarded willows or under rocks. They will also readily adapt to suburban and even highly urban situations like central London. 'Young were bred in a roof garden on a 1933 store in Kensington High Street, in a flower-box on the roof of Canada House 150 feet above Trafalgar Square and on a high block of flats near Baker Street Station with ducklings apparently able to survive the falls to the pavements below.'[112]

In some instances a duckling's journey to the security of open water can be a marathon tramp of several miles, a death-defying leap or even the bird's maiden flight:

My Peterborough office is part of three rectangular buildings separated by completely enclosed courtyards, mostly paved and planted with ornamental shrubs. Not the ideal place to raise a brood of ducklings, but one female mallard thought otherwise. Unnoticed she flew in, laid her eggs, incubated them and obviously commuted to feed without once being spotted. Then one Monday morning in May 1997 she proudly appeared with her ten newly hatched ducklings in an open space without food, water or escape route to the outside world, except by flight.

What were we to do? Emergency rations were obtained from the staff restaurant and a colleague provided a large metal pan which served as the 'village pond'. Over the following weeks the ducklings grew up with only one loss (it was 'replaced' by a plastic duck so mother wouldn't notice!). Then came the moment when the ducklings had to discover a world beyond their own! After some hilarious mis-adventures all managed to respond to mother calling from the roof and fly away, except for two laggards captured and released in the car park. By mid August they were gone and we prayed that they wouldn't all return to breed the following year![113]

Mallard families on the move have given rise to most of the modern road signs warning of the dangers of pedestrian wildfowl, while a crocodile of fluffy ducklings is a regular cause of traffic queues. The naturalist and broadcaster Eric Simms remembers his routine super-vision of mallard families in their safe transit through London streets. When the birds nested in Gladstone Park near the Edgware Road, the mother had 'to usher them some three-quarters of a mile to the Brent Reservoir at the bottom of Dollis Hill':

I would then shepherd the group over three minor roads, across the No. 16 bus route and finally the two lanes of the North Circular Road which involved holding up the traffic. The ducks' average speed was 2 mph and this must have put a considerable strain on the physical reserves of the newly hatched ducklings. Once I was nearly hit by a car so after that my daughter and I netted the duck and put the young in a

Almost everyone will pause for a mother and her passing troupe of ducklings, even at Buckingham Palace.

box. I then drove them down to the Brent Reservoir and launched the family on the water from a yacht-club slipway.[114]

Mallard behaviour that evokes a good deal less sympathy occurs slightly earlier in the season, usually just after the male deserts his partner and she retires to incubate the eggs. If the sitting bird leaves the nest, to feed with the rest of the mallard flock, she can arouse the attention of unattached drakes. Up to 20 will sometimes pursue her relentlessly through the air or on the ground and if the unfortunate duck is overtaken the drakes try to mount her. If the attack takes place on water she runs a risk of being trodden under and even drowned. Although it is 'natural' and regular behaviour, the mallard 'gang-rape' is a distressing experience and has given rise to historical odium and modern offence.

In the *Parlement of Fowles* Chaucer described the drake as a 'stroyer of his own kind'. However Mrs Beeton felt that it was human interference which had caused the mallard's ruin: 'It is to be regretted that domestication has seriously deteriorated the moral

Now part of a vanished sense of British interior design.

character of the duck. In a wild state, he is a faithful husband, desiring but one wife, and devoting himself to her; but no sooner is he domesticated than he becomes polygamous, and makes nothing of owning ten or a dozen wives at a time.'[115] In fact the background to the rape scenario is a numerical imbalance between the sexes. The greater mortality of females during the breeding season, from other quite natural causes, leads to a surplus of unattached males and these are often the birds harassing the females.

The Liberal statesman and aristocrat Edward Grey, who kept a large wildfowl collection on his Northumbrian estate at Fallodon, shared a disdain for the 'uninvited and unwelcome' mallard as a type of avian social climber. 'Beautiful as the drakes are in their season, they have a coarse appearance among the other kinds of wildfowl. The females especially are common and underbred in appearance and vulgar in manner. They are clever at finding the food that is meant for choicer birds, and their appetite is large.'[116]

The go-getter's success is reflected in the present British and Irish total of about 125,000 pairs. There has been an upward trend for the last 40 years, although the current population almost certainly represents a decline from the bird's historical numbers. Both Britain and Ireland have experienced a massive loss of wetland and this would have been ideal habitat for the most adaptable of ducks. But a more eloquent comment on its former abundance is the harvest of wild mallard in earlier centuries.

Throughout the Middle Ages they were a favoured target of the falconer's peregrine, but this form of hunting was mainly a pastime indulged for its test of skill and of the harmonious alliance between man and hawk. Catching mallard for the table was primarily the business of the rustic fowler, using a wide variety of nets and traps. For more than a thousand years it was a highly organised industry, a point well illustrated by the supply of 4000 duck in 1465 for the banquet in honour of the Chancellor of England, George Neville, during his investiture as Archbishop of York. This total, which included teal (see page 90) as well as mallard, represented over a quarter of all birds served at the meal and outnumbered all menu items except rabbits.

Young birds were particularly popular for their tenderness and because they were flightless and thus easier to catch, although even adult duck become vulnerable during their summer moult when they shed the main wing feathers. The males also lose the conspicuous breeding dress and assume the more camouflaged colours of the female, a condition known as eclipse plumage. Throughout the Middle Ages hunters took advantage of this period of flightlessness and trapped the 'flappers', as they were known, in large organised drives.

The usual method in places like the Lincolnshire Fens was to assemble high walls of netting towards which men in boats would slowly corral the duck. They used long poles to knock down escaping birds and eventually pushed the flock to a point where the nets narrowed into a series of tunnel traps. The technique was occasionally condemned, and was even legislated against in 1534 and 1710 because of its sheer brutal efficiency, but it was still being used in the eighteenth century in the Fens, where Willughby had previously seen and described it. With 'the day for fowling set, there is a great concourse of men and boats . . . To one fowling sometimes you shall have four hundred boats meet. We have heard that there have been four thousand Mallards taken at one driving in Deeping Fen [near Crowland, Lincolnshire].'[117]

The basic principle of nets tapering to a narrow trap was further developed in Holland into a permanently sited system involving specially dug flight-ponds, which were made attractive to wildfowl by their secluded location or with bait. From the central pond a series of up to eight channels curved away to the sides and tapered to a covered capture area. From the air the entire water body resembled a giant starfish and the trick was to lure the ducks into one of the limbs and under the 'pipes' of netting enclosing it on all sides.

To achieve this, the fowlers exploited an innate aspect of wildfowl behaviour. When an animal like a fox or dog comes down to the water's edge near swimming mallard, the birds will move towards the predator rather than swim away. This somewhat surprising reaction echoes the behaviour of small garden birds when they locate a roosting owl, or indeed the way in which antelope follow a lion walking through the herd. The alarm calls and visual contact that they maintain with the predator presumably reduce the chances of any one member of the flock or herd becoming a victim. But wildfowlers were able to work with this anti-predator response and lure the ducks into the trap using specially trained dogs.

It was a technique involving enormous skill, and further refinements included wicker screens to let the fowler watch his decoy pipes without being seen; the use of sawdust to deaden his footsteps; burning peat to disguise his scent (actually duck have little or no sense of smell); and the presence of tame 'coy duck' to help persuade the wild birds to settle. In Britain the system became known as a 'decoy', from the Dutch name *Eendekooi*, meaning duck-cage.

Among the first to be built in this country was one on the east coast of Norfolk at Waxham in 1620, although a better-known prototype was in St James's Park, London, which was assembled for Charles II in 1665. After these pioneering efforts they gradually caught on and by 1886 there were 200 decoys operating throughout Britain, with particular concentrations in the Lincolnshire Fens, Norfolk and on the Essex coast.

Through its complex architecture, the fowler's keen acumen and the instinctual understanding between man and dog, the decoy blossomed into a major institution of the British countryside and an integral part of the regional economy. It was in essence a factory of the wetland landscape, converting wild birds into food for the British dining table, and the principal quarry was the mallard, which for several centuries must have provided more protein for the nation than any other wild species of bird. The overall total is unknown, but it certainly involved many millions of birds. A statistical survey of 1790 suggested that London alone was receiving around 200,000 during each six-month season.[118]

There are a number of accounts confirming the extraordinary productivity of individual decoys. Around the Lincolnshire village of Wainfleet, for instance, in the late eighteenth century, 10 decoys recorded a combined total of 31,200 duck in a single season.[119] At nearby Ashby, in the 34-year period from 1833, the single decoy caught 95,836 wildfowl, while Thomas Southwell recounted the huge bag taken at Fritton, near Great Yarmouth on the Norfolk/Suffolk border: 'When John Fisk (the old decoyman, previous to 1848) made what he called a "good haul", Col. Leathes [the owner] says, the

The sign for the Decoy Tavern at Fritton, Norfolk, reminds us of the trap's principal quarry.

stone pavement in the court-yard at the hall, used to be covered from end to end with ducks taken in one day; it took six hundred fowl to do this, and he would average two hundred ducks per day often for weeks.'[120] Today the most prominent legacy in Fritton village is the 'Decoy' pub, with its emblematic image of a drake mallard.

One of the most famous and enduring decoys in Britain, Borough Fen, near Peakirk in Cambridgeshire, was operated by the Williams family for 300 years and declared an ancient monument in 1976. Janet Kear, one of Britain's foremost experts on ducks, describes in her book, *Man and Wildfowl*, the fine-honed transportation network that shifted the daily harvest to the capital:

Until the coming of the train in the middle of the [nineteenth] century, birds had been sent to London via the Great North Road, meeting the 'stage' at Norman Cross 16 miles away, to which point they were carried by horse. Birds caught in the afternoon at Borough Fen would be on the stalls in the capital's Leadenhall Market the next morning. They were packed in hampers . . . [and] with their necks expertly dislocated, birds were in better condition for market than those that had been shot, and were preferred by London cooks as looking neater and keeping fresh longer.[121]

The nineteenth century may have been the heyday of the duck decoy, but its demise followed swiftly in the

'Water off a duck's back' is just one of the mallard's many gifts to our language.

twentieth. The scale of their harvest, combined with the great losses in wetland habitat, may have been part of the same self-defeating syndrome that has more recently eliminated so much of Britain's fishing fleet. It is also certain that advances in gun technology and a large increase in duck shooting had a double impact on a fowling method which relied so heavily on undisturbed conditions. The decoy literally went out with a bang.

By 1918 there were just 19 still in use, and in 1936 only four. However, their extinction has by no means signalled the end to the killing of mallard. Janet Kear has provided the most recent estimate of the numbers of duck being shot in Britain and she suggests that of the annual bag of around a million wild birds, *Anas platyrhynchos* accounts for up to three-quarters, or 700,000–750,000.[122]

In view of the mallard's history of mass slaughter, it hardly seems surprising that our stock phrase for a thing exhausted of life, interest or enthusiasm is a 'dead duck'. It is only one of the bird's numerous contributions to the English language, probably the most familiar of which is the classic euphemism for rain: 'good weather for ducks'. The connection between wildfowl and wet conditions is obvious, but their powers to forecast rain have a pedigree dating back to the ancient Greeks. The philosopher Theophrastus thought that ducks plunging under water were a sign of showers, and this finds a more recent echo in the Victorian couplet: 'When ducks are driving through the burn/That night the weather takes a turn.'

There are also a number of associations with games such as the old pastime of skimming stones lightly across the surface of the water, known as 'ducks and drakes'. Another is the 'duck' in cricket, originally known as a 'duck's eggs', whose shape was thought to resemble the nought scored by the unsuccessful batsman. Finally, a slang expression drawn directly from the mallard's

plumage, is the 'duck's arse' or 'DA', a layered and heavily oiled hairstyle beloved of 1950s Teddy Boys, rockers and greasers, but also, more recently, of the late Princess Diana.

Northern Pintail, *Anas acuta*. This remarkably long-necked, elegant bird ranges across almost the entire northern hemisphere and is, or was, a candidate for the world's commonest duck, with an estimate of six million birds for North America alone. While it has suffered a recent steep decline in many countries, the pintail still has a very large global population. From these millions, just a little over 30 pairs nest annually in Britain and Ireland, making it our rarest resident dabbler.

Breeding was not proven until the late nineteenth century and its establishment may well have been helped by the release of feral birds. Exactly why it should be so rare is not fully understood, although the limiting factor appears to be highly specific habitat requirements: 'it consistently selects shallow aquatic habitats in open grassland areas, most frequently eutrophic waters. Such habitats are subject to most threat from modification through drought, disappearance of temporary pools, pollution, late-spring flooding and drainage.'[123] The 30 pairs are spread very thinly across Britain and Ireland, with concentrations on the Inner Hebridean island of Tiree, the Orkney archipelago and the Ouse/Nene Washes.

In winter about 20,000–30,000 arrive from north-west Europe, representing more than one-third of the total regional population. These congregate mainly at coastal

The pintail is renowned for its huge global population, but not in Britain and Ireland where there are fewer than 30 breeding pairs.

sites, particularly in north-west England, with spectacular flocks involving thousands of birds on the Dee, Mersey and Ribble estuaries, as well as Morecambe Bay. The pintail was once a favourite target of punt-gunners and was considered good sport because of its speed – 'by far the fastest of our duck', according to one authority – but it now forms only a minor part of the wildfowlers' bag.

Garganey, *Anas querquedula*. People regularly mispronounce the name, sounding one or the other 'g' (or even both) as soft. Rightly they should be hard as in 'gargoyle'. It is said to derive from an Italian name, *Garganello*, itself echoing the female's gruff monosyllabic note.

The more arresting sound is the male's advertising call – a curious hard creaking that has elicited some wonderfully imaginative descriptions: 'recalls crackling noise of breaking ice'; 'quite closely resembles drumming of woodpeckers in acoustical structure and spacing; if taped call played at quarter speed sounds like pleasing tune of even spaced notes tapped out on wooden xylophone or wooden blocks'; 'a dry wooden rattle, swaying a little in pitch . . . like running a fingernail across a comb'.[124] It was also once thought to resemble the stridulations produced by some grasshopper species, hence an archaic name used in southern England, 'cricket teal'.

Unique among British and Irish wildfowl, it is a summer visitor to these islands, which are on the edge of its massive Eurasian range. Just 130 pairs are spread thinly across the whole of the country, with a definite bias towards eastern and southern England and with the largest concentration in the Ouse Washes. Here they favour rushy marshland and wet meadows intersected by water-filled ditches, where these quiet and unobtrusive birds can quickly vanish among the lush vegetation.

Northern Shoveler, *Anas clypeata*. 'Scopperbill', 'shovel bill', 'shovelard', 'spoonbill', 'spoon beak', 'whinyard', 'stint', 'beck' – the list of old names for this odd-looking duck is testimony to the feature that has most captured our attention. Its 'de-Bergerac-like bill' is longer than its head and twice as wide at the tip than at the base; it is by any standards an extraordinary appendage.[125] The German, French, Spanish, Swedish and Italian names all celebrate the peculiarity. So, indeed, do the Irish (*Spadalach*, 'spade bill'), Gaelic (*Gob-leathan*, 'broad bill') and Welsh (*Hwyaden Llydanbig*, 'duck with a broad bill') versions.

In some ways the most intriguing of the old names were 'sheldrake' and 'spoonbill', because they give us a fascinating insight into historical attitudes towards wildlife. Prior to the development of ornithology as a science, there was no need or concern to separate each

The shoveler's extraordinary de-Bergerac-like bill is celebrated in most of its European names.

bird unambiguously. Instead a number of species were referred to by a single name, especially when they shared striking characteristics. So we find 'sheldrake', referring to a duck with a strongly variegated plumage, used for both shoveler and shelduck.

The fact that 'spoonbill' served equally well for a duck and a bird closely allied to the herons (see page 60) is stronger evidence for the old fowlers' complacency. It could sometimes result in a lack of clarity, as in the Elizabethan statutes giving protection to spoonbills (*Platalea leucorodia*). In the wording of the Act it was felt necessary to list alternative names so that 'no loophole was left for an offender to escape his fine'.[126] Fortunately in the late seventeenth century John Ray accorded the two birds the different names used to this day.

The choice was fitting because, while the spoonbill usually immerses and sweeps its long bill through the water, the duck is much more willing to shovel directly in the mud. In both birds the bill is similar in structure. The edges of the upper and lower mandible bear a sequence of tiny corrugations, known as lamellae, superficially like the teeth of a comb. These enable the shoveler to filter out seeds and plankton, but it is also one of the most carnivorous of the dabbling ducks and not particularly valued by wildfowlers on that account: 'Shoveler are comparatively easy to shoot, and in my opinion, scarcely worth shooting, for the flesh, though quite eatable, is muddy to taste.'[127] Another wildfowler, F. B. Simson, wishing to express his distaste for a now-extinct Indian bird, the pink-headed duck *Rhodonessa caryophylhacea*, said that he would rather eat any other type of wildfowl, *except* the shoveler.[128]

The bird prefers shallow mud-fringed wetlands over deep lakes and shows an aversion to areas regularly

As a name, 'common pochard' accurately reflects the widespread winter flocks, but come spring fewer than 600 pairs remain to breed in Britain and Ireland.

subject to frost. The climatic cooling associated with the 'Little Ice Age' (1550–1850) probably caused its decline in Britain during that period, while the amelioration in the twentieth century coincided with a gradual recovery. Today about 1250 pairs breed in Britain, mainly distributed east of a line between Glasgow and the Isle of Wight, and with a large concentration in the Ouse/Nene Washes (sometimes as many as 350 pairs), where they nest in wet meadows or grassland, adjacent to water-filled ditches and other pools.

Before shoveler pair off in the spring they sometimes perform an elaborate collective ceremony involving dozens of birds:

> One February [at] Holkham Park in north Norfolk I saw a mass display of some forty shoveler on the lake in which all the birds were packed into a raft on the water no bigger than a kitchen table. All the birds, drakes and ducks, were head to tail, and progressing in a fairly rapid clock-wise movement, giving short, subdued 'hnuk-hnuks'. From time to time some birds would shoot off at a tangent as if thrown out by

centrifugal force, and then would hurry back again into the milling throng.[129]

Aside from the deep resonant courtship calls, shoveler also produce a distinctive drumming rattle with their wings when they rise into the air. They also 'have a trick in flight of simultaneously arching the neck and depressing the wings: it reminds me of someone at a theatre raising himself on his elbows to see past the man in the seat in front'.[130]

Red-crested Pochard, *Netta rufina*. This handsome duck was a rare vagrant in Britain and Ireland until the early twentieth century, since when the number of records has dramatically increased. While this may reflect the bird's genuine range expansion on the European continent, it is also undoubtedly a product of its widespread inclusion in ornamental wildfowl collections. There is a total of about 100 in Britain in most years, many of them initially from captive stock, such as the well-established population at the Cotswold Water Parks, in Oxfordshire and Wiltshire. Individual free-flying pairs have now bred in a number of southern English counties.

Common Pochard, *Aythya ferina*. The unusual name is thought to derive from the same root as the verb 'to poke' or 'poach', and to reflect the bird's delving action when feeding. There were two other possible spellings and pronunciations – 'pocard' or 'poachard' – while an alternative, 'poker', was in use in East Anglia until the late twentieth century along with a name for the plainer female, 'dun bird'.

In autumn the small British and Irish population is joined by a large continental influx and rises as high as 60,000, with more than one-third of these (24,000) in one part of Northern Ireland – at Loughs Neagh and Beg in County Down. In the nineteenth century many were taken in nets, although there were longer traditions of pochard-catching in eastern England, where some of the old names like poker and pocard date from the sixteenth century. While the birds were highly prized as a table item, they were a difficult quarry, unwilling to enter the pipes of duck decoys and reluctant to rise off the water for the wild-fowlers' battue, then flying fast and high once airborne.

The best means of catching them, employed at favoured wildfowling sites on the Essex coast such as Mersea, Goldhanger and Tollesbury, was originally a Dutch technique that combined nets with 'flight-ponds':

[Since] these birds ... skim the water for a certain distance before getting into their flight, nets of about 50 yards long by 18 feet deep were placed on poles, so fixed and adjusted by weights that they could be quickly moved up and down by the aid of ropes and pulleys; so that, as soon as the fowl were flushed and made to fly in the direction of the nets, the nets were raised and thus intercepted their flight, the birds tumbling down ... at the foot of the net ... from which they could not escape. Hundreds used to be taken in this way at a single haul.[131]

More recently wintering pochard provided one of the few examples where improved water quality and reduced pollution has had an adverse effect on wildfowl numbers. Until 1978 Loch Duddingston just outside Edinburgh held about 7000 birds, the largest regular flock in Britain. These fed out in the Firth of Forth on the aquatic invertebrates that thrived around a major sewage outflow pipe and on the waste grain pouring from it. When a new treatment works was built, the food supply ceased and so did the pochard. Within seven years the Loch Duddingston flock had virtually disappeared.[132]

There have been just four records of the **Canvasback**, *A. americana*, in Britain. The first of these smartly dressed American ducks presents a classic illustration of site fidelity by an individual bird. The young male was initially found in January 1997 near the Wildfowl & Wetlands Trust reserve at Welney, Norfolk, where it stayed intermittently for seven weeks. The disoriented vagrant then presumably migrated to eastern Europe with Welney's wintering flock of 1400 largely male pochard, with which it closely associated and even more closely resembled.

The following November it flew back to Britain, appearing this time at Abberton Reservoir. After just a week at this Essex site, it dutifully returned to Welney for the rest of the winter, disappearing once again in early spring 1998 with the departing pochard. Thereafter the now fully adult canvasback forsook Welney entirely and all of its subsequent appearances were at (or near) Abberton, where it turned up briefly in April 1999, then throughout the winters of 1999/2000 and 2000/2001. But where precisely this lost American soul passed its four summer holidays on continental Europe no one knows.

The closely related **Ring-necked Duck**, *Aythya collaris*, and **Ferruginous Duck**, *A. ferruginea* (VN: Fudge Duck), are both attractive annual visitors to Britain and Ireland in small numbers. While the first is a North American bird with an expanding range, the second is a Eurasian species severely affected by habitat loss. If their distribution and status could not be more contrasting, in Britain the birds are at least united by birdwatchers' uncertainty surrounding their origins. Both are widely kept in captivity (where they readily hybridise with other *Aythya* species) and the extent to which the birds found here are genuinely wild is part of the age-old problem surrounding rare wildfowl.

Tufted Duck, *Aythya fuligula*. VN: Tufty/ies. These are 'the lovable little diving ducks' grown tame – and plump – on daily handouts of bread in London's St James's Park, and now in most other town and city parks featuring a water body of moderate size.[133] While the mallard may be more familiar to the public, tufties are just as easily identified, especially the dark blue-black males with their golden eyes, floppy top-knot and that 'white patch on each side, shaped much like a Dutch wooden shoe, with the toe pointing towards the tail'.[134]

Their present ubiquity contrasts sharply with their status in the mid-nineteenth century when a breeding record was an occasion for great excitement. The villages of Malham in Yorkshire and Osberton in Nottingham-shire claim equal honours for the first ever definite record in 1849, although it was almost certainly breeding elsewhere in Nottinghamshire during the 1830s.[135] From these pioneer sites tufties began a rapid expansion and may have been assisted by the introduction of an important prey item, the zebra mussel, which was first released into the London docks in 1824.

The duck's general reputation for unpalatability was probably beneficial: 'Tufted reminded one irresistibly – at least such is my experience – of chewing a piece of india rubber, so that the wildfowler pays little or no attention to them.'[136] Of much clearer benefit to its increase was the widespread construction of drinking-water reservoirs in the early twentieth century and the mania for gravel extraction, with its resulting flooded pits. It is now hard to imagine either of these wetland types without its nesting pair, the birds often laying on small islands in the middle of the water. At Loch Leven, Tayside, there is a much more impressive concentration, where an area known as St Serf's Island near the loch's southern shore hosts a colony of 400 pairs (about 40 per cent of the Scottish total). Yet even this cannot compare with an extraordinary winter gathering of over 20,000 tufties on Lough Neagh, County Down, in Northern Ireland.

The present breeding total of around 9300 pairs is spread widely throughout Britain and Ireland, with outposts in the Outer Hebrides, Shetland, Orkney and north-easternmost Grampian. At St Combs, near Fraserburgh, there is Britain's only 'Tufted Duck' hotel, built originally as a shooting lodge for the guests of J. D. Carnegie, whose estate once included the Loch of Strathbeg (now an RSPB reserve).[137]

Greater Scaup, *Aythya marila*. 'Greater' was added simply to differentiate it from the slightly smaller **Lesser Scaup**, *A. affinis*, a vagrant from North America, but 'scaup' itself is a recent shortening of the original name, 'scaup-duck', which derived from an old medieval Scottish word – 'scalp' – for a mussel bed. Mussels and several other types of shellfish are a favourite prey of this autumn and winter visitor.

In the late nineteenth century, the north Lancashire cockle-gatherers used to have a sideline in scaup-catching, taking them with nets staked out at low tide on the sandflats near Flookburgh and Arnside.[138] Another important wintering site where they were also netted in large numbers was on the Firth of Forth.

The birds were attracted by Edinburgh's old Victorian sewage system and the great outpouring of untreated effluent from outfall pipes offshore at Leith and Seafield. This was the basis of a highly productive marine eco-system, and the endlessly bobbing slick of up to 30,000 scaup (80–90 per cent of the entire British population) fed on a 'super-abundance of small worms'. Edinburgh's distilleries and breweries, whose warm, comforting malty odours still waft through the capital's streets, were also an important source of waste grain for the birds.[139]

Sadly, these rafts of handsome sea duck almost completely vanished when Edinburgh acquired a brand-new sewage-treatment plant in 1978 (see Common Pochard,

page 99). The striking irony was not lost on L. H. Campbell, who studied the Firth of Forth scaup flocks for several years: 'as a result of a major environmental quality improvement scheme, the United Kingdom has lost one of its ... internationally important wildfowl sites'.[140] A smaller flock at Invergordon disappeared in similar circumstances, but the species' happy link with British sewers remains unbroken at sites like Largo Bay and Loch Indaal, where the duck also benefit from distillery waste.

Common Eider, *Somateria mollissima*. VN: Dunter (Orkney and Shetland); Cuddy's or Cuddy Duck (Northumberland). This is by a wide margin our heaviest duck, the big males weighing more than 6 pounds (2.9kg) and almost twice as much as their mallard counterparts. The Scottish author and naturalist Gavin Maxwell captured them perfectly when he wrote that eiders 'are heavy, solid, flat-bottomed, ocean-going people; awkward on land, with their legs set too far back for a dignified gait, but deep divers and superb in the momentum of full flight that appears to gain impetus from weight like a runaway lorry on a steep hill'.[141] They enjoy a reputation as the world's fastest bird in level flight, with timed speeds of 47 mph (76 km/h).

Although only a single species breeds, two other eiders from the high Arctic appear occasionally in Britain and Ireland. The males of both **King Eider**, *Somateria spectabilis*, and **Steller's Eider**, *Polysticta stelleri*, are dazzlingly beautiful, the first deriving its name from its 'occasional association with a flock of common eiders, among which this striking bird appears as "king".'[142] At one time the sumptuous golden knob at the base of the bird's bill was bitten off and eaten in Greenland as a powerful aphrodisiac. Fortunately the idea has not taken hold among Britain's birdwatchers and the one or two king eiders that turn up here almost annually are treated more like celebrities.

Steller's eider, discovered and named after the distinguished eighteenth-century German explorer–naturalist Georg Steller, is much rarer, with only 14 in the last 170 years. The most recent record was based simply on a dismembered wing picked up off the beach on Fetlar, Shetland. Far more satisfying was the male that arrived at Vorran Island on the west coast of South Uist, Outer Hebrides, in May 1972, and remained at the site for the next 13 years. Thousands of people made the pilgrimage to see it over that period and 'the visitor's book at the tiny Howmore hostel must read like a Who's Who of British twitching'.[143]

If less handsome than these rare relatives, the drake common eider is itself 'a superb creation', suggesting to Gavin Maxwell the 'full dress uniform of some unknown navy's admiral':

Eider are birds of rocky shorelines in northern Britain and Ireland.

The first impression is of black and white, but at close quarters the black-capped head that looked simply white from far off seems like the texture of white velvet and shows feathers of pale scintillating electric green on the rear half of the cheek and on the nape; the breast, above the sharp dividing line from a black abdomen, is a pale gamboge, almost peach. From the white back the secondary wing feathers of the same colour sweep down in perfect scimitar curves over the black sides adding immensely to the effect of a uniform designed for pomp and panache. The whole finery looks so formal that one has the impression that it must be uncomfortable.[144]

It takes the drake at least three and a half years to achieve this full adult dress, while the sub-adults progress through a truly 'bewildering variety of piebald plumages', so that eider flocks seldom have two young males looking exactly the same.[145] Such is the complexity that in *The Handbook of British Birds* it took more than 2000 words of the densest telegramese – more than for any other species of wildfowl – to give an account of the eider's various plumage stages.[146]

The brown-and-black vermiculations of the female look dowdy by comparison, but ironically her plumage has contributed far more to the species' world renown. This is because of the grey-brown down that she plucks from her own famously soft breast and uses to line the nest. Eider down, for centuries synonymous with the feather-filled quilt that once provided much of the warmth on British and northern European beds, has remarkable insulatory properties and is still widely used in jackets, pillows and sleeping bags. 'The outer edges of the plumules interlock to provide a dense mass that can be compressed and spring out again without damage. Trade figures state that 1.5kg of goose down, which lacks much of the cohesion and elasticity of Eider down, can provide adequate insulation in a sleeping bag at –35°C; eiderdown can provide the same or better, while a synthetic fill is satisfactory only down to –7°C.'[147]

The feathers have been harvested in the northern parts of the eider's range for hundreds, if not thousands, of years. The Icelandic people are particularly successful at encouraging dense colonies of wild birds, sometimes involving thousands of pairs. Sitting eiders are extra-

The female eider's famously soft breast is still regarded as the optimum source of feather down for duvets and pillows.

ordinarily tame and will allow humans to walk carefully among them and even touch them. A single nest yields two lots of down a season and 30 nests are needed to produce a single pound (450gm). Although the industry has now declined, the Icelandic farmers once gathered more than 4 tons (4294kg) for export in peak years: the

down feathers from approximately 280,000 eider breasts.[148]

Exploitation was never so fully developed in Britain, although the name used for the eider by Martin Martin in the seventeenth century was 'colk', and was closely related to an old Gaelic word *colcaidh*, meaning 'a featherbed'.

Fenwick Lawson's bronze sculpture of St Cuthbert is at Lindisfarne Priory on Holy Island. However, it was the protection he offered to the wildlife of the Farne Islands that marks out the seventh-century saint as one of our earliest conservationists. His beloved eiders are still common there today.

More recently Gavin Maxwell attempted to develop a commercial eider colony near his lighthouse home on Eilean Ban, the White Island, a tiny speck just off the Skye coast, in the 1960s. Maxwell visited Iceland and was enthused both by the success of the locals' time-honoured methods and by the high value of the eider down itself; a single pound was then worth £10 (more than £110 today). The author's premature death in 1969 meant that the project never properly materialised.

In the medieval period there appears to have been some harvest of eider down in northern England, judging from the ancient laws instituted to protect the species. There was also a fascinating, long-established association between the duck and St Cuthbert, the seventh-century missionary, whose hermitage was on the Farne Islands off the Northumbrian coast. Cuthbert was an early naturalist and conservationist, giving protection to the abundant wildlife on the Farnes. Tradition has it that he had a special attachment to the ducks sharing his remote island cell and laid down rules for their protection in the breeding season (although James Fisher suggested that this was possibly a subsequent refinement of the saint's history).[149] Yet 'St Cuthbert's duck' was for centuries the Northumbrian name for the eider, and even today 'particularly in the fishing villages from Boulmer to the Scottish Border older residents are aware that Cuddy's Duck or Cuddy Duck were local names'.[150]

Whatever the truth of Cuthbert's relationship, there is little doubt that the birds' identification with the Anglo-Saxon holy man would have conferred a reflected sanctity on them, making the myth a useful conservation tool for an economically valuable species.[151] Today it is also true that at the Northumbrian sites associated with St Cuthbert, particularly Lindisfarne and the Farne Islands, the duck features strongly, like the saint himself:

> Of the eider both pottery and porcelain models are available as tourist souvenirs in Seahouses and on Lindisfarne, and an illustration of a drake has been adopted as the emblem of the Northumberland and Tyneside Bird Club. Although no longer available it was also produced as a metal lapel badge by the club and featured as the cover illustration of *Northumberland's Birds*, the standard county avifauna produced by the Natural History Society of Northumbria.[152]

Yet not all communities are quite so welcoming of eiders. The birds are well known to feed upon molluscs, which they prise from the rocks and then swallow whole. In parts of western Scotland local fishermen have established mussel 'farms' in which the spat (larvae) are encouraged to settle and develop on ropes suspended in the water from anchored rafts. When the mussels are mature, the ropes are simply hauled up and the shellfish harvested. Unfortunately, as Janet Kear has explained, 'Rope-grown shells are thin and free of barnacles, and Eiders like them as much as the clients of London restaurants.'[153] Occasionally, if serious damage is in-

103

The long-tailed ducks wintering in northern Britain and Ireland are a beautiful addition to our coastal wildlife.

flicted, the fishermen can obtain a licence and shoot the offending birds.

Aside from the full breeding regalia of the male, eiders have one more feature to help disarm any animosity – the wonderful, soft, husky cooing note made by the courting drakes. It is a soothing sound and in Berwickshire and East Lothian it gave rise to the local name, 'coo-doo'. Another Northumbrian name, now also obsolete, 'Culvert's' or 'culvert duck', is intriguing because it is usually deemed to be a corruption of Cuthbert. However, 'culvert' is also a vernacular word for the wood pigeon, and 'culvert duck' neatly combines a celebration of the eider's gentle dove-like vocalisations with the more usual saintly connections.

The call itself, often delivered by males in unison and beautifully coordinated with a number of extravagant physical gestures, can also have a rather humorous quality. To me the sound of several drakes calling in concert is rather like a comic exaggeration of north-country women simultaneously scandalised and excited by a piece of choice gossip.

No doubt it was the same sort of associations that led to the array of colourful, now politically incorrect, old names for another of our most beautiful wintering wildfowl, the **Long-tailed Duck**, *Clangula hyemalis*. 'Old squaw', 'old Injun' and 'old wife' – all supposedly garrulous stereotypes – derived from the modulated conversational quality of the calls produced by the male bird (the first of the names, rendered as a single word, 'oldsquaw', survived in North America until the end of the twentieth century).

Yet another old name, 'hound duck', suggests the vocalisation's similarity to distantly baying hounds, but in Scotland or around the Borders, where most of the British birds occur, it is more frequently likened to the skirl of the nation's favourite instrument: 'To my ear it resembles the bagpipes, but whatever it resembles, once heard it can never be confused with the call of any other bird, nor can it ever be forgotten.'[154]

I was down on the rocks very close to them – close enough to see the pale-pink bands on their dark-tipped brown bills and the curious white ellipses round their eyes, and to hear more clearly their musical calls: that broken yodelling in two pitches, tenor and baritone, a diminutive of the Whooper's *gwuk-gwoog*; and, in addition, a higher-pitched repetitive single note, and a guttural quack when one drake 'flew' in anger at another. It was this melody of notes, variously broken and modulated by wind and sea, that produced the effects of bagpipes.[155]

An attempt at transliteration of the commonest four-syllabled call resulted in two local Scottish names, 'col-candle wick' (Fife) and 'col-cannel-week' (Forfar), which are a fairly accurate echo of the sound. The simpler onomatopoeic 'calloo' still survives in Orkney and in Shetland, where 'In the past I have heard it said that spring is coming when the calloos call. In reality it is a courtship call and they do it on nice days from January onwards.'[156]

(Common) Black Scoter, *Melanitta nigra*. This is the classic sea duck off British and Irish coasts in winter, typically congregating in densely packed rafts of hundreds, sometimes thousands, of birds. However even the largest gatherings can be difficult to observe well, as they roll in and out of view with the swell. Whole sections of the flock also vanish intermittently as they submerge to hunt for their shellfish prey and some dives can last up to a minute, with birds recorded at depths of about 100 feet (30m).

In flight they form neat strings of black 'blobs' close to the sea surface, when one of their strongest identification features is the absence of colour and, in the case of males, of plumage contrast of any kind. Another pointer is the sheer speed and directness of their flight: 'I fancy this is the fastest of all the ducks that visit Britain.'[157]

It has been suggested that the odd-sounding name is derived from an Old Norse word meaning 'to move quickly', *sceotan* (whence the English 'scoot'), but W. B. Lockwood favours the idea that it is a misspelling of 'sooter' – the soot-coloured duck.[158] This certainly meshes with many of the old vernacular names, which reflect the bird's monochrome plumage.

Northern Scotland accounts for almost all of the 100 pairs breeding on mainland Britain (there are also about 65 pairs in western Ireland) and a high percentage of the wintering population, for which the Moray Firth is an old traditional stronghold. The areas around Spey and Burghead Bays, as well as Dornoch on the opposite shore, once held 10,000 common scoter, together with up to several thousand of their much scarcer and slightly larger, white-winged relative, the **Velvet Scoter**, *Melanitta fusca*. Unfortunately these impressive gatherings have since declined.

There are also occasional large movements of common scoters off English coasts with a 'staggering' passage of 27,000 seen off Dungeness in Kent on 8 April 1979. of them passed the point in just three hours and Peter Grant memorably described one flock of 1360 individuals as 'an astonishing sight as it crocodiled over the waves like a gigantic sea serpent'.[159]

They may well have been birds returning north from their winter quarters in France, where they gather off the country's Atlantic coast. Thomas Bewick knew of the French population in the eighteenth century and described how local fishermen caught them in nets:

These birds are sold to the Roman Catholics, who eat them on fast days and in Lent, when their religious ordinances have forbidden the use of all animal food except fish; but these birds, and a few others of the

same fishy flavour, have been exempted from the interdict on the supposition of their being cold-blooded, and partaking of the nature of fish.[160]

Scoter-eating during Lent was apparently widespread among northern Catholics, although the rather opportunistic interpretation of the bird's identity was of dubious benefit. 'Rank and fishy' was one verdict on the meat. The noted wildfowler Brian Vesey-Fitzgerald could think of no 'sound reason why either the common scoter or the velvet scoter should be shot'.[161]

The North American **Surf Scoter**, *Melanitta perspicillata*, is a scarce migrant to these islands, mainly off western coasts, and has been recorded almost annually for the last 50 years.

Common Goldeneye, *Bucephala clangula*. The piercing golden eyes and the curiously bulbous, almost triangular head-shape are about the only features shared by the markedly different sexes of this shy diving duck. Although it has long been known as a winter visitor and has acquired a string of local names across Britain and Ireland ('rattlewing' in Norfolk and 'curre' in Scotland are now obsolete), the goldeneye's colonisation as a breeding species is a much more recent and striking development.

They are primarily birds of middle and higher latitudes around the whole of the northern hemisphere, where they breed in tree holes, often occupying the large cavities excavated by black (*Dryocopus martius*) and

During the nineteenth century the Lapps put out nest boxes for common goldeneye in Scandinavia. More recently Scottish environmentalists followed suit and there is now a thriving population in the Highlands.

pileated (*D. pileatus*) woodpeckers in their respective Eurasian and American ranges. However goldeneyes readily adapted to nest boxes in Scandinavia, where Laplanders erected them as much as two centuries ago so that they could harvest the eggs.

In view of the bird's strong tree-nesting habit, the first British breeding record in 1931/2 was treated with a degree of scepticism, primarily because the birds laid in a rabbit burrow adjacent to saltmarsh at Burton on the Dee estuary, Cheshire. The suspicion has remained that they were injured birds pricked the previous winter by wildfowlers.

It was 1970 before the species attempted to nest in Britain again, in the far more likely setting of a small pine-fringed lochan near Aviemore in the Spey valley. Few perhaps could have realised as they watched the female and her four ducklings that the small family group was the vanguard of a remarkable southward expansion. The birds were undoubtedly aided by a local nest-box scheme and as early as 1973 five of the six pairs were using man-made structures. By 1990 around 700 boxes had been erected, and by 1998 of the 52 pairs nesting at the RSPB's Insh Marshes reserve, only five were in natural sites. Goldeneye have now increased to about 200 pairs, mainly concentrated around the Spey valley, although they have successfully bred as far south as the Borders and summered at a number of sites in England, Wales and Ireland.

One of the great pleasures afforded by the spread is the opportunity to watch goldeneye in communal display, during which the immaculately plumaged males perform a striking head-pumping action. It involves:

> a very dramatic leaning of the head back until it meets the middle of its back, then suddenly kicking out with the feet, which not only produces a large amount of spray but has the effect of lifting the rear end of the bird out of the water, while forcing the front end down. Simultaneously with the kick, the bird thrusts its neck and head vertically and gives out a loud and rasping double whistle, which can be heard a kilometre away.[162]

Smew, *Mergellus albellus*. Early ornithologists had real problems with the identity of this scarce winter visitor to our lakes and reservoirs. Sir Thomas Browne named it the 'weasel coot', after the reddish-brown colour of the female's crown (even now females are known as 'redheads'). Later in the seventeenth century John Ray knew it as the 'white nun', which reflected the strikingly hooded appearance of the elegant male.

More than a hundred years later Thomas Bewick diagnosed the trouble when he wrote, 'The Red-headed Smew had long been considered by some ornithologists as a distinct species; while others have maintained that it is the female of the species. It is now, however, ascertained to be the immature male of that bird.'[163]

His statement was both right and wrong. Bewick highlighted the puzzlement arising out of the radically different appearances of the two sexes, but then added his own ha'p'orth of confusion. In fact young smews of both sexes, the adult female and even males in eclipse plumage have the same basic appearance, with largely grey bodies and partly or wholly chestnut crowns.

Our deeper understanding of the pattern of distribution among wintering birds now allows us to understand the earlier errors. In several species of duck, including smew, the females and young winter further south and west than their mates, so that the sexes are to some extent geographically segregated. The early naturalists probably never saw a pair of smew together. In Britain 'redheads' outnumber 'white nuns' by about two to one. In Ireland the males are rarer still.[164] In most years there are seldom more than 100–200 birds scattered thinly, with the highest numbers in south-east England, especially around London. However, hard conditions, as in the winters of 1978/9 and 1996/7, can bring an influx of continental birds, mainly from the Netherlands, with a record total of 453 in the second of these cold spells.

Red-breasted Merganser, *Mergus serrator*. VN: Merg, RBM (birders); Sawbill, Hair Duck (Orkney); Herald Duck (Shetland). Both this bird and its close relative, the **Goosander**, *M. merganser*, have long necks and long flat-backed bodies, which they often hold low in the water to give them an almost diver-like profile. The effect is compounded by a slender and rather un-duck-like red beak, whose serrated inner edges give the two birds and also the smew their group name, the sawbills. Like tiny backward-pointing teeth, these enable the birds to grasp small slippery fish that are their main prey. They also have prominent crown feathers, in the case of the merganser a spiky 'punk's' crest (thus the Orcadian name, 'hair duck'), while the goosander has a richer fuller 'mane' down the back of the nape.

The other striking similarity between the two is their remarkable range expansion in Britain and Ireland during the course of the last 150 years. In the first half of the nineteenth century only the merganser was known as a breeding bird, and in Britain it was confined to Scottish lochs and coastal waters north of the Clyde. In the second half of that century it began to spread south and by 1930 had reached the Scottish Borders, crossing into England exactly 20 years later. Today the species shows

The goosander is a bird of lochs, upland reservoirs and fast-flowing northern rivers.

a strong western bias, but has steadily continued to colonise as far south as Derbyshire and mid-Wales.

The goosander's spread has an even greater sense of drama, given that as recently as 1871 the only breeding birds in Britain were one or two pairs in Argyll and Perthshire. Yet these gradually expanded to all parts of the Scottish mainland and crossed the border into Cumbria in 1950, exactly the same year as the red-breasted merganser. Now the goosander occupies much of Wales and almost all of northern England as far south as Derbyshire, with small populations even in Devon and north-western Ireland. Its British range exceeds that of its close relative and although the last estimates suggested 2700 goosander as opposed to 2900 merganser pairs, these positions may well reverse, since the last major census suggested that the former was still increasing while mergansers had marginally declined.[165]

What makes these two sawbills' recent success all the more extraordinary is that both are widely regarded as a nuisance to fishing interests and the spread has been achieved in the teeth of persecution. The reasons are the sheer efficiency of that saw-edged bill and the two birds' fondness for salmon parr and young trout. Both will take a wide range of fish and eels up to 1 foot (30cm) in length, although on some river systems young salmon and trout may comprise 80 per cent of the goosander's diet. And while their usual prey are smaller than those desired by

anglers, it is argued that the birds take out a large percentage of young stock, suppressing the abundance of the subsequent catch.

Experiments involving young goosander demonstrated that each bird required 72 pounds (33kg) of fish to reach the adult stage, while studies done on Lake Windermere into the diet of the smaller red-breasted merganser indicated that each young bird ate more than 44 pounds (20kg) of fish in 100 days. The overall estimate of fish taken during the summer by the lake's average total of 131 merganser ducklings was 2.6 ton(ne)s.[166]

Water bailiffs and anglers long complained of fish predation and on rivers like the Tay a 20-pence bounty was paid for dead goosander up until the 1970s.[167] As a consequence neither species was safeguarded under the 1954 Protection of Birds Act, while under the 1981 Wildlife and Countryside Act provision was made for licensed shooting of them both. Each licence application is theoretically subjected to a vetting procedure, which establishes that there is a serious economic impact from the damage, that a range of other non-lethal methods have been tried and have failed, and that control measures will not significantly damage the bird's overall population.

Commercial fisheries, including put-and-take angling clubs, trout or salmon farms and the district salmon fishery boards on Scottish rivers like the Deveron and Tweed, routinely seek permits to control goosander and merganser populations. In 2000 almost all of the 26 licences for goosander (357 birds shot) and all 25 for merganser (88 shot) were sanctioned in Scotland.[168]

The issues surrounding sawbill predation of fish are complicated and vexed, not least because adult birds, young and eggs are all still being destroyed illegally; because goosander numbers continue to increase; because salmon have suffered severe adverse effects from rises in sea temperature and over-harvesting by the Irish salmon fleet; and because artificially stocked rivers and lochs create their own ecological syndrome. Mick Marquiss and David Carss have investigated the problems posed by fish-eating birds and outline some of the implications of culling:

> In three of four instances, sawbill numbers were reduced by intensive shooting but the local reduction in subsequent duck abundance was much less than the numbers shot. In no instance were sawbills eliminated, even from small sections of river, because of the persistent movement of ducks into areas where shooting occurred.
>
> These results imply that casual shooting is ineffective in reducing bird numbers but, more importantly, that where shooting is sufficiently intensive to be effective, it will have impacts on the bird population over a much wider area than the fishery concerned. Stated simply, if shooting birds to protect fisheries is to be effective it presents a potential conservation problem because it involves a cull of the wider population.[169]

Whatever the truth of their impact on fish stocks, there is no doubting the sawbills' predatory ability. They can dive for up to 45 seconds and there is one extraordinary claim for a merganser submerging for two minutes. Both species will also swim along with just the head and neck underwater as they search for prey, while another technique is to drive a fry shoal in unison, the birds moving in a loose front and diving constantly to snap up the disoriented fish.

For all the controversy, it is also hard to imagine a more beautiful 'pest' than a male goosander. The head is a glossy bottle-green with hints of amethyst, while the whole of the white underparts are suffused with pale salmon-pink. The birds spend long periods asleep or loafing on the water and on a cold, bright winter's day there are few more lovely visions than a group resting in a backwater, their smooth contours and patterns mirrored in the river's surface.

Ruddy Duck, *Oxyura jamaicensis*. With its plasticine-blue beak, crisp white cheek patches and rich chestnut body the colour of fresh conkers, the male ruddy duck is a bird of undeniable physical charm. However, its most arresting characteristic is present on both sexes and in all ages – a long, often erectly held tail, from which *Oxyura* ducks gain their generic name, 'stifftails'.

Originally a North American bird, the species has gained a footing in this country more rapidly, more securely and more controversially than any other exotic wildfowl. Its half-century residence in Britain and the more recent establishment of British birds on mainland Europe, where they are presumed to be a significant threat to the closely related but globally threatened white-headed duck *O. leucocephala*, are subjects more hotly contended by ornithologists than almost any other bird-related issue.

Like many painful disputes, it started quite innocently when three pairs were imported to the Wildfowl & Wetlands Trust headquarters at Slimbridge in 1948. The birds seemed almost immediately at ease in an Old World setting and began breeding the following season. However the young ducklings were so adept at diving that each year some of the broods eluded the curator's best efforts to catch and pinion them. As a consequence a full-winged population was soon established and was escaping from the Trust collection as early as 1952. A handful slipped the net each year until 1957, when there was a mass break-out of 20 birds. By that time the ruddy duck's feral future was well under way.

Given that some environmentalists view its subsequent history as a tale of dangerous promiscuity, they may well unearth something darkly significant in the fact that the small caucus of males that had established itself at the Chew valley and Blagdon reservoirs in Somerset in the late 1950s was very soon 'displaying – albeit in a restrained manner – to each other and, on one occasion, to a female mallard and to a mallard drake in eclipse plumage'.[170] Under normal conditions ruddy-duck breeding behaviour is often accompanied by 'intense hostility' between the sexes and territorial aggression towards other species.[171]

Since the Wildfowl & Wetlands Trust is now at the forefront of efforts to eliminate the present population, the current staff must rue the day their predecessors helped to ensure the ruddy duck's establishment. In 1961 Slimbridge personnel turned out several young females at Chew to mate with the love-lorn drakes, although it is almost certain that escapee birds had already bred for the first time the previous summer.

Chew valley and Blagdon reservoirs have remained very important wintering sites for ruddy duck ever since. However the birds' real fortunes were made to the north in the West Midlands, where they dispersed over the

British ruddy ducks are now under a death sentence from environmentalists.

The genetic threat presented to the look-alike white-headed duck of Spain is the main reason for the ruddy-duck cull.

region's numerous new man-made reservoirs and gravel pits. The success of these small isolated breeding populations was best revealed in winter, when the birds congregated in large flocks at the Staffordshire reservoirs of Belvide and Blithfield.

Every attempt to monitor the bird's progress has returned with evidence of dramatic increase. During the course of the first nationwide census of bird populations from 1968 to 1972, ruddy duck more than doubled their breeding population to 25 pairs. By the time of the second in 1991 it had exploded, with an estimated 570 nesting pairs and a national total of 3400 birds. Throughout the 1990s it was increasing at an annual rate of 10 per cent and by the end of the decade a population of 5000 birds was widely spread from central Scotland to the Channel coast.

While they were confined to British shores, ruddy ducks were not perceived as a serious problem. They exploit a largely vacant ecological niche, and as recently as 1976 their release and colonisation were accepted without serious objection: 'it must be conceded that no harm appears to have been done to any native species or habitat, nor is there any danger of this essentially aquatic species becoming an agricultural pest.'[172] Its apparent attachment to the English Midlands was also fully

reciprocated by local birdwatchers, who in 1975 chose it as the emblem of the West Midlands Bird Club. Its vice-president, Alan Richards, explains the decision:

The government's redrawing of county boundaries in the early seventies made a bit of nonsense of our previous emblem, which was an outline sketch of the club's area – the counties of Warwickshire, Worcestershire and Staffordshire. When the committee got together to choose a replacement, we had a couple of candidates. At the time in question the Marsh Warbler was a speciality of the region, however, it was such a nondescript bird that once reduced to a simple design we realised no one would have a clue what it was meant to be! The other option was the Little Ringed Plover, which was just beginning to colonise, especially in north Warwickshire. Unfortunately we learned that the Middle Thames Naturalists had already bagged it for their logo. So that was out.

However, a bird which was beginning to make itself noticed in the Club's area was the Ruddy Duck. It was turning up at various waters, nesting and quickly becoming part of the West Midlands ornithological scene. As an adventurous, go-getting species, which epitomised the region's dynamic approach to life, it

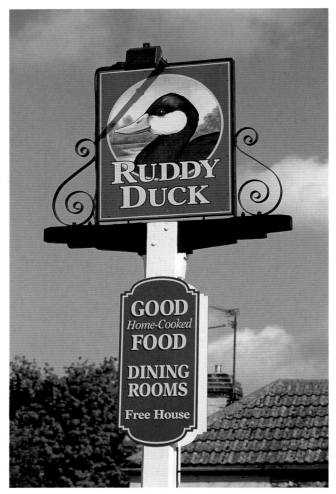

Britain's only Ruddy Duck pub is in Peakirk, Cambridgeshire.

was agreed that the Ruddy Duck was the perfect choice. Also, with its physically distinctive appearance it could be recognised in even the simplest motif form. Everyone agreed it was a wonderful choice – if only we had known then what controversy was around the corner![173]

Peakirk in Cambridgeshire, the location of a WWT reserve, was an early destination for some of the surplus ruddy ducks from Slimbridge. Shortly after the transfer the title of the village pub was altered from the 'Black Bull' to the 'Ruddy Duck', although the precise background to the name-change is in doubt. While Sir Peter Scott's gentle influence with the brewery has been suggested, the locals insist it was a grass-roots decision. Whatever the real reason, it is Britain's only Ruddy Duck pub, complete with a handsome hand-painted sign and, for a long time, a display case featuring a stuffed male bird.[174]

The far less positive attitude towards ruddy ducks began when birds presumed to be of British origin started to colonise mainland Europe. In rapid succession they appeared in the Netherlands (1973), France (1974) and Belgium (1979), and subsequently began to breed, possibly joined by local escapees. However, the main problem was identified when they eventually surfaced in Spain. The white-headed duck is an Old World relative of the ruddy duck and has suffered massive decline throughout much of its range as a consequence of hunting and habitat loss. The history of the Spanish population was typical of the species' wider fortunes. By 1977 it was down to 22 birds, although a dramatic recovery to a present population of more than 2000 birds has made it a symbol of Spanish conservation in a way comparable to the avocet in Britain.

The ruddy ducks appearing in Spain in the late 1980s were soon in association with their closest relatives. By 1991 up to 30 were arriving each year, while male birds were breeding with female white-headed ducks and producing hybrid young. To date Spanish environmentalists have shot 98 ruddy ducks and 58 hybrids. This development has raised the spectre of the rare European bird being genetically swamped through interbreeding with its more aggressive, more successful American relative. The near-extinction of the New Zealand grey duck, *Anas superciliosa superciliosa*, as a consequence of hybridisation with the introduced European mallard is the precedent cited by most environmentalists.

Britain rather than Spain has become the focus of control measures, because this country is thought to be the main source of birds appearing in Iberia. A radical programme was devised under mounting pressure from eight European countries and in compliance with Article 8h of the 1992 Convention on Biological Diversity, to which the UK government is a signatory. Its proponents argue on the basis of a strict precautionary principle: whatever the true impact of ruddy ducks on their rare relative, there is no margin for error. They further emphasise that the window for effective action is small. Should ruddy-duck populations become as well established in Europe as they have in Britain, there will be little or no likelihood of ever controlling the bird.[175] To date the plan has involved a trial cull costing about £800,000 to assess the feasibility of the total elimination of British ruddy ducks. The experimental work involved shooting them in three areas – Anglesey, Fife and the West Midlands – and by 2002 a total of 2500 had been killed.

The plan itself (and the rationale behind the slaughter) is complex and raises a whole suite of environmental issues, including the validity and 'rights' of introduced species; the feasibility (and morality) of eliminating a bird's entire population; the responsibility that Britain bears for animals native to other countries (the white-headed ducks of Spain and eastern Europe). While it might be an ornithological controversy, many responses have been framed in overtly anthropomorphic language: 'The culling programme of Ruddy Ducks which is now underway is nothing short of "ethnic cleansing".'[176] And 'It should be up to them [the white-headed ducks] with which other birds they wish to mate. Will we take the scenario one-stage further and ban interbreeding between races of the human species?'[177]

A recurrent facet of the debate is the extent to which the ruddy duck's human-induced establishment in Britain and Europe alters our sense of its 'legitimacy' and confers a status outside that enjoyed by the rest of nature. Those on both sides of the argument point out the anomalies that this introduces:

Why is it that some people are up in arms about culling a species wrongly introduced by man, when we have been doing it for years to nearly universal approval? It seems OK to remove rats, cats and stoats from small islands to prevent [them] wiping out endemic birds, but not to stop Ruddies wiping out White-Headeds.[178]

This single fact [its deliberate introduction] is central to the muddled thinking that has characterised much of the debate to date: the rather 'Victorian' notion that Man is somehow 'outside' nature, and that any of his actions are therefore 'not natural'.[179]

If the bird's 'unnatural' status is a central justification for culling it then, as one commentator notes, it begs a difficult question: 'If by some (albeit remote) chance the original pair had arrived in Europe under their own steam, would we still be thinking about eradicating them? After all the threat would be exactly the same.'[180]

The issue of controlling an introduced bird also merges imperceptibly with our larger, more persistent anxiety over race and racism. A number of stereotypical attitudes seem to be at work, such as our routine distaste for outside interference, particularly in the form of political demands from Europe: 'The fact that they [ruddy ducks] are a relatively recent introduction here does not make them any less valuable – they are sentient beings and should not be massacred just because Spanish conservationists are offended by a small handful of "genetically impure" hybrids.'[181]

A key theme concerning critics of the policy is its cost and the diversion of British money towards a policy whose success will mainly benefit another nation's birds:

For the Department of Transport and the Regions, supported and endorsed by many UK conservation bodies, to commit £800,000 of 'conservation' money for regional trials alone to such a biological non-threat is a folly bettered only by the hundreds of millions of pounds of taxpayers' money spent on that function-less appendage in London, the Millennium Dome. Perhaps some cash could be better spent educating Spaniards as to the improbability of gene swamping of their study species. How many UK seabird islands could be cleared of harmful alien mammal species with a budget of £800,000? Most, I would say.[182]

A central objection – strikingly anomalous given the long history of exploitation of wildfowl – is the method of the cull itself by six professional marksmen.

Moving targets such as ducks may be wounded and left to die in pain and at the mercy of predators. One duck put in this situation is one too many.[183]

I am angry that shooting is the method chosen to cull the Ruddy Duck as often birds are not killed outright.[184]

. . . Arguments used for killing of Ruddy Ducks in the UK are scientifically 'wobbly', and the method of execution verges on the banal. How much illegal 'wilful disturbance' will shooting create at sites where Ruddy Ducks occur alongside Schedule 1 species? While the DETR, the RSPB and others are happy to commit their/our money and support to the Ruddy Duck fiasco, there are many local conservation projects deserving funding.[185]

I go birding at Blithfield Reservoir, Staffordshire, where in winter 2000/2001 the shooting of Ruddy Duck occurred six times . . . The amount of disturbance caused to so many birds by the cull is catastrophic.[186]

Despite the ruddy duck's 'plucky' character and the undeniable affection that it enjoys in some quarters, the precautionary principle adopted by the British government and its agencies will prevail. In July 2002 a green light was given to the bird's total elimination. However the question remains: can they truly get them all?

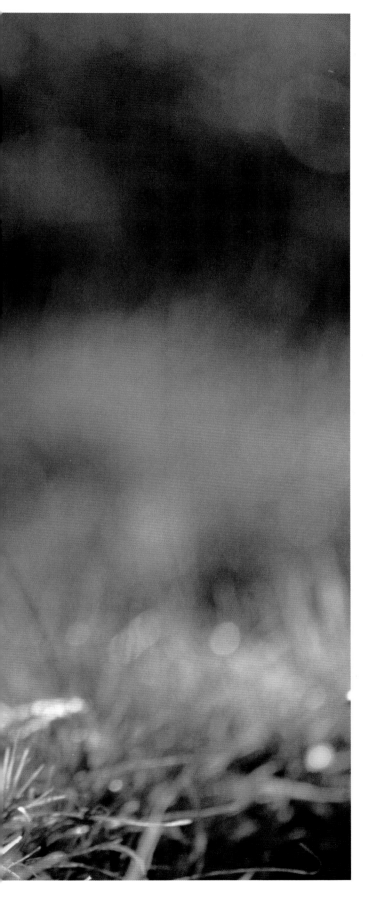

Birds of Prey *Accipitriformes*

European Honey-buzzard, *Pernis apivorus*. Leslie Brown, the great scholar of the world's raptors, once noted that this scarce summer migrant is badly named, given that it is neither a buzzard (not even closely related to the buzzard genus *Buteo*), nor does it eat honey.[1] The old name, 'bee hawk', was closer to the facts, since the bird is predominantly insectivorous and the shortness of its stay in Britain – it arrives as late as June and leaves just 12–16 weeks later – flows from a dependence upon the grubs and adults of wasps or bees.

The bird's past status and distribution in Britain are clouded with uncertainty, partly because of confusion with common buzzard, although Willughby had listed it as a British species by the seventeenth century and Gilbert White accurately noted key identification features when a pair nested in Selborne Hanger in 1780. 'When on the wing,' he wrote, 'this species may be easily distinguished from the common buzzard by its hawk-like appearance, small head, wings not so blunt, and long tail.'[2]

Another factor in the under-recording is its unobtrusive behaviour. Honey-buzzards spend large amounts of time on the woodland floor digging out wasp nests, when their excavations are sometimes so deep that they disappear down the hole. The bird is equipped with long stout toes and claws for raking the earth, while scale-like protective feathering on the long slender head is a defence against possible stings. The bird itself is unperturbed by the enveloping cloud of angry workers, but the insects will sometimes vent their frustration on other animals, including unfortunate ornithologists who just happen to be in the vicinity. Leslie Brown suggested that birdwatchers thus assailed should persevere. They may find a honey-buzzard at work.[3]

Despite the bird's harmless nature, it often fell victim to game interests in the past and its scarcity inevitably fuelled the passion of egg thieves. That redoubtable old character Colonel Richard Meinertzhagen adopted imaginative tactics to protect one pair from disturbance in 1957. He erected signs around their woodland nest warning of unexploded bombs. He also reassured the landowner and keeper that they would not take pheasants but promised them two shillings and sixpence

Eurasian honey-buzzards are one of the few large insectivorous birds of prey. They spend long periods on the woodland floor digging out the nests of wasps and bees to eat the larva-rich comb.

a bird should they stray. 'The wretched birds,' he later claimed, 'took forty-seven pheasants.'[4]

More recently honey-buzzards appear to have expanded their range and numbers, with 50–60 pairs nesting widely across Britain, and they may be one of the beneficiaries of global warming.[5] Sometimes the breeding birds are further increased by wind-drifted migrants from Scandinavia on their journey south. The year 2000 was notable for an autumn passage of almost 2000 honey-buzzards, 10 times the usual annual total, with individuals turning up in the oddest places: 'I am a long-time fan of Tranmere Rovers and often feel torn by the conflicting lure of Prenton Park or going to look for birds. Yet on occasions the two interests do combine. The best bird I can recall at a Tranmere match was a honey-buzzard over St Andrews during an away game with Birmingham City. (I don't remember the score.)'[6]

Red Kite, *Milvus milvus*. With its bright colours, unmistakable shape and languid mastery of the air, it would have commanded our attention even had it been one of our commonest birds. The red kite's rarity has simply conferred upon it an additional layer of glamour, while its recent rise from mere handful to several thousands is among the great success stories of modern conservation. Ian Carter, at the heart of the kite recovery programme for the last decade, argues that the 'bird has been hugely successful in helping to reconnect people with the landscape and encouraging a greater interest in wildlife'.[7] Testimony to its flagship status is a recent RSPB poll which ranked it with the golden eagle and song thrush in the nation's list of favourite birds.[8]

The dramatic spread has hinged on a reintroduction scheme at six sites in England and Scotland using kites originally taken from Spain and Sweden respectively. The English releases began in the Chilterns in 1989 and when these had achieved a healthy stable population, subsequent introductions were made in Northampton-shire (1995–8) and Yorkshire (1999–2003) using mainly English-reared birds. The Scottish releases (around the Black Isle on the Moray Firth, 1989–93; Stirling and the Trossachs, 1996–2001, and Dumfries and Galloway, 2001–3) have resulted in new populations totalling more than 50 pairs. Altogether there are now around 3000 kites in Britain, while the Chilterns population alone has topped 1000 and their breeding success well exceeds the productivity of kites in central Wales, which for most of last century was the species' only location in Britain.

The Welsh birds remain an anchor for kite fortunes in Britain and their own hard-won increase over more than a century represents a major triumph in its own right. In 1903 a species that had once been considered as 'common as the Carrion-crow' was estimated at just five breeding

The village sign designed by schoolchildren in Culbokie on the Black Isle, Ross-shire, reflects the way that red kites have been swiftly embraced by local communities.

pairs. The formation of a 'Kite Committee' by members of the British Ornithologists' Club in the same year was a last-ditch effort to avert extinction. Enduring for more than 90 years and 'without parallel in the annals of bird protection anywhere in the world', the committee was central to the bird's recovery. In the first decade a major problem was what Abel Chapman called 'that fungoid excrescence on science' – the egg collector – with a single kite clutch fetching as much as £5 (more than £300 by modern values).[9] Deliberate persecution of various kinds, along with the Welsh weather, myxomatosis and inadvertent poisoning continued to blight the project, but after the Second World War the population finally started to gain momentum. It may have been one of Britain's rarest birds of prey, but in places like Tregaron or Devil's Bridge in the upper Tywi valley, the kite seemed almost common and so became virtually synonymous with the region.

'Kite Country', as it is now widely known, lies virtually at the physical heart of Wales and is a place of 'hidden

The long slender wings and deeply forked tail are features unique to red kites.

hamlets with unpronounceable names, of deeply-cut valleys, thick with hanging oak-woods, of whalebacked hills and grassy sheepwalks'.[10] For almost a century anyone wishing to see kites was obliged to make a pilgrimage to this beautiful area. In return, the bird's unique association was reflected back in tourist brochures, business logos and in the signs of cafés, restaurants and hotels. The emblematic status was eventually appropriated by Welsh nationalist politicians, who saw in it an enduring symbol of Celtic identity.[11]

However, there is a fascinating twist to the recent symbolism. The red kite is not inherently a bird of the Welsh hills. If anything, it is most at home in the English lowlands. The rapid expansion of the Chiltern population indicates the suitability of the gentler conditions. Most ironic of all, the kite was not historically associated with wild landscapes of any kind – English, Scottish or Welsh. It was a bird of the medieval townscape, where its status alternated between valued scavenger of edible refuse and bothersome opportunist snatching titbits from the poultry yard. For the Elizabethans, the kite's carrion-eating habit carried darker associations of cowardice and baseness. When the king wished to insult the scheming Goneril in Shakespeare's *King Lear* (Act 1, Scene 4), he could think of no deeper insult than 'Detested kite! thou liest'. The bird's present status as majestic icon of natural wilderness has thus involved a cultural journey through 180 degrees.

In Tudor times the classic location to see kites would have been in the streets of the English capital. The visit of a Flemish naturalist, Charles Clusius, has left us with a remarkable image of their numbers. Clusius thought the bird more common in London than in Cairo and he described flocks hovering overhead to snatch scraps off the ground and even out of the Thames. A near-contemporary described them stealing fish out of women's hands and this was echoed in an earlier account of 1496: 'the Kites . . . are so tame, that they often take out of the hands of little children, the bread smeared with butter, in the Flemish fashion, given to them by their mothers'.[12] The London population of kites was protected by statute for its valuable refuse-disposal service,

The red kite's curious habit of adorning its nest with scraps of fabric, including handkerchiefs, underpants and even teddy bears, has been well known since Elizabethan times.

and according to one source, killing kites was punishable with the death penalty – although this sounds improbable.[13]

Is it possibly the kite's former reputation as the bird for devouring leftovers that explains a presumably old Midlands saying:

My mother-in-law, a lifelong resident of Brigstock in east Northamptonshire, would always say to our one-year-old son whenever he finished a hearty meal, 'Bless your kite.' It was always said with a note of surprised approval and being Maltese I believed it was a proper end-of-meal expression to be used at every opportunity. Instead it was often received with raised eyebrows and hints of mild offence.[14]

The answer may lie equally in an old northern dialect word, 'kyte', meaning belly or paunch.

and was conclusively *not* the bird seen above the London skyline, since these were known to be residents, while European black kites are only summer visitors.

The red kite never suffered the indignity of its relative's nickname, but it was well known for many centuries either as the 'glede' or 'glead' (from a Saxon word for 'glide'). Gleadthorpe in Northamptonshire and Gleadless and Gledehill in Yorkshire are place names that honour connections with the red kite.[16] An alternative was 'puttock' or 'puddock' (also used for buzzard), a word of obscure origin, but assumed to be another reference to the powers of flight.[17]

The bird's long, loose wings are strongly angled at the carpal joint and, with a deeply flexible forked tail, give it unparalleled manoeuvrability. If necessary kites can remain stock-still in mid-air with only the tail twisting in relation to air flow, like a rudder. Their bread- and fish-snatching tricks derive from a capacity to drop to ground or water level, then return instantly skywards. In parts of the Chilterns some villagers have taken to feeding their local birds: 'throwing out scraps of meat and watching, spellbound, as the kites dive down like "Stuka bombers" to snatch up the food within feet of the kitchen window'.[18]

There is often an obvious playfulness to the aerial activities, particularly when the birds gather in flocks of up to several hundred at traditional night-time roosts. Their spectacular chases and mock fights are little understood, except perhaps as a recreational trial of their flying skills, and are known to kite watchers as 'circuses'.[19] Sometimes the play extends to other species, and birds have even been recorded flying in tandem with motorised hang-gliders: 'He was outclimbing me so I opened the throttle to keep up. I then let him outclimb me and last saw him at about 1200 feet and still turning. It was a wonderful thing to happen.'[20] They are also attracted to model radio-controlled gliders, with up to five birds following the plane and getting so close that the pilot feared a mid-air collision.[21]

There seems to be a touch of sport in another of the red kite's more unusual habits – its penchant for adorning the nest with all sorts of scraps, from animal dung and old corpses (including, once, two dead kittens) to items off the washing line.[22] The habit was famously mentioned by Shakespeare in *The Winter's Tale* (Act 4, Scene 3), where the character Autolycus, a self-confessed 'snapper-up of unconsidered trifles', says, 'My traffic is sheets; when the kite builds, look to lesser linen.' As long ago as the second century AD the Roman author, Aelian, wrote that London birds had a habit of plucking hair off men's heads to weave into the nest.[23] Other unlikely items have included handkerchiefs (off hedgerows and out of the

Historical images of marauding city flocks led several modern observers such as Richard Meinertzhagen, familiar only with the tiny enclave in deepest Wales, to argue that 'the red kite is not and never has been a proletarian, assuming the role of the sanitary squad'.[15] Instead he thought the London birds were more likely to have been **Black Kites**, *M. migrans*, scavengers familiar in many European cities and infamous to British service-men posted to Egypt or India as the 'shite-hawk' (for its coprophagous habit). Although black kite is an occa-sional visitor to Britain (308 records), it has never bred

Red kites are probably more common in Britain now than at any time since the early eighteenth century.

The initial birds used for release in the red-kite reintroduction scheme came from Spain and Norway.

hand), gloves, paper bags, newspaper, straw bonnets and other head coverings (some stolen directly off the wearer – one local name was 'hat bird') and mutton bones (from the Welsh hills after the dreadful winter of 1947).[24]

This habit of stealing has by no means decreased with the passage of time. The nests of recently reintroduced birds have been 'found to contain underwear with surprising regularity. Other traditional items include children's soft toys, as well as more modern offerings such as crisp packets and supermarket bags and in one the polystyrene-encased data-gathering box from a weather balloon.'[25] Seton Gordon told the lovely story of a Scottish keeper who took off his socks to wade across a river, which he then started to fish. When he recrossed to retrieve the stockings, they were nowhere to be seen, but they turned up later that year 'forming a nice warm lining to the kite's nest'.[26] The novelist Henry Williamson wrote a short story entitled 'The Flight of the Pale Pink Pyjamas', which describes a 'kite's predatory assault on a clothes-line in Devon'.[27]

It was not the bird's love of lesser linen that fuelled the long, slow, methodical war against kites between the seventeenth and nineteenth centuries. A more likely *casus belli* was its reputation as a poultry thief. (One explanation for the name 'puttock' is that it is a contraction of poult-hawk.[28]) The onset of kite persecution also coincided with improvements in urban sanitation: the birds' clearance of offal and other organic waste would no longer have such value. Equally critical was the elevation of partridge, pheasant and grouse as the central totems of British rural life, which cast all birds of prey as the enemy-in-chief. Unfortunately the kite's tolerance of human presence and its scavenging habits made it an easy target.

Writing in 1921 Norman Ticehurst offered a revealing glimpse of the campaign waged at parish level, in this case at Tenterden on the Kentish Weald. There the church wardens offered bounties of one to two pence for a kite's bill. In the period from 1677 to 1691, 380 kite bills were delivered for reward, with 100 killed in the single twelve-month period of 1684/5. An equally telling picture is created by a list of vermin, including 275 kites, killed on the Duke of Sutherland's estate at Glengarry between 1837 and 1840.[29] Together the details indicate the bird's nationwide abundance, but they also graphically illustrate just how a common species could have been reduced to five breeding pairs by 1905.[30]

Although the diet of the current kite population has been shown to include pheasants, they are almost entirely scavenged carcasses, many of them road victims or killed by disease. So far the reintroduced kites have steered clear of chickens. However, this probably reflects the changed ecology of domestic poultry, rather than any modification to the kite's hunting methods. Hens and their chicks would once have scratched their living on every village green and presented easy pickings in the more open landscapes of pre-enclosure England, particularly to an agile opportunist like the red kite.

Ian Carter speculates that the species, an arch-generalist, has already demonstrated its ability to thrive in the British countryside and, given time, could easily recover much of its former range and numbers:

> If the densities of birds now found in the Chilterns are to be repeated across the rest of lowland Britain then the red kite will once again be one of our most common and familiar birds of prey. A population in excess of 50,000 pairs, more than double the current world population, is by no means impossible. Although at current rates of increase it will take many decades for it to return to all its former haunts. This British success is in marked contrast to the situation across much of Europe, where numbers are in steep decline. Ironically even in places like Segovia province in central Spain, which once had very high densities and was a source of birds for the Chilterns, numbers have plummeted. The situation is so serious that we may even find we have to repay the favour and help them with their reintroductions using birds from England.[31]

The one possible factor that could frustrate the red kite's return to its former abundance is its vulnerability to poisoning:

> It is alarming to find that by far the highest cause of mortality amongst the released kites has been from poison baits, administered either deliberately or placed in the countryside to kill crows and foxes. In England it is estimated that illegal poison has resulted in the deaths of several hundred birds since the start of the project. In Scotland the problem is even greater with poison baits being used almost routinely in association with management of grouse moors in some areas. Indeed this is the main reason why the Scottish kites have not enjoyed the success of their English equivalents. All the kites face an additional risk of accidental death when scavenging on rats killed by modern anticoagulant poisons (up to 600 times more toxic than warfarin). The introduction programme has brought into focus just how extensive is the use of poison in our countryside and highlights a threat which affects not only kites but other birds of prey and predatory mammals.[32]

Over the centuries the species has had many different qualities projected on to it. It would be a sad day if the present kite population became a new symbol for a poisoned landscape.

White-tailed Eagle, *Haliaeetus albicilla*. VN: Sea Eagle. It is difficult to judge which is the more exciting conservation achievement – the reintroduction of this magnificent bird or of red kites. By wingspan and weight, this is the largest eagle in Europe and one of the biggest of all birds in Britain. However, if the species itself is on

The eminent Scottish conservationist Roy Dennis with one of the last young Norwegian white-tailed eagles to be released on the Scottish west coast.

a grand scale, the size of the reintroduced population is tiny and the pace of increase agonisingly slow. Almost 30 years after the species was first released there are just 23 pairs holding territory, and from 17 occupied eyries in 2001 no more than 11 young fledged. At the same time, even these bare facts suggest the obstacles that have been surmounted in order to give life to the long-held dream.

The project was first mooted in the 1960s by environmentalists, including George Waterston, after the bird had been exterminated more than forty years earlier. The initial small-scale attempts in Argyllshire (1959) and on Fair Isle (1968) both failed, but they provided valuable information for the larger releases that took place on the Inner Hebridean island of Rhum. These involved a remarkable team effort by various UK environmental groups, Eagle Star insurance, the RAF and the Norwegian Air Force, as well as the Norwegian conservationists who organised the capture of the donated birds. Between 1975 and 1985 they released 82 eagles (39 males and 43 females) from a special holding area on Rhum. Eight were since recovered dead (one from illegal persecution), but in 1983 came the first breeding attempt.

Two years later a pair of white-tailed eagles produced the first British-born chick in 69 years and every subsequent breeding season has seen a small incremental improvement. There is now an established breeding nucleus spread between the islands of Skye and Mull as well as the adjacent mainland, and their recent history suggests that the white-tailed eagle's increase will continue throughout north-west Scotland.

The common alternative name for the bird, 'sea eagle', reflects a strong bias in the species' distribution in Europe. The scientific name *Haliaeetus* is derived from two Greek words, *hals* 'sea' and *aetos* 'eagle'. White-tailed eagles often nest on coastal cliffs where seabirds, fish (dead and alive) as well as other strandline offal, including cetacean and seal carcasses, are important elements in the bird's diet. In the past their willingness to eat carrion led to an almost moral differentiation from 'the great and noble' golden eagle, which is more inclined to hunt its own prey.[33]

In the Scottish highlands and islands, sheep carrion is a staple of white-tailed eagles and they are still occasionally accused of taking lambs, although research suggests that their impact is marginal. The vast majority of lambs eaten by eagles are already dead and most of those still alive at the moment of seizure are likely to have been already weakened in some way. An Argyllshire study showed that 15–20 per cent of all the lambs died usually within the first week. Of 252 carcasses examined, three-quarters of them had never even suckled and just 7 per cent appeared to be healthy prior to death.[34] However occasionally rogue eagles can become habitual predators of live domestic stock and a system of management payments is offered to sheep crofters where breeding eagles are present.

In the past the bird's notorious reputation as a lamb-killer gave no grounds for tolerance and it was persecuted throughout its range, which once extended into Ireland, north-west England and many parts of Scotland and the outer isles. Even in southern England it was a well-known winter visitor. Sir Thomas Browne wrote in the seventeenth century of the regular occurrence in Norfolk of what he named 'Fen Eagles'.[35] Two hundred years later William Yarrell thought this species 'much more common' than golden eagle and noted specimens taken as close to London as Wimbledon Common or Epping Forest.[36]

The intriguing evidence contained in English place names suggests that at one time white-tailed eagles also bred in heavily wooded parts of England as far south as Devon. The Anglo-Saxon word for eagle was *erne* or

earn, and Margaret Gelling has examined 30 place names in 14 English counties that contain an 'eagle' element. Our other breeding eagle species is eliminated as a candidate because of its almost universal preference for uplands. Yet Gelling found consistent associations with habitats and landscapes suitable for white-tailed eagle, such as *earn-leah*, an Old English name for 'eagle wood'

A fishing white-tailed eagle is the very essence of raw power and finely tuned precision.

(e.g. Arley, Cheshire; Earley, Berkshire; and Earnley, Sussex); *earn-wudu* (e.g. Arnewood, Hampshire; and Earnwood, Shropshire) and *earn clif* (e.g. Arncliffe and Yarncliffe, West Yorkshire; Arnecliffe, North Yorkshire). Most of the woodland names cluster around major river systems like the Severn (e.g. Ayleford, Gloucestershire; and Areley, Worcestershire) and the Thames (Earley, Berkshire). In the case of the latter site, white-tailed eagle bones were found just 20 miles (33km) away at a fifth-century archaeological excavation.[37]

The white-tailed eagle's reputation as a lamb-killer was the reason for its eventual extermination as a breeding bird by the early twentieth century.

Another eagle place name listed by Gelling is the somewhat confusing Heron Crag in Cumbria, widely viewed as a corruption of *erne-cragge*. Although the Lake District is now the only English region with breeding golden eagles, either species could have been associated with this site, and the white-tailed eagle certainly bred there until the eighteenth century. It was then widespread and judged 'so destructive to the interests of the shepherds, that their extermination became absolutely necessary'.[38] In other areas where sheep and white-tailed eagles overlapped, the pattern of persecution was similar. Orkney crofters, for instance, operated a reward system of a chicken (or eight pence) from each household in the parish for anyone killing a bird.[39]

The Highland Clearances of the early nineteenth century and the subsequent conversion of much of the region to sheep farming had major implications for a supposedly lamb-eating raptor. A bounty of up to five shillings per adult's beak could significantly boost a shepherd's income and, while there are eye-witness accounts from Skye of 40 white-tailed eagles gathered on a single carcass, the same place produced claims from keepers of 57 eagles shot on a single estate.[40] In his forgotten classic, *A History of Fowling*, Hugh Macpherson recounted the extraordinary tale of a 104-year-old Skye shepherd, Angus Macleod, who could recall killing 'more Eagles than any man of his acquaintance'. His strategy was to shoot the parents and then climb down to the eyrie, into which he plunged tar-soaked rags to burn or smoke out the eaglets.[41] The final breeding pair on Skye in 1916 was also the last in Britain, and when an albino female failed to return to nest cliffs in Shetland after several solitary barren years, her disappearance marked the start of the species' 70-year absence.

It was not just the eagle's mutton diet that inspired opposition. Domestic pets also appear in the list of prey. There is a record of an eagle struggling off with one poor dog weighing 24 pounds (11kg), while another of 33 pounds (15kg) proved just too heavy. Even more extraordinary was the old legend, recorded as long ago as Pliny and surviving for 1800 years, that eagles threw dust in the eyes of deer and drove them blind over the crags.[42] Observations of released birds on Rhum may offer insights into this old myth: 'Some foolish young eagles have been seen to attack them [red deer]. In one such incident . . . the eagle was seen to be carried along several metres with its talons firmly embedded in the back of the hind. It is easy to see how old wives' tales arise, of eagles riding the back of a deer and using its wings to blind the panic-stricken beast until it falls over a cliff and is killed to become carrion for the crafty eagles.'[43]

Perhaps the most intriguing and controversial of all the sea eagle's prey items is ourselves. In the Anglo-Saxon poem 'The Battle of Brunanburh', celebrating the Saxon victory of King Aethelstan over the Scots (AD 937), the subsequent carnage is powerfully evoked: 'They left behind them the dark-coated, swart raven, horny-beaked, to enjoy the carrion, and the grey-coated eagle, white-tailed, to have his will of the corpses.'[44]

At an even earlier date some Scottish communities seem to have taken advantage of the bird's scavenging habit to prepare their dead for burial. At Isbister on the Orkney island of South Ronaldsay a large, important neolithic burial site has been discovered where there are thought to be the remains of 342 individual humans. The manner of interment indicates that the bodies were laid on platforms (the bones show no signs of gnawing by terrestrial carnivores, which would have followed placement on the ground), probably to be eaten by birds. The defleshed skeletons were then disarticulated and placed in the chamber, but along with these archaeologists have found 35 carcasses of large birds of prey, two-thirds of which are white-tailed eagles.[45]

The relatives' inclusion of the very creatures that would have joined the earlier feast of human flesh suggests a ritual – possibly a spiritual – attachment to the eagles (the discoveries at Isbister may well also shed light on how the raven acquired its enormous symbolic importance; see page 424). The site also indicates how the Orkney communities enjoyed a level of domestic intimacy with these huge raptors that will take many decades to recreate in modern Britain.

Today we have only a dying echo of the bird's taste for humans in a number of toe-curling stories about eagles flying away with babies. In the seventeenth century the Scottish naturalist Sir Robert Sibbald included children in the bird's diet, and one of the most authentic-sounding accounts was given by Martin Martin in 1695:

> a native in the isle of Skye, called Neil, who when an infant was left by his mother in the field, not far from the houses on the north side of Loch Portree, an eagle came in the meantime, and carried him away in its talons as far as the south side of the loch, and there laying him on the ground, some people that were herding sheep there perceived it, and hearing the infant cry, ran immediately to its rescue, and by good providence found him untouched by the eagle, and carried him home to his mother.[46]

It should be added that either eagle species could have been involved in the incident. It is also worth noting that the Hebrideans had much the same approach to personal names as the native peoples of North America, because the child was known ever afterwards as Neil Eagle.

Another account, which is probably the last-recorded British example, dates from 1790 and was part of Shetland oral tradition until the end of the twentieth century. In the 1960s the local ornithologist, Bobby Tulloch, recorded the details from a resident of Fetlar, where much of the action was said to have taken place. The eagle apparently picked up a baby girl in the north of Unst and then flew to its eyrie on the neighbouring island. The child's father and other Unst crofters chased to the shore and rowed across the sound to Fetlar, where they eventually lowered a young boy down to the nest ledge. Remarkably, the baby was completely unharmed because of a thick shawl wrapped around her. Both adult and young eagle had been unable to get through the covering and had actually become entangled in the woollen threads.

The wealth of detail supporting the story is intriguing, but it stumbles at several major points. First, the pursuing men would have had to run 10 miles (17km) and row 4 miles (7km), which makes a minimum journey time of around four hours. One wonders how an infant could have survived unharmed when confronted with two hungry eagles for that length of time. Second, if one accepts the woollen shawl as an effective barrier to their razor-sharp talons and beaks, then it is difficult to see how the teenage rescuer might have grappled with two huge frustrated raptors while simultaneously securing the baby on the eyrie's narrow ledge.

Yet the most serious doubts centre on the eagle's ability to carry a very large prey item over such a long distance. One cannot imagine a baby weighing much less than 20 pounds (9kg) being left unattended for a period that would have allowed the bird its opportunity. By contrast, it is precisely the brevity of the flight in the case of Neil Eagle

Behind this famous pub sign in Oxford lies an extraordinary tale of foundling offspring, infidelity, and nesting eagles. But was any of it actually true?

on Skye – and the bird's subsequent abandonment of its bundle – that lend credibility to that story. A further unsupportive detail in the Fetlar tale is the fact that it appears to have taken place at harvest-time (probably September), when no eagle should have had a chick still in the nest. And a final element that seems to gild the tale and elevate it from natural historical account to something resembling myth is the eventual marriage between the rescued infant and her gallant teenage saviour.[47]

The story's end hints at another possible function for eagle-and-child stories, which is explicit in the legend embedded in the family history of the Earls of Derby, the Stanleys. One of their fourteenth-century ancestors stage-managed the 'discovery' of his own illegitimate child as he walked the estate with his wife. The foundling had been placed beneath a tree where eagles nested and he managed to persuade his wife to accept the baby as their own. The eagle and child still feature on the Stanley crest, but the most conspicuous reminders of the legend are the country's 26 'Eagle and Child' pubs, many of which are located close to historical or existing Stanley lands

The food pass by nesting marsh harriers, when a male supplies his mate with prey, involves a miraculous display of aerial coordination.

(including the famous example in Oxford, once the drinking hole for C. S. Lewis and J. R. R. Tolkein). One can perhaps see how these tales of majestic bird and baby could be a convenient way of retailing the gossip, without mentioning the more mundane facts or indicting the principal players. With the passage of time the euphemised and romantic version might endure, but as if it were genuinely true.[48]

Yet this interpretation of some of the eagle-child stories does not exclude the possibility that at the root of the whole tradition, in a remote past, there were authentic cases of baby-snatching eagles involving real heroism and possibly real tragedy.

Eurasian Marsh Harrier, *Circus aeruginosus*. There is a depressing familiarity about this reedbed specialist's extermination at the hands of nineteenth-century game interests, matched only by a comparable sense of drama over its recent recovery.

In the early 1800s it had been common in both Britain and Ireland but was quickly reduced to a minuscule rump in Norfolk by the 1870s. For ornithologists of the period there then followed a half-century of unfulfilled hopes as marsh harriers made occasional nesting attempts that either failed or were further blighted by the attentions of egg and skin collectors.

Then in 1915 Jim Vincent, the conservation-minded keeper at Hickling Broad, stumbled upon a nest containing five eggs, the first confirmed breeding attempt for almost 20 years. While the Second Battle of Ypres and the Allied landings in Gallipoli rose to their futile climax,

Vincent's employer, Lord Lucas, took advantage of a period of military leave and, in his keeper's words, 'dashed home to see the sight, for he adored the birds of prey. As we sat on the grassy bank and saw the Marsh Harrier go down to its nest on our right hand, and on our left a Montagu's Harrier settle on her eggs, his lordship turned to me with a sparkle in his eyes, and said, "By Jove! Jim, this is the next greatest sight to the War."'[49]

Even this historic moment was followed by disappointment. The nest failed and it was another six years before the birds returned again to breed successfully. While they gradually increased and spread to a number of other widely spaced localities – Kent, Dorset and Anglesey – marsh harrier remained Britain's rarest diurnal bird of prey. They also suffered a second dangerous 'bottleneck' in the 1960s as a consequence of organochlorine pesticides. By 1971 there was just a single breeding pair at Minsmere RSPB reserve in Suffolk.

The withdrawal of the agrochemicals eventually paved the way for harrier numbers to rise at an annual rate of almost 20 per cent, and by the end of the millennium there were 206 breeding females (to talk of 'pairs' is misleading, since males often form bigamous relationships). More than half are concentrated in three eastern counties – Lincolnshire, Norfolk and Suffolk – but their success in places as widespread as Orkney, Kent and Somerset is just as heartening as the ever-rising total. One would probably have to look to the eighteenth century to find a time when marsh harriers were commoner.

Alongside their population recovery they have also shown some striking changes in behaviour. One important innovation is a willingness to nest in arable crops wherever their traditional reedbed habitat is in short supply. It first occurred in west Norfolk in 1982 and is now widespread in several counties.

Even more remarkable are the marsh harriers that remain in Britain for the winter. Although most books still list the species as a summer visitor from Africa, some individuals have completely abandoned this long migration. A winter ritual for the resident harriers is the nightly return to a communal roost, usually in extensive areas of reedbed. There are several large examples, particularly in East Anglia, and by far the most impressive is at Horsey Broad in Norfolk. On most winter evenings, just a short distance from where Jim Vincent found his historic pair in 1915, it is possible to see more than 30 marsh harriers floating together on their characteristically upraised wings.

Sadly the same cannot be said for its smaller sibling, the **Montagu's Harrier**, *C. pygargus* (VN: Monty's). It is our rarest breeding raptor (just 9–16 pairs) and, in some ways, more troubling is the fact that numbers were

Nesting hen harriers and their offspring are still routinely persecuted by game-shooting interests.

substantially higher in the mid-1950s (40–50 pairs). Yet it is on the very edge of its range in this country, to which it is only a summer visitor.

It was not properly identified from its close relative the hen harrier until 1802, when Lord Montagu accurately diagnosed the confusion which had reigned previously. People had once assumed that the largely pale-grey males of both hen and Montagu's harriers were one species, called 'hen harrier', while the predominantly brown females of both species were considered the two sexes of another bird called the 'ringtail'.

In flight Montagu's harrier is the most refined of an elegant family. John Walpole-Bond nicely captured the floating grace of their movements when he wrote:

The normal flight of all these birds is very low, exquisitely easy, usually leisurely and always lovely to look at. They generally proceed by a series of three or four limp, if deliberate, flaps, followed on the instant, each instalment, by a brief but beautifully buoyant glide, wings half-raised the while; and frequently when hunting, do they quarter again and again the same section of their beat, floating methodically to and fro, hither and thither, light almost as the air itself.[50]

Hen Harrier, *Circus cyaneus*. It was first recorded as a native bird by William Turner in the sixteenth century, who also noted that it was called 'hen-harrier' (or 'harroer') 'among our countrymen from butchering their fowls'.[51] While the reasons for the antagonism may have changed over the centuries, the fact of human opposition to hen harriers has not. It is still 'one of the most reviled, most persecuted and controversial of our raptors'.[52]

In the nineteenth and earlier twentieth centuries it faced a classic pincer movement from the gamekeeper and collector. As one shot, trapped and poisoned the adults, the other hounded their eggs and nests for trophies. There are grizzly tales from two grouse-shooting estates in south-west Scotland of 351 harriers being killed in a four-year period. While the imprecise recognition of raptors in that period may overstate the size of the bag, it is clear that no bird of prey could withstand such a systematic cull. Some landowners even adorned the killing with quasi-judicial ritual. The Marquess of Bute made his keepers swear, 'I shall use my best endeavours to destroy all Birds of Prey, etc., with their nests, etc. wherever they can be found therein. So help me God.'[53]

Of a dozen key target species – 'vermin' to the men taking aim – the hen harrier was among the easiest to

125

The smaller and lighter male hen harrier has a predominantly white and pearl-grey plumage of almost gull-like purity.

control because the birds nest on the ground and are tenacious in defence of the young, so allowing a close approach with firearms. In the past their opponents took advantage of the adults' parental devotion by killing all the offspring except a single chick, which they tethered to a post. This individual could not leave the nest even after fledging and so continued to be fed by the parents until these too could be shot at a more convenient moment.[54]

The bitter relations between keeper and bird are exemplified by the way the harrier's national fate ran in inverse proportion to the fortunes of its human antagonists. At the turn of the century and at the height of game shooting in both countries, control efforts had caused its virtual extinction on the British and Irish mainlands. Then, as keepering declined between and during the two world wars, when able-bodied men were called up for military duty, harriers managed to re-establish themselves on mainland Scotland. The advance south slowly continued, and wintering birds now visit large parts of southern England where they favour open habitats like lowland heath, rough grassland, dunes and grazing marsh.

However, the breeding range, with much the same basic outline as two other moorland specialists – short-eared owl and merlin – is confined to upland areas north and west of a line between Middlesbrough and Cardiff. Both the population size and distribution are strongly shaped by direct persecution. The present total of about 670 pairs in Britain is thought to be well below half the potential figure if illegal destruction were stopped.[55] Since 1997 no birds have nested successfully on English grouse moors, while in Scotland up to one in six of all hen harriers is killed every year. Their illegal slaughter is one of the most contentious and persistent wildlife crimes in Britain and during 2004 the Association of Chief Police Officers launched 'Operation Artemis' to highlight the hen harrier's protected status with relevant landowners and moorland managers.

Where game interests see only a major nuisance, others celebrate a scarce but integral member of the upland bird community, a consummate exponent of low-level search-and-pounce hunting techniques and a species of great beauty, particularly the smaller, lighter male whose pearly grey, black and white plumage has a gull-like purity ('Of all the predators, none is more immaculate than the Hen Harrier').[56] What environmentalists are sometimes less willing to confront is the fact that hen harriers regularly kill red grouse and sometimes kill them in large numbers.

Between 1992 and 1997 a specially commissioned inquiry, entitled the 'Joint Raptor Study', took place in south-west Scotland to examine the impact of raptors on grouse moors and included a representative panel from both sides of the argument. It concluded that raptors were very unlikely to be responsible for the long-term decline in red grouse (see page 153). Grouse bags have been falling since the 1930s, when harriers were completely absent, and have continued to fall during periods when harrier numbers have been stable. However birds of prey can and do sometimes take a substantial proportion of a local grouse population and the challenge they pose is how to reduce their impact without resorting to illegal poisoning or the legalisation of lethal control methods, given that hen harriers are rare in Britain and declining across half their European range.

Part of the answer lies in the management of the moors themselves. The study established that harriers in particular settle to breed in areas where there are sufficient meadow pipits and voles and, in turn, these prey species are dependent on the amount of grassland on a heather moor. The harrier's main prey species decline in relation to the extent of heather cover. The conclusion drawn is that better management of heather – itself directly beneficial to the red grouse, which feed almost exclusively on one plant species – discourages both the harrier and its food.

Another novel experiment was to examine the impact of supplying the harrier brood and their parents with a mixture of day-old hen chicks and laboratory mice as an alternative to them hunting wild prey. Trials showed that this diversionary feeding can reduce grouse predation by 86 per cent. It is proposed by environmentalists as a possible short-term measure to neutralise the impact of breeding harriers, until wider improvements in heather condition and moorland management take effect and discourage the raptors' presence. The feeding policy can also be underpinned in some cases by government support grants. However the new solution demands that moorland managers and gamekeepers overcome their ancient visceral reflexes. Instead of trying to shoot or poison hen harriers, as some have done hitherto, it requires that they locate and take a food supply to the vicinity of the nest. So far, unfortunately, bearing gifts to the old enemy seems to have little appeal.[57]

Northern Goshawk, *Accipiter gentilis*. VN: Gos. The name of this huge version of the sparrowhawk is occasionally mispronounced as '*gosh*-awk', which is in some ways highly appropriate, given the sense of occasion accompanying most observations. It occurs thinly across many well-wooded parts of the country, although whether it was originally a native species is an issue mired in confusion, partly because the name – a contraction of 'goose-hawk' – was once widely used for the peregrine.[58]

It is certainly true that goshawks were kept for centuries and were so highly regarded that ownership was a privilege reserved for nobility among both the Normans and their Saxon predecessors.[59] The present scientific name, *gentilis*, means noble and is a further indication of the high esteem in which they were held.

The technical name for one who keeps and trains the species is an austringer and the most famous exponent of the art was T. H. White, author of *The Goshawk* (1951). The book explored in detail White's painstaking efforts to convert a raw young hawk, known as an eyas, into a seasoned hunter. Birds that are inadequately trained sometimes fail to return to their owner and are thought to be an important source of Britain's wild goshawk population. Together with birds that were deliberately set free and genuine colonists from the Continent, goshawks have steadily increased to 250–350 pairs.[60]

Despite its local scarcity, the goshawk is a highly cosmopolitan species occurring right around the northern hemisphere. However one place it does not occur is on the Azores, which is ironic given that the islands are named after it. The original Portuguese colonists saw birds of prey on the mid-Atlantic islands and misidentified them as goshawks, called *Açor* in Portuguese (the Spanish name is *Azor*). The birds turned out to be

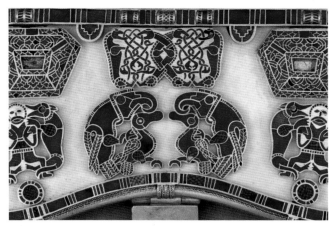

The Sutton Hoo Treasure from the seventh century includes a purse depicting two goshawks fastening on to their duck prey.

common buzzards – the only diurnal raptor occurring – but the name *ilhas dos Açores* stuck and a goshawk now appears on the islands' flag.[61]

Eurasian Sparrowhawk, *Accipiter nisus*. VN: Hawk, Sprawk, Spazz. In his book *British Birds of Prey*, Kenneth Richmond recounted the extraordinary tale of a sparrowhawk he once found on its kill. Playing a game of grandmother's footsteps with the preoccupied raptor, Richmond managed to inch forward each time it looked down to eat until he was almost on top of the bird:

> Exposed to the fury of that lunatic, pitiless glare I halted in my tracks. Impossible to think that any creature, let alone one with the razor-sharp mind of a hawk, should fail to recognise the imminence of danger – but there it stayed knitted to the flesh . . . One step more and I would have trodden on it. What now? On a sudden impulse, thinking to catch it with my bare hands, I bent down. Too late. Quicker than thought, the hawk whipped over my shoulder . . . and there at my feet, its guts trailing in the grass, lay a partridge . . . Half eaten alive, and yet the wretch would have flown if it had been given the chance.[62]

Richmond's grizzly anecdote captures the characteristics that make the species one of the most controversial birds in Britain and Ireland. On the one hand there is the captivating intensity of the sparrowhawks. Leslie Brown suggested that it 'gives an impression of nervous tension and capacity for sudden swift movement unequalled in any other raptor'.[63]

His claim will no doubt trigger memories for many people: the vision of one weaving through the washing lines in a row of terraced backs; the brown blur out of the

127

corner of an eye as it rides parallel with the car and then flips effortlessly over the hedge; or the missile down the lane ahead of the vehicle, suddenly veering at right angles, without any apparent adjustment on its part, to descend into a yard or sail through a five-bar gate.

While birds form almost the entire diet of the sparrowhawk, it takes an enormously wide range – in the wild more than 120 species have been recorded – from the smaller members of the tit family to black grouse.[64] The sexes exhibit the largest size difference of any raptor, with the size of their prey strongly divided along gender lines. The female is up to 25 per cent larger than her mate but often twice as heavy. Game birds, particularly smaller immature birds, as well as lapwing, wood pigeon, collared dove and jay, are all well within her capabilities.

The adult male is seldom much above 5 ounces (150gm) and is the true flyweight of British raptors, with a prey range usually below 2 ounces (50gm). Yet even he will sometimes kill birds as large as himself, and he was by no means despised in the age of falconry. Traditionally he was a hawk for the priest and was known as a 'musket' (probably from *mosca*, the Latin for 'fly'), from which the medieval age derived its name first for a type of crossbow bolt and then for the newly developed hand guns carried by the infantry (whence musketeer). The compliment was repeated in the twentieth century, when the plane manufacturers Gloster named one of their models the 'Sparrowhawk'.[65]

Wild sparrowhawks are classic opportunists and will avail themselves of any kind of assistance. In the age of bird-catching, the fowlers often found one in their nets after it had stooped at the decoy finch.[66] They will chase prey into blind alleys, and sometimes into a house through an open door or window. Nor are they afraid of the occupants, even in very large numbers.

It has been claimed that a person gives off heat equivalent to a one-bar electric fire. I'm not sure what the thermal total might be for 30,000 such fires but I would suggest it's enough to satisfy a soaring sparrowhawk. Towards the end of the 1994 season at Manchester City's Maine Road at least one spectator was distracted by a sparrowhawk circling over the ground. Perhaps the crowd created a local thermal, aided possibly by the vortex of wind produced by the configuration of stands. Latterly a replica sparrow-hawk was hung from the roof to scare birds away from re-seeded turf. The club claimed the exercise was a success, but I suspect credit should go to the real thing, present when the stadium was empty.[67]

Sparrowhawks have also learnt to exploit the daily

handouts of food on the birdtable to obtain their own dietary requirements, and gardens have become one of their favourite killing fields:

Wildlife garden textbooks often advise planting shrub cover for smaller birds as a refuge, but it would seem

The sparrowhawk's routine assassination of songbirds on the birdtable is a vision that stirs great controversy. So far there is no evidence to support the widely held notion that the predation is driving the decline of species like the song thrush or bullfinch.

urban sparrowhawks are ahead of the game. Our neighbours possessed a thick, well-trimmed holly in which local sparrows would take shelter. One day I was drawn to a commotion in the tree, sparrow alarm-calls being especially loud, and after a couple of minutes a sparrowhawk emerged – with prey.[68]

The male sparrowhawk is a glorious mixture of rusty orange and deep blue. By weight he is also our smallest bird of prey.

Emphasising how little notice sparrowhawks pay to thorn bushes, Richard Meinertzhagen described a male he once found with blackthorn spines embedded in its chest.[69] However the most damaging of all garden images of the sparrowhawk is the bird stooped over a fresh-plucked songbird, with wings cowling the victim like a vampire's cape. Unfortunately it brings the predator–prey relationship to the kitchen sink and can be deeply distressing to see and hear, especially if the witnesses think of the casualty as one of 'their' garden birds:

> Recently my wife came steaming downstairs shouting 'Your bloody eagle is frightening *my* small birds!' Translation – the local sparrowhawk had nipped over the hedge and had taken a sparrow from the bird-table. I told her that was what sparrowhawks do, not daring to add that I was sorry I'd missed it! As long as he spares the finches, tits and blackcaps I'm not too bothered.[70]

This type of encounter has hugely increased in parallel with the bird's recovery from the effects of organo-chlorine pesticides in the 1950s and 1960s. These highly toxic agrochemicals were either directly poisoning sparrowhawks or causing them to lay eggs with unnaturally thin shells, which the incubating female then cracked. The resulting decline was so severe that fears

were expressed for the species' ultimate survival. 'In the 1960s, the population was so low that the RSPB bought Coombes valley in Staffordshire as the only site in the Midland counties where they bred.'[71] However the pesticides were later withdrawn and, with increased legal protection, the sparrowhawk has now exceeded its former level of abundance.

This rise in numbers coincided with declines in a suite of formerly common farmland birds, some of them important prey species for sparrowhawk, such as the skylark, song thrush, tree sparrow and bullfinch. A number of people have assumed that the two trends are closely linked and the issues are hotly contended in the national media ('The ruthless predator [sparrowhawk] many birdwatchers love to hate is enjoying a population explosion'; *Daily Express*, 6 February 2001). The letter columns of regional newspapers have also made it a favourite source of debate – 'Raptors destroying small bird population' (*Eastern Daily Press*, 7 August 1995); 'Bird population decline not due to sparrowhawk' (*East Anglian Daily Times*, 28 March 1996).

There is in fact little evidence to support a causal relationship between raptor increases and songbird declines. On the contrary, the sparrowhawk's dis-appearance in the 1960s, particularly in the eastern half of England, was not matched by any corresponding surge in songbird numbers. Similarly, long-term studies of woodland birds in Oxfordshire and Surrey revealed that 13 common songbirds showed no appreciable differences in population either when sparrowhawks were absent (1960–72) or during the years before and after their decline. Great tit, robin, greenfinch and collared dove – regular prey species for sparrowhawks – have all pros-pered alongside the predator itself.

Rather than predation the main factors in songbird declines, particularly in the case of skylark and song thrush, have been massive land-use changes, intensive use of pesticides and loss of habitat, but the notoriety of sparrowhawks sails on regardless because it is not based in objective fact. It is probably more securely grounded in the dismemberment 'horror show' so graphically described above by Kenneth Richmond.

The extent to which it is a relative, culturally deter-mined response is suggested by the unassailable popularity of three other birds of prey: barn owl, tawny owl and kestrel. These three feed largely on small mammals, particularly voles, whose populations are thought to be declining, like those of the song thrush and skylark. Yet they arouse no parallel opposition from the public. What separates kestrel from sparrowhawk is not its differing impact on its respective prey, but *our* different cultural responses to the prey itself. Song thrushes and skylarks excite our affections and our pity in a way that short-tailed field voles do not. Ironically, if we wished to find proof of our powerful attachment to birds then it is in the demonisation of sparrowhawks.

Common Buzzard, *Buteo buteo*. VN: Buzz-hawk (Wales); Tourist's Eagle. The sight of buzzards, sometimes four or five birds together, planing effortlessly over a woodland canopy is an increasingly commonplace occurrence. Yet the species' large size, free-floating movements on broad wings and wild high calls still have a capacity to capture our attention and imaginations. It is generally regarded as 'the-next-best-thing to the Eagle' and for many it is more than that, since it is the species most often mistaken for the genuine article, hence the vernacular name Tourist's Eagle.[72]

It is the one large raptor most people are likely to have seen, since buzzards now have a wide distribution across western parts of Britain and northern Ireland. In some areas of central and northern Scotland, the Lakes, the Welsh hills, the New Forest and the English south-west they are positively common. After 150 years of constant persecution, the buzzard has also begun to reoccupy large swathes of the Midlands and has even ventured into eastern England. A recent UK estimate of about 50,000 pairs, which makes it the commonest of all our raptors, is a measure of a huge ongoing increase and invites a vision of a future countryside free from persecution where buzzards soar above almost every stretch of woodland.

The bird's recovery is not just a matter of population. It also shrugged off a rather ambiguous moral image, which may have been partly the eagle's shadow. The initial impression of large size and aerial fluency seems to hold out a promise of real power that the bird seldom demonstrates. Nineteenth-century authors, even those sympathetic to the bird, frequently expressed their disappointment and characterised it as a 'dull stupid, heavy bird . . . a lazy, sleepy, cowardly fellow who [dozes] away half his time on some old rotten stump'.[73] In *A History of British Birds* William Yarrell wrote: 'Bulky in appearance and rather slow in flight, it remains for hours watching from the same tree, appearing to prefer the accidental approach of an animal . . . rather than find it by a laborious search . . . Its courage too, as compared with others of the *Falconidae*, has been questioned, since it is known to attack such animals as are either young or defenceless.' As if wishing to compensate for his criticism, Yarrell extolled the buzzard's powerful maternal instinct and illustrated his point with the remarkable tale of a captive female that incubated and reared broods of hen chicks year after year.[74]

One cannot help thinking that some of the insults had more to do with linguistic custom than direct field observation. 'Buzzard' has a long history as a term of

The common buzzard has now displaced the kestrel as Britain's most numerous bird of prey.

abuse. Dictionaries list an older meaning that dates from the age of falconry as 'a useless kind of hawk'. The asperity is evident in a lost proverbial expression, 'between hawk and buzzard' – a put-down for those historical oddities like the governess or tutor who were not deemed the social equal of their master or mistress, but were more important than a simple servant.[75] Even today, 'old buzzard' is a well-oiled insult.

The negative connotations of the word are probably most familiar to us from Hollywood westerns of a particular vintage. 'Them buzzards' were the classic stage props to indicate a human corpse was at hand and referred to the gloriously ugly carrion-eater of North America, the turkey vulture, *Cathartes aura*. Eating roadkill (or the by-products of an Apache raid) has always been lowest in our register of raptor morality.

In real life the British buzzard is the arch-opportunist and its current success is partly a consequence of its sheer adaptability. While it will take fresh roadkills, it can easily strike down its own prey as large as adult rabbits, crows, pigeons, coot and duck. Sometimes even humans can testify to its lethal powers:

A few years ago my colleague and I picked up what we assumed to be a dead buzzard at the roadside intending to pack it off for post mortem to confirm the cause of death and to assess pesticide residues in the liver. A couple of miles down the road the 'dead' buzzard sprang to life and after flying around the inside of the car it alighted in my lap, where it proceeded to embed its talons. After an extremely anxious few moments the buzzard was removed. No lasting damage had occurred, not to me at any rate as I now have a daughter.[76]

Some landowners still insist that the buzzard is a predator of game birds, particularly chicks and, despite the species enjoying legal protection since 1880, keepers have long targeted it. Today in Scotland it is one of the most frequent victims of wildlife crime, especially illegal poisonings. Even in 1955, when the population was a quarter of the present total, it was estimated that in just three small areas 400 buzzards were shot during that winter.[77] Ironically the myxomatosis virus, which had just then been unleashed into the British hedgerow, was about to demonstrate the true nature of the buzzard's main diet. As the disease ravaged rabbit populations, so the bird declined in parallel, and even this new plight was turned to the species' disadvantage by those who wished to legalise shooting them. Colin Tubbs, author of *The Buzzard*, wrote: 'At one stage the national press became interested in the controversy and, with its usual capacity for reporting exaggerated accounts at face value, printed stories of starving buzzards attacking such improbable targets as farm workers on tractors, shepherds, sheep-dogs, full-grown ewes, a lorry driver and – inevitably – a small child in a perambulator.'[78]

The following contribution to *Birds Britannica* suggests that we have lost little of our capacity to mis-judge the bird, even when pursuing its most innocuous feeding techniques: 'A well-to-do lady from a big house near Dumfries phoned me up to say that she was very concerned that there were "FIVE buzzards stalking about in her field and it was like bloody Africa out there and what on earth were they doing." She really felt threatened by them and was only slightly comforted when I told her that they would almost certainly be feeding on earthworms.'[79]

Fortunately buzzards are more likely to make an impact as an integral element of many wilder parts of the country. Their ability to ride thermals almost without a wing flap is a quality that has evoked consistent praise: 'a spirally flying Buzzard is the very poetry of motion'.[80] Others have waxed more lyrical: 'What would a Welsh valley be without its Buzzards? – or Ullswater? ... If only this eyecatcher's value were to be reckoned in terms of the pleasure it has afforded to many a bus-load of casual tourists and holiday-makers ... so aimless-looking, so carefree in its aerial manoeuvrings, answering to each and every suggestion of breeze, yielding to it, heeling away to turn and master it, testing it, feeling its uplift ... adrift in a cloudy heaven.'[81]

The buzzard's 'curious, weirdly beautiful cat-like cries', known as mewing, are another feature with an enormous capacity to evoke the spirit of place:

On the Dartington Hall Estate near Totnes, Devon, two miles of footpath have been adapted to the needs of blind or partially sighted walkers. To one side of the path lies Queen's Meadow, a broad water-meadow patrolled by egrets and herons. On the other side, steep frowning woods rise dramatically. How to convey this celebrated landscape to pedestrians who could not see it? This was the task confronting me when I designed an audio guide to accompany the walk. The answer lay in directing attention to the cry of buzzards, wheeling and squealing from the heights above the wood. That watchful, lordly and command-ing call powerfully evokes all the history and wildness of high and ancient places.[82]

Rough-legged Buzzard, *Buteo lagopus*. VN: Roughleg. This scarce winter visitor to Britain and Ireland is a touch more impressive than its commoner relative, partly because of its greater size and partly because it carries with it a hint of its tundra breeding grounds largely beyond the Arctic Circle. It is another northern raptor strongly dependent upon lemmings and the cyclical collapse in these rodent populations every four to five years triggers a small influx of roughlegs, largely to lowland south-east England, with sometimes as many as 237 in a winter (1994).[83]

Golden Eagle, *Aquila chrysaetos*. VN: Goldie. There are really two categories of golden eagle in Britain. The first is the wild bird, which has long held the reputation among ornithologists as 'the most magnificent of all British birds of prey'.[84] The second is the form that most people are familiar with – the eagle as symbol in art, literature, mythology and commercial life. In Scotland the two types converge since nearly all the British population breeds there, but it is also the creature most frequently invoked to convey the wild rugged peaks and glens of the region.

There are about 420 pairs in the Highlands and these have been held in check for the last two decades by intense over-grazing, which has reduced its natural prey, and by various forms of persecution mainly from game interests,

With the raven and the dove, the eagle completes the holy trinity of European bird symbols.

as well as from sheep farmers and egg collectors. Crofters have long feared eagles of both native species for their supposed depredation on livestock, and it was the goldie's reputation as a lamb-killer that drove its extermination in Ireland, Wales and most of northern England by the mid-eighteenth century. Eagles will certainly take sheep and deer carrion and occasionally lambs are carried back to the eyrie, but most of these are stillborn and the bird's contribution to overall lamb mortality in spring is negligible (see also White-tailed Eagle on page 120).

As an emblem, few birds are either as widespread or as revered as the eagle. Josephine Addison has well summarised its many meanings: 'The eagle symbolizes ascension, aspiration, empire, faith, faithfulness, fertility, freedom, fortitude, generosity, immortality, inspiration, keenness of vision, majesty, power, swiftness, storm, victory, splendour and strength. Alternatively it symbolizes evil, discord and rapacity.'[85]

Our commonest association of eagle imagery is with the apex of political power. Eagle motifs dating from 3000 BC were found above the doorway to the royal palace at Lagash in the Euphrates valley, and thereafter passed from the Sumerians to the Babylonian and Hittite empires and on to an almost continuous succession of European civilisations and dynasties. To the ancient Greeks the bird signified their paramount deity, Zeus, and in the age of Rome an eagle was liberated over the emperor's funeral pyre to carry his soul heavenwards.[86]

An eagle ensign had led the Roman armies into battle for 400 years by the time Constantine the Great introduced the double-headed eagle to symbolise the twin sovereignty of Church and State in the Byzantine empire. Almost ever after European conquerors seeking to identify their own political aspirations with the earlier glories of Rome adopted the same bird imagery. Great individual conquerors like Charlemagne or Napoleon had eagle crests, as did the ruling dynasties in Russia, Austria, Germany and Poland.

While eagles might have been dominant in the European lexicon of bird symbols, the British state and military, with the exception of the modern Royal Air Force (whose badge features a somewhat innocuous-looking bird), have seldom favoured this species. As a consequence its image tends to be more closely associated with our traditional enemies, assuming its most sinister connotations during the Second World War.

Persecution drove the golden eagle from Wales and northern England by the eighteenth century. Most of the British population is now confined to the Scottish Highlands, where the bird is often used as the classic motif for this wild and beautiful region.

In fact the conflict's chief architect must have brooded much on world domination with a severely angular Art Deco eagle image perched literally on his forehead.

Many of our most enduring images of Adolf Hitler include the symbol either on his peaked cap or his sleeve. Similar motifs were omnipresent in Nazi iconography, and in almost every subsequent English-speaking film or television progamme with a war setting the party's eagle

The eagle was often used as a symbol for St John and this accounts for its routine incorporation into church lecterns, like the striking example in Hereford Cathedral.

Right: The Eagle of St John depicted in the Lindisfarne Gospels (c. 700AD).

crest – the bird dangling a swastika in its all-powerful talons – is a standard shorthand image to convey the malignant power of the whole regime.

A more recent expression of the eagle's highly ambiguous symbolism occurred with the British-assisted US invasion of Iraq in 2003. It was one of many wars where, in the realms of symbolism, eagle clashed with eagle. And if one accepts that the bird on the flag of

The ospreys at the RSPB's Loch Garten reserve have done more to promote the cause of conservation than any other dynasty of birds.

Saddam Hussein's Baathist state was a direct descendant of the eagles in ancient Sumeria, then it also involved the eagle's oldest and most recent adherents.

The American bird, however, is not the golden eagle, but the **Bald Eagle**, *Haliaeetus leucocephalus*. This species has appeared twice on this side of the Atlantic (two other British examples involve birds of unknown origin), on both occasions in Ireland. Their treatment perfectly encapsulates our highly divergent attitudes towards the eagle-as-symbol and the real creature that lies behind it. The first occasion was in 1973 at Garrison, County Fermanagh. A juvenile bird allegedly attacked a farmer's poultry, and in obedience to a long, barren tradition, the man shot and killed it. The skin now resides in Ulster Museum. However a second exhausted bird was taken into captivity in November 1987 and, following its identification as a young bald eagle, it was repatriated to its American homeland and released back into the wild.[87]

Osprey, *Pandion haliateus*. The return of this rare fish-eating raptor is one of the great environmental stories of our age and sheds light on almost the entire spectrum of attitudes towards birds and the wider environment in the last half-century. Its status as an icon

took off in 1959 with the inspirational decision (pioneered by Scotland's then RSPB chief, George Waterston) to allow public observation of breeding ospreys at Loch Garten, then considered the only pair in the country. To date they have drawn in two million visitors and cemented the interests of tens of thousands of people. No single dynasty of birds has done more to engender positive responses towards nature.

Extreme rarity was certainly part of the osprey's initial appeal, but was by no means the sole reason. In fact such is the success of 'Operation Osprey' that the bird is no longer so scarce and in 2003 there were 160 occupied eyries.[88] (Four hundred pairs by 2025 is considered a very realistic estimate, and eminent Scottish ecologist Roy Dennis posits a potential British and Irish population of 1500 pairs.) The bird itself is intrinsically impressive, second only in impact and size to the two eagles, with a wingspan of 5½ feet (1.7m). It is unique among our birds of prey for an exclusively fish diet, which it captures in a trademark dive beneath the water that rivals the peregrine's stoop for sheer theatre.

As with most catchers of fish, the genuine powers have long been supplemented with make-believe. In the 1960s a dramatic photograph apparently depicting a dead

Trout fishery managers are often happy to donate a few of their fish to ospreys, especially if the paying public comes to witness the spectacle.

osprey locked by its claws in the body of a 10-pound (4.5-kg) carp was subsequently shown to be a hoax involving a buzzard skeleton.[89] A more enduring myth held that fish were so mesmerised by the predator that they simply turned belly-up in a shiver of feminine surrender. Hence Shakespeare's lines in *Coriolanus* (Act 4, Scene 5) as Aufidius and his lieutenant ponder whether the eponymous general will capture Rome:

All places yield to him ere he sits down,
. . . I think he'll be to Rome
As is the osprey to the fish, who takes it
By sovereignty of nature.

A contemporary reference in Holinshed's *Chronicles* suggests that the Elizabethans tried to capitalise on the bird's magical powers: 'We have also ospraies, which breed with us in parks and woods, whereby the keepers of the same do reap in breeding time no small commodity: for so soon almost as the young are hatched, they tie them to the butt ends or ground ends of sundry trees, where the old ones, finding them, do never cease to bring fish unto them, which the keepers take and eat from them.'

Since he added as colourful detail that ospreys possessed one webbed foot and one taloned foot, it is difficult to know how to interpret Holinshed's other claims.[90] More certain is the fact that James I kept otters and ospreys with cormorants that had all been trained to fish (see page 37), but the isolated nature of his efforts with ospreys suggests that the experiment was a failure.[91] One can appreciate the attempt, however. There have been many records of fish up to 2¼ pounds (1kg), although the birds find these difficult to carry and typical catches are 10–12 ounces (280–340gm). Opreys will also exploit a wide range of freshwater and marine species, depending on season. Mullet are an important prey during the bird's winter stay in Africa and on migration, hence an old West-Country name, 'mullet hawk'.[92]

The osprey's presumed role as competitor for Scottish trout and salmon was one of the many motives driving human persecution of the bird in the nineteenth and early twentieth centuries. Another was the Victorian obsession with displaying dramatic predators in the drawing-room cabinet. Some individuals like the notorious egger, Lewis Dunbar, played a key role in the osprey's eventual extermination, although armchair naturalists who never set foot in the Scottish Highlands were also part of a

chain of supply and demand driving the trade in souvenirs. At least men like Dunbar risked their lives to obtain the trophies and one could almost celebrate their undoubted courage, if not for the depressing nihilism at the root of their exploits.

In one famous raid in May 1851 Dunbar walked overnight to a well-known osprey eyrie on a castle in the middle of Loch an Eilein, just a few miles from the Loch Garten site. He then stripped and swam out at three in the morning in the midst of a snowstorm. Securing two eggs, he realised he had forgotten to bring anything in which to put them and, having tried one in his mouth and found he was unable to breathe, he swam on his back with an egg in each hand. He blew them immediately on his return, washed out the interiors with whisky and promptly sold them to a well-known English egg collector, John Wolley.[93]

The relentless efforts of the trophy hunters worked through to their bleak and inevitable conclusion by 1916 when Scottish ospreys were considered extinct. In fact they may have continued to nest occasionally throughout their 'exile' period.[94] What is not in doubt is the slow pace of social change in Britain, because the moment ospreys showed signs of breeding 40 years later, exactly the same persecution threatened the recolonisation. From 1955 to 1958, a solitary pair in Strathspey and Loch Garten had their nests robbed. In the last of the years Philip Brown, director of the RSPB, was himself on duty as part of a round-the-clock guard when thieves made an attempt on the nest. The stolen osprey eggs were smashed in the chase, but the thieves had already replaced the genuine clutch with two chicken eggs daubed with boot polish to deceive both ospreys and osprey watchers until the getaway was complete. The measures suggest the forethought and determination of the thieves.[95]

Fortunately they were not as determined as their opponents. The following season the bird's new nest tree was swathed in barbed wire, its lower limbs amputated and primitive electric alarms installed around the base. George Waterston also took the bold step of making the ospreys public property. The broadcasting of the nest site brought 14,000 visitors to Loch Garten in seven weeks and the figures rose each year, encouraged by wide press coverage of breeding successes. Operation Osprey eventually became an institution with important symbolic and social functions.

The osprey eyrie at Loch Garten was cut down by vandals in 1986 and rebuilt by the RSPB staff. One wonders if the birds would have so galvanised the public imagination if the story had not neatly translated into a tale of heroes and villains.

Speyside residents have long embraced their most famous bird neighbours.

It received national media coverage, with regular BBC television items on the highs and lows in the osprey's year. Notable 'lows' in the soap opera were the moment in 1964 when vandals tried to cut the nest tree down, and a further theft of the eggs in 1971. After the first incident the RSPB had 'to strap up the tree with 4 huge iron bars secured with eight-inch coach-bolts'.[96] The news relating to this 'pair' – in fact it was an evolving dynasty of birds – was often presented as if it were the only one in Britain. The Speyside ospreys thus performed another key function, drawing attention away from birds elsewhere in the Highlands that were quietly breeding beyond the spotlight.

Mike Everett, who was central to managing the young Operation Osprey, recalls the romance of these pioneer years:

In the early 1960s it was my job to oversee recruitment of about 140 volunteer wardens – nine a week for something like sixteen weeks of the bird's breeding season. It was the first time anyone had ever run anything like this in Britain, probably in Europe. By modern standards it was a rather primitive, almost military-style camp but with an air of make-do enthusiasm you'd find in any pioneering operation. It was a wonderful time and one of my greatest memories is the people, who ran the entire spectrum of British society from grandmothers to raving

People were once so awed by the osprey's fishing skills they thought it cast a spell over its victim, causing the fish to surrender itself belly up.

Marxist students. There was a lot of support from local Scottish people as well as visitors from as far away as the USA. It was also a training ground for the nation's new conservationists, with what seemed like half those involved today in ornithology coming through at one time or another.

Camp itself was a matter of old-fashioned tents but at its heart was the mess caravan, where huge quantities of food were served by volunteer cooks on a strictly maintained timetable. It was a wonderful place full of coffee, cigarette smoke, endless talk and laughter – sometimes lasting all night – huge games of Scrabble and amazing political arguments or philosophical discussions. You didn't mind the cold-water washing and all the usual aspects of life under canvas because people were having such a good time.[97]

The operations have become ever more sophisticated, with new permanent premises for staff and a large visitors' centre where the public can view constant live video footage of the nest interior. The identity of the surrounding area is now intimately associated with the birds. 'The neighbouring Boat of Garten is known as "The Osprey Village", with prominent signs featuring the totem species. Osprey business logos are widespread locally and nationally, while the birds have benefited from the wonderful support of landowners and game-keepers, on whose estates most of the pairs now nest.'[98]

Media fascination with ospreys has also remained high, although the positive benefits of so much publicity hinge on a striking paradox. Indeed Operation Osprey is itself born of paradox. It is perhaps the most intense expression of conservation effort targeted at a single bird species. Yet it flows in large part from the diametrically opposed attitudes of egg collectors and vandals. One wonders, even, if the bird would have so captured public imagination if the story had not as neatly translated into an epic battle of heroes and villains.

New developments in the osprey story have largely involved the efforts of Scottish ecologist Roy Dennis, who has been central to their conservation for nearly 40 years. One innovation was artificial nest construction. It drew on experience on the other side of the Atlantic, where egg collecting has no place in North American culture and where ospreys will nest side by side with humans, even in bustling ports. They can be tempted to breed by placing cartwheels horizontally on quayside poles, and in Scotland more natural-looking eyries have been widely used to encourage ospreys to colonise new sites. One such nest was involved in a successful breeding attempt in 2001 at Dodd Wood, near Keswick, the first in the Lake District for at least 150 years. The eyrie, constructed by staff of the Forestry Commission and the Lake District National Park Authority, was sited with public access very much in mind. Tens of thousands of visitors have viewed the occupants at a special centre in Whinlatter, but there is also a camera link relaying live osprey images on to a giant video wall.

Translocation has been another successful feature. Ospreys have bred at Rutland Water in the English Midlands since 2001, following a six-year programme of release managed by Roy Dennis (Highland Foundation for Wildlife), Anglian Water and the staff at Rutland Water Nature Reserve. In 2003 two pairs reared five young – the first breeding ospreys south of the northern uplands since 1848.

Now the techniques have taken to cyberspace, with the fitting of radio transmitters to wild migrating birds. These have enabled the monitoring of osprey habits, while generating huge publicity as Internet users track the birds' daily movements on the Rutland Water website (www.ospreys.org.uk). Some of the revelations resulting from telemetry have been remarkable. Adults tend to make south-easterly journeys, hugging the European coastline and following the west African coast to their winter areas in Senegal, Mali and Guinea. Yet some young ospreys from Scotland show a troubling westerly trend in their route, and one radio-tagged bird made a remarkable non-stop 600-mile (1000-km) journey from Ireland to northern Spain. Another adult female from Scotland ended up just a few miles apart from her own offspring at the same Senegalese wetland, yet the juvenile had taken a completely separate trans-Saharan route on its first journey to Africa.[99]

Common Kestrel, *Falcon tinnunculus*. VN: Moosie-haak (Orkney), Kes, Kessie, Windhover. This falcon is the bird of prey *everyone* will have seen, although it is often ascribed to completely the wrong family, and not even great poets are immune to the error, witness Ted Hughes' poem, 'The Hawk in the Rain':

> . . . the hawk
> Effortlessly at height hangs his still eye.
> His wings hold all creation in a weightless quiet,
> Steady as a hallucination in the streaming air.
> While banging wind kills these stubborn hedges.

Until recently the kestrel showed the adaptability to

'High there, how he rung upon the rein of a wimpling wing In his ecstasy!' (Gerard Manley Hopkins, 'The Windhover')

thrive in modern Britain and Ireland. It has since suffered a troubling decline and has been overtaken by the buzzard as our commonest raptor, yet its hovering cruciform is still an everyday sight over many road verges and has led to its secondary name as the 'motorway hawk'.

It has also managed to find a secure home in the midst of urban sprawl. In the countryside it occupies tree holes or old nests built by other birds, but city-dwelling kestrels seem to require little more than a sense of the dramatic in their choice of site. 'In 1991 I found a pair of nesting kestrels in Portsmouth city centre. The location was a galleon-style weather vane, which still rotates, above a dome of the university building. The ship was used in subsequent years but a second pair had a more conventional site – a hole in the side of the same building.'[100]

London also has a good kestrel population, with birds seen regularly in the 'Square Mile' and breeding attempts on the British Museum, the Broadgate Centre, the Britannic Tower and the Tower of London (where they stole choice cuts of meat from the ravens).[101] In the pre-war period they were known to nest on the Palace of Westminster and Westminster Abbey.[102]

I used to watch from the BBC director general's office the ornate façade of the corporation's Langham Hotel across the road, where kestrels regularly nested in a ventilator hole which had lost its protective grille. Other nests have been built on office buildings, large hotels, churches, gasworks and power stations. From a tall office block above Ealing Station I used to watch a kestrel leave the ledge of my window and glide down without any wing movement to snatch an unsuspecting house sparrow hopping in the gutter.[103]

Sparrows were once a mainstay of the London population but since their huge decline in the capital (see page 441), kestrels have switched to other birds, including juvenile feral pigeons.[104] The choice demonstrates the species' striking versatility, given that their usual diet is small mammals, particularly voles. It was, incidentally, the mushrooming of small mammal populations along the strips of undisturbed grassland on either side of most motorways that explains the kestrel's familiar roadside performance.

Its gift for adaptability has sometimes cost the kestrel dear. In the age of game shooting the fact that it will sometimes take birds and, very occasionally, young game birds, led to many being unjustifiably shot or trapped. (However rare the bird-taking habit, in some individuals it can become routine. At Great Yarmouth the productivity of the largest little tern colony in Britain was severely reduced when kestrels took 147 – possibly 271 – tern chicks in 1995.[105]) Ironically in an earlier epoch when falconry was widespread, the kestrel was condemned for the reverse failure: they had a reputation as little more than a good mouser. As a consequence it came lowest in the feudal hierarchy of trained 'hawks' and was prescribed as the bird of the servant or knave.

More recently the novelist Barry Hines borrowed the phrase for his popular work, *A Kestrel for a Knave*, which describes a young boy's efforts to rear and train a foundling kestrel. It later became the basis for Ken Loach's 1969 film, *Kes*, and in both portraits the species' rather lowly historical reputation is turned on its head. The eponymous bird becomes a symbol for the individuality and spiritual longing of its central character – the V-flicking victim of working-class Barnsley life, Billy Casper, who was brilliantly played in the film by untrained actor David Bradley. (*Kes* also triggered an unfortunate rise in kestrel-nest robberies, as would-be Billy Caspers tried to emulate his uplifting experience.[106])

The one activity for which the species has always been celebrated is the art of remaining aloft and stationary for what can seem like minutes on end. The hovering kestrel is as inspiring a vision of avian perfection as a peregrine in its headlong dive or a fishing gannet. In the early 1960s Hawker Siddeley paid homage to it when they named their newly developed vertical take-off jet fighter the 'Kestrel'. They then rebranded the production model using a larger, more impressive raptor and the plane achieved subsequent fame as the Harrier.[107]

Yet the hovering kestrel has indubitably given rise to the most famous bird-of-prey poem in the language, Gerard Manley Hopkins' 'The Windhover':

I caught this morning morning's minion, kingdom of
daylight's dauphin, dapple-dawn-drawn Falcon, in his
riding
Of the rolling level underneath him steady air, and
striding
High there, how he rung upon the rein of a wimpling
wing
In his ecstasy! then off, off forth on swing,
As a skate's heel sweeps smooth on a bow-bend: the
hurl and gliding
Rebuffed the big wind. My heart in hiding
Stirred for a bird, – the achieve of, the mastery of the
thing!

Hopkins exploited the bird's cruciform shape as it hovers to convey the notion that a wild creature in fulfilment of its true being expressed a near-divine perfection. Yet the poem is also simply a beautifully observed evocation of a kestrel's effortless suspension followed by that languid turn as it moves to hover over a different spot, which is the bird's classic mode of operation. Almost 70 years ago Bernard Tucker addressed the common fallacy that the kestrel is not really moving. In fact, 'the hovering bird is only stationary with reference to the ground; actually it is moving forward at a pace adjusted to the speed of the wind in the opposite direction'.[108]

A more modern discovery arising from Dutch film studies of hunting kestrels is that the bird achieves maximum focus on the ground below by allowing its head to move 'less than 6mm in any direction' despite the body and wings being buffeted about 'like a flapping rag'. A bird will also cease fluttering its wings and allow itself to be blown backwards a few millimetres but compensates by stretching the neck forwards. Then it flaps again to bring the body forward and so allow another glide. The whole cycle takes less than a second and requires 'almost unbelievable coordination'. The use of both techniques saves 'an estimated 25–44% of the energy that would have been required for continuous flapping flight at that wind speed'.[109]

Other raptors like common buzzard, rough-legged buzzard and two vagrant falcons – **Lesser Kestrel**, *F.*

In the Middle Ages the male merlin was renowned as a lady's falcon. One can imagine him being sported on the bejewelled glove like a medieval fashion accessory.

---

naumanni (18 records), and **Red-footed Falcon,** *F. vespertinus* (738 records) – all hover, but none is so reliant on the technique and perhaps only the last has developed it to the same level of perfection. It is strange then that we should have discarded the bird's most distinctive attribute in giving it a name. 'Kestrel' is of French origin (*faucon crécerelle* is the current name) and draws on the high, rather metallic rattling call (*crécelle* is 'a rattle' or 'harsh voice').[110] The scientific name *tinnunculus* has much the same meaning (from the Latin *tinnire*, 'to ring').

'Stondin 'ork' – the Midlands dialect for 'standing hawk' – is an interesting local variant and seems to be a reference to the kestrel's motionless flight.[111] Yet Lockwood argues that while it may have incorporated these associations, it is in fact derived from an older version, 'stannel' or 'stanniel', which is onomatopoeic in origin. *Stangella* meant 'stone yeller' in Old English.[112] We are thus left with 'windhover' – and today it has a rather mannered, self-conscious ring – as the only reference to the peerless flight. At one time the species was known as 'wind bibber', 'wind cuffer', 'wind fanner' and the rather remarkable 'windfuck' or 'wind fucker'. However the last two seem to have had none of the contemporary vulgar associations and may simply have drawn on an old word meaning 'to beat'.[113]

Merlin, *Falco columbarius.* VN: Peerie hawk (Shetland). In length this is our smallest bird of prey. The male, traditionally known as a jack, is sometimes just 10½

inches (25cm), shorter than a mistle thrush. At a fraction over 5½ ounces (160gm), he is also a featherweight – although the average male sparrowhawk is even lighter – but is a bird of enormous energy and dash.[114] At rest merlins look compact and muscular, although one seldom enjoys prolonged views of them simply because they move so quickly and so often.

The usual flight is a low-level sortie and involves light deft wingbeats interspersed with glides, when the overall impression is one of hectic intensity. Should the wings close completely during a stoop the bird mutates to a missile and it is the ferocity and speed of attack that enables it to down prey four times its own weight. An old North American name was 'pigeon falcon', a connection enshrined in the scientific version *columbarius* (literally, 'of the pigeon'). The name 'merlin' is itself of unknown (if ancient) origin, but it has nothing to do with the wizard of Arthurian legend.

In the golden age of falconry the species was acknowledged as a lady's bird and was much valued by huntress monarchs like Mary, Queen of Scots and Catherine the Great. The male has striking blue-grey upperparts with rich rusty tones to the buff and dark-streaked breast, and one can imagine that, like a medieval fashion accessory, it was as highly regarded on madam's bejewelled glove for its aura of ferocious chic and its 'elfin falsetto' as it was for any genuine sporting prowess.[115]

In a later age of field sports, merlins were ruthlessly

A detail from the fourteenth-century Devonshire Hunting Tapestries shows a falcon on a lady's gloved hand.

suppressed and their love of favourite look-out perches – walls and posts – made them very susceptible to the pole-trap. Although they will take large birds, including grouse and partridge chicks, the vast majority of victims weigh around 1 ounce (28gm), and the bird has a heavy dependence on skylarks and meadow pipits. The anxieties and resulting persecution of gamekeepers were thus completely unjustified. Yet one researcher of this otherwise little-studied raptor noted in the 1920s that merlins returned to an area of heather moor for 19 years, and each season the keeper shot them so that not a single egg was hatched.[116]

Fortunately the pressure has largely lifted and about 1400 pairs are now spread across parts of Ireland and the British hill country north and west of a line between Durham and Bristol.[117]

Eurasian Hobby, *Falco subbuteo*. The scientific name, *subbuteo*, simply means 'smaller than buzzard'. For much of the last century the word was familiar to generations of schoolboys, probably without many being aware that it referred to a bird at all. 'Subbuteo' was a hugely popular model football game and acquired its trade name in the following manner.

Peter Adolph, the inventor of the game, was demobbed in 1945 and formed a natural-history business, but trade was slack in winter and so to supplement his earnings he produced a football game and placed an advert in the *Boy's Own* magazine to test the market. While he was away on a business trip to the USA to evaluate a collection of birds' eggs, Adolph's mother was swamped with postal orders for the game (£7500 in 7s. 6d. orders). In 1948 Adolph applied to register 'The Hobby' as a trade mark because this had been his favourite bird of prey as a child. When it was rejected he used the Latin name instead. There is a Subbuteo crest with the bird's head on it, but it doesn't seem to have been designed or used until the late 1970s.[118]

The English name arises from an old French verb *hober*, meaning 'to jump about' (the current French name is *faucon hobereau*), apparently a reference to its agile movement. Built 'like a bijou … Peregrine' or 'a giant Swift', the bird has long slender tail and wings, which are framed in flight like a rakish scimitar bow, while the wingbeats are simultaneously deep and economically precise.[119] It is the only British raptor with the aerial flexibility regularly to catch swifts, hirundines and even bats on the wing. It seems strange that modern plane manufacturers have never exploited this prowess in the naming of their own products, although there was an early type of slender cannon known as a robinet, which drew on an old, rather confusing name for a hobby, the robin.[120]

It usually tackles only small birds and among the early falconers it was used in the sport of 'daring' larks. Otherwise it had a reputation as a young man's bird, perhaps before he graduated to a larger adult model like a peregrine.[121] However, hobbies are impressive even in pursuit of prey as small as dragonflies or beetles, which form a major component of their diet. Up to 20 birds gather over particularly rich feeding sites and pluck them from the air at a rate of one every 7–10 seconds.[122]

There is an aura of almost studied casualness as the bird swoops down with a few leisured beats, then turns at the last moment to take the insect with claws uppermost. Hobbies eat the prey as they fly. In fact the curious cycling motion, as the indigestible chitinous parts are stripped and the soft body transferred from talon to bill, is the only momentary inelegance in the whole operation. Then down it goes again to kill with the same remorseless grace.

The English population was once strongly associated with southern heathlands, yet in the last 30 years it has been found to thrive perfectly well in ordinary farmland, enjoying at least a thirteenfold increase over that period. One estimate suggests nearly 2000 pairs spread from Cornwall to Northumberland.[123]

Gyr Falcon, *Falco rusticolus*. The largest, heaviest and, in its white morph, most spectacular falcon in the world is a scarce visitor to Britain and Ireland from Iceland, Greenland and northern Scandinavia. A large female can weigh more than 4½ pounds (2.1kg) and in the wild the bird has the ability to overpower prey as large as swan, capercaillie and snowy owl.

Testimony to its remarkable strength is the story of a Greenland specimen watched by a local cottager as it killed a gull on Anglesey in January 1949. With all the dismal animus of his age, the man then set about baiting two steel gin-traps with the remains of the gull carcass. On its return the falcon was caught by the foot in one of these, but it was still able to rise into the air, gin-trap and all, and pull 'the anchoring pin clean out of the ground'.[124]

Fortunately gyr falcons now have pulling power of a very different kind. 'In 1986 I heard about a white morph bird at Berry Head, Devon, whilst at Port Stanley the day before I was due to leave the Falkland Islands. I arrived back at Brize Norton in Oxfordshire the following day, but as my mother wouldn't take me straight to Devon I had to go back to Stoke-on-Trent – for the quickest welcome home party you've ever seen – and drive overnight to Devon. After seeing the bird first thing in the morning I went to my car and slept for six hours.'[125]

An 8000-mile (13,300-km) chase may appear a quintessentially modern response to the bird, but our sense of its specialness dates back more than a thousand years. It was traditionally the sporting bird of royalty and much cherished by the doyen of all Europe's falconers, the Holy Roman Emperor, Frederick II, who kept a polar bear as well as his white Arctic falcons. There are also accounts of English monarchs possessing gyrs right back until the mists overtake recorded history with Ethelbert II, the Saxon king of Kent. More famous sovereigns like Henry II and his son, John, owned and flew them at herons or cranes (see page 184).[126]

White birds were the most prized and for the power jetset of medieval Europe they functioned as an alliance-building currency, in much the same way that thoroughbred horses or parcels of caviar might do today. There are stories of the King of Norway sending native gyrs to Edward I, who in turn dispatched birds to the King of Castille. And the gyr's legendary status spanned civilisations as well as continents. The high-mettled cacking call of the Arctic falcon would have echoed down the corridors of the Alhambra as it did in the palaces of the Mongol emperor Kublai Khan, who was said to have 200 of them.[127]

One catches glimpses of a highly lucrative trade in the commercial records of Norfolk-based boats sailing to and from Iceland in the Elizabethan period. One vessel named the *Susan* came back to Blakeney in 1598 with 14 gyr falcons, which would have been as precious a cargo as the hold full of salt cod and ling.[128] Despite current international protection, gyrs are still illegally traded, mainly by bent German falconers and petro-dollar millionaires, some of whom are said to have paid as much as $100,000 for a white male.[129] Yet this was probably less than the king's ransom apparently offered by the French monarch, Philip Augustus, for a white bird that he lost during the siege of Acre in the Third Crusade.[130]

Peregrine, *Falco peregrinus*. VN: Perry. Kenneth Richmond suggested that 'Anyone who tries to do justice to this prince of Falcons must first dip his pen in superlatives.'[131] As well as mountain crags and sea cliffs – and now also high-rise inner-city buildings – the peregrine inhabits a secondary human landscape that combines a dense forest of historical reference with an elevated plateau of high praise. One devotee, tipping his hat towards its key rival as predator-in-chief, wrote, 'Begging the Golden Eagle's pardon, the Peregrine Falcon is our most splendid bird of prey.'[132]

The bird's strength, beauty, sheer success and adaptability cement its status as one of Britain's, if not the world's, most impressive animals, although perhaps the key launch pad for our imagination is its remarkable speed. This Ferrari of the bird world has the reputation of being the world's fastest species. In level flight the

More purple ink has probably been spilt on the peregrine's stoop than any other avian manoeuvre.

maximum is consistently estimated at 60 mph an hour (100 km/h), but the peregrine's legendary dive as it stoops at prey has inspired wildly differing results, if not outright exaggeration. Claims range upwards to a mind-boggling 270 mph (430 km/h) although mathematical calculations of the bird's maximum terminal velocity suggest no more than 240 mph (380 km/h) is possible. And it is questioned whether this theoretical figure could ever be reached.[133]

It is not so much the true rate attained by a diving peregrine that is important, but rather our perception of an apparent contradiction: uncontrollable speeds exercised under supreme control. It is perhaps this ultimate expression of aerial mastery that inspired the claim by one of the peregrine's great champions. Richard Treleaven, author of two books on the species, writes, 'Of all wild creatures the peregrine is the most truly symbolic of freedom.'[134]

The other less quantifiable element in the peregrine's mystique is its élan as a predator. There is a large difference in the average size of males and females, with the former weighing as little as 60 per cent of their partners. In the past the cock peregrine was known as a 'tiercel', from the French *la tierce*, 'a third', because he was assumed to be a third smaller. A big female can be 2 pounds 14 ounces (1.3kg), the equal of an average grey heron, a bird twice its length. The size of prey caught by the two sexes reflects their own size differences, but both overlap in their love of pigeons, and in Britain these birds form the majority of the diet. In inland Wales, northern England and south Scotland pigeons represent 50–80 per cent of the prey items taken.[135]

Yet it is those rare anecdotes concerning less usual prey items, which range upwards from goldcrest to greylag goose, heron or great black-backed gull, that illustrate the peregrine's exceptional proficiency and strength as a predator. A much-repeated story, first told by William Macgillivray, concerned the remains of a black grouse and pheasant found in an eyrie on the Bass Rock in the Firth of Forth. The remains invoked a scenario in which the female falcon carried her own body weight for at least 3 miles (5km).[136] An even more extraordinary image is the individual that chased a skylark down the shaft of a lead mine to a depth of 360 feet (109m).[137] Such determination allows peregrines to include other lesser raptors, such as kestrel, merlin and short-eared owl, in their diet.

Traditionally considered birds of the northern uplands and coastal cliffs, peregrines have recently extended their range and now breed in the centre of several large cities.

In the fourteenth-century Devonshire Hunting Tapestries the party of falconers loose their birds after wildfowl.

Sometimes even predators larger than itself can fall victim to the peregrine. In the twelfth century Giraldus Cambrensis recorded a remarkable contest between a Welsh bird and a 'hawk' belonging to Henry II, which sounds like a goshawk (or, just possibly, even a gyr falcon):

> When Henry II, King of the English spent some time in this neighbourhood making preparations for his journey to Ireland, he occasionally went hawking. By chance he saw a noble falcon perched on a rock . . . and then loosed at it a huge and carefully bred Norwegian hawk which he had on his left wrist. At first the falcon seemed slower in flight. Then it lost its temper and in its turn became the aggressor. It soared to a great height, swooped fiercely down and gave the hawk a mighty blow in the chest with its sharp claws, striking it dead at the King's feet.[138]

Henry II was apparently so impressed with the Welsh bird that he requested peregrines from the same area ever afterwards.

Falconry had been known in China since 2000 BC and reached Britain in the ninth century, surviving as both recreational sport and practical hunting technique until the reign of George III. Throughout, the pre-eminent weapon of choice for most wealthy falconers was the peregrine. The art was surrounded by a vast body of lore and tradition, fragments of which obtrude still in our own age. It bequeathed us words like 'cadge' (the wooden frame on which falcons were carried, and the servant who carried the cadge itself), 'booze' (from an original word, *bouse*, referring to the hawk that overdrank), and 'hawk', in the sense of to sell.

Falconry is also deeply embedded in the history of the English capital. The narrow rows of London dwellings that run down the back of many larger streets and are known as 'mews' have their origins in the detached premises where the household birds were once confined. To mew was an old word meaning to moult and it was gradually transferred from the birds to their cage, and then from the cage to the building that housed them. After falconry fell from fashion, a mews described the same building but with a new purpose – they were the stables where horses were kept. Richard II had his own bird-filled mews constructed in Charing Cross, while Charles II had a new royal mews built on the site where the National Gallery now stands.[139]

The medieval love of falconry was directly dependent upon a healthy population of wild peregrines, and some of the first conservation legislation enacted in Britain – in Scotland during the twelfth century – concerned the preservation of native 'hawks'. In 1621 in Scotland the fine for stealing a bird was raised to £100, which was a strong reflection of the trained falcon's enormous value. The Scottish monarch James IV (1473–1513) is said to have paid £189 for one bird.[140] The breeding cliffs of wild peregrines were intimately known and jealously guarded, and sites like the Great Orme in north Wales were said to have yielded first-rate falconers' birds since the occasion when a local family presented James I with a collection of peregrines worth £1000. In the 1770s Thomas Pennant referred to another traditional eyrie on the South Stack in Anglesey, a site now owned by the RSPB and still a wonderful location to observe the cliff-nesting birds.[141] The records indicate Welsh sites that have been continuously occupied for hundreds of years, and behind the facts lies the more inspiring speculation that some have held peregrines for far longer.

It was perhaps inevitable that the qualities which made it the nonpareil for falconers would damn it as competitor-in-chief once firearms replaced the bird on the gloved fist. By the second half of the eighteenth century a reversal in attitudes was well under way, and in a 1767 letter to Thomas Pennant, Gilbert White bore witness to the falcon's increasingly dismal lot. Unable to identify a dead bird he found, White sent it to Pennant with the accompanying note: 'It haunted a marshy piece of ground in quest of wild ducks and snipes: but when it was shot, had just knocked down a rook, which it was tearing in pieces . . . I found it nailed up at the end of the barn, which is the countryman's museum.'[142]

The period of about 150 years after White's telling reference represents the nadir for the peregrine's cultural status in Britain. Derek Ratcliffe, one of the bird's pre-eminent biographers, has written of the era:

The gamekeepers' onslaught on this raptor . . . was waged with unremitting vigour throughout the nineteenth century. Indeed, a perceptible slackening of this warfare did not begin to show until quite recent years, and it is by no means over. Anyone who browses through the literature of the Peregrine cannot fail to be struck by the sickening refrain of ruthless killing . . . The carnage was greatest on the moorlands of the north and west which had become extensively preserved for Red Grouse, and included any adjoining seacliff haunts, but in the lowlands, any coastal eyries close to Pheasant and Partridge ground suffered similarly.[143]

The period should perhaps be viewed less as the typical state of affairs and more as an aberration. Today the peregrine has reclaimed much of the lost ground in terms of national range and population, and one may have to go back to the Middle Ages to find a time when it was more numerous. Ironically, its renaissance in Britain was preceded by a short period when peregrine numbers fell to probably their lowest level since the last ice age.

During the Second World War the peregrine's depredations upon pigeons were deemed a threat to the military effort because so many homing birds were used as message carriers. Private breeders supplied 200,000 pigeons to the armed services, and many bomber crews – particularly those operating over the Atlantic, North Sea and Channel – took birds with them on raids in case they had to bail out. It was hoped the pigeons could return to Bomber Command with a message indicating the crew's location and trigger a recovery search (see Rock Dove, page 264).[144] In 1940 the government issued a Destruction of Peregrine Falcon Order, and the Air Ministry implemented the cull with great thoroughness. As many as 600 birds were killed, while many nests were also raided for eggs and young. In areas like Cornwall and Devon peregrines were almost completely wiped out and it is a measure of the bird's remarkable resilience that once the pressures were lifted they quickly recovered.[145]

Yet barely had the threat receded than another, more severe challenge arose. Ironically awareness of the problem surfaced only after complaints by pigeon-racing groups from South Wales, who claimed that the peregrine was causing major losses among their birds. In 1960 they delivered a petition to the Home Office seeking removal of legal protection for the falcon, to which the government responded with a full peregrine census to establish the truth of the claims. Rather than returning with confirmatory evidence of a huge increase, BTO census workers compiled a picture of massive losses. Derek Ratcliffe, the organiser of the Peregrine Inquiry, wrote:

The once flourishing population of southern England had all but disappeared and that of Wales was greatly reduced. In the north of England, numbers were well down on their normal level, and in coastal southern Scotland few falcons remained . . . Breeding success was low amongst the remaining Peregrines and numerous territories were occupied by birds which failed to rear young, or even to lay eggs . . . over the country as a whole a large number of nesting places once held regularly by Peregrines seemed to be totally deserted, in many cases for the first time ever known.[146]

As the decline intensified, evidence was gradually assembled to prove that newly introduced pesticides were at the root of the problem – particularly the recently synthesised organochlorine compounds with proprietary names like Dieldrin, Aldrin, Heptachlor and Lindane. These were used as seed-dressings and were building up to sub-lethal levels in granivorous birds and were then passed on when these species fell victim to a bird of prey. The effect of the toxic agrochemicals was to poison the raptors outright, although a secondary factor in the peregrine's decline was only unravelled after a brilliant piece of detective work by Derek Ratcliffe.

Dichloro-diphenyl-trichloro-ethane (better known as DDT) had been manufactured in large quantities during the war and represented a major breakthrough in the control of insect-borne disease. Its subsequent use as an agricultural pesticide coincided with an unusual development in peregrine behaviour. From the late 1940s Ratcliffe had observed an increasing propensity among the nesting falcons to damage their own eggs. In 1966 he suggested that the likely cause of these inadvertent breakages was a thinning in the egg shell. He then tested the hypothesis by weighing and measuring peregrine eggs taken both before and after the introduction of various pesticides.

Egg collecting was illegal by the 1960s, so once Ratcliffe had examined all the legitimately held assemblies, he had to find a way of gaining access to more dubiously obtained stock. The solution was found by his friend, Desmond Nethersole-Thompson, himself a former collector, who 'promptly poured his tremendous energy into "opening the door of the underworld"' to Ratcliffe's inquiry. The opportunities this gave to the government scientist to work 'through the mahogany drawers with their cherished loot from the wild places of Britain' represented one of the most unlikely and bizarre alliances in conservation history. Yet the outcome was dramatic.[147]

The causal link between DDT, thinner shells and nest failure was proven and the offending product was eventually withdrawn. Almost for the first time, society woke up to the unforeseen but insidious impact of industrial and agricultural chemicals upon nature. 'Miracle' products like DDT, which had initially been heralded as a way to eliminate mosquito-borne scourges like malaria, were not really solutions at all. On the contrary, the poisons leached into our water systems

contaminated the land and killed everything from fish to birds. The challenge to reduce or eliminate their destructive consequences is now central to our understanding of the environment and is manifest in the huge growth in organic products in our supermarkets.

In the USA and in Britain, where wildlife was equally affected by pesticides, the peregrine was a key symbol for our confrontation with the Frankenstein's monster of industrialisation. In the 1960s and 1970s it was even classified as a Red Data Species – a bird at possible risk of global extinction – which was all the more extraordinary given that it is one of the most widespread of the world's raptors. Peregrines occur on six continents from latitudes 76° N to 55° S.

One response to the crisis in America was the appearance of several major environmental books such as Rachel Carson's bestselling *Silent Spring* (1962), a 'devastating and well-informed indictment' on the follies of indiscriminate pesticide use.[148] In Britain an expression of the heightened sensitivity to this bird icon was J. A. Baker's *The Peregrine* (1967), one of the most outstanding books on nature in the twentieth century. Baker was a retired librarian, who devoted 10 years to the study of wintering peregrines on the Essex estuaries near his home. Rewritten five times before finally being published and winning the Duff Cooper Memorial Prize, Baker's book is a mixture of detailed observation and his idiosyncratic prose-poetry. There is an occasional metaphysical density to the language, but more often he described the falcon's actions in passages of radiant lyricism that both express his own burning obsession and restate all the qualities that make the bird such a totem species:

Rain began, and the peregrine returned to the brook. He flew from an elm near the bridge, and I lost him at once in the hiss and shine of rain and the wet shuddering of the wind. He looked thin and keen, and very wild. When the rain stopped, the wind roared into frenzy. It was hard to stand still in the open, and I kept to the lee of the trees. At half past two the peregrine swung up into the eastern sky. He climbed vertically upward, like a salmon leaping into the great waves of air that broke against the cliff of South Wood. He dived to the trough of a wave, then rose steeply within it, flinging himself high in the air, on outstretched wings exultant. At five hundred feet he hung still, tail closed, wings curving far back with their tips almost touching the tip of his tail. He was stooping horizontally forward at the speed of the oncoming wind. He rocked and swayed and shuddered, close-hauled in a roaring sea of air, his furled wings whipping and plying like wet canvas.[149]

An atmosphere of greater awareness and enhanced protection eventually allowed Britain's peregrines to increase and expand their range. From the 1962 low of about 350 pairs, they have climbed to 1400 by 2002, occupying sites where they had not been observed for decades, if not centuries. The more unusual locations for their eyries include the Newton Building at Nottingham Trent University, Chichester Cathedral, London's Battersea Power Station and, most unlikely of all, a lighting maintenance platform for a chemical works, where the nest was within 13 feet (4m) of a conveyor belt carrying 1200 ton(ne)s of limestone every 24 hours.[150]

Many conspicuous eyries are intensively watched, not merely because of the peregrine's public appeal, but because the bird continues to be persecuted. A small number of pigeon-fanciers, who accuse the falcons of killing their birds, place pigeon carcasses laced with poison close to their nests. In some instances the frustrations are perhaps understandable, given that in areas like the south Wales valleys domestic pigeons are the most important component of the falcon's diet during the breeding season, and more than 90 per cent of these are racing birds.

For conservationists matters have come full circle. Rather than fending off the charges made against the peregrine for its predation of racing birds, they recognise that domestic pigeons may be critical to the falcon's healthy population. One study concluded: 'Raptor predation is cited as a contributory factor in the decline of pigeon racing and changing the racing season is potentially one way in which peregrine predation may be reduced. The adoption by pigeon fanciers of a strategy in which there is a hiatus in the race programme and pigeons are confined to their lofts for a period during May/June could have profound, inimical effects on peregrine breeding success.'[151]

Yet elsewhere the illegal persecution of peregrines is still causing a serious reduction in their numbers, particularly where eyries are close to keepered grouse moors. One study estimated that in the early 1980s in south-east Scotland interference at peregrine nests was causing the loss of almost a quarter of productivity, while in central Scotland it was reduced by almost one-fifth. Yet some suggest that matters may also come full circle here. Derek Ratcliffe speculates:

During its long association with humankind, the peregrine has acquired a varied symbolism. More recently it heralded the new age of environmental concern, particularly through its central role in highlighting the dangers of pesticides. Having fought a long campaign to rescue it from oblivion, its

Modern falconers deploy peregrines at airfields to frighten off birds that might come into collision with aircraft.

champions are not going to stand idly by while old enemies, in the form of game-shooting interests, seek to turn the clock back to the Victorian era of ruthless predator destruction. This time, it is the wildlife protagonists who will be on the offensive, and from as simple a position as that of the opposition, but one with greater moral force. Whereas the shooters derive enjoyment from killing birds, the bird-of-prey enthusiasts find pleasure in seeing the creatures alive and celebrating their existence as marvels of evolution. If the professed 'sportsmen' cannot tolerate other natural predators sharing their domain, then the pressure will increase to close down their sport completely. Today there are many more people who enjoy watching birds than enjoy shooting them, and if it turns into a contest between the two groups, the watchers will win. The peregrine could become a new symbol for the passing of a field activity which, however long its traditions, is no longer acceptable in the twenty-first century.[152]

Grouse family *Tetraonidae*

Red Grouse (Willow Ptarmigan), *Lagopus lagopus*. VN: Muir-hen (Orkney). Even when just 12 days old and no bigger than thrushes, grouse chicks have acquired the powers of flight as well as the characteristic plump-bodied, small-headed shape of their parents. Yet the adult plumage varies considerably. The ground colour ranges from warm tan through to a deep, dark vinaceous brown, and this is blended with differing amounts of black barring, 'frosty' white feather-tips and variable white patches on the flank and belly. Two constants are the whitish 'stockings' of the completely feathered legs and feet and the crimson comb above each eye, most prominent on the adult male.

W. H. Hudson memorably described the cock as resembling 'a figure cut in some hard dark red stone . . . red gritstone, or ironstone, or red granite, or, better still, deep-red serpentine, veined and mottled with black, an exceedingly hard stone which takes a fine polish'.[1]

The red grouse is the only family member to be widely shot in Britain and Ireland, and where the entire game stock is derived from wild birds. For the shooter, it is a wily contender with a capacity for high, fast, jinking flight and an apparent gift for learning from its experience as a target. The exacting trial of marksmanship in some of the most beautiful upland country – an open heather landscape that has been specifically shaped in its name – makes grouse shooting a premier sporting event and has earnt the grouse a reputation as 'the King of Game Birds'.

As if aware of its social rank, there is an imperious quality to the loud, harsh, very human '*go-bak, go-bak, go-bak*' call, issued as the grouse rise in vocal challenge above the moor. There is also a wonderful, almost regal theatricality in some of the bird's ritual behaviour: 'What a marvellous picture of pompous rage the cock can be! He struts, stamping down his feathery feet and toe nails stiffly as he approaches another cock. He is big, almost blown up like a balloon ready to burst. His throat swells and vibrates as he bursts out a staccato gurgle of angry calls, snaking out his head towards you in the car.'[2]

Brian Vesey-Fitzgerald also found an element of comic self-importance in the male's courtship display: 'There is a formal pattern in which the cock advances towards the hen with a rather high-stepping mincing gait – rather as if he were walking on hot bricks and hoped no one would notice that he was not very comfortable – with tail fully fanned and erected, wings drooped and the neck stretched out to a positively astonishing extent.'[3]

The challenge presented by the high, fast twisting flight of a red grouse is a key part of its reputation as the King of the Game Birds.

While they have been the focus of much human aggression, red grouse are not incapable of turning the tables. During the breeding season cock birds are well known for their vigorous defence of territory. A hand-reared bird at Tomintoul would attack all who entered its area including the local postman, 'who was daily thrown from his bicycle' until the council bought him a van for protection.[4]

I have personally known three aggressive red grouse over the years. Roughly fourteen years ago I was phoned up by the *Manchester Evening News* about a 'psychopathic' red grouse terrorising walkers on the Pennine Way near Edale. It emerged that it was a male which reacted to the colour red and attacked red hiking socks, red coats, red rucksacks.

Another was in Northumberland in 1984 that used to hurl itself against my red VW Polo, but didn't seem to react to other non-red cars. The third was last year on Langsett Moors, which also attacked walkers. I have a poor photograph of the grouse hanging by its beak, attached to my son's red baseball cap which was in my hand. As I was holding the cap, the grouse and the camera at the same time the photo is a little blurred.[5]

Grouse are remarkably hardy birds, their feathered tarsi (from which they get the scientific name *Lagopus*, 'hare-footed') being an adaptation to the freezing conditions of the northern uplands. They routinely breed at an altitude of 2000 feet (600m) and occasionally occur up to almost 3000 feet (900m). Throughout the year the diet is dominated by *Calluna vulgaris*, making grouse extremely reluctant to leave heather moorland. They will burrow under the snow to reach it and ringing schemes have found that almost 90 per cent move less than 1 mile (1.6km) from the place of capture.

Yet they occasionally make longer journeys. One famous story, which sounds rather more like a good after-dinner tale, involved a tame grouse from Cawdor, Aberdeenshire, at the turn of the century. Its party trick was to strut down the dining table, pecking at plates as it went and calling to the guests. Eventually a visitor persuaded its owner to part with the bird and it was taken back with him to Henley-on-Thames. Two weeks later the grouse was discovered to be missing. Thinking that it had been killed, the new owner wrote to Cawdor explaining his sad loss. A reply instantly came back announcing that the bird had beaten the original letter north by a day.[6]

Genuine evidence of grouse migration includes a flock that was observed crossing the 11 miles (18km) of the Pentland Firth from Hoy in Orkney to the mainland, while the great Scottish naturalist John Harvie-Brown saw grouse cutting across a 40-mile (67-km) stretch of the Moray Firth.[7] More unusual was a covey that landed on the deck of HM destroyer *Ophelia* in December 1917, about 30 miles (50km) off the Shetland coast.[8]

The red grouse enjoys a lingering renown as Britain's only endemic bird. In 1907 its unique status was honoured by the founders of the monthly journal *British Birds*, when they chose it as their logo. A full run of 97 volumes is still distinguished by a corresponding number of golden grouse running in line down the shelf. Unfortunately the peculiarity of *L.l. scoticus* has since been downgraded by its redesignation as a subspecies of the circumpolar willow ptarmigan. Yet this is immaterial to the affections in which it is still held. Although it has been a major quarry species for fewer than 200 years, during that period it has acquired a richer social and cultural history than almost any other British bird.

The current total of about a quarter of a million pairs represents a massive decline from its heyday, when the summer population could soar to five million. These numbers would collapse just as dramatically when the Glorious Twelfth launched the slaughter of as many as 1.5 million brace. There are still 1 million acres (405,000ha) of grouse moorland in England and Wales, and twice that amount in Scotland. With the exception of the common pheasant, no other single bird has so shaped the British landscape or continues to receive such preferential treatment. Yet both habitat and grouse shooting are in long-term decline. In order to understand

the bird's impact upon us, we should turn to its illustrious past.

The moorcock or moorfowl, as it was once known, was always a bird for the pot, but there was originally no cult of sportsmanship attaching to its capture. Snares and traps would have been the most effective way to take it, and there was little or no concern to develop the bird's habitat. Grouse flourished where low temperatures or a high water table or grazing pressure maintained the open treeless country that they need. They were particularly common in parts of Scotland. In 1773 Samuel Johnson noted that 'moorgame is everywhere to be had' in the Hebrides, and when he had earlier stayed at James Boswell's Edinburgh home, his loyal friend expressed patriotic attachment to the bird: 'We gave him [Johnson] as good a dinner as we could. Our Scotch muir-fowl, or growse, were then abundant, and quite in season.'[9]

The date for the first recorded shooting of grouse in flight is usually given as 1650, achieved by a Mr Wilson of Broomhead, Yorkshire. However, until the eighteenth century it was customary to shoot them 'over dogs', usually pointers and setters specifically trained to mark crouching birds. Otherwise it was a case of 'walking up' the grouse, a method that involved small groups tramping the moors with their cumbersome muzzle-loaders and then picking off a small bag as they exploded from the heather. Red grouse are remarkably tight-sitting birds, occasionally refusing to move at all: 'Walking once through deep heather on a Yorkshire moor, I trod on the back of a red grouse on a nest. She squawked and flew away, undamaged, as were the eggs, and I sat down to recover from the shock. I can still recall that squidgy feather feeling when I think about it.'[10]

The system we all now envision when talking of a 'grouse shoot' – the army of beaters and flag-waving flankers purposefully guiding the birds towards a line of manned shooting butts – acquired wide popularity only in the second quarter of the nineteenth century. In Brian Martin's detailed history of the bird, *The Glorious Grouse*, he points out that prior to 1825 there was no record of letting a grouse moor, in 1837 just eight Scottish grouse moors were for rent, but by the end of the Victorian era the figure had risen to several thousand.[11]

The development of the driven grouse shoot is closely tied to a number of nineteenth-century technological advances. One crucially important breakthrough was the French invention of a breech-loading shotgun in 1847. The new fowling piece was lighter to carry and quicker to load, paving the way for the competitive element that became such a key feature of the grouse moor. However, its greater convenience did not eliminate the need for practice. Henry Douglas-Home, brother of the former

Tory Prime Minister, recalled the traditional preparations made by his Victorian relative:

> One June morning in the early thirties ... I was summoned by my uncle Brackley – Lord Ellesmere – to have a drink at his palatial residence in St James's, Bridgewater House. I arrived about 11 o'clock to find him and the butler dodging about behind a pile of furniture practising the art of loading with two guns: a one hour exercise they performed every day throughout the summer to keep in trim for the shooting season ahead.[12]

Another major technological change, which made an August holiday in northern England or Scotland such a pleasant prospect, was the completion of the British railway network. By 1863 the line had reached Inverness, rendering some of the most remote Highland moors accessible in under 24 hours, while the uplands of northern England could be reached in considerably less. By the twentieth century trains were the key vehicle for the great grouse exodus, with the rail companies laying on a number of special departures to meet the rush north.

August Twelfth was an anomalous date for the opening of a game bird season, given that most start and end on the first of the month. In fact, 1 August was the original date for grouse, but in 1752 the British government finally accepted the Gregorian calendar system, which had been used widely on the Continent for almost 200 years (supporters of the euro take note). At the time of its adoption, the old British Julian calendar was running 11 days behind the true season, and when 2 September was followed by 14 September, there were street riots by people who thought they had been cheated of 11 days' pay. Once the new system was in place, 1 August fell on what had previously been 21 July and very close to the end, or even in, the grouse-breeding season. So a new date corresponding to the old 1 August was chosen and thus it became the Glorious Twelfth.

The interlocking elements that made grouse shooting so popular also made it an important boost for local employment and, in the case of Scotland, even a factor in the national economy. Writing in 1910, George Malcolm conservatively estimated that the rents alone from Scotland's 3157 grouse moors amounted to £789,250 (more than £46 million in modern values).[13] And this was only one strand of an economic web that touched almost everything, from core essentials such as the employment of domestic staff, beaters or gamekeepers, to the huge seasonal trade in fashionable extras: tweed and Burberry, guns and cartridges, shooting sticks and hip flasks, smoked salmon and single malt. One advertisement even suggested that 'marksmanship was improved by a regular intake of Eno's Fruit Salts'.[14]

Unlike other game species, there is no satisfactory method of hand-rearing grouse, although the growing popularity of the sport led to the deliberate introduction of grouse during the nineteenth century to areas outside the bird's natural range. Releases failed in Suffolk (1854), Norfolk (1864) and Surrey (1871), but met with greater success in Shetland and the Outer Hebrides, as well as on Dartmoor and Exmoor (1915/16). (Sadly, in the last 30 years the species has endured a marked range contraction with severest losses in Ireland, Wales and the west country.)

The rental values of Victorian grouse moors were closely linked to the size of the bag, with the result that owners and managers alike did everything possible to boost bird numbers. Some of the statistics of nineteenth-century shoots are remarkable by today's standards. In 1872 at Grandtully in the Tay valley the Maharajah Duleep Singh set a record of 220 brace in a single day, contriving the feat by riding from drive to drive, and using several guns with a number of personal loaders and scores of beaters.[15] During the same year on the Yorkshire moors of Wemmergill and High Force, the season's total reached 17,074 and 15,484 respectively.[16] The second figure was achieved in just 19 days of drives.

In its early years, driving grouse was condemned by some critics, notably Lewis Clement, the founder of *Shooting Times*, on the grounds that it was unsporting and that the person in the butt need have no genuine understanding of his quarry. In 1877 Clement complained: 'Truly the poetry of shooting is going, and going very fast ... Game is now shot with a solemnity that would be in its place at a funeral; it is now performed in the same business-like style, and with that want of fire and enthusiasm that must perforce accompany the necessary operation of fowls' throat-cutting, on the eve of market days.'[17]

Although driven grouse are reckoned to be the most challenging test of marksmanship, the competitive urge among some of the top shooters at times descended into an obsessive mathematics of slaughter. Lord Walsingham's record in 1888 of 1070 grouse in a day fully justified Clement's sharpest comments. He achieved the feat on his own Yorkshire estate at Blubberhouse Moors, motivated partly, it was suggested, by the Prince of Wales' rejection of his offer to shoot there. Walsingham had kept a detailed breakdown of his 12½-hour marathon, meticulously recording that in the 18 minutes between 07.10 and 07.28 he shot 79 birds. It meant that at his peak he was extinguishing the life of a grouse every 14 seconds. John de Grey, his half-brother, recalled that 'The stone passages of the farmhouse where we were staying were stacked with grouse three and

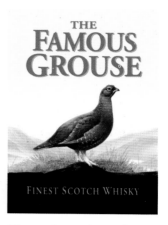

The perfect end to a day on the moors.

Archibald Thorburn's paintings of the totem bird found a lucrative market amongst the grouse-shooting fraternity.

four feet deep. For a fortnight the place was swarming with the lice left behind'.[18]

Another annual competition was the rush to get grouse on to the table of fashionable London restaurants. The ultimate was achieved in 1922 and duly reported in the *Shooting Times*: 'For the first time actually on the Twelfth itself, grouse was served at luncheon at the Savoy Hotel on Saturday last. Some of the earliest shot on a well-known moor near Ripon were carried away by motor car and transferred to an aeroplane, and thus reached London in the forenoon.'[19]

Except perhaps for the peregrine and other species of raptor used in medieval falconry, no bird has inspired such romantic attachment among Britain's landed classes. The week preceding the Glorious Twelfth was a moment of high excitement in the capital, 'when everyone who was anyone left London for the Grouse moors ... Marvellous pictures from the thirties show the great London Termini littered with Labradors and bristling with burberrys as the city took to the North.'[20]

Just as anticipation of the moor could strongly influence the metropolitan mood, so were the fortunes of Scottish landowners dependent on London's affairs. The exact summer timetable in the Houses of Parliament could make or ruin an entire year's work.[21] In the summer of 1915, aside from the dearth of able-bodied men to act as beaters and loaders, their lordships were finding the Great War a severe strain on their sports shooting. Just as the debacle at Gallipoli was reaching its climax, Lord Lovat guided a bill through the House of Lords giving dispensation for the grouse season to open on 5 August. It was widely condemned as a measure designed to guarantee

aristocratic recreation irrespective of severe wartime pressure. It was rejected in the House of Commons amid shouts of 'We want to shoot Germans, not grouse.'[22]

Those filled with an out-of-season nostalgia for the moor and its panoramas of flowering heather formed a large market for a range of barely related products, like grouse tiepins or cufflinks and jewellery items featuring portions of grouse anatomy: 'A popular Victorian bangle was made from the foot of a Grouse with its feathered claws, which was mounted in silver with a cairngorm. My mother often wore one of these in her church-going hat before the Second World War, fascinating her very young son.'[23] However, perhaps the best-known product of all, available still on most supermarket shelves and complete with its image of the totem bird, is 'Famous Grouse' whisky.

There was also a good market for a popular brand of game-bird painting. The leading exponents of these large oil canvases were the great bird artists Archibald Thorburn and George Lodge. Images of the nation's favourite sporting bird in beautiful upland landscapes, and routinely softened by a romantic Scots mist, were sold to hundreds of wealthy clients, including royalty.

Although the red grouse lay at the heart of a great body of outdoor ritual, historically grouse shooting had a mixed impact on the upland environment itself. A desire to maximise grouse bags led to the elimination of everything else considered to be a threat. Vermin control included much of the bird and mammal fauna for which the habitat is now celebrated. On the Highland property of Glen Garry, for example, between Whitsuntide 1837 and 1840 the estate keepers killed 11 foxes, 198 wild cats, 352

The old tradition of a couple of guns walking up grouse with dogs (left) was eventually replaced with the formal drive involving beaters, shooting butts and a much larger bag (right).

martens and polecats, 67 badgers, 48 otters, 98 peregrines, 78 merlin, 462 kestrels, 475 ravens, 285 buzzards, 3 honey buzzards, 15 golden eagles, 27 sea eagles, 18 ospreys, 63 goshawks, 275 red kites, 68 harriers and 109 owls.[24] The total number of birds of prey was 1501.

On the estates of the Duchess of Sutherland the figure for slaughtered raptors between 1831 and 1834 was 1055 birds.[25] This pattern was replicated across almost all Scottish sporting estates, leading to the extinction of several species, including red kite, osprey and sea eagle, and a severe reduction of everything else.

Even in the nineteenth century the artificial manipulation of much of the British and Irish upland ecosystem in the interests of one bird had its critics. The famous naturalist Lord Lilford wrote:

I have had my full share of days on the heather in pursuit of Grouse . . . but as a lover of birds in general, I would put in a word of protest against the destruction, I may say the extermination, of many of our most interesting native birds in favour of the Grouse; I allude specially to the Golden Eagle, the Peregrine Falcon, the Merlin, and the Buzzard . . . I do not like to believe that there are many who deserve the name of sportsmen who would deliberately connive at the death of either Falcon or Eagle for the sake of a few more Grouse or pounds stirling.[26]

The thorny issue of raptor persecution is still with us today (see Hen Harrier, page 126), although now the number illegally poisoned or trapped is far smaller, and enlightened attitudes are taking root among estate owners and keepers.

Modern grouse management focuses much more closely on the maintenance of optimum habitat, which involves burning one-tenth to one-fifteenth of the moorland on a rotational basis. The mosaic pattern of burnt areas and new growth is a classic feature of a well-managed grouse moor and provides the birds with a balance of young and old heather. Grouse bags are strongly determined by geology. Moorland on base-rich rock, which influences soil fertility and the nutrient quality of the heather itself, provides the highest densities of grouse, while moors overlying granite or a thick peat layer are less productive.

The bird is also prone to population cycles as a consequence of grouse disease, a condition caused by an infestation of threadworm. During the nineteenth century mysterious fluctuations in numbers were blamed on poachers and vermin predation. It is a measure of the grouse shoot's social importance that the puzzle was finally solved by the work of a parliamentary committee of inquiry. The team included Dr Edward Wilson, who had previously travelled with Robert Scott in the Antarctic and who would later die during Scott's ill-fated expedition to the South Pole. But in 1907 Wilson visited almost every major grouse moor in Scotland and personally dissected 2000 birds.

The inquiry discovered that the real culprit was not the hooded crow or hen harrier, but a tiny nematode called *Trichostrongylus tenuis*. These dirty-white threadworms are ingested as eggs from the young heather shoots and then build up in the grouse's caecum, sometimes as many as 10,000 in a single bird. The parasite is always present in grouse at low background levels, but greater grouse densities often serve to trigger a more serious outbreak of the condition. So record bags are often followed by a crash in grouse numbers, like a cycle of famine and plenty.

Rock Ptarmigan, *Lagopus mutus*. British ptarmigan are considered a distinct race, *millaisi*, a title honouring the wildlife artist John Millais, fourth son of the better known Pre-Raphaelite painter of the same name. Compared with other European forms, our birds are slightly smaller and purer grey in autumn. They are inhabitants of high mountain tops and, although in the eighteenth century they were found as far south as the Lake District, they are now confined to the Scottish Highlands, with main concentrations in the Grampians and around the Cairngorm massif.

The strange name with its silent 'p' is a pseudo-classical construction coined by the seventeenth-century physician and antiquary, Sir Robert Sibbald. The spelling still proves baffling today: 'I used to have great difficulty as a child trying to say Ptarmigan. I seem to remember thinking they were called Partamanigans for years.'[27] The word comes from the Gaelic name *tarmachan*, meaning 'croaker', a reference to the bird's dry rattling call, which is said to be 'not unlike the winding of a clock or ticking of a fishing reel'.[28]

They are unique among British birds for the male's four distinct seasonal plumages – with three in females – including an ermine-like transformation to pure white in winter. They favour the boulder-strewn, lichen-rich arctic-alpine heath up to an altitude of 4000 feet (1200m) and share this beautiful if barren landscape with just five or six other birds, including snow bunting and dotterel. Yet none of the others withstands the rigours of winter. Ptarmigan, however, are renowned for their hardiness. 'It has been suggested that when the sun's fire burns low and ice creeps further across the earth the ptarmigan will be the last bird left alive.'[29]

They seldom drop below 2000 feet (600m) and an especially dense plumage gives extra insulation, while highly modified thick feathering on the feet creates a fourfold increase in the load-bearing surface – the equivalent of miniature snowshoes. During winter they usually roost in snow hollows and even in May, when much of the ground is clear, birds concentrate around the remaining white patches. The ecologist Adam Watson has seen ptarmigan during severe storms fly to roost on ridges where a human could barely stand up. Each bird finds a hole on the leeward side of an exposed rock, past which the snow drifts but does not accumulate.[30] 'Many climbers, fighting their way apprehensively in gathering darkness in a blizzard, have envied the ptarmigan preparing to spend a comfortable night on the exposed summits.'[31]

While the bird's wings stay white in summer, the body turns lichen-grey. The subtly beautiful patterning harmonises perfectly with the open boulder fields, where

Ptarmigan in winter plumage.

moving ptarmigan are said to resemble 'running stones'.[32] The slightly duller hen on a nest is almost impossible to find and shows remarkable courage if approached. The Scottish naturalist Seton Gordon, who rated a covey of ptarmigan turned golden by the evening sunlight as the most beautiful vision he had ever witnessed in the Highlands, recounted a wonderful example of the female's spirit: 'we lately heard a story of a stalker who discovered, after lunching on the hill-side, that he had been sitting on a stone immediately above the spot where a ptarmigan had been covering her eggs, and that he had actually been dropping crumbs on to the back of the brooding bird!'[33]

Outside the breeding season, ptarmigan rely heavily on their subtle crypsis and when disturbed by walkers they prefer to run rather than take wing, moving 'with rounded back and depressed tail and often with a sort of nautical roll'. Yet they are extremely strong fliers. John Millais witnessed them 'shooting up or down a precipice of several hundred feet without apparent effort'.[34] The chicks' powers of flight are also remarkable, and Seton Gordon saw 'a covey of these mountain grouse no larger than larks fly cheerfully over a precipice some 1,000 feet deep'.[35]

Sportsmen once knew ptarmigan as 'white grouse' or 'white game' and in happier times they were occasionally driven, with a record bag of 122 set as long ago as 1866. Nowadays their low numbers and the athleticism required to reach ptarmigan country mean that they are shot in only a handful of locations. Golden eagles are their more frequent enemy and ptarmigan 'will take flight at greater distance from an eagle than from a man, even where they are often shot'. Adam Watson has seen an eagle put up scores of birds from hillsides where earlier there had seemed to be none at all. He has also recorded two occasions when ptarmigan flew towards humans while being chased by goldies: 'the Ptarmigan partly closed its wings, dropped in a near-vertical twisting dive to within a few metres of the ground, and then ran to crouch among boulders only ten metres from me and my companions. On the first occasion the eagle flew away after the Ptarmigan dropped. On the second it followed the falling Ptarmigan ... pulling up only 20 metres above our heads.'[36]

The more recent decline in parts of their range is thought to be a consequence of overgrazing by sheep and of habitat destruction. On areas popular with skiers, like Cairngorm, birds also collide with ski-lift wires, while the greater volume of litter and tourist debris have drawn in hooded crows, which predate the eggs. Yet at this heavily visited spot ptarmigan become highly accustomed to human presence, sometimes nesting close to the chair-lift pylons and disputing territorial boundaries just outside the aptly named Ptarmigan Restaurant near the summit.[37]

Black Grouse, *Tetrao tetrix*. VN: Black Cock, Black Game (mainly game shooters). This beautiful grouse is remarkable both for the seemingly irreversible downward trend in its population and for the complex breeding display performed by 'lekking' males.

A spring visit at dawn to one of the species' traditional parade grounds, known as a lek, still provides what is unquestionably one of the most stirring visions of the northern uplands. As many as a dozen males gather and adopt a highly ritualised posture, in which the head, crowned by a pair of flaring crimson 'eyebrows', is thrust forwards and downwards. Air sacs in the chest are inflated and the neck feathers are raised to intensify their silky blue-black lustre. The whole performance is accompanied by a low soothing dove-like note known as 'rookooing'; but, for all its softness, it is a remarkably penetrating sound and can carry for more than ¼ mile (400m). As birds strut towards their rivals, the flight feathers droop, revealing a sequence of white 'studs' on the leading edge, while the undertail coverts are raised above the bird's back to create a white bustle framed within a lyre-shaped spread of jet tail feathers.

Each male has his own territory and the closer he stands to the centre of the lek, the higher his status and the greater his likelihood of mating with the females, which unobtrusively visit the lek at intervals. At the height of the breeding season copulation is a frequent element in all this testosterone-charged theatre. 'David Lack once watched a Blackcock mounting a stuffed hen Black Grouse 56 times in 45 minutes.'[38]

Lekking black grouse create one of the most impressive spectacles in the northern uplands.

Some of the oldest leks are known to have been in continuous use for 50–60 years and in places have become embedded in local geography:

The Forest of Bowland in Lancashire is littered with places that were obviously named after animals. Wolf Fell, Catshaw Greave, Raven Scars, Hawks Heath and Grizedale Fell (Grize = wild boar) are just a few examples. However there are several places that I believe were named after black grouse. These are Moor Cock, Cockley Bank, Cocklet Hill, Cocket Moss and the amusingly named Cocklick End [see also Woodcock, page 216]. All are in the eastern part of Bowland, which is the area where black grouse persisted until recently, and the only part of Bowland where they have ever been recorded. 'Let' and 'lick' sound like a corruption of lek, although the word itself is apparently a recent addition to the English language, possibly from the Scandinavian *leka*, 'to play'.[39]

Lekking black grouse are now to be found only in parts of the Welsh uplands, the northern English hill country centred on the Pennines and the more sparsely inhabited parts of Scotland. This charismatic bird has therefore gone entirely from England south of the Humber and the disappearance comes with a double twist. While the decline of the bittern or corncrake is an event that has touched the national consciousness, black grouse are vanishing without any corresponding sense of public alarm. Worse still is the fact they have been dwindling since the nineteenth century and ornithologists have charted their passing with great accuracy, but for a long period they knew insufficient about black grouse ecology to halt the process.

Blackcock (strictly this name refers to the male, separating it from the smaller, dowdier 'greyhen') were once widespread and common from the Highlands to the Home Counties and, as Chris Mead put it graphically, 'Birdwatchers in London could find leks within a few dozens of miles of home a century ago!'[40] They were a routine bird of the southern heaths from Kent to Berkshire and across the south-west between Dorset and Cornwall. However, the exact extent of the species' natural range and the pattern of its decline were obscured by frequent releases of captive stock by gamekeepers and their masters.

Blackcock were valued as sporting birds and relished as a roast. Mrs Beeton recommended that after hanging them for a few days to tenderise, 'Put them down to a brisk fire, well baste them with butter, and serve with a piece of toast under, and a good gravy and bread sauce.'[41] Yet even the great mistress of the Victorian kitchen knew more than simply how to cook them: 'culture and extending population,' she noted, 'hav[e] united in driving it into more desolate regions.'[42] By 1905 black grouse were almost extinct south of a line between the Wash and Severn estuaries, except for isolated colonies around Dartmoor and Exmoor. While these held out until the 1970s, reinforced by fresh releases, it was exclusively a northern bird thereafter and the shrinkage in range continues even now.

Black grouse are essentially birds of the temporary habitats that exist where upland woods and moorland meet. Unfortunately they have been trapped by the improvements made to both these classic northern landscapes. The drainage of marginal farmland, the overgrazing of heather moorland and blanket afforestation with exotic conifers are all implicated in the loss of blackcock country. Over the twentieth century, the total population loss has been estimated from a fall in game bags at 95 per cent.[43]

If blackcock are long gone from the London hinterland, they are at least still present just a few dozen miles from the Scottish capital. The Borders hill country south of Edinburgh holds good numbers, as do large parts of the Highlands. It is still legal to shoot the species, although the daily game bags involving scores of birds and the nineteenth-century records of flocks numbering 200–300 will almost certainly never be seen again.

Yet the blackcock's former distribution has left a rich and rather intriguing legacy in terms of upland watering

One for the pub quiz – black grouse are regularly depicted on the signs of pubs called the Moorcock, despite there being very little evidence that the bird was ever known by this name.

holes: 'There is a pub three miles SW of Monmouth in South Wales on the road to Trelleck called The Gockett (an old name for Black Grouse?). It has a fine portrait of Black Grouse on its sign. The bird was presumably found in the area at one time (there are remnants of heathland habitat amongst the farmland and conifer plantations), but probably eighteenth century at the latest.'[44]

Tim Melling, RSPB conservation officer for the north-west region, believes that a good number of pubs in northern England signify former black-grouse areas:

I have long had an interest in pubs named after birds, particularly those called 'The Moorcock'. There are thirteen that I know in northern counties and many, if not all these, have signs illustrating black grouse. Yet the word is usually only recognised in the literature as an old country name for the red grouse. It would be interesting to know if there was an unacknowledged folk tradition of using 'Moorcock' as a name for both grouse species and whether the pub's choice of title reflected the former presence of black grouse themselves. Certainly we know that several of them are within the black grouse heartland. For example, one at Eggleston in County Durham still has black grouse in the surrounding fields. Another on the edge of the Peak District near Macclesfield is in an area that held black grouse within living memory.

There are also at least four former 'Moorcocks' at Saddleworth, Gt Manchester, Coverham, N. Yorks, Drighlington, W. Yorks and Denshaw, Gt Manchester. At the last of these, a pub which is now sadly closed, they had obviously commissioned an artist to paint a moorcock. He clearly looked it up in a book and found it wasn't there, but presumed that it must be the same as a moorhen *Gallinula chloropus* and so the sign depicted that species![45]

Jim and Joy Farms have helped tease out a few more of the facts: 'The term moorhen is more appropriately reserved for the female of the black grouse which is, in turn, known as the moorcock. There are several inns called "The Moorcock" and "The Bonnie Moorhen" is the name of the marching song of the oppressed lead miners who took industrial action in the nineteenth century. This is the reason, I believe, for its adoption as the title of the magazine of the Durham Bird Study Group.'[46]

Western Capercaillie, *Tetrao urogallus*. VN: Caper. This magnificent turkey-like bird is even more restricted in range than the black grouse, and almost entirely confined to mature Scots pine woods of the east-central Highlands, especially remnants of the old Caledonian forest. It is the biggest grouse in the world, and British males weigh anything from 7½ to nearly 10 pounds (3.4–4.4kg) and are as much as three times the size of the hen.

The name is a mystery. It has been known by a wide variety of spellings. 'Capercalze', 'caperkalze', 'caper-cailzie', 'capercally', 'caperkally', 'caperkellie', 'capercaleg' and 'capercaili' are all Anglicised versions of the old Gaelic name, *capull coille*, literally 'horse of the woods'. This is thought by some to draw on the equine quality of the male's frenzied and bizarre advertising call; if so, it invokes a strange kind of horse. The more reasonable suggestion is that the opening notes resemble the sound of hooves on cobbles. However, the most likely association is with the bird's huge size: 'The horse element . . . is probably used in a figurative sense meaning "big" (*cf.* horse-radish and horse-lark, the latter a local name for the Corn Bunting, *Emberiza calandra*). Curiously enough a similar figurative use appears in the scientific name *urogallus* (*urus* = bull, *gallus* = cock), a parallel in English being found in the name "Bullfinch".[47]

Possibly an insight into the *capull* part of the original name is offered by a similar English word 'cob', which describes both a stout kind of horse and, according to the *Oxford English Dictionary*, a great, big or leading man (and also, of course, a male swan). *Capull* may have carried parallel associations with a dominant male of any kind, and *capull coille* may have meant something like 'great cock of the woods'.

This would certainly capture an important aspect of male capercaillie behaviour – its imposing breeding display. During April and May males occupy a temporary parade ground, although capers seldom show the same loyalty as

'Goat of the woods' or 'Horse of the woods'? The exact origins of the Gaelic name capercaillie have long been debated.

black grouse to a traditional communal lek. Often it is just a solitary male in a woodland clearing. Yet the posturing is no less formal and the display itself is, if anything, even more impressive. Birds strut with neck and head stretched skywards, the wings drooping and the tail cocked and spread turkey-style, when a delicate band of white patterning across the black feathers can look like fretwork on a Spanish lady's open fan. In this awkward posture and 'with the aid of a part of his oesophagus that inflates like a toy balloon', the bird launches into a remarkable vocal performance, 'commencing with a resonant rattling sound (the clip-clop of hooves), which is followed without a break by the noise of a cork being drawn from a bottle, it concludes with the impression of water being squirted from a siphon, followed by the sound of a muffled knife-grinding'.[48] The last element has also been likened to a scythe against a whetstone, dwindling to a muffled whisper or a vigorous sucking in of breath.[49]

The intensity of the bird's exhibition could at one time be the cause of its own undoing: 'When the climax of the song is reached the bird closes its eyes and is completely absorbed in its performance, and the classical method of hunting the bird is to play the old game of "Grand-mother's Footsteps", during these brief periods of blindness and deafness.'[50]

Occasionally, however, the hunted becomes the hunter. Displaying male capers, which must be one of Britain's most aggressive wild animals, will threaten and attack human observers and some of these rogue

A cock capercaillie in rampant mode seems to think no intruder too large for him to confront.

individuals have given rise to a great body of stories and have acquired near-legendary status:

> I was told of one bird that held a territory at Tilyfourie in 1982. It remained in the area until the early summer, attacking any large moving object that strayed into its path, including vehicles. Reputedly it met its end when it attacked a verge trimmer! Another individual held territory in Glen Tanar for several years and again attacked just about any moving being (animate or not) that entered its patch. I also heard of another that laid siege to an occupied house in a Deeside glen and actually had to be forcibly evicted to a remoter part of the forest. In Finland I was once shown a bird that we were told had flown directly at a forestry worker, knocked him flat and fractured his collar bone in the process. To the credit of the company and the injured party they let the bird survive. We had to run away from this bird when we finally located it.[51]

A bird in Rothiemurchus forest attacked children going to school and ladies wearing silk stockings. For four years another individual living in a small wood near Brechin attacked vehicles, people, horses and sheep, but never dogs. The keeper could summon the bird with his Land-Rover's horn and its peck could be felt through wellington boots.[52]

However, one of the most notorious recent British examples was a male that held sway over a section of the RSPB's Abernethy reserve in Speyside during the 1990s and was known with great affection – laced with considerable respect – as Mad George or Mad Max:

> My wife and I had an encounter with a caper at Forest Lodge a few years ago nicknamed Mad George. Although I was keen to see it, my wife wasn't, so I told her a little white lie and said it was down a different path, but just in case, I walked in front. I saw no sign of the bird as we wandered up until I heard a scream behind me. George had waited for us to go past, then dropped down from a tree on to the path behind us as if to cut off our retreat. Despite everything you read about how big they are, nothing quite prepares you for a bird in full aggressive display hissing and popping just behind you and it's fair to say it put the willies up both of us. (I have a feeling that the bird was radio-tagged and the appearance of an aerial sticking out of it only added to the 'Robo-bird' feel.)
>
> Mad George had been a constant topic of conversation among the Speyside birders and various

stories were doing the rounds. The bird had apparently launched itself at several mountain bikers and knocked them over. People were going up to and grabbing the bird and swinging it round their head while the wife took photos. Everyone's favourite story, though, was that Mad George had taken out an Aussie tour leader twice. Apparently the tour leader had decided to show his group a really close encounter and went right up to the bird. MG flew at him and knocked him over. Not wanting to lose his macho Aussie image, he claimed to his group that he had slipped. He then stood up, went in and the bird took him out again. All this was happening at a time of some high-profile 'silly' lawsuits in the States and there was much speculation as to what would happen if it attacked some litigious Americans.[53]

The day before another notable encounter in 1997, the caper had 'landed on the bonnet of a Land-Rover, stubbornly refused to get off and chipped the paintwork in the process. So we knew that it was "around"':

As we reached the site we began to look anxiously on either side of the track, peering through the tall pines and snow flurries. After nearly quarter of an hour we had not seen anything and were beginning to think that it had used up too much energy on yesterday's Land-Rover attack.

But then we heard a guttural croaking and sneezing, a whirring of wings and a large turkey-sized bird was flying low through the forest towards us. The bird landed on the centre of the track about 50 metres away. With its throat feathers erect like those of an angry raven, wings drooped and tail spread like a huge fan, it began strutting back and forth on the road. Throwing its head back it made a series of bizarre popping and clicking calls which became louder and faster, rising to a mad crescendo.

We slowly knelt by the side of the track, quickly set up our cameras and began taking photographs. However, the bird was soon 'enlarging' within my viewfinder, and as I looked over the top of my lens I could see that it was purposefully moving towards us, head stretched menacingly forward. When it was less than 10 metres from us we decided that a dignified retreat was in order. As we turned and crept backwards away from it, this seemed to be the cue for Max to charge – it dropped its wings again, raised its tail feathers almost vertically, and ran straight at us, snapping at our legs and tripods. We retreated to a safe distance and watched as Max then triumphantly strutted back and forth on the track, almost goading us to come back for more![54]

Part of the cock caper's testosterone-charged display involves a dramatic flutter-jump into mid-air.

Male capers inevitably fight with each other and regularly bear scars or cuts from these encounters; they occasionally die of the wounds. Small wonder, perhaps, that some Gaelic scholars think the real source for its name was *gabhar coille*, 'goat of the wood', a reference to the male's ragged 'beard' and his sexual aggression.[55]

Unfortunately, capercaillies have not translated their physical potency into sustained breeding success. They are one of the few birds at risk of a second extinction in Britain and the present population is now thought to be 1000 birds at most. Fox predation, the birds' fatal collision with deer fences and degradation of the woodland understorey, through over-grazing by deer and sheep, are all cited as contributory factors. Another key background reason may be climatic change: spring rains, particularly in June, are a major cause of chick mortality.

The free-fall in population from a 1970s total of around 20,000 birds has led to a sharp change in attitudes towards capercaillie. It has been removed from the list of legitimate game birds and its former status as a serious pest of new conifer plantations is now overlooked or forgotten. Although they still nip out the leader buds on young trees, gone are the days when foresters used to drive 'along the forest roads to shoot them with .22 rifles at point-blank range out of their car windows'.[56]

Even more remote seems the age when capercaillies

were considered a bird for the table. Yet the extinction of the original Scottish and Irish capercaillie population in the eighteenth century was produced by a combination of over-hunting and clearance of the old Caledonian forest. The species had probably gone from most of England and Wales before the seventeenth century, while the Irish population was exterminated around 1760. The date given for the last of the original Scottish birds is 1785: two shot near Balmoral Castle in Grampian 'on the occasion of a marriage'.[57] Of this indigenous population only a single specimen now exists, held in the Hancock Museum in Newcastle-upon-Tyne.

The capercaillie's return to Britain is almost entirely due to the nineteenth-century triumvirate of the Welsh naturalist Llewelyn Lloyd, his cousin Sir Thomas Fowell Buxton of Northrepps Hall in Norfolk, and Lord Breadalbane of Taymouth Castle in Perthshire. In the 1820s Lloyd had sent a pair of capers to his cousin in Norfolk, but the birds failed to prosper. However, the idea of reintroducing capercaillie had taken root and in 1837, in gratitude for a prolonged visit at Breadalbane's Scottish home, Buxton organised the transportation of 49 birds to Taymouth Castle, followed by 16 more the following year.

These birds instantly settled down at their new home and numbers were further boosted by putting caper eggs under brooding greyhens. Within 25 years Breadalbane estimated 1000 birds on his estate, while the head keeper thought there were twice as many. Various other successful releases followed and capers spread both north-east and south-west, reaching their greatest extent in the early twentieth century, when they occurred from the Dornoch Firth south to the Clyde and Forth estuaries. A good indication of their former numbers is the record bag of 150 birds in a single day near Kincardine in 1908.[58]

There were also numerous nineteenth-century attempts to reintroduce capercaillies at English sites, some of which look like mere pipe-dreams, such as the releases in Buckinghamshire and at Lord Derby's Knowsley Hall, then in Lancashire. Even in the late twentieth century there were attempted reintroductions at the Forestry Commission's Cannock Chase, Staffordshire, and at Grizedale Forest, between Coniston Water and Windermere in Cumbria. Sadly both these projects also failed.

This wonderful bird is now very much a flagship species of Scottish conservation. Recent grants of £750,000 from the Scottish Executive and of £4.5 million from the EU Life Fund, which are aimed mainly at the control of predators, the marking or removal of deer fences and the enhancement of its forest habitat, offer the best hope for securing its long-term future.

Partridge, Quail and Pheasant family *Phasianidae*

Red-legged Partridge, *Alectoris rufa*. VN: Redleg, Frenchman, French Partridge. There is a faint echo of Agincourt in some of our attitudes towards this introduced game bird, especially in the past. Sportsmen used to criticise the 'Frenchman' as a 'foreign plague', not only for its preference for running over flying (thus presenting a poor target), but also for the bland flesh and its displacement of that fine flavoursome sporting beast, the 'English' partridge.[1]

In 1879 a Somersetshire naturalist C. Fry Edwards complained of the redlegs released in the east of the county: 'The birds spread and drove the grey birds [partridges] till they became so strong that to preserve any of the old species it was resolved to exterminate the foreigners. This was done and the grey birds [partridges] were restored.'[2] Redlegs were also accused of corrupting the native partridge, by encouraging them to run away, rather than lying for the dogs as they had done in the past.[3]

All of this was completely untrue, but some of the old myths persist, particularly because grey partridges have catastrophically declined almost nationwide while the redleg has flourished. Yet the success of one has not been based on the ousting of the other, as in the case of grey and red squirrels. In fact in territorial disputes, despite a small size advantage, the redleg is usually sub-dominant to the grey. The main factor behind the loss of the native species is agricultural change, particularly the widespread use of agrochemicals, which deplete the insects of arable land on which young partridges feed. For some reason the redleg is less affected by the problem, and its numbers are further boosted by the female's ability to lay a second clutch of eggs, which is incubated and reared by the male.

Its presence in Britain dates back to the reign of Charles II, who was anxious to introduce the bird to the royal parks at Windsor and Richmond, partly because of the over-hunting of native partridge. Despite these efforts, redlegs achieved no lasting presence in mainland Britain until a century later. In 1770 the Earl of Hertford imported large numbers of eggs from France – thus the enduring Gallic association – and put them under brooding hens on his estate near Orford, Suffolk.

After this success many other landowners followed suit and the bird has gradually colonised most of England, with a heartland in the arable districts of the drier south and east. Its distribution is closely associated with areas enjoying annual rainfall of less than 35 inches

The 'French' partridge is often assumed to be the bird perched in the pear tree in the famous Christmas song, but the matter is by no means beyond debate.

(84cm). However, large-scale releases of hand-reared birds (up to two million) are annually superimposed upon its 'natural' range in Britain, so that redlegs can be found almost anywhere from Land's End to John O'Groats. The moorland edges of many upland estates are now heavily stocked with redlegs and the species may eventually displace the red grouse as the principal quarry species.

Adults are fine-looking birds with black, white and chestnut crescentic bars on the flanks and a delicately black-speckled breast beneath a white throat. They are easiest to see in winter or early spring when cereal crops are still short, but they also have a fondness for perching on hillocks or posts to deliver a 'monotonous piston-like' song, which was frequently likened to a 'labouring steam engine'.[4] In 1953 Derek Goodwin noted 'at some little distance it is often hard to believe that it is a bird and not a locomotive making the noise', although the loss of steam trains has rendered the comparison a little less meaningful.[5] Sometimes the redleg's song-post can be the roof of a building, including the top of a supermarket and a church in the middle of a small town.

They will also perch in trees, and many people have assumed that the partridge given on the first day in the famous Yuletide song 'The Twelve Days of Christmas' is a redleg. The song's presumed French origin also seemed to strengthen the notion that the bird in question would be the 'French' partridge. But this is a false argument, because both partridge species occur in France and in that country greys still outnumber their relative by almost two to one. (In fact the real stronghold for the redleg is not France but Spain, with more than three-quarters of the world's 3.5 million pairs.) In one French form of the song the partridge is simply described as flying ('*Qui vole et vole et vole*'), a characteristic that

nineteenth-century sportsmen most closely associated with grey partridge.[6]

Yet if we must interpret the pear-tree-perching behaviour as a strictly accurate piece of natural-historical data – despite the fact that the meaning of the song has never been satisfactorily explained and despite the obvious element of fantasy running through the verses; and disregarding a 1951 Hertfordshire record of three grey partridges perched 30 feet (10m) up in an oak, and a 1976 account of 10–11 in a Warwickshire holly – then it may be safest when you sing the carol next, to think of the bird in question as *Alectoris rufa*.[7]

Grey Partridge, *Perdix perdix*. VN: Common Partridge, English Partridge, Englishman. In the last 60 years the species has been known by three 'official' names. Until the Second World War it was the common partridge; thereafter it was reduced simply to the partridge; by the time of the *New Atlas of Breeding Birds* (1993) it had become the grey partridge. In many ways the changes reflect the species' evolving fortunes, because during the twentieth century the population has become a ghost of its former self, with a decline of around 80 per cent in Britain and almost complete extinction in Ireland.

Much of the reduction has occurred since the war, although in some areas a fall had been noted as early as the nineteenth century. At one time it was widespread across the entire archipelago, except for the wettest north-western districts of Ireland, Scotland and Wales. The ornithologist Max Nicholson estimated that a 2000 acre (809-ha) farm could hold about a ton(ne) of birds, and until the 1950s he knew of coveys less than 6 miles (10km) from Hyde Park Corner.[8] Given that it was the most abundant bird on many East Anglian farms and among Britain's 10 commonest species overall, with at least one million pairs, it represents as serious a loss as the disappearance of the corn crake.

Ironically, as the numbers have dwindled to just 75,000 pairs, our native partridge has never been better understood. Thirty-five years of research have made it one of the most exhaustively studied birds in the world. The investigations have identified agrochemicals as a principal factor behind the decline. Herbicides have killed off the arable weeds which, in turn, supported the insect life (particularly sawfly larvae) on which young partridges rely in the first weeks of life.

Fortunately measures have been devised to reverse the decline. 'No other farmland bird arouses such passion amongst farmers. In some places, such as Norfolk and the Cotswolds, they have set up their own "partridge groups" to help conserve the bird.' The key remedial steps include providing good nesting habitat.

This can be created by placing tussocky grass margins around fields and beetle banks (grass strips across larger cultivated fields). When the chicks hatch, they need a plentiful supply of insects to eat and this can be provided by creating conservation headlands – weedy cereal field margins – which attract large numbers of these chick-food insects. All of these options are now funded under the Government Countryside Steward-ship Scheme to help farmers with the cost of implementing these features; however, the money available is not enough and the paperwork and red tape involved are a turn-off for many landowners.[9]

While the red-legged partridge is seldom seen in anything other than pairs, grey partridges are much more sociable birds. In late summer and autumn the adults and young form small groups of up to 20, which are known as coveys. But the more intriguing collective, formed in fading light and seen by very few people, is the grey partridge's 'jug' or 'juk' or, historically, 'jouk'. Of French origin and serving equally as verb and noun, the word refers to the bird's habit of roosting in a collective huddle with heads facing out. The positions adopted by jugging partridge are often revealed by the configuration of their droppings, although gamekeepers occasionally come across the real thing:

I have seen partridge jugging (jukking), but only after dark with the aid of a spotlight. The birds gather towards dusk, calling a lot, then at last light fly towards the centre of the field well away from thick cover. They prefer a ploughed field or open broken ground where they can settle for the night, usually in a slight depression so they are not exposed to the wind, which they dislike. The classic image of a jug is with each bird of the covey facing outwards like the

The grey partridge is a bird of subtle, understated and rather 'English' beauty.

spokes of a wheel, but I've only ever seen this formation on 1–2 occasions, i.e. on a very calm night. Normally what you get is the birds collected in a reasonably tight group each facing the wind.[10]

Partridge families with young under five weeks never jug in this manner but roost in thick cover for protection. As an added defence both parents will feign injury, fluttering ahead of any potential predator in a classic broken-wing display that distracts attention from the chicks. Occasionally they adopt a more aggressive technique:

I had just been looking for marbled white butterflies on a tiny patch of hilltop downland near the south Kent coast and was walking back to the road across a stubble field. Suddenly a covey of some 7–8 grey partridges exploded from amongst a pile of straw. One of them – I had the sense that it was the largest and possibly the father of the rest (distinct chocolate belly patch) – flew deliberately and directly at me from about three metres and struck me a heavy thump right in the chest. He bounced off on to the ground in a flurry of feathers, pulled himself together and flew away, leaving me amazed and slightly winded![11]

Archibald Thorburn's painting of jugging grey partridge is presumably a work of imagination, because the real thing is extremely difficult to observe. The birds usually adopt their roosting formation after darkness has fallen.

The usual clue to the presence of grey partridge is their wonderful rasping dissyllabic call, which until recently was a part of the soundtrack to almost any agricultural landscape. The emphasis is on the first syllable, with a slurred creaking middle section: '*skiErRRRRRek*'. It is most frequently delivered at dawn and dusk and is sometimes likened to a swinging gate with rusty hinges or to a key turning in a rusty lock.

Grey partridges are sometimes described as dull and predominantly brown, but their plumage has a delicate complexity, with both sexes showing chestnut flank bars cross-hatched with pale streaks and fine grey vermiculations on breast and throat. Males also sport an ochrous wash on the face and an inverted horseshoe of dark brown on the belly. Some people divine in the very different types of beauty exhibited by our two partridges an expression of their stereotyped 'national' identities: 'I am a gamekeeper concerned with grey partridge and it's interesting to see how people, whenever they get an opportunity to see the bird closely, comment on its subtle, understated and very "English" beauty. This is especially evident when in contrast with the gaudy colours and bold patterning of the "French" partridge.'[12]

Grey partridge rely heavily on their camouflage to avoid detection and explode from cover only at the very last minute, when the loud whirr of wings compounds the rather alarming effect. Despite their inability for sustained flight, partridges rise rapidly and speed off with a deft twisting action and were highly regarded as sporting birds. They are also extremely sedentary and may pass their entire lives in just two or three fields. Today there are perhaps no more than 50 estates in Britain that are managed for their grey-partridge shoot, although at one time thousands of English farms held sufficient birds.

Hampshire, Norfolk and Suffolk were long considered the optimum areas for both the bird and its associated sport. At the Grange in Hampshire, Brian Vesey-Fitzgerald listed a number of extraordinary bags, with 4109 birds shot in four consecutive days of 1887 and 3533 taken on three days in 1897. These records fall squarely within the period recognised as the grey partridge's heyday – and shared with Britain's four native grouse species – which ran from 1880 until the outbreak of the First World War.

During the Victorian and Edwardian eras, for some of the landed classes the grey-partridge shoot formed part of a well-established round of sporting activity. In high summer there was the anticipation and practice for the coming season. In August there was the familiar journey north for the grouse moor and the Glorious Twelfth. September opened with St Partridge's Day, and a return to the lowlands to walk up a few birds before the big driven partridge shoots at the end of the month. With November and the turn of season came the first gatherings in the English pheasant woods. For a quarter of the year these three game birds literally shaped the social and, in many cases, the professional lives of tens of thousands of people.

The slump in population has led some to call for grey partridge to be taken off the quarry list to conserve the remaining birds. However Peter Thompson, Field Officer for the Game Conservancy Trust, points out the hidden dangers:

> The large sporting estates such as Holkham and West Barsham in Norfolk and Castle Raby in Durham have the highest populations in Britain. These estates specifically manage the land for grey partridge and employ keepers to look after them, only shooting them in years when there is a 'surplus', thereby managing a sustainable population. Remove grey partridge from the quarry list, however, and at a stroke all this positive effort would be eliminated.[13]

Many people still regard the grey partridge with particular affection, not only for the excellent sport, but for its fine qualities as a roast. Young English partridge is often considered the best eating among Britain's game birds, although an old proverb suggested that there was one more piquant still: 'If the partridge had the woodcock's thigh/'Twould be the best bird that ever did fly.' This couplet had its inevitable corollary: 'If the woodcock had but the partridge's breast/'Twould be the best bird that ever was dress'd.'

Common Quail, *Coturnix coturnix*. VN: Fey Fool (Unst). An important key to understanding the character of Europe's only migratory game bird is its sheer unpredictability. Max Nicholson once wrote that 'to go in quest of quail is one of the most baffling of ornithological enterprises'.[14] Barely greater than a skylark in length, the species is heard far more than it is seen. The classic view is often obtained in a state of mild shock, when something like a long-winged game-bird chick explodes from beneath your feet, then speeds off with buzzing flight, banking and twisting as it goes, and in a matter of seconds

Close views of quail are extremely rare and usually achieved by accident.

plumps back down to earth, when it vanishes completely almost irrespective of the vegetation length.

The best indication of the presence of quail is the distinctive whippy three-note song of the male, which is conventionally rendered as 'Wet-my-lips'. An older version was 'Quick-me-Dick', while in his poem 'Summer Moods' John Clare records an alternative that alluded to the quail's status as a prophet of rain: 'While in the juicy corn the hidden quail/Cries "wet my foot" and hid as thoughts unborn.'

All of them convey the song's unstressed middle syllable, but none can indicate the extraordinary and often maddening ventriloquial qualities of its delivery. 'This ability was very evident to me . . . when, as I was cycling slowly along the side of an oat-field, a Quail began to call apparently about twenty yards in from the road. I continued along the road at about eight miles an hour and the call appeared to keep level with me right to the end of the field.'[15]

In previous centuries it was standard practice to exploit the call in order to catch them. Quail-pipes or quail-calls, variously constructed to produce sounds similar either to the male or female notes, were used in Britain and can still be found in parts of mainland Europe:

> I live in Italy where migrant quail are common in most years and the local bird-catchers use a 'quagliarul' – a small pipe with a bag on the end of it (a sort of hand bagpipe) – and a landing-net. You strike the bag with the side of the right forefinger, holding the pipe upright between the thumb and forefinger of the left hand, the bag blocked against the palm of the left hand. The call you should aim for is a double 'wit-wit' or 'quick-

quick' in rapid succession that is said to imitate a soliciting female. The male (apparently) goes barmy, running around your feet looking for the female and is easily bagged. Traditionally the pipe is made from a cat's thigh-bone, although any bone will do – as long as it's c. 8mm in diameter.[16]

Reg Moreau described the soft sound of a Belgian female pipe as in top A-flat, while an Italian male quail-call produced a more percussive note in top D-flat. A seventeenth-century British account confirms the quail's responsiveness to these pipe notes: they 'will most busily come about you and never leave till they finde the place whence the sound cometh, to which when they do approach they will stand and gaze and listen till the nette be quite cast over them'.[17]

Modern birdwatchers also appreciate the value of mimicry, no matter how modest the likeness:

Some years ago a friend was desperate to see Quail, so three of us went out to a site near Canterbury where I'd heard them a few days previously. We heard the bird easily enough, but we looked long and hard without seeing a thing. Frustrated by our lack of success I walked out along a footpath and tried my pathetic Quail imitation – a deeply unconvincing 'wet-my-lips' whistle. So effective was my attempt that the bird which had been calling somewhere on the nether part of the field promptly stopped. No wonder the other two chuckled at my imitation. I've rarely felt quite so foolish.

However, as I turned to walk back up the path the quail rocketed up from the ground a few inches from my feet! As it flew it disturbed a skylark and the two birds flew down to opposite corners of the field. Inevitably, the person who had never seen quail followed the skylark and the chap who'd seen quail before locked on to the right bird![18]

Quail show a strong bias towards calcareous grassland or cereal areas of southern England, although they have a talent for suddenly appearing almost anywhere across the whole of Britain and Ireland. This is particularly the case in what are known as 'quail years', when numbers dramatically increase. Exceptional influxes have occurred in 1870, 1893, 1947, 1952/3, 1964, 1970, 1983 and 1989, the last being the highest on record with approximately 2690 calling males, compared with the more usual 200–300 birds.

Despite this recent influx, the anecdotal evidence from game bags and game legislation indicates that the bird was once far commoner than it is now. Early sixteenth-century price regulations for poulterers placed a value of threepence on a quail, which was the same as the much

larger mallard or rabbit, and twice the cost of a teal. The tariffs suggest that the quail was something of a treat, but by no means exceptional. Even in the late eighteenth century Gilbert White wrote that both the birds and their catchers were locally commonplace: 'Quails crowd to our southern coast, and are often killed in numbers by people that go on purpose.'[19]

The real collapse began about the middle of the nineteenth century and coincided, somewhat curiously, with a sudden increase in Irish records. Not only were quail appearing in the summer pastures but birds also seemed to be resident in winter. In 1841/2 a Belfast game-dealer handled an average of three dozen a week, while from November 1849 to March 1850 a single gun in County Down shot 240 quail within a radius of 3 miles (5km). Thereafter, however, even the Irish birds declined and by the 1880s the species was virtually extinct in that country.

The cause of the losses in Ireland and Britain was almost certainly the over-harvesting of migrating birds as they passed through the Mediterranean. Sudden and massive influxes have been known in that region since biblical times and were famously described in Exodus, when they proved a timely bounty for the Jews as Moses led them through the wilderness. They also appear in the book of Numbers, but here as a curse from God, which probably drew on the quail's ancient status as an erotic symbol. In each instance their huge numbers were obvious: 'And there went forth a wind from the Lord, and brought quails from the sea, and let them fall by the camp . . . and as it were two cubits high upon the face of the earth' (Numbers 11:31). A 'fall' of quail covering the ground to a depth of 44 inches (106cm) (calculated to involve some 1000 million birds per square kilometre) sounds like Old Testament exaggeration, but Pliny claimed that quail flocks migrating across the Mediterranean by night could crash into the sails of vessels and so swamp the decks that the boats eventually sank.[20]

The dramatic spring arrivals of quail on the Mediterranean shores were a natural focus for hunters, and birds were taken in massive quantities. Mrs Beeton recounts a single day's slaughter of 100,000 birds within a 4–5-mile (6–8-km) stretch of southern Italy. For decades Egypt was a major centre for trapping north-bound birds and in 1913 alone 1,858,000 were exported. This level of slaughter was completely unsustainable and the catch had fallen sharply to under one-third of this total even by the 1930s.[21] It is hardly surprising that less than a generation later, Brian Vesey-Fitzgerald wrote of British quail, 'Family parties – bevies is the correct term – stay together until the autumn, and it is said that migrants arrive in small parties. I have never heard of anybody in this country putting up a bevy of quail.'[22]

Pheasants are enjoyed as much for their exotic beauty as their sporting opportunities.

Common Pheasant, *Phasianus colchicus.*

On 5th October 1952 about two miles south of Dunbar, I noticed a hen Pheasant sitting out at sea on a small isolated rock which was half awash. Between it and the shore were about a quarter of a mile of rock and rock pools, as well as 20 yards of open water. Presently a wave washed it into the sea and, after floating for a second or two, it took off from the surface and flew successfully to land. This is probably the only known case of a Pheasant doing something interesting.

Professor M. F. M. Meiklejohn[23]

This passage from *British Birds* represents one of only about a dozen similar very brief references to the species that have appeared in the journal during the last 55 years. In those many thousands of pages no other wild bird has been so ignored, and Maury Meiklejohn's comic riposte typifies a widespread attitude towards the pheasant. Despite its thousand-year history in this country, some birdwatchers even now refuse to consider it a British bird.

There is some justification. Every year approximately 20 million pheasants are reared in conditions not far removed from the production of free-range chickens. These are then released in woodland across almost the whole of Britain and Ireland, and before natural predators like foxes can devastate these semi-tame easy pickings, around 12 million of them are brought down by the shooting community. More than half of all game birds

killed in Britain are pheasants. The extraordinary levels of artificial production and slaughter help to explain ornithology's indifference and the game community's passionate devotion.

No bird has had a greater impact on the English landscape, while in Ireland and Britain as a whole, only red grouse has had anything like the same level of influence. Love of pheasant shooting continues to shape the attitudes and management practices of many landowners. For its devotees, gathering for the shoot at the woodland edge on a crisp autumn morning is one of the highlights of the year, and for a single day's sport they will pay hundreds (and occasionally thousands) of pounds. The whole season, from 1 October until 1 February, drives a multi-million-pound industry and at its heart is an introduced bird whose natural range comes no closer than the eastern shore of the Black Sea.

The scientific name *Phasianus* derives from the River Phasis (now called the Rioni), just as *colchicus* comes from the region in the ancient world known as Colchis, which was the heart of its western range. From there the Greeks first brought pheasants back to Europe, and the Romans eventually took them to Britain, although it is unknown whether these birds established a feral population. The first reliable written reference to the species concerns pheasants eaten at Waltham Abbey just prior to the Battle of Hastings. It is thought that once William the Conqueror was established on the English throne, the Normans' Sicilian connections would have led to the bird's increased importation.[24] During the Middle Ages they gradually spread, but the species remained an

169

Surveying the day's achievements.

expensive table item until at least the seventeenth century. Only with the rise of the gamekeeper and the era of organised covert shoots did pheasants become anything like as commonplace as they are today.

The most popular form of shoot involves birds being driven by beaters and then forced to fly, preferably as high as possible to test marksmanship, over a line of guns assembled in a woodland clearing. Major advances in gun and transport technologies (see Red Grouse, page 153) meant that for the Victorian landed classes, pheasant shooting became a major part of their social calendar from the mid-nineteenth century.

It is impossible to over-emphasise the sport's historical importance. The artificial boosting of pheasant numbers involved time-consuming and expensive management of woods and maintenance of rearing pens, carried out by an army of gamekeepers and helpers. Small wonder perhaps that keeping up the shoot bankrupted several large landed families. There was a Victorian adage reflecting the associated costs: 'Up goes a guinea, bang goes a penny-halfpenny, and down comes half a crown.'[25] Today little has changed in pheasant economics. On some Scottish estates it

can cost the guns as much as £27 per bird to shoot 1000 pheasants; at the end of the day's sport, the carcasses are so numerous and of so little value that they are buried.[26] However such disregard for the pheasant's culinary potential is rare. The meat is highly prized and its preparation is as steeped in ritual as most other aspects of the shoot. Opinions differ on the length of time pheasants should be left to hang and few tastes are quite as cultivated as the household where: 'My father used to say you should wait until you could hear them crying from the cellar.'[27]

The environmental historian Oliver Rackham has assessed the consequences of devoting so much of our landscape to the interests of this Asian bird. On the one hand 'pheasants filled a vacuum which the decline of woodmanship was leaving'. In turn 'the gamekeeper kept alive many otherwise disused woods that might have been grubbed out; they also kept up the coppicing' which was beneficial to so much woodland wildlife. Today pheasant keeping maintains the fabric of the countryside and by providing an alternative crop 'it limits the excesses of prairie farming'.[28]

Yet Rackham also argues that gamekeeping 'more than any other activity up to that time . . . corrupted country life and produced ill-feeling between landowners and other folk':[29]

[gamekeepers] took it upon themselves to persecute beasts and birds of prey and to exclude the public from woods. This need not have been so. France, Germany, and Switzerland are equally good shooting countries, and yet ancient woods are everyone's heritage; in Britain alone we have lost that birthright, and with it our knowledge and love of woods. A generation of people grew up who, except in such fortunate areas as south Essex, had never been in a wood and could easily be persuaded that woods had merely an economic function. People who have been rudely expelled from a lime-wood are unlikely to oppose its destruction.[30]

Modern gamekeeping plays a valuable role in suppressing foxes and crows, which are key predators of all ground-nesting birds. Unfortunately for more than a hundred years almost everything else considered a threat to the cherished pheasant and its chicks was ruthlessly eliminated. Species like red kite, buzzard, peregrine and raven are only just recovering parts of their former ranges, and the historical activities of some gamekeepers defy belief. W. H. Hudson insisted on the authenticity of one story concerning a 'keeper who shot all the nightingales because their singing kept the pheasants awake at night'. Another destroyed an old heronry 'because their cries frightened the pheasants', while a third incident personally witnessed by Hudson featured a keeper and team who systematically worked their way through a wood. 'All the nests found of whatever species, were pulled down, and all doves, woodpeckers, nuthatches, blackbirds, missel- and song-thrushes, shot; also chaffinches and many other small birds. The keeper said he was not going to have the place swarming with birds that were no good for anything, and were always eating the pheasants' food.'[31]

The object of all this excessive care was to maximise pheasant bags and it is little surprise that most of the records were set during the keeper's heyday, which waned with the Edwardian era. That monarch was himself a passionate devotee of the shoot and was instrumental in widening its popularity, but it was his son and grandson, George V and the future Edward VIII, who established the British record when their party killed 3937 birds in 1913. 'Perhaps we overdid it today,' the king was recorded to have said. However, the apotheosis of this anally retentive psychopathy was achieved in the second Marquess of Ripon who, in a long career as a sportsman, killed 556,813 birds. Nearly a quarter of a million of these were pheasants.[32]

In the 1880s the Old World passed its sporting pleasures to the New, and pheasants were introduced to the Willamette valley in Oregon. The species quickly flourished in America, to the point where it now occurs in 35 US states – some of which have populations numbering several million – nine provinces of Canada and a north-western fragment of Mexico. Worldwide as many as 50 million pheasants are released annually in places as far-flung as Cuba, the Bahamas and New Zealand.

In some of these locations, particularly continental North America, pheasants mean something very different to those who hunt them. Peter Robertson, the author of *A Natural History of the Pheasant*, has argued that:

In contrast to the British system, with its emphasis on intensive management, high numbers and formalised arrangements, most pheasant shooting in North America is conducted by small groups of hunters on a fairly informal basis. This is partly due to the different traditions of hunting. Compared to Europeans, North Americans are closer to their subsistence hunting roots and a much higher proportion of the population is involved. In some rural areas over 50 per cent of the male population hunts at some time during their lives.[33]

In Britain there has also been a form of subsistence pheasant hunting and, though it is entirely distinct in terms of its social and cultural milieu from the formal

Unlike the bowler hat, roast pheasant is still a popular British tradition. These birds hang in a butcher's window at Leadenhall Market, London.

shoot of the landed classes, it is parasitic upon the latters' intensive pheasant-rearing efforts. It was – and to some extent, still is – the shadowy, unlawful, romantic world of the poacher.

The rural hardships that once motivated old-style poaching have now largely vanished. So too have the shark-jawed mantraps and the mark of subversive criminality, which once stained the poacher's character and inspired magistrates to draconian punishments. Transportation and even the death penalty were sometimes imposed. Today attitudes have softened to the point where poaching is even treated in children's fiction, such as Roald Dahl's *Danny the Champion of the World*. In this the father-and-son team set out to steal the local landlord's pheasants, using raisins spiked with sleeping tablets.

Dahl's wonderfully comic story is part of a long tradition of tales in which poaching is invested with a Robin Hood-style morality. Taking from the rich is justified if it feeds the poor. And if the formal pheasant shoot tests the marksmanship of the upper-crust sportsman, the working-class poacher expresses his own talent through an ability to outwit two opponents, pheasant and keeper. There was even at times a bond of kinship between the two types of pheasant man. Brian Vesey-Fitzgerald, former editor of *The Field*, wrote that a 'gypsy poacher friend of mine' could 'bring down two cock birds, roosting next door to one another, one after the other, with a long whip, a weapon he used in the manner of a lasso with great dexterity'.[34]

Other poaching techniques are legion:

I know a man who in his youth used to go to a pheasant roost with a cocoa tin filled with hot coals. He would put rock sulphur into the tin and place an inverted funnel over it with the narrow end inserted in a long piece of rigid pipe or hollow bamboo. He then placed the end of the pipe under the front of the pheasant as it roosted. The bird got knocked out and fell off its perch. I believe that people today use an air rifle – not as romantic but possibly a lot less hassle.[35]

Another technique involved putting raisins in a paper bag and then smearing the inside with gum or treacle. The bird took the bait, but the bag remained glued to its head and the pheasant was left blindfold and stationary until 'rescued'. One particularly cruel method involved raisins threaded with horsehair so that the pheasant choked. Far more benign were the raisins laced with alcohol so that it fell into a stupor.

A more expensive technique was attempted by 'a chap (since died) who was driving along and saw a pheasant in the road ahead of him and thought, "Right, I'll have this," and tried to knock it over with his front wheels. Instead it went through his radiator and into the engine and did over £200 worth of damage. This was over 15 years ago, so it must have made a mess!'[36]

Other roadside efforts have been more successful:

In the early '60s the lure of Norfolk's birds drew several regular caravans of birdwatchers north from Cambridge and the London area. The routes varied with intent; for some it was a straight dash for Cley. But one team with a Morris Minor Traveller added a culinary stratagem to the day's tactics, the harvesting of pheasants from the quiet lanes of the [Stanford] 'Battle Area' north of Thetford. Their method was 'sporting rustic'; the birds were swotted with hockey sticks flailed from the front windows.[37]

In some rural areas, pheasants reverse the roles and present hazards to motorists. In recent years reared birds have tended to get heavier and are incapable of sustained high flight. Modern sportsmen complain of the lack of challenge offered by these obese creatures, and their poor aerial performance may also help account for the large number of birds that crash into car windscreens. In some parts of the country dead pheasants litter the road every few hundred yards and this new abundance of high-quality, albeit high-risk, protein may have a major impact on the ecology of Britain's road network. However in the dead of night these roadkills provide a host of nocturnal predators – including some of the gamekeeper's main enemies – with their easiest pickings.

The preferred habitat for Britain's 'wild' population of pheasants is deciduous woodland with a dense scrub layer. 'I have heard a story of a game adviser who, while training an apprentice, used to send him into a wood. He would then judge how attractive it was by the state of his assistant's clothes when he came out the other end.'[38] In these thick coverts the female pheasant's brown chequered plumage is good camouflage, and even cock birds can be suprisingly difficult to see.

The male pheasant is a gloriously beautiful creature. As well as the red fleshy 'goggles', many have a prominent white collar between the iridescent green head and bronze body. This feature was absent from the original Caucasian stock in medieval Britain. It derived from the nineteenth-century importation of the hardy Chinese race *torquatus*, known as the ring-necked pheasant. There are about 30 races recognised worldwide and the genes from many of these are now so mixed in Britain's pheasants that they exhibit a huge range of plumage variation.

One constant feature is a tail that is sometimes as much as 20 inches (48cm) long and more than the length of the body. When moulted, the main black-banded copper tail-feathers are a cherished find for children and adults alike on any outing and were once a routine feature of the countryman's (or woman's) hat. For the poacher, however, they were less welcome: 'I used to take all the long feathers out so they didn't stick out of my pocket . . . and if there was water I used to throw them all in so they floated away.'[39]

Cock pheasants are seen at their best in early spring, when the dominant birds attract a harem of broody females. 'He is all attention then, capering round each bride in turn with trailing inside wing and half-spread tail canted towards her; shaking his crescents and spangles, setting his emerald ear-tufts and vermilion wattles at her.'[40] The male also performs a striking territorial display out in the open field, when he raises his tail and cranes his head upwards to deliver a loud, harsh '*gokk-gokk*' call, immediately followed by an audible drumbeat of the short stiff wings.

It is remarkable how a bird of such tropical colours as the golden pheasant can be so elusive in an English winter wood.

Other displaying males, and even loud noises or disturbance, can stimulate a cock pheasant into a response. It was claimed that one of the first indications of the First World War's Battle of Jutland was the agitated calls of pheasants across East Anglia, as the huge naval guns blasted away in the North Sea.[41] During the Dunkirk evacuations of 1940, Kent pheasants were said to be similarly aroused, and Brian Vesey-Fitzgerald wrote, 'At the time of the first big daylight blitz on London, I heard cock pheasants crowing in Hampshire, though I could not myself hear the bombing.'[42]

Even by late October male pheasants will crow in territorial fashion, particularly as the sun is setting and often as ground mist fills the valley floor. W. H. Hudson argued that in the season's richer colours 'the pheasant no longer seems an importation from some brighter land . . . and out of harmony with the surroundings'. In East Anglia, as each cock bird answers its neighbour, the calls ricocheting across the fields until they die away in a distant landscape, the sound can seem the very essence of the English autumn at dusk.

Golden Pheasant, *Chrysolophus pictus*. Like Lady Amherst's pheasant (see below), this introduced species was accepted on to the official British list in 1971. It seems improbable that the gorgeous plumage of the males could look anything other than unnatural amid the sombre tones of the British landscape. Yet the birds in this country are not only intensely shy, but remain concealed in dense conifer plantation or thick deciduous scrub. In the dappled conditions of the undergrowth the brilliant colours often appear as little more than an occasional, tantalising flash as the cock birds slip effortlessly from sight. The careful stalk normally required to obtain even moderate views compounds an impression that you have just seen a truly wild species and one that has found a reasonable alternative to the dense bamboo thickets of its native central China.

Although a viable, if localised, population has been present since the 1890s, little is known about the golden pheasant's ecology or breeding behaviour. This is partly on account of its secretive manner and also the sheer difficulty involved in finding an incubating female. Observing

The Lady Amherst's pheasant is one of the world's most beautiful birds, but some environmentalists are happy to watch it slide into extinction in Britain because it is an introduced 'exotic'.

captive birds, Derek Goodwin established that one hen never moved on the nest until the chicks hatched. He was able to verify this remarkable fact partly because there was a spider's web just 2 inches (5cm) above her tail and another about 'half an inch away on one side. These webs could hardly have remained intact had the pheasant moved to any appreciable extent, and certainly any attempt on her part to turn round would have broken them, yet they remained intact during the whole period.'[43]

Another major reason for a lack of hard information is the general prejudice shown towards introduced exotics. Ironically the neglect of golden pheasant is likely to end just as the bird seems to be slipping away. Most recent census work indicates a steady decline in its three main areas: the Breckland of Suffolk and Norfolk, the South Downs of Hampshire and Sussex, and the Galloway Forest Park. All are the product of regular releases of captive stock, which continued until at least the 1960s. The Breckland population, originating with birds put down on the Elveden estate

near Thetford, is both the largest and best known.

Five birds radio-tagged by Stephen Browne, Mark Rehfisch and Dawn Balmer appear to be extremely sedentary, moving 'a maximum of 1,250 m from one end of the home range to the other over a year'.[44] Another striking discovery was the fact that recently hatched chicks were not accompanied by their radio-tagged mother, but by the cock pheasant, presumably while she recovers from her marathon incubation.[45]

Lady Amherst's Pheasant, *Chrysolophus amherstiae*. VN: Lady A, The Lady. The curious philosophical limbo suffered by some of our introduced animals is perhaps more intensely expressed in the case of this bird than any other non-native species. Its credentials as a 'Briton' are about as good as the now widely accepted little owl, yet both its behaviour and conservation requirements have been almost entirely ignored for more than a century. (It is now illegal without a licence to make further introductions yet the equally non-native common pheasant is bred and released on an industrial scale.)

William Beebe's assertion in 1926 that 'Our ignorance of the wild habits of the Amherst Pheasant is about as complete as in the case of its golden congener' is still essentially true.[46] Even more disturbing is the fact that some consider the bird more exquisitely beautiful than its close relative, yet it joins the long list of British game birds now in serious decline, with a total of just 94 pairs confined mainly to mixed woodland on the Bedfordshire/Buckinghamshire border.

The feral populations established on the Isle of Bute (1890s), Bedfordshire (1890s–1930s), Hampshire (1925) and Surrey (1928/9) were acts of striking generosity by their original authors. A pair sold at auction in 1873 at the Zoological Gardens of Antwerp went for the equivalent of £160 (well in excess of £10,000 by today's prices).[47] However, only the descendants of birds from Woburn and Whipsnade survived and spread into the wider countryside. Away from its native home in the montane forests and bamboo of north-east Myanmar and south-west China, this area of southern England is possibly the only place in the world with a feral population. Unfortunately not all local landowners feel particularly honoured:

> Since most people visit to see the Lady in the winter, which coincides with the pheasant season, game shoots are often disrupted by 'wandering bird-watchers', resulting in the poor Lady being eradicated in end-of-season vermin shoots. More than one keeper has said to me that the two main reasons for shooting them out is, 'trouble with them bloody trespassing birdwatchers', and the fact that the birds won't fly – more than one beater has been peppered by an old duffer taking aim and firing at a running Lady![48]

One of the few features shared by its Chinese and Bedfordshire homes is the presence of dense rhododendron scrub, in which these brilliant and enormously long-tailed birds are very difficult to observe:

> The Lady's unwillingness to fly is legendary – in fact all the years (over 20) I've been snooping around Woburn woods I've only see them 'fly' once, and that was no more than two feet off the ground as they scrambled for cover. A good ploy for watching them, once located by the call, is to lay down with your head into the plantation and wait. It's surprising how often this works; I've had cracking views of cock pheasants 'lekking' in front of hens.[49]

William Beebe kept a bird in a stable covered with straw, and it hid so well that he once went for more than 15 days 'in the belief that it was dead'.[50]

Rail, Crake and Coot family *Rallidae*

Water Rail, *Rallus aquaticus*. VN: Watter Rail (Yorkshire). From its bizarre squealing call to its occasional penchant for impaling wrens with a spear-thrust of its long bill, the water rail is one of the genuine oddities among British birds. Many of its antics have a capacity to engage us, partly because almost every observation of this reclusive species seems tinged with a sense of unexpected revelation.

'Its plumage, a mixture of browns, greys and buffs, camouflages it well, and every movement it makes seems to be considered beforehand . . . and carried out with stealth.'[1] Yet on occasions water rails can be remarkably bold and venture right into the open, where they appear to act as if they are still invisible. Sometimes they can even be lured out: 'One of my previous jobs was to check water quality, which involved lowering a sensor into a tube until it reached the water table and beeped. The sound turned out to be remarkably attractive to water rails and to this day it is the only time I've observed them at close quarters.'[2]

In 50 years just 80 nest-record cards have been submitted to the BTO, reflecting the acute difficulties in

Unpredictable, reclusive, yet strangely noisy, the water rail is one of the true eccentrics of British nature.

Lord William Percy trained one weird water rail to jump for worms on his improvised fishing rod.

locating their nest, yet at Loch Lomond a pair once bred out in the open near a main road where neither 'bird seemed in the least disturbed by the noise and bustle of the scores of holiday-makers, hikers, and cyclists'.[3]

Water rails normally nest in thick vegetation. At Leighton Moss they have taken to nesting both under and inside bearded-tit nest boxes. These reed 'wig-wams' obviously providing suitable cover. On one occasion a brood of bearded tits was succesfully reared in the nest box while a nest of water rails hatched successfully under the box, only the wooden floor and about 10cm separating the two nests![4]

Absent from most upland areas, they are widespread but thinly distributed across much of Britain and Ireland. Two centuries ago Thomas Bewick accurately described the water rail as a bird of 'low wet places, much over-grown with sedges, reeds and other coarse herbage, amongst which it shelters and feeds in hidden security'.[5] Its strongholds are a south-easterly belt from Hampshire to Norfolk, in the English West Midlands, in southern Scotland near the Forth and Clyde estuaries, and especially in central Ireland, in which country there are almost twice as many water rails as there are in all Britain.

In the last 30 years wetland loss seems to have caused a marked reduction in range, although the findings may be distorted by the many obstacles to an accurate census. Some believe the present population figure of fewer than 2000 pairs is a serious underestimate. David Glue noted that 'Atlas recorders consistently place the Water Rail among the "Top Ten" most elusive of birds.'[6]

The best means of locating a water rail is by its strange voice. An old name for the bird in Norfolk was 'sharmer', and 'sharming' has since become a standard description for the bird's delivery of its piercing call. It is usually likened to squealing piglets, although water rails have a large repertoire, evoking a wide range of colourful descriptions: 'heart-rending and fearsome groans'; 'a curious rolling note . . . between the purring of a cat and the croak of a frog';[7] 'incessantly uttered purring noise, likened to the purring of contented squirrel';[8] 'their wheezy grunting . . . the sort of noise a hedgehog makes when grubbing in the dusk';[9] 'a remarkable note (apparently rare) sounding like a klaxon horn'; and finally 'a subdued sort of grunting not unlike the "cluck" of a recalcitrant cork being repeatedly and forcibly drawn from a bottle'.[10]

Given the striking character of the voice, and the water rail's routine invisibility, it is surprising that most of the old names celebrate the bird's movements, which have an almost rodent-like character. Its body is laterally compressed so that it 'finds no tangle of vegetation too dense'.[11] A white flash of undertail coverts vanishing into reeds or a grey shape scuttling down a drain are typical sightings, and something of the nervy, mouse-like speed is conveyed by the old West-Country name 'skittycock' or 'scittycoot', while 'velvet runner' and 'brook runner' are in the same vein. Another ancient strand of names – 'weircock' or 'warcock' (weir = pond or pool) – has given rise to Warcockhill in Lancashire, which may well be the only place name in Britain to commemorate the species. (Crakehall and Little Crakehall in north Yorkshire and Crakesmarsh in Staffordshire may come from this species, although corn crake is just as likely.)

Like many water birds, they are severely affected by intense frost and it can drive them towards some of their most eccentric behaviour. They are reluctant and appear ungainly-looking fliers, yet one strategy to avoid adverse conditions is to migrate. A personal observation of this unlikely phenomenon in October 1998 involved a water rail scuttling around the funnel of the P&O ferry as it steamed south just off the French cape of Finistère. When the bird finally flew off over the Atlantic, legs trailing and rounded wings barely longer than a house martin's, it was undoubtedly among the strangest sightings in 30 years of ornithology.

Cold weather also helps trigger a latent predatory behaviour that seems out of character with the water rail's largely insectivorous or vegetarian lifestyle and with its usual timidity. Yet it has been known to take nine other types of bird, and will attack species as large as knot. One modus operandi is to run the bird through with its stiletto-like bill; another is to seize the live prey and then drown it. Both methods almost certainly benefit from the victim's failure to recognise the bird as a threat, and chance opportunity seems to form a large part of the behaviour. A water rail and three twite were once found on Fair Isle in the same catching-box of a trap, where two of the three twite had been killed and partly eaten. Another water rail introduced to a large aviary was seen to eat or kill a greenfinch and a Chinese quail, *Coturnix chinensis*.[12]

Bird ringers working in reedbeds are especially wary of leaving their nets unattended, because water rails are well known to help themselves to a ready-caught meal tangled in the lowest shelf of the net. At the RSPB's Leighton Moss reserve, the former warden John Wilson and his team routinely scattered 200–300 sprats during exceptional cold spells as supplementary food for wintering bitterns, but found that many of these were being taken by an equally hungry band of water rails. They also used baited traps to try to catch bitterns as part of a radio-tracking study. Their efforts were thwarted because water rails took all the fish bait. 'Even placing the fish at a height, which it was thought only bitterns could reach, did not work because water rails learnt to jump up and grab the fish off its hook, so activating the trap.'[13]

Sometimes chance conditions can reverse the pattern of predation. For macabre spectacle, few sights can compare with the vision produced at Parkgate, on the Dee estuary, Cheshire. The area sometimes attracts hundreds of wintering water rails and on 29 December 1974 the birds 'were seeking shelter from the incoming tide in rafts of floating vegetation. Small groups of herons landed nearby, seized water rails in their bills and then flew to shallow water, where they drowned their prey. At one stage, we saw four herons each devouring a rail.'[14]

Spotted Crake, *Porzana porzana*. Of our regular breeding birds, this starling-sized rail is among the two or three most difficult to census. It has a shifting range that stretches from Scotland's outer isles to western Ireland, yet in any year there are seldom more than 60 singing males. Only minuscule populations in the Spey Valley and the Cambridgeshire Fens maintain anything like a consistent spring presence. The bird has a highly characteristic whiplash call, delivered in sequences of 55–90 a minute, audible as much as 1.2 miles (2km) away and best transliterated as '*hooid*' or '*whitt*'; 'we could imitate the noise by whipping the top point of a fly-fishing rod quickly through the air'.[15] Unfortunately it is

The Baillon's crake found in 1989 at Mowbray Park, Sunderland, was so tame it would occasionally walk over the feet of the assembled crowd.

usually given at night and as soon as the male pairs, he ceases to advertise his presence, 'confining the census "window" to but a few weeks or even days'.[16]

The spotted crake appears to have been much commoner historically, but British birds suffered a serious decline in the first half of the nineteenth century, probably because of the loss of their very specific habitat of open meadows, marshes or fens dominated by various sedges and inundated to a depth of less than 1 foot (30cm).

Baillon's Crake, *Porzana pusilla*. This sparrow-sized European crake with its disproportionately long feet has all the creeping mouse-like ways of its family. It was once reported widely in Britain as a rare migrant and there were even a handful of breeding records in the nineteenth century, the last from Sutton Broad, Norfolk, in May 1889. Yet in the last half-century there have been just 13 occurrences.

Both this species and its congener, the marginally larger **Little Crake**, *P. parva*, can be remarkably skulking, and even identification of their vocalisations poses problems because of their similarity to various amphibians. A bird believed to be a little crake was heard over several evenings at a small pool near Newton Abbot, Devon, in June 1984, until it was identified correctly (from tapes) as the call of a European tree frog.[17]

However, there was no mistaking a little crake seen in

Seldom seen but easily heard, a corn crake can make its harsh 'arp-arp' call 20,000 times in one night.

the Cuckmere valley, East Sussex, in March 1985, which reversed the family norms and was so confiding that it fed from the hand and was 'quite oblivious of the furiously clicking cameras'.[18] If anything, a Baillon's crake, which appeared in Mowbray Park in the centre of Sunderland in May 1989, was even more extrovert. It fed completely out in the open along the cobbled edge of an artificial lake, at times a matter of inches from hundreds of observers. Sometimes it even walked across their feet. The editors of the rare-bird report in the journal *British Birds* noted wryly that for those vetting the record, 'tangible evidence' was on this occasion a literal reality.[19]

Corn Crake, *Crex crex*. The almost complete disappearance of this summer visitor from the British mainland is one of the saddest developments of twentieth-century ornithology. Its remaining toehold in parts of western Ireland, the Orkneys and Hebrides involves just 799 calling males, and this 1998 figure represents a significant increase on numbers a decade earlier.

It is hard now to imagine that Mrs Beeton knew it as a bird for the pot (under its old alternative name, 'land-rail'), recommending a dish with four birds roasted on a skewer. It is harder still to believe that in her day it was as widely distributed as any other British species and 'that corncrakes in the meadows on a summer day were part of the unchanging order of things'.[20]

Yet one need not travel so far back in time to encounter personal memories of birds living right among us: 'My uncle (John King) died aged almost 80 in 1998. He lived for over seventy years in the same house in North Shields, now very much built up and surrounded by traffic and industry. He remembered being kept awake as a boy by corn crakes calling in the meadows around this same house.'[21]

In truth, this dark-streaked grey and rusty-barred rail was probably seldom seen even in its heyday. It is a classic skulker, notorious for its refusal to show and, 'more like a rat than a bird', it burrows into the grass at the slightest disturbance.[22] Yet on occasions it can overcome its natural timidity. 'A woman on Tiree had a corncrake come to her house five summers in a row which would walk in through the front door and feed on kitchen scraps. In 1999 a bird also wintered on Barra and when the farmer threw out the chicken feed, the corn crake would come out for its turn once the hens had finished.'[23]

Usually, however, the bird's presence is given away by

its distinctive voice. The scientific name echoes the sound fairly accurately – a mechanical harsh, dry *'arp-arp'*, which is as monotonous and ventriloquial as it is persistent. Although males sometimes call while snaking through the grass and even occasionally in flight, they normally stand on a slight rise and stretch the neck skywards, with head almost vertical and bill wide open.

The bird can be heard from as much as 1 mile (1.6km) away and may continue almost without pause for six hours. In the course of a night it can repeat itself 20,000 times, although the main calling period is between midnight and 3 a.m. Small wonder, perhaps, that in the late 1930s during the first major investigation into the causes of its decline, several correspondents asked how they could get rid of them![24]

With its virtual extinction south of the Scottish border not everyone has retained an ability to recognise the corn crake's distinctive call: 'A farmer in north Wales recently called out the National Grid because he could hear a pylon "shorting" in his field. An engineer arrived and went to investigate the problem pylon, only to have a bird with rufous wings fly out. The sparking then recommenced in the middle of the field. This led to the discovery of Wales's only breeding corn crake that year.'[25]

Ornithologists have devised several artificial means of reproducing the sound. Bernard Tucker recommended 'drawing a piece of wood such as a foot-rule across the teeth of a comb or, still better, across a strip of wood or bone with a succession of notches cut in it'.[26] The materials and cultural resonances may have changed since the 1930s, but the basic technique remains much the same in the twenty-first century: 'Conversing with Corncrakes using an old credit card and a comb can produce fascinating results . . . If only from bemused onlookers!'[27] And stranger still: 'I have heard of notched "Corncrake sticks" being used to lure calling birds. This was adapted to good effect by colleagues, using the edge of plastic bank cards and a comb to induce birds to call. A variation on this in the absence of a comb was running the edge of a card against the zip-fastener on a pair of jeans – quite a bizarre sight seeing several people doing this on a field edge in Kent in 1994.'[28]

The first sign of the bird's disappearance was noted in the middle of the nineteenth century, and by the first decade of the twentieth it was largely absent from Buckinghamshire, Essex, Hampshire, Hertfordshire, Middlesex, Suffolk and Sussex, with only a handful in Berkshire, Kent, Lincolnshire and Norfolk. The inquiry of the 1930s found compelling evidence for what ornithologists had long suspected: it was a major victim of agricultural progress, particularly the development of mechanical mowing machines.

Contrary to its name, the bird is also closely associated with hay meadows, as well as fields of potatoes, turnips, oats and even nettles. Until the 1850s most grass crops were cut almost entirely by hand, but machines started to displace manual methods, particularly when a movable cutter bar was developed, which allowed the blade to adapt itself to the rise and fall of ridge and furrow. By 1875 roughly a quarter of all mown grass east of a line between the Humber and the Severn was cut by horse-drawn machine. At the outbreak of the First World War that figure had risen to 90 per cent and it coincided almost exactly with the corn crake's virtual absence from the region as a breeding species. Thereafter there was a close relationship between the technology's slow spread north and west and the species' parallel retreat.[29]

Anecdotal accounts from various parts of the country, and those submitted to the corn crake inquiry, graphically illustrate how this switch from hand-scythe to machine transformed the bird's fortunes:

There were seven or eight Corn-Crakes' nests in a six acre field of meadow being mown. Not one escaped. Chicks, recently hatched out and too young to run from danger, were butchered wholesale, while in a few cases eggs not yet hatched out were crushed by the cutter-bar of the mower. (J. Connell, Co. Meath)

I have continuous notes regarding this species, more particularly relating to the Sheffield and Barnsley areas and extending over a period of 45 years. I am convinced that there has been a very considerable reduction in numbers and that this is chiefly due to the machine cutting, which undoubtedly destroys many nests and birds, both old and young, of which fact I have a number of indisputable proofs. (A. Whitaker)[30]

The problem was not just the indiscriminate nature of the cutting action; it was also the pattern of the cut, which was from the perimeter steadily inwards in an ever-decreasing circle. Any escaping birds were ultimately trapped in the last stand of hay at the field centre, whereas scything by hand had allowed them ample time to escape into neighbouring fields. It is no coincidence that the corn crake found a last refuge in the extreme north-west, where agricultural mechanisation was slowest to arrive and where the crops are harvested latest in the season. Otherwise in grass meadows used for silage, which is cut in early summer, the mortality rate for chicks is 95 per cent.

Another hazard encountered arises out of the bird's return each winter to tropical Africa. Although it takes to

The moorhen is one of the most successful and widespread of our wetland birds.

the air reluctantly and gives the impression of little flying ability – 'it flutters a short distance in a desultory way . . . with legs dangling and hurried feeble-looking wing action suggesting that of a young bird' – it is more than capable as a migrant. An old French name for the bird was *roy de caille*, 'king of the quail', and these two secretive ground birds regularly move in association. Unfortunately nets set for one also capture the other, and in Egypt as many as 9000 were taken in 1993, with 14,000 the following year.[31] The corn crake now has the dubious distinction of being the only bird breeding in Britain and Ireland that is considered at risk of extinction throughout its global range.

Common Moorhen, *Gallinula chloropsis*. VN: Moggyhen, Moggy/ies, Wa(t)ter Hen (widespread); Woggy Hen (County Durham); Watter-hen, Moran (Orkney). Although moorhens lack the size-12 boots of the common coot, they have disproportionately thick green legs and long toes, with a jaunty, high-stepping gait as if the digits are too large to allow more dignified progress. The outsized feet are also part of an underlying humour, which seems to colour much of the bird's everyday behaviour and seems to be reflected in some of

its vernacular names. 'On shooting days I have watched them fly up to the tree-tops and perch uncomfortably on bare swaying twigs; craning their silly necks to look down on the guns and beaters; while others hide in the bushes and let dogs pick them up.'[32] But few tales of the moorhen's eccentricities can match the individual observed surfing on a pond.

Near my home in Newbury, Berkshire, I watched a Moorhen swimming near a small piece of floating timber about 30 cm long. It . . . then climbed on top of it . . . started to flap its wings, and in so doing propelled itself across the pond. My first impression was that it was trying to get its balance, but, when it turned around on the board and proceeded to flap its way across the pond again, I felt that it must be doing it deliberately.[33]

Moorhens in regular contact with humans become quite confiding, although they generally exhibit a nervous disposition. Swimming birds dive when threatened and can remain submerged for up to a minute, sometimes holding themselves under by gripping aquatic vegetation.

One very odd Cornish moorhen was even observed to walk underwater right across the bed of the River Fowey.[34]

Even when relaxed, the bird maintains its nervous twitch: an anxious up-and-down tail flick, which flashes a double 'scut' of white outer tail-feathers. If alarmed while on land, it trots away with head and neck pumping rhythmically at every step, and when danger is imminent it will quickly return to water – a departure usually accompanied by a sharper, pared-down version of the more typical '*krrrruk*' call, which is one of the classic sounds of British wetlands.

Despite this comic bent, the moorhen is a remarkably successful and adaptable species, with a near-global distribution across five continents. Next to the mallard, it is Britain's most widespread waterbird and is only absent from the extreme north-west of Scotland. There are about 240,000 breeding pairs, while migrants from Scandinavia boost the winter population to around one million birds. It occupies almost every form of freshwater habitat, from weed-fringed lakes down to muddy ditches or large garden ponds.

It is very much at home in the town park, where its untidy platform of water vegetation is usually highly visible and often represents the first bird's nest that many children ever encounter. The dark-speckled fawn eggs were also a favourite target for many childhood nesting expeditions, which were not illegal until 1954, nor were they by any means an act of thoughtless vandalism. 'In Suffolk, collecting waterhen's eggs was done by tying a dessert spoon to a length of bamboo, then scooping the eggs out one by one. This was only done if the pond or stream was too deep. Otherwise it was a case of socks and shoes off and wading in. Waterhen's eggs we used to fry up, while pheasant and partridge eggs mother would use in baking cakes.'[35] In Lincolnshire 'local lads would take the eggs home to be fried with bacon'.[36]

The nest itself is almost always positioned on, over or close to water, but occasionally moorhens will build as much as 26 feet (8m) up in the crown of a tree, or will occupy the abandoned nest of a wood pigeon, magpie, rook or jay. 'I once came across a nest in an overgrown hedge at least four feet above the ground and half-a-mile from the nearest water.'[37] Moorhen pairs often make more than a single nest, one for the eggs and others simply as brood platforms, which can be assembled in double-quick time:

I was watching a family of two adult and three almost fully grown young Moorhens on a small pond in Burnley, Lancashire. Suddenly a tremendous storm broke and torrential rain began to raise the water level … Four small young Moorhens, obviously the

Despite the moorhen's largely aquatic lifestyle, it will climb into bushes to feed and will nest high in a treetop.

second brood, were in a brood nest which was rapidly becoming swamped. The other five Moorhens began to build another brood nest, using part of the original and incorporating several potato-crisp packets and waste paper; within 15 minutes, the young were safely in this second nest and the first was beneath the surface of the pond.[38]

Nest-building birds seem to have a liking for discarded human objects. A brooding moorhen was observed in heavy rain covering itself in a small polythene sheet so that it draped the body like a tiny cape.[39] Richard Fitter recounts an incident in Kensington Gardens, London, when a moorhen inserted two old pink-and-blue omnibus tickets into the fabric of the nest, while at St James's Park, London, W. H. Hudson found a moorhen nest that incorporated four peacock 'tail' feathers, which were 'so arranged that the broad tips stood free above the nest, shading the cavity and sitting bird, like four great gorgeously coloured leaves'.[40]

The high visibility of moorhen nests no doubt helps explain why the species suffers such severe levels of nest predation. A study undertaken at 42 ponds in Hunting-donshire found that 44 per cent of clutches were lost to predators.[41] The range of animals taking the eggs is large and includes rats, mustelids, corvids, coot and even its smaller shape-shifting cousin, the water rail. Feral mink eat moorhens of all ages and may be one factor in the recent decline of some populations. 'On Harris, mink fur farms were established in the late 1950s, and the first feral mink reported by 1969. By 1988 there were estimated to be up to 7,500 females on Lewis and Harris. Prior to the arrival of fur farms, 60 pairs of Moorhens bred on these islands, but by 1982 the species was extinct.'[42]

The moorhen's status as a table bird is very old. In Norfolk there is an account of one being shot with a gun in 1533.[43] Even today it is 'not to be despised as a shooting mark and it is often the first species of water bird to be shot by the young gun'.[44] Country people valued the bird, particularly during the Second World War, when the strong dark meat was viewed as a welcome supplement to the strict rations. 'We used to go out once a fortnight and catch about half a dozen. Waterhens were taken by scaring them into swimming under water then pressing them into the bank of the dyke with a crotched stick. Then they were pulled out of the water by hand. Their necks were wrung when we got home and they were skinned rather than plucked. Mother would make a stew with vegetables and much the same was done with pigeons.'[45]

In other European countries, such as Greece, moorhens are still hunted and in these circumstances the bird undergoes a striking personality change. From the gauche tail-flicking creature of the English town park, it becomes a shy recluse that hardly ever offers a decent view. Until very recently some of the large Cypriot community in north London maintained their traditional liking for the bird. 'I often look in at my favourite Greek butchers in Harringay to see what wild birds they have on display. Until a couple of years ago I was always mildly surprised whenever I found a few moorhens swinging from the hooks among the rows of pheasants, partridges, mallard and occasional snipe and woodcock.'[46]

Common Coot, *Fulica atra*. VN: Cooit (Yorkshire); Snyth, Snysin (Orkney). While full-grown birds are unmistakable with their uniform charcoal plumage, white fleshy bill-shield and huge feet, younger birds are not obvious. Sub-adults are a washed-out olive-grey and have pale cheeks, but lack the distinctive white bill and blaze. Even more confusing are the newly hatched young. These are not the moorhen's 'feathered balls of soot', which so captivated W. B. Yeats ('Meditations in Time of Civil War'). Coot chicks are rather unappealing creatures with bare claret and blue facial skin and a tatty ruff of 'dyed' gingery down around the neck.

The white bill shield explains the expression 'as bald as a coot'.

The adult's white blaze is the source of the two surviving Orcadian names, 'snyth' and 'snysin'. (*Sny* in the islands' now-vanished Norn language referred to a white spot on a horse's face.[47]) The featherless shield also explains the phrase most frequently associated with the bird: 'as bald as a coot'. However it is more difficult to account for the once equally common and now vanishing 'queer as a coot'. It may possibly have acquired some of the modern homosexual associations although the coot has long had a reputation as a foolish bird (e.g. 'silly coot'), and 'queer' in this instance originally meant no more than 'odd' or 'strange'.

What precisely struck our ancestors as queer about the bird is more difficult to ascertain. Certainly those multi-coloured many-lobed toes impart an element of comedy to some of the coot's actions. On dry land the feet look a serious impediment and result in a 'twisting walk and awkward waddling run'.[48]

Yet overlaying any humour is the bird's deserved reputation for quarrelsome and aggressive behaviour. Coots form large flocks outside the breeding season, but nesting pairs are highly territorial and are frequently involved in boundary disputes. During these, birds will face one another and almost lie back on the water as they flail out with feet and wings. The fracas is invariably accompanied by much splashing of water and a clatter of loud metallic calls. Occasionally they will kill or drown intruders like moorhens and even young coots from other families.

One possible origin for the phrase 'as queer as a coot' is the bird's 'peculiar' penchant for aggression, both amongst its own kind and towards other species.

During the breeding season rogue birds will occasionally stray from their normally vegetarian diet and eat young ducklings or the eggs of great crested grebes and other birds.

At Leighton Moss, where black-headed gulls nest close to the hides, coot have been seen on occasions to systematically eat many clutches of black-headed gulls' eggs. The reaction of the gulls was interesting, only the pair being predated mobbed the maurading coot, while the neighbouring pairs continued with normal nesting activity. This was in complete contrast to the behaviour when a carrion crow or heron approached the colony. They evoked a mass group response to try and drive off the potential predator.[49]

In spring 2002 at Titchwell RSPB reserve, Norfolk, one very queer coot completely demolished 18 avocet clutches, as well as the contents of several black-headed gulls' nests, before finally descending into cannibalism and eating the young coot reared by its neighbours.[50]

These deviant ways may have been familiar to country people and may explain the queer/coot association. However the most frequent source for a bird's reputation as a fool was the ease with which it was caught (see Dotterel, page 199). At one time coot were widely eaten in Britain, and Brian Vesey-Fitzgerald offered a relatively recent judgement on the flesh: 'Young moorhen are very good eating, but I would infinitely rather have a coot.'[51]

There were traditional coot shoots at several large British wetlands, but the one at Hickling, Norfolk, survived longest and dated back until at least 1825. Huge winter flocks numbering several thousand were commonplace. The nineteenth-century naturalist Richard Lubbock wrote: 'On Hickling broad, a fen-man, to whom I put the question, What quantity of Coots might there be? returned for answer, "About an acre and a half." '[52] These birds were the focus of a major sporting event and over a 62-year period betwen the winters of 1894 and 1956, a total of 55,269 birds were killed.[53] The annual harvest seemed to have little appreciable effect on coot numbers and the birds vanished only when water pollution eventually destroyed the aquatic plants on which they fed.

Coot take to the air only reluctantly, but they are much stronger fliers than other family members, and the Hickling birds were driven by lines of punts until they rose high above the broad. At the end of the day as many as 1200 birds (and seldom fewer than 900) were gathered together, laid out at Whiteslea Lodge, then all given away in just 60 minutes. The ritual dispersal of the birds to local residents was on the basis of one per household member. Coot were skinned rather than plucked, and several birds were on the dining table in almost all the local houses for many days to come. Hickling's famous gamekeeper, Jim Vincent, believed that over his 20-year period he had given away 24,000 coot to his neighbours.[54]

Crane family *Gruidae*

Common Crane, *Grus grus*. This magnificent creature is undoubtedly a bird of superlatives. It is our tallest breeding species and has the greatest wingspan, longer even than either of the British eagles. The sonorous bugling calls produced by migrating flocks were likened in the *Iliad* to the sound of armies advancing into battle, which is surely one of the earliest specific references to a wild bird in Western literature. The enormous voice that so captivated Homer is a product of a highly elongated trachea and can be heard from as much as 3½ miles (6km) away.

While the ancient Greeks attached to cranes some of the fertility symbolism normally associated with the white stork, in Europe the bird never enjoyed the semi-religious aura surrounding crane species in the Far East. Instead the more utilitarian West honoured it as the ultimate quarry for the falconer. It is in this guise that Britain's cranes occasionally loom into view from that remote and often silent landscape – the Middle Ages. We know, for instance, that as early as 754 King Ethelbert II of Kent wrote to Boniface, the Bishop of Mayence in Germany, asking to be sent a pair of gyr falcons, the only species with the size and strength to overpower a crane.[1]

In the strict feudal hierarchy associated with falconry, gyr falcons were reserved for royalty and successive British kings, including King John, who was particularly fond of the sport, kept the birds to fly at cranes, In 1209, disappointed by a lack of game, he is said to have issued legislation to control poaching, although a less punitive, possibly more persuasive measure was his offer to treat a number of subjects in proportion to the crane bag seized by his hawks. After one successful crane-hunting expedition he is said to have feasted 100 paupers on bread, meat and ale.[2]

A fifteenth-century recipe gave advice on how to display so grand but ungainly a roast: 'Let a crane bleed in the mouth as thou didst a swan; fold up his legs, cut off his wings at the joint next the body, draw him, wind the neck about the spit; put the bill in his breast: his sauce is to be minced with powder of ginger, vinegar and mustard.' Not everyone rated roast crane. A sixteenth-century physician, Dr Moffet, thought it 'hard, tough, gross, sinewy ... yet being young, killed with a Goshawk, and hanged two or three daies by their heels, eaten with hot gelatine and drowned in sack, it is permitted unto indifferent stomachs'.[3]

However, it seems that on the medieval banqueting table size really mattered. Crane was the equal in cost and

Cranes featured regularly in medieval manuscripts such as the Sherborne Missal (c.1400). The birds were also a favourite roast on the banqueting table.

exclusivity to swan, bustard or peacock. At George Neville's gargantuan feast of 1465 (his inauguration banquet as Archbishop of York) crane was clearly de rigueur. An extraordinary 204 birds are listed on the menu – a figure that was already considered 'more than the fowlers of England could supply'.[4]

Habitat loss and over-exploitation took a heavy toll and while cranes continued to be caught well into the next century, the species dwindled rapidly as a breeding bird and possibly died out even before 1600. It certainly seems significant that when Elizabeth I visited Kirtlinge in Cambridgeshire in September 1577 only a single crane was presented at the royal board, compared with 70 bitterns, 28 grey herons and 12 spoonbills.[5] In the late seventeenth century Willughby wrote of 'great flocks of them' in Cambridgeshire and Lincolnshire, but these almost certainly involved passage or wintering birds

The crane's unaided recolonisation of Britain after an absence of 350 years is one of the most heartening developments in recent ornithological history.

coming to Britain during the autumn from northern Europe.[6]

These migrant birds may have played just as prominent a part as the breeding population in the legacy of crane place names that are spread right across England. Simon Boisseau and Derek Yalden have drawn up a list of nearly 300 place names including towns, villages, rivers and other land features that bear the association. These show a bias towards wetland areas (e.g. Carnforth, 'cranes' ford', in Lancashire; Cranmere, 'cranes' mere', in Shropshire) or landscapes with wide open horizons (e.g. Cranwell, 'cranes' spring', in Lincolnshire; Cranborne, 'cranes' stream', in Dorset). Yet the sheer spread of sites across more than 40 counties in Britain and Ireland suggests an almost nationwide presence.[7]

The exact origin of some place names is complicated, because Boisseau and Yalden argue that once the crane was extinct in Britain, the word for the species was then attached to the only similar large bird in the region, the grey heron. The Anglo-Saxon name for crane – *cran*, and less commonly *cron* – was of very ancient pedigree and written accounts often specifically mention both birds (heron was *hragra*), indicating that our ancestors were able to distinguish one from the other. Even so, Cornwood ('cranes wood') in Devon has the ring of a grey heron breeding site (perhaps we should note that in Spain cranes will feed in an open oak-wood habitat known as *dehesa* and a similar kind of wood-pasture may have been occupied by birds in Devon). Other names, however, are indisputable.

The origin of the place-name of (Great) Cransley village in Northamptonshire is 'Cranslea' in 956 AD and Cranesley/lea in 1086 AD meaning 'Crane's clearing' (or possibly 'island') – probably referring to a nearby marshy area, now the site of Cransley Reservoir. Cranes are also represented in the medieval stained-glass window in the village church, and also in the 'Three Cranes' village pub sign, which recalls the coat-of-arms once belonging to the manorial owners.[8]

It is perhaps surprising that East Anglia has few crane place names and those that exist – Cranwich, Cranworth (Norfolk) and Cransford (Suffolk) – are located some distance from the bird's old breeding stronghold in the Fens.[9] Yet at least one has some continued validity:

Twitching sixties-style for Houbara bustard near Westleton, Suffolk.

I lived for seven years in the tiny village of Cranwich, near Mundford in the heart of Breckland. A local history book told me that Cranwich means 'the bog where cranes breed', though of course they have not done so for very many years. In May 2000 I moved from Norfolk to Bedfordshire. Standing in the back garden of my Norfolk house, waiting for the removal van to arrive, I happened to look up to see, circling above me . . . a crane! It was the last bird I saw from that house.[10]

The modern Swedish name for crane is *Trana* and in its ancient Norse form it is found in the largest of Britain's crane localities, Tranmere ('the cranes' sandbank') in Cheshire. The Norse name also appears in a more local context: 'A number of years ago I was at Malham Tarn. I was told that there was a local tradition that in days of yore cranes nested at a local farm called Trana Farm. Before the Norman invasion much of the north-east was settled by Vikings and Norse names abound in much of the area.'[11]

There are a further 23 *Trana*-derived place names in Yorkshire.

For much of the twentieth century cranes were little more than occasional wanderers to these shores, so the re-establishment of a tiny breeding population during the 1980s was all the more remarkable. Two birds took up residence in the Horsey/Hickling area of east Norfolk and were gradually joined by others, until in 1982 there were five, including a pair that reared a young male chick – the first proven breeding success for three and a half centuries. In the following two decades cranes bred successfully in seven other years (1983, 1986, 1988, 1997, 1998, 1999 and 2001) and 'flocks' of up to 17 birds have now been seen. Whether this nucleus can consolidate and spread will depend upon the cranes finding sites similar to Horsey, where they enjoy a blend of extensive wetland, undisturbed conditions and a guardian as devoted as Horsey's owner, John Buxton.

Bustard family *Otididae*

Houbara Bustard, *Chlamydotis undulata*. This striking desert bustard has been recorded on just five occasions in Britain, the first four records all in the nineteenth century, all on the east coast and all in October. The last was a young male, which stayed for over a month, and was initially identified as 'a small, sandy "turkey"' by a local farmer near Westleton, Suffolk, on 21 November 1962.

In many ways this individual marked a new era in British birdwatching. The landowner and gamekeeper, rather than shooting the celebrity, as had been the custom for more than a century and a half (see Cream-coloured Courser, page 196), devoted themselves to its protection.[1] The houbara was also one of the earliest rarities to be 'twitched' in Britain. One of these observers, Ron Johns, found that the bird behaved in close accordance with the ornithological textbook:

> Although lacking precise directions for the location of the bustard, I soon found the correct spot when I came across a 'crowd' of twenty or so birders on a minor road at Hinton watching this wonderful eastern rarity. Throughout the next few hours the houbara performed in front of its admiring audience, casually walking about just a couple of hundred yards from the road in a small field of mustard, occasionally picking off and eating the leaves. I later read the account of Macqueen's Bustard – as the houbara was called in *The Handbook of British Birds* – including a fascinating snippet that in India this species feeds regularly in mustard fields.[2]

Recent DNA studies suggest that the houbara bustards of eastern origin are a different species to birds from North Africa, and a proposed 'split' may reinstate the bird's old name. So the last five records of houbara may become the first five examples of the Macqueen's bustard.

Great Bustard, *Otis tarda*. Nothing speaks more eloquently of the former wildlife riches of the British landscape than the past presence of this globally threatened species on the chalk wolds and open heaths from southern Scotland to the Channel coast. The collective noun for great bustards is a 'drove', which aptly suggests a creature on the scale of farmyard livestock. Bernard Tucker echoed the idea in his lovely remark that 'At great distances on [the] open plain a flock presents much the appearance of sheep.'[3] However, in classical Greece the association with domestic animals was

Great bustards ceased to breed in England in the 1830s. They are now the subject of a reintroduction scheme in Wiltshire.

thought to go further. Some believed that bustards bred with horses and chewed the cud.[4]

Great bustards are magnificent creatures and one of the world's largest flying land birds, with the biggest males weighing 39 pounds (18kg) and up to six times more than the females. This bird is equally impressive in flight, its huge, largely black-and-white wings beating with a deep constant rhythm. The *tarda* element of its scientific name, which originated with the term used for the bird by Pliny, *avis tarda*, draws on this apparent slowness in all its actions. On the ground the gait is measured and deliberate, while the head is often carried with bill uptilted to give it a suitably regal bearing.

If bustards are slow in their actions, they are also supremely difficult to approach and were seldom an easy target for the hunter. 'Extremely sagacious' was the judgement of the old Cambridgeshire warreners; 'nervous and mistrustful' was a more recent ornithological observation.[5] Their requirement for a horizon with clear views of ⅔ mile (1km) or more on at least three sides is a measure of their cautiousness and gives a clue as to why British bustards were driven to extinction.

Their disappearance by the end of the 1840s was preceded by an intensive period of agricultural enclosure. The breaking up of southern England's ancient heaths and commons and the erection of thousands of miles of field boundaries were all likely to bear heavily on a huge bird of the open plain. The areas long considered their natural stronghold were the chalk downs of Sussex, Dorset, parts of Kent and Wiltshire, particularly the area around Salisbury Plain. In the north they once extended into southern Scotland around Berwick (where they were probably extinct by the eighteenth century), while the wolds of Yorkshire and Lincolnshire formed another known site.

Unfortunately the bird combined large size with a reputation for good eating. The meat apparently tasted somewhere between turkey and goose and was deemed a 'rare union of gastronomic excellence'. Until the eighteenth century, roast bustard was a customary centrepiece in the inaugural feast for the mayors of Salisbury, although the bird's extreme wariness required some form of subterfuge. On the Spanish plains a stalking horse was used to get close enough for a shot, but in Suffolk the hunters contrived an equivalent:

This 'Crib' is a sort of rude cabin about three feet high, covered with furze and bramble. It moved upon four wheels; in its centre a windlass was fixed; and at different parts of the fen posts were firmly planted, attached to which were ropes having their connection with the windlass. The fowler, seated in the 'Crib', when he saw the Bustard alight and sufficiently engaged, would gradually wind the 'crib' towards the direction of the bird, and when within shot, let fly.[6]

The combination of agricultural change and hunting were insupportable burdens upon the remaining English populations, and at a certain level of scarcity a third factor interlocked with these downward pressures: the nineteenth-century passion for collecting. It worked in a fatal syndrome. The bird's ever-increasing scarcity gave an additional gloss to the possibility of owning such a rare trophy. This in turn guaranteed that high prices were paid for both the birds and their eggs. A single egg, for instance, could go for as much as a guinea, which represented a small fortune to the ordinary country worker. It meant that the birds were collected at every opportunity, and a market for bustard trophies continued right until the moment of extinction.

It fell to two men, the Reverend A. C. Smith and Henry Stevenson, authors respectively of the *Birds of Wiltshire* (1887) and the *Birds of Norfolk* (1870), to narrate the bird's obituary. In Wiltshire and neighbouring areas of downland the huge, flavoursome game birds inspired a particular form of sport when they were run down by greyhounds. Although over-hunting undoubtedly played a subsidiary role, the bustard population around Salisbury Plain was largely a victim of agricultural development, and Smith judged them to be extinct around the year 1820.

The lesser population of East Anglia lingered for another generation, and gave small hope of the bird's survival. In around 1812 one Suffolk eye-witness could recall 'peeping over a warren bank, at Eleveden ... just after harvest', and seeing 'quite close to him a drove which might have consisted of forty birds, "large and small", which sat there preening their feathers'.[7] Sadly they were faced with a formidable array of opponents and in his account in the *Birds of Norfolk*, Stevenson was both saddened by the bird's premature extinction and scathing of the destructive part played by men like George Turner.

This gamekeeper rigged up a battery of four duck guns, aligning their fire on an area strewn with turnips. To the triggers he then attached a cord that stretched for about ½ mile (0.8km). One day in 1812 this lethal device killed seven birds in one go, and although it fell to another farmhand to pull the trigger, Stevenson castigated Turner as a 'notorious *otidicide*'.

The great nineteenth-century ornithologist Alfred Newton contributed generously to Stevenson's account of the East Anglian bustards, including a description detailing the experiences of a Mr Thornhill of Riddlesworth Hall, who in August in 1832, 'while walking one hot day across Icklingham Heath, came upon a place where it was evident that some large bird had been rolling and dusting itself in the sand. On examination, he found close by a bustard's feather, and looking round him he perceived a hen bustard not many yards off.'[8] The almost casual circumstances of the encounter belie its significance. This was the last ever sighting of a native bird in Suffolk.

While a final bustard drove survived in west Norfolk, this too was gone within a decade. It is entirely in keeping with the species' wider British history that the last ever verified native bird, a female containing a well-developed egg at Lexham, Norfolk, in 1838, was also shot and subsequently stuffed. Since that date the great bustard has been no more than an increasingly rare and irregular visitor, with just 20 records in the last 45 years. The final appearance, involving at least seven birds, was in the winter of 1987.

Such a large and majestic bird was bound to have left an impression in the areas where it had most frequently occurred. Thus we find it on the county crest for Cambridgeshire, although it is probably Wiltshire where the bird has the largest symbolic presence:

A male, wings aloft, sits atop the Wiltshire crest, and in this pose is exhibited at every council establishment from schools and libraries to offices and rubbish dumps. Another male bustard makes a remarkable job

Great bustards appear in the Wiltshire (left) and Cambridgeshire county crests, reflecting the two areas where the birds were once common.

of holding a truncheon with its three forward-facing toes on the heraldic crest and banner of the Wiltshire Constabulary. A county badge of a great bustard is used by both the Wiltshire Girl Guides and the Wiltshire Army Cadet Force. The Royal School of Artillery and at least one village school have used this most impressive and stately of birds as their badge.[9]

Aside from at least three Bustard pubs in the bird's traditional heartland – including one at South Rauceby near Sleaford, Lincolnshire, and a further two on Salisbury Plain (in one at Rolleston a stuffed little bustard, *Tetrax tetrax*, is still displayed) – the species' key legacy was a profound regret that so magnificent an animal could have been allowed to slip away. In 1900 in Norfolk this was translated into an early, though failed, attempt at reintroduction. A second, more concerted effort to bring bustards back to Britain was made in the 1970s, centred on the MOD lands around Porton Down, Wiltshire.

Despite the failure of this second project, the notion of returning bustards to Britain retains a powerful attraction for some people. In 1999 the Great Bustard Group came forward with a fresh scheme that has recently (2004) come into effect. This relies upon obtaining rescued eggs or fortnight-old bustard chicks from a secure Russian population. After transportation to Wiltshire, the birds are held in a fox-proof open-topped pen until they reach a free-flying condition. The plan is for about 25 birds to be released annually for at least five years into the large area of grassland centred more or less on the Bustard pub at Rollaston.[10]

In his play *Summer Day's Dream*, set in 1975, J. B. Priestley imagined a Britain whose towns had been devastated by a third war. The only blessing upon this depopulated and shattered landscape was the return of great bustards to England's southern downlands. It would be pleasant to contemplate more agreeable circumstances for the bird's return.

Waders *Charadriiformes*

Eurasian Oystercatcher, *Haematopus ostralegus*. VN: Oik, Kleeper (northern England); Shelder, Shelter, Sheldro, Chalder, Cholder, Cholard, Skeldro, Scottie (Orkney); Shalder (Shetland). It is ironic that the most inaccurate of the names listed above is the modern English version. Oystercatchers eat cockles, mussels and earthworms, but seldom if ever eat oysters. The name for our bird was borrowed from the New World in the early eighteenth century, where the American oystercatcher, *H. palliatus*, will occasionally take them. However, early British ornithologists also suggested that the birds once widely ate oysters here, before our passion for the aphrodisiacal shellfish reduced them to extreme rarity.[1]

Most of the vernacular alternatives are accurate reflections of the 'biggest, brashest and noisiest' of our waders, drawing particularly on the loud 'cleeping' call or the graphic black-and-white plumage, which seems tailor-made as a business logo:[2]

The oystercatcher's ability to prise apart closed shells with its bill is a source of frequent admiration and occasional controversy.

Oystercatchers and knot in the high-tide roost at Snettisham, Norfolk.

Oystercatcher is still known as shalder in Shetland and is one of the most widely used local names. There was even a local bus company named Shalder Coaches (with the appropriate symbol). Unfortunately they have recently been bought out and the symbol is now an Eagle! Shalder is supposed to come from the Old Norse name Tjalder, and compares with the name, Tjaldur, used in Iceland and Faroe, and Tjeld in Norway.[3]

'Skeldro', an Orcadian name used for both the wader and for shelduck, comes from an archaic dialect word, *sheld*, meaning pied or piebald. 'Scottie', too, is a reflection of the bird's plumage and finds its echo in the second element of a modern Swedish version, *Strandskata*, literally 'beach magpie'. This is very close to the old English name 'sea pie', which survived in common usage until the eighteenth century.

Oystercatchers can be remarkably long-lived. Robert Pinchen, an early warden at the tern colony on Blakeney Point, Norfolk, claimed that the male of an original pair present when he first arrived in 1900 was still breeding when he retired 31 years later.[4] Another individual was caught on the Wash in 1967 and was retrapped at Wainfleet, Lincolnshire, in September 2002. At 35 it holds the longevity record for any wader in Britain.[5]

The bird artist Eric Ennion, usually fastidious in his ornithological observations, wrote of the oystercatcher's 'blunt vermilion bludgeon', which slightly exaggerates the bill's orange-pink colour.[6] But there is no disputing its enormous physical strength, which enables an oystercatcher to prise open a mussel shell's heaviest armour or to hammer limpets clean off the rocks.

Their largely shellfish diet once confined oystercatchers to coastlines and they are still very much birds of tidal estuaries and rocky shores. However, in the eighteenth century, breeding oystercatchers began a steady advance along inland waterways, particularly in Scotland, where a very high percentage of Britain's 38,000 pairs breed. They are now widespread across almost all of the country and northern England, where they will even nest on grazing pasture well away from water. In the English Midlands they are regularly found on old gravel pits, and in East Anglia oystercatchers have steadily colonised arable land along the river valleys.

A more recent adaptation is stranger still: the habit of nesting on rooftops as occurs in Aberdeen and other Scottish towns:

In the early 1970s I used to watch Oystercatchers nesting on the gravel-covered roofs of the Aberdeen Royal Infirmary. Here was a synthetic beach if ever I saw one. Even today the habit continues in Aberdeen with some 250 pairs nesting on school and hospital roofs. Chicks do not always remain to the full free-flying stage before leaving. Some may throw themselves off the roofs as baby mallard will do and only very small ones survive.[7]

In winter the resident oystercatchers are joined by as much as 45 per cent of all Europe's population, when their numbers can swell to 300,000 birds. Spectacular concentrations occur on a number of estuaries such as Morecambe Bay and the Wash, and during the last century they were sometimes viewed as serious competition for the stocks of cockles and mussels taken in human fisheries. The classic conflict situation arose in the 1960–70s on the Burry Inlet near Llanelli in Carmarthenshire. Alarmed by a growth in the estuary's oystercatcher population, the local cockle gatherers claimed that the birds were damaging their harvest and demanded a cull.

It seemed as if they had a strong case. An oyster-catcher can take a cockle every 72 seconds and eat a daily total of around 500 shells and more than 11½ ounces (330gm) by weight. Despite a massive public outcry, the Ministry of Agriculture eventually gave way to the fishing interests and implemented a cull between 1972 and 1974. It is a perfect measure of how the relationship between a bird and its prey can be completely misunderstood that, following the elimination of 10,000 birds, the cockle stocks also collapsed.

In the 1990s in the Wash a more enlightened attitude accompanied the severe decline of oystercatchers from a previous total of 45,000 to just 10,000 by 1998. This was found to be triggered by a failure of both cockles and mussels in the estuary, itself attributed to the insidious hydra-headed impact of global climate change. Fortunately on this occasion the birds and fishermen have worked out a happier modus vivendi. Oystercatchers benefit from the human movement of young mussels from the sub-tidal areas on to beds in the intertidal zone. This brings the shellfish within reach of the feeding waders, which then perform a reciprocal service – selectively 'weeding' the smaller shells and reducing overall densities, thus allowing a healthy crop of harvestable mussels to develop.[8]

Sammy the black-winged stilt is one of Britain longest-staying rarities and now unofficial mascot for the RSPB's Titchwell reserve.

Black-winged Stilt, *Himantopus himantopus*. Proportional to its size, this is the longest-legged bird in the world. It has occurred in Britain and Ireland on more than 300 occasions, mainly as a spring and autumn vagrant from southern Europe. However, there have been surprise records of nesting stilts, most unusually in 1945 when certainly two, and possibly three, pairs bred in Nottinghamshire.

Perhaps even more exceptional is the individual male bird that appeared in Norfolk in August 1993 and eventually took up residence at Titchwell for the ensuing decade. He has been observed by tens of thousands of observers and has endeared himself to visitors and RSPB reserve staff alike, who eventually christened him 'Sammy'. The bird is now deeply embedded in the life of the reserve:

In recent years Sammy has become our unofficial mascot. Visitors to the reserve shop can now commemorate their sighting by buying polo shirts, hats, bodywarmers and a sweatshirt bearing his image or perhaps a limited-edition print of him in the company

Beautiful and delicately built, the avocet is also heroic in defence of its nest and young.

of the local avocets, by Robert Gillmor. So well known is he that in an advert for new RSPB members in the July 2002 *Birdwatching* magazine, Sammy was shown saying that he liked RSPB reserves so much he had never gone home to the Mediterranean![9]

His unwillingness to leave north Norfolk has sparked occasional controversy and it was rumoured that he may have escaped from a local bird collection. The more intriguing possibility is that Sammy was one of two young birds raised by a stilt pair which nested at Holme in 1987. As the stilt flies, Holme is just 2 miles (3.3km) from Titchwell, and it is suggested that Sammy's decade-long visit may have arisen out of loyalty to his natal area. Unfortunately British residence comes with its own complications: 'Each spring, as the sap rises up his long legs, Sammy's thoughts turn to sex and his attentions to the local oystercatchers, who can sometimes be seen looking worriedly over their shoulders when Sammy fixes his attention on the only other black-and-white bird with long pink legs to be found in Norfolk.'[10]

Avocet, *Avosetta recurvirostra*. With its refined black and porcelain-white plumage, needle-sharp uptilted bill and long legs, this is one of our most elegant waders. The odd name derives from an Italian version, *Avosetta*, whose meaning and origin are obscure, but it seems far more suited to so delicate a bird than many of the old coarse English alternatives like 'barker', 'clinker' and 'crooked bill'.

For all its refinement, the avocet was pushed to extinction in the nineteenth century by a combination of marshland drainage, over-shooting, the collection of its feathers for fishing flies and its eggs for the table. On the Norfolk coast a local Salthouse wildfowler recalled that 'in his young time he used to gather avocet's eggs, filling his cap, coat pockets, and even his stockings; and the poor people thereabouts made puddings and pancakes of them. The birds were also as recklessly destroyed, for the gunners, to unload their punt guns, would sometimes fire at and kill ten or twelve at a shot.'[11]

As the late Chris Mead mischievously pointed out, we owe the avocet's modern breeding presence in Britain to Adolf Hitler.[12] The flooding of vulnerable sections of the East Anglian coastline, and six wartime years completely without disturbance, formed the perfect background to the species' recolonisation. This was further helped by parallel circumstances on the coastlines of the Low Countries, where avocet populations underwent a

Left: The avocet is probably the most wide-spread bird symbol in Britain.

Right: This British Rail poster by R. B. Talbot-Kelly shows how the Havergate avocets quickly moved from top-level secret to tourist attraction.

Avocets and Ringed Plover, Havergate Island

SUFFOLK

SEE BRITAIN BY TRAIN — BRITISH RAILWAYS

similar revival. Today there are at least 650 pairs breeding along the east and south coasts of England from the Humber to Dorset, which represents a more-or-less complete recovery of its old eighteenth-century range.

Despite the upturn in its fortunes, the avocet is probably still most familiar to us as an icon rather than as a living creature. It has been the RSPB logo for half a century, initially in full silhouette (approved by the Society's council in October 1955) and then as the stylised head-and-shoulders image (1987) that we see today. The society's adoption of the symbol is rooted in a deep involvement in the bird's post-war recovery. Both Suffolk sites used by avocets as a bridgehead for recolonisation are still in RSPB hands, while Minsmere is widely considered the organisation's premier reserve.

The birds returned in the early spring of 1947 (a surprise appearance of two breeding pairs at Wexford in south-east Ireland in 1938 was never repeated), when four or five pairs settled at Havergate, a dune/shingle island just landward of Orford Ness. In the words of Gwen Davies, author of *The Return of the Avocet*, the RSPB offices were 'electrified by the news'.[13] It is a measure of the pioneering spirit among the early conservationists that voluntary wardens were rushed to the Havergate site, where the four men, including Philip Brown (future executive head of the RSPB) and the author Lieutenant-Colonel J. K. Stanford had to sleep top-to-toe in a small tent, living on wartime rations cooked on a single primus stove.

Simultaneously four pairs also arrived at Minsmere, but such was the secrecy surrounding the parallel events that neither set of guardians informed their colleagues. The birds themselves were referred to by a code word, 'zebras' – Zebra Island was a nickname used for Havergate itself – and when written accounts appeared in *British Birds* (1948 and 1949) and *The Times* of January 1950, entitled 'The Return of the Avocet', the true location remained undisclosed.[14]

Like much of the east coast, the island of Havergate was devastated by the huge surge tide on the night of 31 January/1 February 1953. The reserve's warden, Reg

Partridge, recalled that the avocets' nesting ground was covered by 'a vast reservoir of more than a hundred million gallons of water ... to a depth of five feet or more'. Remarkably, temporary repairs involving tens of thousands of sandbags ensured that the next avocet breeding season went off largely without a hitch, and the following winter the sea walls were completely rebuilt.[15]

In his fictionalised story describing the events surrounding the avocet colony at Minsmere, *Bledgrave Hall*, J. K. Stanford wrote of the birds in the highest possible terms: 'There is no wader which will sit so devotedly through floods and gales, even when a rising tide has lapped against the nest for hours and wrapped it in foam-flakes ... I know, too, no wader which is so wary or so heroic when breeding, dashing off with its shrill cry into the blue to attack a heron, or a crow or marauding gull.'[16]

With an increase in numbers, the avocet's image has lost a little of its original sheen. At some of the Norfolk reserves with large avocet colonies, the birds are notorious for their aggression. 'At Cley some people occasionally refer to them as Exocets – a play on words referring to the way, during the breeding season, they launch themselves and promptly chase off any and every interesting migrant wader that dares to come on to their pool!'[17]

Stone Curlew, *Burhinus oedicnemus*. VN: Norfolk Plover, Willy Reeve, Goggle-eyed Plover (East Anglia). The awkward scientific name derives from the Greek *bous* (an ox) and *rhis* (the nose); the second word is a combination of *oidos* (a swelling) and *kneme* (the knee). A loose literal translation ends up with the rather clumsy 'bull-nosed swollen knee', but it effectively captures two of the dominant features of this bizarre-looking wader – the short bulbous-tipped bill and the swollen tibiotarsal or 'knee' joint, from which the bird also takes its family name, thick-knee.

The other striking characteristic is better conveyed in an old piece of Norfolk vernacular, where it was once called the 'goggle-eyed plover'. Stone curlews are famous for their bright, or 'malevolently glaring', or even 'coldest and most cruel-looking straw-yellow eyes'.[18] These equip them well for a nocturnal lifestyle, but also gave rise to one of the strangest pieces of bird folklore in the European canon. From the time of the ancient Greeks possibly until the Middle Ages, it was believed that the look of a stone curlew could cure jaundice. Sir James Frazer, quoting directly from Plutarch, referred to it in *The Golden Bough*: '"Such is the nature . . . and such the temperament of the creature that it draws out and receives the malady which issues, like a stream, through the eyesight." So well recognised among bird-fanciers was this valuable property of the stone-curlew that when they had one of these birds for sale they kept it carefully covered, lest a jaundiced person should look at it and be cured for nothing.'[19]

Aside from their strange looks, the birds also produce a loud quavering call that is often transcribed as '*cour-lie*', and which explains their false association with the unrelated Eurasian curlew. The notes are often repeated with mounting intensity to convey an extraordinary and climactic sense of excitement or distress, and when a group of birds begins wailing in concert at dusk, they create a powerfully haunting atmosphere. Yet the vocabulary is large and varied, and wildlife-sound recordist Eric Simms discovered that the birds are also capable of more tender vocalisations:

In the summer of 1952 I recorded ten separate calls used by adult stone curlews and their young. I concealed a microphone by the nest. After some exploratory pecking, which came over the loudspeaker as a series of deafening bangs, the hen bird accepted it without demur. I recorded change-overs and conversations at the nest. Then at 8 p.m. on 15 May I listened in amazement to faint vocal sounds coming from the chick inside one of the egg-shells that I knew was still unbroken. I recorded the actual conversation that then ensued between the hen stone curlew and the unhatched chick. The clucking notes of the hen became more rounded and mellow as the chick's faint 'Qu'eeks' grew stronger. The steady alternation of calls between mother and baby showed that it was a real conversation.

Simms suggests that it 'must have been a unique event in the history of wildlife sound recording'.[20]

Stone curlews are primarily birds of treeless, stony steppe or grassland and reach the north-western edge of their large trans-Eurasian range in Britain. Few people have more accurately or lovingly conveyed this rather bleak habitat than John Walpole-Bond, who described it as 'wild wastes sown broadcast with jagged flints, interspersed with low rank weeds and maybe a few starveling elders, thorns and brambles. Next . . . come more or less hog-backed ridges, now sparingly, now strongly, studded with thorn, elder, gorse, bramble and perhaps particularly juniper, with mole hillocks, stones, a sprinkling and fragments of dead wood marring the smoothness of the virgin sward.'[21]

Despite the open character of such landscapes, stone curlews are remarkably difficult birds to spot. Their dark-streaked sandy plumage is usually perfect camouflage against the stony short-cropped vegetation. Even the bright-yellow legs blend with the usually pale-toned substrate, so that 'from a distance, a thick-knee can look like simply a head and body moving smoothly, effortlessly and mysteriously forwards'.[22]

Abroad, stone curlews are often close neighbours of the great bustard (in fact, early ornithologists like George Montagu divined in their similarities of lifestyle a family relationship, and Pennant referred to the curlew as the 'thick-kneed bustard'). In Britain the two birds once shared much the same distribution, and stone curlews are still commonest in the bustard's former strongholds, around Salisbury Plain in Wiltshire and the East Anglian Breckland.

Early in the twentieth century they also ranged more widely across England south of a line between the Wash and Humber. Agricultural improvements saw the range steadily contract, and the more northerly Yorkshire and Lincolnshire populations were extinct by the 1930s. A nadir was reached in the 1980s, when there were only about 130 pairs nationally, but a highly intensive programme managed by the RSPB has since brought about a modest recovery.

Two small teams of roving field workers were first

The stone curlew is the focus of an intensive conservation initiative and has now doubled its number in twenty years.

employed in the 1980s to locate stone-curlew nests across Breckland and Wessex. If the birds are sitting in arable fields, the staff alert the farmer to the nest location and can be present to help if agricultural activity requires that the chicks or eggs be temporarily moved. Field workers also now measure the weight and size of the eggs and, by using a standard mathematical formula, can predict fairly accurately the date of hatching. This enables the farming to be planned around the birds, and the success of the project owes much to the willing cooperation of farmers and landowners.

Rob Lucking, RSPB conservation officer with responsibility for Breckland, writes:

The overall achievements during 20 years have been encouraging, with stone-curlews reaching 250 pairs by 2000. The single most important factor in the increase has been the field workers' direct intervention, but there have also been important statutory developments aimed at encouraging further increases. In 2001, English Nature designated over 14,000ha of arable land in the Brecklands as a Site of Special Scientific Interest for stone-curlew. The designation not only gives additional protection to those nesting on arable land, but also pays farmers to carry out special management prescriptions, such as creating nesting plots within fields or spraying off areas of growing crops that threaten to engulf the stone-curlew nest. In due course, this land will form part of the Breckland Special Protection Area to be designated under the EU Birds Directive.

The ultimate aim is to increase the UK's stone-curlew population to 300 pairs by 2010 and encourage birds to breed in more secure semi-natural habitats, rather than in arable crops. This would not only reduce dependence on direct intervention, but stone-curlews nesting on good quality Brecks heathland tend to be more successful and nest at higher densities than their arable-nesting compatriots.[23]

Unfortunately the birds themselves have their own ideas on what constitutes a suitable nest site:

No one could have predicted the events of 2001 when a pair of stone-curlews happily nested in the herbaceous border of a Breckland garden. Thanks to the under-

Stone curlews are encouraged to breed in high-quality heathland but, like this pair that nested in a Suffolk garden, birds have a habit of doing the unexpected.

standing of the householder, gardening and other activities were kept to a minimum. The stone-curlews were, however, nesting to a tight deadline as the householder's daughter was to hold her wedding reception in the garden less than a month after the nest was first found! Fortunately the stone-curlews managed to hatch two chicks which were large enough to be transferred into adjacent cow pasture before the big day.[24]

While an annual productivity per pair of just 0.65 chicks will maintain the population growth, and while stone curlews are long-lived birds with ringed individuals known to reach 18 years old, they are reluctant to expand beyond their core area. They remain dependent upon concerted human intervention when nesting on arable land and are highly vulnerable to any deterioration in their heathland habitat. Typically, they are adversely affected by the recurrent epizootics of myxomatosis and potentially by the rabbit haemorrhagic virus in the future. These diseases decimate the mammals whose endlessly grazing incisors maintain the short-cropped grassland that the birds love.

It may be many years before stone curlews form the kind of pre-migration flocks that were once such a feature of the Breckland area each autumn (in the early part of the twentieth century congregations of several hundred birds were recorded), although a flock of 97 at Gooderstone Warren, Norfolk, in autumn of 2001 gives strong grounds for hope.

Cream-coloured Courser, *Cursorius cursor*. This elegantly long-legged and desert-toned wader is an inhabitant of the arid steppes of North Africa and Central Asia and has occurred on just 33 occasions in the last 200 years. The most recent was on Scilly in September 2004.

Thomas Hardy referred to one of the earliest records in a passage in *The Return of the Native*. The individual was seen in Dorset in 1853 by the Earl of Ilchester, who rather predictably ordered his keeper to shoot it. In the novel Hardy describes its slaughter at the hands of 'a barbarian', perhaps intending that the fatal visitation of a lost bird stand as an oblique symbol for his tragic heroine Eustacia Vye, who is similarly doomed and out of place amid the brooding primal landscape of Egdon Heath.[25]

One of the more remarkable among the subsequent courser records was a long-staying bird seen at Blakeney and Ormesby in Norfolk from 18 October until 15 November 1969. The bird became exceptionally tame and would even take maggots from the hand, until it was finally found dead at Ormesby and its skin was preserved at Norwich Castle Museum.[26]

Little Ringed Plover, *Charadrius dubius.* VN: LRP (birders). With its black necklace and shining golden eye-ring, this dainty plover has a massive world range across the whole of Eurasia, from Japan westwards to the Atlantic palm-fringed wadis of North Africa. While Britain also lies on the western edge of its range, the LRP is now found so widely across England and Wales – with recent outlying toeholds in southern Scotland – that it is difficult to recover the enormous buzz of excitement it once generated.

Yet it started to breed only 65 years ago, and prior to that moment it had been nothing more than an ultra-rare vagrant. The first-ever nest was found at Hertfordshire's Tring Reservoirs in 1938, but the species only resumed its UK invasion just as the Allies were readying themselves for the Normandy beaches. In 1944 it returned to Tring and to a gravel pit in the Ashford district of Middlesex, where a pair nested 'near a narrow-gauged railway on which a locomotive and trucks passed to and fro with loads of washed gravel. Dozens of children were playing, sailing boats, and throwing sticks into a pool which was within the little ringed plovers' territory.'[27]

The blend of heavy plant and continuous disturbance seemed unlikely conditions for a rare bird's breeding success, but they have been a constant background to the colonisation. LRPs have flourished best amid the detritus of twentieth-century industrial society. In fact their favourite nest sites read like a catalogue of the country's most unloved and unlovely landscapes: refuse dumps, sewage works, industrial tips, ash lagoons at power stations, flashes in the vicinity of mining subsidence, flooded slag or spoil heaps associated with open-cast mine complexes, gravel pits, man-made reservoirs, disused airfields, quarry and brick clay pits, factory dumps and, 'in Metropolitan Essex, on clinker among junked car bodies'.[28]

It is perhaps the deep contrast between the bird's initial jewel-like rarity and the industrial grime which it frequented that helped to stir people's imagination. This was perfectly captured in Kenneth Allsop's novel, *Adventure Lit Their Star.* A John Llewellyn Rhys Memorial prize winner in 1950, the book describes both the bird's unexpected adaptation to the English industrial scene and the intense excitement that this engendered. Its hero Richard Locke, a convalescent RAF pilot, is also an embodiment of the extreme protectiveness shown by

The little ringed plover is one of several bird species benefiting from industrial gravel extraction.

many local birdwatchers towards the LRP's pioneering efforts. Locke is particularly determined to foil the intentions of an elderly man in 'pepper-and-salt tweed' suit, called Colonel D. E. R. Goodwin, who is a notorious egg collector and the novel's stagy villain.

Wilful disturbance and egg theft remain a constant menace today, but this has not prevented the bird's steady spread which, for several decades, maintained an annual average increase of 15 per cent. By 1950 there were about 30 pairs, by 1962, 158 pairs and 230 just five years later. John and Eileen Parrinder, who assembled all the national records and published them in a sequence of papers over four decades, noted an almost exact correlation between the LRP's advance and the post-war building boom.[29] This was manifest in a 200 per cent increase in gravel and sand production between 1944 and 1962, particularly in a belt of southern England between south Suffolk and Berkshire, which was the bird's initial bridgehead. In a paper in 1964 John Parrinder suggested that a doubling of gravel production in Wales was likely to presage the LRP's arrival as a breeding bird. Sure enough, his prediction was quickly borne out and there are now more than 50 Welsh nest sites and, nationwide, in excess of 1000 breeding pairs.

Ringed Plover, *Charadrius hiaticula*. VN: Ringedy (Yorkshire); Sandy Lu/Sandy Lo (Shetland); Sand Lo/o, Sanloo, Sain Lo, Sinloo, Sand Laverock, Sand Lark, Sandy Lavro (Orkney). Colin Harrison perfectly captured the now-you-see-me, now-you-don't manner of this brightly patterned, highly vocal plover:

This is the small worried wader that tends to suddenly appear on an apparently empty beach, making the conscientious holiday-maker almost scared to lower a foot, for fear of crushing a nest that is too well camouflaged. It is small, squat and rounded, the dark eye almost hidden in the bridled head patterns. In spite of this bold patterning, it is not conspicuous. The dark face-patch provides false countershading that turns the bird's head into two rounded pebbles that are lost on a shingle beach.[30]

The ringed plover is a species of sub-Arctic and Arctic coastlines on the south-western edge of its world range in Britain and Ireland. The main breeding concentrations are on the open sandy flats known as machair on the North and South Uists in the Outer Hebrides. They are also common in Orkney and Shetland, where the wide range of local names pays homage to the bird's beach-loving lifestyle (*lo* being the Norse word for plover).

In spring the species can be found on most areas of British and Irish coast where there are stretches of sandy or shingle beach. Ringed plovers are easiest to see when they perform a curious, slow-winged 'butterfly' display flight accompanied by a call that resembles the sound of a wheezing pump. The eggs are laid in a shallow scrape hollowed from the sand, are pebble-like in colour, beautifully camouflaged and, as a consequence, highly vulnerable to the trampling feet of unwitting holiday-makers. During the twentieth century ringed plovers were victims of our growing passion for seaside recreation. Their numbers declined steeply on some coasts, particularly in Wales and south-west England, although the species has partly compensated by occupying many new inland sites such as reservoirs and gravel pits.

Kentish Plover, *Charadrius alexandrinus*. VN: KP (birders). There is a melancholy irony in the name, because Kent is not a county where it continues to breed; rather it is the place where the bird was hounded to extinction. Now Kentish plovers are no more than annual visitors in very small numbers. They last nested in 1979 – in Lincolnshire, where two young were raised – and this isolated pair ended a 23-year absence from the mainland.

Yet in the nineteenth century the species had been relatively numerous on the coasts of Kent and Sussex. Dr John Latham discovered the British population when specimens were sent to him from Sandwich Bay. Sadly, its separation from the similar ringed plover drew the attention of taxidermists and egg collectors. They doggedly pursued the highly localised birds, particularly at their stronghold on the shingle stretch between Dungeness and Rye Harbour, and many hundreds were killed or robbed of their eggs. Full legal protection only came into effect in 1904, when just a handful of pairs remained. These gradually built up to around 40 pairs, but a second decline set in with the development of seaside tourism on the Kentish coast and by 1931 the birds had gone completely.[31]

Contrary to its parochial name – it is known as the snowy plover across the Atlantic – the bird is highly cosmopolitan and has a world range spanning five continents. It breeds widely on the other side of the Channel coastline, but even here disturbance seems to be driving a long-term decline.

It has an unusual habit of burying its eggs, point downwards, in the fine beach material on which it nests. The loose sand and shell fragments apparently fall on the eggs as the sitting bird rotates its body, although elsewhere in Europe Kentish plovers have been observed to deliberately scrape sand on to the clutch, both to disguise it and to keep the eggs cool.

Greater Sand Plover, *Charadrius leschenaultii*. It seems an extraordinary coincidence that the first records of this extremely rare bird and of its twin, the **Lesser Sand Plover**, *C. mongolus* – neither of which normally approaches closer to Britain and Ireland than the Red Sea coast of Africa – were both at Pagham Harbour in Sussex. The former species appeared in December 1978, the latter 19 years later in August 1997.

Dotterel, *Charadrius morinellus*. One of our most beautiful and endearing waders is probably best seen among Britain's highest upland landscapes, such as the Cairngorm massif. In late spring it is possible to find dotterels on the short heath-like vegetation of the plateaux tops, where there is an additional twist of pleasure in seeing their lovely summer colours. For once these are brightest not on the male, but on the adult female.

Dotterels reverse the usual gender roles, the cock bird assuming almost all of the duties of incubation and chick rearing, while the hen performs the normally masculine functions of courtship. As well as being more brightly coloured, she song-flights to attract her dowdier mate and, on laying the clutch of eggs, often abandons their care entirely to him or occasionally takes a second partner.

Dotterel is one of the very few birds to nest on the arctic-alpine heath of Britain's highest mountains, such as the Cairngorms.

In Britain the prolific student of upland birds, Desmond Nethersole-Thompson, was the first to uncover this polyandrous behaviour. In June 1934 he found a dotterel nest in the Cairngorms and instantly recognised the uniquely patterned eggs of a female that he had christened 'Blackie'. A few weeks later he found a second clutch of Blackie's eggs being incubated by a separate male partner.

Nethersole-Thompson's studies, which continued over five decades and involved 'camping for hundreds of nights on the roof of Scotland', and which also engaged the independent efforts of his wife and six children, culminated in a classic book, *The Dotterel*.[32] Its author noted that dotterels were particularly attracted to nest on peaks with broad backs and long ridges, and advised

those seeking the bird in western Scotland to watch out for hill crests looking like stranded whales.[33]

Nethersole-Thompson's pursuit of our highest-breeding species – Scottish birds seldom nest below 3000 feet (900m) – was made a little less arduous by the creature's remarkably confiding manner. The second element in the scientific name, *morinellus*, means 'little fool', while 'dotterel' itself (which has the same linguistic root as 'dotard' and 'dotty') dates from at least the early fifteenth century and carries similar pejorative associations. It reflects the great ease with which bird catchers once trapped it (although W. B. Lockwood has also argued that the first syllable 'dot' is an onomatopoeic re-creation of its single-note call).[34]

The full extent of the bird's supposedly foolish

character was outlined by the Elizabethan poet, Michael Drayton:

> The dotterel, which we think a very dainty dish,
> Whose taking makes such sport, as no man more could wish:
> For as you creep, or cower, or lie, or stoop, or go,
> So marking you with care the apish bird doth do;
> and acting everything, doth never mark the net,
> Till he be in the snare which men for him have set.[35]

Subsequent studies have never borne out these mimetic habits. In fact, quite the reverse. In the seventeenth century John Ray described how Norfolk bird catchers worked in teams to drive dotterels into nets, adding that 'The birds ... do often stretch themselves, putting out a Wing or a Leg and in imitation of them the men that drive them thrust out an Arm or Leg for fashion sake, to comply with an old custom.'[36] It begs the question whether the real fool was human or avian.

Yet there are undoubtedly many stories to confirm the species' extraordinary fearlessness. The Swedish photographer Bengt Berg wrote a book entitled *My Friend the Dotterel*, in which he published images of a bird incubating its eggs as they and the nest lining were held on his hand, while resting in his lap.[37] Scottish birds have shown themselves to be no less confiding. The naturalist and wildlife sound recordist Eric Simms recalls trekking into the central Grampians to capture the calls of dotterels. He placed his parabolic reflector microphone close to a nest, where there was:

> a conflict between the female who was interested in laying the second egg and the male who wanted to brood the first. It was blisteringly hot on the mountain top. The male finally got his way and his mate stood close by panting in the heat. She then walked over to the reflector, studied it closely and realised that it was the only bit of shadow on the whole mountain top. She squatted down within six inches of the reflector completely in its shade and remained there for three-quarters of an hour. How wonderful it was that after lugging this strange object some 3500 feet up a mountain that I should see it used as a sunshade by one of the rarest birds in Britain![38]

The dotterel is thought to be a relict species from a much colder era, when it was far more widely spread. Now it has a highly fragmented range, which appears on a world map as a far-flung archipelago of small, high-altitude 'islands'. In southern Europe there are localised populations in the Romanian Carpathians, the Austrian Alps and the Monte Maiella massif of central Italy. Yet the heart of the main breeding area is more than 1700 miles

Dotterel was long considered a delicacy and the migrant birds were regularly hunted at their resting spots, such as the chalk heaths near Dotterell Hall in South Cambridgeshire.

(2875km) away in northern Scandinavia, while the Scottish highlands represent the bird's westernmost outpost.

In the last two decades the British birds have significantly spread, both in number and distribution. There are now irregular breeding records from the Lake District and North Wales, while a recent national estimate of 630 pairs represents a sixfold increase from a census in the 1970s. This may well be as much a recovery of former haunts as it is a true expansion, since dotterels were persecuted, particularly in the nineteenth and early twentieth centuries, owing to their reputation as a table delicacy and for their feathers, which were highly prized in the making of fish-flies.

However, the traditions of hunting dotterel go back until at least the late Middle Ages. Most were taken as the migrant flocks, or 'trips' as they are known, passed through England on their way to and from North Africa. Sometimes involving scores of birds, the trips were highly faithful to a number of stopover localities and these often acquired the name of 'dotterel fields'. One old haunt near Reighton, Yorkshire, is said to have 'attracted gamekeepers from a wide area, prompting the building of the "Dotterel Inn" to accommodate' them.[40] The pub survives to this day.

South Cambridgeshire is another area with a deserved reputation for the bird, and has a Dotterell Hall near Balsham with a Dottrell Hall four miles north-east of Royston.[41] The whole community around the second town was said to turn out for 'Dotterel Day' in the second week of May, when the birds were a choice item in the marketplace. King James I maintained a hunting stables near Newmarket and was a regular on the high chalk country around Royston, especially 'at ye season for shooting dotterails'.[42]

Record-breaking flight – an argument about how fast golden plovers can fly was the background to The Guinness Book of Records.

Although these sporting traditions have long since lapsed, it is extraordinary how true dotterels are to their ancient routine. In 1972 the fields around the Dotterell Hall near Balsham hosted a trip of 20 birds, many arriving within hours of their designated 'Dotterel Day' of 12 May.

European Golden Plover, *Pluvialis apricaria*. VN: Goldie (widespread); Plivver (Orkney and Shetland); Plooti (Shetland). Golden plover seem to come in two guises. In spring and early summer it is the solitary, yellow-spangled, black-bellied bird, whose mournful fluting cadence seems to express the essence of wilderness in the British uplands. Yet by autumn it has become a rather plain-looking, green-toned wader gathered in nervous flocks on English pasture or stubble and given to sudden 'dreads', when it whistles across the sky in large fast-moving formations.

The goldie's wing is much more narrow and pointed than a lapwing's, while the flight is correspondingly more direct and the impression of speed underscored by a rather shallow flickering wing action. Quite how fast the birds fly has been a matter of some significance. In 1951

an Irish shooting party hotly disputed whether the golden plover was Europe's fastest game bird. Three years later at Castlebridge House in County Wexford the debate was resumed, this time centring on which was quicker: a red grouse or a goldie. One of those involved in both controversies was inspired to commission a book to settle just such pointless arguments. His name was Sir Hugh Beaver, managing director of the Guinness brewery, and the work he inspired has since become one of the world's bestselling titles, *The Guinness Book of Records* (now entitled *Guinness World Records*).[42]

In winter the British and Irish goldies are joined by large numbers of birds from Iceland and Scandinavia. Although there are several impressive concentrations at major wetlands, such as the Wash and Carmarthen Bay (16,000 and 7000 respectively in an average winter), most birds are gathered on inland areas, particularly south of the Humber or east of the Severn, while roughly equal numbers are spread across the Irish central and southern inland counties. These continental influxes have previously led to British and Irish totals of 600,000 birds, although a deterioration in the quality of their winter habitat – particularly the 'improvement' of old pasture – has led recently to much smaller national totals.

Wintering goldies are often found in association with lapwings, and the whole flock may include a liberal sprinkling of black-headed and common gulls. All these birds feed on worms, although only the goldies and lapwings are involved in the direct act of catching them. The gulls get their quota by chasing and stealing them from the waders (see Common Gull, page 236), particularly the golden plovers, which are partly compensated by the increased vigilance of their assailants.

The bird's appearance in autumn may have helped cement the plover's generic reputation as a harbinger of bad weather. 'Many fowlers maintain that golden plover move off before a frost and that their departure foretells hard weather.'[43] 'Plover' in both modern and historic European languages reveals an association with rain. In French it is *pluvier* (*pluie*, rain) and in Latin it was *ploviarius* (*pluvia*, rain). The current scientific name *Pluvialis* means 'bringing rain' and underscores the *ex post facto* reasoning that permeates much bird folklore. Since birds like goldies appeared in autumn – the season of rain and storms – they eventually acquired a causal link with the weather conditions.

The goldie's capacity to foretell the future once intertwined with the more sinister legend of the 'seven whistlers', an old superstition from Wales and western counties of England, in which six unidentified birds were said to call constantly during their search for a seventh. The birds were taken as an augury of death or disaster, while in Shropshire it was held that on finding their lost companion the seven whistlers would foretell the end of the world. The Victorian folklorist Charles Swainson argued in favour of the goldie as the bird behind the myth. There is certainly a haunting melancholy to golden-plover vocalisations, but tying the legend to any single species overlooks a number of other candidates (for example, wigeon, whimbrel and curlew) and ignores the fluid, imprecise character of most of these myths.[44]

Grey Plover, *Pluvialis squatarola*. If the golden plover's plaintive note expresses the soul of our northern uplands, then few sounds better evoke the windswept space of a winter estuary than the mournful trisyllable of the grey plover.

This bird is an almost exclusively coastal wader compared with its moor-dwelling relative, but both are often treated together as 'tundra plovers', while Abel Chapman included them in another wader group, which he christened the 'globe-spanners'.[45] Grey plovers fully justify the title. The circumpolar breeding range embraces the northernmost lands on earth, yet wintering birds can be found along almost the entire coastline of the whole southern hemisphere, and even down to Australia's Macquarie Island, beyond the 54° S meridian.

The bureacratic anonymity conjured by 'grey' plover understates their striking appearance, and the French and Dutch names, which both translate as 'silver plover', more accurately capture the delicate patterning of the white-spangled upperparts. The name used in America, 'black-bellied plover', refers to the beautiful pied breeding dress, and birds are regularly seen in this condition in Britain. The species' long-distance migration entails an arrested moult for some populations and adults can be found in almost full summer plumage right into early winter.

Northern Lapwing, *Vanellus vanellus*. VN: Green Plover, Peewit, Pewit (widespread in England and Scotland); Pie-wipe (Norfolk); Pee-wee (Lincolnshire); Chewit (Lancashire); Lappy (Yorkshire); Tuefit (County Durham); Toppyup (Borders); Peasiewheep (east Scotland); Teeack, Teeick, Teeo, Teewhup, Teewhuppo, Thievnick, Thievnig (Orkney); Plivver, Peeweep, Peeweet, Ticks Nicket, Tieve's Nacket (Shetland). Few birds have created as large a cultural legacy in Britain as the most beautiful of our plovers. Certainly none has more surviving vernacular names. These, together with an even longer list of obsolete versions (assembled in Ken Spencer's classic account of the bird's social history, *The Lapwing in Britain*), are testimony to its eye-catching spring display, its unforgettable vocalisations and our historical attachment to its flesh and eggs as food.

It looks essentially black and white at any distance, but the lapwing's dark upperparts resolve into a rich bottle-green glossed in parts with bronze and magenta iridescence at close range. The species is as distinctive in shape as it is in colour, and Francesca Greenoak has noted how the broad, almost owl-like wings give the flight an appearance of being 'flappy and unmanageable', when it is in fact 'beautifully controlled'.[46]

The *Oxford English Dictionary* indicates that the bird's common name is a reflection of the striking flight action, although W. B. Lockwood considers it a combination of two Anglo-Saxon words, *læpi* ('crest'), and *-wince* ('a word having a primary sense of moving up and down'). Thus, lapwing is a name where a part – the bobbing crest – stands for the whole.[47] The exact origin is possibly beyond etymological proof, although we know for certain that the two characteristics lie behind a number of archaic alternatives: flight ('flopwing', 'flapjack', 'wallock', 'wallop' or 'wallopie wep') and crest ('horneywink/s' or 'horny wick', 'hornpipe' or 'hornpie').

The lapwing presents us with another fascinating conundrum. The species is so intimately associated with every kind of farmed countryside, from the Scottish

From Pewit to Teewhuppo, the lapwing probably has more regional names than any other British bird.

Highlands and Welsh sheep hills to the arable plains of south-east England, that we have almost a shared ecological history. For more than 2000 years the lapwing's annual cycle has marked the seasonal round in the rural landscape. It is, for example, the classic herald of spring and in modern times few birds are more popular:

When I was farming in North Lincolnshire during the 1960s there were plenty of nesting lapwings and I was delighted to hear their calls and watch their aerobatics. The ploughmen would always carry the eggs from a nest in their path to a safe spot in a newly turned furrow.[48]

Whenever I hear lapwings it immediately takes me back to being a child on North Ronaldsay [Orkney]. I love to hear them. It always strikes me as joyful and life-affirming. It's the sound of late spring, of people ploughing or working out in the fields.[49]

I grew up on a small 50-acre family farm in rural Aberdeenshire. Lapwings and oystercatchers success-

fully raised young on our fields year after year. I can still sense the joy all this time after the event. When their nests contained eggs, we used a marking system to pinpoint their location and it helped us to get on with disking the over-wintered ploughed ground without destroying them. Disaster did strike once when the marker disappeared from view. As a boy of around 10, I was totally inconsolable at what happened that day.[50]

One of my own most treasured childhood memories is of lying in bed with the window open, listening to the sound of lapwings in mid-March. The male birds continued to perform their looping sky-dance long into the moonlit Derbyshire evenings and not only could I hear those high, slurred, wheezy notes on which so many local names play, but also that delicious creaking throb from the bird's outer flight feathers – a sound aptly described by Desmond Nethersole-Thompson as the bird's 'wing music'.[51]

In his meditation on the importance of grass in human culture, *The Forgiveness of Nature*, Graham Harvey suggests that 'No other plant family has played such a dominant role in the advance of the human species.' He goes on to argue that grassland is the habitat in which we feel our deepest sense of physical and spiritual freedom, an echo of the time when we first moved on to the African savannas from the forest.[52] It would seem fitting that two of the most benign birds of British grassland, lapwing and skylark, should be part of this positive response. Given that both species benefited from the felling of hundreds of millions of acres of Europe's wildwood, the birds' airborne displays were, in a sense, a hymn to neolithic man's agricultural triumph. There is certainly a long tradition of treating skylark song as almost synonymous with joy, yet for hundreds of years lapwings were viewed in a very different light.

'The false lapwynge, ful of trecherye' was Chaucer's verdict in the *Parlement of Fowles*, while John Gower called it 'the bird falsest of all'.[53] In the fifteenth century William Caxton described it as a 'foul and villainous bird'[54] and Shakespeare has his womanising fop, Lucio, boast in *Measure for Measure*, (Act I, Scene 4)

> . . . 'tis my familiar sin
> With maids to seem the Lapwing, and to jest
> Tongue far from heart . . .

Prostitutes and deceitful women were known in the seventeenth century as 'plovers', while betrayal was added to the lapwing's list of vices by the Protestant Covenanters of Scotland, who claimed that the bird's

Despite a huge decline in the breeding population, a wheeling black-and-white line of lapwings is still a common winter sight in many parts of Britain.

calls gave away their whereabouts when they were hiding from their pursuers. Even now the habit dies hard. While it may be an exaltation of larks, the collective for lapwings is a 'deceit', and in Shetland the current vernacular name, 'tieves' nacket', means the thieves' imp.

The long history of reproach hinges on the lapwing's distraction display in defence of its eggs and young, when it may drag its wings along the ground as if injured, or simply call hysterically to lure the attention of possible predators. Lapwing eggs were popular as food and, while it seems deeply unfair, our ancestors condemned the bird for its efforts to protect them.

The harvest of eggs appears to have been an ancient, widespread and systematic practice. Thomas Bewick records a price of three shillings a dozen in the 1820s, while early eggs could command as much as eight pence each, the equivalent of 20 gull eggs, which were by no means disregarded at high table. Lapwing eggs were undoubtedly prized both as a delicacy and for their aesthetic appeal.[55] It was apparently traditional to serve them hot or cold, complete with their shells in a basket lined with moss, which no doubt emphasised their

beauty. Another form of presentation was to peel and pile them up in a dish surrounded by a ring of aspic jelly.

They were also valued for their high nutritional qualities:

In 1937 I was 6 years old and living in Colne, Lancashire. During the spring I had a severe chest infection. My father and uncle searched for a tewit's nest and brought home two eggs which were beaten with milk and sugar for me to eat raw. These eggs were believed to be 'stronger' than pullet's eggs. It was also believed that although birds could not count, two eggs should be taken to avoid desertion of the nest as the parent would notice a change from odd to even, or vice versa.[56]

London was the main market for lapwing eggs over a wide area of southern England, and they were particularly heavily collected in places like east Norfolk, then transported to the capital, even long before the arrival of the railways. A single operator, Isaac Harvey, was moving 600–700 eggs a week during spring and early summer in the 1820s. Another egger working the marshes around Potter Heigham took 160 dozen (1920 eggs: a minimum of 420 clutches), while a Yarmouth game dealer sent 600 dozen eggs to London in 1834 (including many similarly coloured eggs of redshank, snipe, ruff, black-headed gull and possibly black tern).[57]

These high levels of harvest were often completely unsustainable, as indicated by figures produced by C. B. Ticehurst from a Breckland estate near Thetford. In the 1860s, 3360 eggs were being taken annually. This had fallen to 720 by the 1880s and dropped again to just 72 by 1902. In 1915 there were only 20 lapwing pairs left.[58] Although the taking of lapwing eggs declined in the twentieth century, it was briefly revived during the Second World War:

> I remember going with my father to collect birds' eggs. These were mainly lapwings but also the occasional curlew. I think we were allowed to take such eggs up to 14 April. These were then taken by a man from the Ministry of Food to be used in the making of a dehydrated egg powder which was part of the 'egg ration'. I never saw money change hands but I'm sure that Dad wouldn't have done this for nothing.[59]

Lapwing eggs can still be collected under licence, although this is now exceptional and the open season ends on 15 April, thus ensuring that any harvested clutches can be replaced. However, an echo of the old egging days survives in a piece of vernacular from northeast Lincolnshire:

> The local name for lapwing in Grimsby used to be pyewipe and there's an area to the west of Grimsby Docks bordering the Humber estuary called Pyewipe, which is good for roosting curlew and black-tailed godwit these days and presumably, at one time, for lapwings.
>
> When I was a child, if I asked a daft question like 'where's mum?', my dad or pretty well any other adult would answer sarcastically 'gone eggin'' which I never understood at the time. The full version was 'gone eggin' back o' Doigs', with 'Doigs' being an old shipwrights on the dock. So 'back o' Doigs' would have been referring to the West Marsh or Pyewipe area. When I've thought about this more recently, it's occurred to me that the saying may well have referred to poor folk hunting for plovers' eggs and those of other wild birds on the marshland in bygone days. It was quite a common saying in the town and I bet it's still used in some families.[60]

The adult birds are no longer legal quarry, although at one time they were also killed in vast numbers. In Mrs Beeton's *Household Management*, she suggested that in

Lapwings are so eye-catching at all seasons that they have become embedded in local place names. This sign is on the outskirts of Grimsby.

the mid-nineteenth century the London market was 'sometimes so much glutted with them that they are sold very cheap'.[61] The practice survived well into the last century and Billy Bishop, the former warden of Cley Marshes in Norfolk, recalled in his autobiography that 'Of all the birds that were eaten by such families as mine, there is none to compare, in my opinion, with the Lapwing or green plover. Plover pie was a real treat.'[62]

One of the main sources of lapwings was in the Fens, where the washmen killed them with punt-guns. Some of the record bags from a single shot suggest a very high harvest: near Whittlesey in Cambridgeshire a father-and-son team killed 58 and 65 plovers with two shots.[63] Another standard method was to use clap-nets. The wildfowlers maintained artificially flooded scrapes, which were particularly attractive to lapwings if the surrounding levels were dry. These traditional plover-netting sites, with local names such as Snushall's Plover Hole, Hugh's Hole and Peak's Plover Hole were passed down within families through the generations.[64] In her biography of Peter Scott, who lived on the Nene Washes in the 1930s, Elspeth Huxley gives an account of their methods:

> The plover-netter spread his net on water just deep enough to conceal it and beneath the flight-paths of flocks of plovers coming in at dawn to wash themselves after feeding in muddy potato fields. Tempted by the decoys, they alighted on the water, and when twenty or thirty of them were in the right position, the man would jerk the rope which released the springs that controlled the poles, and the net rose and folded over the birds like the pages of a book. The

netter quickly killed the birds, extracting them from the net, flung them into a sack and set the trap ready for the next lot. Plovers were there in tens of thousands in those days. One of the last surviving Fenmen, Ernie James recalled his record morning's catch of 240 birds. As a boy, he cycled six miles to the railway station with a sack of plovers over each handle bar, each sack containing up to a hundred birds, to catch the London train. Back came substantial payments from Leadenhall market dealers, who had no trouble selling plovers to restaurants whose customers accounted them a delicacy.[65]

Scott was impressed by the skills of the plover-netter and adapted the methods of one old wildfowler, Berney Shawl, for more benign puposes – to catch geese so that they could be ringed. This eventually set him on the road to developing his rocket nets, which are still used by the Wildfowl & Wetlands Trust today (see Pink-footed Goose, page 72.

Direct persecution may have ended, but unfortunately lapwings have not prospered in the modern farming environment. The population has undergone a dramatic slump, with a virtual halving of breeding numbers in just 11 years. The disappearance of this agricultural totem is thought to be driven by the loss of mixed farming, increased agrochemical use and the switch from spring to autumn sowing of cereals. In Wales, where a decline of 75 per cent is the worst in Britain, the subsidy-driven over-stocking of the traditional sheep hills is considered a major factor. In England there is now a pronounced north–south divide, with lapwings surviving best in the uplands. So the village of Tewitfield near Lancaster is more likely still to support its eponymous bird than the beet-and-barley prairie around two other lapwing place names, Tivetshall St Mary and Tivetshall St Margaret near Diss, Norfolk.[66]

The scale of the decline is partly masked by a large influx of continental birds during winter. The sight of these lapwing congregations moving in perfect unison is one of the real treats of the winter countryside and all the more lovely when set against the featureless regiment of ridge and furrow presented by a bare field of earth. A more recent development in the lapwing's flocking habits is the post-breeding use of the roofs of warehouses and other commercial or industrial premises. It was first noted in 1984 (possibly as early as 1972) in Rochdale, but has since been recorded around Bolton, Bury, Oldham, Salford, Stockport, Wigan, Leeds and Bradford.

Rooftop flocks have even been recorded in busy town centres. The birds are thought to enjoy greater protection from predators, shelter from wind, and warmth from the building below. They also show a marked preference for

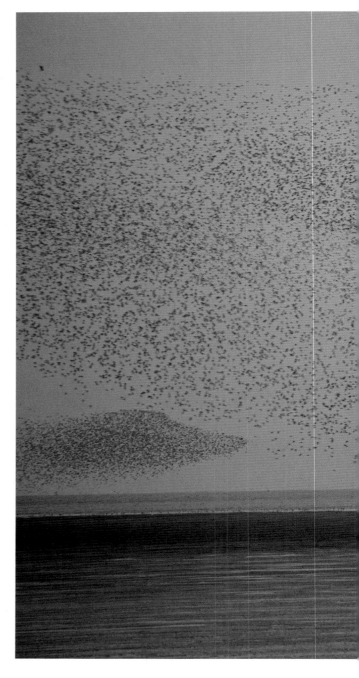

grey roofs – a choice that is closely paralleled by the lapwing's partiality to grey or brown fields on which to nest. The habit has since passed to other populations, with roof assemblies noted in Basingstoke (Hampshire) and Cumbernauld (Clyde), while breeding has even occurred on a factory roof at Hazel Grove near Stockport.[67]

Lapwings are particularly sensitive to low temperatures: 'The old names I remember my grandfather used to call lapwings was horneywinks and when it was very cold he would say, " 'tis cold enough to kill a horneywink".'[68] Frost and snow can trigger westerly movements of British lapwings to Ireland and France, a response that helped

The aerial movements performed by a flock of knot involve a mesmerising blend of seemingly telepathic coordination and volcanic energy.

cement the bird's former status as an omen of bad weather. It was exactly these conditions that have brought about some of the most extraordinary lapwing occurrences in America, where it is a rare vagrant. In December 1927 there was an unprecedented hard-weather movement of several hundred birds, which overshot Ireland and arrived in Newfoundland, one of them having been ringed as a chick at Ullswater in Cumbria the previous spring.[69]

Red Knot, *Calidris canutus*. The common name has long been thought to honour a connection with King Canute, although it probably also echoes the bird's odd monosyllabic call. 'Red' knot is something of an anomaly in Britain, because the glorious terracotta of its breeding plumage is usually seen only in late spring among a handful of final stragglers, just prior to their northerly migration. The species nests in Greenland and Arctic Canada amid barren stony plateaux that represent some of the most northerly terra firma on the planet.

Sanderling are the Keystone cops of the British seaside.

In Britain and Ireland knot are invariably in drab winter plumage, when singletons can be a pitfall for unwary observers. Medium-sized, with mid-grey upperparts and bill, and legs of anonymous colour and moderate length, the knot is best recognised by its lack of striking features. En masse, however, they present few identification problems. They are famous for the huge flocks that build up on a number of major English estuaries, such as the Thames, Ribble, Dee and Mersey, Morecambe Bay and the Wash. At the last as many as 150,000–200,000 were estimated at a single high-tide roost on 16 October 1993, which must be among the largest single-species groups of any bird (other than starling) recorded in Britain.[70] It is rather surprising that these congregations, which, in flight, look like mobile rain storms or mesmerising swirls of dense smoke, have not given rise to a collective noun.

Knot was once deemed 'really excellent eating' and was a great favourite among the old wildfowlers, particularly because they could bring down large numbers with a single shot.[71] The former warden at Cley Marshes in Norfolk, Billy Bishop, recalled an occasion when a Blakeney father-and-son team each fired their punt-gun at a dense knot congregation and downed 618 birds, including six dunlin and nine redshank.[72]

Nowadays, at places like Morecambe Bay and the Dee estuary, they are more valued as one of the great natural spectacles of the English seaside – a blend of seemingly telepathic coordination and sheer volcanic energy:

In autumn in the Cheshire Dee I borrowed a hide to put at the end of Middle Hilbre Island. Soon the rocky shelves of the island were being covered by water. As the birds rained down a grey mass of knots spread around the hide. More and more thrashed the air looking for spaces in which to drop and finally landed on the heads and backs of birds already down. I could have put out a hand and picked some of them up. There were some 5000 knot around the hide. The concert of bird calls deafened the ears but then the birds settled down to sleep. Twice I saw every bird swing its head from under its scapulars and look upwards. So rapid and simultaneous was the movement that a strange sensation ran up my spine. Was it a peregrine flying high above the island? As the waters receded, the great flock began to melt away. Should they be frightened, they take off with a roar of wings like the sound of an express train bursting forth from a tunnel.[73]

Sanderling, *Calidris alba*. With their purged surf-white bellies and palest grey upperparts, sanderling have an almost ghostly pallor as they dash along the wrackline of our winter beaches. Their high-speed action has all the mechanical rhythm of a clockwork toy. The manner in which they first scurry away from an incoming surge, then instantly reverse to follow it back out, also has something of the quality of those speeded-up cop chases popular in the silent-movie era.

Yet the comic note belies their heroic migration, which closely resembles that of the curlew sandpiper. There is evidence to suggest that birds breeding in northernmost Siberia can winter as far away as South Africa, a round trip of around 17,700 miles (29,500km).

Although they can be found on almost any British and Irish shoreline with intertidal mud or sand, they are most frequently found on the east coast of southern Scotland and England, and on the west coast between Cumbria and north Wales.

Semipalmated Sandpiper, *Calidris pusilla*. VN: Semi-P (birders). This rare transatlantic vagrant has been recorded on more than 100 occasions, and annually since 1980. The first ever was found by Peter Clarke at Cley, Norfolk, in July 1953. A subtle feature that separates it from most waders – other than the similar, but even rarer **Western Sandpiper**, *C. mauri* – is the palmation between the toes (hence its name). One of the more original measures taken to secure an accurate identification was Richard Richardson's plout across Arnold's Marsh in order to examine its footprints. Sadly the mud was too liquid to leave an accurate impression.[74]

A far more convivial version of the exercise was attempted for the second Irish record, when it was trapped at Ballymona, County Cork, on 16 October 1966. 'It is reputed to have been walked on the head of a pint of Murphy's stout in order to demonstrate the palmations when the bird was being examined in a local pub.'[75]

Little Stint, *Calidris minuta*. During their migrations to and from breeding grounds in Arctic Russia, these tiny sparrow-sized waders are regular spring and autumn visitors to a wide variety of British and Irish wetlands. They are probably most often found on large coastal freshwater lagoons, where their feeding action is characterised by a high-octane nervous energy, the fine bill working across the soft, muddy substrate like a sewing-machine needle.

If anything, the **Temminck's Stint**, *C. temminckii*, is a shade smaller than its relative, while its shorter legs give it a more crouching, mouse-like posture. No more than a few score birds pass through annually on their migration to Arctic Russia, but since the mid-1930s a handful has also been proved to breed sporadically in northern Scotland. In the last 20 years a regular nucleus of up to four pairs has been found.

It is remarkable how this unobtrusive bird of passage changes into a loud-trilling extrovert with moth-like display flight once it reaches the Scottish moors. The Temminck's stint's love-life is also highly complicated, with both sexes routinely mating with more than a single partner. The female will lay double and even triple clutches (and up to 12 eggs in 16 days), her mates brooding the first nest or nests while she incubates the last-laid eggs.[76]

Curlew Sandpiper, *Calidris ferruginea*. VN: Curly Sand (Yorkshire). Essentially this is an autumn visitor in small numbers mainly to the east coast, where it can easily be overlooked among larger flocks of dunlin. With their longer bill and legs, however, curlew sands are more elegantly proportioned birds and often the adults retain some or, occasionally, all of the rich russet underparts from their breeding costume.

Along with the sanderling, they perform one of the great migrations among British waders. The birds that arrive in Britain during autumn spend their winters in West Africa, yet they breed no nearer than the Taimyr peninsula in coastal Siberia, beyond the 80° E meridian and further east than the Nepalese capital of Kathmandu. From Mauritania to this vast tundra region and back is a round trip of 10,600 miles (17,000km) every year. Some Siberia-breeding curlew sands migrate as far as southern Australia, a one-way journey of 8375 miles (13,400km).

Purple Sandpiper, *Calidris maritima*. VN: Purp, Purp Sand (Yorkshire); Grollick (Fair Isle); Deafie (Shetland). Apart from a handful of pairs that have bred in northern Scotland in most years since 1978, this compact, dark, rock-loving wader of the Arctic and subarctic rim is mainly a winter visitor to the English north-east, the west coast of Ireland and Scotland, in particular the Outer Isles. It is remarkably sedentary in its habits and loyal to particular stretches of shoreline. A bird ringed on the Isle of May was retrapped there 14 years later, and was thought to have spent every winter during the intervening period in the same place.[77]

Although strictly coastal in distribution, purple sands seldom feed on the open beach, like turnstones. They are much more attached to boulders and rocky outcrops near the tideline. However, they will make an exception of certain man-made structures. On the Orkney island of North Ronaldsay, which holds one of the largest British concentrations (about 400 birds), they feed on the old cobbled slipways running down to the sea. In other areas they have adapted to the huge concrete blocks in breakwaters and, when their normal roosts are over-topped by high tides, they regularly resort to the pier head or its underlying metal struts.

At any distance the upperparts look brown-black, although good views reveal the purplish sheen from which the bird takes its name. It is seldom difficult to make a close approach to a purple sandpiper. An old Scottish name, 'blind dorbie', and the Shetland alternative, 'deafie', derive from the bird's seeming inability to recognise danger.

Dunlin, *Calidris alpina*. VN: Plover's Page (Orkney and Shetland); Tang Snipe (Shetland). With approximately half a million visiting us each winter, this is our most abundant shoreline bird – the commonest constituent in many wader congregations and the comparative baseline for the separation of similar family members, such as the two stints, curlew sandpiper and even the many transatlantic species of calidrine sandpipers that turn up here as vagrants, and which the Americans call 'peeps'.

Yet the recognition of dunlin itself is far from straightforward. At least three races occur in Britain and Ireland, *alpina*, *schinzii* and *arctica*. These differ considerably in appearance and size, with some runt specimens being almost as small as little stints. The confusion is compounded by striking seasonal plumage changes. While the summer bird is a dapper creature of high moorland, with almost fox-red upperparts and a sharp black oblong across a linen-white belly, by autumn it has metamorphosed into the anonymous mud-grey wader of our winter estuaries, where its most striking characteristic is the sheer intensity of its feeding action.

The dunlin's complete change of personality confounded early ornithologists. William Turner wrote nothing about it in the sixteenth century, while more than a hundred years later Ray and Willughby believed they were dealing with two distinct species, the 'summer dunlin' and the 'winter dunlin', which Linnaeus later classified as *Tringa alpina* and *T. cinclus* respectively. Even Bewick, referring to it by an old East Anglian name imitative of its trill-like call, declared: 'The purre leaves this country in the spring, whither it retires to breed is not yet known.'[78]

In fact nearly 10,000 pairs breed in Britain and Ireland and it was almost certainly more numerous in Bewick's day. The disappearance of many wetland habitats in historical and recent times has led to widespread losses. Abel Chapman recalled an occasion at the end of the nineteenth century when he and his brother made a 10-day trek from the Tweed right across the Cheviot tops, down to the west coast on the Solway estuary, 'putting up by nights at shepherd's houses or wherever we could get shelter'. As well as noting that 'Few people . . . (even in the north) have the faintest conception of the extent and wild character of this mountain-land which lies

The dunlin has two distinct personalities – the anonymous grey wader of winter estuaries and the beautiful black-patched songster of the northern uplands.

betwixt England and Scotland', Chapman 'observed dunlins, at wide intervals, all along'.[79]

This revealed an altitudinal range in the birds' English breeding distribution of 2700 feet (820m) – in Scotland they will nest even higher – although today the dunlin nesting on the coastal saltmarsh at the western end of Chapman's transect have largely gone. As, indeed, they have from much of south-west Scotland, Wales, Cornwall and Devon (where the dunlin breeding on Dartmoor are the most southerly in the world).

Their present breeding strongholds are the high moors of the Pennines, the Scottish Highlands, Shetland and especially the Outer Hebrides, where the birds become semi-colonial, with nests sometimes just a few feet apart on the coastal machair of the two Uists. Sutherland and Caithness hold similar densities, but here dunlin face a newly manufactured challenge. More than 3800 pairs (roughly two-fifths of the British population) nest among the fragile, quaking mosaic of peat bog and acid pool that we know as the Flow Country. The ill-judged afforestation of this highly aquatic landscape, which often comprises fewer solids than full-cream milk, has triggered a reduction in dunlin numbers of 17 per cent, possibly because the dense conifer stands have enabled nest predators like crows and foxes to get a foothold in an otherwise treeless landscape.[80]

Most people involved in censusing dunlin on their upland breeding grounds freely acknowledge the scale of the challenge. In the Borders, Chapman found that they were 'scattered so widely in sporadic pairs, or groups of pairs, that one may search for a week without seeing a sign of their presence. Year after year they return to the identical moss or flowe – it is perhaps a mile in circuit, and that great, flat featureless area is tenanted by but a single pair of dunlins. Very likely there is not another haunt within 10 miles.'[81] In *The Atlas of Breeding Birds in Britain and Ireland* the author of the dunlin account agreed that it was 'remarkably easy to overlook breeding sites', but suggested that sometimes 'a useful clue can be obtained by listening to the local Skylarks ... which, when Dunlins are nesting nearby, frequently include an excellent imitation of the trill in their songs'. Another tip was to search for the larger and more conspicuous golden plover, in whose company dunlin are often to be found.[82]

This is an interesting example of ornithologists being slow to grasp what had long been a part of general country lore. In western Scotland the dunlin was known as the 'plover's page', while in Orkney and Shetland the name is still used, but its significance was almost completely overlooked until Clifford Oakes recorded several instances of the two waders performing a bizarre double-act. Each time the golden plover moved, its dunlin attendant followed, but when the goldie flew off to land on a wooden post, it triggered a bizarre cameo. 'The plover alighted first and its faithful attendant, with legs down and wings fluttering in its efforts to obtain a lodgment, actually succeeded in landing beside it! The post was, unfortunately, only tenanted for a few moments, but in this space of time the two birds, both in full breeding dress, made a unique picture.'[83]

Not only does the plover's page often shadow the goldie's every move, but it will also call in response to the other's vocalisations. Sometimes up to six dunlin will batten on to a single host, and occasionally they will form the same attachment to a greenshank or dotterel.[84] While this appears like subservience on the dunlin's part (in Iceland the dunlin is known as *loupall*, 'the plover's slave'), the golden plover can seldom shake off its attendant. In fact the relationship is more akin to parasitism, with the smaller bird greatly benefiting from the goldie's higher responsiveness to potential predators.[85]

A ruff lek involves all the aggression and posturing theatre of a heavyweight title bout.

Ruff, *Philomachus pugnax*. Ruff are remarkable for the lekking behaviour of the males when they gather at a special display locality known as a 'hill', to outdance their rivals for the attention of the smaller dowdier females, known as reeves. These aggressive bouts, which can involve the spilling of blood, are considered one of the most spectacular birdwatching events that Britain has to offer:

They scuttle round with half-spread wings and ruffs expanded, whirling for all the world like Devil Dancers of Tibet ... First one and then another suddenly stops and crouches, mantling prostrate on the ground with bill-tip touching it, trembling all over now and then. They crouch face to face, or facing a reeve, mesmerised for a minute or more before they relax. Then several of them break away in crazy bull-necked flight, or mince among the rushes, after the reeve. Presently one or other of them mates with her; it doesn't seem to matter to her which.[86]

At the heart of the pageant is the male bird's summer dress, with its sumptuous ear tufts and a thick, Aztec-like corolla of plumes encircling the head. It has an almost human quality of ostentation, and the impression is reinforced by the individual colours and pattern variations in every cock bird's plumage.

One might imagine that the ruff gave us the word for those exaggerated collars of Tudor fashion, but in fact the reverse is the case. The first mention of the present name – which, along with rook and smew, is the shortest for any of our birds – was in 1634. For at least 200 years it had been known by a word that was even shorter: 'ree', or alternatively 'reeve'. The exact origin of ree is lost, but it may draw on an Old English word *hreoh*, describing the aggression of the male's courtship display. The second version may have suggested itself to our medieval ancestors because the bird's arresting plumage evoked the formal costume of the high-ranking feudal official, the reeve.[87]

It is as the 'ree' that the bird appears in that extraordinary catalogue of dishes served at Archbishop Neville's enthronement banquet in 1465. According to John Leland's chronicle, 2400 were served at the feast, the greatest number of any single species to be itemised, which seems entirely in keeping with the high-flown extravagance of the entire celebration. Ounce for ounce, ruff was one of the most expensive birds on the medieval banquet table.[88]

Waders of saltwater marsh generally had a mixed culinary reputation (see Eurasian Curlew, page 223) compared with those like dotterel and ruff, which feed almost exclusively on freshwater or away from wetlands of any kind. Both the latter species were esteemed great delicacies, and the combination of popularity and high price fuelled a constant harvest across the entire range from Northumberland to south-west England.

However, East Anglia was always the bird's stronghold. When Thomas Pennant made a visit to the Lincolnshire Fens in 1769 he came across a fowler who had netted 72 ruff in a single morning. The man explained that he trapped the birds as they lekked, using clap-nets 14 yards (12.7m) in length and 4 yards (3.6m) in depth, often luring others in with stuffed birds or 'stales'.[89] Between April and Michaelmas (29 September) he could expect to take 500–600, which were kept in holding pens, where they were made even more piquant on a diet of bread and milk mixed with hempseed. The fowler could make between two shillings and half a crown per bird, and 48–60 guineas for his entire bag.[90] In the Lincolnshire town of Spalding, Lord Montagu interviewed a ruff-trader called Towns, who included George II among his clients and claimed that his family had been fattening the birds for 100 years.[91]

Such levels of harvest were clearly unsustainable, particularly after wetland reclamation took away much of the bird's most suitable habitat. When nineteenth-century trophy hunters joined the chase for Britain's last few, the ruff's decline soon became terminal. By the 1850s they were gone as a regular breeding species, and it was more than a century before they started to make a tentative return. In the interim, well-intentioned ornithologists tried to speed up the process by putting ruff eggs of Dutch origin under nesting redshank at Hickling (1925, 1936) and releasing wing-clipped reeves at Cley Marshes (1956). While these Norfolk projects brought only temporary success, free-flying birds started to lek at a handful of sites, such as the Ouse Washes in Cambridgeshire and Norfolk, but their testosterone-fuelled pageantry is still a highly localised event.

Common Snipe, *Gallinago gallinago*. VN: Horse Gokk/Gowk (Orkney and Shetland); Snippo, Snip, Water Pleep (Orkney); Snippek (Shetland). If the plumage of an essentially brown, black and buff wader lacks variety of colour, it more than compensates with the extraordinary complexity of its patterning. The counter-shading of pale and dark lines gives this secretive bird superb camouflage and, since the creature often refuses to move until almost trodden upon, the classic snipe encounter is a mildly alarming experience. Suddenly it explodes at your feet and announces an erratic, twisting departure with a couple of harsh *'scaap'* calls. It is probably only in the late twentieth century, with the development of high-powered optics and wetland hides, that many people have been able to enjoy the sight of a living bird on the ground.

The combination of dramatic speed and unpredictable take-off made snipe one of the ultimate challenges for the sportsman for more than two centuries. Its collective name, a 'wisp', perfectly evokes the unpredictable thread-like patterns produced by a small flock in flight. Yet the original motive for hunting the 'palate pleasing snite', as the Tudor poet Michael Drayton knew it, clearly lay in the realms of gastronomy.

The plucked carcass weighs just a few ounces, but snipe were probably a common table item for nearly a thousand years. Most commercially caught birds were taken in nets or in a horsehair snare known as a spring, springe or sprint. In the late thirteenth century the birds were priced at four for a penny, and while this increased slowly to fourpence each by 1633, the similarly sized ruff was seven times more expensive. That snipe were cheap over such a long period indicates just how common they once were.[92]

In his poem 'To the Snipe', John Clare accurately described it as a 'Lover of swamps/and quagmire overgrown/with hassock-tufts of sedge'. However, all the bird really needs is damp ground sufficiently soft for it to probe for worms with that extraordinary bill – pro-

The common snipe's captivating display is a vanishing part of our country experience, particularly in southern England.

portionately the longest of any British bird. This kind of marshy cover was once found virtually everywhere. Typically, in the 1830s snipe were still being taken in central London on a marsh where Belgravia now stands.[93] But such were the joys associated with this wader that gentlemen would travel to Ireland or Scotland and pay good money to rent a patch of bog for the privilege of shooting them.

The bird was known as the 'full' or 'whole' snipe, to distinguish it from its continental relative, the **Jack Snipe**, *Lymnocryptes minimus* (VN: Jack; and once called the 'half snipe' by fowlers), which visits Britain only during the autumn and winter. Both birds were shot, although the jack's smaller size and habit of diving back to earth quickly after take-off made it less appealing sport, and recent declines have now seen it removed from the quarry list altogether.

Around 85,000 common snipe are still shot, although this represents a small bag in comparison with the huge numbers taken during the nineteenth century. In 1881, for instance, some marksmen claimed bags of 1000 birds each. Such levels of slaughter probably caused temporary declines, but across the region had little impact. Even today the bird still merits its 'common' tag, with an estimated 20–30 million snipe arriving in western Europe from Russian, Scandinavian and Icelandic breeding grounds.

Snipe nesting in Britain and Ireland has unquestionably declined, mainly as a consequence of habitat loss, especially in the area south of a line between the Wash and the Severn. This means that many people in southern England now seldom hear or see the bird perform its captivating territorial display, which can continue long into the night on warm, still summer evenings.

The male bird rises high above the nesting ground and, for as long as an hour, gives an airshow-like demonstration of its flying skills, sometimes looping the loop or undertaking a series of angled switchback manoeuvres. As the bird performs repeated steep descents, it also produces two highly distinctive sounds: either a rhythmic '*chicka-chikarr*' call ('with a kind of hollow, wooden quality and rising and falling in strength') or a strange, rising tremulous noise that rather resembles the bleating of a sheep or goat, and which is usually described as 'drumming'.[94]

Although the word 'snipe' – and originally 'snite' – derives from the long thin bill, it is this unforgettable sound that accounts for most of the bird's vernacular names, not just in Britain but across Europe. In Ireland it is still known in Gaelic as *gabharín reo*, 'little goat of the frost', while the extant 'horse gokk' used in the Outer Isles is meant to reflect its similarity to a neighing horse.

The means by which snipe produce this sound was little understood for centuries and was the source of enduring debate. A Swedish ornithologist first demonstrated that it was, in fact, produced by the two outer tail feathers, but it fell to Philip Manson Bahr to convince the ornithologists of this country, when he gave a lecture to the British Ornithologists' Club in 1912. His methods involved a memorable demonstration with a snipe's two outer tail feathers inserted at precisely the right angle into a cork on a long string, which he then whirled around the club's regular London watering hole called Pagani's, 'a somewhat sleazy Italian restaurant where even the waiters' coats were stained with grease and the food abominable'.[95]

His lecture explained the physiological background: 'That they are definite musical instruments there can be no doubt ... The radii of the inner web of these feathers are firm and stiff and fashioned as the strings of a harp. To keep them taut during the performance and to ensure their vibration when acted upon by aerial resistance, a band of specialised muscle-fibres runs to each of these feathers, so that when the tail is spread they project beyond the others.'[96] Several years later the editor of *The Field*, Eric Parker, confirmed Manson Bahr's ideas by attaching the same feathers to an arrow which he then fired from a bow – the arrow duly produced the snipe's drumming sound when it fell.[97]

Eurasian Woodcock, *Scolopax rusticola*. VN: Cock (mainly wildfowlers); Muckle Snippeck (Unst, Shetland). The woodcock's plumage has been described as 'one of the best examples of camouflage in the world of nature'.[98] The rich rusty-brown patterning on this most unwader-like of waders has the same kind of complexity as that on an owl or nightjar. The woodcock also shares their night-feeding habits and undoubtedly has something of their indefinable magic, which may have to do with the nocturnal bird's inverted regime, particularly the daylight hours of trance-like stillness.

Woodcocks often rest up in dense tangled cover such as brambles but will also sit out on the woodland floor, where their large eyes – set far back on the sides of the head – command 360 degree monocular vision. As a further safeguard the beautifully marbled plumage renders them virtually invisible:

Once, in Ashridge Forest, Hertfordshire, while watching a shimmering Wood Warbler singing ... I caught sight of movement among the leaf litter. There was a Woodcock feeding only yards from where I was sitting, its camouflage such that when it paused it became invisible to the naked eye.[99]

During the long hot summer of '95 working with fifty volunteers and local people, [we] built a traditional

Part bat, part frog, part nocturnal bird – the woodcock's roding display is a wonderful and mysterious feature of our woodlands in spring.

cruck barn at Lanternhouse, our centre for celebratory and vernacular arts in Ulverston, Cumbria. Great bendy oaks from the Graythwaite Estate were felled on the shores of Windermere as part of the forest management. The head forester carted out trees by tractor. One day, stepping down, he accidentally trod on a woodcock's nest, cracking an egg. Previously he had been driving over it, his axles spanning the hen and her eggs.[100]

I have only once seen the nest of a woodcock and found that simply because I noticed what appeared to be a shining black berry among dead leaves on the floor of a wood in Kent. The berry was the watchful eye of a sitting woodcock.[101]

Despite its air of mystery, it is also a creature of strict routine. A classic instance, reported by Thomas Bewick, was a white bird (a continental migrant) that was seen in three successive winters in the same Glamorganshire wood.[102] Equally remarkable site fidelity was demonstrated by a resident woodcock dynasty in Hampshire, seen by Brian Vesey-Fitzgerald. 'I remember well a bird that nested within a few feet of a path down which I used to walk every day. She nested out of cover, and yet I was unaware of her presence . . . until one day I took a dog and he put her up. That was in 1924, and there has been a nest within a few feet of the place every year [probably until 1944 or 1945].'[103]

Another of the woodcock's dogged habits is a refusal to walk over fallen branches or other obstacles on the woodland floor. Fowlers exploited this to guide birds into their snares, known as springs or springes. The ease with which they could be tricked earnt it a reputation as a foolish species, and Woodcock is said to have passed into usage as a surname after being originally applied as a nickname for a simple-minded or naive person.[104]

It is as a synonym for stupidity that the woodcock

appears regularly in sixteenth- and seventeenth-century verse. In 'Calasterion', Milton (whose second wife, incidentally, was called Catherine Woodcock) refers to the 'incogitant woodcock', while in 'The Owl', Michael Drayton's bird is 'witlesse'. Shakespearean references to the species are usually incorporated into images invoking follies of the heart. In *Love's Labour's Lost* (Act 4, Scene 3), when Berowne discovers that he and his three friends have all fallen in love despite their vows to the contrary, he calls them 'four woodcocks in a dish'. In *Hamlet* (Act 1, Scene 3) Polonius dismisses the prince's protestations of love for Ophelia as mere 'springes to catch woodcocks!'.

Other characteristic behaviour that was heavily exploited was the bird's winter routine of going out to feed in the open fields just after sundown, then returning to the woods in the pre-dawn hour. Despite an agile and twisting quality to the flight, woodcocks also use a very precise route through the trees, and bird catchers cut corridors through the wood, then slung wool-mesh nets on poles across the open rides. Some nets were 100 feet (30m) long and were manned at dawn and dusk, when the waders would crash into them in the semi-darkness. The avenue cleared for the purpose was known as a 'cock-shoot' and the word eventually passed into usage as a local place name, such as Cockshoot Broad near Woodbastwick, a reserve now owned by the Norfolk Wildlife Trust.

British woodcocks have been eaten at least since Roman times, and their economic importance has led to their being commemorated in a number of other place names, particularly in the simplified form evident in 'cock-shoot', which is still a regular alternative. Examples include Cocklaw or Cockle Park (Northumberland) and Cockley Cley (Norfolk).[105] Yet it is not always possible to eliminate other derivations. Ken Spencer, examining Lancashire place names around Blackburn and Burnley writes:

Many names incorporating the word 'coc' have an element of doubt about their connection with woodcock. According to various authorities, 'coc' can mean such diverse things as 'boggy ground', 'a clump of trees', or 'a hill', or it may derive from a personal name 'Cocca'. Some of the place names in the following list, however, I like to think, do genuinely derive from woodcock:

Cock Hill, near Longridge
Cock Hill, near Colne
Cocklet Hill, near Slaidburn
Cockleth House, near Slaidburn
Cock Leach, near Colne
Cockley Bank, near Slaidburn
Woodcocks, near Lanho
Cock Bridge, between Portfield Bar and Clayton
Cockridge, Thursden Valley
Cockden, near Harle Skye
Wildcock House, near Chipping
Cockshutts Part, near Slaidburn.

The last five – and indeed several of the others – lie close to the kind of bracken-and-timber country where woodcocks dwell or used to dwell.[106]

Irrespective of any place-name ambiguity, there is no doubting the bird's abundance in winter and its great popularity as a roast. In 1772 Thomas Pennant found that dalesmen around Lake Windermere were sending large numbers of spring-trapped birds up to London on the Kendal stage, while netting operations in Devon were transporting as many as 30 dozen in weekly consignments via the Exeter coach. An even more compelling statistic is given by George Owen in *The Description of Pembrokeshire*, published in 1603. The author claimed that 'I haue my selfe oftentimes taken vi at one fall, and in one roade, at an eveninge taken xviii, and yt ys no strange thinge to take a hundred or sixe score in one woodd in xxiiii houres if the haunt be good.'[107]

Because it was customary to take woodcocks at dusk, the bird's cropful of worms from the previous night was usually well digested and the stomach empty. 'Many times,' wrote Gilbert White, 'have I had the curiosity to open the stomachs of woodcocks and snipes; but nothing ever occurred that helped to explain to me what their subsistence might be.'[108] One consequence of the woodcock's empty stomach is a culinary tradition of roasting the bird, guts and all. As Mrs Beeton noted, epicures 'considered the entrails a great delicacy'.[109]

Another highly valued piece of woodcock anatomy was the pin-feather, the small pointed plume at the base of the leading primary on each wing. Although much of the traditional lore surrounding them has been lost, several specific uses are recorded. It was the implement employed to draw the gold stripe down the side of a Rolls-Royce car, for putting lines down bicycle frames, painting oval-shaped miniatures on ivory and the detail on small model soldiers. Thousands of them were also made up into decorative fans or incorporated into fishing flies, while a quasi-medical function was as a delicate instrument to remove motes from people's eyes.

Woodcock or snipe pin feathers are also essential equipment for the aficionados of the smaller moths or Microlepidoptera. To identify and distinguish externally very similar species of these, one often has to dissect out

The woodcock's pin feather was once a prized instrument of watercolourists. Colin Woolf of Betws-y-Coed in Wales is the only British artist to maintain the tradition.

the hard structures of the abdomen, particularly the genitalia, which very often provide excellent diagnostic characters. For these very small moths a mounted pin feather provides an ideal implement for clearing the softened (heated in caustic potash) abdomen of soft tissue and scales to reveal the hard structures.[110]

By far the most exotic use was invented in the Far East, where they were made into an early form of sex aid – mounted in a silver stick and used to stimulate a woman's clitoris.[111]

Pin-feathers were also prized by watercolour miniaturists, despite the fact that they hold little paint, are resistant to water and quickly wear down at the tip. During the twentieth century the tradition of painting with them lapsed until the watercolour artist Colin Woolf revived the practice when he was given one by a gamekeeper:

It is an extremely difficult implement to use and it took me ages to really master it, but I'm glad I persevered. The technique intrigues people of all backgrounds and rather fittingly, my paintings of

woodcock are in constant demand. I think people are fired not simply by the unusual character of their creation but by the magic of the bird itself, which is naturally one of my favourites.[112]

He is now Britain's only exponent of the art, and a lovely touch is to insert into each finished painting the feather used to complete it. His most famous image, auctioned for charity in 1999, was done with a 150-year-old pin-feather once owned by the Victorian miniaturist Lady Letitia Louisa Kerr.

In the mid-nineteenth century many pin-feathers were obtained from migrant birds since woodcock only started to breed in the 1820s. (In previous centuries it was either unknown or extremely rare.) The bird subsequently achieved a rapid colonisation of both Britain and Ireland and is now a widespread resident across the entire region, although declines have occurred in recent decades, particularly in Ireland. Today a combined total of about 36,000 is still boosted by an autumn influx of several hundred thousand birds from northern and eastern Europe, and these migrants feature strongly in

The woodcock, like this one in the Bird Psalter (1280-1300AD), was regularly depicted in medieval manuscripts because of its renown as a table delicacy.

the shooter's bag. Many are brought down during the course of pheasant drives, although there is a perception among some in the sporting community that wintering numbers have fallen, and some shooters exercise a voluntary ban.

Yet there are still a handful of dedicated shoots, particularly in the bird's traditional winter strongholds in Cornwall and south Wales, where coverts of rhododendron and laurel were specifically planted for woodcock in the early 1900s. At these sites it is not unusual to see between 70 and 150 birds in a day:

> Having been accustomed to flushing the odd bird on winter walks and seeing three or four flighting from a local wood at dusk, I was astounded by what I saw on one of the renowned Cornish shoots. As the beaters set off through the wood with their Cocker and springer spaniels there was a cry of 'cock' every few minutes followed by a blur of mottled brown as a woodcock flipped across the top of a ride. On several occasions birds flew straight at us, having turned sharply into our ride and then, on seeing us, jinked rapidly from head height to canopy level and disappeared over the wood. Each short drive held between five and 20 woodcock and by dusk we had been treated to glimpses of more than 170 birds.[113]

While the total woodcock bag has probably fallen since the Victorian era, the skill required to shoot the bird has not diminished. Its zigzagging flight through the trees makes it one of the most difficult prizes and even now there is an exclusive Woodcock Club, sponsored by the whisky company J&B Rare, for those exceptional marksmen who have shot birds with a left and right.[114]

Between Michaelmas and Christmas the woodcock hunters relish the prospect of an east wind which, as if by magic, seems to conjure the birds from the woodland floor. In fact, it helps to carry the migrants safely across the North Sea, where in adverse conditions woodcock have been known to land on ships or pitch into the water. The collective name is a 'fall' and accurately reflects the way birds occasionally plump down anywhere in an exhausted condition.

Another classic migratory trigger for woodcock is frost, because it prevents them from feeding. The Celtic fringe is the usual refuge for these westering birds, yet many also fall victim to the cold. In the infamous winter of 1962/3 (the worst since 1740) only seven species suffered higher levels of mortality than the woodcock, based on the number of corpses found (609). In the Siberian conditions the starving birds threw off their usual secretive manner and were found feeding in gardens and town centres.[115] Some even ate bird seed, as the manufacturers of a brand called 'Swoop' were proud to announce in their advertisement.

However, it is in spring that woodcocks normally reveal themselves most fully, particularly at a full moon, when the males perform a repeated flight circuit high over the woods at dusk and, to a lesser extent, at dawn. As it orbits the canopy, often merely as a heavy round-winged silhouette, a roding woodcock expresses something of the bird's wider sense of mystery. Yet the performance can also be remarkably reliable:

On a mad impulse I went to view a Victorian house that was for sale. It was a cold, wet November afternoon. The house had retained its original name of Woodcock Cottage and faced a copse that, on old maps, was called Woodcock Covert, stemming from its time as part of a nineteenth-century hunting estate. Two birds flew past in the fading light – two woodcock. Surely this was a good omen and I bought it! As the house seems to be on a regular roding flight path and as their first evening flight is dependably a set time after sunset, give or take a minute or two, it is easy to impress dinner guests. Between courses, a casual stroll into the garden can produce displaying woodcock almost immediately.[116]

As it flies the bird makes a distinctive call, the first note a curious gruff, frog-like sound, followed by a high, far-carrying '*twisick*' note.

Occasionally females can also be seen, but they are far more secretive, especially during incubation, which they alone undertake. An intriguing aspect of the female's breeding behaviour is a habit of carrying the young, when they are threatened with danger.

I was once in Norfolk walking through a wood when I saw a woodcock fly up from the ground in a hunched position and, on looking closely, I noticed it was carrying a chick between its legs. This strange occurrence happened a second time about ten years later when I was in a Hampshire wood and a repeat performance was enacted before me. I've never met anyone else who's witnessed this.'[117]

The event is so rarely seen that it was long surrounded by controversy, but it has since been established that a mother woodcock normally carries the young tucked between legs and body, often with the tail as additional support. More unusually, she transports them gripped by her claws, but chicks have also been seen secured in the bill. Rarest of all is the vision of a mother flighting off with a youngster nestled on her back.[118]

Black-tailed Godwit, *Limosa limosa*. VN: Blackwit (Yorkshire). In breeding plumage, black-tails are a

Black-tailed godwits winter increasingly on British and Irish estuaries.

striking chequerwork of black, white and brick-red, and dense pre-migration flocks can form sumptuous pools of colour against the lush spring vegetation. During recent years increasing numbers have also taken to wintering in southern England and Ireland, although the greater drama is the bird's recolonisation as a breeding species in the mid-twentieth century. This followed a hundred-year absence, and even now there are only about 50 pairs in Britain. When the first nesting birds were found by an Ely schoolteacher, E. J. Cottier, in 1952, the episode was surrounded with the utmost secrecy.

Such was the cloak-and-dagger atmosphere that it was six years before the godwit's return was first revealed in print, and even a decade after the discovery, a written account entitled 'The Return of the Black-tailed Godwit' disguised Cottier's identity under the pseudonym 'Mr Cullen'.[119] It was only in 1969 that the original breeding site on the Cambridgeshire/Norfolk Ouse Washes was finally disclosed.

For three successive seasons between 1968 and 1970

two pairs of black-tailed godwits attempted to breed at the Norfolk coastal reserve at Cley. This exceptional occurrence inspired similar secrecy and an intensive wardening effort, although not even round-the-clock guards could save the birds from the vagaries of weather and natural predators. All of the nest attempts failed, although one undisputed benefit was the wealth of new information that was assembled on their behaviour. In the second season alone, the team of wardens clocked up 300 hours of detailed observation. The main watcher, Richard Richardson, later converted his notes into some of the most memorable descriptions of the species, which captured both the parent godwits' and his own forlorn dedication to their breeding attempts:

> Male C relieved his mate at noon and sat as if petrified throughout the afternoon, becoming progressively wetter as the minutes dragged by. Huddled in the nest, with white eyelids tightly shut and swallowing the raindrops as they trickled down his bill, he was the epitome of dejection. His mate became long overdue and at last he could bear it no longer, staggering to his feet, stiff-legged and saturated, before flying off to find her. She came back at once but after pecking about round the nest for several minutes, refused to sit and went away.
>
> . . . I decided not to wait and, seizing an old newspaper, waded waist-deep through the Main Drain and out to the island.
>
> The four eggs were almost afloat and the faithful male had been trying to brood them in an inch of water!
>
> I placed the eggs on my woollen cap on higher ground nearby and set to work with balls of newsprint to soak up the water. The island had been made of non-porous clay which prevented the rain from seeping away . . . The job took nearly an hour and after refurbishing the nest with a lining of dried grass we withdrew to the Hide to await developments with fingers crossed.

The parents returned to incubate, but sadly the eggs were already chilled and the nest failed. Matters have changed little, despite British godwits expanding their range from Kent to Shetland. In 2001 the 28 pairs in the Ouse Washes hatched 76 eggs, but reared just 16 young.[120]

Given the bird's enduring reputation as a table delicacy, black-tailed godwits must once have been widespread breeding waders across large parts of England. It was partly over-harvesting by bird catchers (together with the other usual suspects: wetland drainage, Victorian trophy hunters and egg collectors – for the table as well as the display cabinet) that eliminated the birds in the first place.

There are regular historical references to godwit as a special food item. Sir Thomas Browne judged the bird to be 'the daintiest dish in England; and I think, for the bigness, of the biggest price'.[121] One of Browne's near-contemporaries, Dr Thomas Moffet, wrote that 'nobleman, yea, and merchants, too . . . stick not to buy them at four nobles a dozen' (a noble being a gold coin worth 10 shillings).[122] The godwit's status as a gourmand's delicacy is perfectly captured in a passage from Ben Jonson's *The Alchemist* (Act 2, Scene 1), where Sir Epicure Mammon boasts that:

> My footman shall eat pheasants, calvered salmons,
> Knots, godwits, lampreys: I myself will have
> The beards of barbel served instead of salads;
> Oiled mushrooms; and the swelling unctuous paps
> Of a fat pregnant sow, newly cut off
> Drest with an exquisite and poignant sauce.

Bar-tailed Godwit, *Limosa lapponica*. VN: Barwit (birders). A visitor from its Arctic European and Siberian breeding grounds, the bar-tail is almost exclusively a bird of coastal areas, with large concentrations on the Wash, Ribble and Thames. These three estuaries hold more than half of the 60,000 birds wintering in Britain and Ireland.

In flight bar-tails are notable for the speed and playful eccentricity of their manoeuvres. 'At times they perform intricate gambols in the air, plunging down from a height, shooting upwards and then down again, dashing hither and thither, wheeling, twisting, and side-slipping with an abandon quite distinct from the drill-like evolutions of the smaller shore-birds.'[123]

It is very similar in appearance to the black-tailed godwit, but the bill shape is one of several subtle differences. While the black-tail's is longer, there is a pronounced upturn at the tip of the bar-tail's beak. Yet both possess an extraordinary appendage, which enables them to penetrate deep into soft sand and mud. Often it is pushed in right to the base, when bar-tails leave a trail of deep probe points across the sand wherever they have been feeding.

An archaic name used by the Essex wildfowlers for the bar-tail was 'preen', which was an old term for a long bodkin or dagger. It is, incidentally, from the same linguistic root that we have acquired the word used to describe the feather-care performed by all birds.

Eskimo Curlew, *Numenius borealis*. If it still survives at all, this bird is among the rarest in the world. Remarkably it was once considered one of North America's most abundant shorebirds, but the annual spring slaughter of migrants pouring through to breeding grounds in northern Canada and Alaska brought it to the brink of

The bar-tailed godwit is a widespread winter bird of coastal estuaries.

extinction by the end of the nineteenth century. Ironically as this orgy of killing was at its height, there were six eskimo curlew records from Britain and Ireland, between 1852 and 1887, spread between Aberdeenshire and the Isles of Scilly.

The bird's more usual migration to the pampas of northern Argentina was the unlikely subject of Fred Bosworth's 1955 novel, *The Last of the Curlews*. The book contrasted the epic scale of a single bird's life journey – particularly its long, lonely quest for a mate – with the species' wider history of decline as a result of human greed and folly. Bosworth's blend of technical natural-historical detail and simple poetic narrative was enormously successful and made *The Last of the Curlews* one of the most important early catalysts for public awareness of environmental destruction. It was translated into 13 languages and sold more than three million copies worldwide, while a 60-minute Hanna-Barbera animation film won an Emmy in 1973.[124]

On this side of the Atlantic, with a probable global population of fewer than 50 individuals, the position of the **Slender-billed Curlew**, *N. tenuirostris*, is barely less perilous. It is indisputably the rarest bird in Europe, breeding only at unknown locations in western Siberia. No nest has been found since 1924 and no more than a handful of sightings are reported each year. Thus the record of a first-year bird at Druridge Bay, Northumber-land, on 4–7 May 1998 – the first ever for Britain and Ireland – was truly remarkable. Eric Meek considered it 'one of the most (if not *the* most) outstanding records ever to come before the BOURC [British Ornithologists' Union Records Committee] … giving some faint hope that the species may be able to cling to existence'.[125]

Whimbrel, *Numenius phaeopus*. VN: Peedie Whaup, Tang Whaup, May Bird (Orkney and Shetland). This smaller darker version of the curlew breeds only in the northernmost tip of mainland Scotland, in Orkney and Shetland, with all but 5 per cent of 530 pairs nesting on the latter archipelago. In these areas it has the characteristically positive image associated with the advent of spring. Its old Gaelic name, *Eun-Bhealltuin*, translates as 'Beltane bird' and reflects its appearance in northern Scotland around the date of the ancient Celtic festival (1 May). There is a modern echo in the Orcadian alternative, 'May bird'.

Elsewhere in Britain and Ireland it is a passage migrant of spring and autumn, when the bird's highly distinctive seven-note call can be heard by day or night almost anywhere, even in the centre of large cities. The unique structure of the call makes it fit most closely with the old ominous, if ambiguous, legend of the 'seven whistlers' (see Golden Plover, page 202). However, if the whimbrel was ever credited with such darkly prophetic powers, these did not prevent the bird ending up on the dining table: 'In the York City Art Gallery there is a painting by the Dutch artist Frans Snyders, dating from about 1625. It is entitled the "Game Stall" and depicts fourteen bird species. Clearly identifiable (by the coronal stripes on one bird) is a brace of whimbrels. This must surely be one of the earliest paintings of the species ever done in Britain.'[126]

Eurasian Curlew, *Numenius arquata*. VN: Whap/ Whaup (Scotland). Although there have been recent declines in breeding numbers, there are still 47,000 pairs of curlew in Britain and Ireland (some estimates suggest almost twice this figure), while in winter there is a major influx of European birds.[127] Aside from the lapwing, it is the most familiar of our waders and perhaps best known of all for its powerful, mood-creating voice.

This is undoubtedly at its most beautiful when curlews combine the long drawn-out trembling spring song with an aerial display that Desmond Nethersole-Thompson has perfectly described as their 'air dance', when they rise up above their territory and fall to earth on uplifted wings. Yet curlew calls are just as evocative of the winter estuary. At times the sound suggests a haunting melancholy, and as late as the early twentieth century it was capable of unnerving the superstitious. Like the whimbrel, it was long implicated in the doom-

The powerfully atmospheric calls of curlew evoke the glories of the northern uplands in spring, as well as the windswept emptiness of coastal marsh.

laden myth of the seven whistlers, but curlews also provoke a diametrically opposed response.

Robbie Burns wrote that he had 'never heard the loud solitary whistle of curlew on a summer noon . . . without feeling an elevation of soul'. Almost every subsequent writer has shared these positive sentiments, including the late Ted Hughes ('Curlews in April/Hang their harps over the misty valleys . . . A wet-footed god of the horizons').

'Of all bird songs or sounds known to me,' wrote Lord Grey in *The Charm of Birds*, 'there is none that I would prefer to the spring notes of the curlew . . . The notes do not sound passionate: they suggest peace, rest, healing, joy, an assurance of happiness past, present and to come. To listen to curlews on a bright, clear April day, with the fullness of spring still in anticipation, is one of the best experiences that a lover of birds can have.'[128] Hearing them on moonlit nights as they migrated over central London, Nethersole-Thompson placed them among the 'most romantic waders'.[129]

The curlew's voice also has the distinction of featuring in one of the earliest bird references in British literature. 'The Seafarer', a bitter-sweet meditation on the life of the sailor, appears in a manuscript dating from about

AD 1000, but the poem itself is of much earlier date. It includes the lines:

> I took my gladness in the cry of the gannet
> and the sound of the curlew instead of the laughter of men,
> in the screaming gull instead of the drink of mead.[130]

James Fisher translated the second line as 'And whimbrels' trills for the laughter of men', on the basis that the smaller wader's call 'is perhaps better laughter than the curlew's music'.[131] However, he conceded that the Anglo-Saxon word *huilpe*, from which we derive the modern Scottish name 'whaup', could refer to either bird.

From well before the time of the 'The Seafarer', the curlew was valued as food. It is our largest wader; females are the bigger sex and have noticeably longer bills. They can be 3 pounds (1.36kg) in weight and were much sought after by country people, as evidenced by the old proverb: 'Be she white or be she black/The curlew has ten pence on her back.' An alternative version ran: 'A curlew lean, or a curlew fat/Carries twelve pence on her back.'[132] 'In the 1950s I was a keen wildfowler and once managed to shoot a curlew on the Solway estuary.

Eric Ennion's painting perfectly captures the exhilarating intensity of spotted redshank as they dive after a shoal of fry.

Knowing of its inclusion on medieval menus, I decided to sample its culinary delights. The meat was dark and firm, not unlike snipe and woodcock, and the taste reminded me of overdone beef. It was certainly not fishy.'[133]

Brian Vesey-Fitzgerald considered curlew 'really good eating' in September but thought winter birds taste 'a bit kippery'.[134] Their diet was probably a major factor in this variable flavour. 'To Wells town folk [north Norfolk coast] born 1920–30, who had to live partly by the gun, there were two different types of curlew – one that lives on the saltmarshes and another that lives on the land and flights back to the saltmarsh only to roost. The land curlew is good eating, whereas the marsh curlew is not.'[135]

Although it was removed from the quarry list in 1981, the bird has lost none of its innate sensitivity to human disturbance: 'The curlew has rightly been labelled "the wariest of shore birds".'[136] A close approach is almost impossible and, when mixed wader flocks are feeding out on the estuary mud, curlews are usually the first to fly and give alarm.

Spotted Redshank, *Tringa erythropus*. VN: Spot-red, Spotshank (birders). Few birds undergo the same seasonal transformation as this species. In spring spotted redshanks look almost completely black – thus its older alternative name, dusky redshank – but outside the breeding season they are an anaemic mixture of white and cold iron-grey. Nesting in the high tundra of northern Scandinavia and Russia, spot-reds mainly occur in Britain during spring and autumn passage, with about 200 birds remaining through the winter. At this season they can be separated from the common redshank by the overall paler plumage, longer bill and legs and a quicker, more intense feeding manner.

Often birds will wade up to their bellies and sweep the bill rapidly back and forth through the shallows, almost like a spoonbill. Occasionally they will even take to the water, with as many as 70 birds combining in tight packs to up-end like ducks, collective feeding behaviour that is exceptional among waders. It is characterised by the birds' almost frenzied manner and can be triggered by high concentrations of fish fry, which are possibly herded and disoriented by the waders' combined actions. J. H. Taverner, who made observations of this behaviour over a 30-year period, wrote:

> They then move quite rapidly backwards and forwards as a group, each individual most of the time with its bill, head and neck under water . . . so that the flock usually appears as a mass of tails pointing skywards . . . All the time the flock is feeding, there is a constant babble of noise, the note . . . a quiet quacking . . . The only conclusion that I can reach, unlikely as it may seem, is that the waders continue to utter the note when their heads are under water.[137]

Common Redshank, *Tringa totanus*. VN: Watery Pleep (Orkney); Ebb Cock (Shetland). It vies with the curlew as our most nervous wader. It is associated with a wide variety of wetland landscapes, from open mudflats and saltmarsh to industrial sites such as sewage works and slurry ponds. Yet in all settings it remains one of the noisiest, most restless and vigilant birds.

Breeding redshank often fly above any intruder, threatening or otherwise – even cows can be harassed – maintaining a constant high, fluting four-note alarm.

When eggs and newly hatched young are at stake the ceaseless volley of calls acquires a neurotic intensity. This is at times mildly irritating, but highly effective. When danger appears to have passed, the birds will return to earth but often land on a convenient fence post as a look-out and maintain a body posture suggesting continued anxiety. You realise that the old names of 'yelper', 'warden' and 'watchdog of the marshes' were all well deserved. Ironically, redshank is something of a misnomer, since the legs are actually bright orange.

The redshank's parental anxieties extend to weaving a kind of canopy over the nest, both as camouflage and possibly also to prevent the eggs being washed away in a high tide.[138] On hatching, the young are carefully steered towards suitable safe feeding areas. W. G. Hale, for whom redshank was a favourite bird from the age of seven, and who has made a lifetime study of the species, once found a redshank family that had walked a mile from the nest site. In so doing they had negotiated three drystone walls (and probably a fourth), 'two roads, two tall, thick hedges and a wide ditch with a rush-covered fence'. Hale concluded that, while 'in all probability the young walked most of the way, they must have been carried over the walls and rush-covered fence'.[139]

Common Greenshank, *Tringa nebularia*. This elegant bird is most commonly seen as a spring and autumn migrant, when it passes through many coastal and freshwater wetlands in good numbers. A few remain

'Yelper', 'warden', and 'watchdog of the marshes' were old names for redshank that nicely captured the bird's noisy response to intruders.

in winter, especially along the isolated bays and strands of the Scottish and Irish west coasts, while 1350 pairs of greenshank – the most westerly sub-population in the world – breed in northern Scotland, largely beyond the Great Glen, as well as in the Outer Hebrides and, more recently, on Shetland. Yet, without question, the most intensively studied greenshank community is that occurring on the Flow Country of Sutherland.

These birds were given world renown through the efforts of a single ornithological dynasty, the Nethersole-Thompsons (the second generation are known simply as Thompsons), whose eight members have studied the species continuously for more than half a century. For six weeks of every summer from 1964 to 1978, all the family, plus their guests, lived in the Greenshank Camp, largely comprising a wooden fishing hut 15 foot (4.5m) long and 10 foot (3m) wide.

At the heart of this extraordinary project was the eminent naturalist and family patriarch, Desmond Nethersole-Thompson, who was once judged to have 'spent more hours watching birds than any ornithologist'.[140] Infamous for his early years as an egg collector, Desmond compensated for any youthful folly by a lifetime devoted to the birds of northern Scotland.

Greenshank were his first love and formed the subject of two separate monographs in 1951 and 1979, the latter written with his second wife, Maimie. Part of the bird's undoubted appeal was the challenge it presented to the old nest hunter in him. One Edwardian egg collector wrote: 'after all these years I consider the nest the most difficult to find of any species nesting in the British Isles'.[141] An occasional clue is provided by the bird's habit of breeding near a 'mark', a prominent slab or rock and occasionally a fragment of dead wood or tree stump. The Nethersole-Thompson family is unique in having located 300 nests by 1978. Many of the individual birds were known in intimate detail and acquired pet names such as Old Glory, Old Knoll, Tiger and Tigress. During their studies in the Spey valley, the Nethersole-Thompsons found the eggs of a female called Elizabeth in 13 consecutive seasons.

Green Sandpiper, *Tringa ochropus*. This rather shy, medium-sized wader breeds in northern Eurasia's boreal forests, where it has the exceptional habit of laying its brown- or purple-spotted eggs in old thrush or crow nests and abandoned squirrel dreys. In Britain and Ireland it appears mainly as a long-staying passage migrant (several hundred remain in winter), when it is usually associated with freshwater lagoons, sewage works, the muddy edges of reservoirs, farm ponds or ditches, and even large garden ponds well away from general wetland areas.

At any distance its dark white-flecked upperparts simply look black, and in flight the combination of white rump and dark wings suggests a large house martin. Perhaps its most distinctive feature is the manner in which it rises steeply when flushed, amid a salvo of unmistakable '*klu-weet-weet*' calls. As migrant birds pass overhead they can be heard on clear quiet evenings, sometimes above large cities. During mid- to late July those ringing notes have a rather melancholy death-in-life resonance signifying, even in the very heart of summer, that the nights are turning cold on the sandpiper's northern breeding grounds, while the bird itself is already well into its migration towards Mediterranean latitudes or further south.

Wood Sandpiper, *Tringa glareola*. It is smaller, less vocal and less shy than its relative described above. It is seen mainly during autumn as a passage migrant in a wide variety of freshwater situations – sewage works, the marshy edges of reservoirs, gravel pits, quiet reed-fringed pools and open coastal lagoons.

It was probably more common in the nineteenth century before the drainage of many suitable wetlands. There was even an old breeding record from Prestwick Carr, Northumberland, in the 1850s, but it was more than a hundred years before another nest was located. This was found in northern Scotland in 1959, since when a tiny nucleus has expanded to as many as 15 pairs at nine widely spread localities.

Common Sandpiper, *Actitis hypoleuca*. VN: Sand Lark (Orkney). This is the small brown migrant wader of upland rivers and lochs, with the curious bobbing and tail-pumping habits and a shrill whistling call. Even more striking is the way in which several common sands will flight-display together, the birds often skidding low across the water on stiff, bowed wings with rapid beats. The species has made a long slow withdrawal to the north and west since the 1850s, while the Irish population now breeds in less than half its former range, but it is still a widespread, common bird in northern England and Scotland, with around 16,000 pairs.

Ruddy Turnstone, *Arenaria interpres*. VN: Staneputter, Steenie-putter (Orkney); Stanepecker, Ebb Picker, Ebb Pikki (Shetland). These are essentially birds of rocky shorelines in winter, where the tortoiseshell pattern of the upperparts gives them perfect camouflage among the tide-abandoned jumble of flotsam and seaweed. Even the bright-chestnut and black-and-white plumage of summer can be remarkably cryptic. The first sign of their presence is usually the querulous chattering call, but often they act as if they are far too absorbed in their shoreline rummage to worry about a human intruder.

Their communal lifestyle and busy, fearless manner

The eccentricity of the turnstone's diet embraces chopped garlic, Lifebuoy soap and human flesh.

make them birds of enormous character: 'A gust of wind dislodges a dry tangle of bladderwrack, sending it bowling away; in a split second the spot is alive with turnstones, bellies to ground, scrambling for sand-hoppers like children after pennies at a fête.'[142]

They have short orange legs and a stout chisel-like bill, whose trademark is a capacity to lever up stones and other seaside objects in the search for shoreline invertebrates. They have regularly been observed working in concert to turn over heavier rocks and even dead fish, digging the sand around them the better to flip them over.

Versatility is the keynote to the turnstones' feeding behaviour and they are particularly willing to exploit a wide range of man-made opportunities. They are partial to crumbs – both brown and white – and have been noted persistently chasing a sparrow on a Hugh Town beach in Scilly in order to steal its large piece of bread.[143] The Cornish birdwatcher Bernard King observed them picking through a gutter on a Newlyn warehouse roof and chiselling gull excrement off a concrete path.[144] Frank King, however, pipped his namesake for observations of sheer eccentricity. At Dun Laoghaire in County Dublin he watched eight turnstones (with three purple sand-pipers) devour a whole bar of Lifebuoy: 'the waders fairly pushed and knocked each other over as they absolutely gobbled the soap'.[145]

As well as a more conventional diet of sandhoppers, beach-dwelling insects, molluscs, crabs and other small crustaceans, turnstones have been seen eating sea anemones, the eggs of terns and gulls, as well as the eggs of their own species. They have been recorded to consume raisins (seedless), freshly chopped cloves of garlic, oat- and cornmeal, pearl barley, cracked wheat, dogfood, cheese, potato peel, apple cores and fish remains. On St Kilda they joined the starlings and herring gulls to forage for scraps around dustbins at the army kitchen.[146]

Colin Selway and Michael Kendall once found a turnstone busily feeding inside the thoracic cavity of a sheep carcass, while other carrion has included a dead wolf (on Canada's Ellesmere Island), a cat and various birds, as well as a human corpse on an Anglesey beach, off which five turnstones stripped 'small shreds of flesh' from the facial muscles and neck.[147]

Red-necked Phalarope, *Phalaropus lobatus*. This family of dainty and colourful waders is famous for the habit of swimming on the water's surface like a miniature

The red-necked phalarope is one of the few British birds in which the female is the more colourful sex.

The minuscule ½-ounce (4-gm) chicks have been described as 'lovely little objects looking little longer than bumblebees'.[148] Despite the apparent fragility, young phalaropes are anything but, as revealed by a delightful anecdote from the Inner Hebridean island of Tiree:

Years ago, one of a full clutch of four phalarope eggs failed to hatch, and was abandoned by the male; Henry Allison, a retired artist and ornithologist, took the stone-cold egg to his hut and left it on his table. Imagine his surprise when, apparently revived at the 11th hour by the warmth of the sun streaming in through the window, a tiny chick hatched out on the table top! The little waif was coddled and fed throughout the following night, but by morning was apparently dead. It was, in the course of preparing breakfast, pushed 'out of the way' into the still-warm oven (space was at a premium in Allison's microscopic kitchen), where it made a second dramatic recovery! Henry Allison took it to the loch that morning and gave it to a second male who already had four chicks in tow, and apparently it survived to leave with the others at the end of the short breeding season.[149]

The odd name phalarope derives from the Greek for 'coot-footed', referring to the lobed structure of the toes, which equips the wader for its highly aquatic lifestyle. It feeds by stirring bottom sediments – and in the process constantly spins itself round on the water – and pecking at the displaced invertebrates with its needle-fine bill.

The bird's cork-like buoyancy enables it to occupy a winter niche that is unique among waders. After spending the summer in the Arctic and sub-Arctic tundra, red-necked phalaropes migrate to live at sea off the southern tip of Arabia, where about 100,000 birds have been encountered by a passing ship in a single day.

Their close relative the **Grey Phalarope**, *P. fulicarius*, is wonderfully misnamed, since it turns brilliant terracotta during the breeding season (in North America it is called the red phalarope). However, it is only a scarce autumn-passage migrant off British and Irish shores, when its winter plumage is suitably nondescript. Occasionally vigorous Atlantic depressions drive exceptional numbers on to our shores, and in September/October 1960 there was an influx of several thousand.

Like its relative, the grey phalarope endures an entirely pelagic winter, the Atlantic population settling in the waters off west Africa. In some oceanic areas grey phalaropes have been seen feeding in the wake of whales, even riding on their backs and taking parasites from the mammal's skin.[150]

duck. The red-necked has a circumpolar breeding range largely beyond the 60° N meridian and is on the southern edge of its range in far northern Scotland. Around 20–30 pairs normally breed (there were just 13 in 2000), mainly on the Shetland island of Fetlar, where they favour shallow pools and flooded peat diggings.

To talk of phalarope pairs is misleading, since the species is often polyandrous and the sexes are famous for the role reversal encountered in dotterel. The females are the brighter larger birds, they song-flight to attract their mates, will initiate both courtship and copulation (which invariably takes place on water) and fight each other to secure the attentions of the duller-plumaged males. The latter, by contrast, perform all the incubation and tend the young, while their mates often take second partners.

Skua family *Stercorariidae*

Pomarine Skua, *Stercorarius pomarinus*. VN: Pom/Pom Skua (birders). The strange name is often thought to have an association with Pomerania, the Baltic region shared between Germany and Poland. In fact it is a word of Greek origin – *pomato* (lid), *rhinos* (nosed) – referring to the thin plates that overlay the base of the bill on all skuas. Until the mid-twentieth century the bird was known by the more accurate and even more cumbersome name of 'pomatorhine skua', but the shorter corrupt version eventually triumphed.[1]

Its increased usage by modern seawatchers reflects a parallel rise in British records as the birds make their way to northern circumpolar breeding grounds. They are most often seen in late spring from the north-west coasts of Scotland, and during autumn along the British east coastline or off the south-western promontories of Ireland. Usage has also rubbed off even more of the name. Field birders now seldom refer to these birds as anything other than 'poms', and the most sought-after is a pom with 'spoons' – the blunt-ended and curiously twisted central tail feathers on a summer-plumage adult.

Arctic Skua, *Stercorarius parasiticus*. VN: Scootie Allan, Skooty Alin (Orkney and Shetland). Skuas have been described as 'seabirds of prey', although in some respects they outshine their terrestrial counterparts. Rob Hume suggests that the Arctic skua's physique is 'one of nature's most perfect bird shapes. The body is sleek and tapered, muscular about the chest but long towards the tail, beautifully streamlined. The wings are quite long and slender, angled at the wrist and then tapered to a sharp point: falcon-like is not quite a true description, as there is more flexibility, more curve, more elasticity about a skua than a falcon.'[2]

These physical accomplishments equip them, in the words of their most devoted researcher, Robert Furness, 'for a life of robbery with violence'.[3] The Arctic skua harasses terns, gulls or auks until the distraught victim, intent on quickening its escape, disgorges any recently caught fish. The manner in which the bird shadows every deviation in the prey's flight is 'reminiscent of a First World War dogfight'.

It is perhaps not surprising that plane manufacturers drew on the bird's aggressive action as inspiration for one of their creations: 'The aptly named Blackburn Skua was the British Fleet Air Arm's first naval dive-bomber. In September 1939 it had the distinction of shooting down

Arctic skuas are fearless in defence of their nest sites.

the first enemy aircraft of World War Two. But the Skua's day really came in April 1940, when 16 of them flew from Orkney to Norway and sank the German cruiser, *Königsberg* in Bergen harbour. This was the first time that a major warship had been bombed and sunk in wartime.'[4]

Arctic skuas breed in northernmost Scotland, occurring no further south than Jura in the Inner Hebrides, while the majority – more than 90 per cent – of 3200 pairs nest in Orkney and Shetland. Most people enjoy their dashing piratical antics when the birds make their spring and autumn migrations along the whole of the British and Irish coastlines. Autumn skuas are especially prone to lingering on southern estuaries, where they can parasitise the large numbers of terns and gulls.

If our ancestors had enjoyed modern optical equipment, the bird might have been spared an undignified assortment of old names, like those surviving in the northern isles. Even the modern Welsh name for the related bonxie (see Great Skua, below) is a variation on the same theme. *Sgiwen fawr* translates as 'dung skua', while 'scootie/skooty' and, originally, 'scoutie' literally mean 'shitty'.[5] (The scientific name, *Stercorarius*, similarly originates with a Latin word for 'dung'.) They all hinge on an old misconception that skuas chased other seabirds in order to catch and eat their excrement.

The scatological associations seem completely inappropriate for such an impressive creature, and even more so for the **Long-tailed Skua**, *S. longicaudus*, whose elegance and beauty exceed those of its close relatives. It is the scarcest of Britain's four regularly occurring species and is the least parasitic in its feeding habits. Instead it has a marked dependence upon lemmings and other small rodents, whose cyclical abundance on the northern tundra closely controls the long-tail's own breeding success.

British Arctic skuas are also on the southern edge of their breeding range in Europe and numbers have recently declined, possibly as a consequence of the over-fishing of sand-eels around Orkney and Shetland. Yet the current total represents a huge increase on the nineteenth-century population. If early observers were somewhat myopic when it came to foraging skuas, Victorian landowners were blind. They shot them as a threat to game birds, and only with the lifting of this persecution did the skuas start to recover, particularly in strongholds like the Shetland islands of Fetlar, Unst and Yell.

The ornithologist and former BBC sound recordist Eric Simms judges the Arctic skuas' 'penetrating and shrill yodelling, the bird call most evocative of wild places.'[6] With their swooping and diving displays over the coastal moorland, they are a prominent feature of the Shetland landscape. On Yell one traditional breeding site is called Alin Knowes, 'skua mounds'.[7]

They breed in loose colonies, which are virtually no-go areas in high summer because of the birds' vigorous territorial defence. They often work in pairs, accompanying their attacks with loud screaming calls, and routinely hit the intruder – whether it is a sheep, dog, pony or human. In areas where the nests are near settlements, skuas provide the islanders with a distinctly northern type of sport: 'Orkney and Shetland children love to induce attacks from skuas. Toddlers at peat banks may be frightened by unexpected swooping birds, but as soon as the bairns are old enough to go out and play themselves they tease the skuas, attempting to catch them as they swoop.'[8]

On Fair Isle and Foula, Robert Furness has watched children 'deliberately cycling backwards and forwards along a short stretch of road through Arctic Skua territories purely for the excitement of being dived at'.[9] Even Shetland sheepdogs can get a buzz from these aerial assaults: 'some of the experienced ones clearly enjoyed the game of snapping at skuas'.[10] While most crofters are highly tolerant of the birds, the skuas' harassment of sheep has been more controversial. During the 1980s on Fair Isle the locals illegally shot Arctic skuas because their dive-bombing behaviour was said to prevent stock from grazing particular areas and occasionally drove the sheep over the cliff edge.

Great Skua, *Catharactes skua*. VN: Bonxie (widespread). The word 'bonxie' provides the best example of a localised vernacular name assuming nationwide ascendancy over the official version. This is especially true in an oral context, where few birdwatchers would use anything else. It possibly derives originally from the old Norse word *bunki*, whence came the Shetland term 'bunksi', for a dumpy, untidy, or heavily dressed person (often a woman). However, as Francesca Greenoak notes, it 'makes a good sturdy name for a formidable bird'.[11]

Bonxies are a heavy-set, barrel-chested species with short, broad, powerful wings, characterised by a startling white crescent at the base of the primaries. Although they feed largely in the piratical manner of Arctic skuas, they are also ferocious predators and will kill birds far bigger than themselves, such as gannet, great black-backed gull, grey heron, as well as other gulls, terns and even skuas. The blend of compact size with power and aggression has led to regular anthropomorphic judgements, even among ornithologists: 'a particularly mean assertive character'; 'squat in build, thick-necked and thuggish-looking'.[12]

Bonxies are relatively recent arrivals in Britain's northernmost islands, initially breeding on Unst and Foula, where they were described by the Reverend George Low in 1774. These pioneer colonies probably did not pre-date the middle of the eighteenth century and were first welcomed by the Shetland crofters because the skuas drove away other predators of their sheep, such as ravens and white-tailed eagles. Low wrote of 'Bunxies' being 'cherished by them with the greatest veneration and kindness; and nothing hurts their feelings more than to see the death of their favourite bird'.[13]

Sadly, the relationship turned sour when bonxies were found also to take lambs. Shetland people then combined vermin control with profit, by catching and tethering young bonxies around the croft as they were fattened up for the table. The birds were eaten until the twentieth century, while the illegal consumption of eggs continued on Foula until the 1970s. In conjunction with the efforts

Bonxies are specialists in robbery with menace.

of taxidermists and trophy hunters, these population pressures forced bonxies to the brink of extinction. However, with legal protection in the early twentieth century, the species has made a steady recovery. Some decades saw a doubling of their numbers, and the current population of 8500 pairs is almost two-thirds of the world total, while the 3000 pairs breeding on Foula forms the largest bonxie colony on earth.

One of the reasons for the rise in numbers is the increased availability of discarded fish from local trawlers. Bonxies are as willing to scavenge as they are to parasitise or predate other birds, and it has been calculated that between 1976 and 1986 fishing boats dumped enough offal and unwanted fish to support around 200,000 seabirds.[14] Their increase has not been without controversy. The 1980s crash in their main food source, the sand-eels they take from other seabirds, has led to a dietary shift towards direct predation of other species. Robert Furness estimated that by 1996 British bonxies were killing around 200,000 kittiwakes – half of them adults.[15]

Gull family *Laridae*

Modern profiteers of human waste, gulls are among the birds we love to hate.

VN: Cob (East Anglia); Sco(u)rie/Sko(r)rie, for immature birds (Scotland). The gull family enjoys a consistently bad press. Rob Hume argues that our antipathy contrasts starkly with the highly positive attitudes towards their close relatives: 'Terns are the elegant seabirds, the ones that everyone likes . . . Gulls are the good-for-nothings of the bird world, often ignored, disliked even, and frequently described as either "boring" or "too difficult to bother with".'[1]

Only crows have a more ambiguous reputation, and it is notable that most members of both these bird families enjoy minimal legal protection. It is similarly striking that they were jointly demonised in Hitchcock's film *The Birds*, and also noteworthy that the original short story by Daphne du Maurier was inspired by her vision of gulls following a tractor and plough near her Cornish home.[2] Yet it would be more accurate to see their portrayal in *The Birds* as a symptom rather than a cause of the gulls' present status. The old Greek name, *laros*, means 'ravenous seabird'; today gulls are frequently condemned as 'flying rats'.[3]

Gulls form the one bird family with equal mastery of land, sea and air, and an underlying element in our regret may be this sheer adaptability. Could we possibly project on to them some of the unconscious regret that we feel at our own relentless ecological dominance? Are they perhaps too successful, too numerous – too human – for their own good? Certainly gulls are the main beneficiaries of modern living, profiteers on the rubbish dump and familiar even with our most unusual, intimate products. 'When I was about 16 I went to school in South Shields and while walking on the beach a group of us saw a seagull flying along with its foot in a condom. Thereafter in our sixth form we used to refer to condoms as "seagulls' wellies".'[4]

Sometimes the intimacy comes at a high cost. 'I once recovered a great black-backed gull . . . that was literally bound up like a parcel with three hooks and yards of line from an abandoned paternoster.'[5]

One evening at the Chasewater in Staffordshire, with several thousand gulls across half a mile of water and more pouring in, a gull tangled up in plastic tape flew in from a tip and tried to join the roost. Seeing a bird with a 15-foot streamer behind it, all the others flew up in a panic. Each time the gull with the streamer tried to join them, thousands of gulls milled around in the air or flew to the other end of the lake, to be followed by the outcast, only for the whole performance to be repeated.[6]

There is perhaps an irony that the bird most likely to be cast in the role of avian lager-lout is precisely the one that most frequently falls foul of the beer six-pack. 'Whenever I buy a pack of cans it is routine for me to cut every single strand of the plastic hoops, leaving a collection of bits and pieces which can never act as a gull's necklace like you see so often in the photographs.'[7]

Not all of us display such environmental sensitivity. The gull habit most likely to inspire antagonism is their willingness to nest on our rooftops, sometimes in the most urban locations. The first signs of the trend were observed in Devon and Cornwall in the 1920s, but it started to spread during the Second World War. In Dover, for example, a large colony of herring gulls was partly located in sections of the town damaged by the Blitz.[8] Since then the behaviour has passed to three other species

Gulls somehow dignify the most unsightly human landscapes with their intensity and colour, as well as their often overlooked beauty and grace.

and occurs around much of our coastline, with colonies as far inland as London.

In addition to the smell and constant loud noise, rooftop gulls are discouraged because their nest debris, dead chicks, food carcasses and piles of acidic droppings, routinely choke the drains and cause floods. Even more problematic are the protective measures adopted by adults, should chicks fall on to the roads below. Sometimes even this stimulus is not required. A 'slightly psycho herring gull' nesting above a quiet London mews in 2003 assaulted the local postman, apparently agitated by the sight of his red mail bags.[9]

In the same year, in a scene straight out of *The Birds*, a woman was rushed to a Devon hospital with deep head-wounds after a gull had attacked her, while in Brixham a Yorkshire terrier was killed by a nesting pair.[10] In neighbouring Cornwall roof-dwelling gulls are guilty of stealing takeaway meals and – that quintessential act of heartlessness – snatching ice cream from children's hands.[11]

Yet for some, the bird's sheer aggression is part of their dynamic appeal. 'It is a fine spectacle to see the gulls descend to feed on some large tip, rising up . . . when one

of the garbage trucks comes too near and then descending in a screaming, snatching, threatening, rummaging, grabbing, tugging, gulping throng when it has dumped its load.'[12] Occasionally the appreciation is based simply on the gulls' much-overlooked but undeniable beauty:

A flock of geese against a sunset is an emotional image that thousands of people react to, not least me. A swirling flock of gulls disturbed from a roost, flying against a copper sky at dusk, is every bit as appealing but barely gets a second glance. Even birdwatchers ignore them. I've watched gulls flying across rainbows, filling the scope in bands of colour with gleaming white birds passing in front in a stunning display. Gulls lit by low winter light take on vivid orange and white highlights against strong blue shadows. Leaden skies and falling snow seem poor conditions, but pale grey and white gulls shine in such weather as if lit with an inner light, their subtle tones and patterns crystal clear.[13]

Even rarer still today is the highly personal, almost

spiritual attachment to their company, which was once a commonplace response of Britain's maritime communities:

My brother Andy has followed a family tradition of fishing since his early teens and one day he and his crew went four miles offshore to haul some crab pots in a 20 foot open-decked Norfolk crab-boat. Severe north-westerly gales had been forecast for the following day, but they appeared to have a chance to get their gear during the calm before the storm. However the wind soon strengthened, the sea began to build and the storm came much earlier than predicted.

They got back through the rough sea towards the harbour mouth, but it was extremely dangerous to turn into the entrance because the breakers would have filled and sunk the boat. They had to head westwards along the coast in order keep facing into the waves in the hope of finding a chance to turn across the waves, then ride the heavy sea into harbour, which they managed to do with the coastguard waiting on standby.

Talking about the incident some years later, one of the crew remarked that as the weather turned nasty, a large gull appeared and began to follow above the boat stern and remained with them over the next few hours, and immediately they were in the safety of the harbour mouth it left. It is often said that big gulls are the spirits of old fisherman and he felt that this was our grandfather, a lifelong Wells fisherman, seeing his grandson safely into the harbour.[14]

Mediterranean Gull, *Larus melanocephalus*. Med (gull) (birders). 'Mediterranean' is something of a misnomer because the bird's main breeding grounds are in the Black Sea region. It was once an exceptionally rare species in Britain and Ireland, with only a dozen records prior to 1940.

A highly illuminating tale attaches to the second of these. On Boxing Day 1886 a Breydon wildfowler, unable to remove a damp cartridge, casually discharged his gun at a gull while docking the boat. Neither he nor his colleagues could identify it, and when they sought the opinion of a local Yarmouth bird dealer called George Smith, he pretended only slight interest and snapped up the skin for five shillings. Yet Smith's hunch that it was something special was fully confirmed, and at a later meeting of the Zoological Society he tried to profit from 'his' find by raising the price for the skin with each offer he received, even refusing a bid from Lord Lilford of £300 (more than £18,000 in modern values). The

collectors eventually tired of Smith's grasping tactics and the skin sold for less than one-third of Lilford's offer, while the deception of the initial finder angered local gunners and many refused to deal with Smith thereafter.[15]

Since the 1960s Med gulls have become regular, if scarce, visitors to most coastal areas and to many inland reservoirs and lakes. In 1968 a pair reared two young in the black-headed gull colony at Needs Oar Point in Hampshire, which proved the vanguard for a gradual colonisation. By 2000 there were at least 90 pairs at 28 sites spread from Kent to Cumbria, while a pair at Wexford in 1996 proved the first breeding record for Ireland.

In winter, Meds wander to many parts of the coastline although some show remarkable fidelity to a single spot. A bird has been returning to the same small harbour on South Gare, Teesside, since 1982. In the time-honoured tradition of long-staying birds, it has been given a personal name after the small harbour called Paddy's Hole, on whose small jetty it spends one to three hours most days. In 2002 Paddy was at least 23 years old and a candidate for the world's oldest Med gull.[16]

Little Gull, *Larus minutus*. The smallest gull in the world was a rare bird until the 1930s, but it is now a regular visitor, with several hundred wintering off British and Irish shores each year. The adults are birds of delicate beauty with black hoods, pearly grey upperwings and a striking charcoal underside, while some spring birds show a rosy flush on the breast. The tiny size and the habit of hawking for aerial insects over water, often dipping to pick them from the surface, are more reminiscent of a marsh tern than a gull.

Black-headed Gull, *Larus ridibundus*. VN: BHG (widespread); Petch (Lancashire); Black Hatto, Black-heided Baakie, Heidi Craa, Rittick, Ritto (Orkney); Hoodie Maa, Peck Maa, Hoodie Craa, Tirrick Maa, Scoth Maa, Hoodie Pikk Maa (Shetland). Black-headed gull is the classic misnomer, given that the head is actually chocolate-brown. It is the most common, widespread, versatile and familiar of all the gulls. In summer it has the contrasting dark hood and, at any other season, when the breeding population is joined by as many as 2.5 million visitors, the combination of small size, raucous voice and white blaze along the forewing make black-heads easily identifiable. In many cities and suburban areas it is now very much a garden species, its greater manoeuvrability compared with larger gulls enabling it to come down even on the smallest back lawn or to take scraps from the window ledges of high-rise flats. It is the one gull adept at perching on telegraph poles and even on wires.

Black-headed gulls are routine visitors to the lake in most town parks, where they are usually the most

Black-headed gull is a classic misnomer, given that the summer hood is chocolate brown.

successful, if not the most welcome, contenders for the handout of bread. Yet in other contexts they give enormous pleasure – particularly sunlit flocks wheeling in linear formations behind a tractor and plough, which has become one of the classic images of the British countryside.

It may surprise some people to discover that the bird's widespread year-round presence inland, particularly in built-up areas, is a relatively recent development. Gulls were only noticed travelling up the Thames to feed in the capital during a succession of harsh winters in the 1880s and 1890s.[17] In fact it was their older status as a coastal inhabitant that led people to regard gulls flying overland as a reliable omen of bad weather. Yet these storm-driven flocks were quickly embraced by Victorian London. W. H. Hudson dated the habit of feeding gulls on the Thames to the severe winter of 1892, when 'working men and boys would take advantage of the free hour at dinner time to visit the bridges and embankments, and give the scraps left from their meal to the birds. The sight of this midday crowd hurrying down to the waterside with welcome in their faces and food in their hands must have come "as an absolute revelation" to the gulls.'[18]

With the bird's gradual metamorphosis over the last century from 'sea' gull to urban scavenger, there has been a parallel transformation in its status as a table item.

Today, except for the collection of eggs by a few individuals, nobody looks on black-headed gulls as a source of food. Yet this represents a major departure from our past. For hundreds of years black-heads were valued both for meat and eggs. Young birds particularly were eaten, while established colonies and the associated rights of harvest were managed as important economic assets.

A famous commercial gullery, notable for its inland location, was near Norbury, Staffordshire, and was long managed by the Skrymsher family. The birds were known rather confusingly as pewits or puits, probably an onomatopoeic version of the adults' breeding calls. A month after the eggs had hatched, teams of catchers would erect great walls of rabbit netting and drive the brown and rather ungull-like youngsters into pens. Sometimes almost 3000 were caught, and the sale of the total crop could realise £60, at a rate of five shillings a dozen. A seventeenth-century account of the Norbury gullery by Staffordshire naturalist Robert Plot suggested that the birds were by no means despised at the best houses: 'the generous Proprietor usually presents his Relations, and the Nobility and Gentry of the County … which he constantly does in a plentifull manner, sending them to their houses in Crates alive, so that feeding them with livers, and other entrals of beasts, they may kill them at what distance of time they please'.[19] This specialised diet was intended to counteract what one author described as the birds' 'raw gust of the sea'.[20]

Another well-known commercial gullery was at Scoulton, Norfolk, where the traditions may have dated back to the thirteenth century and were certainly known in the sixteenth. The harvest continued well into the early 1900s and once involved as many as a thousand eggs a day and 14,000–18,000 during a whole season.[21] From the Middle Ages the control of Scoulton Manor carried an obligation to act as larderer to the crown, a service that probably involved the supply of young gulls.[22] Certainly Sir Thomas Browne knew of Scoulton birds supplying English cooks as far away as London, although the eggs – as many as 44,000 in 1840 – were mainly used in puddings. Almost a century later Leadenhall Market was still handling 300,000 eggs a year.[23]

The eggs are beautifully patterned and highly variable, with ground colours ranging from chalky-white to deep brown and marked with even darker scribbles and blotches. Although quite distinct from the eggs of lapwing, the higher commercial value of the latter led to much dishonesty by collectors upon wealthy but ornithologically challenged society hostesses, as indicated in *Law's Grocers' Manual* of 1901:

It was just such a gull throng that inspired Daphne du Maurier's short story, The Birds.

Gourmets have for years been eating eggs never laid by plovers, and paying fancy prices for them. A large section of the gull family, who are farinaceous rather than fishy in their diet, lay eggs precisely similar to those of the plover. These are collected in hundreds on the small islands in the land lochs of north Scotland and sent to London. They are ridiculously cheap (to the collectors) and require no dye or flavour to give them artistic verisimilitude.[24]

According to Ron Murton, this form of fraud continued until at least the 1970s.[25]

The widespread trade in black-headed gull eggs has left its mark in a number of places. Near Harwich, Essex, there are three coastal islands called Pewit, while a gullery near Portsmouth dating from the reign of Charles I is thought to have occupied a site still known today as Pewit Island.

An increase in the population has seen a steady expansion of colonies throughout Ireland and Britain, with more than a quarter of the entire 220,000 pairs at just two massive gulleries: Lough Neagh in Northern Ireland and Sunbiggin Tarn, Cumbria. In England south of a line between the Wash and Severn estuaries there is a bias towards coastal marshes and dune sites, although elsewhere black-heads frequently use moorland pools, upland tarns, disused mining pools and man-made reservoirs.

Ring-billed Gull, *Larus delawerensis*. The first record of this North American gull, which is intermediate in size and appearance between common and herring, did not occur until March 1973. Yet within 20 years more than 600 had been discovered and it now maintains a permanent presence on our shores. It is especially regular around coastal cities like Belfast, Cork, Dublin, Plymouth and Swansea, the last being the original site of discovery. A large population increase on the other side of the Atlantic is a possible background to its future colonisation here. Only the collared dove has more quickly exchanged the status of extreme rarity for that of widespread familiar.

Common (Mew) Gull, *Larus canus*. VN: Cob (East Anglia); Cullya, Whitie, White-ack, White-maa, Whitefool (Orkney); Blue Maa, Peerie Maa, Pikka Maa, Tanyick, Tinna Maa (Shetland). Although the name is not quite misplaced, this is by no means the most common British and Irish gull. Herring and black-headed gulls are nearly three times more numerous as breeding species, while kittiwakes outnumber it by almost eight to one. The present population stands at a

Common gulls have acquired the knack of opening mussel shells.

little over 70,000 pairs and nests almost entirely in Scotland.

In winter the resident birds are boosted by a large continental influx, making the species especially abundant in Scotland and along the eastern half of England. They are widespread inland and are almost as willing as black-headed gulls to follow the plough or feed in arable fields. Nor do they spurn the easy pickings from roadkills, rubbish dumps and inner-city gardens.

Worms form a high percentage of the diet, and common gulls are particularly attracted to areas of close-mown turf, whether it is cattle pasture or the putting green on a golf course. This is also the classic gull of the school sports field, even in highly urban areas, and often simply moves to the touchline when games are in progress. Yet it is far less approachable than the black-headed gull and the bird's call has a lovely wild, lonely quality that is perfectly in keeping with the rugged nature of the Scottish breeding grounds. The wailing sound is well captured by the traditional name, 'mew gull', recently reinstated as the official version.

Of the five gulls widely found in terrestrial settings, the common gull has in many ways the most pleasing appearance. Its large, dark eye and neatly domed head suggest an almost dove-like gentleness, although this is often negated by the bird's aggressive manner. They regularly steal food from smaller black-headed gulls or from each other, while both black-headed and common gulls have a long-standing parasitic relationship with

lapwings and golden plovers. The gulls stand at regular intervals among a plover flock and instantly give chase when they see one of the waders hauling up a worm. Although the plovers lose a substantial proportion of their prey in this fashion, they are thought to benefit from the gulls' early-warning alarms if a predator approaches.

Equally intriguing is the bird's habit of carrying shells aloft to crack them through the impact of the fall. But they are not always successful:

> The concrete promenade and sea defences on the north Wirral shore in Cheshire are used as a hard surface above which common gulls gain height and drop cockles to break them and get access to the insides. I've more than once seen innocent passers-by startled by a falling shellfish and on one occasion saw one drop into a pram while the person pushing it (but not necessarily the occupant) remained none the wiser.[26]

Lesser Black-backed Gull, *Larus fuscus*. VN: Sco(u)rie/Sko(r)rie, for immatures (Scotland); Peedie Baakie (Orkney); Saithe Fowl, Peerie Swaabie, Peerie Baagie (Shetland). It is the smallest and arguably the most handsome of the large gulls, its more slender build and proportionately longer, narrower wings giving it an elegance not often associated with herring or great black-backs. It is also the gull for which Britain and Ireland hold the greatest responsibility, since our 88,000 pairs represent 40 per cent of the European total.[27]

Not that people look more favourably on lesser black-backs than on any other large gull. The birds are routinely killed by a wide variety of interest groups, while their eggs can still be harvested under licence. A huge colony at Tarnbrook Fell, Lancashire, that involves nearly a quarter of the entire British population and is of international importance, is subjected to intensive culling, ostensibly over issues of water pollution. However, this seems little more than an excuse, given that the reservoir supposedly affected already supports a black-headed gull colony of 4000 pairs, which has never been controlled. The more likely reason behind the controversial control measures is the lesser black-back's proximity to prime grouse moor.[28] For several years a licence has permitted the poisoning of 18,000 birds with alphachloralose, but the estate owners have failed to achieve the figure in recent years, partly because of the colony's falling numbers.

Environmentalists are sometimes no more welcoming. At Orfordness, Suffolk, former warden Cliff Waller outlines the problems posed by the birds:

The Orford complex forms the second largest shingle area in Britain after Dungeness, but it's far superior, being the purest example of an unspoilt shingle spit in Europe. It supports a rare shingle heath, comprising mainly lichens and mosses, that can take hundreds of years to establish. A problem arose at Orford because the gulls, which established a colony here in 1963, rose by 1993 to 9000 pair of lesser black-backs and 3600 herring. The birds gather shoreline seaweed or flotsam and other coarse vegetation for nesting material. Together with their guano and food remnants, they are creating a more nutrient-rich environment that threatens to destroy this unique ecosystem.[29]

A more routine source of conflict is the lesser black-back's fondness for nesting on buildings. Compared with the herring gull, it was a latecomer to the habit. The first recorded instance was on factory rooftops in Merthyr Tydfil, Glamorgan, in 1945. By 1970 there were still only 60 pairs nesting on buildings throughout the country, but the tradition has steadily expanded until today some colonies are numerically large and geographically enormous.[30] The biggest in Britain is in Gloucester and extends in a network of city rooftop settings for 9 miles (15km) and involves 2100 pairs of lesser black-backs, as well as 235 herring-gull pairs.

Unlike the other large gulls, lesser black-backs seem less able to face the rigours of the British winter and migrate southwards to the Iberian and north African coastlines. Until the 1950s the autumn exodus involved almost the entire population, and during a winter census of 1953 just 165 birds were located. However the changing climate and the abundance of food provided at landfill sites are thought to be key influences behind growing winter numbers, which presently stand at about 70,000.[31]

Herring gulls developed their roof-nesting habit in the 1920s.

Herring Gull, *Larus argentatus*. VN: White-maa, Whitie, White-ack, Whitefool (Orkney); Maa, Blue Back, White Maa (Shetland). This is the species we automatically associate with the name gull. The bird is also inextricably fused with our sense of the sea – an identification reinforced by the endless repetition of its vocalisations in the context of radio and television programmes with a coastal setting. Most famously, herring gulls call to us during the theme tune for BBC Radio Four's long-running *Desert Island Discs*.

The most memorable and distinctive of their sounds – if not of all British bird sounds – is the long-call or trumpeting-call, when adults deliver a series of loud notes, first with head pointed downwards, then as the sequence intensifies with the head thrown back and bill wide open. At all times herring-gull notes have a decidedly human quality and often a strong, deeply ambiguous charge, sounding almost exactly halfway between manic laughter and an empty, despairing wail. It is the call's ability to express such powerfully conflicting emotions that makes it a popular choice with sound recordists, and also with people in general:

If I was ever fed up as a child I used to go down to the beach. Feeling rather sad and inward, I was always struck how the gulls reflected and complemented how I felt.[32]

The voice of a Herring Gull is wonderfully melodious

Regardless of their widespread image as unwanted scavengers, herring gulls have suffered a troubling population decline in recent decades.

. . . I think there is no finer bird-call than the[ir] clear sturdy resounding cries . . . carried away by the wind along the wide beach or over the undulating dunes.[33]

Herring gulls are the arch-exploiters of human opportunities and have been major beneficiaries from the food bonanzas associated with landfill sites. Their diet is gloriously catholic, extending to rope, bonfire charcoal, matchboxes, greaseproof paper and the rubber seals around car sun-roofs.[34] One young bird was once found with a six-inch-long wooden meat skewer protruding through its neck, presumably swallowed in the hope that it might prove digestible. When the projectile was removed the chick made a complete recovery.[35]

Other favoured food items include molluscs, crabs and hermit crabs inhabiting whelk shells, which the gulls have learnt to open by flying up and dropping until they crack on a hard surface. Sometimes the method carries risks from neighbours, who can reach the exposed morsel before the shell-cracking bird itself, although some individuals have discovered how to outwit even these tactics:

About 3 years ago I was in Exmouth, where herring gulls carry mussels to above the main esplanade path. They often need many goes before the shells break, but if they fly higher to increase the impact, the dropping mussels are caught by lower gulls and stolen. One individual worked out that if he flew lower, but then 'lofted' the mussel (which he did with tremendous energy, snapping his head back and achieving about another 15–20 feet in height for the shell), he not only enjoyed quicker smashing of the mussel, but also introduced enough confusion about its trajectory for the bird to evade the robbers. He was also very clever at predicting the landing spot, so he could easily win the race to the food.[36]

However, these shell-cracking strategies sometimes involve less intelligence than they seem to imply. Niko Tinbergen once observed a gull drop a shell 39 times into shallow water.

Herring gulls have spearheaded the family's general invasion of terrestrial habitats, but they still show a strong coastal bias in choice of breeding ground, with the only notable gap along the low-lying shores of Lincolnshire and East Anglia. Generally they favour rocky coasts, where they occupy low-lying cliffs or boulder-strewn offshore islands. The present population of 205,000 pairs represents a massive increase on pre-war numbers, yet there has been a troubling downward trend for the last 30 years, with the British coastal population virtually halved since 1969.[37] The bird's susceptibility to botulism, the loss of feeding opportunities with tighter regulations over waste disposal, and fox predation are all thought to be factors in the decline: 'Half a mile from where I live on the north Devon coast there used to be over 300 pairs of herring gulls nesting along the clifftop. Within two years the foxes cleared the lot. We picked up thirty-six pairs of gull wings around a fox's earth.'[38]

The development that has brought the species into closest contact – and often direct confrontation – with humans is the habit of nesting on buildings. Herring gulls were the original pioneers in the 1920s and are still the main roof-nesting species, with almost 10,000 pairs breeding in urban settings by 1994. Their presence is often unpopular and, to some, deeply alarming. The *Aberdeen Press and Journal*, for instance, recently carried a nightmare headline: '3 million pairs of gulls invade coastal towns'.[39] Unfortunately Sue Raven, source of the original information, writes: 'for reasons best known to themselves the reporters added three zeros to the numbers given in the press release'.[40]

Another story reported in *The Times* is more rooted in fact, but still has a strong hint of Hitchcock's famous film, or perhaps its sequel, *The Revenge of the Gull*:

When Don Weston found a young gull squawking pathetically on the ground in his car park he knew he had to help. Tenderly, he picked it up and put it on top of his hut . . . A few hours later it flew away and Mr Weston went home with the warm glow that comes from a good deed.

Now that warm glow has turned to cold terror. For the past three years Mr Weston has been the target of a bloody vendetta run by a crazed seagull – the very one, he believes, whose life he saved. By way of gratitude it has pecked his head, bombed him with droppings and vomit, stalked him through the city by air, divebombed him and terrified him with its blood-curdling screams.[41]

In addition to their undoubted aggression – invariably from adults with well-grown young, rather than from the immatures – there are frequent complaints concerning the noise, their feeding assaults on rubbish bags, and the blizzard of guano. The methods used to deter them, which are often in vain and occasionally ridiculous, have included pricking or hard-boiling the eggs, tying fireworks to the ends of broom handles and firing them at the birds, employing eagle owls or other birds of prey to patrol the city and feeding them contraceptives or narcotic sandwiches. 'In . . . South Shields the herring gull alarm call was broadcast throughout the town in an effort to deter nesting birds. This measure, which increased noise disturbance considerably for a while, served to scatter the nesting birds over the town and thereby actually facilitated the increase.'[42]

A more successful strategy in Arbroath involves the council's employment of two builders, who patrol the rooftops to collect gull eggs and then combine pest control with gastronomy. 'I like them myself,' one of them admitted. 'They make good omelettes. A doctor told me there's six times more nourishment in them than in a hen's egg.'[43]

Glaucous Gull, *Larus hyperboreus* (VN: Glauc) and **Iceland Gull**s, *L. glaucoides*. The crystal-white and pearl-grey tones of these two northern birds seem a perfect echo of their ice-bound breeding grounds. They are regular winter visitors to British and Irish shores in moderate numbers, with most appearing in Scotland and its northernmost islands, where the birds favour small fishing ports like Stornoway, Lerwick or Ullapool. There is also a long tradition of records at reservoirs in the English Midlands:

It used to be a bit of a sport, more than a little competitive, to find a glaucous or two in the thousands of gulls on the Staffordshire reservoirs. The big triangle of white at the back end of an adult instantly stopped the telescope on its repeated sweeps through the flock. On memorable days we would have 3–4 glaucous and a couple of Icelands, which look great at any age, whether pristine white-winged adults or oatmeal juveniles. But great big immature glaucous gulls would arrive and float over the roost like giant barn owls.[44]

Sometimes the birds are highly faithful to one particular winter location. An Iceland gull returned to Hamilton, Lanarkshire, for at least three consecutive winters from 1950 to 1952. It was habitually to be found on the local rubbish dump, with a short absence every Saturday afternoon and Sunday – the bird timing its departures down the Clyde to coincide with the weekend cessation of dumping operations.[45]

Yet the champion of all Britain's long-staying Iceland gulls was a bird honoured with the strikingly unimaginative title of 'The Regular'.[46] At least it was well deserved.

'Boy George' was one of two glaucous gulls that returned regularly to the north Norfolk coast over a 27-year period.

It returned each winter to the seafront at New Brighton, Cheshire, from February 1957 until 4 May 1985, when it was at least 29 years old. During its long life it came to be known more affectionately as 'Whitey'. It also developed a penchant for stealing molluscs from oystercatchers, as well as a particular attachment to the sewage outflow pipe adjacent to Vale Park and, in later years, a pronounced limp that simplified its individual recognition.[47]

Almost as faithful was a glaucous gull that patrolled the coast between Cley and Weybourne, Norfolk, each winter until 1979, sometimes reappearing at its favourite haunt as early as August. The bird was at least 16 years old when it finally disappeared and was known as 'Weybourne Willie', and latterly as 'George'. Shortly after its last patrol, another adult glaucous gull assumed George's old beat. The second bird's appearance in 1982 coincided with the brief fame of the pop band Culture Club, and it was appropriately christened after the lead singer, Boy George. Except for a three-year gap, the two birds maintained a glaucous-gull tradition in north Norfolk from 1963 to 1990.[48]

Great Black-backed Gull, *Larus marinus*. VN: Geeb (birdwatchers); Blackback, Saddleback (widespread); Land Gull (Norfolk); Big Baakie, Baakie (Orkney); Swartback, Swaabie, Baagie (Shetland). The world's largest gull is one of the most impressive birds of the Atlantic shoreline and is widely acknowledged for its air of glorious villainy. 'If Marlowe had written *The Parlemente of Fowles* he would have made this bird or the Great Skua his supreme figure.'[49]

The chest is deep and the massive head equipped with a heavy, hook-tipped bill. At full stretch the adult's black wings are as much as 5 feet (1.5m) across, and when coming to rest they settle over a body of sea-surf whiteness. Comparison with its largest relatives only seems to emphasise the bird's dominance: 'next to a Lesser Black-backed Gull, not many inches shorter, they can look "twice as big" and they weigh twice as much'.[50] Even the bird's coarse, goose-like notes have a robust muscular quality, while its imposing presence is capped by what Francesca Greenoak has described as its 'maleficent pale-eyed stare'.[51]

The Victorians honoured great black-backs by shooting and mounting them as exhibits for the drawing room, as if it were a top predator (quite unlike other gulls, which were treated as little more than target practice).[52] The birds' large eggs were also gathered until at least the 1960s. Severe persecution steadily reduced the population and for many decades confined it exclusively to the coast. Typically, there were just four records from London during the whole of the nineteenth century.[53] Today it is commonplace.

Despite the general recovery, great black-backs are still shot by farmers for taking sickly lambs or distressed ewes. Even conservationists cull them for predation of vulnerable seabirds – another classic example of the arbitrary cultural blinds that isolate large gulls from 'true' birds of prey. They remain primarily breeding birds of rocky cliffs and offshore islands, with a permanent bias towards western shores, from Cornwall and County Cork to Shetland. In some areas great black-backs can feed their young almost entirely on other seabirds, particularly hole-nesting species like puffin and Manx shearwater. They are also well known to knock tired land birds into the sea as they migrate, or to catch, and then drop, mammals into the water to drown them.

They share the family's attachment to carrion. One of the most impressive testaments to the bird's digestive tract was the vision of two adult great black-backs tearing at the bleached and rotted carcass of a sperm whale on a North Ronaldsay beach, where it had lain for more than six months. Dead dogs and cats, myxomatosed

The great black-backed gull is one of the largest and most powerful birds of the north Atlantic shoreline.

rabbits and a red rubber balloon have all been recorded in the bird's diet, although landfill refuse and discarded trawler fish are the typical staples.

Ross's Gull, *Rhodostethia rosea*, is a small long-winged species of the high Arctic and is named after James Clark Ross, the British polar explorer, who obtained the first specimen in northern Canada during June 1823.[54] Even several decades after its discovery it was a bird steeped in mystery. The eastern Siberian breeding grounds were not located until 1905, and even now its winter quarters are little understood. Although they are thought to lie inside the Arctic Circle, north of its breeding grounds!

The lengths taken to secure some of the first nineteenth-century specimens are testimony to the bird's powerful allure. During an ill-fated American expedition of 1879 the party's main steam vessel was crushed by ice near Henrietta Island (now Ostrov Genriyetta). The survivors were forced to drag or row the ship's boats through leads in pack-ice between the New Siberian Islands, then aross the Laptev Sea and finally to the Lena Delta on mainland Siberia. Throughout this 200-mile (320-km) nightmare ordeal the expedition naturalist, Raymond Newcomb, carried three skins of Ross's gull under his shirt.[55]

By the 1950s there were almost no published photographs, and barely a handful of British ornithologists had seen Ross's gull. However, a slow trickle of sightings began in the 1970s and have now become almost annual. By 2001 there were 74 records, from Shetland to Cornwall and County Cork, but for most observers this delicately rose-coloured gull retains a strong dash of that initial magic.

Some consider the **Ivory Gull**, *Pagophila eburnea*, the only competitor to the previous bird as our most charismatic gull. The British and Irish records (118 by 2001) exceed those for Ross's gull, but it has on average the most northerly range of any bird in the world and breeds to 85° N.[56] The wings are long and the flight noted for its grace and buoyancy, while the plumage of the adults is entirely white – a distinction shared with just three other of the world's polar seabirds. There is a curious twist to all this beauty and purity of colour. The ivory gull is a frequent scavenger at seal whelping grounds for the placental remains, and also devours seal excrement as well as walrus and polar-bear shit.

Black-legged Kittiwake, *Rissa tridactyla*. VN: Kitt (birdwatchers); Tarrock, for immatures only (northern Scotland); Kittick, Rittack, White-maa, Chitty-wekko,

Wekko (Orkney); Weg/Waeg, Rippack (Shetland). It is the most numerous (540,000 pairs) and often considered the most beautiful of Britain's common gulls, although this is possibly as much a statement about the lack of scavenging habits as it is a purely aesthetic judgement. Observers even comment on a more benign appearance, with the dark eye on the rounded white head imparting a certain gentleness. Kittiwakes flying through stormy seas, when the conditions emphasise their aerial grace and the purged whiteness of the plumage, are particularly impressive. On these occasions they seem more closely allied to purely pelagic birds, such as fulmar or gannet, than they do to other gulls.

This is the family member that best warrants the name 'sea gull'. Kittiwakes are highly marine birds, coming ashore only in spring and summer to breed in their large cliff colonies. These spectacular sites – famed for their noise, the mesmerising activity and the smell – are found all around the British and Irish shores, with a notable gap in south-east England and a marked concentration along the north-east coast between Shetland and Yorkshire. Although it has the least contact with humans, the kittiwake makes a concession when it comes to its choice of nest site. Since 1931 it has found a perfect substitute for a coastal cliff in warehouse window ledges, pier structures, harbour walls and various seaside buildings. Perhaps the most famous and controversial sites are in north-east England:

> The most inland nesting colonies in the world are located on both the Gateshead and Newcastle quaysides of the River Tyne, with 160 pairs nesting on the

iconic Tyne Bridge in 2002. A seabird colony on this cast-iron cliff at the heart of the regional capital is a wonderful wildlife spectacle, but down below the once-derelict quayside is now lined with fashionable restaurants and wine bars. These smart new colonists don't appreciate the neighbours' evocative 'kitty-waak kitty-waak' calls nor the showers of droppings, and the city council has sought to net the Tyne Bridge to prevent gulls nesting.

Unfortunately the Geordie kitts are victims of gentrification on both banks of the river. Their former stronghold was a giant grain warehouse known as the Baltic Flour Mills where they became firmly established in the 1960s. But not for long ... With a £46 million lottery grant, the site has been transformed into the BALTIC, the biggest contemporary art gallery in the UK outside London. The bird's whitewash was not considered art and their nests were cleared from the window ledges. An artificial nest platform was erected downstream where 100 'tarrocks' fledged in 2002. But the displaced colony headed north as well as east – and it's these birds that settled on the Tyne Bridge in 1997.

Alongside the BALTIC gallery is the brand-new Sage Music Centre, a mini Sydney Opera House alongside the mini Sydney Harbour Bridge. This was the launch pad for Newcastle and Gateshead to mount a joint bid for European Capital of Culture in 2008. Sadly the civic worthies neglected to appreciate that the kitti-wakes are part of the cultural mix, a wildlife wonder with which no other city can compete.[57]

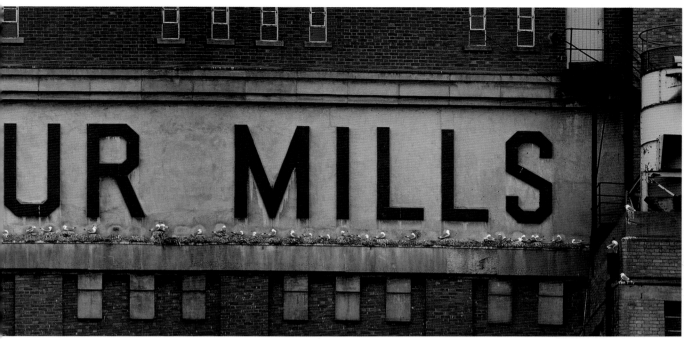

A vision of an older Gateshead. The flourmill – home to the world's most inland kittiwake colony – has now gone and been replaced with the BALTIC, Britain's largest contemporary art gallery.

At a personal level, the presence of kittiwake neighbours can be much more highly valued.

During the 1970s we lived near Lowestoft harbour in a four-storey hostel for ex-offenders of which I was warden. We had many kittiwakes nesting on the house, so their calls would be the first thing we heard in the morning and the last at night. I know the name is meant to represent the call, but to our ears, given our peculiar situation, it always seemed more like 'Let Me Out'. Yet I still love the sound and whenever we go somewhere like Bempton Cliffs I always find it magical, and am instantly reminded of our happy times in Lowestoft and some of our residents shouting 'Let Me Out'.[58]

While kittiwakes are not often direct beneficiaries of human action, they are frequent if inadvertent victims. It is commonplace to see a bird with its normally pristine underparts sullied brown with oil. Colonies nesting in Orkney and elsewhere in Scotland have also declined as a consequence of over-fishing of sand-eels and one major source, the Wee Bankie fishery off east Scotland, was closed in 2003 precisely on the grounds of its impact upon kittiwakes. In Shetland the decline of sand-eel stocks has been a double negative, reducing breeding success and causing bonxies (see Great Skua, page 229) to change their feeding habits towards direct predation of

kittiwakes. In combination, these have caused numbers to halve since 1981.

Although these downward pressures are relatively new, the human toll of kittiwakes has a long and melancholy history. Sir Robert Sibbald judged the flesh 'as good as a partridge', and in the nineteenth century both birds and eggs were taken in large quantities at ancient breeding stations like Ailsa Craig and along the Yorkshire coast between Flamborough and Bempton. The harvest at these 400-foot (120-m)-high cliffs continued until the 1950s, with the collectors, known locally as 'climmers', sending great basketfuls of various seabird eggs up to the top on ropes.[59]

There was also a huge trade in kittiwake skins for the millinery trade, the birds' wings being worked into nineteenth-century hat designs. The young birds with their striking M-shaped black patterning on the wings were particularly valued. The colony on Lundy island, which supplied a dedicated cottage industry in the adjacent Devon village of Clovelly, was devastated by the trade. Birds were also horribly abused, the plumage hunters 'often cutting their wings off and flinging the victims into the sea, to struggle with feet and head until death slowly came to their relief'.[60]

Even more indefensible was the slaughter of kittiwakes merely for sport. From the 1830s onwards, shooters hired steam vessels to take them under the cliffs at Flamborough Head. The captain would then sound

Kittiwakes are the species most truly deserving the name 'sea gull' and can feed on fish discarded while trawlers are still far from shore.

the siren, causing the seabirds to make a mass exodus overhead, when they were brought down in large numbers. One 'so-called sportsman' shot 80 birds in an hour for a bet, while an army officer in Ireland is reputed to have killed 500 during a day in pursuit of a similar wager.[61] A key development in the history of environmental protection was the Seabird Preservation Act of 1869, which was passed in an attempt to halt these forms of abuse. It set in train the gradual recovery that has seen the Bempton–Flamborough population blossom into one of the largest colonies in the North Atlantic region.

Tern family *Sternidae*

Sandwich Tern, *Sterna sandvicensis*. VN: Sarnie, Switch Tern, Eric (birders). 'The loveliness of the Terns, like all beauty in the bird world, is accompanied by a deplorable voice, cries always ugly, dissonant, and often, literally, a "scream".'[1] George and Anne Marples captured the central dichotomous character of the sandwich tern, which is one part elegant grace, one part grating racket. While acknowledging the disharmony, Rob Hume suggests that tern calls 'help create the essential atmosphere' of the British and Irish coasts and are 'singularly appropriate for birds of their salty, stormy, wide-skied realm'.[2]

The adult's main note has been likened to 'an unoiled cart wheel', which is an equally good description of a duet routinely performed by parents and offspring.[3] The classic scenario occurs in late summer, when a fish-carrying adult is pursued by its hungry full-winged chick. To each raucous '*keeryuk*' (or '*Eric*' as some people prefer) delivered by one, the other instantly appends a squeaky begging note, '*keee*'. Together they create one of the most unforgettable sounds of the British seashore. Remarkably each chick is able to identify its parent's voice – to us an anonymous noise – even above the cacophony of the nest colony.

Sandwich is the largest and heaviest of the British breeding species and in the Farnes it was the bird known as the 'tern', while its more delicate relatives were always referred to as 'sea swallows'.[4] The bigger bird is surprisingly timid in defence of its nest and seldom launches the violent assaults upon intruders made by common or Arctic terns. Of all of them, it perhaps best justifies James Fisher's assessment of family character: 'extremely capricious, nervous and sociable'.[5]

Breeding colonies are widely scattered with clusters in western Ireland, Anglesey, along the Hampshire and Sussex coast and in the Firth of Forth, although the distribution seems to obey few discernible rules. There are, for instance, several colonies throughout the Orkney archipelago, yet none has ever been recorded in seemingly suitable Shetland. Britain's largest sandwich tern population is on the north Norfolk coast and rises at times to 4475 pairs (2001), about a third of the national total, although 70 years earlier no more than nine pairs had ever been found together in the county. The colony alternates between two main sites – Scolt Head and Blakeney Point – according to the availability of good feeding areas. The terns are also highly susceptible to

Sandwich terns nest in dense noisy colonies like this one on the Farne Islands.

disturbance or predation and, sometimes it seems, to mere whim. Hence Rob Hume's telling remark: 'Buy a Sandwich Tern colony and make it into a nature reserve and they will probably repay you by nesting somewhere else the following year.'[6]

The common name commemorates the Kentish seaside town, where the bird was originally discovered by William Boys in 1784. The gradual uncovering of a massive oceanic range, from western Canada and Argentina to the shores of India and Mozambique, now makes the initial choice seem a little parochial.

Roseate Tern, *Sterna dougallii*. VN: Rosie tern (Yorkshire). There is a history of confusion surrounding early records of British terns, primarily because their identification features were so poorly understood. Typically this bird was not recognised until 1812, when several were shot by Dr Peter McDougall and his friends on the Cumbrae islands in the Firth of Clyde. He sent a specimen to Lord Montagu, who honoured the initial finder but mysteriously shortened his surname in the bird's patronymic.

Apart from a delicate rosy flush on the breasts of spring adults, they are distinguished by the overall white-

ness of their plumage, proportionately short wings and enormously long tail streamers. The bird's great beauty has long been matched by a precarious status. An initial plunge towards local extinction was triggered by com-

The roseate tern is one of the rarest seabirds to breed in Britain and Ireland.

This Ghanaian bracelet was made of bird rings taken from terns killed in their West-African wintering area.

Right: Common terns willingly nest on manmade islands like this one at Abberton Reservoir, Essex.

mercial collectors involved in the millinery trade and by taxidermists who rushed to secure a newly discovered rarity. The insidious problem of egg collectors has also spanned the bird's 200-year history in Britain and Ireland.

Yet protective legislation initiated a gradual recovery in fortunes, until a maximum of 3500 pairs was reached in the 1960s. Sadly a fresh collapse quickly ensued, driven partly by new threats in the bird's west African wintering grounds, where they are trapped and eaten by the locals. Otherwise, these elegant terns are kept as bedraggled toys for a few days by Senegalese and Ghanaian children, a striking echo of a time in nineteenth-century Italy when black terns, with their wings ripped off, were 'sold for young girls to use as playthings'.[7]

Most of Europe's roseates now breed in two Irish colonies at Lady Island's Lake, County Wexford (116 pairs), and on Rockabill islet off Dublin (611 pairs). The British population stands at just 63 pairs, with the largest colony at Coquet Island, Northumberland (57 pairs in 2002).[8]

Common Tern, *Sterna hirundo*. VN: Sea Swallow (widespread); Peerag, Pickie, Pickie-terno, Rittack, Ritti(c)k, Ritto, Sheer Tail (Orkney); Tirrock, Tarrock (Orkney and Shetland). Contrary to its name, this is not the most abundant tern but it is the one most commonly seen. Although twice as numerous, Arctic terns breed mainly in north-western Scotland, far away from contact with most of us. The common tern is found widely in the south and is the only one of the twins willing to inhabit inland freshwater locations. It is the tern species regularly seen in town or city centres, even floating high over the terraced streets of London and occasionally nesting on factory roofs.[9]

A major spur to its colonisation of non-coastal counties such as Leicestershire and Buckinghamshire is its adaptation to often small, newly created gravel pits or reservoirs. At some sites common terns are encouraged by local conservationists, who provide floating rafts or man-made islands where the birds can breed in relative safety. At Breydon estuary, Norfolk, a substantial colony (197 pairs) has taken to four artificial platforms, the first of which was floated in 1977. Each couple is provided with a ½-foot (46cm) square breeding compartment, but these reached capacity in 2001 and four pairs even doubled up to gain a toehold on the highly desirable residence.[10]

The complete duplication of vernacular names for common and Arctic terns is a good measure of their historical and, in many ways, continuing inseparability. 'Sea swallow' was long used as a name for the family, but Linnaeus cemented its association with this bird in 1735 when he called it *Sterna hirundo*, the 'swallow tern'. Ironically, when he drew up the description it is likely that he was looking at the skin of an Arctic tern.[11] Even today some birdwatchers shy away from the challenge of their identification and prefer to log them as 'commic terns', a catch-all term for both species. The differences are subtle but numerous, the Arctic tern being darker, smaller, narrower winged, proportionately longer tailed, shorter legged and with a beak of deep blood-red, as opposed to the black-tipped orange-crimson bill of its twin.

Visitors to the Farne Islands run the gauntlet of an Arctic tern colony.

The swallow is an apt comparison for both species, given their elongated tails, slender bodies, summer-only residence and aerial refinement. Perhaps the clearest testimony to the inspirational qualities of their aerodynamism is the number of small private sailing boats named after them. Birds are a constant theme in boat names – probably more than any other life form – and perhaps we should perceive in them the associations of physical and spiritual freedom that we project on to birds and sailing boats alike. *Sea Swallow* seems to carry the most obvious, fundamental connection between the two.

Arctic Tern, *Sterna paradisaea*. VN: Sea Swallow (widespread); Peerag, Pickie, Pickie-terno, Rittack, Ritti(c)k, Ritto, Sheer Tail (Orkney); Tirrock, Tarrock (Orkney and Shetland). Even though endless repetition has reduced them to a cliché, the vital statistics of this 4-ounce (113-gm) bird cannot fail to move us. Its summer presence on British and Irish shores, which mark the southern edge of its breeding range, seems nothing less than extraordinary, given that it passes the winter off the Antarctic pack-ice. Its annual migration thus involves a virtual circumnavigation of the planet, and in the process the bird enjoys eight to nine months of perpetual daylight every year. One bird ringed on the west coast of

Greenland on 8 July 1951 was found dead in Durban harbour, South Africa, having covered the minimum 8700-mile (14,500-km) journey in less than three months.[12] Small wonder that every textbook attempting to convey the miracle of migration cites this species.

To boot, they are beautiful birds. A dense breeding flock rising off the beach, amidst a cacophony of grating calls, and with their underwings and streamers gleaming like silver blades, is one of the most stirring visions of the northern summer. Except for a large southern outpost in Anglesey, they are almost exclusively Scottish in range – even Ireland has only 2000 pairs – with a major stronghold in Orkney and Shetland (about 30,000 pairs in more than 800 colonies).[13]

Arctic terns share the whole family's notoriety for sudden, arbitrary changes in breeding location, in some years building up dramatically or just vanishing completely. At Papa Stour, for example, in Shetland, there were just 400 pairs between 1969 and 1979, but numbers rose to 3000 in 1980 and more than trebled again the following season.[14] The factors that can influence tern distribution and breeding success are

The Arctic tern performs the longest migration of any British bird.

many and varied, not least the vagaries of the Scottish weather. But a major anxiety in the last 15 years has centred on the over-fishing of sand-eels, which underpin the marine ecosystem in the northern isles. 'In 1990 there was considerable debate amongst Shetland's . . . ornithologists about whether even one Arctic Tern fledged from Shetland's 500+ colonies.'[15]

Terns also fall victim to a wide range of nest predators, including human-introduced feral mink and hedgehogs, while on Foula in Shetland another improbable cause of mortality is the island's sheep, which bite the heads, limbs and wings off young birds in a presumed quest for calcium. Although this is not thought to be a serious check on breeding success, in 1975 the number of sheep-nibbled tern chicks was 200. (This strange behaviour by a ruminant has an interesting parallel on Rhum, where red deer eat young Manx shearwaters.)[16]

Fortunately the parent birds are ferociously determined guardians of their eggs and young, and will not shrink from attacking possible nest predators as large as humans. George and Anne Marples, authors of a forgotten classic, *Sea Terns*, cite an occasion when the former was struck 28 times in succession during a visit to a tern colony. 'Dazed and bewildered, he beat a hasty and undignified retreat.'[17] Where breeding Arctic terns are a major attraction, the wardens and visitors are obliged to take extreme precautionary measures:

On the Farne islands in Northumberland there should be a sign on the quay which reads, 'You are entering a hard-hat zone.' Regular visitors and the National Trust wardens know the drill but you can always spot first-time visitors. They're usually day trippers from Sea Houses who climb out the boat wearing flip flops, Bermuda shorts and puzzled expressions that say: 'Why are people putting on construction workers' helmets?' The puzzlement soon turns to dismay then terror as they approach the first tern nests. '*Kik kik kik kaa kaa kaa*', the Arctic terns home in like vengeful Valkyries, divebombing the intruders. They hover by people's faces and stab at their heads, and a bill that deftly plucks sand-eels from the sea can easily pierce human skin. An umbrella is a good deterrent, so too a telescope and tripod strategically carried above head height. But withstanding the onslaught is well worth it. This is England's Masai Mara – a huge wildlife concentration in a small area.[18]

Lesser Crested Tern, *Sterna bengalensis*. This large, yellow-billed tern is a bird of tropical waters and usually comes no nearer to Britain than the Mediterranean. By far the most noteworthy of just eight previous records was a female known as Elsie (from the initials LC), which first appeared among the sandwich tern colony on the Farne Islands, Northumberland, on 4 August 1984. The initial visit proved part of a faithful routine that Elsie maintained for 14 years until August 1997. During this period she became a well-known attraction enjoyed by thousands of observers and provided a good deal of additional income for the Farne boatmen. Elsie even succeeded in mating with a sandwich tern and reared four hybrid young, one of which also bred at the site.

During her summer visits to Britain she is thought to have accounted for a long string of records, ranging from locations as far apart as Lothian and East Sussex. It was also assumed that a lesser crested tern found in the sandwich tern colonies at Blakeney and Scolt Head, Norfolk for several weeks during August–September 1983 was none other than Elsie prospecting for her future summer headquarters.

One of the 26 records of **Sooty Tern**, *S. fuscata*, another rare wanderer from tropical latitudes, followed a remarkably similar pattern of movements along the English east coast. It was first seen on the scrape at Minsmere RSPB reserve in Suffolk on 11 June 1966 and then commuted between Scolt Island and Blakeney Point from 14 to 19 June, before finally appearing on the Farne Islands two days later.

This beautiful black-and-white species has an extraordinarily aerial lifestyle akin to that of a swift and enjoys a legend as the world's longest-flying bird. Most of its life is passed far from landfall over the open sea, where it sleeps on the wing and feeds by picking items off the surface, rather than plunge-diving (the feathers become waterlogged if soaked). Young birds do not breed until at least their third year, most will not do so

Our modern love of seaside recreation has widely evicted the beach-nesting little tern from its breeding areas.

before their sixth, and some individuals may not return to the nest island before they are 10.[19] It is thought possible that some sooty terns may never land at all during these non-breeding years.

Little Tern, *Sterna albifrons*. In some ways this is the least elegant member of its super-elegant family. The long narrow wings produce a purposeful flight, but they look disproportionate against the tiny body and stubby tail, and when beating fast they can appear like curiously over-sized paddles working in mid-air.

To many people the little tern's diminutive scale (it weighs just 1½–2 ounces/40–60gm) makes it particularly endearing. Simon Barnes described it as 'how you would expect a Black-headed Gull to look after it has gone to heaven'.[20] Its elfin character is all the more touching when set against the power and frequent hostility of the bird's coastal habitat. There is also an affecting daintiness in its breeding rituals:

I once watched the fascinating courtship ballet performed by a pair of these exquisite little birds on the island of Tiree. It was truly one of the most moving things I have seen in nature. The hen stood on the sandy shore, the cock just behind with a sandeel in his bill. After an almost imperceptible shiver of her wings her invitation was accepted and the cock lightly hopped on to her back. Immediately she turned her head and took the eel while he positioned himself to perform his role with the utmost delicacy.[21]

Unfortunately the little tern is as vulnerable as it looks and, with just 2800 pairs breeding in Britain and Ireland, it is one of our rarest seabirds. It nests in a marginal, highly dynamic landscape often within a few yards of the high-tide mark. Freak storms or spring tides frequently swamp whole colonies, and although the adults replace lost clutches until late summer, the list of nest predators is depressingly long and varied: rats, foxes, squirrels, hedgehogs, stoats, cats, dogs, gulls, oystercatchers, kestrels and magpies. Humans too, either inadvertently or deliberately, can affect breeding success. The ⅓-inch (32-mm)-long eggs are still robbed by collectors and were at one time even taken for food. Bert Axell, creator of the RSPB's flagship reserve at Minsmere, confessed that the first wild-bird eggs he ever tasted as a boy were from this species.[22]

The larger and more persistent problem is that humans share the bird's love of open sandy beaches. The access restrictions on our coasts between 1939 and 1945 probably meant that little terns had a good war, but the subsequent increase in our leisure time led to major losses of their favourite breeding areas. C. G. Gibson-Hill suggested that 'The growth of bungaloid settlements on previously deserted coast sometimes displaces the Little Tern, but often the birds merely move to another site.'[23] Unfortunately the author, writing in 1947, had little grasp of the finite beach space in our overcrowded islands. By the 1960s colonies in north Wales, Anglesey and along the south coast between Hampshire and Kent were being squeezed out.

Today little terns flourish best where access is restricted, as on nature reserves, and in some cases, where areas of seashore are temporarily cordoned off to protect the breeding colony. A classic example of an apartheid beach is at Great Yarmouth, Norfolk. An original little-tern colony had flourished on an area that had been mined during the war, but in 1983/4, parallel conditions recurred in a fenced-off section where a sewage pipe was being installed. A nucleus expanded to become the largest little-tern colony in Britain, with 277 pairs in 1991.

However, high concentrations of eggs and young seem to trigger their own problems. Two seasons later at least 90 young fell victim to four cats. Even worse, in 1995 kestrels were thought to have killed as many as 271 chicks, despite the fact that RSPB staff kept the falcons' own young well supplied with dead mice. A partial answer has been found in giving the terns their own form of air-raid shelter: 6-inch (15-cm) lengths of plastic piping camouflaged with the help of sand and glue.[24]

Black Tern, *Chlidonias niger*. The strange-sounding generic name is actually a misspelling of the Greek *khelidonios* – 'of, or like, a swallow' – a reference to the bird's airy grace. There is also a rare word *khelidonias*, a spring wind, so named because it carries the swallows with it.[25] Presumably it also bears this beautiful marsh tern, which winters in Africa and breeds widely in mainland Europe. Now it appears only as a migrant over British wetlands during high spring and autumn, accompanied occasionally by one of its two rarer siblings, the **Whiskered Tern**, *C. hybridus* and **White-winged Tern**, *C. leucopterus*.

Black terns are at their loveliest in May/June when there is a warm dusty bloom to the black-and-grey parts of the breeding plumage. It is possibly this that accounts for the old East Anglian name, 'blue darr'. Another archaic version was 'carr swallow', reflecting the bird's preference for inland freshwater sites rather than the coastal locations of the *Sterna* species. It is one of a suite of British birds – spoonbill, common crane, ruff and black-tailed godwit are others – pushed to extinction through loss of wetlands and, in particular, drainage of the East Anglian Fens. Pennant's 1769 description of 'vast flocks' which 'almost deafen one with their clamours' seems almost unbelievable, given that there has been only a handful of breeding attempts since the mid-nineteenth century.[26]

Black tern and their eggs were taken commercially for the table, the latter passed off as 'lapwing' eggs, in which there was a lucrative trade (see page 204).[27] Taxidermists and trophy collectors then made sure that the final few birds never supplied a core of survivors for a subsequent recovery. Typically the last Norfolk breeding pair in 1858 was thwarted when the eggs were taken and the adults shot. Even a nesting attempt near Nottingham in 1975 failed because of egg collectors.

Eric Ennion, writing about a Dutch breeding colony, gives a full sense of what we have lost:

I could lie by the hour watching the black tern's flight. It is at once sensitive and strong. One wingbeat sends the black and silver body ten yards through the air, but the bird can stop dead, twist, or pivot on a wingtip in a split second as the hazards of flycatching demand. They must be able to turn somersaults, or something between a somersault and a roll. The exact details are too rapid to follow but one moment the tern hangs almost upsidedown to jab at a fly passing beneath its tail, and the next moment is gliding ahead with the fly in its bill.[28]

Auk family *Alcidae*

Common Guillemot, *Uria aalge*. VN: Aak (Orkney); Loom, Longvi, Longi, Lungvi (Shetland). Guillemots defend the smallest nest territory of any bird (at times just 2 inches/5cm square) and form in consequence some of the largest, densest breeding bird congregations in Britain.[1] Altogether there are more than 1.2 million birds in these islands, and in Scotland there are at least 28 colonies each with more than 10,000 birds. The largest on Handa Island contains almost 100,000.[2]

Peering down over a sheer edge on to these massed ranks huddled against the cliff – 'like rows of milk bottles on doorsteps' – their harsh growls and trumpeting calls distinct even above the sea surge, is one of the most memorable and powerful experiences in British nature.[3] Part of the satisfaction lies in the clear linkage between the ancient and the present. The ledges are often spread across the cliff walls in step-like formation and may well have originated in fault-lines laid down even before the original strata broke the earth's crust. Hundreds of thousands, probably millions, of years have passed for them to achieve their present structure. The infinitely slow geological forces are clearly instrumental not only in the birds' presence but in the colony's exact con-figuration – the lines of incubating auks clustered into the narrowest fissures:

[they] . . . greet every occasion of interest, curiosity or excitement with snaky cranings and bowings of neck and vary their marital and family preoccupations with squabbles with their neighbours, filling the air with a vast chorus of raucous notes which reverberates from the cliffs in astonishing waves of sound. All around is kaleidoscopic activity, with birds swarming like insects in all three elements, coming and going in a constant succession between rocks and water or sweeping along the cliff-face, out over the sea, and back again . . .[4]

Along with their intense sociability, auks share with their unrelated southern counterparts – penguins – an upright stance that has cemented their image as the bird families most similar to humans. The cliff-face auk colony can also evoke a high-rise block of flats or comparable structure. 'The rows of black and white birds rising in tiers up to near the top, and the ghostly noise of the[ir] combined twitter . . . made it seem as if one was in a vast opera house, packed with crowds of people in

Britain and Ireland's seabird cliffs, with their dense colonies of guillemots, are of international importance.

white shirt-fronts and black tails, all whispering comments on each other and rustling their programmes.'[5]

Another element in their almost comic persona is the range of seemingly affectionate and very human gestures in their social relations. Edmund Selous, one of the pioneers of bird behavioural studies, described the pair-bonding of guillemots thus:

> With the tip of his long pointed beak he, as it were, nibbles the feathers . . . of her head, neck, and throat, whilst she, with her eyes half closed, and an expression as of submitting to an enjoyment – a 'Well, I suppose I must' look – bends her head backwards, or screws it round sideways towards him, occasionally nibbling with her bill, also, amidst the feathers of his throat, or the thick white plumage of his breast.[6]

Their gruff conversational calls gave rise to an original onomatopoeic name, 'murre' (pronounced 'myrrh'), still used for several of the auk family across the Atlantic. Guillemot, however, was a word of French origin, a pet form of *Guillaume*, and this finds its echo in 'willock', an old name that may yet survive in northern Scotland.[7]

It is the largest of the four breeding auks and comes in three forms. In Britain and Ireland the paler brown-backed southern race *albionis* occurs as far north as St Abb's Head on the east and Islay on the west coast. Thereafter it is replaced by the northern nominate black-backed subspecies, *aalge*, among which there is a distinctive 'bridled' variety that shows a white line along an indented crease behind the bird's eye. In England the latter form accounts for less than 1 per cent, but this proportion increases further north, with one in four birds showing a bridle in Shetland.

The adult guillemot's toleration of the densely packed conditions of the loomery – the name for an auk colony – is well matched by the adaptations of the single enormous egg. Proportional to body weight it is one of the largest produced by any British bird. It also exhibits the most striking variations, with a wide range of base colours and an infinite pattern of squiggles and blotches. For these reasons it was, and sadly still is, a great favourite among collectors. But the function of the individual markings is to aid recognition in the anonymous conditions of the cliff ledge. One consistent feature is the extreme pyriform structure. The narrow end ensures that

Oil pollution is just one in a long list of human activities that has had a detrimental impact on guillemots.

the eggs roll in a tight circle rather than veer off the bare rock sill, although sometimes parents are panicked by the sudden appearance of a predator and can drag the egg with them when they take flight.

Another common characteristic is the egg's high nutritional value, with a very high fat content as a result of having a larger yolk than the eggs of most terrestrial birds.[8] It is hardly surprising to find auk eggs featuring strongly in the past diet of many coastal communities. The most celebrated were the inhabitants of St Kilda, who gathered huge numbers from the seabird cliffs fringing their tiny islands. In his seventeenth-century account, Martin Martin estimated that the number of eggs provided for him and his crew amounted to 16,000 in just three weeks – a staggering average of 762 eggs a day – and added: 'without all doubt the inhabitants, who were treble our number, consumed many more eggs and fowls than we could'.[9]

A nineteenth-century eye-witness of St Kildan practices recorded the islanders visiting the offshore Stac Biorach, where they hoisted down to the boats 17 baskets containing 400 guillemot eggs apiece:

These eggs are very good eating when fresh. After they are incubated for a few days most of the egg appears, when boiled, to be changed into a rich thick cream, and in this condition they are also relished. Sometimes eggs, not only of this species but of some others which have not been hatched, are found late in the season. Some of these when cooked look like a piece of sponge cake, have a high gamey flavour, and are esteemed a great delicacy.[10]

Eggs were taken widely around English and Scottish coasts, although it was indiscriminate shooting by sportsmen that led to the guillemot's local extinction at sites like Beachy Head, Sussex, to which the bird has never returned. Another famous source of eggs was the Yorkshire coastline around Flamborough, the site of England's largest guillemot colony. The practices of the local 'climmers' involved leaving cliffs 'fallow' once they had been heavily worked and ceasing operations at a certain point in the season to allow the auks, as well as the gulls, to re-lay.

A degree of sustainable husbandry permitted an almost continuous harvest at the site from the seventeenth century until the 1940s, with an annual offtake rising at times to 130,000 eggs.[11] Yet the combination of egg collecting and shooting for sport eventually triggered a steep decline in numbers. The recreational battues, amounting to little more than purposeless slaughter arranged by local boatmen and sometimes involving special trains to bring in the participants, are well described in a *Guardian* article of November 1868:

On a strip of coast eighteen miles long near Flamborough Head, 107,250 sea-birds were destroyed by 'pleasure parties' in four months; 12,000 by men who shoot them for their feathers to adorn women's hats and 79,500 young birds died of starvation in emptied nests. Commander Knocker . . . who reported these facts, saw two boats loaded above the gunwales with dead birds, and one party of eight guns killed 1100 birds in a week.[12]

More recent causes of auk mortality include contamination from oil. The sight of a scrawny carcass, unrecognisable even as a bird, in its thick coat of black slime, first became familiar during the oil disaster of the *Torrey Canyon* in 1967. Today it is the classic image of industrial pollution, but oiling of birds was a serious problem long before the Second World War. Ironically it has become less significant today because of far stricter controls over procedures on oil tankers.[13]

Another modern threat arises from the huge extended nets used in fishing operations. Diving auks become entangled and drown in these 'walls of death'. One minor benefit is a better appreciation of the bird's swimming capabilities. Feeding auks studied in Scotland had an average dive time of more than a minute, with a maximum of 202 seconds.[14] The all-comers' record is a dive to a depth of 600 feet (180m), the equivalent of a bird swimming down almost the entire height of London's Post Office Tower.

Razorbill, *Alca torda*. VN: Aak, Coulter-neb (Orkney); Wilkie, Willock (Shetland). Both guillemot and razorbill have short stiff wings that double up as underwater flippers once they plunge beneath the surface. In the northern hemisphere they occupy much the same niche that penguins fill in the southern, and in France the name for the razorbill is *petit pingouin*.

The key difference between a penguin and an auk (except for the extinct great auk; see below) is the latter's powers of flight. In the case of the razorbill, however, these often seem poorly developed, although they are happily counter-balanced by an extremely robust constitution. 'I have seen Razorbills flying down from a bad take-off trying to gain airspeed. Eventually they strike the rocks about 30 feet below, bounce off and continue on their way as if nothing had happened.'[15]

The bird is compact and heavy bodied, while the wings are short and narrow. It has a distinctly energetic buzzy flight, giving a sense of speed that is largely illusory. Great black-backed gulls regularly pursue and kill razorbills. With long, deep, slow wingbeats, the gull looks ponderous in comparison with the whirring missile-like trajectory of the auk, but it can quickly overhaul its victim and knock it to the sea surface with a single hammer-blow of the bill.

Razorbills are no more than occasional winter visitors to the low-lying coasts of south and east England. For breeding purposes they need sea cliffs, boulder fields or undisturbed talus slopes on offshore islands, a requirement that tilts their distribution towards the coasts of Wales, Scotland, Ireland and western England. The spectacular colonies formed with other auks and seabirds are one of the few elements in our avifauna to lure continental birdwatchers across the Channel. But their significance is far higher than a simple tourist attraction; in the case of the razorbill, around two out of every five razorbills in Europe nest on our shores.

Although they occur virtually side by side, guillemots and razorbills occupy subtly different niches. Razorbills prefer lower cliff slopes for nesting and usually lay their egg in a covered crevice, underneath a boulder, between rocks, or even take over a rabbit or puffin burrow. Unlike guillemots they never breed on top of an exposed stack. The razorbill's egg reflects the subtle differences in location, being more oval in shape and lacking the strongly pyriform, roll-resistant structure of the guillemot egg.

Yet there is the same wide variation in pattern to aid individual recognition and it is, if anything, even larger in size than its close neighbour's. A razorbill egg can weigh more than 3 ounces (90gm) and one-seventh of the mother's entire body weight. To give some sense of her

The female razorbill lays an egg that is one-seventh of her body weight.

ovulatory achievement, a 9-stone (57-kg) woman would have to have an 18-pound (8-kg) baby to achieve the same weight ratio; and all this on a narrow cliff ledge with the waves crashing below.

Great Auk, *Pinguinus impennis*. The infamous story of two birds strangled on the small Icelandic island of Eldey in June 1844 is usually cited as the world's last sighting of this magnificent species, but 1852 is now accepted as the date marking the bird's extinction. This flightless species – one of only two flightless birds of the northern hemisphere – may have been gone for more than 150 years, but it has lost none of its symbolic potency. It is the dodo of British ornithology, if not of the whole North Atlantic, and it still galvanises our imaginations around the appalling consequences for nature when folly and greed are given free rein.

Typical of our continued preoccupations are Jeremy Gaskell's recent book *Who Killed the Great Auk?* (2000) and Errol Fuller's exhaustive monograph *The Great Auk* (1999). Fuller has called his subject 'one of the true stars of extinction. Its story rises and falls like a Greek

Errol Fuller's beautiful and atmospheric recreation of a great auk colony breathes fresh life into our image of this extinct bird.

tragedy.'[16] His book includes his own superb paintings, which have stripped away much of the limerick-like unreality of early portraits and breathed a new sense of living proximity – and, ironically, of fresh tragedy – into our image of the species.

Standing about 30 inches (76cm) tall and five times the weight of a common guillemot, the great auk well deserved its name, although previously it had been known by a bewildering variety of alternatives. To British and Spanish sailors it 'was the *original* penguin and its name was simply transferred . . . to the *Spheniscus* penguins of the South Seas' when mariners subsequently encountered them. (Off southern Newfoundland there is still a group of islands called the Penguin Islands.[17]) In Britain another traditional name was 'garefowl', deriving from the Norse *geirfugl*, spear-bird, in honour of the strange razor-like bill.[18]

The species' history of exploitation includes 13,000 years of sustainable harvesting by the Boethuk Indians of the Newfoundland coast. But to Europeans of the early modern period the great auk's extreme tameness and flightless condition simply confirmed its role as God's 'admirable instrument for the sustenation of man'.[19] The feathers and flesh were taken in industrial quantities, with hundreds of thousands being killed on Funk Island off Newfoundland. Almost all of the bird's by-products were utilised. In Greenland great-auk stomachs served as harpoon floats, while on St Kilda, where the bird once bred in good numbers, it was prized for its huge 5-inch (12.4-cm)-long eggs – 'as big almost as those of the Ostrich'. The St Kildans also stuffed a great-auk stomach with its own fat, hung it in the chimney to be cured by the smoke and then used it as a type of medicine.[20]

Until the late medieval period the bird was probably a regular visitor to British and Irish shores, especially during the winter. There are bone remains or records from localities as far apart as Counties Antrim, Donegal, Clare and Waterford, Durham, Orkney, Caithness, and both Inner and Outer Hebrides. The last-known British breeding pair was seen on Papa Westray, Orkney, in 1812. The birds were well known to the locals as the 'King and Queen o' the Aaks', but the female was soon stoned to death on her nest, while the male was killed the following year. St Kilda lays claim to what was probably the final British example, a bird seen on Stac an Armin in 1840, where it shared the same sorry fate as the Orkney pair. It was killed on the tragic presumption that it was a witch or demon.

Ironically it was not superstition but the explosion in interest in natural history that sealed the great auk's fate. Wealthy collectors and their agents were relentless in pursuit of a final few birds, driven forward by the outrageous prices paid for skins, eggs and similar relics. For example, a single egg exchanged hands in 1832 for £15 15s. 6d. 'at a time when the average annual income for a skilled worker was about £9 10s'.[21] Similarly, it was a collector called William Bullock who had provided sufficient financial incentive to orchestrate the killing of the male bird on Papa Westray. This he subsequently sold for £16 5s. 6d.

As the century came to a close there were thought to be just 70 great-auk eggs left in the world (a survey in the 1960s added five more), along with 81 skins, 10 skeletons and the detached bones from a further 120 birds. With the growing realisation of the bird's extinction, and the loss of any further opportunity for fresh skins, prices soared accordingly. In 1895 a single egg went for £350, while five years later a fine skin fetched £330 15s. 6d. at auction (the equivalent in today's prices of more than £20,300 and £19,200 respectively). During the same period even plaster-cast replicas sold for the not inconsiderable sum of £5 each.[22] One auction house, Stevens' of Covent Garden, became so closely associated with the inflated sales of these relics that its telegraphic address was simply 'Auks, London'.[23]

During the last hundred years the bird has become less an object for our obsessive acquisitive instincts; instead modern commentators have focused on its environmental symbolism. The great auk's history provides the ultimate example and benchmark for all concerned with the future of natural history in Britain. It is in this context that one can appreciate the cairn and monument erected in Papa Westray in 1988, 175 years after William Bullock's male bird had been killed there. They were built by the junior members of the Orkney Field Club at Fowl Craig in the RSPB's North Hill reserve. Ralph Faulkner, the driving

Black guillemots bring a dash of character and interest to many small harbours on the Irish and west Scottish coastlines.

force behind the monument, recalled: 'We couldn't count Great Auks or draw them or plot their nests. The monument cairn . . . was the only thing I could think of':

> A potter modelled a half-size replica of the Great Auk; a plaque on the cairn made the commemoration a public statement; a time capsule placed in the cairn looked to the future; every child was given an enamel lapel badge of a Great Auk . . . [Ralph Faulkner] remembers the uplifing emotion at the reading of a dedication . . . The hushed crowd of children asked the future citizens of the world to remember the Great Auk and to care for the planet which these children would be handing on to them.[24]

Black Guillemot, *Cepphus grylle*. VN: Tystie, Tyste (Scotland, especially the Northern Isles). This is another good example where a piece of local vernacular has been taken up virtually nationwide, particularly by bird-watchers.[25] 'Tystie' is the northern name for what Ken Williamson described as 'this most lovable of all seabirds'. Versions of it are still used in the Faeroes and Iceland, and all are thought to derive from an Old Norse word, *þeisti*, describing the call.[26] The sound is a high, clear, piercing whistle that can attain frequencies well beyond the range of the human ear. It is quite unlike that

of any other auk or, in fact, any other seabird, and it can take you completely by surprise as it rings out from some unseen source amidst a jumble of coastal rocks.

The black guillemot is the least numerous of our four resident auks, with a population of fewer than 40,000 adults, three-quarters of which occur in the Hebrides, Orkney and Shetland. (It is one of a select band of birds that has found its way into Shetland place names, with Teisti Geo, along Clift Sounds near Lerwick.[27]) Yet it also breeds widely around Irish shores, down the west coast of Scotland and the Isle of Man, while a relict population in Anglesey represents the southernmost British colony. In some areas these are the easiest auks to see, breeding close to small harbours where they often fish alongside the boats moored in the quay. Most nest in loose colonies, occupying crevices on lower cliffs and scree slopes, rabbit burrows or under boulders close to the beach. They have also adapted to a number of human-created situations such as holes in wooden piers, harbour walls, ruined buildings and, most original of all, down the barrels of old cannons.[28]

Apart from the scarlet legs and a lovely, rather intriguing vermilion lining to the mouth, a black guillemot's most striking features are the flashing white areas on the upper- and underside of each wing. These mirror-like patches seem to intensify the whirring action

255

Storm birds – little auks are regularly blown on to British and Irish shores by autumn gales.

of the bird's stubby wings and perhaps explain why one ornithologist felt that it resembled 'a giant bumble bee'.[29]

One of the most unlikely birds ever to occur in British waters is the single – and only – example of the **Ancient Murrelet**, *Synthliboramphus antiquus*, a diminutive auk never recorded even on the Atlantic coast of North America, and whose normal breeding range lies entirely within the Pacific, from the Commander Islands and the Kamchatka east to Alaska and Washington state in the USA; it was found on 27 May 1990 on Lundy Island, Devon, where it took up residence with the colony of breeding auks for the next three springs.

Little Auk, *Alle alle*. VN: Rotchie (Shetland). This tiny species is no larger than a starling and vies with Wilson's petrel for the title of the world's most numerous seabird. It breeds almost entirely beyond the Arctic Circle, with some Greenland sea cliffs holding several hundred thousands. A rare witness at one of these inaccessible sites observed that 'in the comparatively birdless landscape of the far north the huge colonies ... are extraordinarily impressive'. The birds were once widely eaten by the locals and were particularly enjoyed when 'high' – 100 auks being stuffed into a blubbery sealskin and cached under a rock pile.[30]

Only a fragment of the Arctic hordes ever reach Britain, mainly as a result of northerly gales in late autumn or winter. Unlike other British alcids, little auks feed almost exclusively on planktonic crustaceans and their snow-bound nest sites are often dramatically streaked with the resulting red guano. Autumn storms can force the crustaceans to depths beyond the little auk's reach, when the birds are compelled by starvation to make desperate journeys far from their normal range and habitat.

Known as 'wrecks', the dispersive movements have been noted since the early nineteenth century, but the most recent were in 1982/3, 1990 and 1995. The last was one of the largest ever recorded with an estimated 40,000 birds past Flamborough Head, Yorkshire, during the first half of November.[31] They often involve a few disoriented strays wandering inland, sometimes after they become caught up in flocks of migrating starlings and other land birds.

The tiny seabirds can then turn up in the oddest places, with records of birds plumping down among a flock of chickens, or on to a house roof (Tredington, Gloucestershire), and in one instance on to a street in central Bristol.[32] C. A. Gibson-Hill tells the story of a man who was desperate to see this Arctic speciality and hired a boat to travel to Svalbard. When he returned to Cambridge he discovered that two had turned up near the city, driven inland by autumn gales.[33]

The lack of context and the tiny size of these storm-driven waifs only seem to compound the sense of oddity: 'it can look more like a child's toy than a seabird'.[34] (Curiously the adults even sound rather like a squeaky toy, although en masse their calls have been likened to 'hysterical witch-like laughter'.[35]) 'The body shape is a hunched oval, blunt at both ends and beetle-like ... On the water an exhausted Little Auk is hunched and dejected, its neck withdrawn and bill so small as to be insignificant, creating a frog-like facial appearance.'[36]

The scientific name of the nominate race is *Alle alle alle*, deriving from the Latin for a great toe, *allex*, the 'x' being omitted to designate that the hind toe is missing on the bird itself. The strange name was once the source of a fabled prank played by Ernst Hartert as he walked through the bird room at Lord Rothschild's private museum in Tring, of which Hartert was curator. Finding the work of a 'rather pompous ornithologist' open at the little auk, he altered the account so that it read *Alle alle allelujah*.[37]

Atlantic Puffin, *Fratercula arctica*. VN: Tammy Norie, Norie, Sea Parrot (northern Scotland). Few birds are more completely enfolded in an aura of humour and affection than this species. Testimony to our attachment are the special tourist excursions to puffin colonies in places like Lundy or the Scilly Isles, the boat trips often involving people who would otherwise take little interest in natural history. Where puffins are present with a host of other seabirds, as at Bempton Cliffs or the Farne Islands, they are singled out as the endlessly photogenic star-attraction.

But why exactly should a highly seasonal inhabitant of remote islands and headlands so captivate us? Some of the charm is surely a result of what the poet Norman MacCaig described as its 'mad, clever clown's beak'. Equal in depth to the head and banded with blue, red and yellow plates, the bill makes the puffin look part seabird, part tropical parrot. Ornithologist Colin Harrison also notes that the 'false triangular eyebrow over a red-rimmed eye . . . gives it an air of earnest bewilderment. This is accompanied . . . by deep conversational *aah*'s in what sounds like a rural human accent.'[38] Equally endearing are those curious downturned yellow 'hinges' at the corner of the mouth, which increase the impression of human dejection and, equally, the air of comedy.

Yet puffins seem to have other physical properties that predispose humans towards them. Kenny Taylor points out that they are about the height and bulk of a 1-pint (½-litre) milk carton, and 'Psychological studies have shown that people often respond to creatures that have rounded features . . . The reason for this behaviour is probably linked to the rounded features of human babies, but the response can be activated by other species – and the puffin's rounded features are a good example.'[39] We love puffins, it seems, because these funny little birds remind us of our infant selves.

Certainly, if you scan the shelves of soft toys, you find that few birds are considered as cuddly or as appropriate for children (except perhaps owls and the puffin's southern counterpart, the penguin). It is striking that

The all-comer's record for one puffin's beakful of fish is 62.

Noel Carrington and Allen Lane came to the same conclusion on puffin appeal in 1939, when they devised a brand name for their children's list at the better-known publishing house of Penguin. Puffin Story Books was launched in 1941 and is today the largest children's publisher in the UK and throughout much of the English-speaking world. The logo has passed through six versions en route to its present smiling avatar, but throughout the images have retained one central characteristic – the bird's sumptuous rotundity.

Our sense of amusement at puffins has a long history. 'Pope' was an old name that Willughby and Ray encountered in seventeenth-century Cornwall, where it may still

Lundy Island off the north Devon coast derives its name from the old Norse for 'puffin'.

Banded with blue, red and yellow plates, the puffin's bill makes it look part seabird, part tropical parrot.

survive.[40] Its current scientific name, *Fratercula*, similarly means 'little friar'. The bird's plumage suggests the white surplice of clerical costume, but one imagines that the mock-serious associations were a way for coastal folk to satirise religious authority, as well as the puffin's own air of bumbling solemnity.

There is a similar dash of acid in another West-Country name. 'In Cornwall puffins are apparently called "Londoners". The reason given by locals is that they see puffins standing on the cliff looking mindlessly out to sea and they are reminded of the countless visitors from London who seem to do exactly the same.'[41] 'Londoners' is a highly intriguing name because of its similarity to the original Norse word for puffin, *lunde*. Although the rationale may have been worked out in purely contemporary terms, nevertheless one wonders if the linguistic affinities are ancient. More certain is the fact that the original Norse survives today in Lundy, the

Together with penguins and owls, puffins are the birds most often found in the baby's cot.

Bristol Channel islet where there were once huge numbers of puffins. *Lunde-ey* meant 'puffin island'.

Our sense of comedy and emotional engagement may have existed in the past, but they were no barrier to exploitation. The bird's plump carcass was considered good eating, just as the dense colonies were once valued as important economic assets. There was a large puffin population on the Scilly Isles, which the islanders harvested in part to pay their annual rents.[42] The trade was widespread and driven to some extent by a questionable papal dispensation that allowed the clergy to treat the bird as fish and thus suitable for consumption during Lent.

Many methods were devised for trapping the birds and were probably most advanced on St Kilda, Britain's last bastion for the hunter-gatherer lifestyle until the twentieth century. Puffins handed the old fowlers a comfortable head-start through their exceptional tameness and highly gregarious behaviour. Most of them were taken with a specially designed puffin-gin or puffin-snare, which was described thus by one eye-witness:

> It consists of about a fathom of stout cord to which hair nooses, about nine inches long, are fastened at intervals of three or four inches. This is stretched out on any boulder . . . and fastened at the ends. The nooses along the sides are then carefully opened out to a diameter of about an inch and a half. The birds which have been disturbed are soon back again, and, being restless little fellows, it is not long before some of them have got their feet entangled in the nooses . . . Sometimes very many more are caught, for the puffin is a very pugnacious little fellow, and when he finds himself caught attacks his neighbour. In this way a general fight is started, during which many are caught. On a suitable day a person with four or five of these snares, which are as many as he can attend to, may kill several hundreds.[43]

Observers of St Kildan life marvelled at the huge numbers killed. Some estimates suggest an annual catch of 90,000 birds, many of which were eaten throughout the summer. They were also taken for their yield of 4800 pounds (2177kg) of feathers, which were transported to the mainland to be used as mattress and pillow stuffing. Although the harvest was vast it hardly affected the puffin's incredible abundance on St Kilda. People likened the huge wheeling flocks of summer birds to locust swarms, while Richard Kearton said that 'the clouds of birds . . . made a sound like a whirlwind whipping up a great bed of dead rushes'.[44] One author estimated a total population of three million birds.[45]

If this calculation was accurate – and no less an authority than James Fisher thought it was – then puffins

The massive puffin flocks wheeling around St Kilda in summer create one of the most powerful visions in all British ornithology.

have declined dramatically in the intervening years. There are now fewer than one million pairs in Britain and Ireland combined, possibly as a consequence of sea temperature rises, which do not suit this cold-water northern species.

Yet puffins are still common seabirds and a visit to a large breeding colony is among the most captivating experiences offered on the coastlines of Britain. Unlike the rather dangerous conditions and awesome spectacle of a loomery, a puffin colony is normally on a gentle grassy slope and provides a far more relaxed setting. In fact a visitor often feels inclined to sit or lie down in order to get on more intimate terms with its pint-sized occupants. Yet this micro-environment still has a distinctive atmosphere that assaults all the senses.

The puffin's pickaxe-like bill enables it to dig easily in most substrates, and it can even cut a tunnel into soft sandstone. (However, its most extraordinary excavations must surely occur on Funk Island, Newfoundland, where the cap of 'soil' in one part is made up of the decomposed bodies of millions of seabirds laced with great-auk bones and egg fragments. The organic material was the by-product of decades of exploitation by New World fowlers. The tragic irony is not lost on Kenny Taylor: 'The puffin's cradle is the great auk's grave.'[46]) In Britain burrows are often sited on deep beds of peaty soil and the ground is correspondingly spongy, with a close rabbit-cropped turf that is softened further with waxy cushions of sea pink or thrift.

Above the constant sea-sounds you can invariably hear the wail of marauding gulls, while from the earth itself rise the deep groaning notes of puffins in their subterranean chambers. Along with a rich fishy stink, the birds' abundant guano gives rise to a distinctive burrow-rim flora of sorrel, scurvy grass, mayweed, mosses and liverworts. Taylor notes that when viewed from a puffin's eye-level, 'the variety of colours and textures of these tiny plants – emerald green, acid green, tawny and deep red, velvety, crinkled or hung with drops of rain – has a delicate and astonishing beauty'.[47]

He also captures what it is like to pass through a puffin colony where many decades of occupancy have given rise to a distinctive stepped structure to the site:

> Walking up a terraced puffin slope is like climbing a gigantic flight of grassy stairs, but to the puffins that live there it must be more like an enormous multi-storey block of flats. Immediately behind each level, sheep- and puffin-flattened step is an upright band of soil, like the riser on a staircase or a floor in the apartment block . . . Stepping over this burrowed riser takes you to the next terrace – one floor up, but close enough to the previous storey that a puffin sitting there could lean over and touch the head of a bird on the floor below.
>
> In big puffinries, a single turfy slope can shelter thousands of burrows . . . Birds at the top of the slope may be more than one hundred 'floors' above the burrowers at the foot. I counted 131 'floors', for example, on one slope, in part of a Hebridean puffinry . . .[48]

The nest burrows are slightly longer than a person's arm, which may explain why old fowlers caught the free-flying adults, and the chamber rises slightly at the far end so that water drains away from the single chick. Although few people ever get to see a young bird ('like an egg-sized powderpuff . . . mostly charcoal grey, but with creamy feathering on the chest and belly'), its existence can be inferred by the presence of an adult with what Norman MacCaig called 'a six-fold whisker of tiny fishes'. In fact six is a modest catch. The specially hinged mandibles, which are able to open in parallel, and the backward-pointing serrations in the mouth, enable a bird easily to take 4–12, while the all-comers' record is 61 sand-eels and a three-bearded rockling.[49]

The young bird feeds on the abundant protein for about seven weeks in the sanctuary of the burrow until the adults finally abandon it. It must then make its way to sea alone at night, where it may see its parents for the first time. Ironically the blackout conditions of the nest chamber mean that neither the parents nor the chick have ever made visual contact and, as a consequence, will never recognise each other thereafter.

The Pallas's sandgrouse is one of the blue-ribbon rarities for British twitchers.

The street-dwelling version of the rock dove is probably the only wild bird most people will ever have touched.

Sandgrouse family
Pteroclididae

Pallas's Sandgrouse, *Syrrhaptes paradoxus*. Subtle but exquisite beauty and a range centred between the Chinese province of Sinkiang and the Gobi Desert of Inner and Outer Mongolia are only part of the reason why this is one of our most mythic of rarities. The other element is the strangely irruptive pattern of migration, triggered by extreme winter conditions, that brings a bird of the inner Asian steppe to these islands.

There were two dramatic invasions in 1863 and 1888, with smaller numbers in seven years between 1859 and 1909. The largest 1888 irruption comprised several thousand birds spread from Kent to Shetland, while more widely they reached as far as the Faeroes and southern Spain. Remarkably the episode also involved two British nesting records – at Culbin Sands, Grampian, and near Beverley, Yorkshire – and a piece of specially enacted legislation aimed at controlling the relentless fusillade that greeted so many of the birds.[1] In Norfolk alone about 186 were killed.[2]

No one really knows why the irruptions ceased, but analysis of the sandgrouse appearances indicates that most birds occurred in May. The penultimate record was even on the Isle of May on 11 May 1975, while the last ever individual was at Loch Spiggie, Shetland, on 19 May 1990.

Pigeon and Dove family
Columbidae

Rock Dove (Pigeon), *Columba livia*. VN: Doo/Dow (Orkney, Shetland). This species is *the* pigeon, one of the best known, most cherished and yet, paradoxically, most frequently persecuted members of our avifauna. It is the one and only wild bird many people will ever have touched.[1] Its appearance has become so variable and the physical shape so elastic through centuries of selective breeding that it is almost impossible to offer a generalised description. Charles Darwin estimated 228 named varieties. (Darwin was himself a keeper of pigeons, prompting George Bernard Shaw's description of him in *Back to Methuselah* 'as an intelligent and industrious pigeon fancier'.)[2] Yet true wild rock doves, the ancestors of all domestic and feral strains, usually feature a white rump and double black bar across the pale-grey inner wings.

The species' image involves a reverse pattern to the one evident in carrion and hooded crows (see page 418). Instead of being two birds with a single cultural profile, it is one species with a split personality or, more accurately, with multiple personalities. It is the feral pigeon that struts the city street; the wild dove of northern coastal cliffs; it forms the semi-domesticated flocks kept for centuries in the dovecote or pigeon loft. It is also the brave, defenceless homing bird beloved as a messenger by Egyptian pharaohs and English generals alike.

Perhaps more important than these practical roles, the

rock dove is, along with the eagle and raven, part of a great trinity of bird symbols for Western civilisation. Indeed its emblematic status is as old as civilisation itself, dating back to the city-states in the Tigrus–Euphrates valleys. It was an ancient sign of fertility sacred to the Sumerians and Hebrews. Later it became an image of the Christian Church and of spiritual love, while more recently it has come to embody, virtually for all human-kind, the ideal of peace on earth. In its pure-white form it is also a symbol of romantic love that is endlessly reproduced on modern valentine cards and wedding imagery. No species has featured more often or has worked harder for us – metaphorically and literally – in art, religion or our daily lives. It is worth bearing these thoughts in mind when you next stand on a city street with the humble bird itself at your feet.

The distribution of the wild and feral populations spans almost the entire northern hemisphere, yet the rock dove has, in its various forms, outflanked the eagle and raven in establishing colonies in three southern continents, primarily in areas of highest human density. British colonists, for example, took pigeons with them to Australia, New Zealand and South Africa, where they rapidly made a bid for freedom. Antarctica is still pigeon-free, but the bird's range now stretches from inside the Arctic Circle to Ushuaia in southernmost Argentina.

In Britain and Ireland the wild birds were primarily inhabitants of rocky coastlines, as they still are today. However it has become almost impossible to disentangle the feral from the original wild birds and, while the former can resemble and behave like wild rock doves as far south as the Yorkshire coastal cliffs, few if any are of unalloyed native stock. Those found on the remote north-western coasts of Scotland and in the outer isles are usually considered the purest examples. Yet the rock dove once occurred right around British and Irish coasts, leaving a wide legacy of place names, such as Culver Hole (Gower peninsula, Swansea), Doos' Cave (near Tingwall, Shetland) and Duhol (Papa Stour, Shetland).[3]

The birds often live on sheer cliffs and nest in remote sea caves, but are not averse to our company or to man-made food opportunities. In the eighteenth century Thomas Pennant wrote of rock-dove flocks involving thousands of birds in the Orkneys and Hebrides that did 'great injury to the rick-yards'.[4] It is also noteworthy that the St Kildan population died out once the human inhabitants abandoned the islands in the 1930s.[5] Those birds reared by hand quickly become habituated to our presence and rock doves were thought to have been kept as early as 4500 BC, making them a possible contender, along with the red junglefowl, for the world's earliest domesticated bird. More certainly the Romans kept them

Dovecotes, like this fine octagonal example at Culloden, Invernesshire, were once a major source of protein in Britain.

for the table in a specially designed breeding house called a *columbarium*, better known as a dovecote.

For 700 years British dovecotes functioned as a major source of protein and there were still 2059 surviving examples in 1995, although at the height of their importance there may have been as many as 26,000. A visitor to Britain in the seventeenth century said that 'No kingdom in the world has so many dove houses'.[6] Some surviving examples, like the circular rubblestone structure at Dunster in Somerset, are thought to have been built at the time of the Norman conquest. Ownership rights were a privilege of the feudal overlord, to whom dovecotes were an important economic asset.

Most followed a basic structural pattern. They were round or rectangular multi-storey buildings proofed against vermin at the lower levels, with closeable apertures in the roof to give the birds access, plus an entrance and ladders to enable the owner to harvest the squabs. The interior was often dimly lit and its upper walls pierced with recessed ledges to create nesting conditions that closely mimicked those in the wild dove's breeding caves. Some large buildings could hold

The Willington dovecote, Bedfordshire. There were once as many as 26,000 dovecotes in Britain.

Jacob Epstein's sculpture from 1914-15 captures the ancient sexual symbolism associated with doves.

thousands of birds, such as the National Trust-owned double-chambered Willington Dovecote in Bedfordshire, which had accommodation for 1500 nests. The buildings also had a good supply of drinking water in the vicinity because, like many grain-eating birds, rock doves are well known for their strong thirst, which they will find any means to satisfy. 'I was watching wildfowl on the River Great Ouse when I heard a swish of wings above me. A group of six racing pigeons circled overhead then three actually landed on the water's surface (like seagulls), had a drink, flapped their wings, lifted off and joined the others still circling overhead. They then got their bearings and were gone.'[7]

Although it went into decline by the eighteenth century, the dovecote was an ingenious institution. Pigeon meat, particularly that of the nestlings, known as squabs, was long considered good eating. Mrs Beeton recommended that pigeons were broiled, stewed, roasted or baked in a pie with three of their feet sticking out of the top to identify its contents.[8] In previous centuries the bird was a delicacy fit for the royal table. In 1387 Richard II's Christmas dinner involved 1200 pigeons, along with

16 oxen and 120 sheep.[9] The feathers were also gathered as a stuffing material. The droppings were valued as fertiliser and as an ingredient for softening leather in the tanning industry, while a third function involved a nice irony: the guano from our archetypal emblem of peace was known to be rich in potassium nitrate, an important ingredient of gunpowder.

One of the great virtues of the multiple harvest was that it so quickly reproduced itself. Pigeons breed as many as six times a year throughout the calendar, a genuine fecundity that goes a long way towards explaining the bird's history as a religious and cultural symbol. In the Judaeo-Christian tradition and earlier Asiatic religions the dove was the classic motif for fertility, birth and rebirth. Doves were said to draw the chariot of the Roman goddess of love, Venus. They were the birds sacred to Aphrodite and her earlier Asiatic equivalents, like the female deity Astarte. Far better known is the bird's appearance in Genesis, when a dove bearing an olive twig to Noah signals the Earth's reappearance after the Flood (8:11). In many contexts, the life force symbolised by the dove had both sacred and profane connotations, which are perfectly illustrated in the Christian legend of the immaculate conception. Mary was thought to have been inseminated by the holy spirit, manifest (according to the early Christian fathers) in the form of a dove that escaped from Joseph's groin, or alternatively from his staff.[10]

More recently the associations of physical or spiritual rebirth converged with the living bird itself in the Palestinian skies on the stroke of midnight on 31 December 1999, when 2000 doves were set free above Bethlehem. Few people worldwide would fail to recognise the symbolism inherent in the gesture. Yet how many would have known that this act of celebration drew on a tradition older than the Assyrian cult of Ishtar, whose temple prostitutes were known as 'doves'?[11]

Today the fertility associations are usually even more prosaic and are generated by courting pigeons, the mate with neck feathers ruffed out, strutting a railway platform or station concourse. With its 'mean-looking eyes . . . as cold, secretive and shrewd as that of a CIA agent', no other species better conjures a sense of the city.[12] It is the London bird *par excellence*, with its traditional dual concentration at St Paul's Cathedral and Trafalgar Square. More recently it has been cleared from its latter domain, along with the sellers of birdfeed, by the present London council. The eviction, together with the opposition it aroused, perfectly expressed our ambivalence towards feral pigeons, which are seen as both urban companions and foul curse. American film director Woody Allen famously described them as 'rats with wings'.

Among birdwatchers, however, the species has a simpler history of more-or-less complete neglect, which parallels a similar indifference to the common pheasant (see page 169). An extreme expression of this was a private nickname I once heard for the feral pigeon – 'winged shit'. Few people are quite so dismissive and Richard Fitter, author of *London's Natural History*, believes the species has been 'unfairly and cavalierly treated . . . just because it happens to be descended from birds escaped from captivity'.[13] He also points out that it has a venerable tradition in the capital dating back to the fourteenth century. Another devotee, Derek Goodwin, who has probably observed Greater London's pigeons more carefully than any other person, believes that they derive from the old type of dovecote bird, while new populations in provincial towns are likely to have originated from lost or stray homing pigeons.[14]

There are about 250,000 pairs in British and Irish towns and cities. Part of their success is undoubtedly their gloriously catholic diet, which includes ice cream, waste from fast-food outlets, cheese, potato, bacon rind, cooked meat, apple, chocolate, peanuts, pulses and, of course, breadcrumbs. Another key to their urban success is the ability to recognise not only our own physical gestures when we feed birds, so that they can instantly be on hand for the bonanza, but also people who have fed them two or three times before. Often pigeons can single them out among scores of other people. Derek Goodwin notes that the 'mutual recognition tends to be gratifying to the person and hence rewarding to the pigeon' and suggests that it is particularly important to injured or deformed feral pigeons, which may survive on these handouts for several years despite their disability.[15]

A goddess with her sacred birds. A sixteen-year-old Elizabeth Taylor feeds the pigeons in London's Trafalgar Square.

Metropolitan pigeons have also acquired typically metropolitan talents, such as negotiating the Underground:

I was travelling west-bound on the District Line where the stations are sometimes above and sometimes below ground. A pigeon was on the platform when the doors opened and deliberately walked on to the train, but not in a way that suggested it had spotted a food item. It didn't react when the doors closed but simply walked up and down between the seats. The next two stops were underground and the bird didn't attempt to leave. It only approached the doors as the train emerged into the daylight at the third stop, where it walked on to the platform as unhurriedly as it had got on.[16]

I watched a street pigeon foraging for scraps on a platform at Marble Arch station . . . far below ground. The bird had mastered the difficult flight down many steps with right-angled turns, through the booking hall and down a long escalator shaft to the platforms below. I have often seen street pigeons feeding at night in Paddington, Victoria and Waterloo stations.[17]

It has recently been estimated from studies in Bristol that it requires 67 people to support a single feral pigeon,

Racing pigeons is still a hugely popular hobby. 'Lost' birds are an important source of recruitment for the urban-dwelling pigeon population of our towns.

while the city's total population of 7440 birds was estimated to be consuming over one-fifth of a ton(ne) of grain each day.[18]

However the major problem with city pigeons is not what they take, but what they leave behind. It is the species most likely to give rise to the superstition associating bird dirt on our clothes with good luck. (I was intrigued recently to find in West Africa the same belief attached to another urban dweller, the fruit bat.) But not everyone feels blessed by pigeon faeces. In 1990 the Bristol Bus Company stated that it was required to meet around 100 claims a year from passengers seeking the dry-cleaning expenses for their soiled clothes, which amounted to an annual bill of £1000.[19]

The cumulative impact of pigeon dung is far more serious. In 1961, 50 ton(ne)s of pigeon droppings and debris were removed from the roof of the old Foreign Office, while the acidic content has a corrosive impact on many ornamental structures, statuary and historical façades.[20] It is this inadvertent soiling and destruction, which the London council claimed was costing £100,000 a year, that caused pigeons to be exiled from Trafalgar Square and their favourite perch, Nelson's Column.

Yet their nuisance impact to the great admiral should be offset by their invaluable service to other military figures. Birds were used by the Duke of Wellington to carry military information, just as they helped to broadcast the coronation of Rameses III in 1198 BC. The value of messenger pigeons was particularly recognised in the Second World War, when 200,000 were supplied to the British armed services. These birds helped save numerous lives. Eric Simms, author of *The Public Life of the Street Pigeon*, recalls that when he flew Lancasters for Bomber Command his plane carried two pigeons in case they ditched into the North Sea.[21] Fortunately they were never needed, although *The Times* of 19 August 1943 carried the story of a bomber crew picked up from a life raft in the Mediterranean after their carrier pigeon notified the authorities of their position and a rescue launch safely located them.[22] No fewer than 26 pigeons have received the Dickin medal, the animal equivalent of the Victoria Cross.[23]

One of the most remarkable journeys was performed by a message-bearing pigeon that belonged to the Duke of Wellington. In 1845 it dropped dead about 1 mile (1.6km) from its London loft, having allegedly flown 7000 miles (11,265km) in 55 days.[24] Yet perhaps even more extraordinary is the journey made by a pigeon described in this story from a Staffordshire family:

My brother-in-law adored his pigeons, but sadly one Sunday morning he had a fatal heart attack while attending to them in his allotment. His wife, my sister Jean, looked after them but later gave them to a friend, keeping only a pale blue pigeon, which her husband had named after her. One day before she died in tragic circumstances, Jean told my wife that she would come back and visit us as a pale blue pigeon.

On my way home from work some time later I met my wife in a frantic state. A pale blue pigeon had flown into the kitchen and wouldn't leave. After a long time I got it outside and it flew on to the bedroom windowsill. The following dawn it woke us up by tapping on the bedroom window. My sister had a slightly turned-in right foot and I noticed that the pigeon had a turned-in right claw. It stayed for a week then flew away. Very strange, but very true.[25]

Stock Dove, *Columba oenas*. Although the turtle dove usually claims the laurels as the most beautiful British member of the family, the stock dove runs it a close second. It has none of the pale-eyed 'meanness'

The stock dove has a soft, subtle beauty and an intriguing gift for anonymity.

occasionally suggested by the wood pigeon but has large dark irides and, in combination with a perfect round head shape, these give it a deeply benign appearance. Nor does it attract any of the resentment often heaped on the more conspicuous feral pigeon. Instead it has an intriguing gift for anonymity.

Birdwatchers routinely pay stock doves little or no attention and sometimes fail even to identify them, despite their wide distribution and increasing numbers (270,000 pairs). They can look similar to feral pigeons and are easily overlooked among large flocks of wood pigeons. Testimony to this is the failure of ornithologists to recognise the stock dove's presence in Britain or Ireland until the early nineteenth century. After its discovery the species appeared to spread north and westwards across Britain, first breeding in Scotland in the 1850s, although the rise in records may simply have been a function of increased awareness.[26]

Stock-dove vocalisations are like the bird itself – easy to overlook. They lack the clear separate notes of wood-pigeon and collared-dove songs, which somehow commend themselves to our memories as fragments of human speech. Instead, this bird produces a rhythmic, almost pumping, throaty coo that is often lost in the context of other bird vocalisations: 'it's not so much a song as a comforting background noise, like the sound of central heating coming on on a winter's afternoon'.[27] For some it has a 'hollow moaning' quality, although W. H. Hudson judged it the most attractive of all the pigeon songs.[28]

The 'stock' part of its name refers to the tree trunk in which the species regularly nests. In Britain it previously had a marked attachment to holes in elm trees, but has a wide repertoire of alternatives that have compensated for the impact of Dutch elm disease. Nest cavities in coastal sand-dunes, hayricks, sea cliffs, rocky outcrops, quarry faces, church towers and old buildings have all been recorded. Stock doves also like the thick entangled ivy that often cloaks abandoned buildings or 'witches' broomsticks' – the epicormic outgrowths – on the sides of lime-tree trunks.[29] Rabbit burrows are another well-known alternative, and in East Anglia the old warreners had a habit of sealing over the nest entrance with cross-sticks so that the parents could continue to feed the young, but the chicks could not escape until their captors wished to retrieve them for the pot.[30] A more unusual site is in the sides of wells or pits, in one instance 23 feet (7m) underground, and once on the floor of a concrete building at the end of a jetty, half a mile (0.8km) from shore in the Thames estuary.[31]

The lengths to which stock doves will go in order to find suitable nest holes is an indication of their relative scarcity, and this probably explains an interesting occurrence at Sway, Hampshire. In late February a tawny-owl nest was found with three eggs in an ash-tree hollow. A month later the owls had deserted, but stock doves had proceeded to raise the first of five broods, constructing their own nest on top of the owl clutch.[32] Even more extraordinary was the discovery of the remains of 25 stock doves in a hollow elm tree at Fleet, Hampshire, along with the bones from 90 jackdaws, 13 starlings and six green woodpeckers. In this instance it was suggested that the mass-grave was a result of birds dying while roosting in conditions of severe cold, especially during the arctic winter of 1946/7.[33]

It is the breeding stock dove's need to secure or defend a highly desirable tree hole that occasionally compels it to throw off the self-effacing persona. It has been known to attack jackdaws, break the leg of or even kill a little owl, and scrap violently with neighbours.[34] 'Two pairs will sometimes fight fiercely over a potential nest hole until all four birds are tottering with exhaustion and too weak (temporarily) to deal another peck or cuff.'[35]

Common Wood Pigeon, *Columba palumbus*. VN: Woody, Wood Pig, Ring/ed Dove (widespread); Culver (England); Cushat (northern England and Scotland); Cushy-doo (Scotland); Dow (Orkney, East Anglia); Quist (Midlands); Ringdow (Essex); Stoggy/ies (north-east England). With a population of more than three million pairs, this is our commonest pigeon. In fact it is the most numerous, large, truly wild bird in Britain (heavy individuals weigh well over 1 pound/500gm), as well as our most serious agricultural bird-pest, a good source of sport and protein, and a garden familiar of considerable beauty: 'the patches on the side of the neck glistening white, the head more blue than grey and the breast a delicate vinous, while the iridescent violet and green feathers of the neck add immeasurably to its charm'.[36]

It is hardly surprising that such a conspicuous and abundant species was once known by several titles. The present official version only triumphed over its main rival, 'ring dove', in the last century, which was fortunate given the subsequent arrival of the similarly named collared dove. Yet vestiges of the Old English word for wood pigeon – *culfer* or *culfre* – still survive in Britain. It gave rise to 'culver', while another Saxon word, *cusceote* or *cuscote* (pronounced 'cushat'), has led to other dialect names, including the Scottish 'cushy-doo' and various English alternatives. 'In the 1970s my paternal grandfather and maternal grandmother (both from north Worcestershire) referred to wood pigeons as "quice". I've never heard the name since, but "quist" was used in Gloucestershire.'[37] 'Cushat' is also enshrined in the name of one of the Cheviot Hills – Cushat Law – in Northumberland, and there are five other wood-pigeon place names just across the Scottish border, including Cushatgrove, Cushathill and Cushat Wood (Dumfries and Galloway).[38]

While it has always been very much associated with woodland, the species was once far less common or widespread. Today it breeds as far north as the Outer Hebrides and Shetland, where it will occasionally nest on the ground. This almost universal presence is strongly linked to the expansion of arable agriculture during the last two centuries, which created a new food supply that is of particular importance in winter. The wood pigeon's diet is almost entirely vegetarian and includes a variety of wild fruits and seeds, particularly those of oak, beech, hazel, ivy, hawthorn and bramble. Yet neither its taste for cereals and greens nor its capacity is in any dispute. 'In our family we used to call them J. Edgar Hoovers for the way these greedy devils used to wolf down the food.'[39] Single pigeons have been examined whose crops and stomachs have contained 1020 grains of corn, 198 beans, or 20 small potatoes.[40] As long ago as 1780 Gilbert White wrote:

> of late years, since the vast increase of turnips, that vegetable has furnished a great part of their support in hard weather; and the holes [the wood pigeons] pick in these roots greatly damage the crop. From this food their flesh has contracted a rancidness which occasions them to be rejected by nicer judges of eating . . . They were shot not only as they were feeding in the fields, and especially in snowy weather, but also at the close of the evening, by men who lay in ambush among the woods.[41]

The wood pigeon's white half-collar gave rise to a widely used alternative name, ring dove, which survives even today.

At the end of the breeding season there may be as many as 10 million woodies in Britain. These resident birds are remarkably sedentary and most ringed wood pigeons are recovered less than 3 miles (5km) from where they were trapped. Occasionally northern continental birds pass through on their way to southern Europe, and in 1959 flocks detained in their migration by bad weather had congregated on the Kent coast, where they were so numerous that 'the white cliffs of Dover assumed a blue appearance'.[42]

With a touch of our hereditary suspicion for continental influence, British sportsmen once held that we were subject to large influxes of European wood pigeons and that they could separate the foreign birds by their darker plumage and larger size. Both claims have since been proved to be untrue.[43] Yet I would testify to a very distinctive impression created by some migrating wood pigeons. Large numbers spend the winter among the Iberian cork-oak woods and are widely shot as they pass south on both sides of the Franco-Spanish border. These autumn migrants move in high, fast, nervous formations through the Pyrenean valleys and seem to belong to a

When wood pigeon flocks suddenly take flight they produce a distinctive clattering noise with their wings. A breeding male incorporates the sound into his display, when he rises up and claps the wings sharply together above his back before gliding back down.

very different, far wilder species than the birds that lumber complacently – and often too slowly – from our country roads.

Another widely held notion among game interests that proved false was the belief in shooting to control pigeon numbers. In the 1950s government-funded culls were organised to reduce the population and the damage to vulnerable crops. They took place in the early part of winter to fit in with the sporting calendar. Yet R. K. Murton, long-term observer of the species and author of *The Wood Pigeon*, demonstrated that many of the birds shot would have died naturally from food shortages later in the winter. He argued that it was this which operated as the major check on population growth. Murton's conclusion 'caused scepticism among many shooting men who could not apprehend that causes of death are compensatory, not additive. Only if more birds are shot than will be lost in any case can shooting become a controlling factor.'[44]

One element Murton had not considered in his research was the partly compensatory pleasures derived from hunting the wood pigeon. Although it has never

enjoyed the status of red grouse or pheasant, at least one authority thought it excellent sport because it is 'extremely wary, flies high and flies fast'.[45] It is also widely considered good eating and falls victim to a number of strategies:

They say a pigeon can only count to one. If you want to get some, walk three people into a hide and leave two inside while one walks away. They'll soon come straight back. We used to shoot them when they were feeding on sprouts and you could knock them down like billy-o. You don't pluck pigeons, you skin them. My wife cooks them in a pie with a crust top. Add a couple of hard-boiled eggs and a couple of slices of bacon to give them flavour. Delicious![46]

Equal ingenuity, if less effort, was employed in taking the squabs.

Before and during the war we used to keep young wood pigeons in the nest so the parents would keep feeding them. This was done by tying a string to the leg and to a branch. The nest had to be visited at least once a day to make sure that the young pigeon hadn't fallen out.[47]

Between 1947–52 I did my apprenticeship with a man who used to go out in summer with his twelve-bore shotgun to look for 'floppers' in the nest. A full flopper was a young pigeon just ready to fly. He would shoot them through the nest and take them home to his wife, who would skin them and, taking only the breasts, would dip them in egg and bread crumbs, and fry them for his supper.[48]

However, full-winged pigeons have usually been the main target and the numbers taken in some areas, such as the 130,000 killed between 1862 and 1870 in East Lothian, argue for the success of the methods.[49] The total also implies the sheer size of some winter populations.

The food shortages that Murton identified as the key source of wood-pigeon mortality can have an even greater impact when combined with intense cold. In the winter of 1962/3 the bird was the most frequent victim of the freeze, based on the number of corpses recorded (3749), which was almost a quarter of all those found.[50] Desperation occasionally led to extraordinary concentrations. In one 20-acre (8-ha) field of kale near Fordinbridge, Hampshire, 3000 birds were shot, while in a ¼-mile (400-m) stretch of road, 47 corpses were counted – birds killed during their forlorn search for food and grit. At nearby Cranbourne, '30 were found frozen to the branches of one oak tree, as if they were still sleeping'.[51]

In rural areas where wood pigeons are regularly shot, they are extremely wary. Birds caught by surprise while feeding deep within the foliage often burst out in panic and hurtle away, with much crashing of vegetation and grey feathers spiralling down behind. The nervousness compounds the impression of a rather clumsy species, and in late spring when males tussle for territorial control they can be heard in the tree tops, their wings thrashing as each struggles to displace his rival and retain his balance during the contest.

Yet W. H. Hudson thought the wood pigeon was usually a bird of graceful dignity. One of the most distinctive gestures is the slow raising and lowering of the tail a few moments after it alights, which appears 'to indicate that the bird is sufficiently at ease to have "decided" to have remained where it is'.[52] Woodies have a slow measured gait on the ground, while feeding birds can show great agility, some hanging completely upside down, wings and tail spread, to get at inaccessible fruits

or acorns. Just as impressive is the wood pigeon's ability to land on open water to drink, where it floats and takes off again without any apparent difficulty.

The birds are completely at home in inner-city areas and often become remarkably tame, taking bread from the hand or entering houses for scraps, and even perching on their human benefactors. Richard Fitter records a highly telling anecdote about a Scots gamekeeper who was asked in the 1930s 'on returning home from a holiday in London, what had impressed him most about the city, and replied, "Seeing the cushie-doos in St James's Park eating from a man's hand." '[53] London's wood pigeons were heavily persecuted during the war because of their pest status, but it seems that at least some have resumed their trusting habits. Audley Gosling, a more recent visitor to St James's, found that several allowed themselves to be 'stroked not only on the head, neck and breast, but also on the back and flanks, with the cupped hand actually imprisoning the wings, which, incidentally, they often allowed me to extend'.[54] Even after Gosling had been prevented from visiting the park for six months, 'his' wood pigeons flew instantly and alighted on him.[55]

City gardens usually require tall trees to encourage wood pigeons to breed, although the nest itself 'is absurdly small for the size of the bird'.[56] It is seldom more than a skimpy platform of twigs and is among the easiest of bird nests to find, sometimes with the eggs and chicks visible through the latticework. If conditions are suitable wood pigeons breed even in winter and birds have been recorded to lay in every calendar month, while the discarded white shells are among the first wild-bird eggs that many children ever see.

The adults also give themselves away with a distinctive and persistent song, which can occasionally be too persistent:

We have a wide variety of birdlife around the house and garden with an impressive dawn chorus. Last summer it was loud and long. A particular culprit, a wood pigeon, would start 'murmuring' at about 4.30 in the morning which led to some especially early risings (I've been known to be gardening by six!) and became something of a family joke. 'That bloody pigeon' became a part of breakfast conversation.[57]

The true song comprises five husky notes, which have been interpreted in many ways: 'A mnemonic I use to help people remember the song is: "Who cooks for-you, Oh", which they repeat 3–5 times, before ending with an abrupt "Who?" '[58] W. H. Hudson noted the 'depth and singularly human quality' of the voice, which helped to

Wood pigeons clambering amongst ivy bushes for the ripe berries is a classic sight of late winter.

convert the notes into 'a passionate complaint'.[59] He cited an old mnemonic from East Anglia – 'My toe bleeds, Betty' – that was in keeping with the sense of distress. However perhaps the best-known interpretation of all, in England at least, is 'Take two coo, Taffy' or 'Take two cows, Taffy', which plays on an old offensive stereotype of the Welsh as a nation of cattle thieves. (Yet wood pigeons also feature in the Welsh repertoire of insults: 'A Welsh name for the bird, "ysguthan", pronounced skeethan, is also a derogatory remark for an unpleasant woman. Rather than say "She's a real cow", one might hear a Welsh speaker, especially in North Wales, saying "Hen sguthan" – "Old wood-pigeon"!'[60])

Since the wood pigeon's breeding season is longer than that of almost all other birds, the song really comes into its own when most rivals have fallen silent. The drowsy conditions of the late-summer landscape then seem somehow amplified in that long, slow, soporific phrase. 'In the profound stillness, on a windless day . . . ,' wrote Hudson, 'these sonorous notes [have] a singularly beautiful effect.'[61] The poet Katharine Tynan Hinkson exploited the song's somnolent quality in her poem of age and decay, 'The Doves':

The house where I was born,
Where I was young and gay,
Grows old amid its corn,
Amid its scented hay.

Moan of the cushat dove,
In silence rich and deep;
The old head I love
Nods to its quiet sleep.

Where once were nine and ten
Now two keep house together;
The doves moan and complain
All day in the still weather.[62]

Eurasian Collared Dove, *Streptopelia decaocto*. Its half-century in Britain is perhaps too brief a period for the species to have acquired anything resembling a vernacular name. (In Germany, however, it has become known as *Die Fernsehtaube* 'the television dove', because it always calls from the aerial on the roof.[63]) In Britain there are more private nicknames: 'Some time ago I titled it "the Evostik bird", as its call sounds like *E-vo-stik*. The name is now catching on locally.'[64]

The collared dove's familiarity is now beyond question. Since the first pair bred in 1956 collared doves have spread as far north as Orkney and Shetland, while their numbers have rocketed from a handful to at least 230,000 pairs.

Today the RSPB lists it as the seventh most frequently seen bird in British gardens, having risen six places even in the last decade.[65] The dove's almost unavoidable song has lost some of the initial gloss through endless repetition. In 1959 David Bannerman spoke of a 'pleasant tri-syllabic *coo, coo-coo*'.[66] Less than 30 years later it struck a more jaded ear as a 'mournful, penetrating and monotonous *kuk coo ku*'.[67] 'For me it perfectly conjures up a bored football fan chanting "*U-ni-ted, U-ni-ted*". The mnemonic has all the more personal meaning, given that I support Northampton Town and their great local rivals are Peterborough United.'[68]

However dull it may seem now, that sound evokes an astonishing story. The collared dove has achieved a more rapid spread through Europe than any other recorded species. Until the early part of last century it occurred only in south-eastern Europe, particularly in the Balkan areas previously under the rule of the Ottoman Turks. The dove's status as a great favourite of the Muslim inhabitants has been proposed as a possible factor in its subsequent spread.[69] By 1932 it had reached Hungary, and by 1936 Czechoslovakia. It is a striking irony that the archetypal symbol of peace achieved much of its territorial expansion during the Second World War. Sometimes the dove's movements closely shadowed those of the German panzers. In 1940 it arrived in Poland. Fortunately its own conquests were much more permanent, and within a decade it had reached the edge of continental Europe and was poised to cross the English Channel.

The eminent birdman James Fisher documented the dove's extraordinary history up to that point in a short 15-page paper that represented the distillation of more than 250 references in nine European languages. Yet Fisher found space amid his extraordinary scholarship for the charming tale of the collared dove's scientific name: 'A poor maid was servant to a very hard-hearted lady, who gave her as wages no more than eighteen pieces a year. The maid prayed to the Gods that she would like it to be made known to the world how miserably she was paid by her mistress. Thereupon Zeus created this Dove which proclaims an audible *deca-octo* to all the world to this very day.'[70]

In 20 years its range had shifted 1000 miles (1600km) and in twice that time-span it had occupied almost 1 million square miles (2.5 million sq km). The exact mechanism triggering the spread is not fully understood, although genetic mutation is one theory, while the bird's propensity for multiple broods has certainly aided the process.[71] Typically, once it had crossed the English Channel in 1955 (and possibly in 1952) the first pair raised three broods the following summer.[72] More recently, as many as nine clutches of eggs and five

No bird has more quickly exchanged the status of extreme rarity for that of garden familiarity than the collared dove.

successful broods have been recorded in a single year.[73] In the early period of its British residence collared doves were doubling their numbers annually and, while the increase has slowed, the expansion continues both nationally and internationally, with a substantial population, originally from released birds in the Bahamas, spreading across the southern USA.

In Britain they are habitual visitors to human environments that offer access to their grain-based vegetarian diet, including chicken runs, farmyard cereal bins and stores, parks, zoos, wildlife collections, open-air cafés, food kiosks, suburban or city gardens and even upper-floor flats: 'Last year to my thrill and amazement a pair of collared doves had built a nest in between two plant pots outside my door on the second-floor balcony walkway. They regularly sit on the railing waiting for me to get up and feed them.'[74]

Collared doves have also become habitual visitors to the garden birdtable, although the following stories suggest that the species has lost none of its original popularity with increased numbers. On the contrary, our deepening acquaintance with this gentle biscuit-toned bird has cemented a sense of domestic companionship:

Several years ago collared doves nested in our holly tree. One morning I was amazed to find a baby dove fast asleep beneath the nest, two feet from the sleeping cat. With the bird in one hand and the telephone in the other I called a local bird expert, who told me to put it in a hanging basket close to the nest. I did this and wrapped it in an old woollen sock with just its head showing. The parents started feeding it almost immediately. Even when fully grown it was smaller than the others, so we thought it was a girl and called her 'Beauty'. After the parents left her to fend for herself I would feed her twice a day. When I stood on the edge of the local park and called 'Beauty' she would suddenly appear at my feet. Sadly I have not seen her this year but I do not think I will ever stop searching the sky for her.[75]

My new neighbour felled an elder tree and that afternoon he called for me to come and see what he described as a buff-coloured baby bird. I went around and there sitting on the side of its upturned nest was a collared dove squab. It was nearly feathered but still had the yellow chick fluff attached to the plumage. Off

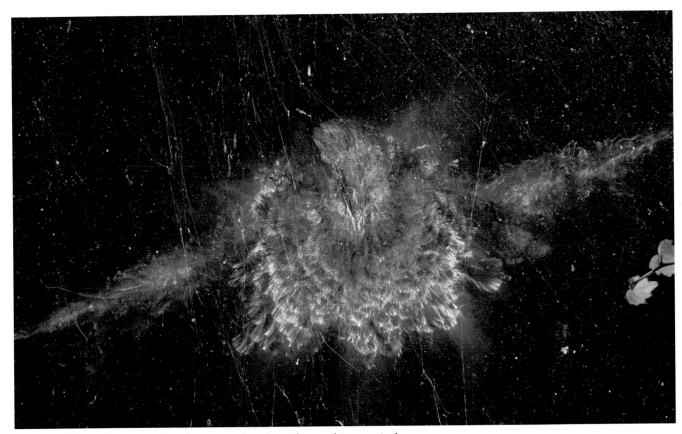

A collared dove leaves its ghost image on the glass after striking a window.

I went to the chemist to get some baby food, then to the pet shop to get some shelled sunflowers that I would mix in the baby food once crushed. I only had to open his beak and feed him via a syringe a couple of times, then he had got the idea and took the food readily from a bent teaspoon. 'Bibbles' went from strength to strength and started to become quite frightened of humans and was ready to go. My mother, brother and daughter were all there to watch the maiden voyage. My brother got him in his hands and threw him up, when Bibbles' wings opened and he flew on to the top of my neighbour's pigeon loft. After a few more minutes he flew in a huge circle around us before we lost sight of him. We never saw him again, but there is one collared dove who never flies away when I bike past him at the end of our avenue. I wonder . . .'[76]

European Turtle Dove, *Streptopelia turtur*. This classic emblem of marital tenderness and devotion has appeared as a motif in English poetry since Chaucer. It is the most apt dove to be so characterised, because in real life the bird's pair bond can extend from one breeding season to the next and because it is the 'smallest and loveliest of the British pigeons'.[77]

It is the only migrant dove in the region, a fact that was recognised as long ago as the Old Testament. The Song of Solomon (2:12) includes the lines:

The flowers appear on the earth;
the time of the song of birds is come
And the voice of the turtle is heard in our land.

Odd as it may seem, that voice is echoed in its somewhat anomalous English name. 'Turtle' has no association with the reptile, but is a modification of the original French word, *tourterelle*, which is closely onomatopoeic of the song. The male's soporific purr is not especially loud or far-carrying and is partly ventriloquial. Yet it is highly evocative possibly because it makes its strongest appeal to the subconscious. Repeatedly observers note its ability to awaken memory or feeling: 'the low crooning of the turtle dove – one of the most soothing sounds in nature';[78] 'It is associated most pleasantly with warm still summer days in the South of England . . . which would be incomplete without it.'[79]

It also has a capacity to summon more specific recollections: 'The very mention of it takes our memories

Turtle doves were once a standard metaphor for marital tenderness.

back to a lowland waste of sandy heath, with scrub and thorn-bushes dotted here and there, for it was in such country that we first encountered this bird.'[80] 'It reminds me of the long hot summer of 1976 when I first heard turtle doves in Suffolk – happy memories of golden days and balmy evenings.'[81] For all its benign and reassuring associations, the song can also have a gentle mournfulness, a quality that Shakespeare exploited in *The Winter's Tale*, when Paulina announces at the play's end (Act 5, Scene 3):

> I, an old turtle,
> Will wing me to some wither'd bough, and there
> My mate, that's never to be found again,
> Lament till I am lost.

Turtle doves spend much of their lives in Sahelian Africa and in the 1970s massive concentrations were recorded, with 450,000 at a single Senegalese roost site and an estimated million birds at another in the Gambia.[82] Periodic drought and creeping desertification in the region are now considered major factors in the bird's recent almost Europe-wide declines, although turtle doves are remarkably tolerant of the heat. They have been observed to feed in direct sunlight until temperatures reach 113°F (45°C).

The north-bound migrants face another great hazard once they reach the Mediterranean, where they run the gauntlet of European hunters. A heavy toll has been exacted for several centuries, and in Malta alone the seasonal slaughter involves an estimated 100,000 birds.[83] Yet as long ago as the 1920s the old Portuguese dove hunters were lamenting their quarry's decline.[84] In combination the two fragments of information suggest first the sheer numbers of turtle doves once present in Europe, and second the devastating scale of the harvest. The tradition is so deeply embedded in rural Mediterranean life that it continues despite being outlawed by EU legislation. Shooting in the Mediterranean has long been listed among the causes of turtle-dove declines in Britain (the bird has no more than a toehold in Ireland), although agricultural intensification unquestionably exerts another important downward pressure on the species. It has lost three-quarters of its population and a quarter of its range in the last three decades.

The nightly gathering of thousands of rose-ringed parakeets at Esher Rugby Club, Surrey, is one of the more unusual and most recently established of our avian spectacles.

Parrot family *Psittacidae*

Rose-ringed Parakeet, *Psittacula krameri*. This handsome grass-green parrot is one of the latest, most surprising and most successful additions to the British avifauna. It has a long history as a cagebird, both in this country and abroad, and escapees are assumed to be the main source of the first feral birds seen in and around London in the 1960s. It first bred in 1971 (possibly two years earlier) and was accepted on to the British list in 1983, when it was thought to number 1000 birds, with records from 50 counties. The first national census of 1992 at least doubled the population estimate and 10 years later numbers had risen again to almost 6000.[1]

The rapid expansion has been attributed partly to the ready-made winter meals that parakeets get from garden birdtables, which see them through any prolonged cold spell. The abundance of handouts is also thought to be a major factor in the parakeets' ability to breed from January onwards. Their successful adaptation to British latitudes – they are the most northerly parrot population in the world – has rung some alarm bells, given that the species is a serious agricultural pest in much of its African and Asian range. Nowhere is it more common or more troublesome than in India, where Salim Ali described it as 'one of the most destructive birds'. India's great ornithologist fleshed out his theme with the following:

> small parties . . . often band together in enormous swarms to raid ripening crops . . . and orchard fruit. The birds clamber about among the twigs and gnaw into the half-ripe fruits, one after another, wasting far more than they actually eat. Or they descend in swarms upon ripening fields of food crops . . . Rabbles of these parakeets commonly gather at wayside railway stations and goods sheds, clambering amongst the sacks of grain and groundnuts awaiting entrainment, biting through the fabric and helping themselves to the contents, or they waddle about comically on the ground . . . to pick up the spillage.[2]

While he felt there were 'no compensating virtues from the economic viewpoint', Ali also described the mesmerising flocks that fly to their evening roosts in 'battalion after battalion, from all points of the compass'. These flights produce a cacophony of loud screeching calls and are an integral part of the colour and passion of

Since it first escaped in the 1960s, the rose-ringed parakeet has benefited hugely from offerings on the bird table.

the Indian dusk, even in the centre of large cities. In fact they are almost synonymous with India. It is impossible to see television footage of the northern subcontinent without rose-ringed parakeets calling in the background. The birds are, for instance, recurrent atmospheric extras in Richard Attenborough's classic *Gandhi* (1982) and David Lean's swansong, *A Passage to India* (1984).

Remarkably, the London suburbs have their own version of this Asiatic ritual. Esher Rugby Club in Surrey is home to the largest parakeet roost in Europe:

The average man in the Esher street seems strangely unaware of their presence. This despite the vast squadrons which stream low over our rooftops each evening on the way to the roost (a row of large poplars in the rugby club grounds). To live in the area is a nightmare. The noise generated by the flocks of 300–400 birds is loud to say the least (especially at five o'clock on a summer's morning!). When I moved to Walton in 1994, just down the road from the rugby club, the roost totalled a mere 600 birds. Since then the population has increased by over 1000 per cent, given that 6918 were counted leaving the roost this August (2003).[3]

Cuckoo family *Cuculidae*

Common Cuckoo, *Cuculus canorus.* VN: Gowk (northern England and Scotland); Gokk (Orkney); Gok (Shetland). With a song that is as far-carrying as it is unmistakable, the cuckoo has made a deeper cultural impression on us than all but two or three other summer migrants. The nightingale, with its richer literary tradition, is almost exclusively a bird of the south and only the swallow (now perhaps replaced by the swift) rivals the cuckoo as the nationwide badge of summer. However the swallow has always been far commoner, and our close neighbour. The cuckoo, by contrast, is thinly spread and highly secretive, which suggests that the arch-simplicity of the song is the key to its emblematic dominance.

The Reverend C. A. Johns observed that 'No bird in a state of nature utters a note approaching so closely the sound of the human voice.'[1] The one spring sound that no one could mistake was clearly best placed to serve as *the* signal for the change from winter to spring, and for some people there is still no spring without a cuckoo. 'It is very important to me to hear the cuckoo every summer. This is something I have caught from my mother, because she and I drive out into the surrounding countryside once May arrives to listen for it and we are not satisfied until we have heard one.'[2]

The species usually appears in most areas of Britain by April and the average for the southern half of the country is 18 April, while in the north it falls in the last week of the month.[3] Yet on Scotland's outer isles the first males are often not heard at all before May. In the last 50 years the earliest record ever was a bird seen and heard on 20 February 1953 at Farnham, Surrey.[4] An adult noted (and later shot) at Delamere, Cheshire, on Boxing Day 1897 or 1898 was not so much early, as late: it had a defect that had prevented it from returning to Africa.[5] But perhaps the most inexplicable of all cuckoo records is the emblem of spring seen on the winter solstice: a singing male (heard by six people) at Milford, Pembrokeshire on 22 December 1954.[6] Some have tried to make sense of these anomalous occurrences by pointing to the coincidental arrival in Britain of the first collared doves, a cuckoo sound-alike that regularly catches people out.

The most famous location for the registration of first dates is without doubt the letters page of *The Times.* Typically, the paper's three published volumes of correspondence are entitled *The First Cuckoo, The Second*

The cuckoo is the classic emblem of spring, adultery and the correspondence pages of The Times *newspaper.*

Cuckoo and *The Third Cuckoo*. The sheer spectrum of observations, reflections and amusing anecdotes dating back to at least 1839 is almost impossible to convey here, but the following samples suggest how the bird has become both leitmotif and time-honoured institution for the paper.

> While gardening this afternoon I heard a faint note which led me to say to my under-gardener . . . 'Was that the cuckoo?' Almost immediately afterwards we both heard the full double note of a cuckoo . . . There is not the slightest doubt that the song was that of a cuckoo.
>
> R. Lydekker, FRS, 6 February 1913

> I regret to say that, in common with many persons, I have been completely deceived in the matter of the supposed cuckoo of February 4. The note was uttered by a bricklayer's labourer at work on a house in the neighbourhood . . . I have interviewed the man, who tells me that he is able to draw cuckoos from considerable distances by the exactness of his imitation of their notes, which he produces without the aid of any instrument.
>
> R. Lydekker, FRS, 12 February 1913[7]

For many years each spring I have tested the cuckoo's

notes with a piano, and have found that they are always within a tone of D and B, or D and B flat (treble stave). It is of interest to observe that Beethoven . . . when he introduced the imitation of the cuckoo at the end of the second movement of his Pastoral Symphony, gave the two notes D and B flat . . . As Beethoven was at the time deaf one wonders whether it was by chance he selected the correct notes . . . or whether his memory of the bird's song had survived after he had been unable to hear it for some years. If the latter, it is fascinating to realize that the cuckoo has not altered the pitch of his notes for over a century.

> Reverend K. H. MacDermott, 25 May 1934[8]

> Last night (June 1) about midnight, shortly before the storm broke, my husband and I, and a friend who lives nearby, distinctly heard the cuckoo . . . I have never before heard the cuckoo at night. Was the bird disturbed by the impending storm?
>
> Rosemary Samson, 14 June 1983

The following letters demonstrate how the correspondence has its own self-perpetuating dynamic:

> Mrs Rosemary Samson's letter on the night cuckoo reminds me of my childhood in wartime Somerset,

when anti-aircraft guns once set a cuckoo and a nightingale singing together.

Pamela Priest, 18 June 1983

Is Mrs Rosemary Samson not aware that the *Cuculus canorus* ... has a marked tendency to behave in an eccentric manner whenever it senses the presence in the neighbourhood of a *Times* correspondence column contributor?

Douglas Vernon, 18 June 1983[9]

While the male's calls have been logged and mytho-logised for centuries, the female's equally remarkable hinny or bubbling note has received far less attention. It consists of a 'single, clear liquid cry of about 15 notes on a descending scale and lasting about three seconds'.[10] Other writers have called it a 'water-bubbling chuckle'; 'half way between a yaffle's laugh and a dabchick's trill';[11] 'rather like a sudden rush of water through a narrow-necked bottle'.[12] Even the young have unforgettable calls – a snake-like hiss to deter potential predators and a loud begging squeal, to which the foster parents and even other adult birds simply passing by cannot fail to respond. However, contributors to *Birds Britannica* have dwelt on another increasingly dominant aspect of cuckoo sounds: the ever-widening, disconcerting silence as the bird declines:

My mother, who lives in rural Worcestershire and always hears the cuckoos, hasn't heard one this year and neither has anyone else I have spoken to around rural Warwickshire.[13]

I have memories of cuckoos calling, two or three at once, around Limpsfield Common, Surrey, in the early 1950s. They sang as lustily at Addiscombe on the suburban fringes of Croydon. At my present home in south Devon, where hedgebanks are flailed twice yearly to keep them low and crippled, I haven't heard a cuckoo call in six successive springs.[14]

In Britain the bird's vocalisations gave rise to two main name traditions. The Old Norse word was *gaukr*, cognate with the Old English *geac*, which accounts for the various vernacular names spread from Lancashire northwards (see above). The more common version is of French origin, *cucu*, and came to Britain with the Normans. The word appears in what must rank as one of the most enduring folk songs in the language, whose opening lines run: 'Sumer is icumen in/Lhude sing cuccu'. The spellings may have changed over the centuries but this secular hymn to the joys of summer,

written by a thirteenth-century monk of Reading Abbey, still flourishes, and I well remember learning it in infant school. The name resurfaced as 'cokkow' in Chaucer (c. 1381), 'cuckoe' in the seventeenth century and in its present form by the eighteenth. It is similarly striking that the pattern is almost Europe-wide: *koekoek* (Dutch), *coucou* (French), *kuckuck* (German), *cuculo* (Italian), *kukulka* (Polish), *cucu* (Spanish); and even beyond, as *koku* (Persian), *kuku* (Kashmiri), *kukku* (Sikkim), *akku* (Bhutan).

The word itself passed into English in all sorts of other contexts. Cuckoo-spit, for example, is the white froth generated by the bugs known as frog-hoppers and is so named because it is found at much the same time as the bird itself. Some people even believe that there is a direct relationship between the two. 'I knew a Nottinghamshire girl who married and settled in north Cumbria. She insisted that the cuckoo was a dirty bird and the source of all that cuckoo spit on the hedgerow plants. Nothing would convince her that the spit was produced by insects as a protection against enemies.'[15]

The cuckoo-bee and cuckoo-wasp have acquired their names from their parasitic exploitation of near-relatives. The cuckoo-flower is another name for lady's smock, and derives from its appearance at the same time as the migrant. Cuckoo-pint (better known as lords-and-ladies) has similarly acquired the name from its seasonality, but it literally means 'cuckoo penis', a reference to the phallic character of the plant's spathe and to the many sexual resonances associated with the bird.

Most of these are anthropomorphic in origin and hinge on an interpretation of the cuckoo's complex reproductive system as being akin to sexual infidelity between husband and wife. The word 'cuckold' has come to be associated with the betrayed husband and, less frequently, with the wife, in the word 'cuckqueen'. Cuckoo itself was also synonymous with a fool. Yet in all three usages the order of things had been completely reversed, given that it is the cuckoo perpetrating the trickery. In his dictionary, Samuel Johnson suggested that 'cuckoo' was originally shouted by passers-by in order to warn a husband of an approaching womaniser, but in time it was transferred from deceiver to deceived.[16] And so it continued to be used, especially by English playwrights, for many centuries.

However the bird's public-image problems have a long pedigree. The Roman naturalist Pliny claimed that a young cuckoo repaid its foster mother's loving attention by eating her when it was full-grown.[17] Chaucer echoed the charge in the *Parlement of Fowles*, where he described the cuckoo as 'ever unkynde' and a 'mortherere of the heysoge', murderer of the dunnock.[18]

In previous centuries it was believed that the young cuckoo repaid the tender devotions of its foster parents by biting off their heads.

The idea survived at least until Shakespeare's day, judging by the Fool's imagery in *King Lear* (Act 1, Scene 4):

> For you know, nuncle,
> The hedge-sparrow fed the cuckoo so long
> That it's had it head bit off by it young.

Even the genuine aspects of its breeding behaviour were cause for recrimination. Gilbert White felt that 'This proceeding of the cuckoo . . . is such a monstrous outrage on maternal affection . . . and such a violence on instinct; that had it only been related of a bird in the Brazils, or Peru, it would never have merited our belief.'[19] White's judgement might well have been worse had he known the full facts. Yet it was not until 1788 that Edward Jenner, the originator of the smallpox vaccination, documented the efforts of the newly hatched chick to heave its foster parents' own eggs and young from the nest by means of a special hollow in the middle of its back. Awareness of this brutal reflex-drive only seemed to harden the attitude of later observers. As recently as 1943 a nature writer suggested, 'There is no more scandalous bird than the cuckoo. By no standard of conduct, whether human or animal, can its habits of life be condoned.' The female author reserved special scorn

for the birds of her own sex, which were lazy, idle, languid, flirty, promiscuous and reprehensible.[20]

The problem for the cuckoo was the bird's own secretiveness and the fact that its human observers tended to fill any gaps with their own invention. Typically one key mystery was not unlocked until the first three decades of the twentieth century. It centred on the exact method by which cuckoos place their eggs in the host's nest, a subject that eventually became one of the most heated and amusing controversies in all British ornithology. The most baffling aspect was the manner in which the female cuckoo seemed able to gain access to tiny domed nests or those in tree hollows, buildings and even to swallows' nests squeezed against the upper beams in a barn.

Part of the answer lay in the cuckoo's remarkable extrusible cloaca, from which she literally squirts the egg in a matter of seconds. But without these details before them, ornithologists of the period developed rival theories that were often contested in blazing arguments. Many were between members of the British Ornithologists' Club at their London meetings in Pagani's restaurant on Great Portland Street, which was infamous then for the awful quality of its expensive food. Two of the main protagonists in the cuckoo debate were the Reverend F. C. R. Jourdain (known to friends and enemies alike as 'Pastor Pugnax') and Percy Bunyard, both of whom were notorious as egg collectors even in an age when egg collecting (or oology as they preferred to call it) was a respectable branch of ornithology.

Bunyard, a fruit grower and market gardener, studied the bird at a Kentish site and was strongly convinced that females laid their eggs on the ground, swallowed them and later regurgitated them into the host's nest. The idea was widely held but Bunyard clung to it with particular zeal. He once stated that the rival theory, which claimed that the egg was placed in the nest by normal oviposition, 'has no scientific data to support it, is economically unsound, and physically impossible'.[21] Jourdain was another who did not mince his words and often savagely abused his opponent in the most colourful terms. Bunyard was perhaps fortunate in being 'as deaf as a post' and often struggled to hear what was being said against him. Otherwise he would aim a 'long-handled hearing aid' in the direction of the reverend vicar's stream of invective. Whenever the two were seated opposite one another at table there was a rush by other BOC members to get ring-side seats for the almost inevitable 'Bunyard–Jourdain scrap'. Matters became so heated that bloodshed was feared and eventually the mention of cuckoos was forbidden at BOC meetings, although a classic British compromise was sought in the appointment of a committee to investigate the subject. This august body's achievements are not recorded in the club's literature.[22]

It was another BOC member who finally discovered the cuckoo's egg-laying secrets. Edgar Chance was a fanatical egg collector, who used his industrialist's wealth to employ several assistants as well as a professional photographer, Oliver Pike, in a ground-breaking piece of field research. Between 1918 and 1925 Chance intensively studied a cuckoo population that habitually exploited meadow pipits breeding on a Worcestershire common. He was eventually able to show that the female laid with enormous regularity every two days, usually in the afternoon or evening between noon and eight p.m.

The bird selected the host nest after careful scrutiny, sometimes extending over several hours, yet the moment of egg laying itself was extraordinarily brief. All in a matter of seconds the female was observed to land at the nest, remove a host egg to allay the pipits' suspicions and then clamber onto the nest rim to squirt her replacement egg into it. In fact it was so fast that even when Chance captured many details on film for the first time and gave a lecture and demonstration at a BOC meeting in 1922, not all could overcome their prejudices or believe the evidence of their eyes. Even after watching the film, some still thought they could see the egg in the cuckoo's dis-

tended throat.[23] Chance dismissed these diehard sceptics as the 'beakers' and 'regurgitators'.[24]

The early BOC disputes may have been acrimonious and often highly personalised but they spurred the participants to unravel the facts, and other biologists have since built on the work of men like Edgar Chance. Cuckoos are now very well studied and yet, if anything, their breeding behaviour, known technically as 'obligate brood parasitism', seems even more extraordinary than was first thought. They have been recorded to use more than 100 different species as host in Europe, while more than 50 have been noted in Britain alone. Of these, six birds are central to cuckoo reproduction: robin, pied wagtail, sedge warbler, meadow pipit, dunnock and reed warbler.[25]

One of the most remarkable adaptations shown by the different cuckoo populations (known as 'gentes'; singular 'gens') that are attached to a specific host is their capacity to produce eggs that closely mimic those of the parasitised species. The robin-cuckoo gens, for example, produces red-speckled eggs, while pipit-cuckoos' eggs are mottled brown. The only gens whose eggs are strikingly different from the host eggs are dunnock-cuckoos. Their dark-spotted eggs look nothing like the pale-blue clutch produced by dunnocks, and this lack of adaptation is thought to indicate that the dunnock is a relatively recent host and there has been insufficient time for mimetic cuckoo eggs to develop.

The cuckoo's choice of host shows significant regional variation, with the dunnock serving as a common foster parent in south and central Britain. Meadow pipits are the main dupes in the north, just as reed warblers are used in East Anglia. The three species together account for 80 per cent of all recorded cuckoo breeding events, and in the second half of the twentieth century the reed warbler has substantially increased its importance as host, which may be linked to a corresponding fall in the British and Irish populations of meadow pipit and dunnock.

These population declines are among several reasons cited for a parallel fall in cuckoo numbers. The species occurs from Shetland southwards to Kent and County Kerry and is adapted to a wide variety of habitats, from open woods to dense reedbed and montane moorland, but is also spread very thinly (about 24,000 'pairs').[26] It has a highly specialised diet, feeding almost exclusively on caterpillars, many of which are hairy and sometimes toxic. It is said that the dissected gizzard of a cuckoo is often covered with these caterpillar hairs so that it looks like a dense lining of fur.[27] Such a specific diet, which has been severely affected by half a century of intensive insecticide use, may be another factor in the cuckoo's decline. It also explains why the totem bird of the British

Above: The hawk-like appearance of the flying cuckoo partly accounts for the old belief that it turned into a sparrowhawk during winter. Right: The number of times the cuckoo sang was the focus of many fortune-telling games about romance and wealth.

summer makes such a brief visit to this country and then so quickly returns to warmer latitudes where caterpillars are still abundant.

The cuckoo's extreme seasonality has given rise to almost as large a body of folklore as its song or its extraordinary reproductive system. One contributor recalled 'the old children's country rhyme':

In April I open my bill
In May, in May I sing night and day
In June I change my tune
In July away I fly
In August away I must.[28]

A Lancashire version runs along similar lines:

Comes in Mid-March
Sings in mid-April
Stutts in mid-May
And the first cock of hay
Frightens the Cuckoo away.[29]

The bird's association with spring was once ritualised across England in various forms of festival that some believe were of ancient and possibly pagan origin.[30] At one long-established celebration in the village of Gotham, Nottinghamshire, the proclaimed intention was to pen the bird in a wooden enclosure and so prolong the good weather that the cuckoo brought with it. Underlying the hopeless task was undoubtedly a more

straightforward wish to make the most of spring's arrival. The timing of such festivities varied but they were usually held to coincide with the cuckoo's first dates: at Heathfield (East Sussex, 14 April), Crewkerne (Somerset, 15 April), Tenbury Wells (Worcestershire, 20 April), Towednack (Cornwall, the Sunday nearest 28 April) and Gotham (Nottinghamshire, 29 April). All of them have now lapsed, although Gotham retains its Cuckoo Bush pub and the site of the traditional penning ceremony is still known as Cuckoo Bush Hill.

The only living cuckoo festival is a recently revised event at Marsden in West Yorkshire, which takes place in the last week of April. However, it draws on a very old local legend, once widespread across northern England and similar to the penning traditions of further south, that if the cuckoo could be walled in, then the good weather could be extended. It has been running for 12 years and was originally arranged by the National Trust, owners of the adjacent 5000-acre (2025-ha) Marsden Moor. As well as organised walks to see and hear the totem bird, it combines typical spring activities – maypoles and morris dancing – with more specific details, like a specially brewed local ale: 'Cuckoo Spit'.[31]

The bird's sudden vanishing act in high summer – adults often leave in July – was another part of its complex life history that was little understood. One historical theory held that cuckoos passed the winter deep inside a hollow tree, and there were occasional confirmatory stories of birds flying unexpectedly out of winter log fires after their secret resting place had been felled and burnt as fuel. Even more common was the idea, based on no less an authority than Pliny (Aristotle mentioned but dismissed it), that cuckoos transformed themselves into birds of prey in autumn. The species does strongly resemble a sparrowhawk and the similarities were confusing, at least until fairly recently. 'In the winter of 1956 a quarryman pointed out a Sparrowhawk swooping over a wall bordering a plantation and said, "Thad bugger'll be back i' th' spring bawlin' 'is bloody hed off Cuck-oo, Cuck-oo."'[32]

The physical similarities between cuckoo and sparrowhawk are now considered to arise from a form of aggressive mimicry, which has a protective function when the birds are conducting their long, stationary vigils in search of suitable host nests. Yet they do occasionally fall victim to hobby, merlin and peregrine. These recorded cases tend to dispel the idea that the cuckoo's diet of toxic hairy caterpillars renders the birds themselves inedible. So too does the cuckoo's culinary status in Italy, where young birds are considered a delicacy. Yet perhaps the most intriguing case of predation was recorded by Richard Meinertzhagen, an ornithologist now infamous for his parasitic 'use' of other people's books and skin collections, who claimed to see the classic kleptoparasite, Arctic skua, take and eat Britain's ultimate brood-parasite, the cuckoo, in Shetland.[33]

Great Spotted Cuckoo, *Clamator glandarius*. This large beautiful cuckoo of southern Europe and Africa parasitises comparably bigger hosts like magpie, carrion crow and European roller. The young bird does not usually seek to evict the host's offspring and sometimes up to five great-spotted-cuckoo eggs can be found in the same nest. The cuckoo chick compensates by hatching sooner, growing faster and having a mouth-lining more attractive to its foster parents even than that of their own offspring. As a result the smaller cuckoo out-competes its rival step-siblings for food.[34] In Britain it is no more than a rare vagrant with just 42 records by 2001.

The **Black-billed Cuckoo**, *Coccyzus erythrophthalmus*, and **Yellow-billed Cuckoo**, *C. americanus*, are New World species that quite regularly make it across the Atlantic (13 and 57 records respectively). Most of them have occurred in Cornwall and Scilly, with the latter hosting more than any other European location. Sadly they share the common cuckoo's caterpillar diet and the autumn dearth causes many to die in a matter of days, even hours. They buck the usual family trend by rearing their own offspring, but their nests are infamous for their shoddy construction and in years of plenty they will lay surplus eggs in other birds' nests.

Owls *Strigiformes*

As one contributor put it so memorably, 'Owls carry upon their backs the whole weight of English folklore.'[1] While they have now shed most of their negative baggage, they are still richly freighted with cultural associations and still have the power to raise the hairs on the back of some necks.

I was amazed when, during the hard winter of 1981–2, a number of owls converged on our modern housing estate in search of food. It was at times possible to see tawny, barn and little owls hunting passerines out of their shrubbery-bed roosts along adjacent streets. My amazement stemmed not so much from this behaviour, as from the reactions of various people. They were convinced that the proximity of so many owls meant death and disaster. Mind you, if you ever get an opportunity to really study an owl at close quarters, you will perhaps feel like I do that they are not merely wise but positively knowing.[2]

In modern television drama or film the momentary image of an owl taking wing – or merely the sound of a tawny owl – is still a standard (if rather hackneyed) device to indicate mystery, darkness, suspense and the presence of evil. It is a modern response but it has a long history and, while it embraces all owls, the two British species most often invoked in these televisual representations are barn and tawny. In literature the owl-as-symbol often combines features of several species and for this reason a general family preface is appropriate. Even John Clare, a poet noted for natural-historical accuracy, repeatedly wrote of the 'grey owl', which seems a curious midway point between the barn owl's creamy buff and the tawny's darker tones. His poem 'Crowland Abbey' opens with the lines:

In sooth, it seems right awful and sublime
To gaze by moonlight on the shattered pile
Of this old abbey, struggling still with time –
The grey owl hooting from its rents the while;
And tottering stones, as wakened by the sound.

One senses that Clare invoked his indeterminate bird (take your pick: neither is grey, and tawnies hoot, but barn owls inhabit old buildings) more as a symbol of desolation than as a genuinely observed occupant of the abbey.

One could go on indefinitely drawing on a vast 700-year

canon of owl imagery in English literature, but two good examples will have to stand for the entire tradition. Samuel Coleridge's poem of the supernatural, 'Christabel', contains a perfect expression of all that owls symbolised in the past. The poem opens with the lines:

> 'Tis the middle of night by the castle clock,
> And the owls have awakened the crowing cock;
> Tu-whit! – Tu-whoo!
> And hark, again! the crowing cock,
> How drowsily it crew.

In the contest between the quintessential symbols of darkness and light, it is the sound of the owl and its omen of doom that triumphs over the day-heralding cockerel. Coleridge thus set an immediate scene for his (sadly unfinished) poem about the seductive power of feminine evil.

The early twentieth century was the moment when British owls started to lose most of their dark associations, and it is typical that Edward Thomas, the great poet of English nature in the period, should so accurately reflect this new symbolism. In 'The Owl' he described his arrival at a cosy firelit inn, from which:

> All of the night was quite barred out except
> An owl's cry, a most melancholy cry
>
> Shaken out long and clear upon the hill,
> No merry note, nor cause of merriment,
> But one telling me plain what I escaped
> And others could not, that night, as in I went.
>
> And salted was my food, and my repose,
> Salted and sobered, too, by the bird's voice
> Speaking for all who lay under the stars,
> Soldiers and poor, unable to rejoice.

His bird is freed from much of the old ghoulish superstition, but its intrinsic power to evoke the alien qualities of night-time for a largely diurnal primate like ourselves is beautifully delineated. It is this irreducible mystery in owls, both troubling and captivating, that compels our attention and has more recently awakened our affections.

First, however, we should ask what led to the owl's long dark past as an emblem of malevolence and death. The answer surely lies partly in their remarkable calls. The most vocal species produce a wide range of bizarre hisses, screeches, wails and moans – all sounds that are either completely inhuman or resemble humans only at their most intense moments. Purified of visual distraction

Barn owls are the classic inhabitants of old farm buildings, church towers and of English poetry dealing with themes of darkness, mystery and the macabre.

Barn owls sometimes look like huge pale moths as they quarter the fields at dusk.

or context, they make audible all that is unknown and seemingly hostile about the darkness. The sense that these are direct, if ambiguous, communications with ourselves is borne out by the appearance of the bird itself, with its upright two-legged stance, staring binocular vision and prominent human-shaped head and face. It somehow resembles a human, if humans ever had bird form. It is striking that in parts of Britain the tawny and barn owl were once known as 'seraphim' and 'cherubim', suggesting a nature that was part spirit, part human.[3]

What is most striking about the fearful response to owls, from which we are even now emerging, is its universal character. The Finnish ornithologist Heimo Mikkola is one of the great authorities on owls and he suggests that the common pattern of attitudes towards them across societies is an indication of the age of our relationship with them. According to Mikkola, the similarities between owl mythologies in Europe, Native America and in Africa derive from the fact that the beliefs travelled outwards with the first human exodus from the African savanna. Even if Mikkola is wrong and there is no single geographical origin for the vast network of

Barn owls are masters of the silent search-and-pounce hunting technique.

mythologies, the fact that they resemble each other in such detail is itself compelling evidence for humanity's shared heritage. Whatever the differences of place, species and context, the owl family has inspired the same responses in each separate community.

To walk through the hot malodorous fetish markets of west Africa, where owls are widely sold today for use in magico-medicinal practices, is to encounter in the most unforeseen way aspects of our own culture. When the witches stirred their broth of trouble in Macbeth's eleventh-century Scotland (*Macbeth*, Act 4, Scene 1) – or, equally, in Shakespeare's Tudor England – they chose exactly those ingredients still on sale in the African markets:

> Eye of newt, and toe of frog,
> Wool of bat, and tongue of dog,
> Adder's fork, and blind-worm's sting,
> Lizard's leg, and howlet's wing –
> For a charm of pow'rful trouble,
> Like a hell-broth, boil and bubble.

Yet even long ago owls were far more than simply an ingredient for the hell-broth. Their wide-eyed expressions and the slow-motion eloquence of the head movements either suggested profound intelligence or dull stupidity. 'Wise' is one of the adjectives most frequently yoked to owl, yet 'owl' itself is also defined as a word for 'the solemn dullard'.[4] To these we now have to add more modern connotations, such as the mothering bird of the Brownie troupe, 'Brown Owl'.

Another good indication of our collective pre-occupation with owls are the three recent monographs on the barn owl alone. Among British birds, only the puffin has attracted the same level of coverage and it is note-worthy that both share important characteristics (see also page 257). Their small rounded shapes and stature are thought to mimic the proportions of our own offspring, and toy owls now vie with penguins (or puffins) as the birds most likely to be found resident in the baby's cot. In addition to cuddly toys, owl images have extended their range into every room of the house as paperweights, sculptures, textiles – in fact as every conceivable knick-knack or household object. No family of birds is more frequently represented and this new-found popularity hinges on our final realisation about owls.

Although now drained of the fear and anxiety which we once poured into them, owls' strange calls still define

Young barn (and tawny) owls are strangely prone to drowning in troughs, water butts and ponds.

The RSPB's 1950s poster by Charles Tunnicliffe highlighted the need for barn-owl conservation. It was taken too literally by some and resulted in birds being delivered to police stations.

the limits of our sunlit domain. They remind us that we share this land, even our gardens and outbuildings, with creatures that are completely other than ourselves. In turn, these beautiful if elusive companions reassure us that there is mystery still in our everyday lives.

Barn Owl, *Tyto alba*. VN: Billy/Willy Wix (East Anglia); Ginny Ollit (Yorkshire); Screech Owl, White Owl. This is one of the most popular of the family, especially since the melancholy glamour of rarity has descended upon the species. There are just over 5000 pairs in Britain and Ireland, less than half the number in England and Wales alone during the 1930s.[5]

It is hard now to imagine the superstitious persecution that the barn owl suffered until about the 1950s: birds nailed spread-eagle to barn doors to ward off storms; or skinned and attached to firescreens with the facial disc pinned between the outspread wings like a central rosette. Presumably the bird's longer history as a magical defence against thunder and lightning was assumed to work against the lesser flame of the household hearth, although no definite explanation for this old domestic fashion has survived.[6]

The past maltreatment of owls now seems incomprehensible, but this is the species that most completely conveys the otherworldly aura that stirred our hostility. With their wide repertoire of 'hissing, snoring, raucous shrieks and other weird noises', barn owls far better deserve a vernacular name that they share with the tawny: 'screech owl'.[7] Although not an especially loud noise, it can be remarkably penetrating and unnerving: 'During the 1920s a Herefordshire villager, knowing that I was interested in birds, brought a basket of young barn owls to the house. The result was that we and our neighbours were kept awake by the parents' outraged shrieks. This was quite amazing as the nest was in a tree several miles away. Next morning I took the owlets home.'[8]

It is easy to see why they had such a strong effect in a more remote past. Gilbert White said that he had known of whole villages 'up in arms on such an occasion, imagining the church-yard to be full of goblins and spectres'.[9]

To reinforce the impression, barn owls are also the

most ghostly in appearance. At times, when caught in car headlights they seem almost to glow and occasionally they actually do: when owls nesting in hollow trees come into contact with the phosphorescence of certain species of fungi. More typically the bird looks as John Clare described it: 'the owl on wheaten wing,/And white hood scowling o'er his eyes'. The upperparts are a rich golden-buff studded with black-edged white flecks and touches of grey, while the underparts are white and buff with sparse black spots. At any distance barn owls look all creamy-white or simply white, and one is more likely to mistake it for a gull than any other bird. Although the confusion is only momentary since their 'flopping, unbalasted, aimless' moth-like flight is unforgettable.[10]

In the nineteenth century the Reverend C. A. Johns described:

> how stealthily they fly along the lanes, dipping behind trees, searching round the haystacks, skimming over the stubble, and all with an absence of sound that scarcely belongs to moving life. Yet, though by no means slow of flight, the Barn Owl can scarcely be said to *cleave* the air; rather, it *fans* its way onwards with its down-fringed wings, and the air, thus softly treated yields to the gentle force and retires without murmur to allow it a passage.[11]

Although the barn owl is well named and agricultural buildings are among the commonest sources of nest and roost sites, it will also use hollow trees, old ruins and particularly church towers. While the loss of prey-rich grassland habitat is an important factor in the species' decline, barn conversions and the steady tidying away of derelict buildings from the British countryside, or the absence of access points to otherwise suitable rural structures, also limit the bird's presence. We now go to great lengths to provide good alternatives. Owl boxes are an important substitute, and the Hawk and Owl Trust has erected 1000 such homes that are now regularly occupied. At Horsham Business Park in Sussex, where owls were found to be nesting in an old water tower due for demolition, the contractors erected a special 28-foot (8.5-m) owl tower costing £30,000.[12]

Eurasian Eagle Owl, *Bubo bubo*. One of the world's most spectacular owls has a chequered history as a British species. In 1996 it was removed from the UK bird list, despite numerous old sightings spanning 300 years from the length and breadth of the country. There have also been several breeding records, but these are now all considered to involve birds escaped from captivity. Even today the eagle owl is 'almost as easily obtained as a budgerigar and as common on council housing estates as

Rottweilers'. In England, Scotland and Wales, more than 2000 licences to hold pet eagle owls were applied for between 1998 and 2003.[13]

The most recent controversial occurrence of birds in a 'wild' state is a pair in north Yorkshire, which has bred since 1996 and reared young in every year except one until 2001. By then 13 British-born eagle owls had fledged. While many birdwatchers would dearly love this supreme predator to establish itself, the enthusiasm is by no means universal. The first published account of the pair's breeding success triggered a wave of media interest and public alarm.

The issue causing concern is the eagle owl's diet. The largest individuals weigh more than 6½ pounds (3kg) – the heaviest owls in the world – and combine the power of a real eagle with the terrifying impact of an owl's nocturnal strike. In 'Eagle Owl' the poet Peter Walton explores the devastating combination:

> Either of these names alone
> Would be enough: the talon
> Bare, or gloved; death dealt by day
> Or dusk. In fierce duality
> They make force shaded, power
> Mysterious; and life less sure.[14]

The lives made a little less sure include those of mammals the size of roe deer fawns and birds as large as eider. Another dietary speciality is other predators, particularly smaller owls and even diurnal raptors that are formidable in their own right such as goshawk. More troubling is the occasional tale of eagle owls taking cats and dogs. In February 2000 *The Times* included the story of a pet dog bearing 2-inch (5-cm) scars after being dropped by an attacking eagle owl. The alarmist headline ran 'Owl "threat to babies"'. Yet several ornithologists, including Derek Goodwin, have noted the manner in which 'eagle owls in London Zoo "come alive" when some toddler comes near their cages, especially if the child goes on all fours and makes high-pitched sounds as little children often do'.[15]

Snowy Owl, *Nyctea scandiaca*. This magnificent white bird is primarily resident beyond the Arctic Circle, where it was once eaten by the Inuit and its feathers used to fletch arrows or as a type of brush to sweep the igloo.[16] More recently it has achieved fame as Hedwig, the post-carrying messenger for Harry Potter in J.K. Rowling's series of novels and the films they inspired.

Snowy owls were regular visitors to Orkney and Shetland during the nineteenth century, and individuals still appear and will occasionally stay for the summer in both archipelagos, as well as visiting the Outer Hebrides

When a male snowy owl eventually ceased to return to the Shetland island of Fetlar in 1976 he left his two female partners 'widowed' for seventeen years.

or the high tops of the Cairngorm massif. Rarer is the stray that reaches England, Wales or Ireland. However their wanderings to these shores have become less frequent, possibly as a result of climatic amelioration.

The all-white male is a huge owl with barrel-shaped body, rounded head and staring yellow eyes, while the even larger female is covered with narrow black bars and crescent-shaped spots. The species has something of the family's feline character and shares the generic owl name in Shetland, 'catyogle'.[17] Although the upright stance and overall proportions have led many observers to note the resemblance to a 'child's snowman' as they stand out boldly in the landscape.[18]

In 1967 there was huge excitement when a pair was discovered to be nesting on the island of Fetlar by Shetland's multi-talented naturalist, photographer, raconteur and fiddle-player, the late Bobby Tulloch. That year five young were reared and in the ensuing eight years a further 15 owlets fledged. In 1972 another female appeared and the pair became a *ménage à trois*, although the nesting efforts of the new bird were never successful because the male just could not find enough food to keep both broods alive.

Human factors had a bearing on their fortunes, for both good and ill, throughout the whole of the 30-year stay. Myxomatosis, for instance, was introduced and wiped out the owls' main prey in 1970, which prompted the RSPB wardens to provide supplementary food in four of the breeding seasons. They also took into custody young owls injured by barbed wire and treated the male for an eye infection.[19]

The bird's possible colonisation of Shetland was dealt a fatal blow when the bigamous male, having chased off all the other immature males, vanished himself in 1976, never to return. Yet one or two females, sometimes more, continued to appear and eventually inspired a vigorous debate in ornithological circles on the wisdom of importing a suitable partner for them. 'There is surely no great ethical problem,' wrote one commentator, 'in rectifying one of nature's minor oversights: to wit a male owl to woo the female owls.'[20] Eventually it was decided to let nature take its course, but not without much heartfelt sympathy from the thousands of people who made the pilgrimage north during the females' many summers of unfulfilment.

In 1989 an immature male found exhausted on an oil platform was released on the island, but sadly he soon put 'distance between himself and the "widows" of Fetlar'.[21] Two years later the Rare Birds Breeding Panel noted ruefully, 'If birds experience loneliness, only the Black-browed Albatross in a Shetland gannetry [see page 10] may be as lonely as this female Snowy Owl.'[22] Remarkably in 1991, when they had been male-less for 15 years, the editors added: 'And still they hang on, waiting for "Mr Right" to come along.'[23] Sadly he never did and after 1993 the females' long Penelope-like vigil came to a close and they returned no more.

Little Owl, *Athene noctua*. This owl had major cultural significance in the eastern Mediterranean and was a symbol of Pallas Athene, goddess of wisdom and patron deity of ancient Athens – hence the scientific name, which means literally 'Athene by night'. British holidaymakers encounter the bird's stylised image in Greece where it is still a ubiquitous motif, but the mythology has little resonance beyond that region.

In Britain the little owl is no more than a naturalised 'exotic'. Yet perhaps this country is a better measure of the species' huge intrinsic character, because even here it has acquired its own special sense of place. The birds show a particular attachment to pockets of dereliction, whether among old farm buildings or hollowed-out veteran trees in parkland, or simply rotten stumps in the hedgerow. In fact it would be hard to imagine many parts of the Welsh and English countryside without the little owl's distinctive piercing calls at dusk, or its round pocket-sized silhouette crowning a wall or telegraph pole.

It is primarily a nocturnal hunter, but it can be seen and closely approached even in broad daylight, the bright-yellow eyes glaring at any intruder. It also has a pair of white 'eyebrows' that meet in a knot on the forehead and impart a facial expression either of total surprise or intense irritation. The bird will often bob its head vigorously but without losing eye contact, an action that rather suggests a person adjusting the angle of their vision over a pair of bifocals.

Little owls were successfully released into the English countryside in the early twentieth century and now seem an integral part of our bird community.

They are capable of taking prey far bigger than themselves, including moorhen, young lapwing, wood pigeon, cuckoo and magpie, as well as mammals up to the size of rabbit or brown rat. They are equally noted for pursuing the quarry with great vigour and across their huge Eurasian range birds have been observed chasing small mammals through their desert burrows. When pulling up earthworms, British birds will occasionally fall over backwards when the force of their efforts prevails unexpectedly.[24]

The little owls' hunting prowess was at the heart of a major controversy in the early part of last century as game interests accused them of wreaking havoc among hand-reared pheasants and partridge. The sense of grievance was all the more intense given that the bird was an unwanted 'foreigner' in Britain. Exotics have a long history of causing disruption to native flora and fauna, but the point at which ecological disapproval becomes a simple dislike for the 'other', akin to racism, is often difficult to disentangle. The fact that alternative names for little owl from the 1920s included the Belgian, Dutch, French, Spanish and Indian owl hints at the crossover between the two types of prejudice.[25]

One commentator called the bird a 'scourge for the game-preserver ... courageous and bold, even to the verge of impudence, and ... exceedingly prolific'. He urged legislation to prevent further releases, heavy penalties for infringements and instant extermination for the introduced stock.[26] In addition to the principal charge of killing game, the owls were alleged to store up surplus carcasses in a larder and to create charnel houses that lured in beetles, of which they were also very fond.[27]

In fact prior to the introduction, little owls had been widely kept as household pets for their prowess as cockroach killers. British records occurred as early as 1758, possibly involving genuine wild migrants from Europe, but they had never bred before the nineteenth century.[28] The owl's first liberator in the 1840s had been the pioneer environmentalist Charles Waterton, but his Italian-caught birds did not take to his Yorkshire estate at Walton and the project failed.

Much of the credit (or blame!) for the little owl's eventual spread should go to Edmund Meade-Waldo. He was one of two double-barrelled naturalists – the other very English surname belonged to Alice Hibbert-Ware – who championed the species during its early years of naturalisation. Over a quarter of a century Meade-Waldo carried out releases in Kent and Hampshire and, together with the similar efforts of Lord Lilford on his own Northamptonshire estate near Oundle, succeeded in creating several breeding centres. The birds quickly expanded and by the 1920s they were nesting widely across southern England and Wales, much to the consternation of game breeders who, caught in 'a wave of hysteria', tried just as quickly to eliminate them.[29]

In order to examine whether the allegations were justified, the newly created British Trust for Ornithology launched a major inquiry into the little owl's diet in 1935. After intensive coverage in the press and on BBC radio, it chose as its principal investigator a young female ecologist. Over two years, with 75 helpers in 34 counties, Alice Hibbert-Ware painstakingly assembled her data. These were largely derived from her dissection of 2460 little-owl pellets, from one of which she extracted the remains of 343 earwigs and from another 2000 crane-fly eggs. The forensic detail both demolished the myths of larders and beetle-luring charnel houses, and gave small comfort to those who stigmatised the little owl 'as

The tawny owl and its powerful vocalisations are widely recognised in Britain, but the species is curiously absent from Ireland.

wholesale destroyer of game-chicks, poultry chicks, and song-birds'. Instead she showed that the birds, 'feed almost wholly upon . . . insects, other invertebrates and small mammals'.[30] The black reputation gradually eroded away, and little owls have since spread into western parts of England and Wales and just over the border into southern Scotland.

Tawny Owl, *Strix aluco*. VN: Brown Owl. The long wavering hoot of this bird is the one owl characteristic that has been most resistant to the onslaught of science. It still has strong inexplicable powers over some of its audience, both for good and ill:

Our Devon cottage during my childhood was next to a wood and I loved to sit in my bedroom window and listen to the tawny owls hooting at night when the family were all asleep except me. The magical com-bination of the smell of coming rain and of leaf mould and the sound of tawny owls is still so evocative that I'm transported back to my childhood with a frisson of pleasure whenever I hear them call. I wish I could get a relaxation tape of tawny owls – it would lull me to sleep every time![31]

Yet another contributor observes: 'My husband says a screeching owl presages death.'[32]

Its past status as an ill omen was accepted across most strata of society and even Victorian intellectuals like John Ruskin wrote: 'Whatever wise people may say of them, I at least have found the owl's cry always prophetic of mischief to me.'[33] In his *Bird Life and Bird Lore*, R. Bosworth Smith retold the lovely black comedy of a man who met his gardener and two sons in mourning clothes. Taking it to imply the unexpected death of their wife and mother, he expressed his condolences only to receive the unexpected news that the invalid was not quite dead, 'but an owl had flown, some nights before, over his cottage, and had hooted repeatedly in the back-yard'. The gardener was a man who knew how to interpret the signs.[34]

The standard transliteration of the male's night-piercing call has survived for more than 400 years, since Shakespeare included it at the close of *Love's Labour's Lost* (Act 5, Scene 2) where the song of winter ends with the lines:

Then nightly sings the staring owl: 'Tu-who;
Tu-whit, Tu-who' – A merry note,
While greasy Joan doth keel the pot.

The usually shortened version of 'Tu-whit, Tu-who', which rather distorts Shakespeare's original interpretation, has been a source of some controversy. Richard Fitter argued that the Bard really had in mind a male and female calling in combination. While 'Tu-who' nicely mimicked his long hoot, the 'Tu-whit' element did not, but it was an accurate rendering of her high shrill '*Keewick*' note.[35] W. H. Hudson was also unhappy on the grounds that in the true sound, 'There is no *w* in it, no *h* and no *t*', and suggested it could be better reproduced by 'some wood instrument that resembles the human voice'.[36]

For centuries schoolboys have known that the best instrument for reproducing an owl's hoot is their own cupped hands, into which they blow downwards through slightly parted thumbs. Even the birds themselves cannot apparently tell the difference. In one study in Cambridgeshire, an ornithologist found that 94 per cent of tawny owls responded within 30 minutes (William Wordsworth described the success produced by the same technique in one of his poems).[37]

Tawny is both the largest of our regularly breeding species and the most adaptable, with an almost nation-wide distribution in Britain (yet, strangely, it is completely absent from Ireland). The diet is correspondingly catholic and includes a wide range of rodents, stoat, rabbit, bats and birds to the size of pigeons, even kittiwakes (taken from the nesting cliffs) and other smaller owls, as well as more specialised fare:

I once found an owl pellet with a hawfinch's skull in it. I also saw a tawny owl nest with well-grown young that had been feeding on fully fledged magpie chicks. There must have been the remains of 5–6.[38]

In the summer of 1954 my parents were puzzled to find that the nests of a large colony of house martins under our eaves were being pulled down. One night hearing a noise, my mother looked out to find a tawny owl sitting on the window sill. She then put wire netting up, but to no avail and the martins were wiped out.[39]

Another suite of unexpected food items are plucked from beneath the water surface. Fish are widely recorded and an owl was found at Derwent Reservoir, Derbyshire, that had choked to death on a spawn-swollen frog or toad.[40] However, the record for the unexpected probably goes to the observer who witnessed an owl in full daylight feeding in the wake of a tractor and plough on worms, a food choice that is apparently innate.[41] 'When my brother was at school in Sussex he found a baby tawny owl which had fallen out of its nest and decided to look after it. By the summer holidays "Owlie" had learned lots of new tricks. He had become an enthusiastic gardener and whenever my mother was weeding in her borders he would be there pouncing on any unsuspecting worms or other delectable insects.'[42]

Along with the hen harrier and the two breeding skuas (see page 229), tawny owls are famous for their ferocious defence of nest and young. 'An August memory is of noonday twilight in the underwood that darkly clothes the sea-cliffs below Lyme Regis. A startled owl came rowing towards me with claws extended and I lay with my face to the earth until it broke its way through the over-arching boughs above my head.'[43] Not everyone, however, is so lucky. David Bannerman recounted the tale of a clergyman who was swooped upon and cut across the forehead, while his cap was carried clean off. The next day it was found more than 200ft (60m) from the scene of the attack.[44]

By far the most notorious incident was the attack that robbed the photographer Eric Hosking of his left eye. Hosking was working on a pair of nesting tawny owls at the appropriately named Doldowlod in Wales, in 1938. He had gone in pitch-darkness to retrieve equipment from the hide. 'There was not a sound, not even the whisper of a wing. But out of the silent darkness a swift and heavy blow struck my face . . . I could see nothing. The owl, with its night vision, had dive-bombed with deadly accuracy, sinking a claw deep into the centre of my eye.' Hosking could remember nothing of the journey to London and within 10 minutes of arrival was in the operating theatre of Moorfields Eye Hospital. A fortnight later, when the eye had become infected, he was given a stark choice: remove it or risk losing the sight in both eyes. He was 27. 'What good,' he asked himself, 'was a one-eyed naturalist-photographer? It looked as if the career I loved so much was to end.'

Hosking went on to become the most celebrated

In 1938 the great bird photographer Eric Hosking took this historic image of the tawny owl which robbed him of his left eye.

British wildlife photographer of the twentieth century. In his autobiography, entitled *An Eye for a Bird,* he described how the local keeper wanted to kill the whole owl family, but Hosking refused and within 24 hours of being discharged from hospital he was back in the same hide (but with a fencing mask over his face). 'As I entered it I was trembling from head to toe and my hair literally stood on end.'[46]

Owls remained Hosking's favourite birds. His most celebrated shot, 'one of the best-known bird photographs in the world', was a barn owl hovering momentarily in cruciform, with a vole in its beak. His personal notepaper featured a ghostly palimpsest of the same unforgettable image.[47]

Long-eared Owl, *Asio otus*. VN: Leo (birders); Catyogle (Shetland). Long-eared by name only – since the appendages on top of the head are merely decorative feather tufts – this is the family member most likely to inspire the collective name, a 'parliament' of owls. Anything up to a dozen birds gather in winter roosts (as

many as 200 have been found together on the east Hungarian steppe), where they remain inactive throughout daylight hours and oblivious to any mobbing from angry songbirds, other than perhaps a brief opening of one, occasionally two, bright-orange eyes. The roosts are often in locations that people seldom associate with owls, such as dense thorn scrub, and despite a lack of foliage they can be remarkably difficult to spot.

In a family renowned for camouflage, the long-eared owl is perhaps the most gifted at concealment. This rests partly on its striking plasticity. Although it measures just 1 inch (2.5cm) less than the tawny owl, by weight it can be a half or one-third the size (about the same as a medium-sized orange). At times of anxiety, long-eared owls seem able to sleek their feathers and contract until they assume the shape of a thin branch. When relaxed they re-inflate and assume the family's customary feline amplitude.

It is among the most difficult of all Britain's widespread species to see. The low, rather mournful call – 'a cooing moan rather than a hoot' – is seldom heard and little recognised by most people, while the bird's distribution is very patchy.[47] Large gaps in Wales, the English south-west, the west Midlands and western Scotland are partly shaped by competition with the more dominant tawny owl. The absence of the latter from Ireland almost certainly explains the long-eared's success in that country, where it is the common owl.

Short-eared Owl, *Asio flammeus*. VN: Shorty/ies (birders); Cataface, Catty/ie Face (Orkney); Catyogle (Shetland). It is a bird of high moors and rough grassland and breeds mainly north of a line between the Humber and Mersey estuaries. It reverses the usual family pattern by being largely diurnal and is an owl that people often observe well. Partly as a consequence, it can make a powerful impression: 'The wings are quite astonishingly long for the size of the bird. It appears light-coloured in the sunlight, the upperparts and wings being attractively marbled . . . It flies with a grace and buoyancy unrivalled by any of its kind . . . The sideslips, the hesitant hover as it looks a second time . . . the quick plunge to earth . . . exemplify the practised skill of a peerless flier.'[48]

Short-eared owls are capable of sustained journeys and routinely migrate from continental Europe in late autumn, often making landfall in Britain with influxes of other classic October migrants like the woodcock. It is this association that explains archaic east-coast names such as 'woodcock owl' or 'pilot owl', and an attached myth that migrant goldcrests hitched a lift in the larger bird's plumage. It is completely untrue, but the owls themselves are not above catching a ride on passing ships, while some birds have been reported to linger on oil rigs

The short-eared owl is the most diurnal of its five family members in Britain and Ireland.

for several weeks, where they survive by catching other tired migrants.[49]

The short-eared owl's principal diet is small mammals, particularly voles, and the bird's numbers have long been observed to fluctuate with the abundance of their prey. A phenomenon unlikely to recur in our age of lethal rodenticides is the occasional plague of voles, which were capable of reducing a landscape virtually to desert. One of the earliest to be described was in 1590 in the marshes around Southminster, Essex, and was so severe that local cattle died of starvation. However, the super-abundance of rodents gave rise in turn to 'such a number of owls as all the shire was not able to yield; whereby the marsh-holders were shortly delivered from the vexations of the said mice'.[50] Another infestation recurred in Essex in around 1620, although far better documented were parallel events in southern Scotland in 1875/6 and more famously in 1891–3.

The second episode, affecting a minimum area of 600 square miles (1660sq km) between the towns of Lanark, Peebles and Dumfries, gave rise to some extraordinary scenes. One eye-witness reported travelling mile after mile with at least a dozen short-eared owls visible at any one time, while 'In Dumfriesshire alone not less than five hundred pairs of breeding birds were estimated':

Probably there were three or four times that number on the vole-infested farms ... the finest sight of all was when at midsummer of 1892 I had a chance of going along the hills at midnight. The night was bright and clear, and very still. The owls were on all sides flying like no other birds I ever saw. The voles were scurrying hither and thither, squeaking and rustling as one stepped over and amongst them. The unfeathered owlets had left their nests, and were sitting blinking their eyes and contorting their bodies in groups on almost every hillock. The parents never troubled to alight amongst their offspring, they simply flew past, and flung the dead voles at their young in the by-going.[51]

No similar concentration has since been recorded, but the establishment of new conifer plantations frequently causes an increase in vole abundance, and the widespread

In winter short-eared owls move off their upland breeding grounds and can be seen quartering coastal dunes and marshes.

afforestation of the uplands has had positive, if temporary, benefits for short-eared owls.

Often the local increases are accompanied by the bird's spread into areas where they would otherwise not be seen:

One hot day in May 1976 I decided to explore the upper reaches of the River Irwell in Salford. In the middle of the day, where the immediacy of the sweltering silence all but negated the distant hum of urban activity, I expected little reward. However, if one bird can make a day, this was it – a quartering short-eared owl appeared, totally unheralded, and passed silently overhead. Given that the multistorey blocks of an overspill estate were only a few hundred yards away, this was certainly not the bird's textbook territory.[52]

Nightjar family
Caprimulgidae

European Nightjar, *Caprimulgus europaeus*. Although the fortunes of this scarce summer migrant have undergone a marked recovery in the last 20 years, and while it occurs as far north as Argyllshire and west into Wales and Ireland, it is mainly concentrated in the counties of south-east England. Here it is closely associated with heathland or young and freshly cut conifer plantations. Yet at one time it was found almost nationwide across a wide range of open habitats, including upland moors, scrubby commons and grazed downland. An old name, familiar to Gilbert White and John Clare, was 'fern-owl', which conjures the bracken-dominated hillsides and woodland breaks it once frequented.

Nightjars feed at dawn and dusk and sleep by day, often roosting lengthwise along a branch or on the ground, where they are protected by an almost impenetrable camouflage. John Walpole-Bond, author of *A History of Sussex Birds*, recorded an occasion when he came upon a nest with the adult's tail feathers all arrayed at the exact spot where she had presumably been trodden on and the tail plucked by an unseeing intruder.[1]

In the past nightjars suffered needless persecution because of the irrational fears associated with many nocturnal animals. Gilbert White, who showed deep interest in Selborne's fern-owl population, wrote: 'The country people have a notion that the *Fern-owl* or *Churn-owl*, or *Eve-jarr*, which they also call a *Puckeridge*, is very injurious to weanling calves by inflicting, as it strikes at them, the fatal distemper known ... by the name of Puckeridge.' Knowing that the condition was in fact caused by the warble fly, whose eggs were laid in the calf's skin along the rump and spine, White added: 'Thus does this harmless ill-fated bird fall under a double imputation ... in Italy, of sucking the teats of goats ... and with us, of communicating a deadly disorder to cattle.'[2]

The more ancient slur is still enshrined in the scientific name *Caprimulgus*, from the Latin *capra* 'she-goat' and *mulgeo*, 'I milk', and recurs in the Spanish (*chotocabras*) and German (*Ziegenmelker*). From classical times it was believed that the birds entered the goat stalls and sucked the nanny's udders, which could eventually cause them to wither and the animals themselves to go blind. No one has convincingly explained how the goat-sucker legend arose, but it was recorded by Aristotle and was probably already ancient in his day. The likeliest background

Left: The distinctive white tail and wing spots of a male nightjar, as well as the species' consummate aerial control, are all captured in Eric Hosking's famous photograph.

Right: James McCallum's painting of a brooding nightjar in north Norfolk.

involves two interlocking factors: the nightjar's habit of feeding in the vicinity of coralled animals where its insect diet would be abundant, and the strong taboos once surrounding domestic stock among pastoral communities. The giving of milk was particularly shielded by ritual, just as an animal going dry was ascribed to all sorts of causes, many of them magical in character.

In the nineteenth century the killing of robins was thought to be a cause of bloody milk in cattle (see page 337).[3] In Shetland the crofters on Unst held that a cow frightened by a snowy owl would be similarly afflicted.[4] In *Tess of the d'Urbervilles*, Thomas Hardy explored the dairying traditions of an older Dorset, where cows were thought to dry up in the presence of strangers or could be coaxed into giving milk with fiddle music, or where the butter would not churn if someone in the house was in love. One can perhaps understand how, faced with strange night birds swooping around the goats and then the failure of their milk in the morning, the early goatherds succumbed to the same sort of rationale. Quite how they added the withered teats and the goat's subsequent blindness is impossible to answer, but William Turner, the sixteenth-century father of British ornithology, accepted the goat-sucking legend in its entirety on the strength of a Swiss herder's personal testimony.[5]

Yet even the most scientifically minded observer would have to acknowledge that there is something powerfully mysterious about the birds, particularly the sudden inverted awakening at dusk, the wildly erratic flight, even the huge eyes and immense rose-pink gape.

In his poem 'Afterwards', Hardy conjured both the eeriness and the absolute silence associated with nightjar movements in a beautifully observed image:

If it be in the dusk, when, like an eyelid's soundless blink,
The dewfall hawk comes crossing the shades to alight
Upon the wind-warped upland thorn.

Hardy, incidentally, may have coined the name, 'dew-fall hawk', after reading John Clare's own writings on the fern-owl ('they make an odd noise in the evening, beginning at dewfall').[6]

If anything the bird's unearthly vocalisations are more arresting than its appearance. The '-jar' portion of the name (whence 'jarring') has an original meaning of 'a harsh, inharmonious sound'. It might suggest the almost insect-like quality of nightjar song but it seriously misrepresents the strange captivating euphony. 'One of life's ambitions has recently been achieved at our Breckland house – to lie in bed on a warm, early summer's evening with the window open and catch the wonderful churring of one of our most enigmatic birds.'[7]

The dry, throaty mechanical notes pour out at a rate of 28–42 a second and every now and then the sound subtly modulates – a shift in pitch and tempo as the bird turns its head, and possibly linked to the nightjar's breathing rhythm. The sound is sometimes compared to the stridulation of the mole cricket but to many it evokes the operation of various mechanical objects. 'Wheel bird' was an old country name because of the closeness of the song to a spinning wheel. For Suffolk birdwatchers of the 1960s the nocturnal hunt for nightjars was sometimes thrown into confusion by 'the distant noise of the water-cooled *Velocette* motorcycle which seemed to be in vogue with the rural constabulary of the area'.[8]

To spot a singing nightjar is never an easy exercise. In the half-light of dusk the males are difficult to pick out as they perform while perched on an exposed tree limb. The sound, which is without any obvious beginning or end, is strongly ventriloquial. The overall lack of fixity makes it seem at times that it is emerging directly from the landscape itself: 'When you are really close to a Nightjar churring, it almost seems that the ground adjacent is caused to vibrate!'[9] Small wonder perhaps that T. E. Lawrence, 'Lawrence of Arabia', Britain's great man of mystery, should have apparently preferred this bird of mystery, 'to the full throated warble of the nightingale'.[10]

Egyptian Nightjar, *Caprimulgus aegyptius*. This pale desert nightjar has been recorded just twice in Britain. The second occasion was in 1984, but to the first attaches an entertaining story. A Nottinghamshire gamekeeper, Albert Spinks, flushed a bird from its resting spot while he was shooting rabbits and, thinking it looked unusual, brought it down with his second barrel. A day later when it started to smell he threw it on to the ashpit near his cottage, only for his ornithologist employer, J. Whitaker, to notice and retrieve the skin. Whitaker sent it to his taxidermist and subsequently had its identity confirmed as an Egyptian nightjar, then he honoured 'his' find by erecting a monument at the site of discovery (Thieves Wood, near Mansfield). The inscription, in which the largest letters spell his own name, was intended to read: 'This stone was placed here by J. Whitaker, of Rainworth Lodge, to mark the spot where the first British specimen of the Egyptian Nightjar was shot by A. Spinks, on June 23rd, 1883, this is only the second occurrence of this bird in Europe.'[11] In fact 'occurrence' was misspelt and the date appears to have been wrongly given as 1882.

The stone is significant as probably the only memorial raised to an individual wild bird in Britain for more than a century (see Great Auk, page 254). Whitaker's mounted skin of the bird is now in Mansfield Museum, but his stone was recently replaced by a simple concrete post with only a nightjar etching and the date, which now forms part of a nature trail through Thieves Wood.[12]

Swift family *Apodidae*

Common Swift, *Apus apus*. For a bird that has such a powerful hold over our imaginations and is so widespread and closely associated with us, it is extraordinary that swifts (apparently) have no vernacular names today. Yet they are still regularly lumped together or confused with the other house-dwelling, sky-trawling species, house martin and swallow. In some ways this is just as extraordinary, given the swift's striking appearance. Except for a small cup of off-white on the chin the bird is all black. The shape is even more distinctive – a combination of long slim swept-back wings with slender body and tail. Together they create a flight silhouette that looks, in Edward Thomas' memorable words in his poem 'Haymaking', 'As if the bow had flown off with the arrow'.

The current lack of alternative names is in contrast to the past, when it was known variously as 'devil's bitch', 'deviling', 'devil', 'devil bird', 'skeer devil', 'screecher', 'screamer' and 'shriek owl'. No doubt the references drew strongly on the black scimitar shape and shrill screaming call, but one would like to know exactly what kind of devils were intended. The species seems not to have had a particularly evil reputation and there is little evidence of persecution, and one cannot imagine a bird genuinely viewed as an agent of Satan being tolerated in the roof space above a rustic cottage. 'Devil's bitch' sounds menacing, but perhaps most of the names were meant to convey nothing more than a small captivating creature, in the same way that we might use 'little devil' for an impish child.

Whatever the resonances once intended, the only devil relevant to today's public image of swifts is perhaps the devil of John Milton, an incarnation of the sheer intensity of earthly life. Swifts are hugely popular and one of the few species to inspire phrases like 'my passion for the birds', 'my obsession' or 'My husband is something of a swift freak'.[1] The following contributions capture the strong emotions that people feel for swifts and the powerful symbolism they carry:

The swifts come back to this part of south Gloucestershire during the first week of May bringing the summer with them.[2]

Our greatest joy is on warm summer evenings watching the swifts fly about the house. Alas, all too soon comes the saddest day at the end of summer when the swifts leave on their long journey. To us it is

A screaming party of swifts is perhaps the most perfect incarnation of summer's energy and passion.

as sad as their arrival is exciting. We can console ourselves, however, that there is always next year to look forward to.[3]

The sounds of swifts take me right back to the long hot summer holidays when I was a child living with my parents. When I hear them, I am there . . . net curtains blowing in the breeze, lying in bed, still daylight, listening to their haunting screams. I'm not a religious person, quite the contrary, but at my funeral the only sound I would like is that of the haunting scream of the swift, to take me back to those long hot summer holidays once more.[4]

Their status as an emblem of summer is intriguing, partly because it is a modern development and partly because one senses they have come to replace swallow and cuckoo in that key symbolic role. Swifts remain here just from May to early August and are 'British' for only a quarter of their lives. Yet compared with the swallow's six-month residence, that 16-week visit seems a more realistic statement about our short season of plenty. Swifts also compensate by making their presence felt to a far greater number of us. They feed at a higher elevation than swallows or martins and are less affected by aerial pollution. They can therefore thrive in urban air space even at the very heart of large conurbations like central London (where swallow is now absent).

The appeal may possibly rest as much on what we do not know as on their familiarity. Swifts are still highly mysterious and, as Max Nicholson noted, 'Paradoxically there are in practice few nesting sites so immune from human disturbance as those under the roofs of dwellings, and the nest of the swift, which is so often this position, must be less often seen than that of any equally common bird.'[5] One of the earliest attempts to investigate them was made by Edward Jenner, discoverer of the smallpox vaccination (as well as the cuckoo chick's technique for evicting step-siblings from a nest; see page 278). He caught 12 swifts at a Gloucestershire farmhouse and clipped two of their four toes off so that he could recognise them. One of them was brought into the kitchen by the farmer's cat seven years after the initial experiment.[6]

The most important modern study of swifts, which is also one of the longest research projects on a bird in Britain, was initiated by David and Elizabeth Lack. Their work was launched in 1947 with the help of a grant from Jacquetta Hawkes, eminent archaeologist and wife of the author and playwright J. B. Priestley. The studies

Swifts have bred in the 'Tower' above Oxford's Natural History Museum for more than half a century.

continue to focus on descendants of the Lacks' original birds which nest in the central spire or 'Tower' of the Museum of Science on Parks Road in central Oxford. The steep roof has special half-cone-shaped ventilation holes giving access to purpose-built accommodation for 80 pairs of swifts, of which 60 are usually occupied.[7]

The project has helped to shed light on many aspects of swift behaviour, such as the chick's capacity to enter a state of torpor, with body temperature and metabolism dramatically reduced when weather conditions are poor. Adult swifts find it difficult, if not impossible, to catch insects in the rain and the young bird's torpid state helps it survive without food for up to 48 hours. Just as remarkable is the parents' ability to overcome the same problem by flying right around depressions. English birds have been recorded feeding over Germany as they move clockwise around low-pressure systems, with some of their rain-dodging excursions totalling 600–1200 miles (1000–2000km).[8] Confronted with eastward-

tracking occluded fronts during summer, British swifts also fly straight towards the unstable air at the rear of the depression, where insects can be present in extraordinary abundance – according to one estimate, 3.5 billion over an area of 1 square kilometre.[9] The birds can then feed in the fine, warm rising air as the front departs and make their return journey nearly 2 miles (3km) above the earth.[10]

The swift's capacity for long-distance flight is nothing short of staggering. Max Nicholson suggested a daily average of 500 miles (800km), which would give a lifetime's total of more than 1.28 million miles (2.06 million km) for Jenner's seven-year-old bird at the Gloucestershire farmhouse; while a swift known to be 20 years old would have flown more than 3.65 million miles (5.9 million km).[11] Equally awe-inspiring is the ability of young birds to roost on the wing, circling for hours in the cold night air at high altitude until morning. It is thought that immatures, which may not start to nest until their fourth year, may remain aloft for the whole of their early lives.

The mystery of swifts impacts upon us most in the late summer when both adults and newly fledged young gather in the evenings to perform wild displays over the city skyscape. These gyroscopes of up to several hundred swirling birds, which are as much an assault on the ears as they are a visual spectacle, are known technically as social screaming-parties. The swift's scream, which to us appears harsh and intense, changes dramatically when slowed: 'At quarter-speed, it sounds like the thrilling vibrated cry of a great northern diver [see page 4] . . . slowed down to a tenth of the natural speed, it is like the clucking and crooning of a domestic fowl.'[12] The function of the displays is little understood, but to earth-bound observers far below swifts give an impression of reckless passion, of avian energy carried to the very limits of physical containment. 'Over many years swifts have pack-raced into our village. So much so that I started to call them the "ton-up kids".'[13]

The intensity is beautifully captured in Ted Hughes' poem 'Swifts':

And here they are, here they are again
Erupting across yard stones
Shrapnel-scatter terror. Frog-gapers,
Speedway goggles, international mobsters –

A bolas of three or four wire screams
Jockeying across each other
On their switchback wheel of death.
They swat past, hard-fletched,

The painting by John Paige of swift's hurtling over an urban landscape is a flawless match for Ted Hughes' poem 'Swifts'.

Veer on the hard air, toss up over the roof,
And are gone again. Their mole-dark labouring,
Their lunatic limber scramming frenzy
And their whirling blades

Sparkle out into blue –

        Not ours any more.

In the weeks just prior to swifts' migration, we are sometimes permitted a more intimate encounter when young birds misjudge their aerial manoeuvres or fall out of the nest hole when not completely fledged. It was once widely held that swifts had no feet, an idea echoed both in the scientific name – *apus* means 'footless' – and in heraldry, where the bird was used as a symbol for a fourth son of the house, a hapless creature unable to plant his feet on the land.[14] Even today not everyone is sure it is merely a myth: 'I once met a farmer who was adamant that swifts did not have any legs. He swears he found a grounded one that had no legs and tried to convince me that none had legs.'[15] A more common assumption is that the birds 'are unable to land on the ground, as their legs are too small and weak'.[16] In fact adults are perfectly capable of taking off from a flat surface, although dazed or young birds often benefit from a helping hand: 'One day we saw that there was a swift on our gravel path. I approached it gently and lifted it up. It lay quite quietly in my cupped hands; its feathers were smooth and much browner than I expected. I lifted it above my head and tossed it into the air, where it joined three companions and then they all flew off together.'[17]

A more unsettling revelation derived from this type of encounter is the swift's routine infestation with a particularly nasty-looking species of louse-fly, *Crataerina pallida*. Some of them are ¼ inch (0.6cm) in length and huge in proportion to the host, as an expert on avian parasites noted: 'a small bird with one or two of these insects creeping about in its feathers can be compared to a man with a couple of large shore crabs scuttling about in his underclothes'.[18] One contributor writes: 'I examined their nest and found, true to the bird books, that the nest material is soft feathers and fluff [all caught on the wing] and that the parasites seemingly dead were ensconced in it like large scarab beetles.'[19]

Kingfisher family *Alcedinidae*

Common Kingfisher, *Alcedo atthis*. VN: Kingy. In his poem 'The Kingfisher', John Clare noted 'that the peacock's tail is scarce as fine'. The bird has long been cemented in popular imagination as the most brilliantly coloured of all our avifauna. Its image is now so ubiquitous – especially on crockery, calendars and anniversary cards – that even people who have never seen one are completely familiar with its appearance. However, first-time viewers are often surprised by its size: it is barely bigger than a house sparrow.

Equally surprising in a bird that is so universally popular is its aggression towards possible competitors, both from other species and its own:

> I was filming a pair of kingfishers digging a nest for several days for the BBC. Just as the nest was finished a second female turned up in the territory. It appeared that she wanted to steal the territory from the resident female and both birds were thus very aggressive towards each other. They spent a day chasing each other and this came to a head on the next day when they attacked each other physically. In one fight the birds grabbed each other by the shoulder and fought in the water as they floated downstream, each trying to drown the other. After a minute it appeared both would drown if they didn't break free and as they attempted this a mink exploded out from under a root system and grabbed the intruding female. The resident bird was just able to fly off.[1]

The British population of just over 6000 pairs is widespread, mainly on slow-flowing lowland rivers as far north as central Scotland, but the kingfisher is nowhere easy to see. Birds spend large amounts of time motionless at the water's edge watching for fish and are often overlooked. The standard view is of a lightning flash of colour as a bird hurtles along the course of a river. Ironically it is on these brief flight views that the brightness is shown to best advantage.

The underparts are rich orange and the wings and crown a deep dark greeny-blue, but when the bird is sitting, the wing coverts and scapulars often mask the even brighter azure running down the back. It is this stripe of magical colour – literally of kingfisher blue – that is on show when a bird streaks past. However brief, it often leaves a lasting impression and frequently a sense of privilege. As one old lady told the bird's chief biographer, David Boag, 'only the righteous ever see the kingfisher'.[2]

Few things better illustrate the doggedly utilitarian attitudes of our ancestors than the past persecution of kingfishers. Their beauty made them equally popular with the Victorian taxidermist and the milliner, who incorporated the feathers into hats and other items of feminine costume. Eighty years ago W. H. Hudson, lamenting the presence of stuffed kingfishers 'in the parlour of tens of thousands of cottages all over the land', analysed the unfulfilled motivation:

> A man walking by the water-side sees by chance a kingfisher fly past, its colour a wonderful blue, far surpassing in beauty and brilliancy any blue he has ever seen in sky or water . . . Forthwith he gets his gun and shoots it, and has it stuffed and put in a glass case. But it is no longer the same thing: the image of the living sunlit bird flashing past him is in his mind and creates a kind of illusion when he looks at his feathered mummy, but the lustre is not visible to others.[3]

More recently David Boag noted that 'each feather on its own is quite a disappointment', since the kingfisher's colours are not pigmental in origin, but are the result of light striking specially modified layers of cells in the feather.[4] The full effect is lost when the plumage is broken down to its constituent parts. One can perhaps better understand the use of kingfisher feathers to make angler's flies, presumably from a hope that some of the bird's fishing talent would magically transfer to rod and line.

Kingfishers have an uncanny ability to find and catch their prey. A pair with a brood of hungry young can catch 115 fish a day. One unfortunate consequence is that the burrow, usually extending into an earth riverbank for 1½ feet (50cm), acquires a mounting deposit of half-digested fishbone and fishy guano from up to 10 young ones. The nest eventually assumes an odour not normally expected in one so beautiful.

One of the more improbable myths once attaching to kingfishers was their ability to predict weather. William Yarrell recorded that in his day they were regularly killed and hung by a thread in country cottages, in the belief that the dangling corpse could indicate the direction of the wind.[5] Ironically, while kingfishers are unable to predict the weather, they are highly sensitive to its impact. Very cold winters, with the inevitable icing over of ponds and rivers, are fatal for all fish-eating species. Fortunately kingfishers have a capacity for large clutches and multiple broods, and quickly recover from these natural disasters. Yet in the 1962/3 winter, 85–90 per cent of our kingfishers were thought to have perished.

Those seeing a kingfisher for the first time are as amazed by its fabulous colours as they are surprised by its small size.

Left: A flock of European bee-eaters hawking insects from the telegraph wires is a treasured sighting of many Mediterranean holidays.

Right: Hoopoe is one of those scarce visitors to Britain and Ireland that often has the power to arouse public interest.

Bee-eater family *Meropidae*

European Bee-eater, *Merops apiaster*. This is one of the most beautiful members from one of the world's most graceful, colourful bird families. It usually breeds no further north than Paris but it occasionally brings a hint of tropical colour to Britain and Ireland, with an annual trickle of records stretching as far back as the reign of Charles II.

There have also been a handful of nesting attempts, including a pair that dug a nest burrow in a sandbank near Musselburgh, East Lothian, in 1920. Given that bee-eaters had previously occurred just 10 times in Scotland, it was described as 'one of the most surprising and intrinsically unlikely events that have ever occurred in the ornithological history of the British Isles'.[1] Sadly the birds' efforts came to grief when a cat ate the male and a gardener imprisoned the female in his greenhouse until it died.[2] The first successful breeding record came when an unprecedented three pairs graced a Sussex sand-pit in the hot summer of 1955 and raised seven young.

More recently bee-eaters returned to the north-east and bred in an old limestone quarry at Bishop Middleham, County Durham, in spring 2003. In some ways an indication that little has changed since the 1920s was the round-the-clock guard to prevent egg thieves. However, the more modern touches were a permanent 'Big Brother'-style camcorder relaying the couple's domestic life to the thousands of visitors, and the 'Bee-eater' signs along the roads giving directions to the site.[3]

The **European Roller**, *Coracias garrulus*, which has never bred and is considerably rarer in Britain and Ireland (about 230 records), is the one Mediterranean bird to run the bee-eater a close second on the issue of tropical colour. The birds are often yoked together as two of the great desiderata among British twitchers – a point well illustrated by the following: 'During the 1980s I felt I was spending more time birdwatching than was good for me and decided that if I saw a roller, a golden oriole and a bee-eater in the UK I'd give up. I eventually saw all three but it didn't stop me – in fact, I think it made me worse than ever!'[4]

Hoopoe family *Upupidae*

Hoopoe, *Upupa epops*. It is the only European bird whose scientific name is as beautifully suggestive of the call – a soft, repeated, bottle-blown '*poop*' – as the English

version. Although it breeds as far north as Estonia and occurs widely along the Channel coast in Europe, there have been only about 40 British nesting attempts.[1] Possibly part of the reason for the failure to colonise was the insatiable appetite of nineteenth-century collectors who harassed hoopoes whenever they appeared. Norman Ticehurst felt that the species' history in Kent would involve 'some of the saddest pages' in the county's avifauna and complained of 'a lengthy and shameful list of acts of wanton destruction'.[2] Fortunately times have changed and the last breeding attempt – in Montgomery in 1996 – resulted in three fledged young. Otherwise the hoopoe is an annual visitor in small numbers (about 100 a year, with considerably fewer in recent times), particularly in spring. Some people divine a religious bias in these occurrences: 'This is subject-ive – from impressions in several county avifaunas – but they seem to have an inordinate preference for vicarage lawns.'[3]

Most Britons first encounter the species during Mediterranean holidays, where hoopoes are routinely seen in hotel grounds. They move across the lawns with a rather crouched posture like a small cinammon-coloured dove, the 'Indian chief's' head-crest usually sleeked down and the long sabre-like bill probing the turf. Only when they take off do they reveal the dramatic colours for which they are celebrated. The wings are broad and rounded, giving the flight a slow butterfly-like quality, an action that seems to exaggerate the strobe-like display of black-and-white zigzag lines.

The hoopoe's graphic possibilities were not lost on the ancient Egyptians, who used it as a hieroglyph and included it regularly in their murals. Today it tops the charts for birds appearing on stamps, with 43 countries featuring it.[4] In North Africa it remains a bird of considerable magico-medicinal power, turning up for sale in the street markets of Cairo, while in parts of Europe the birds have an ancient reputation for uncleanliness because of their strong-smelling nest hole (an archaic name was 'dung bird'). In Aristophanes' play, *The Birds*, the hoopoe was said to construct the nest from human ordure. Yet it is known to make a good pet and the great Scottish ornithologist David Bannerman reared a family of hoopoes during an ornithological expedition to the Canaries. These heraldic birds had a favourite perch on the top of his pith helmet, which he used to wear while preparing skins at his tent entrance.[5]

Woodpecker family *Picidae*

Wryneck, *Jynx torquilla*. It is extraordinary to think that in the mid-nineteenth century William Yarrell described this small bird as a common species that was widely kept as a pet by country children. A fall in numbers was noted shortly after, but it was still described in 1909 as 'plentiful and generally distributed throughout' in *A History of the Birds of Kent*.[1] By 2003, however, for the first time ever, there were no British nesting records at all. The wryneck's gradual extinction has been as painfully slow as it has seemed irreversible and hard to explain, but with the bird suffering declines almost Europe-wide, ecologists have eventually pointed to agricultural intensification and the loss of suitable grassland habitats for its main ant-prey as principal factors.

Rarity is not the only reason for the wryneck's special place in many people's affections. It is one of a handful of predominantly brown-grey species – woodcock and nightjar are two other good examples – that buck the usual convention on bird aesthetics and are renowned for their intricately mottled beauty. A wryneck's most striking features are a chocolate ellipse-shaped stripe running through the grey vermiculations on its back, and a warm ochreous throat patch cross-hatched with fine lines. Yet on a brief flight view, it suggests little more than a large dull warbler and bears no resemblance whatsoever to its other family members.

The bird's generic name – *Jynx* – has a fascinating origin. In ancient Greece and Rome wrynecks were associated with fertility rites that involved a rotating wheel-like charm known as a *Iynx* (or *Iynges* in the plural). The bird was apparently spread crosswise in the wheel as it was spun, when the device was thought to have the power to charm a prospective partner or, according to one source, bring back an errant lover.[2]

On the evidence of Greek mythology, the bird magic worked equally well for both sexes. Aphrodite, for instance, helped Jason win the heart of Medea at Colchis with the aid of a wryneck wheel, while the goddess Iynx worked a similar spell on Zeus so that he fell in love with a beautiful moon-goddess called Io. Unfortunately Zeus' official consort, Hera, learnt of her husband's infatuation with Io and punished her rival by changing her into a white heifer, while the spell-casting Iynx was herself transformed into nothing less than a wryneck.[3]

The question more relevant to ornithology is why exactly should these strange magical powers be vested in a small brown species of woodpecker? The answer lies in

The ant-eating wryneck has all but vanished as a breeding species in Britain because of changes in land use.

the ancient world's genuine observation of wryneck behaviour. The *torquilla* part of the scientific name means 'little twister', an echo of the current English version and a reference to the wryneck's extraordinary capacity to writhe its head round in a highly reptilian fashion. The resemblance to a snake is all the more striking if a wryneck is disturbed in its tree hole, when both adult and chicks will sway their heads, occasionally with their long tongues darting out, and emit a bizarre and disconcerting hiss.

The strangeness of the display is intensified in young birds by their 'extremely large and gargoyle-like heads',[4] while the biological function is well demonstrated in John Clare's beautifully observed poem, 'The Wryneck's Nest'. He described what happens when egg-thieving urchins climbed to the spot:

> The sitting bird looks up with jetty eye,
> And waves her head in terror to and fro,
> Speckled and veined with various shade of brown;
> And then a hissing noise assails the clown.
> Quickly, with hasty terror in his breast,
> From the tree's knotty trunk he sluthers down,
> And thinks the strange bird guards a serpent's nest.

The snake routine has the ability to deter cats and other potential predators. 'Once on Blakeney Point, Norfolk, I saw a wryneck rolling around on the ground going through the neck twisting routine and looked up to see a kestrel hovering overhead. It worked because the falcon flew away.'[5] In the ancient world the wryneck's mimetic behaviour presumably led people to ascribe to the bird the associations of fertility and eroticism which they had long fixed on the snake itself. The bird thus became a potent source of magical power in its own right.

Little, if any, of the wryneck's love symbolism survived the journey north to Britain but, nonetheless, we have 'jynx' – now commonly spelt 'jinx' – as a word for a passage of bad luck, or a type of curse. The bird was also widely known at one time as 'snakebird' in southern England and may still be.[6] Another suite of lost vernacular names – 'cuckoo's mate', 'cuckoo's footman', 'cuckoo's messenger' – carry association with the bird most obviously connected to erotic love. It would be nice to think that some of the wryneck's ancient symbolism was at work in their formation, but they most likely derive from the two migrants' shared arrival in early spring.

Green Woodpecker, *Picus viridis*. VN: Yaffle/r, Yarrow, Rain Bird, Green Pecker, Green Wood (birders). The bird's penchant for feeding at ant-hills makes it the family member we are most likely to encounter on the

If disturbed while hunting for ants on the ground, a green woodpecker adopts a posture reminiscent of a sun-worshipping lizard.

Behind the commercial logo there was a genuine ecological relationship between the green woodpecker and the old English cider orchards.

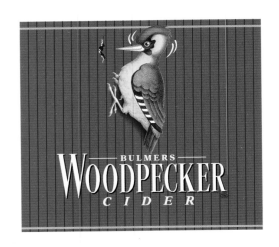

ground. The green woodpecker is usually well aware of us long before we disturb it, but very occasionally it 'freezes' and holds its body in a tense upright position, its cold pale eyes staring and the head lifted so that the bill points skywards. In these moments green woodpeckers look extremely primitive, with a posture reminiscent of a sun-worshipping lizard. More often than not, however, they give us no opportunity to study them and bound away from the ant-hill with strongly undulating flight, bright-yellow rump showing and a loud plaintive call.

The species was at one time surrounded by a complex mythology, and Charles Swainson, in his nineteenth-century book, *The Folk Lore and Provincial Names of British Birds*, unearthed more than 40 vernacular names.[7] Sadly only three of these appear to survive today. The first two are onomatopoeic renderings of the bird's distinctive, high laughing call, but the most intriguing is the last – 'rain bird' – which arose from its apparent gift of foretelling the weather.

In the nineteenth century the idea was widely believed and even William Yarrell was minded to think it was true, suggesting that the bird's feathers acted as sensors of the atmospheric electricity.[8] There was, of course, no substance to it, but the myth survived until the middle of the last century and was itself a final vestige of a woodpecker cult that originated in the ancient Mediterranean. The bird's strong ecological association with the oak, the most sacred of trees, gave it semi-divine status and important powers of augury, hence its gift of foretelling rain. The other final trace of the same lore occurs in its generic name: Picus was an ancient god of fertility.[9]

Great Spotted Woodpecker, *Dendrocopos major*. VN: Great Spot, Greater Pecker, Spotted Woodpecker. This is the most boldly patterned and conspicuous of our four woodpeckers and, with about 27,000 pairs spread thinly throughout the country, it is sufficiently common for the ordinary observer to encounter it regularly, but just scarce enough for sightings to involve a sense of occasion.

Like many arboreal birds it is easiest to see just before leaf burst, when the adults can be located by their mechanical drumming sound, whose dying cadence reverberates through the woodland of early spring and is itself a wonderful statement of seasonal change. Both males and females create the noise and do so by striking their beaks repeatedly against a suitably rotten or hollow branch which acts in turn as a sounding board.

While it is now firmly established that the woodpecker's drum is a percussive sound, there was a period in the early twentieth century when the exact means of production was hotly disputed. It had been claimed that the noise was actually a vocal performance and, in an effort to resolve the issue, an imaginative ornithologist called Norman Pullen took the extraordinary measure of inserting a microphone in a favourite drumming branch of a great spotted woodpecker in early 1943. He established beyond doubt that the sound was a result of contact between bird and tree, and argued further that the loud volume of the drum did not require heavy blows, but rather that the bird attains the correct frequency (since shown to be 5–20 strikes per half-second) to set up the appropriate resonance in the timber.[10]

It was the presumed stress entailed in a bird bashing its head against a tree that led some to think it was achieved by vocal means. In fact, it has since been proved that woodpeckers have a pad of shock-absorbent tissue between the base of bill and skull to neutralise the impact, and research was once carried out in the hope that the woodpecker's anatomy might provide clues for the better design of motorbike crash-helmets.[11]

The protective mechanisms in the skull are sufficient to allow great spots to advance from wooden objects – posts and telegraph poles have long been recorded – to metal poles, even wires, weather vanes, ceramic insulators and, in one instance, to 'a public address system at a racecourse'. It was noted that the bird elected to drum on the one of three large conical speaker horns which was 'pointing directly towards a rival' great spotted woodpecker drumming in a nearby tree. The mechanically enhanced sound was said to be so loud it made its tree-drumming adversary seem 'pathetic' in comparison.[12]

The great spot's adaptation to the man-made environment has been an important element in its recent success. It is the only woodpecker to thrive in inner-city parks, while the colonisation of conifer plantations has eased its spread in northernmost Scotland. However the development that has made it our most familiar woodpecker is its routine attendance at birdtables. It will take a wide range of foodstuffs from peanuts to suet, and occasionally the bird's dietary versatility extends to foraging for mussels on the foreshore, eating grain, raiding peas and stealing the cream from the top of a milk bottle.[13] Sometimes its feeding habits take us completely by surprise:

> I was in a wood near Cambridge and a great spotted woodpecker flew to a 40-foot dead tree with a decent-sized chick in its bill. It then proceeded to do what kingfishers do when they catch a stickleback – bash it several times on a branch. It then flew away, returned about 30 seconds later and flew off in the opposite direction, when it came back with another chick and gave it the same treatment. It was clearly robbing one nest, killing its occupants and taking them to its own chicks as food.[14]

Great spots have been noted regularly to dig out young tits from their own nest holes or nest boxes, and one pair was known to work systematically through a house-martin colony of 35–40 nests, hammering holes through the mud cups and seizing about 100 eggs and young to feed to their chicks.[15]

Lesser Spotted Woodpecker, *Dendrocopos minor*. VN: Lesser Spot, Lesser Pecker (birders). This delightful sparrow-sized woodpecker, largely a species of southern England and Wales, is one of the most difficult of our relatively widespread birds to observe. Even in woods where they are known to breed they are sometimes seen only in early spring, when they can be located by their high-pitched advertising calls and drumming. At other times they are remarkably unobtrusive, feeding high in the uppermost branches where they are all but impossible to spot.

They show a strong attachment to wooded habitats with plenty of dead timber, such as old veteran trees found in the parkland around large country houses. Another former stronghold was in Somerset and Herefordshire, among the cider-apple orchards that were planted at the time of the Napoleonic Wars when con-

Great spotted woodpeckers have increased and spread in recent decades, aided by our own liberal donations via the peanut holder.

tinental wines were unobtainable. As these were grubbed out more than a century later, the lesser spot suffered accordingly, but a more recent boost came with the mass die-off of trees inflicted by Dutch elm disease in the 1970s. Sadly the benefits were neutralised when the old elms fell down or, more likely, were felled.[16]

In the last 20 years lesser spots have undergone a troubling and rather inexplicable slump in fortunes. The species seems to be a bird of an older wooded countryside that acquires subtlety and diversity only with the passing years, while much of England and Wales, shaped by an all-pervasive obsession with landscape management, is now clothed in an ever-quickening succession of young, homogenised vegetation types.

The wood lark is one of the most highly regarded songsters in Britain.

Lark family *Alaudidae*

Wood Lark, *Lullula arborea*. It has never been as widespread or as numerous, nor has it inspired the same level of literary allusion as its better-known relative. Yet the wood lark produces a song that is often highly praised, as one Suffolk-born exile confirmed: 'In my opinion the most beautiful bird song of all. God how I miss it now that I'm in Wales, but it will always be a reminder of glorious sunny mornings on pristine heath.'[1]

For others, the bird's scarcity simply adds to its aura of specialness: 'The song is often a fugitive sound, just around the corner, and when I first heard it as a boy in the 1950s in dawn chorus excursions around Colchester in Essex it was a rare bird, and it still conjures up for me that early sense of discovery, excitement and innocence':

> It is my candidate for the best British songster, surpassing even the nightingale and skylark. The Latin generic name *Lululla* gives a musical clue, as does its French name *lulu*. The song is composed of a series of pure trills interspersed with deeper, yodelling '*luu-luu-luu*' notes, which are structured very simply but with sufficient changes of pace, pitch and volume to allow for almost infinite variation. The result is complex, subtle and piercingly beautiful. The male may sing from a perch on a bush or tree or may choreograph a beguiling song-flight, which will sweep the bird upwards in slow ascending spirals until the song ends abruptly and he plunges silently to the ground. Gerard Manley Hopkins tried hard to capture the elusive music of the phrasing in his poem, 'The Woodlark', which starts:

> *Teevo cheevo cheevio chee*:
> O where, what can that be?

and ends:

> With a sweet joy of a sweet joy,
> Sweet, of a sweet, of a sweet joy
> Of a sweet – a sweet – sweet – joy.[2]

While Hopkins' sprung verse echoes nicely the voice of his subject, the poem that has most intrigued ornithologists is Robbie Burns' 'Address to the Woodlark':

> Oh, stay sweet warbling woodlark, stay,
> Nor quit for me the trembling spray;
> A hapless lover courts thy lay,
> Thy soothing, fond complaining,

Again, again that tender part,
That I may catch thy melting art; . . .

Thou tells o' never-ending care,
O' speechless grief and dark despair:
For pity's sake, sweet bird, nae mair!
Or my poor heart is broken!'

Burns seemed to exploit to great effect the sweet, softly descending cadences in the song in his poem of lost love. Unfortunately in doing so he has given rise to a 200-year-old controversy over exactly which bird he was describing.

Since Burns never went south of Carlisle, and since wood larks have hardly ever been recorded north of the city, people have assumed that the two are unlikely ever to have met.[3] The argument is strengthened by the fact that 'wood lark' was once widely used as an alternative name for the tree pipit (see page 320), a species common in Burns' home area of south-west Scotland. W. H. Hudson believed this to be the bird which the Scots poet invoked, and suggested that the underlying sense of grief Burns had noted in the song referred 'to the languishing notes' at the end of a tree pipit's performance.[4] Yet few have ever suggested that tree-pipit song is a sad sound. On the contrary, it has an almost passionate, life-affirming vigour.

The wood lark's song, however, is characterised as 'extraordinarily mellifluous, melodious, rather melancholy and soulful'.[5] Burns was also noted for the accuracy of his natural-historical observation and the question nags: would he have invoked a happy-sounding bird in a poem of grief? If he was, indeed, describing the song of *Lullula arborea*, then it would suggest that at one time the species extended into southern Scotland.

The issue may well hinge on the differences between ornithological and poetic truth. After all, Hopkins suggested that wood lark song was 'a sweet – a sweet – sweet – joy', so Burns might easily have found the reverse quality in the tree pipit. Yet there is further evidence to support the tantalising possibility of Scottish wood larks. Robin Hull, author of *Scottish Birds*, has unearthed in the *Old Statistical Account*, a passage by a minister at Clunie, Perthshire: 'The notes of the wood-lark are heard, delightful along the banks of the Lunan in spring and autumn; its nocturnal song has a dying cadence peculiarly melodious and has often been mistaken for the song of the Philomel [nightingale].'[6] Unlike tree pipits, wood larks regularly sing at night and in the autumn.

From a 1980s nadir of just 220 pairs, the species has recently enjoyed a decade of unprecedented success, involving a sevenfold increase in numbers. The English birds have now colonised as far north as Yorkshire and

the conundrum posed by Burns' poem may possibly be settled by developments in their distribution during the next few years.

Skylark, *Alauda arvensis*. VN: Lavro, Laverock [also Leverrek, Laverick] (Orkney and Shetland); Skilly (northern England); Lark (widespread). This dull, plump, streaky bird has few notable features except the spiky crest, which it raises and depresses according to mood, but its glorious heaven-sent song is so firmly embedded in our sense of the British landscape that it would make any shortlist of the nation's best-loved species.

The popularity has a long pedigree. In the early nineteenth century William Yarrell wrote: 'The Sky Lark is so abundant as a species, so universal a favourite and its various qualities so well understood . . . as to require little more than a general reference.'[7] Yet for all our totemic attachment, there is a darker side to the relationship that has by no means vanished from living memory. Although each lark seldom weighs more than 2 ounces (57gm), the single-bite size was no barrier to their widespread exploitation as food. 'A land where the larks fall ready roasted' was once proverbial for an epicurean's earthly paradise, while an account written in 1501 indicates how the species more than compensated for its size by sheer abundance: 'The cheefe foode of the Englisheman consisteth in fleshe . . . of wilde burdes these are most delicate, partiches, phesaunts, quayles, owsels, thrusshes and larckes. This laste burde, in winter season, the wether being not to owtragios, dothe waxe wonderus fatte, at which time a wunderful nombre of them is caughte, so that of all others they chefle garnishe menns tables.'[8]

By Mrs Beeton's day, skylarks cost one shilling and sixpence a dozen and she included a recipe for nine birds stuffed and baked with beef, bacon and shallots.[9] An even more exotic-sounding dish graced the tables of the Cheshire Cheese pub in Fleet Street, where Oliver Goldsmith, Samuel Johnson, William Thackeray and Charles Dickens were all customers in their day. At exactly 6.30 p.m. on alternate evenings a pudding was brought in containing a mixture of larks, kidneys, oysters and steak surmounted by a surging billow of pastry.[10] By the end of the Victorian era, lark was largely a preserve of the gourmand and of the celebratory feast, such as the dinner for the opening of the Forth railway bridge in 1890, which included an immense pie of 300 birds.[11]

In Britain two places were particularly associated with their capture: the Sussex Downs near Brighton – the port also serving an important export trade to Paris – and the grass heaths in south Cambridgeshire and around Dunstable, Bedfordshire (the annual catch was estimated at 48,000 and there was even a lark recipe called the

'Dunstable Way'). Most were taken in winter, because of their increased body weight, and were normally caught in some form of net, although traditional practices involved a cow-bell to frighten the birds into crouching. Fowlers working through the hours of darkness carried a lantern and a type of reflector to dazzle them, when the nets could be drawn over the top. On a good night two men might take as many as 180.[12]

When the price for eating birds was high, both males and females were killed for the market, but if prices dropped then the best males were destined to be sold in the cagebird trade. It was the sight of one of these birds that inspired Gerard Manley Hopkins' poem of barely suppressed outrage, 'Caged Skylark', although 'his' lark had not apparently suffered the worst evil associated with the practice. Many were blinded in the belief that they would sing more sweetly. A strong-voiced individual could fetch as much as 15 shillings.[13]

The pre-eminent market for larks in Britain was Leadenhall in London, where in early Victorian times as many as 400,000 were received in a year.[14] If anything the trade gathered pace until the end of the century and only started to decline with the rise of early conservation efforts to have lark-catching banned. This was eventually successful in 1931, when the species was given legal protection, but in the interim those responsible for helping to secure a change of the law left some remarkable images of the harvest in its heyday. Outside one London shop, for instance, festooned with dead birds there was a sign reading: 'Special order, ten thousand larks, one and sixpence a dozen.' By the 1890s 20,000–40,000 skylarks were arriving in sackloads every day at Leadenhall market, and a chief salesman described how he had seen 'truck after truck on the Great Eastern loaded with nothing but larks'.[15]

While these images of mass slaughter were intended to create a sense of alarm, they also sketched for a later generation a background context of the bird's huge abundance, particularly in winter. Ironically it is in our own age of environmental awareness and concern that the bird has suffered its deepest losses.

Skylarks are still widespread throughout the whole of Britain and Ireland and total over one million pairs, but in the last 25 years their population has plunged by almost two-thirds.[16] The decline is even worse in the countryside with which it is most intimately associated. On farmland skylarks have been reduced by three-quarters. The losses closely coincide with Britain's entry to the European Union, whose Common Agricultural Policy has paid subsidies to farmers that have underpinned intensification. Several rapid changes, including the increased use of pesticides and weedkillers, the switch away from spring-sown cereal crops and the autumn ploughing of winter stubbles, have been key elements in the skylark's slump, depriving it of winter food and breeding habitat.

Although grey partridge and lapwing have been even more adversely affected by the changes in land use (see pages 165 and 206), the skylark has become the pre-eminent symbol of our impoverished farmland and has been at the heart of efforts to establish more sensitive approaches to its management. On the face of it, a small mud-brown species would seem an unlikely mascot to galvanise important cultural and political change. Yet this overlooks the massive part played by the bird's voice in our sense of the landscape and our own relationship to it.

Skylarks have inspired a huge cultural legacy and in the realm of poetry only one or two species have generated the same historical depth and volume of reference. Just a sample gives a taste of the bird's exalted place in our literary affections:

'The bisy larke, messager of day' (Geoffrey Chaucer)

'Mighty angel' (William Blake)

'Oh singing lark,
That singest like an angel in the clouds!' (Samuel Coleridge)

'Ethereal minstrel' (William Wordsworth)

'the holy lark' (Elizabeth Barrett Browning)

'Hail to thee, blithe spirit!
Bird thou never wert' (Percy Bysshe Shelley)

The long tradition has developed a self-perpetuating momentum as each new generation aspires to treat the same time-honoured theme. One finds that later poets like Ted Hughes lace their own lark verse with multiple references to their predecessors. And the cross-fertilisation of ideas extends across art forms. The famous celebration of the song by English composer Ralph Vaughan Williams in *The Lark Ascending* was itself inspired by a George Meredith poem of the same title.

The author Francesca Greenoak maintains that Meredith created 'the most perfectly balanced and descriptive imagery which has ever been written about a lark'.[17] Even the appearance of the poem itself on the printed page – 122 lines with just a single break – mimics the structure of the birdsong it celebrates. With good reason the most quoted portion is the opening sentence:

The skylark is one of the most characteristic emblems of British farmland. Recently it has suffered a massive population decline because of agricultural intensification.

He rises and begins to round,
He drops the silver chain of sound,
Of many links without a break,
In chirrup, whistle, slur and shake,
All intervolved and spreading wide,
Like water-dimples down a tide
Where ripple ripple overcurls
And eddy into eddy whirls.

Meredith's image of the song as a 'silver chain of sound', which the bird lowers towards its earthbound audience, is an all-but perfect rendering of the endless, fast-paced and rather mechanical downpour of notes. The whole poem creates a wonderful auditory echo of the bird and explores our implicit identification of the sound with the countryside it inhabits:

The woods and brooks, the sheep and kine,
He is, the hills, the human line,
The meadows green, the fallows brown, . . .

He is, the dance of children, thanks
Of sowers, shout of primrose-banks,
And eye of violets while they breathe;
All these the circling song will wreathe,
And you shall hear the herb and tree,
The better heart of men shall see,
Shall feel celestially, as long
As you crave nothing save the song.

The British landscape in all its complexity and beauty is somehow distilled into a single voice and, since we are products of the same land, the skylark sings of some essence within us.

It is intriguing to observe a reverse process in the case of lark-inspired imagery, whereby our cultural interpretations of the song have helped shape feelings for skylarks themselves. The fact that *Birds Britannica* received no contributions on the bird, but several on lark-inspired music, is symptomatic of how our responses to the real thing and to its human shadows ricochet from one to the other:

Only nightingale song has inspired more poetry than the voice of the skylark.

Hearing Vaughan Williams' sublime music in *The Lark Ascending* always transports me back to my Welsh childhood, lying flat on my back in the gloriously unimproved rough grassland of the Vale of Clwyd, and watching the singing skylark as he soared higher until I wasn't sure whether I could see him or not. Like the real song itself, it evokes a bygone pastoral golden age and the open countryside which the bird seemed once to symbolise – a vital part of sunny spring and summer days, with huge clouds rolling across blue skies and the day, like the inviting patchwork of fields, stretching out before me.[18]

The contribution suggests how we cannot even tell whether the sense of nostalgia is triggered by Vaughan Williams' music, with all its romantic references to old English folk song, or by our memories of the real birds of childhood. A second contributor observes how the orchestral version has become a shortcut both to a sense of lost landscape and to a vanishing sense of national identity:

It makes me furious to observe the decline of the skylark, the very voice of English air and soil. Think of Vaughan Williams' *The Lark Ascending*, used with much the same intention by all sorts of programme makers, from the creators of butter adverts to those producing films on the poignancy of Remembrance Day and the sacrifice of war. I fear the connection between the bird, the land, the music, the suffering and the soil could all be lost for ever, for the sake of weed control, winter ploughing and a larger yield.[19]

It is worth noting that the skylark's seemingly intrinsic association with the British landscape is a human artefact in more than one sense. The quintessential inhabitant of agricultural areas and grassland is unlikely to have occurred in this country before the Bronze Age and early Iron Age clearances of native forest. As Max Nicholson noted: 'even to see a skylark under a tree is quite out of the ordinary, and they are almost equally reluctant to approach hedges'.[20] The species' arrival in Britain was a direct consequence of agriculture and it is tempting to speculate that this shared ecological history lies beneath all our celebrations of lark song. Oliver Rackham suggests that 'To convert tens of millions of acres of wildwood into farmland is the greatest achievement of our ancestors.'[21] For thousands of years the skylark has reflected back to us in its songflight our accommodation with the landscape and our mutual destiny within it.

Shore Lark, *Eremophila alpestris*. A winter visitor in small numbers from beyond the Arctic Circle, it occurs mainly on the British east coast, where it is attracted to landscapes with the openness of its tundra breeding grounds, such as bare ploughed fields, saltmarsh, sand-dunes and tidal flotsam along the beach. Chancing upon a small flock, when shore larks can be told from skylarks by their finer build, silky white underparts and a high, shrill wind-piercing call, is always a cause for celebration during any coastal walk in winter.

On the ground shore larks show lovely markings, including a warm yellow facial patch highlighted by a black chest band and a downward-curving 'bandit's mask' through the eyes. Birds occasionally linger in late spring, when they acquire a striking pair of black feather 'spikes' on the sides of the crown – hence the American name, 'horned lark', which has recently been adopted here. They once showed some signs of establishing a breeding presence on the Scottish high tops, but the first proven record in 1977 has also been the last.

Swallow and Martin family
Hirundinidae

Sand Martin, *Riparia riparia*. VN: Sandy. This plain earth-brown and white martin is the smallest of our hirundines and one of the earliest migrants to return in spring, when it can often be found hawking for insects in mid-March in the blustery cold air space above lakes and reservoirs. It is the most water-loving of the three species, primarily because it requires exposed earth banks in which to excavate its communal nest burrows.

The 2–3-foot (60–90-cm) tunnels are chipped out through the combined action of the sand martins' tiny beaks and weak feet, with a pair proceeding at 3–4 inches (8–10cm) a day.[1] Sand martins would originally have used riverbanks, naturally exposed sand shelves and soft coastal cliffs, but far more now nest in a range of man-made alternatives, such as quarries, railway and road embankments and, more unusually, drainage pipes in the sides of houses or holes in quaysides.[2] Some of the locations are inherently transient, like piles of sawdust at sawmills, heaps of washed sand and even foundation trenches, which are quickly occupied before the construction work gets under way.

Like the great crested grebe (see page 7), the sand martin is one of the chief beneficiaries of the post-war boom in road and house building and the massive parallel expansion of sand- and gravel-extraction sites, which now serve as the most important source of breeding habitat. The birds at these places appear completely oblivious to the industrial activity or noise, while the workforce often feel highly protective towards 'their' sand martins in exactly the way that we prize their house-dwelling relatives. Although sand martins are less colourful, they are just as endearing for their tiny size – each weighing no more than a blue tit – and for the endless 'buzz' around the colony, both audible and visual.

The obvious pleasures of a martin colony have led some to try to recreate suitable nesting conditions, with the earliest known example occurring at Walton Hall, the Yorkshire estate of the nineteenth-century naturalist Charles Waterton. He sank about 50 drainpipes horizontally into a walled bank of his garden and was rewarded with a full complement of breeding birds in his first year.[3] The same basic method is used today, particularly at newly created gravel-pit sites, while a highly innovative approach on an Aberdeenshire farm involves a 15:1 mix of sand and cement set in barrel-

Sand martins originally nested in exposed earth banks but have readily taken to all sorts of manmade alternatives.

shaped moulds. It is then removed and mounted on a steel pipe, where it looks like a huge sand lollipop peppered with ready-drilled holes.[4]

One of the best-known of all these man-made sand-martin colonies is at Minsmere RSPB reserve in Suffolk, 'where a shallow sand cliff was dug out by hand in 1968 in the vicinity of the old carpark'. The history of this enduring site reflects the natural fluctuations in sand-martin fortunes:

In 1987 major earthworks were undertaken to create a much larger sand face and the birds immediately responded with 366 pairs moving in and fledging at least 1300 young. This impressive increase was a mixed blessing, since it also attracted the attention of predators, notably a stoat in 1989 which went systematically in and out of each burrow and wiped out the colony. Despite the erection of an anti-stoat fence the following year, it took the birds until 1994 to 'pluck up courage' to return, since when they've bred

The ornithologist Max Nicholson once noted that a swallow's 'every wing stroke is a pleasure to watch'.

every year except 1997 with a maximum of 121 pairs in 2002.[5]

As well as appealing to other nimble-bodied predators (and not so nimble-bodied, like hedgehog, badger, several species of crow and owl, black-headed gull, kestrel, buzzard and sparrowhawk), sand-martin colonies are attractive to other birds as a nest site, and at least 17 species have been recorded to take advantage of the ready-made holes.[6]

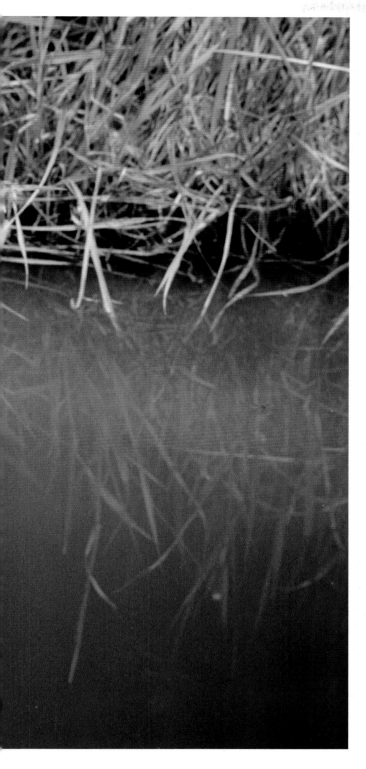

confronted with the following: 'Another intelligent person informed that . . . at Brighthelmstone [Brighton], in Sussex, a great fragment of chalk cliff fell down one stormy winter night on the beach; and that many people found swallows among the rubbish.'[7]

It is more likely that these were dead sand martins left in the holes of an old colony that was broken open by the landslide. Public confusion in identifying the three hirundines and even swifts, is still common today and, given the sand martins' mole-like tunnelling, one can possibly see how the idea might have arisen of them passing the cold months in a subterranean chamber or in the mud at the bottom of pools.

We now know that they return to a broad belt of Sahelian Africa where they occasionally fall victim to drought. In 1968/9 and 1983/4 the British and Irish populations suffered massive temporary collapses. In the immediate aftermath of the second event, which devastated the Sahel region's human populations as well as its birds (and made a latterday saint of popstar Bob Geldof), sand martins may have fallen to just one-tenth of their peak numbers in the mid-1960s. Fortunately they show signs of gradual recovery.

Barn Swallow, *Hirundo rustica*. VN: Swalla (Yorkshire). Our increasingly urban lifestyles have broken the universal link with swallows, but they are still birds viewed with huge affection and among the very few protected by an almost religious respect:

> They are the first birds of which I was conscious in childhood. Their chattering is one of my earliest memories, as is being held up to see the nests in the rafters and the wide-open beaks of the chicks. I was brought up with a clearly defined attitude to swallows. They were welcomed as a bird of great practical use because they ate insects. I believed that they brought good luck and good weather, that the nests must never be destroyed and that swallows only stayed at happy homes, never where there was quarrelling or hatred. I was read *Wind in the Willows*, where the swallows discussed coming back to the House of the Perfect Eaves.[8]

Their popularity is not hard to understand. They have a delightful twittering song that is structurally suggestive of running water and equally soothing. Blue birds also seem to exert their own particular charm over us (see Blue Tit, page 388) and, of British species, only the kingfisher is bluer. There is, in addition, the effortless grace of swallow movements. As one observer noted: 'Each wing-stroke is a pleasure to watch.'[9] Together with the two martins, swallows are the smallest species to

Their remarkable excavations possibly gave a degree of plausibility to the theories once advanced by naturalists to explain the disappearance of summer visitors in winter. Even highly observant figures like Gilbert White entertained the possibility that hirundines might hibernate in hollow trees or earth burrows. Yet he showed an empiricist's natural scepticism when

In late summer swallows frequently spend the night in reedbeds and some roosts can involve many thousands of birds.

incorporate gliding into their flight. Yet the latter's looping playfulness in combination with that elegant streamlined shape distinguish it even from its near relatives.

The bird's image has been repeatedly borrowed as a symbol of physical movement and is, for example, the current logo for Intercity trains. However the impression of speed in swallow flight is often illusory. They are actually rather slow-flying birds – a quality, some might argue, that makes them doubly appropriate as a symbol of our rail service.

At the core of our long relationship is their willingness to occupy our own domestic space. In some instances they are as dependent upon its various structures as we are. Of all birds, the barn swallow seems to have the highest reliance on telegraph wires as a perch, so much so that it is now hard to imagine where swallows would previously have sat. They also feed in the air space immediately about the house, or routinely follow tractor and plough, combine-harvester and livestock, even to the point of riding piggyback. There is an element of symbiosis in the interactions, since the machinery and animals disturb insects on which swallows feed, and the

prey taken are often species that we consider pests such as bluebottles, horse flies and aphids. It is notable that Ireland's largely pastoral landscapes hold high densities of swallows, while declines are steepest in England's eastern arable counties, where pesticide use is heaviest.

The mutual respect between swallow and human extends to a willingness to nest often quite literally just above our heads. Like house martin and swift, the barn swallow was originally a cave-nester that probably made a switch to man-made structures with the advent of brick-built houses in the Tigris–Euphrates valleys during the early Holocene. Occasional pairs show atavistic tendencies and have been found nesting in colliery manholes near Chesterfield, Derbyshire (17 feet/5m below the surface), in the shafts of old Cornish tin mines (a remarkable 56 feet/17m down) and in a disused underground oil depot near Plymouth (40 feet/12m underground).[10]

The swallow's versatility in choice of man-made location is remarkable. William Yarrell recalled one in the half-open drawer of a small table in an unoccupied garret and another attached to a Carlisle paddle steamer that regularly plied the Solway Firth. A nest site with resonances for another *Birds Britannica* account was noted originally by Thomas Pennant. He found a swallow's nest cemented to 'the body and wing of an Owl nailed against a barn' (see page 285).[11]

Individual structures can regularly survive and be reoccupied for 10–15 years and one remarkable example was known to be in continuous use for 48 years.[12] Strong taboos still help to preserve old swallow nests. Typically it was believed in northern England that harming the quintessential bird of the pastoral landscape would lead to the cows giving bloody milk (see European Nightjar for further discussion of bird myths associated with livestock; page 293) or no milk at all.[13] Ken Spencer recorded the survival of such beliefs until well into the 1960s and added one interesting variation: 'maltreatment of Swallows will cause one's hens to go off lay'.[14] A possible factor binding these two birds is the fact that swallows prefer to line the nest with 'small white poultry feathers'.[15] Although in remote chicken-free areas they will improvise: 'This year they built two new semi-detached nests on a beam, lined with duck down from the Aylesburys.'[16]

We may largely have lost the more superstitious fears surrounding swallow nests, but the positive responses to their presence are intact. 'We have to risk rain and rust, on the tools and machinery in the shed by leaving the big double doors open, but we always leave a gap wide enough for them to get through. I remove the most obvious traces of their occupation from the roofs and windows of the cars, but it's a price well worth paying.'[17]

In many ways the historical names we have given the bird have reflected our changing rural architecture and the nesting opportunities it has provided for them. The current version, 'barn swallow', is perfectly apt. It exploits a wide range of agricultural outbuildings, although it also uses church porchways and towers, the underside of bridges or road culverts and even garden sheds. In the nineteenth century and earlier it was called the 'chimney swallow' because of a routine habit of nesting in the big open stacks, which would have been largely smoke-free for the summer months. Most revealing, however, is the name 'house swallow'. The open-door lifestyle of our ancestors would have allowed the birds frequently to share the very same interior space.

It still occasionally happens. Geoffrey and Judy Grimes gave a little encouragement to a pair that had a habit of flying around their bedroom (in one of the oldest houses in Kent). When a nest was built, they kept a diary worthy of Gilbert White on their shared intimacies with the breeding birds:

14 May: As an experiment we cut a shoebox in half, covered the curtains with a dustsheet, and wedged the shoebox on to the rail, balanced

It is hard to imagine where the swallows would all have perched before the invention of telegraph wires.

on some children's building bricks with the entrance viewable from the bed!

18 May: Mud is definitely beginning to appear in the box.

25 May: Nest seems to be completed and the pair roost by it or in it every night.

31 May: Using a hand mirror, we can see that there are three eggs.

3 June: At least four eggs now.

17 June: Great excitement at first light (c. 3.45 a.m.). A tell-tale eggshell on the carpet.

24 June: Another squint with the hand mirror revealed four gapes.

26 June: Parents feverishly bringing in food and taking out droppings. It is quite a cold spell and we wouldn't mind shutting the windows a bit, but we put on thicker pyjamas instead!

9 July: Definite exit of young. All out but back again every evening.

10 July: The excitement of freedom causes premature emptying of bowels. We decide to cover the whole room with a large polythene sheet.

11 July: 4.30 a.m. with polythene sheet under our chins we observe the playful flights of the young. By the time we get up they are out for the day. Scrambling about for clean clothes and a city suit becomes more complicated each day.

4 August: Second brood hatches. The bedroom hasn't seen a duster or a hoover for about a month. It's beginning to get us down.

13 Sept: It seemed that the swallows might have left . . . but they all reappeared!

18 Sept: No bedroom visitors for the first time. Heaved a sign of relief – spring-cleaned the bedroom and closed the window.[18]

The bird's departure is in many ways as much a marker for seasonal change as its arrival earlier in the year. But one senses that the swallow's inability to thrive in urban environments is now altering its proverbial association with spring and summer – a link that is nonetheless Europe-wide and dates back to the ancient Greeks.

As Max Nicholson noted, the swallow's habitat is 'almost entirely invisible', since it 'consists of a rather shallow layer of air from immediately over the land or water up to normally only some some five hundred feet above the surface'.[19] On average swallows take larger prey than house martin or swift and feed closer to the ground than either of the others, and are thus more susceptible to the impact of pollution and pesticides. The swift both eats the smallest prey – known as aerial plankton – and feeds at the highest altitude and is better able to survive in the middle of cities. Perhaps for these reasons the swallow is losing ground to the swift as our modern symbol of summer.

House Martin, *Delichon urbica*. VN: Martin. With their distinctive, almost torpedo-like flight profile and blue-black and white plumage, house martins are one of the most conspicuous of all our summer migrants. They are almost entirely dependent upon aerial insects, yet can tough it out as far north as Orkney (occasionally Shetland), and in mainland Europe they breed well within the Arctic Circle.

This bird is commonly yoked with swallow in the public imagination (the scientific name *Delichon* is simply an anagram of *Chelidon*, Greek for swallow), but our response is far more than affection reflected from its more graceful relative. 'The house martin is a wonderful little bird. I always welcome their arrival with joy and admiration. Joy because they herald the start of spring and admiration because of the huge hazards they overcome on their journey here.'[20]

Our sense of pleasure at their company is in many ways reciprocated by the birds themselves. The half a million pairs in Britain and Ireland have almost entirely forsaken their original nest locations on inland and coastal cliffs for the underside of roof eaves. In *Macbeth* (Act 1, Scene 6), Banquo says of the house martins at Cawdor Castle:

> no jutty, frieze,
> Buttress, nor coign of vantage, but this bird
> Hath made her pendent bed and procreant cradle;

> Where they most breed and haunt, I have observed
> The air is delicate.

No doubt Shakespeare had dramatic irony more in mind when framing the image (since Duncan is soon to be murdered there), but it was almost certainly an accurate observation even for eleventh-century Scotland. By the Bard's own day it is possible that a majority of the population would already have switched to man-made locations. Shakespeare was also correct about their status as indicators of ecological stability. House-martin colonies are a classic feature of long-established, large buildings such as castles, halls, cathedrals, churches, country hotels, railway and road bridges. In some instances the bird dynasty attaching to a building might be as old as the structure itself and should be treasured no less than the original stonework.

Yet house martins will also show the same enduring attachment to the eaves of modern suburban semis or a row of rural council houses, as well as other modern variations: 'I once saw a nest on a burglar alarm outside a jeweller's.'[21]

House martins basking on a sunlit roof are a classic sign of autumn.

It is the birds' faithful return, year in, year out, as well as the ritual pattern of behaviour right up until their departure in September or October that helps cement the house martin's status as a lucky mascot for a building or its area:

> It is lovely to witness their excitement as they examine and clean out old nests or build new ones. As the season progresses we find discarded egg shells which tell us when the first brood has hatched. With a tinge of sadness we then watch them line up along the wires ready for the journey south. They do leave quite a mess, but we overcome it by placing a board underneath the nests and hosing down at the end of season. It would never occur to us to turn them away – I feel honoured that they have chosen our house as a nest site.[22]

A sense of intimacy with the bird is borne out by the personalised name itself. 'Martin', plain and simple, was used until the mid-nineteenth century, but Lockwood identified an earlier and now obsolete diminutive, 'martinet', as the 'oldest known example, by far, of the use of a Christian name to denote a bird'.[23] However one wonders what connotation lay behind the selection in the twelfth century or earlier? As a man's name 'Martin' has its origins with Mars, the god of war, and it is tempting to think that there was an underlying link with military architecture in its use for the bird. Perhaps they showed an early preference for defensive structures (castles, battlements, etc.) or their own nest suggested a miniature fortress in its own right.

The primary requirement for a house martin's nest is a vertical surface immediately underneath a sheltering overhang. The birds can then assemble the mud cup in the angle between the two planes and seal it up, except for a small entrance hole. Construction work requires an average of just over 10 days, depends upon a ready supply of mud in the weeks following the bird's arrival in April and proceeds with more than 1000 beak-sized pellets being glued to one another from the base upwards. It results in a beautifully corrugated outer surface ('rustic work full of knobs' was Gilbert White's description)[24] and the quality of masonry has long been admired, not only by humans.

Old house-martin nests are readily occupied by a range of other birds, but most notoriously by their classic commensal neighbour, the house sparrow (see also page 438). The latter is almost always dominant and usually takes over the nest with impunity just before its completion. Our sense of injustice has led on occasions to direct intervention – the great Norfolk ornithologist Henry Stevenson used to shoot the sparrows! – and to a rich body of comforting mythology. Typically, house martins were believed sometimes to wall up the entrance and trap the brooding sparrow inside, and so convert the misappropriated 'nest into a sepulchre'.[25] One nineteenth-century observer claimed that he had seen house martins gather recruits and then drag an intruding sparrow off to kill it.[26] At times nature imposes its own crude justice:

> The house martins were always welcome when they nested beneath the eaves of our house. So we were not pleased when a nearly completed nest cup became occupied by ill-mannered squatters in the shape of a pair of house sparrows. The consequence was unforeseen by either party. A clutch of eggs was on the point of hatching when the whole structure fell to the ground overnight. A well-fed hedgehog left the scene before daylight.[27]

Gilbert White described the masonry of a house martin nest as 'rustic work full of knobs'.

The constant presence of the birds as they swoop back and forth into the eaves might have created the impression of deep familiarity, but in some ways house martins retain an enormous sense of mystery. While breeding birds usually pass the hours of darkness in the nest, it is thought that part of the population may roost on the wing at elevations in excess of 3300 feet (1000m). Even more remarkable is the fact that we are still not sure where house martins pass the winter. An estimated 90 million birds drain out of Eurasia each autumn into Africa, but exactly where the birds go is unclear. Of the 290,000 birds ringed in Britain and Ireland, only one example has ever been recovered south of the Sahara. It is thought likely that many spend their African months feeding unseen at high elevations, possibly over uninhabited forested areas where they come to earth only to roost.[28]

Pipit and Wagtail family
Motacillidae

Tree Pipit, *Anthus trivialis*. VN. Tree Pip, Tripit (birders). Small, brown and streaky, pipits represent either an expansive pleasure dome for the hair-splitting expert or a baffling *terra incognita* to the tyro. Their dullness is legendary. So to suggest that this one is bright and attractive is to make only a relative claim. Yet there is something rather distinguished about the rich yellowish wash across the tree pipit's black-streaked breast and the contrast between this warm colour and the creamy underbelly. The facial pattern is bold, the legs clear fleshy pink, and it has a delightful wagtail-like habit of pumping rhythmically its whole rear end as it walks or perches on overhead wires.

All three breeding pipits generally conform to habitat preferences indicated by their names. Tree pipits routinely nest and feed on the ground, but they need broken tree cover from which to deliver the song, and the roster of favoured habitats – heath, parkland, young plantations, open woods, scrubby downland, even golf courses and railway sidings – have a common theme of open ground dotted with tall perches. At times even pylons and telegraph poles serve them as an acceptable substitute. In the past tree pipits were favoured by the coppice-with-standards tradition in English woodland, although the decline of these management techniques and a wider loss of the listed habitats have seen the main population shift north of a line between Bristol and York. The species is a summer migrant and, like several other relatively common British woodland birds – tawny owl, green and great spotted woodpeckers – is strangely absent from Ireland.

If the pleasures involved in a tree pipit's appearance are to some extent a matter of taste, there is less dispute about the bird's song. It is as notable for the mode of delivery as for the quality of the sound itself. Eric Simms called it an 'ecstatic vibrant' performance that lifts the heart.[1] A male rises up high into the air and delivers a series of shrill far-carrying phrases that seem to intensify as the bird spirals slowly back to earth with wings outspread, tail fanned and legs dangling. The song terminates with a flourish of descending slurred canary-like notes, but these are normally absent from a less complete version that tree pipits frequently deliver from the perch. In the 1920s Lord Grey felt that he had detected incipient moral decline in tree pipits on the basis that 'this otiose habit . . . seems to have increased'. He went on to express resentment at 'being given the song without the display of flight, to which lovers of tree-pipits feel that they are entitled'.[2]

Historical confusion over the identity of pipits meant that at one time rock, tree and meadow pipits were all referred to as 'titlarks', which literally meant 'small lark'. In the nineteenth century 'woodlark' was another alternative name for the most tree-loving of the three, and John Clare wrote two sonnets entitled 'The Woodlark'. They are so full of beautifully observed detail that most commentators have confidently identified the bird in question as tree pipit:

The woodlark rises from the coppice tree;
Time after time, untired, she upward springs;
Silent while up, then coming down she sings
A pleasant song of varied melody,
Repeated often till some sudden check
The sweet-toned impulse of her rapture stops,
Then stays her trembling wings and down she drops
Like to a stone amid the crowning kecks
Where underneath some hazel's mossy root
Is hid her little low and humble nest
Upon the ground; larks love such places best,
And here doth well her quiet station suit;
As safe as secrecy her six eggs lie,
Mottled with dusky spots, unseen by passers-by.

James Fisher argued that it could not be the real wood lark, on the grounds that Clare's Northamptonshire was north of that species' range, although this was almost certainly *not* the case in Clare's day (see Wood Lark, page 309). His second argument, that a clutch of six eggs favours the tree pipit, was more accurate.[3] Most convincing of all, however, was Clare's description of the bird repeatedly flying up into the air and singing only as it descends – a detail that eliminates wood lark. Tree pipits will rise and parachute down as many as 20 times in half an hour.[4]

Tawny Pipit, *Anthus campestris*. This large sandy pipit is an annual visitor in very small numbers to Britain and Ireland. It breeds in Europe as far north as the Netherlands, but has never managed to do so in England, despite the report of a nesting pair in Sussex in May 1905. The original claimant even maintained that he had shot the birds and obtained their nest and three eggs.

Yet the evidence was later dismissed and the record rejected during the exposure of a notorious fraud case, the largest in British ornithological history, known as the Hastings Rarities. For birdwatchers it has a similar kind of resonance as the Piltdown Man had for palaeontologists. It related to an unprecedented concentration of rare

birds (595 records were subsequently dismissed as unreliable) found in a small area of east Sussex centred on Hastings, mainly between 1901 and 1920. A widespread obsession with collecting specimens of British-caught rarities, for which high prices were paid by wealthy sportsmen, is assumed to have been the motive for faking their discovery.

The bird skins were of American, Asian and European origin and were presumably brought to Britain in refrigerated condition, then passed off as genuine wind-blown vagrants. None of the perpetrators was ever publicly named in their lifetimes, although the finger of suspicion pointed most frequently at a taxidermist based in St Leonards-on-Sea, George Bristow, to whom many of these 'locally found' birds were taken to be stuffed and sold. Since Bristow was himself the 'finder', shooter and (presumably) subsequent vendor of the tawny pipits, this breeding record was expunged with the others.[5]

Remarkably there is another fictional account of *Anthus campestris* nesting in Britain, this one in a quintessentially English wartime comedy entitled *The Tawny Pipit* (1944), to which the eminent bird photographer Eric Hosking served as adviser. It was directed and produced by Bernard Miles and follows the adventures of Colonel Barton-Barrington (also played by a thickly bewhiskered Miles) as he attempts to defend the birds from disturbance by egg collectors, allied military manoeuvres and Cotswold farmers intent on digging for victory. The plot is gloriously eccentric and the humour 'unimaginably genteel', while the wartime propaganda is thinly disguised – Britain is presented as the ideal refuge for birds from Nazi-ravaged Europe. But it seems that the story left a deep impression on some:

My lifelong interest in birds really took off when I was ten and saw a film entitled *The Tawny Pipit* at the local cinema. I was gripped by the interest and excitement shown by those who watched and guarded the nest of this rare bird. I learnt later that the whole thing was fictitious and the nest sequences probably filmed in France, possibly even before the war. Nevertheless this plain but rather elegant bird became for me a kind of birdwatching icon. Yet it was not until 2001 that I went on holiday to the Greek island of Lesbos and on the third day we had good views of two tawny pipits. I was quite happy to go home then, but I'm glad I stayed. On the last day in a hayfield by the shore we saw six tawny pipits really closely. In the same week that I celebrated my sixty-fifth birthday my dream from childhood finally came true.[6]

Meadow pipit is still one of the commonest birds of the northern uplands.

Meadow Pipit, *Anthus pratensis*. VN: Mip, Mipit (birders); Teetick, Hill Sparrow (Shetland); Moss-cheeper (Northern Ireland). It is a typical bird of most forms of open country, from sub-Arctic heath to coastal sand-dunes. Of all its family this is the commonest, the species from which all other members have to be distinguished and the one that most perfectly justifies the expression 'little brown job'.[7] It is gloriously nondescript – a confusing blend of streaks and muted shades of grey or brown that change with the seasons – but meadow pipits have one fairly consistent quality. They manage to convey an impression of physical and almost temperamental fragility.

They are by nature flighty birds and when disturbed they climb up and hang above an intruder in a feeble, loose-tailed dancing motion. The call is also a plaintive, insipid monosyllable that is repeated constantly to com-pound the rather neurotic impression. As Eric Simms notes, when they finally move off, they often 'seem to be blown away rather helplessly downwind like a dead brown leaf'.[8]

For all these appearances, meadow pipits are genuinely hardy birds, toughing it out through the British winter and breeding in some of our highest, most barren country. Above 2000 feet (600m) this is usually the commonest passerine in the landscape. As you walk across a heather moor the birds tend to gather overhead in a nervous band until you leave their territory, when they hand you over to the next anxious meadow-pipit group. In spring and summer the rather sad song – a composition based on the bird's flat call note, which builds during a downward parachute flight to a tuneless accelerando – is part of the eternal soundtrack to the northern uplands. 'Moss cheeper' is a name that may well survive in northern England and Scotland, as well as in Northern Ireland. Lord Grey described the performance as 'a minute but perceptible contribution to the happiness of the day'.[9] Since the bird 'as often as not is the only living thing in sight', the pleasure may hinge on a simple sense of companionship.[10]

Its abundance in such a spartan landscape makes the meadow pipit one of the main building blocks of the moorland ecosystem. The adults are food for a good cross-section of upland predators such as buzzard, peregrine, short-eared owl and raven. Hen harrier and merlin are heavily reliant on meadow pipits and in parts of Wales the bird forms more than three-quarters of the merlin's diet.[11] The young and eggs are taken by fox, weasel and stoat, while breeding meadow pipits are the classic host species for the cuckoo in northern areas. In a 1950s study as many as one in five nests fell victim to the latter's brood parasitism, and cuckoos in the upland environment have a seemingly permanent entourage of anxious meadow pipits.[12]

Rock Pipit, *Anthus petrosus*. VN: Rockit (birders); Shore Sparrow, Tangie/Tangelie Sparrow, Butter Sparro, Shore Lark (Orkney); Bank/Tang Sparrow (Orkney and Shetland); Teetick (Shetland); Stinkle (Fair Isle). This is the large dark pipit found on most British coasts and particularly on the rocky and weed-strewn wracklines of west Scottish and Irish shores. It shares the family's wider reputation for tricky identification, but rock pipits are mottled rather than streaked and grey in the outertail feathers rather than white. However they are best told by the call – a loud, purposeful, almost explosive '*phist*' that is perfectly designed to pierce the strong winds buffeting a rocky beach in winter.

It is one of the most taxonomically diverse of all British birds. There is a separate subspecies entitled

The yellow wagtail is a declining summer bird of wetland grassland and marsh.

meinerzthageni found only in the Outer Hebrides and a further race *kleinschmidti* on St Kilda, Orkney and Shetland. In winter small numbers of the Scandinavian race *littoralis* visit British east coasts, while the **Water Pipit**, *A. spinoletta* – long considered another form of rock pipit and now elevated to a full species in its own right – is a winter regular at coastal freshwater sites and inland locations like sewage works and watercress beds in southern England.

Yellow Wagtail, *Motacilla flava*. VN: Yellow Wag/gy. (birders). In terms of shape this is the most pipit-like of the three wagtails but it has none of that subfamily's usual drabness. In fact its brilliant colours make it one of our most beautiful summer visitors. It is a bird of damp pasture, wet meadow and freshwater marsh, where the male stands out 'as vividly yellow as a dandelion against the green grass'.[13]

In spring yellow wags are particularly noticeable on passage, when small flocks often feed directly at the feet of grazing livestock. Sometimes they get so close they look in real danger of being trampled, and as a bird vanishes down a hoofmark it is easy to fear the worst. But up it pops, the colourful head thrusting forward in typical rhythmic wagtail fashion, until it sallies off to snatch an insect disturbed by the cow's grazing muzzle.

In coastal areas wagtail congregations often include continental forms of the species. The yellow wagtail is a classic example of evolution in progress – 'a bird of vast complexity in systematics and morphology' – with six or seven races from parts of mainland Europe all showing different facial patterns and usually referred to generically as 'flava' wagtails.[14] The commonest of these European visitors is the blue-headed *M. f. flava*, although occasionally long-distance strays turn up in Britain, like the striking Balkan race *feldegg*, which has a glossy black crown. One of my most memorable wagtail visions – which evoked something of the intensity of all bird migration as well as the bright primary colours of all Mediterranean life – was a host of mixed 'flava' wagtails in Crete gathered on a large heap of rotten oranges, the birds darting into a veil of flies wafting perpetually above the sweet-fetid fruit mountain.

The form occurring in Britain, *flavissima*, has started to breed in small parts of Norway, France and the Netherlands, where it occurs alongside the more usual blue-headed wagtails as if they were two different species. If their separate status were confirmed it would add urgency to the current efforts to understand and halt a recent decline in our yellow wagtails. The last Irish breeding colony became extinct before the Second World War and in recent years it has all but vanished from Scotland.

Grey Wagtail, *Motacilla cinerea*. VN: Grey Wag/gy (birders). Although it has long since spread across much of southern England and Wales and is now a routine winter bird around lowland farm buildings or ponds, this truly delightful wagtail is still most often associated with fast-flowing upland streams. It is the one family member that really deserves the old country name 'water wagtail'. It invariably nests in the stream's vicinity, under bridges, in adjacent banks or brickwork, and can often be seen darting along river margins or sallying into the air before returning to a stone midstream. Of the three British species, it has by far the longest tail, which it occasionally splays like a white-edged fan, while the vigorous up-and-down action is a perfect echo of the current's endless motion.

In spring the male is a beautiful contrast of black throat, yellow breast and sulphur-yellow undertail coverts, which are flashed to full advantage as the tail wags. It has a short, rather buzzing high-pitched song phrase, which is almost impossible to dissociate from the background rush of fast-flowing water. The species is often found in man-made adaptations to the riverine environment such as mill streams, weirs, bridges and overflow outlets near reservoirs or trout ponds, where the wider sense of scenic charm and tranquillity feeds into our highly positive response to the bird itself.

Pied Wagtail, *Motacilla alba*. VN: Pied Wag/gy (birders), Water Wagtail, Willy Wagtail (widespread); Peggy Dishwater, Polly Dishwasher, Penny Wagtail (widespread, but especially East Anglia). It is the commonest, and most familiar of the wagtails and shares all the physical panache of its relatives. In the nineteenth century William Yarrell wrote that it was even then 'deservedly admired for the elegance of its form, as well as for the activity and airy lightness exhibited in all its actions. It is ever in motion, running . . . in pursuit of its insect food, moving from place to place by short

undulating flights . . . alighting again on the ground with a sylph-like buoyancy.'[15]

Although it shares the family tendency towards wetland habitats, it is also found in a much broader range of locations. Pied wagtails are common farmland birds and often dignify the midden, the malodorous drain or the scum-topped settle pond. They also bring a touch of living intensity to the otherwise sterile expanses of close-cropped turf in the grounds of public buildings and large houses or on golf courses.

It has a lovely suite of feminine vernacular names and there are various theories about their origins. Lockwood, who also lists the now archaic 'nanny washtail' and 'Molly washer', suggests that the bird's tail-pumping action mimicked the battledore, the club-like stick once used to beat the washing.[16] Eric Simms argues that the bird's constant motion evoked 'a woman scrubbing clothes at a washboard'.[17] However, these explanations take no account of the pot-scrubbing associations commemorated in 'Peggy dishwater' or 'Polly dishwasher' and the element that seems to be missing from both is the context. Women once washed clothes and pots by a stream, garden pump or village well, where spillages would create exactly the kind of wet muddy conditions that pied wags love. The rhythmic actions involved in all forms of cleaning would find their direct visual echo in the lovely motion of the attendant wagtails, and it is this more immediate connection between bird and women washing that surely explains the country names.

While the human context might have changed dramatically, pied wagtails continue to find advantage through association with us. They have been recorded to nest in abandoned machinery or cars, glasshouses, drystone walls and in all sorts of niches and gaps left by missing bricks or roof tiles in large houses, farms and outbuildings. 'I work for the Royal Armouries at Fort Nelson, Fareham, in Hampshire and we had a family of pied wagtails nesting in the barrel of an 1894 battle cruiser gun.'[18]

Their feeding habits involve similar adaptability. 'While waiting at my local car wash, I noticed a pair of pied wagtails flitting in and out. They were eating the dead insects washed from the front of each car. Most surprisingly, they wouldn't touch any insect from a car that had received the full wax treatment.'[19]

In May 2003 I was having breakfast with friends at Reading services on the M4. At 7.00 a.m. we were in an almost empty restaurant when we noticed a pied wagtail running between tables picking up scraps of food. After a while it flew to the entrance lobby and waddled up to one of the closed doors. It looked

A pied wagtail roost located in the centre of Norwich's shopping area was a wonderful natural addition to the Christmas decorations.

slightly up and to our astonishment the door opened automatically and the bird left. A few minutes later the door opened again and in came it or another bird and proceeded to feed. It seemed that it had learnt quickly how to activate the door to avail itself of a ready food supply.

Later that year my ears pricked up when I heard Terry Wogan on the radio reading an email from a listener who, on pulling up at Reading services, noted 1–2 pied wagtails loafing around the carpark. As soon as he stopped his car they flew on to his radiator and started picking off insects which had been trapped and killed.[20]

The habit that brings pied wagtails most dramatically to our attention is their willingness to form winter roosts,

sometimes in large numbers and often in highly urban areas. The most famous roost site is also one that involves the longest occupancy. Pied wagtails have been coming nightly to O'Connell Street in Dublin city centre since 1929, where as many as 3600 birds have been counted in a series of large plane trees. In 1930s Britain, city-roosting pied wagtails seemed to have a curious affinity for the postal services, with major gatherings on the Edinburgh GPO (1930/1) and on the glass roof of a branch post office in Campbell Street, Leicester (1935).[21] Other sites have included a series of commercial greenhouses in Canterbury (occupied for a decade), a power station at Castleford in Yorkshire, the EMI Building at Hayes in Middlesex (1972) and Aberdeen railway station (1976).[22]

At many sites the birds seem to have an eye for secure localities with additional warmth: 'there was a small roost in the municipal Christmas tree in Berkhamsted – after the lights had been switched on'. Few birds can have been more cosy than those sleeping on lagged steam pipes in a Preston factory. The most prestigious address was the roost on Buckingham Palace Road in SW1, while one of the largest ever was by Orpington railway station in outer London.[23]

The attraction at this site was a dense mass of laurel bushes, whose evergreen foliage provided almost perfect cover. The roosting process occupied about an hour and a half from the arrival of the first bird on a near-by roof, to the last one entering the laurels. With just a handful present initially, only my prior knowledge of what was due to unfold kept my attention. Most of the early arrivals stood around, quietly facing into the breeze or foraging for a final snack. Another small group would arrive, then another and as darkness closed in all the nearby roofs would have wagtails on them. One or two then flew down directly into the depths of the laurel bushes and, as if this was a signal, more flew to join them. For minutes they rained into the bushes in tens, fifties and, for a few moments, in hundreds. I would become aware of sustained calling from the birds in the roost, as if they were urging their tardy fellows to join them. It was a true chorus that built in volume, then gradually faded after 10–15 minutes. By now night had fallen, the wagtails would go quiet and the laurel bushes seemed dark and inert. Who could believe they sheltered anything up to 4000 birds? I would close my notebook and head for home.[24]

Michael Warren's painting evokes the inner-city locations beloved of many of our wintering waxwings.

Waxwing family
Bombycillidae

Bohemian Waxwing, *Bombycilla garrulus*. This beautiful bird is essentially warm cinnamon-grey but it has many striking refinements, such as the luxuriant conical hat-like crest, a yellow-edged tail and a slender upward-curving black mask. Strangest of all are the decorative red waxy 'blobs' at the tips of several secondaries, to which it owes its name. The recently added 'Bohemian' is a technical inaccuracy. It derives from an old German name for the bird and simply denoted something foreign and exceptional, in much the same that we once added the word 'French' to several other species' names.

'Bohemian' in the sense of an erratic and unpredictable wanderer is perfectly accurate. Waxwings are inhabitants of the Arctic and sub-Arctic taiga, where their nest and breeding habits remained a mystery until the mid-nineteenth century.[1] The birds' appearances in Britain are triggered by the failure of their usual winter diet, the rowan crop of Scandinavia, and irruptive movements can then occur all along the east coast. If abundant food supplies do not halt their progress, they move steadily further south and west in their quest.

Hawthorn hedgerows are a standard lure, although the horticultural fashion for exotic berry-bearing plants like cotoneaster, pyracanthus and viburnum have had a strong impact on these fruit-devouring visitors. Waxwings somehow discover them even in the middle of town gardens and parks and it has made them something of an urban specialist. Big flocks have been noted in the heart of a number of cities and more recently it has developed a reputation as the 'supermarket' bird, because the red-berried shrubbery is a common feature around many store car parks. Their almost total indifference to human presence means that even in these highly disturbed locations waxwings give maximum pleasure at minimum inconvenience to themselves.

'Invasion years' were noted as long ago as 1685/6, and Gilbert White examined a locally caught bird in 1767 and referred to it as a 'German silk-tail' (*Bombycilla* means 'silk tail' in Latin).[2] During the nineteenth century there were major arrivals in five winters, but many more occurred in the twentieth with 18 notable invasion years since 1937.[3] Possibly the largest ever was in 1946/7 when at least 12,500 birds were recorded. Flocks as large as 1000 have been noted but because they eat such large quantities of berries few areas can support the gatherings for very long.

In recent years waxwings have become something of a specialist bird of the red-berry bushes surrounding supermarket car parks.

The capacity of individual waxwings has been closely observed. One bird feeding at Avoch on the Moray Firth in 1946 ate 500 cotoneaster berries, perhaps three times its own body weight, in six hours. In Norfolk during February 1957 a group of 'seven birds completely stripped a very heavily laden *Cotoneaster* covering 100 square feet of a cottage wall in two days'.[4] But perhaps the all-comers' record goes to a waxwing in Carmarthenshire that consumed between 600 and 1000 berries of the same species in six hours. Just as remarkably – and hardly surprising – it was defecating every four minutes.[5] In a world blanketed by snow, waxwings can produce a display of droppings every bit as colourful as the berries on which they gorge.

Dipper family *Cinclidae*

Dippers are inhabitants of fast-flowing streams in the British and Irish uplands.

Dipper, *Cinclus cinclus*. VN: Water Ouz/sel, Waterhen. It is a measure of the past ambiguities in bird nomenclature that the dipper previously shared names with various rails ('water crake'; in County Mayo, Ireland it is still apparently known as the 'wee water hen'), magpie ('piet') and various thrushes ('water colly', 'water blackbird', 'water ouzel'). 'Dipper' was itself once interchangeable as a name for the little grebe, while 'king's fisher' was applied occasionally to this species as well as to the other water bird of dashing blue.[1]

Whatever name is used there is no mistaking a dipper, which is built like a giant, dark, barrel-chested wren with a gleaming white breast. The graphic simplicity of its appearance has not been lost on environmentalists. For many years a dipper was the logo and name of the newsletter produced by the Devon Wildlife Trust, until it was recently ousted by a badger.

In addition to the hill country of south-west England, dippers are classically associated with the upland landscapes of Wales, Scotland and Ireland, where the sight and sound of tumbling boulder streams seem to feed into our sense of the bird's huge vitality. One of my most memorable sightings was a dipper feeding on an ice-fringed winter tarn in Wales. During half an hour's observation it plunged off the frozen edge or was blown by the biting wind across the ice like a skater and tipped into the near-freezing waters more than 30 times. On each occasion it resurfaced with caddis-fly larvae, whose outer cases were flicked off by a few deft blows on the ice, before it readied itself for the next arctic plunge. It was a perfect exhibition of a dipper's feeding efficiency in the most unfavourable conditions and testament to the bird's endearing hardihood.

The more usual view is of a dark shape whirring upstream with a trajectory that follows the various meanders of a river. The bird normally marks its progress by a sharp '*zik*' note, which seems designed to puncture the constant background sounds of the dipper's world. Otherwise it can often be found standing on a boulder midstream 'bobbing and curtseying in characteristic fashion as if hinged on [their] legs'.[2] Dippers have a remarkable ability to feed underwater, literally walking on the riverbed in defiance of the current and their own cork-like buoyancy to search for aquatic invertebrates. The young are capable of swimming after just a matter of days and are sometimes virtually born underwater, since dippers love to build their large, sometimes football-sized domed nests behind the tumbling curtain of a waterfall.

Breeding birds show a marked attachment to human structures or alterations to the riverine environment, such as weirs, bridges, culverts and embankments, as locations for their nests. More unusual sites include a disused cowshed 300 feet (90m) from the stream, on the wheel of an active watermill, inside a trout hatchery building, the walls of a fish pass and inside the boot of a car dumped in a river in County Tyrone.[3] One remarkable nest found by James Adler in Northumberland could only be reached by parent birds diving beneath the surface, after river levels had risen and left the previously exposed structure trapped in an air pocket. Adults are extraordinarily reluctant to abandon their nests and Adler found another female continuing to incubate her eggs, which were 'steaming on their soaked bed of leaves' after both parent and nest had been thoroughly soaked by flood water.[4]

However the most extraordinary example of a dipper's tenacity was a nest positioned in a section of bridge subsequently treated with a high-pressure spraying of liquid concrete. Not only was the site disturbed while contractors altered the river flow through the two arches of the bridge, but the nest itself received 'numerous layers of light concrete spray from above'. Neither the adult nor the young dippers lost heart and once the concrete set hard the nest became 'an integral part of the interior wall of the bridge'. The freshly reinforced structure was then occupied for at least three further breeding seasons.[5]

Wren family *Troglodytidae*

(Winter) Wren, *Troglodytes troglodytes*. VN: Jenny Wren. It is fitting that one of our smallest species should also have the shortest name (along with smew, ruff and rook) of any British bird. The recently added 'winter' stands little chance of taking root, but it has much more meaning in North America where the bird is a genuine winter migrant to the eastern states of the USA and where the title needs to differentiate it from several other species of wren.

In Britain the name is much more likely to be prefaced with 'Jenny', making it one of the elite group of birds with a personalised nickname. None seems more deserving. Few animals, let alone birds, convey such a sense of indomitable spirit and vitality. The posture and jerky movements suggest constant alertness, the low buzzing flight has an almost insect-like intensity, while the bird's volcanic song generates an aura of energy out of all proportion to its physical size.

The typical fast high trilling phrase, lasting just five seconds and repeated four or five times a minute, is remarkably penetrating. In certain conditions it can carry ½ mile (1km). One wren will often excite a reponse from a neighbouring rival, and in a typical walk through a spring wood one passes through a succession of competing territory-holders, so that wren song cannonades out from the undergrowth from beginning to end. Unlike most other birds it has no off-season – truly 'the only song to be heard any day of the year in Britain' – and whatever the season the impression is of unassailable joy:[1]

Amid the dreariness of dell and thornbush, the song of the wren hidden in the wet branches seems all the more triumphant . . . There is a shameless optimism in it that clothes the bare hedges with something better than leaves. There is no other resident bird so incapable of melancholy. The robin is often pensive, and sings . . . as though he sympathised with us. But the wren never sings except to say that it is the best of all possible worlds.[2]

The wren's inclination to nest in the oddest of locations is matched only by the robin.

A tiny bird fit for a tiny coin – a wren appeared on the old British farthing.

The tiny size and almost mouse-like creeping behaviour mean that it is less conspicuous than most other common birds, but as David Bannerman noted, 'To describe it as "shy and retiring" is absolutely misleading.'[3] Yet nor could it be truly characterised as bold, although the cocked-up tail, which Lockwood argues is at the root of the Old English name *wrenna*, often gives an impression of pert defiance.[4] In the presence of humans, wrens are not so much brave as indifferent and often behave as if we do not exist, or as if they are aware that they are too small and insignificant to be noted. 'We once had a wren that used to help with the housework, eating insects etc. It would come in the back bedroom window of our bungalow and work its way through to the front porch and leave by a window in there. A downside was the droppings on the wardrobe tops and bedspreads but a small price to pay for such a charming visitor.'[5]

The bird's apparent disregard for us is at its most striking in its choice of nest site and William Turner's remark in the sixteenth century suggests that the tradition is hundreds, if not thousands, of years old: 'The nest it makes is outwardly of moss and inwardly of feathers, wool, or down . . . has the form of an upright egg standing on one of its ends, while in the middle of one side there is a little postern as it were, by which the bird goes in and out. It sometimes builds its nest at the back of a house or in sheds thatched with straw.'[6]

The male wren is well known for his industry in the matter of nest construction. Rather than occupying a single jointly assembled dome, the cock builds, or starts to build, a number of different nests and the female selects the one that is best constructed and with the most favourable site. The average number in a male wren's territory is 6.3, although a remarkably hard-working Dutch bird was known to make 40 nests over four successive years (12, 10, 9, 9).[7]

Eccentricity is virtually a speciality of breeding wrens and sites have included the base of a magpie's nest occupied by kestrels, the floral cross on a church pulpit (the bird lining it with moss taken off the lectern) and inside the mouth of a prize pike hanging on a garage wall. Noise and movement are no deterrent whatsoever.

Young wrens were successfully reared from a nest right next to a circular saw (just 8 inches/19cm away) in use eight hours a day, while the young and eggs of another pair made a twice weekly journey from Kent to Covent Garden on the running board of a lorry.[8]

Strong-smelling situations seem to exert a positive attraction, with examples including the lower branches of cabbage and broccoli plants, among the slowly decaying carcasses of crow, jay, sparrowhawk, owl and cat. Not to be outdone by its great rival for our affections, the wren joins the robin on that shortlist of birds known to have built inside a human skull. The folds of a tramp's old shirt draped on a bush combine the attractions of bad odour with the wren's other penchant for human fabrics. Trousers and jackets on washing lines, an old hat in a busy workshop, a scarecrow's pocket and the folds in a church curtain are all on record. More controversial is the legend attaching to St Malo who, returning from work among the monastery vines, found that a wren had built a nest in his cloak and laid an egg in it. E. A. Armstrong, who made a lifelong study of the species, suggested the story may be founded on fact and added, 'Pious imagination may, perhaps, be forgiven for adding one egg so small.'[9]

For all their willingness to exploit man-made nesting opportunities, wrens are in many ways the common garden bird least dependent upon us. The species occupies an enormous range of landscapes, although Max Nicholson pointed out more than 50 years ago that conventional descriptions of habitat are in many ways inappropriate:

> the wren cannot adequately be described as a bird of woodlands, gardens, fields, moors, marshes, cliffs or wastelands – although it is all of these – but must be looked at rather as a bird of crevices and crannies, of stems, and twigs and branches, of woodpiles and fallen trees, of hedge-bottoms and banks, walls and boulders, wherever these may occur. Wrens, therefore, cut across, or rather scramble under, the imaginary boundaries which we are accustomed to draw between different types of country . . .[10]

These subterranean conditions, which explain the scientific name *Troglodytes*, 'cave dweller', can be found virtually anywhere from the seashore to the mountain-tops. Not even coastal cliff faces are out of bounds. On St Kilda the great tumbling wall of granite known as Conachair, the highest in Britain, is home to wrens, while tiny isolated monoliths like Ailsa Crag, 12 miles (20km) off the Ayrshire coast, have habitat enough for them. Along with blue tits and robins, wrens include gannets, puffins and Manx shearwaters among their breeding neighbours. No bird is more widespread.

Nor is there a commoner species although the wren's solitary, even anti-social, lifestyle tends to disguise the total population and its number-one breeding status is a fact still thought sufficiently unexpected for it to crop up routinely in the pub quiz. About ten million pairs are estimated in Britain and Ireland, and they are also notable for dividing into at least five races. There are separate endemic subspecies on Shetland (*zetlandicus*), Fair Isle (*fridariensis*), the Outer Hebrides (*hebridensis*) and St Kilda (*hirtensis*).

The last is by far the most celebrated, partly because of the controversy that arose after its separate recognition in 1884. Victorian collectors paid the St Kildan crofters handsomely for this intrinsically rare bird's minuscule corpse or its bonbon-sized eggs. In 1904 it enjoyed the double distinction of facing apparent extinction at their hands and being the object of a special piece of protective legislation. Yet, as one eye-witness notes, its history is only one element in the bird's renown:

The real importance of the St Kilda wren for anyone who has ever visited these islands is symbolic. The bird is surely the wild spirit of the place. After all it has been there some 5000 years, whereas human occupation is thought to have lasted just about 1000 years. Its loud piercing song can already be heard from among the rocks as you first approach the islands by boat, even above the noise of crashing waves and the cries of a million seabirds. The wren seems elemental – a tiny persistent life in these desolate landscapes governed by the huge impersonal forces of wind, tide and weather.[11]

That dramatic expression of life force, conveyed in one so tiny, is thought to lie at the heart of a folk ritual that has endured for several hundred years. 'Wrenning' or 'hunting the wren' is a mysterious fragment of old bird lore that still survives in parts of western Ireland and, until recently, the Isle of Man. Its full distribution once included much of Wales, most of southern Ireland, south-west Scotland, Hampshire, Essex and Suffolk, and it was possibly spread by its initial Celtic observers.

In its original form, children and adults would go out in fancy dress on 26 December (St Stephen's and Boxing Day) or Twelfth Night. They would beat the hedgerows until they caught or killed a wren, which would then be nailed to a pole or placed in a cage wreathed with winter greenery and ribbons. The tiny burden would then be paraded from house to house, where the 'wren boys' would sing to the occupants and request gifts of food

The St Kildan wren is one of the five separate subspecies in Britain and Ireland.

and drink in exchange for lucky feathers from the bird. Though there are numerous variations, the most commonly cited of the wren-boy lyrics runs:

The wren, the wren, the king of all birds,
St Stephen's Day was caught in the furze;
Although he is little, his family's great,
I pray you, good landlady, give us a treat.

Apart from an event on Sandymount Green in Dublin, most surviving examples of the wren festival are held in parts of western Ireland, particularly County Kerry, Cork or Limerick, and there is a famous wren-boy ceremony held every year on the Dingle peninsula. All

Hunting the wren in County Clare, Ireland in 1967.

of the events remain true to the fancy-dress traditions of earlier times. Many of the participants wear straw hats or garments incorporating straw, and masks feature prominently. It is a measure of Margaret Thatcher's enduring status as a hate figure in Irish society that masks depicting the former prime minister are still being worn at some wren parades. However the killing and capture of the bird itself has long been dropped in favour of a simple glass box or a holly bush in which the wren is symbolically invoked. The ritualised seeking of hospitality or money has also been supplanted by the gathering of donations, either for a general Wren's Ball which all can attend, or, as in Cork city, to help finance the following year's folk festival.[12]

Much ink has been spilt on the exact origins or meaning of hunting the wren. One interpretation hinges on an old legend that the wren betrayed the whereabouts of St Stephen to his persecutors and therefore the bird was ritually stoned – the same punishment meted out to the martyred saint – as a form of Christian revenge. Another popular theory, endlessly recycled in books of British folklore, holds that the wren was a bird sacred to pagan Europe and that its ancient rites were brought north to these islands by our Bronze Age ancestors. The ritual slaughter of the totem bird in mid-winter was a way of giving thanks and of ensuring new life in the coming year.[13]

There is certainly a long tradition of affection towards the bird, which pre-dates the effects of modern environmentalism. Wrens were once protected by many of the same taboos that gave sanctuary to robins (see page 337) and there seems something inherently distasteful in the idea of harming this cheerful mite of the undergrowth. It may also once have been a sacred animal. Much has been made of the fact that in Welsh and Irish the name for the

wren has an apparent connection with the word for druid. In classical Rome the name *Regulus* ('little king') also hints at an exalted status, but references in Latin and Greek literature are highly confusing and may well concern another impressive feathered midget, the goldcrest.

Unfortunately all the various claims that wrenning is a custom with an ancient pre-Christian pedigree stumble at the same hurdle. There is absolutely no evidence for it prior to the late seventeenth century, when it was first recorded in Pembrokeshire. In his study of folk custom, *The Stations of the Sun*, Ronald Hutton argues that hunting the wren was 'a striking demonstration of a festive suspension of norms', which gave licence to merry-making, good-natured mockery of authority and role-play.[14] The ritual parade from door to door in search of hospitality functioned in much the same way that Hallowe'en now presents parallel opportunities for treats to modern children. Few would see Britain's recent adoption of the American custom of 'trick or treating' as the celebration of a pagan deity, and hunting the wren should probably be viewed in much the same light. It is – and perhaps always was – a vehicle for seasonal fun and games, rather than the continuance of a lost pagan rite.

For all its air of vitality, the wren is extremely susceptible to hard weather and bad winters can wipe out much of the total population. In 1962/3 wrens may have declined by four-fifths. Fortunately their capacity for multiple broods and large clutches allows them to achieve equally impressive recoveries. In the ten years following 1964 wrens showed a tenfold increase.[15]

One of the strategies for dealing with heat loss during the long winter night is to gather at dusk in communal roosts, which are all the more impressive given the wren's otherwise solitary anti-social lifestyle. Squirrel dreys (there is a record of at least 17 in one) and old bird nests, including those of swallow, song thrush (12 birds) and house martin (30+ birds), have been recorded.[16] Ten wrens in a coconut shell was more unusual, while the largest ever was a gathering of many dozens between January and March 1979 in the roof eaves of a cottage at Lydney, Gloucestershire. 'Arrivals occurred during a period of 25 to 40 minutes from dusk to almost dark; . . . at times the Wrens arrived in such numbers that they had to line up to enter . . . The highest total was 96 on 15th February.'[17]

Perhaps most remarkable of all, given the confined nature of the space, was a gathering at High Kelling, Norfolk, of over 60 birds in a nest box measuring 5½ × 4½ × 5¾ inches (14 × 11.5 × 14.5cm). This worked out at 2⅓ inches (38cu cm) a bird.[18]

The dunnock's pleasant if rather fragile tinkling song is one of the first sounds to be heard when warmer weather comes in early spring.

Accentor family *Prunellidae*

Dunnock, *Prunella modularis*. VN: Hedge Sparrow, Hedge Spadger. Shuffling in gait, mild in manner and visually rather drab, this quintessential occupant of the hedge bottom has somehow managed to triumph over our affections by sheer self-effacement. A good indication of our long attachment is the list of more than 50 archaic vernacular names, many of them personalised like 'blue Tom' or 'hedge Betty'. Just as telling is the expression 'as mild as a smoky' (referring to the blue-tinged yoke of lead-grey around the neck and throat), which was once proverbial in parts of Northumberland.[1]

Yet the seeming inhibition comes with a delicious twist. So much so that one could easily imagine the dunnock as the kind of bird the poet Philip Larkin should have celebrated. Behind the façade it has an extraordinary private life, described as 'perhaps the most complex known in British birds'.[2] Its mating system includes a good deal of partner swapping and embraces polygyny (two females with a single male), polyandry (a female with two or three males) and polygynandry (two or three males sharing two, three or four females), the first of which is not too dissimilar to Larkin's own arrangement.

In the last 20 years the researches of Professor Nick Davies and others have shown that, in another typical scenario, a 'pair' of dunnocks will tolerate the presence of a second male (the beta male) in their territory. While the alpha male accompanies and guards 'his' partner in an effort to maximise his paternity of any future offspring, the female is equally keen to lose her escort and pair with the beta male. She is partly driven by the fact that an uncopulated beta male may try to destroy her eggs and nest, and so force her to breed again. Also by mating with both birds the female is likely to have her brood fed by two males and so increase their chances of survival.[3]

While dunnocks mate more frequently than has been recorded for any other small bird – once or twice an hour throughout a 10-day period – copulation itself is remarkably brief. In fact the male penetrates the female's cloaca in a fraction of a second as he leaps over her, and

The dunnock's sex life is an arrangement of huge complexity. Here a male pecks at a female's swollen cloaca.

the real function of the movement was overlooked by earlier observers. Another intriguing element in their courtship is the male's pecking of the female's swollen cloaca, which often causes her to produce a droplet of sperm and in turn stimulates him to mate with 'his' partner. For the male too these preliminaries may have a valuable function, since the ejected droplet may well represent sperm from the female's earlier copulation with a rival male.[4]

Our failure to appreciate the sex life of one of our commonest species (still almost three million pairs, although there has been a troubling recent decline) reflects the dunnock's larger capacity to elude accurate observation. Numerous books speak of shyness, but Lord Grey came closer to the bird's true personality when he wrote of habits that 'suggest not so much fear of man as an inclination to apologise for its presence'. Grey supported the case against outright timidity by pointing to the male's love of conspicuous songposts from which to deliver his thin tinkling warble, a performance that he felt had both 'spirit and uplift'.[5]

However for Grey the dunnock's most extravagant acts of self-expression were the species' wonderful blue eggs. Since the dunnock has few other striking attributes and no obvious economic value, Derek Goodwin has suggested that the New Zealand settler who first introduced the bird to the islands did so because he 'wanted his children also to have the thrill of discovering the Dunnock's beautiful rich blue eggs!'[6] If so, he was well rewarded: it thrives in New Zealand to this day.

Our failure to understand the dunnock resurfaces in the question of its taxonomic affinities. An old nineteenth-century name was 'hedge warbler', but far commoner and still surviving is 'hedge sparrow', which even more completely misrepresents its real relationships. Yet the bird's obvious back-yard familiarity and overall sparrow-like dullness explain the error. Dunnocks actually belong to a largely montane ground-dwelling family of subtly coloured birds called accentors. The recent move to introduce the name 'hedge accentor' may provide an interesting example of conflict between familiar usage and technical accuracy. Some human sounds perfectly envelop the thing they describe, as if held by an irresistible gravitational field. Dunnock, literally meaning 'small brown bird' and dating from at least the fifteenth century, seems a word in that category.[7]

A robin singing in the night is regularly assumed to be a nightingale.

Thrush and Chat family
Turdidae

European Robin, *Erithacus rubecula*. VN: Robin Redbreast. Although the bright splash of red makes it instantly recognisable and dominates all our impressions, the robin has other striking features such as the dark eye, which is proportionally larger than our own. Thrushes are also beautifully shaped and have a fullness of belly that is particularly appealing. The robin usually receives the highest praise for this family trait possibly because, when fluffed out, it can look almost ball-like in shape (see Atlantic Puffin for an examination of how shape affects human responses to birds, page 257).

The movements can be equally captivating: 'the robin is a wonderful little bird and seems to brighten everything around. He is so small and yet so full of life.'[1] With a heart rate of a thousand beats a minute, there is genuine intensity in the metabolism and its vivacious spirit seems somehow well captured in the word 'robin'. As David Lack noted, it is surely more than coincidence that the name is given to our favourite outlaw (Robin Hood), our friendliest sprite (Robin Goodfellow), as well as one of the most cherished characters from children's literature (Christopher Robin).[2]

While alliterating with redbreast, the word robin has no association with the colour red. In fact 'redbreast' by itself survived as an alternative name until the twentieth century, and before either of these was an original word, 'ruddock' (from Old English *rudduc*), dating back at least a thousand years and drawing directly on the bird's deep rusty-orange.[3] The much later 'robin' (also once 'robinet') was a diminutive of Robert and was similar in structure to other personalised bird names such as magpie and jackdaw.

One is tempted to think that a creature dressed in the most symbolic of colours is bound to be an important talisman, but another factor is the robin's tameness, which only one or two other species can match. The nest in the plant pot is a standard cliché but the list of sites is truly extraordinary – abandoned kettles, tins, saucepans, peg bags, rolls of wire, an unmade bed (while its owner had breakfast, after which the birds were left to raise young successfully), on a bedroom pelmet and row of

335

The robin is one of the most numerous and widespread of British and Irish birds.

books (three broods over two seasons), a pigeonhole in a desk, in the pocket of a gardener's jacket (built between breakfast and lunch), in a hole made by cannon shot in the *Victory*'s mast, against which Nelson had been leaning when he received his fatal wound (the mast had been resited at Bushy House, London), under the front wing of a sports car ('which limited its use to short trips in fine weather'),[4] in the engine of a Second World War plane at Denham airfield in Suffolk (the nest had initially been destroyed six times; the engine kept the eggs warm while the plane – and nest – were airborne), in the body of a dead cat and in the skull of a man hanged for highway robbery in 1796.[5] A piece of wonderfully tasteless doggerel commemorates the last:

> High he swings for robbing mail,
> But his brain of robin female
> Still is quite full; though out of breath
> The passion e'en survives his death.[6]

The robin sitting on the gardener's spade handle is another stock image of the legendary fellowship of this little bird, but – stock image or not – few people share such moments with our national bird (officially declared in 1960) and are able to remain unmoved. The crowning pleasure for an insular race like ours is the notion – one is tempted to call it a conceit – that continental robins show no such confidence. In fact they will, but the British bird is a separate race, *melophilus*, from the nominate continental form and is marked by a tendency towards warmer brown upperparts and a more confiding nature. The European counterpart, by contrast, is strongly attached to woodland habitats.

The earliest evidence for the British bird's tameness comes from the sixth century AD, when St Serf of Culross in Fife was recorded to feed a robin that perched on his head or shoulder as he prayed. The bird was later killed by some of his disciples and was brought back to life by St Serf's favourite, Kentigern (canonised as St Mungo), the founder of Glasgow Cathedral. The bird's early link with the city and with one of its founding fathers is still commemorated in Glasgow's coat of arms. Almost 800 years later the idea of mutual affection between bird and people was well established, and in his *Parlement of Fowles* Chaucer refers to the species as the 'tame ruddok'.[7]

In the age of imperial expansion the talisman status was confirmed by introductions wherever we thought robins might thrive. While releases in Australia, Canada, the USA and New Zealand were all failures, there was consolation in naming like-coloured birds after the original. There is, for instance, an **American Robin**, *Turdus migratorius* (actually a blackbird-sized thrush, which has even made it as a vagrant to Britain), a Pekin robin (now the red-billed leiothrix, *Leiothrix lutea*, an Asian bird that has established free-flying populations in southern France) and an Indian robin (*Saxicoloides fulicata*).

One has only to turn to European writings to see how different were feelings for the bird on the Continent. Two leading French naturalists, the Comte de Buffon and Georges Cuvier, both dwelt on methods of capture in their accounts, the latter noting: 'redbreasts are more numerous in Lorraine and Burgundy than elsewhere. They are very much sought after there, and their flesh acquires an excellent fat, which renders it a very delicate meat.'[8] A German ornithologist, Johann Naumann, described how his countrymen also killed them in large numbers and took advantage of their willingness to enter buildings by trapping autumn robins in the house and releasing them only in the spring. Throughout their winter confinement the birds served as a highly effective form of natural pesticide.[9] Even now, large numbers of migrant robins are trapped for food in parts of the Mediterranean region.

The British were not entirely averse to eating their favourite bird. There is a sixteenth-century account of its fine savour, but trapping appears to have been small-scale and, although the wild population for centuries was harvested for the songbird trade, this confronted a number of old taboos. The robin remains the classic bird of good omen: 'A saying my mother taught me sixty years ago ran: Good luck to you, good luck to me/Good luck to every robin I see.'[10] William Blake's much-quoted lines – 'A robin redbreast in a cage/Puts all Heaven in a rage' – echoed a long-standing conviction that harming robins was unnatural. Hence the couplet: 'Kill a robin or a wren/Never prosper boy or man.'

If murder were committed it brought all sorts of dire consequences. It was said to cause a man's cattle to give bloody milk.[11] 'As a boy in North Somerset (1940–1950) we used to collect eggs, but not the robin's because one would develop twisted or bent fingers if they were taken.'[12] Similarly during the Siberian winter of 1947, which led Norfolk country people *in extremis* to trap small birds for the pot (see page 352), the capture of a robin was far from welcome. Instead the much-regretted little corpse was buried.[13]

If the archly pragmatic and down-to-earth temperament of the British could be said to allow a sense of the sacred for any bird, then it has to be for this species. Several old rhymes suggest the divine favour:

The robin redbreast and the wren
Are God almighty's cock and hen.

And a Lancastrian variation runs:

The Robin and the Wren are God's cock and hen,
The spink and the Sparrow are the Devil's bow and arrow.[14]

An element in the religious aura may be the robin's recurrent association with dead or dying people, which is itself possibly a variation of the bird's attendance upon spade-wielding gardeners. Any earth-delving exercise, including grave digging or surfacing moles, can arouse a robin's interest. But not all the connections can be so easily explained. 'In December 1978 my father lay dying of cancer in his home. All his life he had been deeply committed to the countryside. Each day a little robin got into the house and perched on a sill above his bedroom door. When he died the visits ceased.'[15]

The ruddock was already a national favourite by the time that the Sherborne Missal was created around 1400.

The most extraordinary bird experience I've ever had was 2–3 days after my father died in a shocking accident during September 1985. An adult robin started coming into the house virtually every day, sometimes even perching on my father's armchair by the fireplace. In some thirty years at the house (with two resident cats) we have never seen a robin indoors before or since. We have made no effort to tame robins and, in any event, this unusual behaviour only lasted a short time.

As a scientist I have tried to find a rational explanation for its behaviour – did it come in because the doors were open more than usual or because there were more visitors than usual? This does not seem convincing since the doors and windows are often open in summer. Possibly it was just chance but what are the odds of a bird choosing this particular fortnight to come visiting out of a 30–year period? Perhaps there is no rational explanation, but an element of mystery that cannot be reduced to the level of DNA and avian science? What I do know, and clearly remember almost 18 years later, is that an apparently unremarkable bird brought a strange sense of comfort and peace to a grieving house.[16]

The traditional legend held that a robin in the house was a harbinger of death but it is striking how often the apparently ominous portent is viewed in a positive light. The Larkins of Loddon, Norfolk, recounted how, on the loss of a father and grandfather, each of five family members had a separate robin experience that same day, including one entering the grand-daughter's stable, another landing in the deceased man's own garden shed and a third going inside the kitchen to take food from a dog bowl at a grandson's house. The daughter, Maureen Larkin, adds: 'When we told each other of all the coincidences that occurred on the day Dad died we were slightly spooked, but we always now associate those robins with him.'[17]

Sometimes the phenomenon is more easily explained. In 1637 a theologian, Dr John Bastwick, was sentenced to life imprisonment, latterly on the Scilly Isles, for his outspoken criticism of church leaders, including Archbishop Laud. A contemporary account reported that on his disembarkation 'many thousands of robin redbreasts (none of which birds were ever seen in those Islands before or since) newly arrived at the castle there the evening before, welcomed him with their melody, and within one day or two after took their flight from thence, no man knows whither'.[18] The dramatic and unexpected visitation was taken as a sign of Bastwick's eventual deliverance, which did indeed come years later. However we now know that large 'falls' of robins, sometimes involving thousands of European migrants, are naturally occurring events especially in October. That one happened on the day of Bastwick's arrival was pure coincidence.[19]

There is a long tradition of robins in religious buildings which, if nothing else, helps to cement its image as the most church-going of our birds. 'Forty years ago I was rector of Hinton Martel near Wimborne, Dorset. During a cold spell I remember a robin and sparrow spent the night in church and were still there for the morning Mass. The robin watched the proceedings until the Consecration prayer, when he actually came and perched on my back. Afterwards he chirruped for some time, as if joining in audibly until the Communion.'[20]

During Charles II's reign a robin regularly entered and sang in Canterbury Cathedral, apparently shaming the Puritan community of Kent by its regular church attendance, while another was reputed to have lived in Bristol Cathedral for 15 years at the start of the nineteenth century. Since the only accurate record of longevity involved a bird that was eight years and five months, the story needs careful scrutiny.[21] More certain, however, since it received nationwide coverage including *The Times* and BBC Radio, was the robin pair that nested in the lectern at Ringsfield church in Suffolk in 1948. The doors were kept open all summer to give them access and sermons were delivered from the chancel steps to avoid disturbing the lectern's occupants. In return the robin would perch in the porch after the service and accompany the vicar to the rectory, or it would fly in during hymns and sit on the piano while it was being played.[22]

Early church writers attempted to incorporate the robin directly into the Christian story by suggesting that it had acquired a red breast by tugging at thorns in Jesus' brow. Although this does not necessarily explain how the most Christian of British species is also, *par excellence*, the bird of Christmas. One possible answer is the robin's winter song. They are persistent vocalists, and have only a short break in high summer during the energy-consuming period of moult. Both males and females then resume shortly afterwards to assert occupation of their autumn territories, which males defend sometimes with great violence. So intense is the territoriality that two migrant birds once found on a ship had taken possession of opposite ends of the vessel.[23] The song resulting from these audible conflicts is all the more conspicuous as autumn proceeds for having so few competitors (see also (Winter) Wren, page 329). The spring voice is richer and more varied, although it has to contend with many other vigorous songsters and is sometimes overlooked. The performance is therefore most compelling in the off-season, when the rather nostalgic quality and wistful structure blend perfectly with a wider atmosphere of decay. Emile Brontë memorably described it as 'wildly tender'.[24]

Sometimes one robin triggers an aggressive vocal response from a neighbour, which is then a stimulus for other robins, but to the ear it simply sounds like a beautiful recession of sound, one song floating above a more distant echo, repeated until it evaporates in the winter woodland. Peter Walton's poem 'Birdsong' explores the impact of these multiple voices, and beautifully echoes the broken arhythmic structure of the performance:

The robin is now an inseparable element of Christmas imagery (left), but its first appearance on the earliest Christmas cards (right) was in the mid-nineteenth century.

Some trouble
Or other, two mornings running, stirred me
At four:
Too late for night, too early for day.
It was
Something I cannot now recall. But what
Afterwards
Kept me awake – though it had not woken me –
Was a bird,
Invisible; no stained breast, no pin-bright eyes,
Just the voice
Of all the robins I had ever heard
Or shall.

Their willingness to perform during the hours of darkness is an unusual aspect of singing robins: 'About four years ago I found that I was hearing birdsong at about 12.30 a.m. At first I just could not believe what I was hearing. No matter what time I got up I could hear the bird. In fact it had a great effect on my sleeping habits. If I couldn't hear it, I would lie awake waiting for it. If I could hear it, I lay awake listening. I was flabbergasted.'

Nocturnal song is by no means a recent development. As our correspondent noted, 'My wife was re-reading *Lorna Doone* and came to the following sentence: "Everyone knows that robins sing all night".'[25] However the advent of artificial street lighting has led to an increase in the habit, and in the numbers of people recording it, although not all recognise what they hear. Since the only species with a reputation for nocturnal song is the nightingale, the sound is regularly assumed to be a performance by this summer visitor, even when heard in winter. The frequency of the error has led some to question whether the 1940 hit, 'A Nightingale Sang in Berkeley Square', hinges on a similar piece of faulty ornithology.

One of the details that has embedded the robin in our current Christmas traditions was first illuminated by pioneer robin scholar David Lack. He noticed that the birds first appeared in the Christmas mail when the custom of sending Christmas cards took off commercially in the 1860s. In the prototype designs the robin was often illustrated bearing an envelope in its bill. Lack suggested that the association hinged on the bright-red coat of the mail uniform, which gave rise to Robin as a nickname for a Victorian postman. He cited a confirmatory line of dialogue from a novel by Trollope, who was himself a post-office employee: '"come in, Robin postman, and warm theeself awhile".' A red-coated livery worn by other servicemen had inspired similar nicknames and Lack concluded that the birds depicted on both Christmas and valentine cards stemmed from the same association.

However robins had been incorporated into Yuletide images, especially among urban artists, since the eighteenth century and, while the robin-postman link undoubtedly cemented the connection, one cannot help thinking that it has deeper roots.[26] The robin's reputation for friendliness is 1500 years old (probably older) and its renown as the bird of winter-cheer long pre-dates the 1860s. There may even be a dash of paganism in our choice of the robin as the bird of Christmas. Like the holly wreath with its bright-red berries, it provides a splash of living colour in a dead world (see *Flora Britannica*, page 244).

The nightingale is one of the few species most people are content simply to hear, which is fortunate since it is a notorious skulker.

Common Nightingale, *Luscinia luscinia*. This bird is extremely difficult to pin down in its favoured habitat of low dense thorny scrub or coppiced thickets. And when eventually glimpsed, it looks little more than a plain grey-brown robin-like bird, with the warmer rufous tones to upperparts and tail obscured by shadows that almost invariably envelop it. Yet few people ever struggle to see a nightingale. It is possibly the only species where most are entirely content to stand and listen (which is not the case with two other invisible vocalists, Corn Crake, see page 178, and Great Bittern, see page 41).

The nightingale's reputation as our foremost songster is both Europe-wide and thousands of years old. It was kept as a cagebird as long ago as the classical period, and Pliny tells us that a noted performer could sell in ancient Rome for as much as the price of a slave. One remarkable white bird is said to have changed hands for 6000 sesterces and to have been presented to the Empress Agrippina as a gift.[27]

Nightingales are right on the north-western edge of their range in this country and, while they were once far more common than they are today, they were never so abundant as in Mediterranean latitudes. Spain, Italy and France each still hold expanding populations of up to a million pairs, but in Britain they have seldom occurred north of a line between the Humber and Severn, and in recent decades have both declined and retreated south-eastwards, with most of our 4000 pairs concentrated in an arc between Hampshire and Norfolk. It has now vanished completely from Wales as a breeding species and has never been recorded to nest either in Scotland or Ireland.

Relative scarcity seems only to have intensified its appeal. The nightingale has almost certainly given rise to a greater body of poetry in the English language than any other species. Even in places where its voice had seldom, if ever, been heard, its renown was implicit in vernacular names for other vocalists. The sedge warbler, for example, was once known as the 'Irish' or 'Scottish nightingale', while the bird that is often ranked number two songster among our summer visitors, blackcap, had a reputation as the 'northern nightingale'.

Yet it was only the real thing that drew the crowds. There are stories of Victorian newspapers giving whereabouts of territorial nightingales and of transport companies laying on special trips to listen to them. A landowner in Cheshire became so irate with the numbers of tourists that he asked for the bird to be scared off his property.[28] Richard Mabey, in his exploration of the cultural importance of nightingales, *Whistling in the Dark*, recalls a poster campaign of the 1920s run by the Metropolitan Railway Company. In the list of allurements which made 'Rickmansworth a Mecca to the city man pining for country and pure air', their advertisement gave special place to the abundance of nightingale song.[29]

During the great epoch of wildlife incarceration, the Victorians attempted to keep the songbird at their own convenience – although, even at the time, this was opposed by a few enlightened souls for its profligate waste of life, since nightingales made poor prisoners. The nature writer Richard Jefferies described them literally beating themselves to death against the cage bars. 'The mortality was pitiable,' he lamented. 'Seventy per cent of these little creatures that were singing a week before in full-throated ease in the Surrey lanes would be flung into the gutters of Seven Dials or Whitechapel.'[30] At least the trade in caged songbirds allowed us a glimpse of the former abundance of nightingales, such as the 100 birds trapped in the last week of May by catchers operating in Harrow in the late 1830s.[31]

Throughout much of the nineteenth century the species was widespread in London, and when the Duke of Buckingham first obtained the land in 1703 on which the main royal residence now stands, it was said to be 'a little wilderness full of Blackbirds and Nightingales'.[32] The most famous of the capital's population was the individual that sang on Hampstead Heath in the spring of 1819 and which was celebrated in John Keats' poem 'Ode to a Nightingale'. Less certain is the twentieth-century claim made in the popular wartime song, 'A Nightingale Sang in Berkeley Square'. From 1900 to 1940 there were just three records from the inner city, and it had long been extinct there as a breeding species.[33]

Although there is undoubtedly a self-perpetuating dynamic to the songster's renown, it is very hard to agree with W. H. Hudson's claim that an excess of praise makes it a disappointment when heard for the first time.[34] The sound of a nightingale is immediately arresting for its range and power. In one study a single male was shown to possess as many as 250 different phrases compiled from a repertoire of 600 basic sound-units. In the passages of song the phrases are drawn together and sequenced in a variety of ways so that each performance is a unique composition, never to be repeated. Many of the phrases are rich and liquid in tone but they are often mixed with guttural croaking noises, unmusical gurgles or chuckling.[35]

Loss of thick woodland understorey and over-grazing by wild deer are thought to be two of the factors causing the current decline in nightingales.

To compound the variety, the phrases can be delivered in totally unexpected ways. A bird may open with a series of long, loud, slow, elongated piping notes, which it steadily accelerates to an almost unbearable machine-gun-like intensity and speed. One senses that it eventually breaks down through the simple physical impossibility of a bird vocalising faster. To listen intently is often to be overwhelmed by the astonishing boldness of the arrangements. When nightingales hold forth, notions like art or conscious invention – ideas that seem at the heart of our own definition as human beings – hover dangerously in the air.

Yet as Edward Thomas noted, the listener is often struck by a diametrically opposite reflection: 'Beautiful as the notes are for their quality and order, it is their inhumanity that gives them their utmost fascination, the mysterious sense which they bear to us that earth is something more than a human estate, that there are things not human yet of great honour and power in the world.'[36]

H. E. Bates touched on another compelling element: the pauses between each newly delivered song phrase. 'It has some kind of electric, suspended quality that has a far deeper beauty than the most passionate of its sweetness. It is a performance made up, very often, more of silence than of utterance. The very silences have a kind of passion in them, a sense of breathlessness and restraint, of restraint about to be magically broken.' Richard Mabey, in whose book the Bates quotation is reproduced, suggests the delivery has 'the extra resonance of *oratory*', an idea that perfectly captures the bird's seemingly conscious mastery of timing.[37]

While nightingale song is intrinsically beautiful – and if not incomparable, then at least comparable to only two or three other birds – the factor which contributes more than any other to our long history of fascination is the nocturnal delivery. Contrary to popular belief, territory-holding males sing almost as readily by day but it is the performances after sunset which explain its dominant cultural role. Even the name itself, used for at least 1400 years and recognisable in the Anglo-Saxon form, *nihtingale*, and meaning 'night songstress' (early writers presumed the female sang), isolates the element dominating our perceptions.

Night-time purifies the voice of any visual interference, heightens its ambivalence and converts it, in Richard Mabey's words, into 'the equivalent of a psychologist's ink-blot test, capable of carrying all kinds of meaning'.[38] It is in many ways the reverse of owl song (see page 281). Instead of embodying the weirdness and seeming enmity of night, nightingales speak of all that is reassuring and wonderful about it. The disembodied prism-like beauty of the song has reflected back entirely different things to different ages, but primarily it has involved those two irresistible fixtures of the dark – love and sex.

'For early English writers ... they were cheerful, engaging birds, the friends and confidants of lovers. In much of Renaissance Europe "listening to the nightingale" became a euphemism for sexual frolicking.'[39] Drawing on a Persian myth, which exploited some of the genuine details of nightingale ecology, English writers portrayed it subsequently as a song full of exquisite pain. As the bird poured forth the sobbing notes, it pressed its breast against a bare thorn to intensify the bitter-sweet sound of unrequited affection.

Eventually the mood swung back: Romantic poets such as Coleridge and Keats reclaimed it as a sound of joy. By the twentieth century, however, the standard associations had become tired and empty. References thereafter tended to be detached or mordant in tone, and in the sequence of liaisons dramatised in T. S. Eliot's *The Waste Land* the quintessential bird of love is invoked with bitter irony; it sings now of the fragmented, loveless character of modern sexual relations.

In our own period it is a consistent motif in British film and television to connote love and romance, sometimes without due regard for its distribution or the extreme seasonality of full song (nightingales are at their best only for a matter of about six weeks from mid-April through May). Often the relationship to which it forms a soundtrack is illicit or doomed, as in the film of L. P. Hartley's *The Go-Between*, starring Julie Christie and Alan Bates, or the Roman Polanksi version of Thomas Hardy's *Tess of the d'Urbervilles* (in the latter it sings as Tess is violated).

If, contrary to the claim of W. H. Hudson, nightingale song seldom disappoints, one can at least appreciate Hudson's case that the bird has been over-referenced and over-versified. Certainly one senses that some of the more contentious claims made for, or even against, the bird have arisen from an urge to say something new. There may well have been an element of shock value in Lord Grey's remark that 'if the nightingale's song is the most marvellous, it is not the most loved of English bird songs ... if we were asked to give up blackbirds and were offered nightingales in exchange, the answer would be an unqualified and unhesitating "No".' 'It is a song,' he concluded, 'to listen to, but not to live with.'[40] Another overwhelmed admirer, Louis Halle, made a similar contentious point:

It is the same with Bach. With Botticelli. Or with Shakespeare.
Sometimes one prays the song will stop.[41]

A completely original celebration of a bird song, unlikely ever to be repeated with any other species, was a series of alfresco performances given by the musician Beatrice Harrison between 1924 and 1935. She persuaded the BBC's first director-general, Lord Reith, to attempt a first live outdoor broadcast of her cello accompanying the male nightingale in her Surrey garden. The bird had acquired the habit of singing along to the instrument, but on the night of the first recording it proved 'a very shy serenader'. Just before they were due to go off air, it decided to join in. Richard Mabey continues the remarkable story:

The broadcast was a sensation. A million people listened in, and the programme was picked up as far afield as Italy, Paris, Barcelona and Hungary – and in areas such as Scandinavia and Scotland where real nightingales had never been heard. Many listened on crystal sets, and those who did not have their own receivers enlisted friends to relay the broadcast to them over the telephone. In some places where the radio (or its loudspeaker) was out of doors, listeners reported the broadcast spurring other real nightingales into song. Over the months that followed Beatrice Harrison received 50,000 letters of appreciation. It was almost

The alfresco cello performances by Beatrice Harrison as she accompanied a singing nightingale are among the most famous BBC recordings ever.

as if the act of broadcasting, putting the nightingale one stage further removed from the listeners, had heightened its already secretive appeal.[42]

Bluethroat, *Luscinia svecica*. This dark elegant skulking relative of the nightingale is always a treasured find for birdwatchers sifting through coastal migrants, particularly when it is a breeding male with a cup of deep blue on the throat. Blue of this intensity is exceptional among the entire European avifauna.

There are usually 100–200 birds a year in Britain and Ireland (numbers have declined recently), most appearing in spring and mainly of the red-spotted form *svecica* from Scandinavia, which bred in Scotland in 1968, with a single repeat performance in 1995. More exceptional was the unprecedented breeding record on Thorne Moors, near Goole, Yorkshire, in 1996. It involved two pairs of the scarcer white-spotted subspecies, *cyanecula*, which

normally breeds no nearer than the Netherlands and eastwards across central Europe.[43]

Black Redstart, *Phoenicurus ochruros*. VN: Black Red, Blackstart (birders). Although this attractive sooty-coloured chat with the bright-chestnut tail is an uncommon spring and autumn migrant around most of our coastlines, it is better known for the small breeding population (seldom more than 100 pairs) centred in south-east England. Like the little ringed plover (see page 197), it has bred mainly in areas of industrial and inner-city dereliction. The grim character of the surroundings often gives an additional serendipitous gloss to any encounter, like the discovery of a jewel on a rubbish dump.

Originally a species of rocky montane habitats, it started to breed in Britain after a long slow colonisation of north-west Europe. The trigger for the expansion was its adaptation, like a number of other crag- and cave-dwelling birds (house martin and common swift are good

343

The black redstart is a bird of inner-city dereliction and economic depression.

examples), to the built-up human environment, where it can find a similar range of niches for nest sites and tall perches from which to feed or sing. Some of the first black redstarts set the trend in the 1920s when they nested on a breeze-block ledge above the roller doors on the old Palace of Engineering, part of the original Wembley Empire Exhibition and close to the famous and now vanished sports stadium.

At least three pairs bred from 1926 to 1941 but their *annus mirabilis* apparently came in the following year, heavily assisted by the German Luftwaffe, which left swathes of the capital in a state of ruin – perfect conditions for a rock-haunting species. The black redstart consolidated its London range and later spread across the south-east and into other towns including Ipswich, Dover, Birmingham and Manchester. It had a reputation first as a 'bomb-site' bird and, when these areas were redeveloped, as a 'power-station' bird (for its occupancy of Battersea, Croydon, Dungeness, Littlebrook and other generating plants). In truth these birds have a taste for most large building complexes, from the classic eyesore to the national monument.

Colonised national monuments have included Coventry Cathedral, Clare College, Cambridge, the Palace of Westminster, Trafalgar Square, Mayfair, Bloomsbury and the Natural History Museum in South Kensington.[44] 'A male used to sing from the flagpole on the Senate House and from 1952 I regularly listened to 1–2 males around the BBC's Broadcasting House.'[45] Many would classify the Millennium Dome as an eyesore rather than an architectural treasure, but a pair of black redstarts bred on the site as it was being constructed. At one stage the birds almost halted proceedings because of their protected status (as a Schedule I species under the Wildlife and Countryside Act) – no doubt there are some who rather wished they had.[46]

Equally long is the list of eyesores favoured by the black redstart – gasworks, sewage farms, railway sidings, marshalling yards, warehouses, timber depots, aggregate and scrap-metal works and industrial wasteground. In 1996 a pair nested on the axle of a disused freight lorry in a second-hand-car dealership, and in the early 1980s they occupied a moving crane in Lowestoft harbour: 'Once the eggs hatched the adults followed up and down the dock to feed the chicks wherever the crane happened to be at the time, sometimes even when it was on the move.'[47]

They have been found particularly to flourish in the vicinity of highly polluted streams. At Tottenham gasworks in north-east London a pair fed on chironimid midges attracted by a brook that received a daily discharge of 40 million gallons (182 million litres) of sewage effluent. In a neighbouring factory an employee maintained an office chart which suggests an eye for natural minutiae rivalling that of Gilbert White. He kept a monthly record of midge faeces on a 10-cm-square section of the office calendar. They peaked in exactly the months when black redstarts breed.[48]

The inner-city wasteland in which the species thrives completely subverts our conventional notions about beauty in landscape. But these unloved places are unique in one respect: almost every other part of the country is intensively managed at a physical level and we are, in some sense, guided towards a particular intellectual and emotional response. Even in nature reserves and national parks our attitudes are largely prescribed. By contrast, urban dereliction is entirely free of these restraints. Uncared for, unmanaged and unintentional – it is, in a way, the nearest thing to true wilderness that we possess. Its key bird emblem is the black redstart, just as the purple lance-like cones of buddleia are its dominant botanical motif. Yet it presents us with a nice dilemma. Would it lose some of its pristine character if we came to cherish it?

Certainly it loses its ecological value once it is redeveloped, as happened in the London dockland area, once a stronghold for black redstarts. It is not surprising to find that the fortunes of both bird and habitat have tended to fluctuate in inverse proportion to the national economy. Both tend to be squeezed at times of boom and inner-city regeneration, and thrive whenever there is a slow-down. The black redstart thus acquires another strange symbolism: it is the bird of economic depression.[49]

The following black-redstart story is not particularly related to the themes above, but it brings us back to our starting point: seeing one can involve an almost magical serendipity.

One overcast Saturday in November 1951 I set off to see a black redstart at Calbourne railway station on the Isle of Wight and add a new bird to my slowly increasing checklist. When I reached Calbourne the station master told me that he had not seen it, but I was welcome to look around. My search produced nothing and after an hour or so I decided that my luck was out. I returned home and went to bed early with a bird book and at about 10.15 p.m. I was distracted by the fluttering of some sort of moth at the window. So I got out of bed and opened the curtains and the huge 'moth' flew into my room – it was a black redstart! I could hardly believe my eyes as the wretched bird flapped madly around the walls and ceiling, perching at times on my bedhead, bookcase or on the picture rail. After a few minutes that seemed an age I heard my parents come in and I dashed out to call them. As I did so my black redstart flashed through the open door to the landing and was rudely shocked to find my father's cap expertly dropped over it. Before it was released into the night our close scrutiny revealed that in the panic it had lost three fine tail feathers, characteristically chestnut red, which I still have as a souvenir of a memorable visitor.[50]

Common Redstart, *Phoenicurus phoenicurus*. This flighty and rather shy inhabitant of upland woods or scrub often allows only a rear-end view as it darts away through the trees. Even the briefest of glimpses, however, betrays the bright rusty-red tail of both sexes, and on closer inspection the male is revealed as one of the most beautiful of all our summer migrants.

It is the splash of departing chestnut that has captivated us most and is honoured in many names for the bird, even 'redstart' itself, the '-start' portion deriving from *steort*, the Old English for tail. The colour also gave rise to most of the (now archaic) vernacular alternatives – 'redtail', 'brantail', 'firetail', 'fireflirt' – and is enshrined in the modern scientific name. *Phoenicurus* is a straight Greek equivalent of the English and dates back more than 2000 years to Aristotle's original description – the perfect measure of how long we have singled out this one feature.

All birds have a capacity to invoke associations with spiritual or physical freedom, but few can have done so as powerfully as this species for John Buxton, author of the New Naturalist monograph, *The Redstart*. The poet and Oxford lecturer studied the species for five years while he was incarcerated in German prisoner-of-war camps. During the spring of 1943 in Bavaria he observed a pair for 850 hours. As the author himself noted, on a nine-to-five basis, it worked out at five solid months of research. 'One of the chief joys of watching them in prison,' he wrote, 'was that they inhabited another world than I. They lived wholly and enviably to themselves, unconcerned in our fatuous politics, without the limitations imposed all about us by our knowledge. They lived only in the moment, without foresight and with memory only of things of immediate practical concern to them.'[51]

In Britain about 100,000 pairs breed, mainly north and west of a line between the Severn and Humber (there are no more than five pairs in Ireland). Elsewhere, it is seen

The classic study of the common redstart was made by poet and scholar John Buxton, while he was incarcerated by the Germans during the Second World War.

on spring and autumn passage, especially on the east coast. It is commonly associated with dramatic arrivals of migrants that are known as 'falls' (see Garden Warbler, page 373). The most remarkable of these was the 'great fall' of September 1965 – an event famous both in literature and in birdwatching lore. It was thought to involve Scandinavian migrants heading on a south-south-west bearing for Iberia, which were then caught up and forced down by a belt of overcast conditions and heavy rain.[52]

Migrants turned up from Fair Isle in Shetland south to Suffolk, but the fall was at its most spectacular in the latter county. On a two-mile (3-km) walk south from Walberswick on 3 September one blessed observer logged 15,000 common redstarts (along with 8000 wheatears, 4000 pied flycatchers, 3000 garden warblers and 1500 whinchats), an average of almost two redstarts for every step he took. There were similar ratios at nearby Minsmere – common redstart (15,000), wheatear (10,000) and pied flycatcher (5000) – while in the 24-mile (40-km) coastal stretch between the towns of Sizewell and Hopton there were an estimated half a million birds. Some were seen 'dropping out of the cloud like rain-drops' and at Lowestoft two people had redstarts land on their shoulders.[53] At Minsmere reserve it was one of the rare occasions when migrants could be seen both outside and *inside* the hides.[54] The birds' almost magical abun-dance, expressed so eloquently in the shivering tails of a hundred thousand redstarts, was the most powerful demonstration of the miracle of migration and among the greatest ornithological spectacles recorded in these islands.

Whinchat, *Saxicola rubetra*. This summer migrant is the less brightly patterned of the two chats and, while it shares the family penchant for exposed perches, a whin-chat working along a barbed-wire fence often chooses to sit on one of the lower strands. The males are striking with their orange-buff throats and dark cheek-patches, but females can resemble stonechats and the similarities between the two may account for Gilbert White's repeated but mistaken assertion that the whinchat was a resident bird.[55]

The problem was compounded by the old tendency for country people to use the same vernacular names for both species. Stonechats and whinchats were once equally known as the 'furze chat' (Sussex–Cornwall), 'furze chuck' (East Anglia), 'furze hacker' (Hampshire) and 'gorse chat' (Yorkshire).[56] At least the gorse association was accurate. The loss of scrubby commons and rough gorse-dominated ground also explains the whinchat's retreat to the upland areas of western Britain and Ireland. In rural Wales, where it is also called the *Crec yr Eithin* (gorse chat), it remains a common bird, with about one-third (5000–6000 pairs) of the British breeding population.[57]

The stonechat is one of the few insectivores to tough it out through the British and Irish winter.

Stonechat, *Saxicola torquata*. Stonechats are one of our few resident insectivores and, like most of the others (see Wren, page 332) they are highly susceptible to bad winter weather. It is this ecological restriction that partly accounts for the stonechat's strong bias towards southern and western coastal areas.

With his curling white half-collar, black face and warm rusty underparts, the male is a bright, conspicuous bird. Both sexes are easy to see because of their strong liking for the crowns of bushes, posts and other prominent perches. They routinely sit on top of drystone walls or isolated buildings and coastal tank blocks, but the species has no clear connection with stony habitats, as the whinchat does with gorse. One wonders, therefore, what should be made of the bird in W. H. Auden's poem 'The Wanderer'?

lonely on fell as chat,
By pot-holed becks
A bird stone-haunting, an unquiet bird.

Possibly Auden knew the old Scottish lore which identified the stonechat as a creature of occult powers, an association that suits the dark imagery connected with the poem's eponymous wanderer.[58] The last phrase also matches the stonechat. When disturbed, it becomes

highly agitated and maintains a constant harsh, scolding call. But it is this tacking sound – like 'two pebbles struck together' – that really explains the stone connections in the name, while the inhabitant of pot-holed becks is usually the following chat, the wheatear.[59] If one had to identify Auden's bird then that species would be a safer bet.

Northern Wheatear, *Oenanthe oenanthe*. VN: Stonechat (Orkney). An unexpected flash of white across the bare fields of early March or the sudden appearance of a bright, buff-throated bird that alternates an almost defiant military stance with a nervous head-bowing action, is usually our first experience of wheatear. And it is often all the more welcome for involving the first summer visitor of the whole season.

Wheatears are birds of enormous character, which seems evident in the extraordinary migration performed by some 'far eastern' populations. They have steadily expanded their Asiatic range across the Bering Strait into Alaska, yet the New World birds still winter in Africa and undertake a staggering two-way journey of 15,600 miles (26,000km). Only a relatively short stretch of tundra now separates the 'eastern' birds from their western counterparts, which have pressed into Arctic Canada from the other direction. Their migration, by contrast, is a mere 7000-mile (11,265-km) odyssey and includes a non-stop transatlantic flight of 1500–2000 miles (2500–3330km). Each wheatear weighs about 1 ounce (28gm).

Testimony to our many responses to the bird is the fact that Peter Conder, former director of the RSPB and the species' chief biographer, unearthed 90 vernacular names. Almost all are now lost but they once covered many aspects of its lifestyle, from the harsh vocalisations ('chick-chack'), the love of open country ('fallow-chat', 'coney-chuck') or upland scree ('stone-chucker') to the distinctive bobbing and bounding behaviour ('clod-hopper') or simply the blaze of white on the rear ('white tail').[60] Its present name, 'wheatear', is a reference to the white rump. It derives from two Old English words, *hwit*, 'white', and *aers*, 'rump' or 'backside'. It may have evolved or been modified to 'ear' when arse acquired its ribald connotations in the seventeenth century. It is notable that subsequent authors invented all kinds of more discreet connections – it was said to have white ears or to depart in the harvest season or arrive at the time of ploughing – rather than confront the earthier Saxon facts.[61]

Today the bird's range is biased towards the western halves of both Britain and Ireland and, while it has always been commonest in stony upland country, it was once found over many lowland heaths and downs grazed

Thrush and Chat family *Turdidae*

by sheep or other herbivores. In the 1950s the deliberate spread of the myxomatosis virus had a destructive impact well beyond the suppurating eyes of its main victim. The loss of rabbits led to a knock-on decline of habitat suitable for wheatears and the bird has been in retreat almost ever since, particularly south of a line from the Humber to the Severn.

Wheatears are further associated with rabbits because they are hole-nesting birds and at one time regularly used abandoned burrows. They will also take to many man-made locations such as drainage pipes and holes in walls.[62] Bert Axell had been fond of the species ever since he found a wheatear clutch in an old tin can at the age of four. During his post-war years as warden at Dungeness in Kent, he provided them with nest sites by part-burying old .303 ammunition boxes in the shingle. He also listed their use of 'a wellington boot, a trilby hat, cardboard boxes, the side of a wrecked dinghy, various parts of flying bombs and destroyed tanks, crevices in broken concrete, various tin cans and . . . under rusty pieces of corrugated iron sheeting'.[63]

Wheatear is one of those small passerines – skylark and ortolan are the two other good examples – whose culinary past is difficult to comprehend and now seems positively obscene. Yet at one time they were eaten in their thousands. Shepherds on the Sussex Downs gained an important supplement to their income by supplying them to fashionable hotels and restaurants in towns like Brighton and Eastbourne. In his tour of Britain in the 1720s Daniel Defoe saw them on sale in Tunbridge Wells: 'they have from the South-Downs, the bird call'd a wheatear, or as we may call them, the English ortolans, the most delicious taste for a creature of one mouthful, for 'tis little more, that can be imagin'd.'[64] Both the Sussex trade and the popularity of wheatears pre-dated Defoe by at least a century. Charles II is reputed to have bestowed a baronetcy on a local family partly for their liberal supply of wheatears to the palace.[65]

The season ran from St James's Day (25 July) until the last week of September, and birds were trapped in horse-hair nooses cunningly placed at the entrance to specially dug shallow pits, which the hole-loving wheatears found difficult to resist. The birds were then sold for around 18 pence a dozen and in a good year a shepherd could expect to earn £4–20. W. H. Hudson suggested that occasionally it could be as high as £40 and repeated the tale of a couple of working traps near Beachy Head, who secured 100 dozen ('so many that he could not thread them on crow-

The northern wheatear performs one of the most extraordinary migrations of any bird in the world.

348

quills in the usual manner'). Instead the shepherd took off his round frock – his wife did the same with her petticoat – and they used them as sacks for the 1200 birds.[66] Sometimes their appetite got the better of some gourmets and they would actively seek recently caught wheatears out on the downs. The custom was to place a penny wherever they took a bird from the shepherd's unmanned traps.

Although it was probably the ploughing of the old downland sheepwalks that triggered the wheatear's permanent decline in southern England, Hudson was passionate in his denunciation of those who ate the birds. 'It is not fair that it should be killed merely to enable London stockbrokers, sporting men, and other gorgeous persons who visit the coast, accompanied by ladies with yellow hair, to feed every day on "ortolans" at the big Brighton hotels.'[67] Eventually enough people added 'amen' to Hudson's sermon and the slaughter was outlawed.

Isabelline Wheatear, *O. isabellina*, and **Pied Wheatear**, *O. pleschanka*, are two eastern European species that occur as extreme vagrants in Britain and Ireland (19 and 44 records respectively by 2001). One of each was involved in a remarkable piece of ornithological good fortune:

On May 28, 1977 Peter Allard found an Isabelline Wheatear at Winterton in Norfolk. Unfortunately it only stayed for one day. It remains the only record for the county. On exactly the same date, one year later, he found at the same place the first county record of a Pied Wheatear, a first-summer male which frequently sang. It too remained only for one day. The following year, you can imagine how many birders turned up at Winterton on May 28, known for several years as 'Wheatear Day'. Unfortunately, the coincidence has not been repeated![68]

Ring Ouzel, *Turdus torquatus*. VN: Rouzel (birders). An unusual thrush for being both an upland specialist and a summer migrant, it occurs almost exclusively in Europe but the range is fragmented and appears on the breeding atlas as an arc of high-altitude 'islands' spread south-east from Ireland to Iran. The winter range of British and northern European birds is even more restricted – the montane areas of southern Spain and north-west Africa.

Fifty years of decline have only added to the cachet attaching to ring ouzels. Whether a chance meeting with a migrant on the coast or a bird located on its breeding grounds, the sense of occasion is often bound up with an initial mistake. The pleasure is watching the blackbird-lookalike steadily resolve into something very distinctive and much more exciting (there are just 8300 ring-ouzel pairs in Britain and Ireland). On close inspection it is bigger than its common relative, longer-tailed, longer-winged and, should it fly, it usually produces a 'stony' chacking sound never made by any blackbird. Even when a bird is facing away, the flight feathers are edged with a lovely pale frosting and when it turns round it declares itself with the bold white crescent (a subtler creamy buff in females).

Encountering the species on its breeding grounds is undoubtedly the most satisfying, since the simple, repeated fluting song is 'full of the *genius loci*' and 'sweetly wild'.[69] The host of old vernacular names ('fell blackbird', 'mountain thrush', 'heath throstle', 'tor ouzel', 'hill chack', 'mountain colley') offers an almost complete roster of its favourite country. It joins an elite group of passerines that will breed up to an altitude of 3750 feet (1140m), although they also occupy the steep gulleys cut by hill streams, abandoned quarries or rough rocky edges of moorland and hilltops. There is an Ouzelden Clough (above Ouzelden Brook) in exactly this kind of country on the west bank of Derwent Reservoir, Derbyshire.

Gilbert White knew the ring ouzel only as a migrant and in 1767 wrote a telling four-line passage: 'Some birds, haunting with missel-thrushes, and feeding on the berries of the yew-tree, which answered to the description of the *merula torquata*, or ring-ousel, were lately in the neighbourhood. I employed some people to procure me a specimen, but without success.'[70] The key sentence is the last (although White got several in subsequent years, describing them as 'juicy and well flavoured').[71] Ring ouzels are unapproachable and unpredictable. A distressed bird can fly away for miles. Their susceptibility to modern disturbance, from hill walkers and even hang-gliders, may be instrumental in their disappearance from old strongholds across the entire Celtic fringe and northern England.

Common Blackbird, *Turdus merula*. VN: Blacky/ie (birders). It is a bird that requires little introduction. There are thought to be more than six million pairs in Britain and Ireland. Wren and chaffinch are the only two species that exceed this total. The wren alone is as universally widespread – from the Hebrides to the outermost headlands of County Kerry and Cork in the west, from Dover to Hermaness in the east.

The blackbird's nest, with the female's bill and tail poking just above the lip, is often a long-remembered detail from the paradise of childhood and our first magical encounter with the reproductive strategy of the whole class *Aves*. In winter the rather crudely

The blackbird has one of the most beautiful songs of all our birds.

constructed bowls of grass and mud are highly visible in the leafless bushes and hedgerows, and even when occupied they can be almost as obvious. Blackbirds will build above doorways, next to windows, in garden sheds, ice buckets, plant pots, lobster creels and a hundred other inauspicious locations:

A blackbird nested in the engine compartment of a working forklift truck over the Easter holiday. When we returned on the Tuesday the hen continued to sit as work resumed, being driven around the site from 7.30 a.m. until 4.30 p.m. on a daily basis. Five eggs were laid and four chicks hatched, which the hen fed by leaving the vehicle whenever it stopped going forward, and returning with food when it was next stationary.[72]

The versatility also extends to construction materials. Eric Simms recalled a blackbird that made a nest at his bomber station in 1944 entirely from the metal strips used to confuse German radar, fragments of which tended to float around the airfield.[73]

If anything, blackbirds are even more experimental in matters of food. They have been known to eat snakes, frogs, small mammals and to clear a whole lily pond of its newt population, while in Scotland an enterprising blackbird learnt how to catch trout hatchlings from the rearing ponds and passed on the technique to blackbird neighbours.[74]

Some years ago a concrete platform across the infant River Welland caused it to drop about two feet where it passes through Medbourne on the Leicester/ Northants border. In the late summer the flow was confined to a channel cut in the middle of the concrete forming a small waterfall. Below this a shoal of fish congregated and at intervals a tiny fish would attempt a 'salmon leap' up the waterfall. Occasionally an unlucky individual would become stranded on the concrete and immediately a cock blackbird would fly down and take the fish. The licencee of the adjacent 'Neville Arms' said it was a regular occurrence at that time of year.[75]

Another individual has been observed behaving like a miniature skua, chasing a kingfisher until it dropped its fish, which the assailant then retrieved.[76] In addition to these more unusual strategies, blackbirds consume a huge conventional range of insects, ground invertebrates and fruits, as well as a spectrum of human foodstuffs from the birdtable.

It is the garden bird most likely to be viewed with feelings of personal intimacy, and such familiarity often leads to a sense of partial ownership: 'We call our resident blackbird "Jet".'[77] Equally striking: 'when I moved into this bungalow I *inherited* [my italics] a very tame blackbird.'[78] The personalised names sent to us for *Birds Britannica* included Billy, Blackie,[79] Mr and Mrs B,[80] Beaky and Fluff,[81] the Alderman ('because the white feathers round his neck looked like a municipal chain of office');[82] Nyja and Nyjella ('after the kitchen goddess, Nigella Lawson')[83] and Nesta, a bird that built and laid eggs in December 1997 in a Christmas tree outside Norwich City Hall (Nesta's story appeared in most of the national newspapers, two local television stations, BBC Radio Four's *Today* programme and Radio Five).

The names testify to widespread affection, which blackbirds sometimes repay with remarkable tameness. Food is often, if not always, the primary motivation. 'He will take raisins out of my husband's hand and walk into the house when the door is open, completely ignoring the cat, who is luckily very short-sighted.'[84] And 'My Grandmother would call to a blackbird by name from her front garden until the bird came to her. It was often

A wide range of fruits are only one part of the blackbird's extremely varied diet.

out of sight and more often than not well across the road. Its reward was always food. The bird also used to nest within cotoneaster bushes on my Grandmother's veranda.'[85]

Recipients of such trust prefer to think it is more than cupboard love. 'Every year I'm compelled to photograph the blackbirds which bring their family into our house and sit quietly on the kitchen mat for a long time. I like to imagine he or she is saying thank you for all the tasty morsels they were given whilst feeding their young.'[86]

Occasionally a bird seems to show awareness of the relationship:

One freezing cold winter's evening, when it had snowed quite heavily, the dogs drew my attention to a noise outside the back door, where I discovered Billy's current mate calling loudly in a very distraught state. I followed her as she flew to the end of the garden where I saw poor Billy hanging upside down, caught by one wing which was impaled on a hawthorn branch covered with frozen snow. Fetching a step ladder, I managed to free him, during which time he made no attempt to struggle or peck me, when released both

birds flew off, but next morning they were back as usual for their food. Undoubtedly the female saved her mate's life that night and knew I could help.[87]

There is unquestionably a mutual sharing in the exchange, if not exactly as the human partner might wish to see it, but its advantages to the birds are perfectly illustrated in Billy's rescue. They are just as striking when expressed in statistical terms. Suburban blackbirds live at densities up to 10 times higher than their relatives on farmland, and the number of fledged young produced per nest is also higher than in other habitats.[88]

The blackbirds' love of our gardens is intriguing for other reasons. Studies of populations in Poland's Bialowieza Forest, some of Europe's last primeval woodland, indicate that blackbirds were originally birds of the high tops, their dark coloration and low-frequency song (which travels better than high-frequency sound in thick vegetation) having strong parallels among canopy-dwelling thrush species of tropical rainforest.[89] The findings indicate first that blackbirds would have been resident in the interior of Britain's own original wildwood long before humans arrived, and second that they would not initially have benefited from the open country created by our agricultural ancestors.

Their complete adaptation to the human environment was, in fact, a relatively recent development. What little evidence there is suggests that the commonest family member throughout Britain was originally the song thrush, while the blackbird only began a steady advance across northern Scotland and into English towns and gardens in the eighteenth and nineteenth centuries. With the song thrush's subsequent decline, the blackbird now outnumbers it by a ratio of almost 4.5:1, but their old respective positions are in many ways borne out in the realms of poetry, where the emphasis was far more on the once abundant song thrush.

Not that the lack of literary references offers a measure of blackbird song. Many consider it equal if not superior to that of its smaller relative. 'The onset of spring for me is represented by the incomparable song of the blackbird, even if it does wake me very early in the morning.'[90] Others share that high opinion: 'Having ruled out close contenders like song thrush and nightingale, my supreme champion is blackbird. I admire the languid excellence and polished ease of a male singing in his third year. I ignore the sometimes poor or scratchy ending. The song is marked by fluent and beautiful fluted notes. It is the epitome of summer in a woodland glade or dusty suburban street.'[91]

The spontaneously composed freshness of the song was once apparently proverbial: 'to whistle like a blackbird' was to do something easily. The many attempts to convey this quality have thrown up a consistent pattern: 'a certain languid ease of delivery';[92] 'The delivery is lazy . . . gives the impression of sleepy contentment';[93] 'trolled out . . . as if by a being at peace and supremely happy'.[94] W. H. Hudson thought its careless beauty came 'nearer to human music than any other bird songs', while the tone was even suggestive of the human voice.[95] People sometimes detect snatches of our own melodies or speech in the performance, while blackbirds often seem to be in conversation with one another. Hudson called them 'blackbird concerts' and Edward Thomas suggested in his poem 'Adlestrop' that the birds could sling their collective net of music across an entire county:

Yes, I remember Adlestrop –
The name, because one afternoon
Of heat the express-train drew up there
Unwontedly. It was late June . . .

And for that minute a blackbird sang
Close by, and round him, mistier,
Farther and farther, all the birds
Of Oxfordshire and Gloucestershire.

I wonder why Thomas drew the line at these counties. Blackbirds are so common and ubiquitous and perform so regularly at both dawn and in the evening, it is more than whimsy to suggest that there are times of day when they form one immense chorus, with millions in voice at the same moment, not only in Britain but right across Europe.

For all its melodic purity, the species is equally renowned for 'a high-mettled nervousness easily touched off by the slightest incident'.[96] The consequences of igniting the short fuse are twofold. A bird will fly away and burrow into the nearest dark cover with a 'sudden, "hysterical", shrill, screaming chatter'.[97] Or it will set up a loud persistent 'chink chink' alarm call, when it stands, tail cocked and its whole body convulsing with each metallic note. It will go on almost indefinitely in response to a threat, real or sometimes imaginary. Owls and cats are classic triggers (cats are major predators). Also apparently alarming is the onset of night, when the irritating chorus seems self-perpetuating, one roost bird setting off another.

At one time blackbirds had good cause to be afraid of the dark because they were hunted in their roosts to provide food for the country table. All of the thrushes were once widely eaten and the price for a dozen (sixpence in 1370; tenpence in 1575; a shilling in 1633) was regulated by statute for centuries. Blackbirds were killed until at least the 1940s and almost certainly later, judging from the testimony of an old Essex poacher, Ted Pearman, who could recall his beat along the Roydon hedgerows, when the birds were dazzled with a torch and stunned with a catapult.[98] In the bitter winter of 1947, cut off from the outside by snow, some Norfolk residents, *in extremis*, resorted to trapping blackbirds and sparrows with mouse traps once the supply of rabbits and pigeons was exhausted. The birds were cooked in a pie along with carrots and bacon.[99] However, blackbird was not always a last resort:

The farmworker we knew had a chicken run and inside this was an inner run. In the winter – we used to have hard winters in those days – he'd leave the door open and scatter corn. Then the birds would get inside and he'd come along and shut the door. He never plucked blackbirds. We used to just cut them down and skin them, taking the breast meat and flesh from off the legs. These would all go in a blackbird pie. Sixty years ago it was a real feast.[100]

The strangest and most famous of all blackbird pies is the one described in the nursery rhyme:

Sing a song of sixpence, a pocket full of rye;
Four and twenty blackbirds baked in a pie.
When the pie was opened the birds began to sing;
Was not that a dainty dish to put before a king.

It was a song of childhood that clearly puzzled some of its audience: 'as a girl I couldn't work out how the birds could have survived the oven'.[101] The answer lay in the timing. Blackbirds – sometimes even mice and snakes – were added live just before the 'surprise pie', an invention of the Tudor kitchen, was served and cut. The birds' escape was supposed to provide entertainment and, as author Josephine Addison notes, probably a good deal of consternation to the guests.[102]

Blackbird bucks the conventional trend in Europe's language of colour by being a black bird that is not generally associated with evil or bad luck. Yet neither is it

entirely free of the taint. In his poem 'A Blackbird Singing', R. S. Thomas felt there was 'a suggestion of dark places about it'. The reference would not be lost in Cumbria where it is held that: 'if a blackbird should peck against your window the impending doom will be either a death in the family or amongst close friends. I am not sure how this originated but can vouch for its authenticity, since it has happened twice to me. Once was on the sudden death of my father.'[103] Miss A. Timbrell tells us that blackbirds were especially suspect for young lovers, and there is an old St Valentine's Day belief that a young woman could tell the career of her future spouse from the first bird she saw (see also Goldfinch, page 450). A blackbird indicated a clergyman, but whether this was viewed as good or bad luck is not clear.[104]

Fieldfare, *Turdus pilaris*. VN: Feltie, Fulfer. Had this northern bird been only a vagrant it would be among the most sought-after rarities on the British list. As it is, roughly a million arrive each year. Yet fieldfares are still held in high regard both for their striking appearance (the Spaniards appropriately call them the royal thrush, *Zorzal real*) and for their status as a classic herald of winter. At that time of year there are few sights more beautiful than a flock of these 'tough, harsh-voiced skewbald' birds head up, chest out, all facing the same direction and spread evenly across a snow-dusted field.[105] Should they take flight, they do so in a flourish of silvery-white underwings and loud vigorous chacking calls.

SING A SONG OF SIXPENCE

1. Sing a song of six - pence, A pock - et full of rye:

Four and twen - ty black birds Baked in a pie:

The surprise pie, which involved concealing live animals and birds under a pre-baked pastry crust, was the origin of this famous nursery rhyme.

The fieldfare is loved as much for its frost-defying toughness as it is for its beautiful colours.

A flock of fieldfares ransacking a hawthorn hedge of its red berries or foraging across a snow-strewn field is a classic vision of midwinter.

The sound is perfectly in keeping with the fieldfare's robust character, which seems all the more impressive in the hard bare winter landscape. 'Fieldfares . . . are strong purposeful birds. I have watched them leave a thicket roost at daybreak in a gale – the wavering curtseying flock bored its way forwards with ease, with a zest in overcoming difficulty, and they flew high, while bigger birds, gulls and wood-pigeons, sought advantage by keeping close to the ground.'[106]

Their routine arrival each autumn has been recognised in Britain at least since Chaucer's day ('Above all the birds of winter, the frosty feldefares') when they were trapped and eaten, a practice made particularly profitable by their highly gregarious behaviour. The notorious old Hampshire sportsman Colonel Peter Hawker gave an account in his diary of 2 February 1831 of how birds could be taken in huge numbers:

An extraordinary influx of fieldfares, not less than 20,000, dispersed round Keyhaven and Westover, and so tame that you might have kept firing from morning till night, though I found it impossible to get more than five at one shot . . . It was quite laughable when the storm ceased this afternoon to see and hear the levy *en masse* of tag-rag popgunners blazing away at

the fieldfare. The whole country for miles around was in one incessant state of siege . . .[107]

Hawker later noted that 'I never ate more delicious birds in my life'. He believed that such a large concentration came only once a century. He was right. In March 1977 there was a comparable roost of 25,000 birds at Brandon, Warwickshire, but autumn groups of fieldfare seldom number more than a few hundred.

Every autumn, the depletion of the Scandinavian rowan crop triggers the fieldfare's nomadic wanderings, which can carry them as far south as the African coast. Once British-bound birds have crossed the North Sea they congregate in open pasture or ploughland to hunt for invertebrates. Further bad weather will push them on west but they also take fruit when the ground is frozen, particularly holly, hawthorn and dog rose. Fieldfares are adept at finding the last hedgerows with a good crop of berries. They will also come to large gardens where late windfall apples are available, and occasionally they resort to not-so-large gardens:

In order to develop our modest 30 × 20 yard urban back garden I planted a large specimen of Cotoneaster, *Cotoneaster cornubia*, to provide a beacon for passing

The song thrush was recently voted Britain's favourite songster.

thrushes. I was not wildly optimistic when a small crop of fruits adorned the branches. However, one frosty morning not long after the turn of the year, there was a fieldfare feeding on the berries. What joy! In barely six months the policy had worked and whilst subsequent winters have seen both fieldfare and redwing nothing will match the sheer delight of that first bird.[108]

Most fieldfares have made the return journey to the Continent by late April, but in 1967 the first ever pair remained in Orkney to nest and raised three young. Since 1973 fieldfares have bred annually except for one season, and in the last 15 years 2–13 pairs have been spread from northern Scotland as far south as Kent.

Song Thrush, *Turdus philomelos*. VN: Mavis, Throstle, Songy. It may lack the improvisatory genius of the nightingale (or Marsh Warbler, see page 367) and the serene meditative tones of the blackbird, but this species is an enormously popular songster. Lord Grey felt that 'if birds were to be regarded as endeavouring to please us by song, the thrush should be put first among British birds'.[109] In an RSPB poll of songbirds that is exactly what happened.[110] And our ancestors clearly shared the opinion, because in the 1860s British settlers took song

thrushes with them to the Antipodes. Although it failed to flourish in Australia in the way the blackbird has done, the song thrush spread quickly and widely in New Zealand and is one of the commonest garden birds throughout both main islands, and also occurs on some smaller offshore islands.

Its song is delivered with a bold, loud, bell-like clarity and the impression created is of happiness pure and simple. Yet the performance itself is by no means simplistic. An individual bird has about 100 different phrases to draw upon, which it does at random and then repeats each unit several times. There is remarkable constancy in some of the song elements, many of them being passed on from one generation to the next. In the 1920s Lord Grey noted that one common phrase resembles the words 'did-he-do-it'. Many song thrushes today incorporate the same fragment into their performance, having borrowed the passage from neighbours. (One wonders, incidentally, to what shaded moment of the Holocene one would have to travel to unearth the Ur I of 'did-he-do-its'?) The resemblance to human phrases compounds the sense of a bird almost directly communicating with us.

Some of the repertoire is also copied from other sources, including man-made objects like trim-phones,

Song thrush chicks often leave the nest before they can fly and are routinely carried indoors by concerned homeowners. Despite the good intentions, these 'rescue' efforts cause more problems than they solve.

while a further pool of borrowed sound derives from neighbouring species. Lord Grey recalled a song thrush at Fallodon that could produce an excellent imitation of a white-faced whistling duck *Dendocygna viduata* in his collection. (I clearly remember a bird 20 years ago at Holkham, Norfolk, that had perfected, by chance – since it could not have copied it directly – the asthmatic call of an Indian game bird, grey francolin *Francolinus pondicerianus*. I could never hear the sound without it awakening some glimmer of mist-filled winter dawns in eastern Rajasthan.)

The memory most often awakened by this unmistakable song is the sound of other song thrushes at other moments and other locations, which have built up layer upon layer in our unconscious. One bird thus taps into an entire memory bank of countryside experience, which is why song-thrush song is almost indivisible from our sense of the British landscape. There is even some taxonomic justification for thinking of British song thrushes differently from their continental counterparts, since most of Europe is occupied by a separate, nominate, race, *philomelos*, which is much more a shy woodland bird.

Before everything, however, it is our sense of the song as a soundtrack to the British countryside – or perhaps, more accurately, the English countryside – that has inspired the long tradition of thrush poetry. The ideas are perfectly expressed in Robert Browning's 'Home-Thoughts from Abroad' ('Oh, to be in England/Now that April's there'), which includes the oft-quoted lines:

That's the wise thrush; he sings each song twice over,
Lest you should think he never could recapture
The first fine careless rapture!

Even better known is Thomas Hardy's 'Darkling Thrush', in which the poet contrasts the bird's 'full-hearted evensong/Of joy illimited' with the exhausted winter landscape. ('The ancient pulse of germ and birth/Was shrunken hard and dry'.) Hardy's emotional responses to the bird hinge on one of those remarkable coincidences in which he excelled. He heard it on the last day of 1900 and the death of the physical environment was extended to the epoch, so that the sense of hope expressed by the thrush became a comment both on that moment and on our shared destiny in the new century. While it is a wonderful evocation of the mood-transforming power of a bird, one cannot help feeling that there is an element of stage management in Hardy's experience.

One intuits much the same of Ted Hughes' extraordinary poem 'Thrushes', which stands well outside the conventional traditions of thrush verse by dwelling on the bird's hunting prowess. Hughes' thrushes are 'Terrifying'. Through the magnifying lens of his imagery, their worm-tugging antics on our back lawns acquire the scale and savagery of a kill on the African savanna. 'Nothing but bounce and/stab/And a ravening second'. Hughes' responses are surely contrived partly for their shock value but, like so much of his nature poetry, are rooted in observation.

Thrushes are truly voracious feeders: 'no thrush ever seems to have had enough to eat,' wrote one commentator, 'I have seen one tip over backwards when a worm it was pulling out of the ground broke and part sprang back into its face.' The young birds in the nest are described as opening their mouths as wide as their shoulders.[111] A contributor who brought up a thrush – 'Precious' – on a diet of cat food wholeheartedly agreed: 'It was amazing how much that bird could eat AND how often. He seemed happiest when fed at least every twenty minutes, which meant I carried bird and catfood with me everywhere. As soon as the dawn chorus started he would let me know it was time for breakfast. An American visitor was heard to remark, "That bird eats more than I do". I didn't get much done that spring.'[112]

Notwithstanding Hughes' accuracy, the great modern poet of the thrush is undoubtedly Edward Thomas and it seems no mere coincidence that his poetic vision was steeped in a sense of the English landscape. Thrushes and blackbirds appear in 15 of his tragically small oeuvre (he produced 142 poems in just two years before being killed on the Western Front) and three poems dwell specifically on the impact of thrush song. Thomas rehearsed many of the ideas discussed above – the feelings of hope and joy inherent in the voice and the sense that it can communicate directly with us – but there is none of the manufactured moment as in Hardy's great poem. Instead the language is plain, (deceptively) simple, even repetitive like the thrush itself, yet without Thomas losing any sense that the song is a powerful statement about all life:

I hear the thrush, and I see
Him alone at the end of the lane
Near the bare poplar's tip,
Singing continuously.

Is it more that you know
Than that, even as in April,
So in November,
Winter is gone that must go?

The song thrush is the only molluscicide we should tolerate in our gardens.

Or is all your lore
Not to call November November,
And April April,
And Winter Winter – no more?

But I know the months all
And their sweet names, April,
May and June and October,
As you call and call

I must remember
What died in April
And consider what will be born
Of a fair November;

And April I love for what
It was born of, and November
For what it will die in,
What they are and what they are not.

Sometimes bird books suggest we are so familiar with song thrush that it barely needs a description. In fact we have a long history of confusing mistle and song thrush (occasionally, we even throw in a strikingly mottled young or female blackbird) and people still talk regularly of *the* thrush as if it were just one bird. The confusion extends to the literature, where it is occasionally difficult to tell which bird is being referred to. Lockwood argues that our ancestors partly resolved the problem by reserving 'thrush' as a name for mistle thrush and another word, 'throstle', to indicate its smaller relative.

'Throstle' goes back at least to the fourteenth century (hence Chaucer's old 'throstel' in the *Parlement of Fowles*) and in modified form gave rise to a group of surnames – Thrustle, Thrussell, Throssell and Thrush –

apparently starting life as a nickname for those as cheerful as the bird itself.[113] The word seems to have the strongest links with the English Midlands. It was used by the Warwickshire poet Michael Drayton in the sixteenth century ('the jocund throstle') and one of our contributors recalls it as a Nottinghamshire name for song thrush until at least the middle of last century. It also appears on the badge of West Bromwich Albion Football Club, and 'The Baggies' is apparently interchangeable with 'The Throstles' as the team's nickname. 'The club's mascot is a huge thrush and for many years until recent ground reconstruction, the electronic scoreboard had a large model of the bird sitting on top of it. The supporters' club is still known as The Throstles.'[114]

The other regional name for song thrush was 'mavis', a word derived from the French *mauvis*, although its

Redwings are winter visitors and are usually first heard as they fly overhead on cold starlit September nights.

fication with me: "It isn't a song thrush, it's a mavis".'[115]

Despite the species' usual billing as a resident bird, Scottish song thrushes and those in northern England are partly migratory, many passing the winter in Ireland. British birds are also joined by the paler, greyer continental birds as they head south for Iberia, where they still run the risk of hunters and the surviving Mediterranean appetite for thrush pâté. However we can perhaps take comfort that thrushes have withstood human pressures since the time of the ancient Greeks. In the *Odyssey* Homer wrote of roosting thrushes caught in nets for the table, while in ancient Rome they were such a prized food that they were trapped and fattened in special thrush-rearing farms.[116]

The British races (there is an endemic race in the Outer Hebrides and Skye, *hebridensis*, distinct from the mainland race *clarkei*) are thought to be only marginally affected by the continental harvest, but are proving highly susceptible to agricultural change. In the last 25 years song thrushes have declined to just 1.4 million pairs, while song thrushes on farmland are down by two-thirds. Another possible threat to the bird is the widespread use of pesticides in back gardens. The commonness of this much-loved species may be an issue that lies in our own hands and turns more precisely on our choice of molluscicide. Do we want the poison in pellet form from a box? Or would we prefer the snail-hammering bird with the spotted chest, the bell-like song and the speckled eggs of 'blue which year in, year out, never fail to prove more decisively than any other fact that spring has really come'?[117]

Redwing, *Turdus iliacus*. Few sounds better reconcile us to the approach of winter than the gloriously atmospheric flight-call of this species. It is often heard on sharp starlit nights in September during the first redwing arrivals, and continues thereafter almost irrespective of conditions or place. It is all the more exciting for being heard in a built-up area where it brings a touch of northern wilderness to the inner city. The novelist John Fowles expressed many of our feelings for the birds when he wrote of them passing overhead during a cold-weather movement (albeit in Poitiers, France, where they are still eaten and apparently more highly regarded than quail or woodcock):[118]

It was three in the morning, the town absolutely silent and deserted and under a slight dank mist. A few street lights. Suddenly I became aware of countless thin voices, the unmistakable whistle of redwings. Everywhere. In the sky. On the roofs of the houses. A curious cry they have; a very thin, high-pitched, *glistening* whistle; an inbreath . . . I kept on thinking of

exact meaning is not clear. It is still used for the bird in Orkney and survives elsewhere in Scotland: 'My father's cousin from Lossiemouth still refers to song thrush as mavis. She seems to be unaware that they are also called song thrushes, since she once argued identi-

the adjective glistening. Like a sudden small gleam of old silver in a dark room. Strange remote beautiful sounds . . . So absolutely unexpected, and so full of special meaning for me; that I, of all the 60,000 people here, should have heard them.[119]

They are classic night-time migrants, although occasionally their movements can be observed by day. Eric Simms judged his experience of a redwing passage in Aberdeenshire on 26 October 1976 one of the great moments in his ornithological life. (Huge movements were noted simultaneously in other parts, with 40,000–70,000 over Kirkwall, Orkney, and more than 900 redwings killed in strikes on the North Ronaldsay lighthouse.[120])

I saw the first parties coming in from the sea. Soon they began to cascade out of the sky pouring like a torrent of dark liquid into the bare canopies of the trees. For four hours redwing were coming into the little Aberdeenshire valley at Cruden Bay in their thousands and by 10.00 hr some of the birds were down on the grass between the trees. Later I found a coastal strip some 24km long and 8km wide where every field, hedgerow, tree, copse and wood was alive with redwings. It was a staggering sight with the total number of birds beyond estimation.[121]

Among the commoner British thrushes, the redwing is second only to the fieldfare in terms of beauty and since the two species often occur together in nomadic winter flocks they provide a double spectacle. Perched birds show a bright rufous crescent along the flank, but the redwing's name really derives from the large patch of rufous chestnut across the whole of the underwing coverts, which are visible only in flight.

Most bird species from the far north have little contact with humans and usually exhibit remarkable tameness, but redwings buck the trend. They are far more flighty and nervous than other British thrushes. At the first signs of danger feeding birds retreat into the nearest trees and if disturbed from this refuge they often burst out, calling constantly and towering high into the sky in a way that suggests almost wild desperation.

Only extreme cold, to which they are highly vulnerable, brings a change in character. During the bitter winter of 1962/3 the only passerine that was a more frequent victim of cold was the common starling, while redwing corpses outnumbered fieldfare by more than four to one, reinforcing a sense of the other thrush's robust character. That winter very few redwings are thought to have survived in England, although some may have done so by

shedding their customary wariness and exploring new foods: they were observed coming to gardens to eat ox tongue, rich tea biscuits, cooked peas and cheese.[122] Even in normal conditions they will visit suburban and city gardens for windfall apples or for berries of holly, cotoneaster, pyracanthus and other exotic shrubs.

In an average winter as many as a million are thought to arrive in this country, although they are highly nomadic and move according to food supply or conditions. Hard frost and snow push them on further west, until the birds make a reverse journey as the weather becomes milder in late winter.

Unlike fieldfares, redwings are notable for singing before they leave in spring, although the off-season song is usually rather rambling, inward and almost self-conscious in quality, as if it was just a pre-performance warm-up. After the 1920s the full version – an even, pleasant liquid twittering – started to be heard in parts of north-west Scotland when a few pairs remained to breed. The population steadily built up over the next half-century until a total of 300 pairs was estimated in 1972. However this was revised downwards to 40–80 by the 1990s and in the last decade there have been no more than the lower figure.

Mistle Thrush, *Turdus viscivorus*. VN: Missie, Storm Cock (widespread); Felt (Northern Ireland). Compared with its smaller garden-dwelling relative, there is something impressive and much wilder about this thrush. It is partly a function of its habitat, which tends to be rugged open country, sometimes at quite high altitude and usually characterised by tall isolated trees. The bird has a habit of flying much higher than song thrush, sailing overhead with a characteristically slow, rolling trajectory. On the ground it is far more unapproachable and maintains a bold, alert stance or moves in a series of long vigorous bounding hops.

Tall trees are famously exploited by mistle thrushes as songposts, from which they deliver a repeated fluting phrase that is one of the earliest signs of spring. They even sing in autumn and are in full voice by late January (which explains a – vanished? – country name, 'Jeremy joy', a corruption of 'January joy'). The bird's complete indifference to the wind and rain at that time of year explains the more widespread vernacular alternative, 'storm cock'. The song is loud and far-carrying, but perhaps it is the acoustics associated with such a high perch that gives it a distinctive 'far-off' quality even when relatively close. Others have thought the delivery 'is suggestive of superciliousness'.[123] In complete contrast to song thrush, there is also a hint of sadness in the song, which somehow fits perfectly with the still, flat atmosphere of late winter.

The mistle thrush is often the first bird to sing on cold, clear days in January.

The mistle thrush has recently suffered declines, especially in agricultural areas, but earlier experienced a widespread and largely unexplained expansion throughout much of the nineteenth and twentieth centuries. It colonised large parts of northern Scotland and Ireland, where it had previously been unknown (now there are 90,000 pairs). While mistle thrushes remain unconfiding, they will enter gardens in autumn and winter in search of supplies of berries. In mainland Europe the bird has a long-standing relationship with mistletoe – thus the common and scientific names (from the plant's Latin name *Viscum*) – but British birds are more commonly associated with holly or hawthorn.

Mistle thrushes have a habit of taking up territory over one richly laden tree and defending the food supply against all-comers, sometimes for the whole of the winter. The bird's loud call – which is not unlike the sound of an old wooden football rattle – is unmistakable and conveys an uninviting mix of irritation and aggression. It usually follows up its vocal threat with dramatic swooping attacks, when the resemblance to a hunting

sparrowhawk may be an additional advantage. The holly connection gave rise to many regional names in Britain: 'holm thrush', 'hollin cock', 'holm cock', 'holm screech' (see *Flora Britannica* page 244) and corruptions of the last, like 'house screech' and 'homescreech'. Other names simply draw on the strident rattling call. 'I can remember my grandfather, who lived his whole life in Gloucestershire, referring to mistle thrushes as "stretchys".'[124] The word probably represents a long slow adaptation of the original Old English name *scruc* or *scric*.[125]

Mistle thrushes are aggressive in defence of territory and food, but even more so when protecting their own nests. Then they routinely chase off much larger birds like crows and magpies. They have even been known to drive away sparrowhawk and buzzard, to knock a barn owl clean off its perch and to attack and kill a jackdaw.[126] Most extraordinary of all is an old report of a peacock that strayed too close to a mistle-thrush nest and was eventually knocked over by the owners' frontal assaults.[127]

Warbler family *Sylviidae*

Cetti's Warbler, *Cettia cetti*. Named after an eighteenth-century Jesuit priest, this is one of the 'characters' of the warbler family. Among its unusual traits are its (unique) brick-red eggs and its tendency towards polygamy, the males mating with up to four partners. The habit of remaining in Britain throughout winter is also surprising, given that it was originally a bird of Mediterranean latitudes as far east as the Indus.

Perhaps most striking of all is the 'robust, abrupt and riveting song' – a series of explosive notes likened to a 'violent outburst of music' and rendered in several mnemonics.[1] The first bird ever to be seen in Britain was thought to be saying, 'is it safe? is it safe? see what you mean, see what you mean',[2] but the version that best expresses its personality was coined by George Yeates: 'What-yer . . . what-yer . . . what-yer . . . come-and-see-me-bet you-don't . . . bet you don't.'[3] Cetti's warblers sing regularly at night and seem to perform with equal gusto in midwinter, even with snow on the ground, when the general absence of bird song makes the sound all the more arresting.

While the vocalisations are loud and obvious, the bird itself is notoriously elusive. The BBC sound recordist Eric Simms thought it one of the most challenging species he had ever attemped to record in 30 years.[4] An unseen Cetti's will burst into song close to an observer, only for it to fall silent and then suddenly start up some distance away. People often think they are confronted with more than one bird and the effect is deliberate. The strategy 'has been named the Beau Geste Hypothesis after the novel by P. C. Wren in which the gallant legionnaire defended a desert fort by propping up dead bodies . . . to make it look as though there were many more defenders'.[5] By moving constantly from songpost to songpost, Cetti's creates the same impression and is thought to discourage possible competitors.

Its history as a British bird is relatively short and it is still no more than a rare vagrant to Ireland. The first record came in 1961 after many decades of expansion on continental Europe, but by the 1970s Cetti's seemed to be everywhere in southern England and at the end of the millennium there were almost 700 pairs, concentrated in Hampshire (171 singing males or pairs), Norfolk (143)

Cetti's warblers have quickly spread across southern England after first appearing in 1961.

and Somerset (90), with outlying clusters as far north as Anglesey.[6]

Zitting Cisticola, *Cisticola juncidis*. Also called the fan-tailed warbler, this tiny wren-sized bird is the only European representative of a predominantly African genus, although this particular species has a massive range across four continents. Its recent expansion northwards through France led to predictions of a Cetti's-like expansion, and in 1977 *British Birds* journal published a paper entitled 'When will the Fan-tailed Warbler colonise Britain?'. Unfortunately its susceptibility to cold winters has frustrated any real advance and to date there have been fewer than 10 records.

Should global warming ease a permanent passage across the Channel, then the zitting cisticola will supplant the reed bunting as chief minimalist (see page 463) among Britain's songbirds. A tuneless, high rasping note, the '*zit*' enshrined in its name, is repeated at intervals in a jerky songflight when the bird climbs as much as 100 feet (30m) into the air and often looks – and sounds – rather like a large flying insect.

Lanceolated Warbler, *Locustella lanceolata*. VN: Lancy (birders). This small relative of the grasshopper warbler arouses great interest among birdwatchers, partly because of its rarity and partly for its extraordinary fidelity to Fair Isle. 'Since the first western European record in September 1908 there have been a further 63 individuals (55 since 1972) of this skulking little treasure on the island. Other parts of Shetland can lay claim to another 14, bringing the county total to an impressive 78, while the rest of Britain has seen just 16.'[7] The concentration seems all the more remarkable given that the distance between the tiny island and the bird's main range east of the Ural mountains is more than 2000 miles (3300km).

Yet the main reason for the bird's hold on our imaginations is its gloriously eccentric behaviour: 'I have seen birds land on shoulders, walk over boots (including my own), and fly through legs. When you see them running along a ditch they have huge feet. It is this ability to run that makes them seem so mouse-like.'[8]

The finding of a lancy at The Plantation Trap, Fair Isle, September 1987 caused enormous excitement. Our £1000 scopes and £500 binoculars suddenly became irrelevant as the assembled masses got down on hands and knees to witness this mouse-like bird creeping about in the grass. Round and round the bowl-like depression in the bottom of the trap it crept, passing within inches of the nose ends of the admiring birders.[9]

On Fair Isle in September 1990 a friend spotted a small bird, which scurried into cover almost from under his

Lanceolated warblers are not so much tame as oblivious to human presence.

feet. I joined him and our odd-looking behaviour, as we walked slowly backwards and forwards peering at the ground, soon attracted others. It was quickly obvious that the bird creeping around like a mouse was a lancy and within a few minutes all the birders on the island were enjoying incredibly close views as it perched on someone's boot and crept across an outstretched hand! It was so confiding that we had to be careful we did not tread on it. We were all completely entranced by the tiny creature and when the time came to ring it, it was simply a matter of picking it up![10]

I had heard about a lancy at the Skerryholm 'tattie' rig and it had continued to show well throughout the day to many people who were leaving on that day's plane. In the afternoon I decided to go down to look at it myself and met several people, all of whom had said, 'They do look very mouse-like, don't they!' With this species that is a typical comment. But I remember thinking to myself that it was much more mouse-like than normal. It appeared again and it suddenly clicked – this WAS a mouse! Fortunately, the *real* bird was then found at the other end of the rig, but how many people in their rush to see a lancy before they left had got mouse on their list?[11]

Despite the bird's name, the song of a grasshopper warbler more closely resembles a fishing reel than an insect.

The far rarer and more skulking **Pallas's Grasshopper Warbler**, *Locustella certhiola*, is almost as much of a Fair Isle speciality as its 'loco' relative. 'This magical speck in the ocean holds a near monopoly on this coveted Siberian vagrant with 17 of the 27 British records. A *Locustella* flushed from a Fair Isle ditch in late September exhibiting a gingery rump and dark tail will always get the heart racing.'[12] The bird's gloriously urbane nickname is PG Tips, a reference to the sequence of pale spots at the end of each tail feather and on the tertials, which help separate it from other *Locustella* warblers.

Common Grasshopper Warbler, *L. naevia*. VN: Gropper (birders). Although still widely found across Britain and Ireland, this species has declined substantially in recent years, possibly through loss of the rough, and often damp, tussocky undergrowth and thickets that it favours. It is a highly secretive bird and few people ever manage to see it without setting out deliberately to find one. The plumage is a suitably anonymous streaky grey-brown, and it is famous for a habit of creeping mouse-like through ground vegetation. Henry Eliot Howard, author of *The British Warblers*, wrote that even birds moving in dense foliage reminded him of 'a stoat-like animal crawling along the branches'.[13]

The bird's mysterious reeling song went unrecognised until Ray and Willughby noted it in 1678, and even in Gilbert White's day people still refused to believe that it was of avian origin. 'Nothing can be more amusing,' he wrote, 'than the whisper of this little bird, which seems to be close by though at an hundred yards distance; and, when close at your ear, is scarce any louder than when a great way off. Had I not been a little acquainted with insects, and known that the grasshopper kind is not yet hatched, I should have hardly believed . . . it . . . The country people laugh when you tell them that it is the note of a bird.'[14]

Despite the bird's various names (White knew it as the 'grasshopper-lark' and *Locustella* means 'little locust') the sound is not especially similar to the stridulations of this insect group. Ornithologists have better expressed its distinctive quality through comparisons with man-made objects and, while the technology has changed down the centuries, the sense of mechanical production has been constant. It has been likened to mill-wheels, saw-pits, miniature spinning wheels, a straw pipe with a pea in it blown with a single breath and, most commonly, the winding mechanism of a fishing reel.[15]

As White noted, the song seems to change dramatically in volume as the bird rotates its head and sprays the sound in different directions. It is also highly ventriloquial, can often be heard throughout the night and can carry for more than ½ mile (1km) in still conditions. Eric Simms studied the song in detail and calculated that it ranged between 4.4 and 7 kHz, a frequency often beyond the capacity of older human ears. He also estimated that it included 1400 double notes a minute, while a bird can sing 250,000 notes during the course of a single night.[16] Although it is probably the least observed of all Britain's commoner warblers, its invisibility does not seem to affect its powers of evocation, nor is it a barrier to public attachment:

Before dawn on May mornings while walking to fish for bass on the south Devon coast I sometimes hear its rasping song, which seems highly appropriate given its similarity to a line being reeled in! That a small, brown nondescript bird, whose presence most people would not even register, may have just arrived from sub-Saharan Africa is quite humbling. I have never seen one of these birds but my knowledge of what that song signifies makes the experience immensely telling.[17]

River Warbler, *Locustella fluvialis*. This large earth-brown warbler has occurred on 29 occasions and at least one-third of the records refer to singing males in spring or summer. They appeared in six consecutive years during the 1990s at localities spread from Fife to Buckinghamshire, raising the possibility of breeding.

The song is a strange, captivating mechanical reel that has invited several colourful descriptions: 'grinding, pulsating sewing machine-like rattle';[18] 'Curious, mechanical, pulsating or rhythmic series of "chuffing" sounds not unlike distant steam engine running at high speed.'[19] It has a completely unbird-like quality and on one occasion a river warbler was observed to sing in direct response to 'a small, hideously noisy tractor', as if it interpreted the engine drone as a competitor.[20]

The song also has a close resemblance to several species of bush-cricket and cicada, which is thought to arise from deliberate mimicry. Some individuals may even copy a diurnal insect by day and then a nocturnal species at night. The mimicry possibly confers a protective advantage by disguising the warbler's presence among the much larger invertebrate population.[21]

Savi's Warbler, *Locustella luscinioides*. This is a large, plain rufous-brown warbler whose song resembles that of the previous two family members, although Eric Simms recommends the value of a simple diagnostic formula: 'Grasshopper rattles, Savi's buzzes and River grinds.'[22] Compared with the first and commoner of its two relatives, Savi's warbler song is also lower-pitched and less sustained.

The laurels for its initial identification went to an Italian teacher at the University of Pisa called Paolo Savi although, in fact, the first specimen ever to be found in the world was taken near Limpenhoe, Norfolk, in about 1819.[23] Sadly this skin was wrongly identified and for more than a decade after Savi's official discovery, Victorian ornithologists failed to notice that the same bird was also breeding sparsely among them, in the Fens and more widely across East Anglia.

Yet the old marshmen were already familiar with a bird they called the 'red craking reed-wren', or the 'brown', 'red' or 'night reeler' to separate it from the ordinary 'reeler', a name they used for grasshopper warbler.[24] The rarer bird produces a distinctive nest with a lower foundation woven from sedge blades or the broad leaves of sweet grass, and it was these enduring structures that the Cambridgeshire reedcutters used to find in the autumn as they harvested the sedge. Unfortunately the British Savi's warblers died out soon after their eventual discovery, probably as a consequence of wetland drainage.[25]

It was almost exactly 100 years before the distinctive mechanical churring song was recognised again at Wicken Fen, Cambridgeshire, one of its old nineteenth-century haunts. Small colonies of Savi's warblers were located in Kent and Suffolk during the 1960s and 1970s, but the population has never exceeded 30 pairs and has now entered a second and possibly terminal decline.

Sedge Warbler, *Acrocephalus schoenobaenus*. VN: Sedgy (birders). Sedge is often linked with reed warbler as a species-pair whose song and appearance require careful separation. Testimony to the difficulty is the fact that British ornithology did not split them until the eighteenth century. Both are summer migrants, but the sedge arrives earlier and, despite recent declines, still breeds far more widely across Britain and Ireland as far north as Orkney. The reed warbler is largely an English and Welsh bird and in choice of habitat is generally true to its name, while the sedge warbler is far more catholic and can occur in areas of bramble thicket or crops of oil-seed rape.

The second element in its scientific name comes from two Greek words, *skhoinos* 'reed' and *baino* 'I walk'. 'Reedwalker' captures the way in which sedge warblers pass effortlessly through the vertical stems of a phrag-

The sedge warbler will often cap its high-energy performance with a striking song flight when the bird rises steeply into the air, then parachutes back to earth with wings outstretched and tail spread.

mites bed. Often they perch on a single stalk, then shuffle to the top to deliver their hectic and magical song.

While both reed and sedge produce long jumbled passages of harsh and sweet notes, sedge warbler song is faster, louder and more varied. A handy pointer listed by a birdwatcher explaining the differences to a group of children was that the 'R' of reed warbler stands for 'regular'. The contrast strikes others as a matter of personality, the sedge being the noisy exhibitionist to the reed warbler's stuttering introvert. Or, as Bernard Tucker wrote, the latter's song has a 'slow and "conversational" manner of delivery, contrasting with [the] quick, noisy,

common sandpipers and greenshank. In a highly original study Clive Catchpole analysed the structure of the sedge warbler's vocalisations and discovered that each bird has a repertoire of syllables and vocal elements which it introduces in random order so that it is never repeated exactly. Each passage of song is thus a unique performance and becomes even more elaborate during the bird's dancing parachute display. Catchpole also found that there was an important function to song mimicry, because those males with the widest and most complex repertoires were also the birds that attracted a female quickest. In other words, the bigger the song, the greater the opportunities for breeding. It seems that in the sexual politics of the sedge warbler, size really matters.[27]

Marsh Warbler, *Acrocephalus palustris*. This is the quintessential 'little brown job' that is the despair of the birding novice and dear to the heart of many hardcore twitchers. More technically, it joins reed warbler in a group known as the 'unstreaked *Acrocephalus*', which also embraces two super-rare vagrants from Asia, **Blyth's Reed Warbler**, *A. dumetorum*, and **Paddyfield Warbler**, *A. agricola* (about 50 records of each). In autumn, when their telltale songs are finished, these species are so similar that they present one of the toughest identification challenges in British birdwatching.

The 20–60 marsh-warbler pairs breeding in England are on the north-western edge of the species' world range and constitute one of our rarest summer migrants. They are also among the latest to arrive, with an average return date for a long-established Worcestershire population of 3 June.[28] Sadly the Midland colony has since vanished and the bird's present headquarters is in Kent, with occasional breeding in 20 other counties, primarily in southern England. Although it shows some preference for wet habitats characteristic of the genus, marsh warbler has far broader tastes, occupying sites without any wetland component and readily breeding in a wide range of tall, fast-growing plants, such as umbellifers, nettles, meadowsweet and willowherb.

The bird's rarity in England no doubt helps to account for the lack of reputation among a wider public, but the almost complete absence of literary or cultural references is extraordinary given the fact that it is one of Europe's most remarkable songsters. (W. H. Hudson is one of the few British writers to dwell on the alchemy of marsh-warbler song, which he ranked 'as one of our four greatest', along with blackbird, skylark and nightingale, while for sheer variety he felt it unsurpassed.[29]) It can sing continuously for more than an hour and in the frenetic stream of sound each individual male embeds an astonishing sequence of near-perfect imitations of other birds.

"declamatory"' voice of its sibling.[26] Sedge warblers also execute a wonderful songflight, in which they rise up chattering incessantly, then spiral downwards on outspread wings and tail to create one of the most distinctive sights and sounds of the British wetland in spring.

The song is also full of wonderfully accurate imitations of other birds' calls and songs, many of them typical of the mimic's wetland habitat, such as reed bunting, swallow, yellow and pied wagtails, wood and

A 1937 portrait of a marsh warbler by the pioneer photographer George Yeates.

Françoise Dowsett-Lemaire, studying a population of 60 pairs near her Belgian home, paid close attention to the marsh warbler's mimetic range. She detected the calls and sounds of many European species in the song, the majority of which reflected the bird's most vocal neighbours in the immediate breeding environment. Yet in Zambia and Kenya she also discovered that marsh warblers continue to acquire new material and that an individual does not complete its full catalogue of borrowed sounds until almost the end of its first year of life. Thereafter it appears hardly to add to the repertoire, but Dowsett-Lemaire established that a total of 212 other birds are copied and that the average male can imitate more than 76 species, over half of them African.

The mimicked species can include kestrel, oystercatcher, redshank and black-headed gull, while the 12 most commonly imitated European birds are blackbird, house sparrow, tree sparrow, whitethroat, swallow, blue tit, linnet, skylark, starling, stonechat, great tit and magpie. Then there are the sounds borrowed from 113 Afrotropical species, many of which are jumbled up with snatches of more familiar mimicry. So a single rhythmic sequence can include the '*spink*' of a chaffinch intercut with the notes of southern puffback, *Dryoscopus cubla* (a shrike-like bird), or a fusion of blackbird with white

helmet-shrike, *Prionops plumata* – a catalogue of sounds learnt at very different moments in the bird's life.[30]

The auditory distillation of its travels is nothing short of astonishing: 'to the human ear many of the songs and phrases are so like the original that one expects an unlikely mixed flock of birds to fly from the bush where the Marsh Warbler is singing'.[31] An ability to recognise the imitations undoubtedly increases a person's understanding of the technical accomplishment, although no expertise is required to appreciate its sheer driving intensity. The range, duration and improvisatory structure suggest parallels with nightingale song and, almost inevitably, marsh warblers include passages of the other bird in their free-style medley. Yet in every other respect the two are astonishingly different. I have written of the only occasion when I heard both singing simultaneously at Walberswick, Suffolk: 'If the nightingale is the avian world's classical composer, then the marsh warbler is its electric jazz equivalent. Occasionally some people suggest the two can sound momentarily and vaguely similar, but the only direct comparison I would make is that the marsh warbler is like a nightingale on acid.'[32]

There is a more serious point. As the bird performs, the bill is held wide open, revealing a bright orange-yellow interior to the mouth, while the head rotates and bobs up and down as if to fire the furious barrage as widely as possible. At times it seems as if a marsh warbler carries bird song, in terms of sheer speed and complexity, to the very limits of its physical production. John Walpole-Bond is one of the few to attempt to convey this aspect: 'It is a song which, at one time somewhat slow, subdued, laboured and even snatchy, suddenly flashes into quick smooth, sustained effortless rhythm – a hurried flow of tune loudly effusive, brilliant and intensely passionate even to the verge of delirium.'[33]

The marsh warbler's preference for tall lush herbage can seem to add an olfactory dimension to the impact of the song: 'I recently heard a super marsh warbler which had included mimicry of blackbird, goldfinch and even a common tern in the performance. The sound was almost fragrant. The bird's syrupy refrains seemed to turn into perfume as they floated across a lush mat of scented meadowsweet, comfrey and cow parsley recently infused by a summer downpour.'[34]

It seems remarkable, given the bird's investment in its vocalisations, that the song appears to have no impact on breeding success. Françoise Dowsett-Lemaire could find no correlation between the marsh warbler's mimicry repertoire and overall complexity of song and the bird's attractiveness to females (unlike the situation with the sedge warbler). Instead the male's ability to find a mate is dependent upon territory size and those individuals

The reed warbler's staccato chattering song is the soundtrack at many southern wetlands in spring.

returning earliest to the breeding grounds tend to acquire the largest territories.

However she did discover that after mating, particularly on sunny days, a male marsh warbler spends a good deal of its off-duty time at the very edge of its territory, where it produces a softer, quieter version of the song. Often three or four males will gather in these sociable song bouts, which appear not to have a strictly territorial purpose. In fact where individual birds hold a territory with an immediate male neighbour who is resolutely silent, the individual will sometimes fly considerable distances to join other social song groups.[35] The lack of evidence for a purely functional interpretation suggests that the marsh warbler's social singing is the equivalent of the raven's sledge ride in the snow (see page 425). They sing simply because they enjoy it.

There is a sad coda to the marsh-warbler story. The small numbers breeding in Kent, which are the mainstay of the bird's national presence, have been the subject of RSPB monitoring since 2001. The species-protection work uncovered a pattern of systematic interference by egg thieves, which is now thought to have played a substantial part in their recent decline:

In the first year of its operation the protection scheme uncovered at least three teams of egg thieves at one site. This kind of criminal activity targeted at rare birds is depressing enough, but in some ways even worse is the way it has been so completely overlooked. If it had been a rare bird of prey like osprey or Montagu's harrier the story would have carried far and wide in newspapers and on TV screens. But because it was a little brown job like a marsh warbler, with virtually no cultural identity, the whole business has gone on with hardly anyone noticing.[36]

By comparison with the musicianship of its congeners the **Eurasian Reed Warbler**, *A. scirpaceus*, seems the poor relation. Its song is far simpler and more markedly metrical, with a higher content of churring and guttural units and 'sounding not unlike a pair of pebbles being rubbed together in a leisurely way'.[37] It shows a much deeper attachment to phragmites reedbed and, although it has recently spread north and developed a breeding presence in Ireland, it is mainly a lowland species south of a line between Bridlington and the Wirral.

At over 7 inches (19cm) long, the **Great Reed Warbler**, *A. arundinaceus*, is the giant of its family and appears at times more like a small thrush. It has an unbeautiful but suitably stentorean voice, with a mixture of throaty gurgling and croaking elements that are often more reminiscent of an amphibian than a bird. It is also

Dartford warblers have increased and spread dramatically in recent years, possibly assisted by climate change.

twice the weight of its namesake and if you fail to see the warbler as it crashes about in a reedbed, the moving vegetation can suggest a much larger species. It is one of the growing band of European songbirds that recent climatic amelioration has allowed to spread north as far as the Channel coast. It now threatens to mount an invasion of Britain and has been recorded singing on numerous occasions, with records even in Scotland; it has also been observed carrying nest material, but it has yet to breed successfully.

Icterine Warbler, *Hippolais icterina*. VN: Icky (birders). Apart from a single breeding record almost a century ago, this is a scarce migrant from eastern and central Europe, where it is a bird of town and garden. The name refers to the pleasing yellow tones to the underparts, which make it look rather like a large, brightly coloured willow warbler. With its more westerly counterpart, the **Melodious Warbler**, *H. polyglotta* (VN: Melody (birders), it forms a distinctive species-pair known jointly to birders as 'Hippos' (after the scientific name).

During the 1960s Ian Wallace was central to unravelling the identification challenge of the two warblers. He recounts the pleasures of watching them in autumn, as well as their characteristic habits:

The excitement of a *Hippo* has never dimmed. You can be working the lees of a hedge on one of the Isles of Scilly, when suddenly there's a heavy movement with a leaf spray tipping like an over-weighted balance. Next you glimpse a clumping warbler, green above,

yellowish below and what a bill! Often it will lunge forward and destroy a berry or insect, the snapping bill approaching 'broom handle' proportions. But which Hippo is it? By the 1960s we'd happily uncovered that both Ickies and Melodies were annual joys while birding Scilly and the south coast. Four decades after our pioneer observations the final perceptions of seven *Hippolais* species are almost secured. Fascinatingly it appears that between themselves all of these birds use specific tail movements to flag their genes – in a kind of avian semaphore.[38]

Dartford Warbler, *Sylvia undata*. VN: Darty (birders). Its warm wine-red underparts make this a highly attractive bird, especially the male. It is about 5 inches (12.5cm) long, although a good half of its length is made up entirely of tail, while the bird itself is no heavier than a wren. (The old country name was 'furze wren'.) George Yeates felt the appendage was 'almost an embarrassment' for such a tiny creature and 'too great a load for the small wings to manage'.[39] The disproportion imparts a characteristic front-heavy quality to the weak flight, and when the bird is perched the tail seems to assume a life of its own, cocking almost vertically or wafting gently from side to side.

Its British presence was not recognised until 1773, when John Latham named the species following receipt of a pair that had been shot on Bexley Heath, near Dartford in Kent. It was later found to occur widely across heathland in southern England as far north as Shropshire, with colonies even on the perimeter of London at sites such as Wandsworth, Wimbledon, Blackheath and Wormwood Scrubs. The bird's skulking manner led to premium prices among the collectors, not only for skins but also for its nests and eggs, which drew scathing condemnation from W. H. Hudson. He blamed the trade for the Dartford warbler's decline in the early twentieth century and predicted its imminent extinction, although the British population has always been subject to two major suppressants: loss of habitat, and cold.[40]

It is confined to just five western European countries as well as the north African littoral, and has the smallest world range of any of our breeding birds. England is on the northern limit of its distribution and the loss of southern heaths and commons through agricultural improvement has fragmented its habitat. It is also a highly sedentary bird and a major cause of decline is its great susceptibility to the cold. The worst case occurred in the two successive hard winters of 1961–3 when the numbers fell from 450 pairs to just 10.

Memories of this calamitous decrease, coupled with the bird's own tiny size and seeming delicacy, have

Common whitethroat is one of our most widespread and numerous warblers, but is subject to a boom-bust population cycle.

cemented our sense of an overarching vulnerability. It is one of the best British examples where a species' local rarity has been assumed to equal almost constitutional weakness. Typical of our pessimism was a 1960s prediction that its breeding range would be virtually restricted to the New Forest 'in the foreseeable future'.[41] There was a similar anxiety in the proposal to trap large numbers ahead of severe winter weather so that they could be safely released the following spring.[42] A few years later it was suggested that the bird was unlikely to increase its 1974 maximum of 560 pairs.[43] After it duly exceeded the total, Eric Simms felt that there was still a 'considerable question mark' over its future.[44]

All the caution is perfectly understandable as an expression of our protective instincts towards a much-loved bird. Yet it sits oddly with the warbler's continuing rise and expansion to a population of 1925 pairs, spread from Devon to Norfolk, by the year 2000. It has undoubtedly been helped by mild winters as well as the intensive management and protection of England's lowland heath, for which it is an important flagship species. Yet the Dartford warbler's recent history illustrates how easy it is to underestimate the resilience of a small rare bird.

Lesser Whitethroat, *Sylvia curruca*. Predominantly grey, brown and white in colour, it is a warbler of rather shy manner and simple appeal. It is technically less colourful than its more widespread namesake, but has a bandit-like mask of dark grey across the ear coverts, which contrasts sharply with the silvery-white underparts, while some birds also show a warm pinkish flush to the breast.

The short, dry rattling song is one of the typical spring sounds of English and Welsh hedgerows, as well as of railway embankments, young plantations and areas of low thorny scrub. More recently the bird has spread into southern Scotland and shows signs of colonising Ireland, where otherwise it is merely a scarce migrant. The slow expansion north and westwards is all the more remarkable, given that the entire European population migrates around the eastern edge of the Mediterranean, rather than taking a direct southerly route into Africa via Spain or Italy.

Common Whitethroat, *Sylvia communis*. VN: Nettlecreeper (Midlands). Although it generally avoids mature woodland, this warbler flourishes in many types of low bushy habitat, such as new plantations, scrubbed-over heath and commons, nettlebeds or roadside stands of umbellifer and other tall herbs. However it was undoubtedly one of the principal beneficiaries of the eighteenth-century Enclosure Acts, and has long since enjoyed an enduring association with hedgerows.

Whitethroats have a habit of making repeated short flights along a country lane ahead of an observer, occasionally rising up in a jerky songflight 'as though suspended on an elastic thread'.[45] Eric Hardy created a nice echo of the main note when he coined the word 'ziggling' for the bird's short scratchy song and pin-pointed it as a classic element of the mid-May dawn chorus.[46] Otherwise whitethroats creep deep into the vegetation as you pass and make their presence felt through a repeated harsh scolding note. The sense of irritation is occasionally reinforced when a bird pops out its head to reveal a pale-eyed 'glaring expression'.[47]

In 1886 Charles Swainson could unearth at least 38 alternative names (including the rather fanciful 'singing skyrocket') to the already long-established 'whitethroat'. Many of them reflected the bird's characteristic behaviour, like the widely used 'nettlecreeper', a name surviving in the Midlands until after the Second World War (possibly still). The richness of this vernacular tradition is strong evidence for the whitethroat's former abundance.[48] It is widespread across Britain and Ireland as far north as Orkney, and until the final third of the twentieth century it was easily the commonest warbler and among the most abundant of all songbirds. Some estimates suggest five million pairs, which is similar to the present-day numbers of robin and far more numerous than the dunnock.[49]

Then in 1969 it suddenly and inexplicably crashed. In a paper entitled 'Where Have All the Whitethroats Gone?' its authors tried to uncover why more than three-quarters of the UK population had simply failed to return. The explanation they converged upon was the impact of drought in the Sahel region, the bird's main African winter quarters. By the date of the paper's publication whitethroat numbers had actually fallen even further to one-sixth of the pre-1969 total.[50] Thereafter they slowly recovered until 1984, when a repeat of the devastating ecological conditions in Africa plunged the species back into free-fall. The boom–bust pattern may well be part of a well-worn population cycle, although recent whitethroat surveys suggest an ongoing recovery.

Garden Warbler, *Sylvia borin*. It is a relatively common grey-brown warbler with a rather heavy body and stubby bill, partly identified, ironically, by the absence of any really striking features. Yet close views reveal an overall gentleness to the bird, emphasised by the smooth rounded head with its large dark eye, which is very different to 'the irascible alertness' detected in the rest of the family.[51]

Its physical anonymity led to a degree of confusion among our forebears. The species was not recognised at all until the end of the eighteenth century and even a generation later Thomas Bewick wrote of it in *A History of British Birds*, 'We have taken much pains to gain a competent knowledge of the various kinds, but confess that we have been much puzzled in reconciling their provincial names with the synonyms of the different authors.'[52] Typically garden warbler shared regional names with common whitethroat ('Billy whitethroat', 'strawsmear', 'small straw') and blackcap ('haychat'), although it became best known as 'pettychap'. Unfortunately another featureless family member, the chiffchaff, had acquired the same name and occasionally ornithologists attempted to assert a higher degree of order by designating garden warbler as *the* pettychap, and chiffchaff as the lesser pettychap (but see also Chiffchaff, page 379).

Today the challenge is separating garden warbler from blackcap by its voice. Their two songs confuse many people and this has given rise to a whole range of mnemonics:

Garden warbler Goes on longer, Blackcap's Briefer.[53]

A birdwatcher I knew in Warwickshire had a dictum that is sometimes helpful: 'if you can see it it's a blackcap, if you can't it's a garden warbler'.[54]

Blackcap has much purer notes than garden warbler, rather like the difference in note purity between song thrush and blackbird (i.e. garden warbler/blackbird has a resonant fluty quality not present in blackcap/ song thrush).[55]

The blackcap hits all the high notes and takes many breaks, singing for about five seconds each burst. The garden warbler has a deeper song and tends to warble on endlessly, never seeming to take a breath. Back in the 1970s I used to say it was like listening to one's mother-in-law endlessly talking, but when I got married I changed my tune and said it sounded like a person gossiping! Such is the impact of political correctness.[56]

Both species are widely celebrated for their musical richness, and Eric Simms detects in garden warbler 'a certain "fruity", often wonderfully beautiful and clarinet-like quality'.[57] Lord Grey, writing lucidly on both in *The Charm of Birds*, found in favour of the blackcap: 'The garden-warbler's song is very good: in one respect it surpasses that of the blackcap; it is more

The garden warbler is one of the plainer and more featureless members of its family except for a rather stubby bill and blue-grey legs.

sustained; but the bird never seems absolutely to clear the throat and let out the sound so pure and free as the blackcap does ... In other words, a garden-warbler's song seems always on the point of an achievement, to which only the blackcap attains.'[58]

The bird's name is singularly unhelpful as an identification aid because only the largest and most rambling gardens include the kind of thick shrubbery and woodland it requires. The garden association may have been more obvious in mainland Europe, where the bird has a reputation for raiding fruit trees. In Portugal it is known as the *felosa-das-figuieras* ('fig warbler'), while in Italy it is called the *beccafico*, 'fig-pecker'. A number of small passerines like robin and blackcap are often included under the Italian term, but the garden warbler has the best claim to be *the* beccafico.

The switch to a partly fruit diet allows the birds to capitalise on a seasonal abundance and gain weight quickly just prior to migration. Bramble patches among dune hollows are favourite sites for garden warblers in autumn, where they can be seen gorging themselves on the heavy drupes. This often results in a characteristically purple-stained mouth, in bright-purple droppings and,

for the ringer of birds in autumn, cloth holding-bags covered in purple patches.

At times large numbers of garden warblers can appear together with similar passerine migrants in what are known as 'falls'. The most famous was in September 1965. Occurring on wide stretches of the East Anglian coastline and involving thousands of garden warblers as well as hundreds of thousands of other birds (see also Common Redstart, page 346), it is considered among the most spectacular events in British ornithology. However these phenomena are closely tied to adverse weather conditions that prevent the birds from migrating, and James McCallum gives a description of a fall that partly conveys the avian point-of-view:

In August 1987 there were classic fall conditions on the North Norfolk coast so I decided to end the day on East Hills, which is only accessible by crossing the main channel into Wells harbour at low tide. Large numbers of passerine migrants like garden and willow warblers were arriving all the time and, carried away with the spectacle, I completely lost track of time. It was only the fading light that told me I should head

Blackcaps have developed a recent habit of overwintering, particularly in southern England, where they are regular visitors to the bird table.

homewards, but when I glanced out towards the channel to my horror the tide was early and flowing fast with the strong winds. To make matters worse, in all the hurry I'd forgotten to tell anyone where I was going.

By now I was soaked right through, so in fading light I picked up bits of polythene and polystyrene to set up a makeshift bed and huddled up to keep warm. As I lay there I could hear the mixture of contact and alarm calls of various small migrants amid the howling wind and hissing rain. Several weather-beaten garden and willow warblers joined me in the shelter of the thick needles and I watched them preening, shaking the rain from their plumage and stretching their wings before fluffing themselves up and tucking their heads into their scapulars to doze. Their presence gave me a strange comforting feeling and also a little insight into the plight of small migrants during their long journeys.

Several hours later I was aware of shouts and torches flashing and the familiar voices of my brothers and my mother, who had rowed out across the stormy harbour to search for me. I tried to slip away from the pine clump as quietly as possible in order not to disturb my sleeping companions.[59]

Blackcap, *Sylvia atricapilla*. The arrival of blackcaps in very early April, or even late March, is one of the best indicators of the seasonal transition. Henry Eliot Howard thought that its song contained 'a peculiar cheerfulness, which alone seems to transform winter into spring'.[60] He went on: 'His rich and liquid notes will bear comparison with those produced by any other known species; it is, in fact difficult to conceive of more beautiful notes being uttered.'

A 'full, sweet, deep, loud and wild pipe' was Gilbert White's much-repeated description, which is one of the most concise and still among the best. White agreed with Howard that the blackcap was the premier songster in its family (the 'King of the warblers' was an old title for the bird,[61] although he considered nightingale song superior.[62]

Its primacy among British summer songsters has been widely accepted for centuries, although there is a suggestion of near-parity in two old country names for blackcap – 'mock nightingale' and 'northern nightingale'. And in John Clare's poem, 'The March Nightingale', the listener cannot distinguish one bird from the other:

while the blackcap doth his ears assail
With such a rich and such an early song
He stops his own and thinks the nightingale
Hath of her monthly reckoning counted wrong.
'Sweet-jug-jug-jug' comes loud upon his ears,
Those sounds that unto May by right belong,
Yet on the hawthorn scarce a leaf appears.

Unlike its rival, the blackcap has the indisputable merit of greater abundance. It is a bird of broad-leaved woodland widespread across Britain and more thinly dispersed in Ireland, but it can survive in far less shrub or tree cover than almost any other warbler. 'I look forward to hearing the first blackcap of spring singing his heart out from a little clump of trees by Harringay station in inner London, only yards from the express trains that thunder along the main London–Scotland east coast line.'[63] The bird's adaptability may be a factor in a recent rise in numbers as well as its spread northwards. Chiffchaff and willow warbler are now the only family members that are more common.

The bird's status as a winter visitor is another recent development. Most of our breeding blackcaps migrate southwards to the Mediterranean areas of Europe and North Africa, but small numbers have long been known to occur at other seasons. In the 1940s and 1950s the average number of wintering individuals was just 22, with most appearing in the milder south-west: 'These birds winter with us in our Falmouth garden. We usually see them in November or December when the white berries of the cordyline appear.'[64]

The south-west bias continues, but blackcaps are now appearing as far north as Orkney and even in 1965 three birds were seen in a large Aberdeen garden, where they took to tapping on the kitchen window to be fed. By the 1970s the average was 380 and a census in the long hard winter of 1978/9 revealed a count of 1714 birds.[65]

Although the year-round presence gives an impression that some birds are resident, the winter population is also migratory, arriving from Germany and Austria just as the breeding blackcaps leave. Today the winter total is estimated at several thousand, a rise possibly linked to our own increased habit of feeding winter birds. Blackcaps regularly eat garden fruits including late windfall apples, cotoneaster, viburnum and ivy, but they

The Mediterranean passion for illegally trapping and eating songbirds, such as blackcaps, is a source of constant controversy.

are also routine visitors to the birdtable for suet pudding, bread crusts, cheese, porridge and meat scraps. Some birds even hang from the peanut bag and are bold in defending the table from regulars like robins, tits and even starlings.

In Mediterranean areas such as Tuscany, Malta and Cyprus, where blackcaps concentrate in large numbers there is a long tradition of hunting and eating them. The sport involves horribly cruel methods, including 'lime-sticks' smeared with extracts from Syrian plums and honey or modern synthetic glues, although mist-nets in conjunction with tape lures are rapidly replacing the older techniques. Across the whole region the annual total of spring and autumn migrants being trapped is estimated at 900 million. The blackcap was once a major source of protein but today trapping is hardly justifiable on subsistence grounds, or, it would seem, for the birds' culinary merit:

In Cyprus large numbers of *ambelopoulia* (primarily blackcaps) are served in restaurants as a delicacy and sell for around £1.20 each. Being migrants they are carrying large amounts of fat, which gives them the required flavour. After the birds are plucked and feet removed they are boiled and eaten whole, apart from the beak which appears to be too tough for the local palate.

I was present in a restaurant in autumn 2001 where diners were arriving from upper-class areas of Nicosia just to feast on this annual harvest. Not wishing to appear out of place and as part of our investigation into bird trapping, we ordered a dozen birds to see what all the fuss was about. They arrived looking like unfeathered blackbird chicks, pale, colourless and to my eye most uninviting. I opened a bird, which I found consisted almost entirely of fat and bone with two patches of darkly coloured muscle no bigger than a child's fingernail, one either side of the breast bone. Put off by the colourless fat, I was only able to taste the richly coloured flesh, which had a very strong meaty flavour relative to its small size.

One bird was enough to convince me that the eating of *ambelopoulia*, like bird trapping with limesticks, is something that has to be learned over many generations.[66]

The Mediterranean trapping of songbirds is illegal under European law and has been the subject of several British conservation campaigns. It is also strongly condemned on moral grounds – 'the slaughter … continues to bring shame to us all' – although mingled with the indignation in our island pronouncements may be a touch of good old Europhobia.[67] A cultural blind seems to allow us to tolerate the killing of many millions of game birds and wildfowl. Equally an estimated 55 million birds are killed by British domestic cats every year and Europe-wide the feline harvest may rival its human counterpart, yet these (partly preventable) losses inspire little more than isolated grumbling. Despite pressures from cats and humans alike, British blackcaps have been on an upward trend for several decades.

Pallas's Leaf Warbler, *Phylloscopus proregulus*. This goldcrest-sized bird is an increasingly regular vagrant that somehow never seems to lose its initial magic. It is often thought of as a 'classic rarity', and 'Siberian jewel' and 'Eastern gem' are the kind of descriptions it inspires, while Ian Wallace's 'striped sprite' is regularly repeated.[68] The last refers to the details that make it easily our most beautiful *Phylloscopus*: two lemon bars across each wing, one through its crown and, above the eye, black-bordered lines of buff-yellow that almost encircle the head. Also unique to this British warbler is a lozenge of lemon-white on the rump, which is occasionally conspicuous as it hovers for aerial insects beneath the foliage of coastal woodland.

The first ever record was at Cley, Norfolk, in 1896 but it was 55 years before a second example occurred at Monk's House, Northumberland. In the subsequent half-century more than 1400 have been seen, mainly on the east coast during October and November.

For some reason Pallas's Warblers make me think of sycamore leaves in autumn.[69]

Pallas's warblers instantly bring back memories of that moment when autumn gives way to winter and of booting around wind-blown sycamore copses and coastal scrub on the Isles of Sheppey and Thanet or down at Dungeness and St Margaret's Bay.[70]

The bird is exceptionally fast-moving. In some cases birdwatchers find it necessary to run through the woodland even just to catch a tail-end glimpse as a bird zips from bush to bush. The foot-slog can sometimes have unexpected rewards:

One day at Bockhill, St Margaret's Bay, Kent we felt the season and conditions were absolutely perfect for Pallas's and were convinced there ought to be one in the area. So we started at dawn, searched all day and eventually found a very mobile, very elusive example mid-afternoon at the furthest end of our 'patch'. We'd headed back to the village for a celebratory cuppa and as we emerged one of our number spotted what he thought was a firecrest. You can imagine how we exploded out the cars when this was corrected to Pallas's. It spent the rest of the afternoon (it was about 3 or 4 by now) singing in the trees or showing brilliantly to ourselves, other birders and passing villagers, who were amazed, and flattered, that so tiny a bird could have flown so far to grace their community.[71]

Although the number of birds appearing each autumn may have increased, the repetitions simply underscore the Pallas's specialness, since each bird, weighing no more than an envelope, has completed a journey of around 3200 miles (5400km).

The other regular visitor from the Far East, **Yellow-browed Warbler**, *Phylloscopus inornatus*, lives a little in the shadow of its more charismatic relative. It is a fraction larger and has occurred in Britain and Ireland at least five times more often than Pallas's warbler. It also lacks a little of the design detail and hummingbird-like intensity of the other bird, although its journey from Siberia is no less extraordinary.

The exhaustion entailed in these formidable distances has resulted in exceptional behaviour by some individuals, like the one that landed near Start Point, Devon, on HMS *Africa* on 10 May 1911. A young rating showed

Wood warblers are famous for having two very different but equally beautiful songs.

exemplary naval discipline when the bird perched on his head during morning prayers ('[he] remained perfectly still, though the vestige of a smile on his face indicated that he was aware of something'), then dropped down his back to settle on his hands clasped behind him.[72]

Wood Warbler, *Phylloscopus sibilatrix*. This is the largest, most distinctive and least common of the three breeding *Phylloscopus* warblers. The generic name is a Greek construction meaning 'leaf-searcher', which nicely expresses the way these slender birds move among the canopy to glean invertebrates from the foliage surface.

This is the most truly arboreal of the three – hence its old name 'wood wren' – and has a distribution weighted towards the oak and beechwoods of western Britain. Yet the bird is most closely identified with tall mature beech trees in spring and summer, Lord Grey specifying May as the classic wood-warbler month at his Northumberland home: 'the soft green and yellow colours of the bird are in tone with the foliage, and its ways and movements . . . animate the beauty of young beech leaves: wonderful and perfect beyond description as this beauty is, the presence of a wood-warbler can still add to it'.[73] W. H. Hudson,

observing birds in the beechwoods of Somerset, also felt that its colours 'harmonised with the tender greens of the opening leaves and the pale greys and silvery whites of the slender boles'.[74]

The wood warbler is unique for its use of two, almost equally charismatic songs, the less frequent being a soft, penetrating repeated whistle – 'like a silver bugle' – that is noted for its melancholic quality.[75] Lord Grey suggested that 'there are tears in the voice'.[76] This could not be more different from the better-known vocalisation, which has some of the passionate intensity of marsh warbler and has inspired poetry, often of purple hue, in a number of authors. Lasting no more than four seconds, the full phrases start with individuated dry 'spitting' notes that gradually quicken and intensify to a loud spluttering cadence. It has been likened to 'a spinning coin on a marble slab',[77] while Eric Simms recalled an old friend's words: 'an image of raindrops scattering among the leaves'.[78] The rain association seems deeply appropriate given the bird's abundance in sessile oak woods of west Wales and Scotland.

Edward Thomas is the one who perhaps best captured the polished, lapidary sharpness of the wood warbler's

The chiffchaff's tuneless two-note ditty is one of the simplest of all bird songs.

cascading notes: 'as if, overhead in the stainless air, little waves of pearls dropped and scattered and shivered on a shore of pearls'.[79] The male caps his performance by throwing the head back and opening the bill wide as he sings, then shivering the wings and his whole body vigorously as each phrase reaches the climax. Hudson identified it as his favourite small bird, noting the almost perfect congruence between physical performance, sound and wider landscape:

> It is a voice of the beechen woods in summer, of the far-up cloud of green, translucent leaves, with open spaces full of green, shifting sunlight and shadow. Though resonant and far-reaching it does not strike you as loud, but rather as the diffused sound of the wind in the foliage . . . a voice that has light and shade, rising and passing like the wind, changing as it flows, and quivering like a wind-fluttered leaf.[80]

Common Chiffchaff, *Phylloscopus collybita*. VN: Chiff/y. Henry Eliot Howard thought this common widespread warbler 'the hardiest of his tribe', partly for its arrival on the February/March cusp, when it can often still feel very wintry: 'no matter what the weather, there, in the tops of the highest trees, he will be, singing intermittently, a restless little fellow, looking, as he sways backwards and forwards, his feathers ruffled with the wind, almost too delicate to stand the cold'.[81]

Howard also noted that as well as being the first migrant to arrive, the chiffchaff was also the last to leave, and nowadays some may not even go at all. There is an expanding population of wintering chiffchaffs, particularly in southern England and Ireland, some of which may have bred in Britain.[82]

Yet it is the bird's appearance in March that arouses most feeling. Wheatear and sand martin sometimes beat it to the earliest date, but without fail it is the first migrant to sing and it is this that freights the sound with such significance. With his infallible instinct for the impact of bird song, Lord Grey captures the essence of the species perfectly:

> Alone of all the warblers, the chiff-chaff has given us the right to expect him in March; he is the forerunner of the rush of song-birds that is on its way to us and will arrive in April, and thereafter enrich our woods, meadows and gardens with still further variety and quality of song. This is why the first hearing of a chiff-chaff moves us so each spring. He is a symbol, a promise, an assurance of what is to come.

Grey felt that the sound itself had a mechanical quality that 'suggests industry, as of the passage of a shuttle to and fro'.[83] It can also be very penetrating and 'audible sometimes to the motorway driver'.[84]

It has the additional merit of being instantly recognisable. Occasionally a flat-sounding great tit catches people out, but the exact structure of the disyllable is rendered in the onomatopoeic chiffchaff. The scientific name is likewise a reference to the song. *Collybita* is a corruption of the Greek *kollubistes*, meaning 'money-changer', because the repeated notes were thought to resemble the jingle of coins.[85] Several old vernacular versions also contain an echo, such as 'chip chop', 'choice and cheep' and 'pettychap'.[86]

There is a small but fascinating mystery attaching to the last and rather odd-sounding of these names. During the eighteenth century and long afterwards, 'pettychap' (also spelt 'pettichap') became established as a name for garden warbler, with its first usage in ornithological literature by John Ray. In 1678 in his edited version of *The Ornithology of Francis Willughby*, Ray associated the bird he listed under this name with a species known in Italy as *beccafico* and *borin*. Both of the European titles were certainly names for garden warbler, and Ray's mention of fruit in the dissected stomach suggests the same species. However, the bird actually described is quite unlike a garden warbler, but remarkably similar to a chiffchaff: 'The colour of its Head, Neck, Back, Wings, and Tail from ash-colour inclines to *green* [my italics], in some dusky with a Tincture of *green* . . . But the quills of the Wing are of a Mouse-dun, with black shafts, and *green* edges. The lesser rows of feathers that cover the underside of the Wings are *yellow* . . . The Legs short, the Feet bluish, and in some of a lead colour.'[87] The description was apparently based on a skin given to the authors by a Mr Jessop of Yorkshire, who 'sent it us by the name of *Pettychaps*'.

Although the word literally means small fellow or, alternatively, small beak, its closeness to other onomatopoeic names, such as 'chip-chop' or John Clare's 'chipichap', raises the distinct prospect that it was initially the name for this species. Judging from Jessop's familiarity with it, it was a folk word in use long before the late seventeenth century and was probably applied generically to all small warblers that people could not identify. Yet it had its origins with the one species whose song was sufficiently simple and distinctive for anyone to recognise. Its later transfer to garden warbler was a product of ornithologists' early and understandable confusion.

Willow Warbler, *Phylloscopus trochilus*. Despite recent declines in parts of its southern British range, this is our commonest warbler and one of the most abundant

The willow warbler is very easy to confuse with its sibling, the chiffchaff.

migrants in large swathes of northern Europe. In the 1970s Reg Moreau suggested, although he offered it merely as an educated guess, that the world total was a staggering 900 million. All of these drain out from a massive Eurasian range during autumn into sub-Saharan Africa, the Far Eastern populations making a journey of around 8000 miles (13,300km).

In Britain its spring arrival is later than that of its lookalike sibling, chiffchaff, although the first male willow warblers reach us long before the end of March. In areas where they are common, the sound of a singing male instantly triggers a response from its neighbours, and according to Henry Eliot Howard it 'results in a concert which no one could fail to enjoy'.[88]

Ian Wallace recreates a spine-tingling moment for any birdwatcher – picking out a Siberian Pallas' warbler (lower centre) amongst the autumn flock of migrant goldcrests.

The full phrase, repeated five to seven times a minute, is a slowly descending cadence, covering a full octave and noted for 'its compelling gentleness'.[89] As 'soft as summer rain' was Lord Grey's memorable phrase.[90] Its emollient effect is all the more compelling in the harsher landscapes of upland Britain where willow warbler is often the only member of its family to breed.

Goldcrest, *Regulus regulus*. VN: Crest, Golden-crested Wren. This much-loved midget is Britain's smallest bird and among the smallest across the whole northern hemisphere. There are at least four full-grown goldcrests to the ounce (28gm), while an individual weighs little more than a five-pence piece (4–7gm). Its eggs are like pale pinkish peas or, according to T. A. Coward, 'children's comfits'.[91] Yet a clutch of 12 represents one and a half times the female's own weight.

The nest, a tiny cuplet of moss and spider's web, regularly overtopped by a layer of insulating feathers, is often considered among the most beautiful constructed by any British bird.

The voice is comparably tiny. Its thin sibilant call has been variously likened to 'the jarring noise made by two branches that cross one another' or 'a damp finger rubbed lightly along a pane of glass'.[92] However the song, 'a wonderful silver-toned tinkle', has a more rhythmic structure that can suggest the turning of a badly oiled wheel.[93] It 'is useful as a standard to test one's hearing, as it is said to be the first song that old age loses'.[94]

The stripe in the bird's self-explanatory name has been described as glittering like 'burnished gold', or glowing 'like a lemon yellow flame', but at times it can be difficult to see.[95] Often the most striking feature is the white wing bar or the large beady eye set within a broad pale eye-ring. Together with a black gape line, which looks like a down-turned mouth, these give goldcrests an endearing but rather vacant or 'surprised expression'.[96]

The species is inextricably associated with conifers, and the huge increase in afforestation has allowed it to occupy almost every part of Britain and Ireland. In the spruce plantations of Killarney in County Kerry it reaches densities of 591 pairs per square kilometre (⅓ square mile).[97] During the last 20 years there have been troubling declines, particularly in southern England, but the goldcrest is unlikely ever to fall to the levels of previous centuries. In his day, Gilbert White thought it 'almost as rare as any bird we know'.[98]

Its highly sedentary lifestyle makes it a frequent victim of cold weather. Eight out of ten birds are thought to die each winter and really severe conditions, like those of 1962/3, can cause a dramatic crash in numbers. Yet the goldcrest is also remarkably resilient and there is something large and impressive about its capacity to survive in the most hostile conditions. It is resident as far north as Shetland, while in northern Europe it can persist at −25°C with just six hours of winter daylight. The long night-time fast is survived by burning up fat equivalent to one-fifth of its body weight.

Another commonplace part of its extraordinary life is the goldcrest's capacity to cross the North Sea during migration. The exodus from northern Europe occurs at the end of autumn in conditions similar to those that bring the first influxes of winter thrushes, woodcocks and short-eared owls. The coincidence in timing gave rise to an old name for goldcrest – 'woodcock pilot' – with the smaller bird reputed to arrive two days in advance of the wader. A persistent legend among wildfowlers was the bird's capacity to hitch a ride in the woodcock's plumage and some alleged they had even seen goldcrests emerge unharmed from the feathers. The same has also been claimed of the short-eared owl.

Much better documented is the goldcrest's remarkable boldness in the presence of humans:

Stacks of fish-boxes on the wharves and other unpromising-looking places are investigated, and not unfrequently houses and greenhouses are entered by these fearless little feathered scraps, hungry after their long journey. Should foggy or misty weather coincide with these migrations, light-vessels and boats off the coast and on the fishing grounds in the North Sea are thronged with these tiny birds, which are well known to the fishermen as 'herring spinks', coming as they do in the middle of the herring season.[99]

Migrant goldcrests have even been known to land on people who happened to be standing still as the bird flitted past. Instead of flying away in instant recognition of the error, the bird has then proceeded to pick among the fabric of their clothes for anything that might be edible.

Firecrest, *Regulus ignicapillus*. With a flaring orange crown (in males) and a brilliant set of stripes across its face, this strikingly beautiful bird was a welcome addition to the list of British breeding species in 1962. It has since consolidated its presence, mainly in southern England and Wales, but the distribution is erratic, while numbers have fluctuated between 22 and 103 pairs during the last 10 years.

Although it may be a 'green and bronze jewel', the firecrest is often overlooked and the song is easily mistaken for that of goldcrest. The birds that have made the largest mark on their human neighbours are in Buckinghamshire, where a small group was discovered at Wendover Forest in 1971:[100]

Four years later there was an incredible peak of 46 singing males, which plummeted to fewer than 20 the following year, probably because of the felling of a large Norway spruce plantation. Numbers remained low throughout the 1980s and declined further to fewer than 11 singing males after the storm of January 1990, which took out more spruce tops. Over the last few years there have been around 5–6 pairs. It's simply a lack of habitat – old stripy just loves those big Christmas trees. And wow, at over 100 foot tall, with stacks of greenery, they are impressive.

Now the Forestry Commission are doing their utmost to preserve what they've got, and have planted loads more, so in about 50 years' time numbers should increase again! They also produce a glossy pamphlet entitled, 'Guide to Wendover Woods'. On the front cover is a picture of our old friend plus a map highlighting, among other walks, the Firecrest Trail. It is waymarked, with an information board, and runs for 3.5km through the forest. It also takes in a hide, which overlooks a part of the canopy.

In the 1990s Wendover's avian celebrity received the ultimate local endorsement with the renaming of The Office pub at Wendover as the Firecrest. 'There is also a picture of the bird on the bar wall and boxes of matches for sale explaining the pub's history, and that of the bird itself.'[101]

Flycatcher family
Muscicapidae

Spotted Flycatcher, *Muscicapa striata*. VN Spotty, Spot/ted Fly. Even the greatest fans of this lovely bird, with its mousy-grey upperparts and whitish breast and belly, would have to admit that it is rather drab. The pale-flecked mantle and scapulars of young spotted flys almost justify the name, but the adults are merely streaked with dark on the breast and across the crown. They have no more than a thin squeaky, microscopically small song. Edward Grey wrote: 'one almost needed field-glasses to hear it – clear vision of the attitude, motions and manners of the bird helps the ear to collect the sound'.[1]

However spotted flys compensate with enormous character. During the first major census of British and Irish birds between 1968 and 1972, 'Atlas fieldworkers very often obtained proof of breeding at farms and country houses . . . since many owners were delighted to show off "their" flycatchers' nests.'[2] The birds are instantly recognisable because of their large-headed, top-heavy shape that is distinctive even in silhouette, and by the habit of returning to the same perch after their agile, twisting, aerial sallies for insects.

They are adept at catching large species like day-flying moths, butterflies, bees and wasps, whose stings they remove by thrashing the victim against the perch. The specialised diet means that they are among the latest spring migrants to return and are now in serious decline because of half a century of intense pesticide use. In the last 25 years their numbers have declined by almost 80 per cent, but they are still sufficiently numerous (155,000 pairs) to be familiar and are often birds of large gardens, churchyards or around farm buildings.

A key element in these human environments is the availability of numerous convenient perches from which to dart for insects. Tree stumps, dead branches in clearings, and wire netting around the woodland perimeter are all popular with spotted flycatchers. Churchyards, with their evenly spaced ranks of gravestones, are also acceptable, as are large gardens, where trellises, tennis-court nets, shed roofs and fence posts form another suite of suitable perches.

Gilbert White enjoyed a pair of spotted flycatchers in his Selborne vicarage garden. One season they selected as their nesting site a highly unsuitable naked bough, which proved fatally exposed to direct sunlight. White believed the half-grown young would have succumbed to the heat, had the adults not improvised a form of air con-ditioning. He described how they resorted to hovering 'over the nest all the hotter hours, while with wings expanded, and mouths gaping for breath, they screened off the heat from their suffering offspring'.[3]

Spotted flycatchers usually resolve this particular problem by nesting in holes in brick walls or other suitable niches, including nest boxes. 'In a small orchard near the farmhouse where I knew these birds were about I took the trouble to make an open-fronted nest box and attached it to a tree. A pair was quick to respond to the invitation and built their nest on the roof of the box!'[4] They have also been recorded to use the old nests of at least 12 other species and, it would seem, occasionally even share the same quarters:

> Some years ago a pair of flycatchers tried to build a nest under our eaves which sloped sharply. They failed time after time and I eventually tracked them down to an old house martin's nest at the side of the house. The martins were late that year and when they did arrive they appeared to be using the same old nest. Sure enough the odd couples continued to co-habit and appeared to feed whatever head bobbed out of the nest when the parents returned. At least one spotted flycatcher and four house martins fledged.[5]

Pied Flycatcher, *Ficedula hypoleuca*. VN: Pied Fly/Flicker (birders, particularly in northern England). This is a hole-nesting bird and has taken to its man-made alternative – the nest box – with even greater enthusiasm than its relative. Until the twentieth century pied flys were highly local birds, breeding mainly in north Wales and the Lake District, but nest-box schemes have aided its spread particularly in south-west Scotland, south-west England, the West Midlands and much of Wales. It can now be the most numerous bird present in some Welsh sessile oak woods, and as a whole that country holds as much as two-fifths of the present British population (37,500). It has also acquired a recent toehold in Ireland.[6]

The male is strikingly handsome and has a strange habit of flicking up one or both wings vertically when alarmed. Pied flys also cock or flick their tails and partly open their wings in tandem with a sharp alarm call, a habit that helps to explain the recently developed birders' name Flicker. It is a shyer species than spotted fly and tends to keep to thicker cover. Even now their exact movements on completion of nesting are little understood. All people know for certain is that, come July, pied flycatchers suddenly disappear from their breeding territories.

Spotted flycatchers are still found widely throughout Britain and Ireland, but have declined alarmingly in recent years.

Babbler family *Timaliidae*

Bearded Tit, *Panurus biamircus*. VN: Beardy. The common name of this beautiful scarce speciality of reedbeds is a classic misnomer given that it is neither a tit, nor is it bearded. The male actually possesses a long pair of mandarin's whiskers or, as Colin Harrison wrote, 'theatrical Victorian moustaches'.[1] However the name is only part of its peculiarity.

It has a remarkable capacity to alter its gut morphology in autumn to accommodate a total change of diet, from insects in summer to seed and vegetable matter during winter. The gizzard thickens and doubles in weight, while bearded tits eat considerable amounts of grit particles (more than 600 per stomach in one analysis) to help grind up the tough fibres. 'At Leighton Moss we've seen autumn parties of beardies collecting grit off the gravel paths and also from special grit trays which we've put out for them in the reedbed.'[2]

The bearded tit is also unique for being Europe's only representative of a large, predominantly Asiatic family called the babblers. Within this it is placed in a subfamily *Paradoxornithinae* (from the Greek for 'strange birds' or 'contradictory birds') usually with a group of species called parrotbills. Several of them share the bearded tit's bright colours, noisy gregarious behaviour and lively bounding manner, but they occupy dense bamboo scrub in the Himalayas rather than lowland reedbed.

The classic bearded-tit encounter involves a family group shuffling to the top of several reed stems, which bend under their weight and give the birds access to the terminal seedheads. They can then remain feeding busily in the open for several minutes, before they shuffle back out of sight, or suddenly take off en masse amid a chorus of sharp 'pinging' or 'twanging' calls, and thereafter you may not see another one well all day.

Although the male has no real song William Yarrell noted more than 150 years ago that the ringing call 'corresponds well with the delicacy and beauty of the . . . birds'.[3] It is perhaps for this striking note – not to mention the lovely colours – that beardies were popular cagebirds in previous centuries.

The bird's high dependence on reedbeds accounts for a highly fragmented range across Europe and parts of Asia. In Britain it was once largely confined to the wetland areas of East Anglia but in recent decades it has undergone a significant expansion. There are colonies in Hampshire, Dorset, on Humberside, in north Lancashire (at Leighton Moss RSPB reserve) and now around

The bearded tit is our only representative of a bird family found mainly in eastern Asia.

Scotland's Tay estuary. The 'engine room' for the spread is thought to have been a brief dramatic surge in the Dutch population following the construction of the 'polders' in the 1950s. The birds then spread outwards into other countries.

Milder winters have also played a part in the bearded tit's recent success. By contrast periods of intense cold can wreak havoc and during the famous snowfall of 1947 the East Anglian population fell to just four or five pairs in Suffolk and a single male in Norfolk. Remarkably, they came through the big freeze of 1962/3 largely unscathed, when the absence of snow is thought to have been the key difference. In the earlier winter period snow completely blanketed the reed litter and prevented the starving birds gaining access to their seed diet.

Another factor in the bird's recent increase is the provision of nest boxes, which was pioneered by the former warden at Leighton Moss, John Wilson:

By weight, the long-tailed tit is one of our smallest birds.

The first nest boxes were wigwam-shaped bundles of reeds with hollow centres and a wooden floor, but we found that almost two-thirds of the pairs preferred to build *underneath* the intended base of the box, resting their nest on the reeds pushed down by the floor. It seemed that amongst bearded tits the true 'des res' was the basement flat rather than a penthouse suite! A new more onion-shaped design is now used and all nest inside the box. In the year 2000 from the 70 boxes we put out we had 66 nesting attempts. All adults were colour ringed and we were able to tell that while a pair might only use a box for the first of their multiple broods, once they left, another pair would take it over for their second brood. With or without nest boxes, beardies are remarkably prolific and will have up to four broods a year. I've even seen recently fledged immatures as late as early October. The high productivity explains all those large 'pinging' family groups which are so characteristic of reedbeds like Leighton Moss in autumn. It also explains their ability to recover so quickly from any disastrous slump during a bad winter.[4]

Long-tailed Tit family
Aegithalidae

Long-tailed Tit, *Aegithalos caudatus*. VN: Barrel Tit/ Tom, Bum Barrel. Although a solitary long-tailed tit is a rarity, family parties of 2–20 birds (very occasionally up to 50) are a distinctive and commonplace sight across much of Britain and Ireland. Outside the breeding season they rove through their communal territory enveloped in a perpetual cocoon of soft, bubbling contact notes. Their movements, which are equally characteristic, are well described by Colin Harrison: 'one is usually conscious of the sudden appearance of a party of them, trees at once alive with small rocketing forms swinging acrobatically on twigs ... then passing on equally suddenly.'[1] The departure of one is normally a trigger for the collective follow-my-leader exodus, during which they resemble a succession of whirring sticks with globular, pink ping-pong-ball foreparts.

Although a long-tailed tit can be almost 6 inches (15cm) from bill to tail-tip and considerably longer than all the other family members except great tit, more than half the length is made up of tail. By weight it is among the smallest of British birds and like other midgets (see Goldcrest, page 381) is highly susceptible to cold weather. And since long-tailed tits maintain a largely insectivorous diet year-round, they find little relief on the garden birdtable.

In very bad winters – 1917, 1947 and 1963 were among the worst – numbers can fall by as much as 80 per cent (although recent mild weather has enabled them to climb to a current total of about 250,000 pairs). One strategy to help them through the long nightly winter fast is to huddle together in a roost, where they form a single feathered clump with numerous protruding tails. The distance between roosting birds decreases in proportion to the severity of the cold. The collective need for winter warmth is suggested as one explanation for their highly tribal lifestyle, which finds further expression in the long-tailed tit's breeding season.

In late winter the family flock breaks down into a series of breeding pairs, and sometimes a couple will receive help in feeding their young from a close relative, particularly if the latter's own nest has failed. In cases where a family relationship has been established, the helper has proved to be the brother of the breeding male. Up to eight helpers have been recorded in attendance at a single brood, where the assistance strongly increases the chances of fledging success. The closeness between nesting adults and the supporting network of 'aunts' and 'uncles' continues after the offspring leave the nest. Thus a tribal group encountered in winter woodland is likely to represent one or more extended families.[2]

Another striking aspect of long-tailed breeding behaviour is the nest itself, which is one of the most elaborate built by any of our birds. It is an oval-shaped dome wedged into a cleft between branches or sited in the middle of dense thorn scrub. It is usually difficult to spot, particularly since the exterior is decorated with a beautiful façade of lichen fragments that blends perfectly with the surrounding vegetation. It is perhaps a measure of the nest-finding capabilities of our rural ancestors that many vernacular names for the species stemmed from the nest itself. Sadly most, if not all, this linguistic invention is now obsolete, but it once included 'bum barrel', 'bush oven', 'feather poke', 'hedge jug', 'jack in a bottle', 'long pod', 'poke bag' and 'pudding bag'. (Equally intriguing is a Cornish name for long-tailed tit recounted to us, 'patiney' or 'patteney paley', which is apparently unknown in the literature.[3])

The nest comprises an intricate mix of wool and moss bound and felted together with spider's web, camouflaged with as many as 4000 lichen flakes (a nest was once seen with a substitute layer of 1500 white polystyrene chippings)[4] and lined with an average of 1500 feathers.

These exquisite structures take more than three weeks to make and were at one time a prized exhibit in the Victorian drawing room or a much sought-after trophy for childhood nesting forays of yesteryear:

As kids growing up in South Shields a gang of us would spend our school holidays exploring the parks, gardens, allotments etc. raiding nests and comparing our egg collections with rival gangs. I always remember being jealous of one gang which had managed to find the fabled 'two-fingered piedy'. Everyone had heard of this little bird that built an oval-shaped nest out of feathers and moss with only an entrance hole big enough for two fingers, hence the name. We looked everywhere and eventually the two-fingered piedy became our holy grail. Then one day I spotted a nest high up in a tree, oval-shaped with a tiny entrance. A two-fingered piedy!

I volunteered to climb up and check the contents while the others waited, drooling with anticipation. I managed to get to the nest, but to my surprise the

The crested tit is a specialist of Old Caledonian forest in the Scottish Highlands.

Tit family *Paridae*

Marsh Tit, *Parus palustris*, and **Willow Tit**, *P. montanus*, are a classic confusion pair that people still find difficult to separate. They are most easily told apart by their calls and, although even these overlap, marsh tit's bright explosive '*pitchoo*' note is diagnostic. The names are misleading since willow tit is the one most often found near water and particularly in damp alder carr or swampy birch scrub. By contrast, marsh tit is an inhabitant of broad-leaved woods.

Another mark of their identification challenge is the fact that willow tit was not discovered in Britain until a century ago. Prior to that all woodland-dwelling black-capped tits had been assumed to be marsh tits. It is intriguing to read nineteenth-century accounts and see the early confusion at work. In William Yarrell's *A History of British Birds* (1845) he wrote: 'Colonel Montagu says he has seen the Marsh Tit excavating the decayed part of such trees, and artfully carrying the chips in its bill to some distance.'[1] It is a precise field observation of an individual creating its nest, but not marsh tit because the species never makes its own hole; yet it describes with great accuracy the willow tit's burrowing technique.

In 1897 two sharp-eyed German ornithologists, Ernst Hartert and Otto Kleinschmidt, finally resolved the long-standing error when they picked out two willow tits wrongly labelled in a tray of marsh-tit skins at the British Museum. In the same year two fresh specimens were collected at Coalfall Wood at Finchley in north London, and willow tit was added to the British list in 1900, the last widespread resident bird to be recognised.

It was later discovered to breed as far north as the Scottish Highlands, but both species are predominantly birds of England and Wales. Neither breeds in Ireland and an attempted introduction of marsh tit at Tipperary in 1909 was unsuccessful. In recent years both birds have gone into steep and rather mysterious declines, particularly the willow tit, and one theory is that they lose out in competition with the other commoner tit species.[2]

Crested Tit, *Parus cristatus*. The crested tit has a tiny relict population of just 900 pairs, largely confined to the areas of Old Caledonian forest or mature Scots pine woods in the Spey valley, around the Moray Basin and along the Great Glen. The sharp restrictions on distribution are helpful in identifying it, although there should be little scope for confusing the country's only small bird possessed of a tall, spiky chequered crest.

entrance hole was at the bottom. Sticking two fingers in and poking around, I was suddenly hit with excruciating pain as if my finger had been stabbed with hot needles. My jaw dropped and the blood drained out of me as a cloud of angry wasps poured out. Needless to say I was down in the blink of an eye. The others had started to leg it, with me and the swarm of wasps in hot pursuit. After a dash through the park we gathered to compare wounds. A couple of the others had been stung, while I got another on the neck that came up like a cricket ball. Needless to say, my nesting days ended with this calamitous encounter and like so many junior eggers I became a fully-fledged birder with a lifelong passion for birds, especially long-tailed tits![5]

Its nearest relatives are in southern Norway or northern Belgium and France and both these populations belong to different races, while the Highland birds have been designated a separate endemic subspecies, *scoticus*. Small wonder, therefore, that the Scottish Ornithologists' Club chose this rare Highland speciality as its badge and emblem in 1947.

Like most sedentary passerines, the crested tit can fall victim to the extreme conditions of the Scottish winter and has been known to leave the woods for garden birdtables. It will also regularly feed 'on the gralloch and skins and fat of shot hinds, particularly those which the keepers have hung up on trees'.[3] The proud emblem of the Scottish Ornithologists' Club will also occasionally resort to feeding from dustbins.

Coal Tit, *Parus ater*. The name – originally spelt 'cole' tit – refers to the black head that is broken by white lower cheeks and a long white stripe through the centre of the nape. It is a specialist of conifer woodland and has increased dramatically in line with the spread of commercial softwood plantations, while also benefiting from the popularity of exotic evergreens in the garden.

Yet coal tits remain less numerous than either great or blue tits and for that reason are welcome visitors at the birdtable as occasional visual relief from their dominant siblings. The species is the smallest and among the most gymnastic of their family and is distinguished by having two endemic races in these islands. The yellower-cheeked Irish birds are classified as a subspecies *hibernicus*, while those in Britain, which have grey upperparts tinged warmish olive-buff, are further separated as *britannicus*.

Blue Tit, *Parus caeruleus*. VN: Tom Tit, Jackie Bluecap. It vies with blackbird and robin as our favourite garden bird and like the latter it is part of a select band enjoying a personalised nickname, although 'Tom tit' is now falling away from regional culture, just as the old generic name 'titmouse' vanished about 50 years ago.

The latter dates back to the early fourteenth century and is a curiously tautologous conflation of 'tit', meaning small or a small creature (hence the old name for a pipit: 'tit-lark'), with 'mose' (later 'mouse'), which signified much the same.[4] The shortened current version was popularised only in the nineteenth century, which is when the word acquired the associations that make it a frequent cause for sniggering among small boys (and girls).[5] It is striking that in both contexts 'tit' carries parallel connotations of roundness and attractiveness.

None of the family is more appealing than the blue tit, whose square-headed shape seems to reinforce the impression of elfin plumpness. We seem to have an intrinsic attachment to blue birds (e.g. kingfisher, bee-eater, roller and swallow) but the blue tit's willingness to

The blue tit is one of the most popular of our bird-table regulars.

feed on birdtables and to breed in substitute nest sites is certainly at the heart of its enormous popularity. In the BTO's Garden Birdwatch scheme it has an almost 100 per cent record in participants' gardens and only blackbirds show a comparable faithfulness.[6]

While great tits are dominant over all other family members, blue tits are often well able to hold their own with their bigger relative and are notably aggressive to other tits. And, on occasions, with other species: two old country names were 'Billy biter' and 'Tom bitethumb' (note the recurrent personalisation), which still resonate with modern bird ringers, as they did with earlier generations of nest-finding boys and horticulturalists.[7] Despite the bird's wide reputation as a gardener's friend (for its voracious consumption of caterpillars in spring and summer), blue tits were often trapped supposedly to protect soft fruits or flowering shrubs. As recently as the late 1950s an Essex farmer boasted of killing 400 birds.[8] Many were also regularly caught by gardeners in mouse traps.[9]

Another habit that earned blue tits a degree of notoriety was their love of removing the foil top from milk bottles and drinking the cream. The practice has now abated with the wider passing of that traditional fixture of the British morning, the milkman, but for several decades few areas of the country were unaffected. Other species learnt to exploit milk bottles, including blackbirds, magpies (see page 405), starlings and sparrows, as well as three further members of the tit family, but blue tits were most widely recorded. In a 1949 study its authors, James Fisher and R. A. Hinde, noted that blue tits accounted for more than 60 per cent of all incidents.[10]

The first ever was reported on a Swaythling doorstep in Southampton in 1921, when a tit was seen to prise wax-board tops from a bottle. By 1935 the practice had acquired two main centres – around London and the Home Counties and in north-east England. The authors suggested that a small group of birds had spontaneously learnt the technique in different parts of the country and thereafter it was acquired by much greater numbers through direct observation. By the late 1940s it was widespread. Birds were known to arrive at the doorstep within minutes of the milkman's departure and even pursue his cart as it passed down the road. Some were recorded to remove tea cloths, tins or jars placed as protection over the milk, and occasionally people found piles of foil caps in shrubbery where the thieves had habitually carried them. Usually only the first 1½–2 inches (3.6–5cm) could be reached, but there are several sorry parables of avian greed – tits that drank too deeply of the cream until they slipped into the bottle and drowned.

Others graduated to a life of wider theft:

In the 1960s we found that the blue tits followed our milk-and-newspaper delivery lady around our south Wales college campus, pecking open the silver top for the cream. She had to put the newspapers over the bottles to beat them to it. The tits also discovered very quickly that students hung plastic carrier bags of butter and other goodies out of their windows to keep them cool and the bags were pecked open at the bottom to gain access for a free-for-all.[11]

The bottle-opening practice flourished for about 50 years until the 1980s, when its demise was observed not without a little fond regret, as RSPB officer Tim Melling records:

Some years ago I received a call from the *Liverpool Daily Post* requesting help with a reader's letter on why blue tits no longer pecked bottle tops. I had noticed myself that they no longer took milk, so gave an instant answer that blue tits only liked cream.

The blue tit's habit of pecking through the foil top has now gone with the decline of full-cream milk and the gradual passing of the doorstep delivery.

During my childhood in the 1960s and 70s everybody had full-cream milk, in which the cream floated to the top. I remember you always had to shake the milk before you opened a new bottle. During the 1980s the nation became more health-conscious and semi-skimmed or skimmed milk became far commoner. The thing I hadn't expected was the huge media interest in the story. First Radio Merseyside wanted to interview me, then the interview was broadcast on all the BBC national radio programmes, and I ended up giving at least 20 other radio interviews the same day. In more than 15 years of working for RSPB this was my busiest media session.[12]

In fact tits lack the necessary enzymes to digest lactose and milk can cause them osmotic diarrhoea. The cream, however (a concentrated emulsion of fat with almost no lactose), was both digestible and energy-dense and this constituted their exclusive reward.[13]

A behavioural adaptation that has lost none of its popularity with blue tits, or with their human hosts, is their willingness to use a nest box. Few streets in Britain or Ireland are without one and in many gardens there are several. The first prototypes were pioneered in the nineteenth century, particularly in Germany, and by 1897 various box formats or platforms had met with success with 20 different British species. The newly formed

The blue tit and the garden nestbox have been an important double act in the development of our national interest in birds.

RSPB played a key role in popularising boxes and was forced to become self-sufficient in their production once the First World War brought an end to the German supply.[14]

By 1935 in a book entitled *Every Garden a Bird Sanctuary*, Emma Turner was dismissing in haughty tones the bird-box equivalent of keeping up with the Joneses: 'Avoid disfiguring your garden,' she warned, 'with the awful atrocities made to resemble Swiss châlets and such stupid, unnatural and rather vulgar counterfeits.'[15] One wonders what she would have made of their twenty-first-century post-modern equivalent – made of predator-proof concrete with a clear plastic 'conical hat'?

From the outset tits were one of the principal beneficiaries of boxes, but are famously catholic in their choice of a suitable site. Cavities in brickwork and pipes,

tin cans, boxes, car dashboards, glove compartments and radiators, letter boxes and street lamps have all been recorded, although not all choices meet with success:

> Some blue tits nested recently in the downpipe on our Cotswold cottage and it seemed cruel to discourage them. However one evening there was a ferocious storm and next morning we took a ladder to investigate. What a sad sight met our eyes: a shallow saucer of a nest containing five tiny eggs and the dead female blue tit sitting on top, her sodden wings still stretched protectively over the nest. We dismantled the pipe and carefully pushed out 23 inches of compressed moss and cow hair, extending from a joint in the downpipe to the summit. My husband picked up the dead bird and the eggs and prepared to bury them, when there was a terrible commotion in the nearby hedge. The cock blue tit was fluttering up and down in a most agitated manner, calling plaintively in a way we'd never heard before. 'He's come to the funeral,' we agreed, and then went to find the spade.[16]

The post-mortem examination and eventual burial of a wild bird are equally telling of our relationship to the blue tit, as is the contributors' wider sense of grief.

Blue tits sometimes obtain more than simply the premises for their nests. 'I was amazed once to look out of our back window and see my husband sitting on the patio with a blue tit on his head pulling out hairs. The bird went to its nest in a nearby box and returned several more times. It also pulled hairs from his legs.'[17] At my own family home we routinely laid out hair after any dog-brushing operations in spring and invariably refound it later in the summer in the tit box.

Just as the little egret played a key role in the development of British bird conservation (see page 50), so must the blue tit – particularly the wide-eyed nestlings staring up from the depths of the nest box – have done more to cement our attachment to birds in general than almost any other species. Along with birdfood, nest boxes are part of a multi-million-pound industry and much of it is geared towards the nation's 3.3 million pairs of blue tits. For reasons that are closely related, the population is still increasing. However not all our garden donations to the bird are so beneficial:

> I remember one warm summer morning, when I was twelve, being aware of our cat, Patch, stalking across the lawn. To my horror I realised he was heading for a blue tit stuck fast to a stale jam tart that had been innocently deposited that morning. I screamed at him but he sped towards the bird and grabbed it. Patch, tart and tit were

heading straight for his favourite escape route through the hedge, but I just managed to get his tail before he disappeared. He finally turned to sink his teeth into my hand, when I grabbed the bird still firmly fixed in the red jam. The only way to remove it successfully was to wash it away under the tap. Luckily the blue tit survived and I put it to dry in the greenhouse until it could be released later that morning.[18]

Great Tit, *Parus major*. With its bold black, white and yellow patterning, its ringing song in early spring and the mixture of intelligence and athleticism on the birdtable, the great tit is as popular with the lover of garden birds as it is with the professional research ecologist. The characteristic that has most endeared it to both groups is its willingness to breed in a man-made substitute for its usual tree hole. The tit family's near-monopoly of the nest-box habit has made their breeding behaviour better known (and more easily studied) than that of any other comparable bird group. However the great tit is known best of all and often listed among the most studied animals in the world. There is a famous research project at Wytham Wood near Oxford (managed by the university) that has been running continuously for 67 years. By the 1990s it involved a population spread across 1125 nest boxes.[19]

If adaptability can be measured in a bird's geographic distribution, then the great tit is as flexible in its lifestyle as it is widespread. Only a handful of British songbirds have a larger natural range. Great tits occur as far south as India, Java and the Indonesian island of Flores, as far east as Russia's Kamchatka peninsula and as far west as the Atlantic coast of Morocco. There is huge variation across the three continents (about 30 different races) with the British and Irish birds receiving separate recognition as the subspecies *newtoni*.

Here it is primarily a species of deciduous woodland and reaches its highest densities in the beechwoods west of a line between the Thames and Mersey estuaries. Beechmast is a key winter staple in its diet. Yet the great tit's ability to thrive in almost any tree cover, including the savagely 'crew-cut' hedgerows of modern farmland or the trimmest shrubberies of inner-city gardens, lies at the heart of its familiarity. Blue tits outnumber it by about 2:1, but both species are equally prominent and equally welcome, even if the smaller bird would probably shave it in a straight popularity contest.

As a vocalist the great tit is a strange conundrum. It has one of the easiest songs for the birdwatching beginner to learn, given that the best known in its large vocabulary is a repeated clear double note, likened to a squeaky bicycle pump and often spelt *'tee-choo'* or

The great tit's attachment to manmade nest sites has allowed it to become one of the most studied birds in the world.

'teach-er'. An old country name was 'saw-sharpener', which might have lapsed from usage but still strikes a chord: 'When I taught birds in evening classes I used to describe the great tit as the "see-saw" bird.'[20]

While the commonest song is simplicity itself, the bird's total output is highly confusing. In a single great-tit population the birds will employ an average of 40 different song types in a year, while each male has an average of four song types delivered in three different tempos. Another standard maxim on the bird's voice – 'If you're in a wood, and you hear an unfamiliar call it's bound to be a great tit' – hints at a complexity that foxes even experienced ears.[21]

One explanation for the variety in their repertoire has been called the Beau Geste theory (see Cetti's Warbler, page 362), after the eponymous hero of the novel who wandered the battlements of his desert fort, propping up dead soldiers to suggest that he enjoyed greater defences than was the case. By a similar vocal subterfuge the great tit is thought to give an impression that his territory is more densely occupied than it is, therefore discouraging competitors. Not all aspects of the theory are consistent, but there is strong evidence that great tits with large vocabularies are socially dominant and breed more successfully.[22]

Another key to the pecking order is the thickness of the black stripe down the centre of the great tit's underparts. In females it narrows and then stops on the lower belly but in males, which are larger and dominant, it spreads as a black patch right to the undertail coverts. As well as this visual 'flag', size is also critical to the great-tit hierarchy, but recent research has revealed some unexpected developments in this variable feature. During the period when one of the species' main predators, the sparrowhawk, was suppressed by pesticide poisoning, the most dominant great tits were also the heaviest. However with the raptor's recovery, the birds carrying the greatest fat were the ones most susceptible to predation and the impact was for dominant birds to lose excess weight and to rely on their social ascendancy to secure access to food resources. They are quite literally the fittest to survive. Subordinate great tits, which may be excluded from food in periods of shortage, are obliged to carry energy reserves for just such hard times and are thus more at risk from sparrowhawk attacks. The overall flexibility in the bird's response to this renewed challenge has ensured that its numbers have not declined despite the raptor's dramatic increase.[23]

With the exception of the European shag, no species offers more opportunity for the double entendre than this family. The following is typical. 'When he was fourteen years old my son always managed to shock me by referring to great tits as Dolly Partons.'[24]

> In about 1984 the RSPB winter sales catalogue was still being produced in-house and was of course full of all those twee products like oven mitts and teacloths we have come to expect. I remember that there was a fashion for naming products after British birds and one that got past the editors and into print that year was 'Marsh Tit Hand and Body Lotion.' Absolutely true.[25]

Nuthatch family *Sittidae*

Wood Nuthatch, *Sitta europea*. The name represents a gradual modification of the original Middle English *nuthak* meaning 'nut hacker'.[1] The earlier version nicely captures the way the bird secures a shell by wedging it into a tree crevice and then hammers through to the kernel with a few blows of the long chisel-like bill. Often the resulting loud taps from these operations give away its location in the trees, although nuthatches are seldom difficult to find. They have a wide range of distinctive calls, including a loud, explosive, liquid '*pwit*' that Gilbert White aptly likened to a stone hitting ice on the slant.[2]

In White's day it was mainly a bird of southern English woodland, but in the twentieth century it embarked on a steady successful expansion to the west and north, occupying lowland areas of Cumbria and Northumberland by the 1980s and breeding in Scotland for the first time in 1989.[3] The spread is linked to an increase in suitable woodland habitat, with a little further help from us in the form of birdtables and nest boxes. Yet nuthatches tend to use man-made sites less often than other hole-nesting birds and routinely use mud to cement the lid to the box or reduce the hole size, as they do when a natural tree hole is too large for their purposes. Emma Turner once found a nuthatch nest in a hole in a wall 'so exquisitely reduced that you could not distinguish the quality of their masonry from the surrounding mortar even when it was scratched with a knife'.[4]

Although they lack the stiff tail feathers of woodpeckers and treecreepers, nuthatches are easily the most versatile of all our bark-dwelling birds. They will just as readily come down a main branch or trunk upside-down as they will shuffle upwards or go horizontally round the boll to take up a position out of sight to an observer. David Bannerman noted the bird's 'irritating habit of remaining at the opposite side of the tree'.[5] However nuthatches are by no means shy and regularly raid tit-feeders and balls of fat from gardens, when their extra manoeuvrability is an advantage . . . and sometimes not:

> I was working in the garden just below the feeders and our robin was helping me, looking for worms. He then stood on top of the steps chittering away and would not stop. I looked up and there was a nuthatch head-first inside a wide-mesh feeder holding peanuts in their shells. He could not get out backward because his wings were caught in the wire. I hastily took the

Nuthatches are remarkable for their ability to climb both up and down the tree trunk.

Wallcreeper family
Tichodromadidae

Wallcreeper, *Tichodroma muraria*. Its long fine decurved bill is uniquely adapted for picking insects and spiders off bare rockfaces, against which the bird's predominantly mouse-grey plumage provides perfect camouflage. Yet once a wallcreeper takes flight, it flashes a double row of white 'eyes' in the dark outer wing and a patch of intense carmine, which have earnt it a reputation as one of Europe's most spectacular species. The languid action of the rounded wings is also reminiscent of a hoopoe and is frequently likened to a butterfly, while in China the wallcreeper is known with equal justification as the 'rock flower'.[1]

In autumn these birds descend from their high mountain tops and frequently substitute the sheer cliffs of summer with the walls of stone buildings. They are regular visitors to hill villages, but wallcreepers also have a penchant for sites that provide a suitably grand setting for so glamorous a bird. These include Neuschwanstein, the Bavarian 'fairy-tale' castle built by Louis II, 'Mad Ludwig' (and the location for the children's film *Chitty Chitty Bang Bang*); the hilltop town of Minerve, the Cathar stronghold in the French Languedoc; and the thirteenth-century Château de Chillon on the edge of Lake Geneva, made famous by Byron's poem 'The Prisoner of Chillon'.[2]

The wallcreeper's autumn dispersal from the mountains has occasionally resulted in birds crossing the English Channel. There have been 11 records since 1792, but the most intriguing was a bird that returned to a private quarry near Cheddar Gorge for two successive winters between 1976 and 1978. An eye-witness account of the Somerset individual only confirms the wallcreeper's ranking among the world's most sought-after birds. 'My memories are that it looked like some big exotic butterfly which danced up the rockface. This appearance was exaggerated when it opened its wings to reveal the exquisite patches of crimson. Quite the most beautiful bird I have ever seen in my life.'[3]

feeder down and my sister held the nuthatch while I cut the wire with wire-cutters from the bird's wings. Once released he made a bee-line for the woods and we were so happy he wasn't injured.[6]

Nuthatches are also great storers of food, which can cause complications. 'A gardening problem we have is retrieving the sunflower seeds that the nuthatches "plant" both between the cracks in the patio and also in the numerous pots my wife has strewn around with all her cherished plants. If we don't find them all we get a plethora of sunflower plants surfacing in the spring.'[7]

Treecreeper family *Certhiidae*

Eurasian Treecreeper, *Certhia familiaris*. Of all our common resident birds (there are about 250,000 pairs in Britain and Ireland) this is the most inconspicuous. The mealy lichen-like patterning of the upperparts renders it almost invisible as it creeps mouse-like up a tree trunk. Without a glimpse of the silvery-white underparts, a treecreeper can look like a moving sliver of bark. The bird's vocalisations are similarly easy to miss and to forget. The call is a repeated insect-like '*see-see-see*', while the song was described by Lord Grey as 'a very sweet little wisp of sound'.[1] It is a tremulous descending ripple characterised by a more vigorous terminal flourish that conjures for me some type of small animal with a whippy tail and writhing action vanishing quickly down a hole.

Although treecreepers are hard to spot, they are not difficult to approach. Young birds have occasionally even been known to shuffle up to a human figure, mistaking it for their more usual habitat. Adults too often behave as if invisible and, when occasionally conscious of being watched, they will freeze 'in a head up position . . . like tiny Bitterns'.[2] They are usually solitary birds and one seldom encounters more than a pair, although it is possible to see larger groups during the winter when they create temporary communal roosts. As many as 14 birds will crowd together for warmth in a crevice or fault in the trunk.

Treecreepers have developed a particular attachment to the huge conifers from California known as wellingtonia, in whose soft bark they hollow out a small roost cavity the size and shape of 'half a hardboiled egg'. The trees were first introduced in the 1850s as a parkland ornament and it was many decades before they reached a size to be of value to treecreepers. Yet birds' partiality for wellingtonia was widely noted in 1923, suggesting that the habit quickly spread through the whole population once the new habitat became available. The practice is now found wherever bird and tree coincide.[3]

Very occasionally treecreepers will utilise a man-made roost site:

> A friend and I were exploring a disused railway tunnel near Bourne in Lincolnshire and as we moved into the darkness with our mini Maglights, we stumbled upon a roosting treecreeper fast asleep and clinging tightly to the heavily-sooted wall. Upon further investigation we also discovered a large number of herald moths, red admiral and peacock butterflies and numerous

A rare photograph of a treecreeper roosting on a tunnel wall.

unidentified spiders all clinging to the same wall surface. We concluded that the tunnel provided a dry safe haven with abundant supplies for a last nightly feed.[4]

Penduline Tit family *Remizidae*

Eurasian Penduline Tit, *Remiz pendulinus*. This tiny bird of southern European wetland thickets and scrub gets its name from the beautiful felted nest made from animal hair and the flossy seed-down from reed mace and willow. The pendulous tubes are remarkably strong, judging by the fact that east European children once wore them as slippers, while the Masai are said to use as a kind of purse the nests made by an African relative.[1] In Britain and Ireland the penduline tit is no more than a vagrant (52 records by 2001), although some of them have remained for several months.

Oriole family *Oriolidae*

Golden Oriole, *Oriolus oriolus*. Few European birds are more beautiful than the male golden oriole. Sadly few are more difficult to see. Despite the brilliant colours they blend surprisingly well with the dense upper canopy of broad-leaved woodland, from which the birds seldom depart. The largely green and streaky female is even better camouflaged and is often only detected by her strange cat-like squalling call.

The species is one of the most spectacular recent additions to the list of breeding birds in Britain, although the existence of an old Somerset name for green wood-pecker, 'woodwall', raises an intriguing possibility. It is thought to derive from *wodewale*, a medieval word for golden oriole, of whose song it is closely onomatopoeic (in modern Dutch it is still known as *Wielewaal*).[1] The name also arises in the anonymously written ballad of Robin Hood and Guy of Gisborne:

> The woodweele sang and wolde not cease,
> Sitting upon the spray,
> So lowde he wakened Robin Hood,
> In the greenwood where he lay.[2]

Golden orioles breed only in a small area of East Anglia.

Chaucer mentions the same bird in the *Romaunt of the Rose* and these multiple references raise the distinct possibility that during the warmer, drier late Middle Ages – when wine-grapes were widely grown in England – golden orioles were also far commoner. Lockwood suggests that when the bird died out with climatic deterioration, so the name was transferred to the only other yellow-green woodland species, the green woodpecker.[3]

There are also intermittent records of golden orioles during the nineteenth century, but the birds were con-stantly persecuted by egg collectors or trophy hunters and a small Kent population probably died out in about 1910. It is easy to understand why the discovery of a new East Anglian colony in the 1960s was a jealously guarded secret for more than a decade.

In 1976 one site on the Suffolk/Norfolk border near Lakenheath became better known and in its heyday was a powerfully atmospheric location. A plantation of mature hybrid poplars, which ran on either side of the Thetford–Ely railway line (and was owned by the match manufacturers, Bryant and May) seemed to ignite in some visitors a vision from childhood: 'Each tree was perfectly symmetrical, the same height and exactly the same distance apart from its neighbour. I had never before seen such absolute uniformity in a wood, but it did strike a chord. Young children often draw over-simplified 'lollipop' trees with bare straight trunks ending in a round mass. The foliage here was slightly pyramidal but otherwise these were the same trees.'[4]

At dawn in midsummer the regimented columns were nicely counter-balanced by a layer of morning mist. In this curiously geometric landscape, itself part of the hottest, driest region in the country, the sense of being in continental Europe (or, at least, anywhere other than Britain) was compounded by the 'ziggling' of abundant whitethroats, the water-bubble notes of breeding cuckoos and, above all, the glorious liquid fluting songs of golden orioles.

The site was subsequently sold and felled (though a small section now forms part of the RSPB's Lakenheath reserve) and the orioles moved to other neighbouring poplar plantations in the Fens basin. This forms the core of a shifting and widely dispersed British population, which has fluctuated between two and 25 pairs in the last 15 years.[5]

Shrike family *Laniidae*

Red-backed Shrike, *Lanius collurio*. The combination of chestnut back, pink-washed cream underparts, black bandit's mask and dusty blue-grey cap make the male one of the most handsome of our breeding birds. However early ornithologists were struck by the contrast between these delicate colours and the shrike's predatory habits. Thomas Bewick suggested that 'their courage, their appetite for blood, and their hooked bill entitle them to be ranked with the boldest and the most sanguinary of the rapacious tribe'.[1] An old country name was 'butcher bird', while *Lanius* derives from the Latin verb *lanio*, meaning 'I tear or rend in pieces'.[2]

The references drew partly on the shrike's practice of impaling surplus food on the spikes of a thorn bush, bramble or barbed-wire fence and, in one instance, the prongs of an upturned garden fork.[3] While most items in the shrike's 'larder' are large insects, such as bees, moths and beetles, it will also take and hang far bigger corpses of birds up to the size of adult thrushes, small mammals and young snakes. Henry Stevenson recorded a more unusual response to the bird's rapacious habits: a retired falconer liked to launch his pet shrike at the flies in his sitting room.[4] Its prey has occasionally included pheasant and partridge chicks, which once ensured that the sparrow-sized predator was added to the gamekeeper's own well-stocked gibbet.[5]

Even relatively recent observers have been offended by the bird's capacity to attack and kill species as large or larger than itself. Herbert Axell, former warden at the RSPB's Suffolk reserve at Minsmere, recalled occasions when breeding shrikes could be seen to enter the holes in a sand-martin colony near the car park and fly off with chicks. When some of the nestlings were subsequently pegged out on the barbed wire, shocked visitors would exclaim, 'Oh, how awful! Why don't you get rid of these beastly birds!'[6]

Possibly some complainants were pleased to learn of the shrike's then impending extinction in Britain. Its seemingly irreversible decline vexed ornithologists for the whole of the twentieth century and, while they were able regularly to assemble data to confirm the shrinking range and falling numbers, they never fully understood the mechanisms that caused it. Climate change in north-west Europe (towards warmer, wetter summers) and the increased use of pesticides are now thought to have been key factors, although these alone do not seem to explain declines in 19 other European countries.

A more local threat to British red-backed shrikes flowed from the bird's beautiful eggs, whose ground colour may be greenish, olivaceous, pinkish, buffish, creamy or almost white, with differing amounts of dark red, purple, grey or brown blotching and speckles. The enormous variety has been a powerful temptation to egg thieves and this is one species where the collectors' systematic depredations may

Egg collecting may have played a significant part in the eventual extinction of Britain's red-backed shrikes.

have played a significant part in its extinction. One notorious figure was H. J. K. Burne, who specialised in locating and taking large series of eggs of stone curlew and red-backed shrike. During a career spanning nearly 50 years he located 175 shrike nests, mainly in Norfolk and Suffolk, containing a total of almost 900 eggs. Many of these ended up in his large collection.[7]

By 1950 a bird that had been relatively common and widespread across England and Wales as far north as Cumbria had gradually dwindled to just 350 pairs. Ten years later the population stood at 250 pairs, and by 1971 it was 81 pairs, with most of them concentrated on the heaths of Hampshire, Surrey, the East Anglian coast and Breckland. As one commentator noted, 'One by one, these last bastions collapsed to the final retreat in the Brecks.' By 1988 there was just a single pair nesting in a popular picnic spot at Santon Downham, Norfolk. The birds were well guarded and well watched – one estimate suggests 10,000 people saw them that year – as they raised three young.[8] However, the following spring only the male returned, and 1989 was logged as the 'first year in recorded ornithological history when Red-backed Shrikes are not known to have bred in England'.[9]

The only glimmer of relief is the sporadic occurrence of 1–13 pairs spread from south-west England to northern Scotland, but the likelihood of a permanent recolonisation is extremely small.

Great Grey Shrike, *Lanius excubitor*. If anything this species is even more renowned for its rapacity than the previous bird. As long ago as the sixteenth century William Turner wrote: 'It lives on beetles, butterflies, and biggish insects, and not only these, but also birds after the manner of a Hawk. For it kills Reguli [goldcrests] and Finches and (as once I saw) Thrushes; and bird-catchers even report that it from time to time slays certain woodland Pies, and can put Crows to flight.'

Turner confirmed his account of its murderous habits with the story of a shrike that once drew blood from his hand through thick protective gloves.[10] Its scientific name *excubitor* means sentinel and refers to the bird's love of high, exposed perches, particularly telegraph wires and poles, from which it searches for prey. Recorded victims range upwards in size to stoat and fieldfare, while injured or immobile grouse and sandgrouse have also been attacked. However insects often form the bulk of the diet.

It shares the red-backed shrike's propensity to store excess prey in a larder, a habit maintained even in the winter territory. Great grey shrikes in Britain are no more than non-breeding visitors – about 150 a year – and their numbers appear to be falling in line with a population slump across much of Europe.[11]

Jay and Crow family
Corvidae

Eurasian Jay, *Garrulus glandarius*. There is great genetic variation across the bird's massive Eurasian range. Typically the British and Irish populations are treated as separate races, *rufitergum* and *hibernicus* respectively. Yet both forms are characterised by the electric-blue patch on the pied wings and a body colour of warm greyish-pink, set off by bold moustaches, black crown freckles and a striking white rump. These lovely corvids were thought by W. H. Hudson 'not altogether unworthy of being called the British Bird of Paradise'.[1] Unfortunately earlier observers were more struck by their showiness. 'Jay' was used as a dismissive term for a flashy dresser or loose woman, while those who have it as a surname must face the possibility that an ancestor acquired the nickname for these qualities or their loud chatter.

The jay call we hear most often is a harsh, grating screech; thus its Welsh name, *Ysgrech y Coed* – 'shrieker of the wood'. Yet it is also capable of a much larger repertoire of vocalisations, some of which are copied from other birds, mammals and even inanimate objects:

> My hand-reared jay was an amazing bird. It could mimic the cat and telephone so well you couldn't tell which was which. 'That bloody phone!' my mother would say – she never swore at anything else. I was certain the jay knew what it was doing. It sometimes repeated words although I doubt it understood those. Its favourite treat was a live beetle. It would send him into rapturous ecstasies, when he would lift his head back and droop his wings accompanied by a muted melodious chortle.[2]

Derek Goodwin kept jays for many years and has observed the function of their mimicry:

> Jays often use copied sounds, alone or together with some innate calls. If one approaches a jay's nest containing young, the parents make their loud screeches of alarm but often these are interspersed by vocal mimicry. In this situation they only use calls of predators such as tawny owl, carrion crow, sparrowhawk and domestic cat and the alarm notes of smaller birds such as blackbird and song thrush; all sounds which might have been associated with situations arousing anger and/or fear in jays. I have often heard

Every autumn jays bury huge quantities of acorns in the ground and any forgotten stores play a highly beneficial role in maintaining our oakwoods.

one utter carrion crow or heron calls when it saw one of these birds flying overhead. My tame jays used to bark if a dog came into the garden and miaow if a cat entered.

Does the jay ever deliberately convey information by means of vocal mimicry? I think it might be possible. Once, when I was keeping tame jays in outdoor aviaries I was awakened by the sounds of disturbance caused by a predator trying to get at the birds. I got out of bed, grabbed a torch and went out where I could dimly see a jay clinging to the wire netting. He looked at me and instantly uttered the 'ker-wick' call of tawny owl, a sound I'd never heard him make before. I was left in no doubt that an owl had caused his original fear but whether he intended to inform me of this is an open question.[3]

The jay is probably the shyest of the corvids and very much a woodland inhabitant, which places a northern limit on its Scottish range roughly at the Great Glen and excludes it from western parts of Ireland and the southern Scottish uplands. Like the other crows it is a recent beneficiary from the decline of game shooting, but it is still a regular item on the keeper's gibbet and previously suffered other forms of persecution.

Its bright plumage excited the interest of milliners, especially the lovely chequered blue-and-black coverts, which were in demand for use in hats or other fashion accessories. In 1880 the Duchess of Edinburgh was castigated when she toured Cannes sporting a notorious muff made entirely from these small wing feathers.[4] The eye-catching coverts were also used to make anglers' flies, which were particularly popular with Irish salmon fishermen.

The current population of about 170,000 pairs represents a striking recovery from former pressures. The birds have benefited from large-scale afforestation projects in Wales and Scotland, as well as their recent adaptation to urban environments. The spread in London is a classic illustration of the bird's expansion. Jays were almost entirely absent until the 1920s, when a pair was suspected of breeding in the grounds of Holland House. By the 1950s they were in Battersea, Hyde Park and Regent's Park, as well as Kensington Gardens. An unusual development was a willingness to nest on buildings, including the Foreign Office (1951), Lancaster

The jay's beautiful azure primary coverts are still used in the making of flies for fishing.

House (1952) and during the early 1960s 'on a ventilator in the porch of a house in Brompton Road, despite the heavy traffic roaring by'.[5] Before the end of the millennium they had acquired the ultimate London address, breeding in the grounds of Buckingham Palace.

Jays have always attracted some of the hostility levelled at magpies (see page 403) for their nest-raiding habit, but this is largely confined to spring adults with well-grown offspring. Although they will occasionally take live prey as large as young rabbits, jays are primarily vegetarian. In winter they are especially dependent on acorns (the second element of the scientific name is from the Latin *glandis*, acorn), although the extent of the species' relationship with the oak was not truly understood until relatively recently.

In the autumn of 1951 M. R. Chettleburgh made observations of a jay population, which is still thriving in Hainault Forest, Essex. Autumn is the one time that this elusive bird becomes briefly conspicuous, when it can be seen flying high over the trees with a characteristically halting, rump-up/tail-down action, which Hudson thought looked more like 'swimming rather than flying'.[6] In the east London outskirts, Chettleburgh studied the intense activities that lay behind these repeated flights – the collection of acorns. Plucking them directly off the trees, the birds carried the nuts in their beaks or in a sublingual pouch, which could be seen to bulge as they flew away.

The acorns are normally cached in natural crevices or holes, often in damp ground and under a thin layer of dead leaves, which are used (along with sticks, pebbles and earth) to disguise the burial site. Chettleburgh noted that each load of three or four acorns required about 10 minutes and, during the most intense phase of the 10-week effort, the birds were averaging 60 flights in a 10-hour day. He estimated that during the whole operation each bird was storing about 5000 acorns.[7]

It has since been established that jays are particularly adept at remembering the whereabouts of their stores, even digging through 16½ inches (40 cm) of snow to retrieve them. Should the supply last until the following spring, they will even feed their young on buried acorns. However it is inevitable that some will never be found and jays play a major role in the maintenance and spread of oak woodland. If one uses Chettleburgh's figure of 5000 acorns per bird, it produces a hypothetical total of 1700 million buried by the present British and Irish population each autumn.

Across the whole of North America and Eurasia several jay species and relatives have parallel relationships with a number of host trees (see Spotted nutcracker, page 406). At this hemispheric scale we can conjure an extraordinary vision of these autumn forests with many millions of corvids gathering and burying many billions of seeds, which should at least mitigate some of the odium occasionally heaped on the family.

The bird's dependence on the oak means that any failure in the acorn crop can trigger substantial influxes of continental jays. These have been noted at least since the early nineteenth century, but two of the largest were in 1957 and 1983. The more recent of these was on an unprecedented scale, with jays observed in East Anglia flying in off the sea. The passage lasted throughout September and October, with most birds heading in a westerly direction. The migrants were thought to include local birds, since the British acorn crop had also failed almost completely. The highest single concentrations were in Cornwall, where more than 1000 birds were recorded on six separate days. One can possibly imagine the sense of alarm experienced by a gamekeeper who witnessed 500 flying past Crafthole, near Millbrook, on 15 October. Two days later a remarkable figure of 1800 jays were seen in an hour at Kenidjack valley, near St Just, while an observer estimated 1500 over his garden at Land's End.[8]

Magpie, *Pica pica*. VN: Maggie/Maggy. Noisy, gregarious and mischievous, the magpie is as characterful as it is unmistakable, with its crisp black-and-white plumage, long tail and a loud machine-gun-like chattering call. The classic encounter is usually a carbound experience, when a feeding bird stands on the tarmac ahead and then rises up from some horribly eviscerated roadkill, such as a dead pheasant or rat. It would be easy to assume from these associations that the guttural-sounding name has some relationship to 'maggot'. An earlier version, used by Shakespeare, was 'maggot-pie' (*Macbeth*; Act 3, Scene 4), but in fact the name has more tender connotations.

The first element is a contraction of 'Margaret' or 'Margot the pye' (borrowed from a French equivalent, *Margot la pie*).[9] More recently the bird has acquired a prefix to become the black-billed magpie (to separate it from an endemic Californian yellow-billed sibling, *Pica nuttalli*), but it is inconceivable that the unwieldy official title will ever take hold among the public. The simple disyllable has a special place in our consciousness and the striking shortage of vernacular alternatives may indicate how well it suits the bird.

Yet one localised name survives in northern England. 'In the first twenty years of my life I was lucky enough to spend most of my holidays in the Holme Valley in the West Riding of Yorkshire. The local name for magpie was – and I can only guess at a formalised spelling – pinette. This was usually pronounced *"pa-arnet"*.'[10] Other spellings include Pyenot, Pianate and Pyenate, and all derive from a northern dialect name dating back to the sixteenth century. This was very similar in structure to 'magpie' itself, combining the word 'pied' with 'Annot', a pet version of Agnes. In the West Riding village of Liversedge there is still a 200–year-old Pyenot Hall, 'as well as a Pyenot Hall Lane, Pyenot Drive, Pyenot Garden and Pyenot Avenue all clustered in an old part of Cleckheaton, about half a mile west of Liversedge'.[11]

Almost in echo of the striking black-and-white plumage, magpies provoke strongly opposed views in many people. At the root of our ambivalence to this species and several other flesh-eating corvids is their long attendance upon carrion, both in the form of livestock and even ourselves (see Northern Raven, page 424). Nowhere is the ambivalence better expressed than in the many rhymes that are popular still with all generations.

'There's one we say at Rainsford High School [Chelmsford] every time we see the birds around the buildings':

One for sorrow, Two for joy
Three for a girl, Four for a boy
Five for silver, Six for gold
Seven for a secret never to be told
Eight for a dream, Nine for a wish.[12]

A sixteen-year-old Birmingham schoolgirl recounts a saltier version:

One for anger, two for mirth,
Three for a wedding, four for a birth
Five for rich, six for poor
Seven for a bitch, eight for a whore
Nine for a burying, ten for a dance
Eleven for England, twelve for France.[13]

A modern alternative, which ended 'Eight's a wish and/Nine's a kiss/Ten is a bird that you must not miss', was lodged in the memories of an entire generation of children in the 1970s. It was part of the signature tune to the enormously popular Thames Television programme *Magpie*, which ran from 1968 to 1980 and has been described as a 'working-class *Blue Peter*'. It was intended to be more up-to-date than the BBC programme and the show's mascot magpie, Murgatroyd, seemed to fit the sharper, more streetwise style and character. There was a series of magpie badges to be won and, rather than requesting children to post the bottletops or old stamps beloved of their rivals, *Magpie* charity appeals asked children to send the 'Magpie Sixpence', which traded on the bird's legendary attraction to shiny objects.

At the heart of the original magpie rhymes, which date back at least to the eighteenth century, was a fortune-telling game. Some of this has been blended into the pastimes of modern city-dwelling children who, until recently, may not have known the bird itself. Iona and Peter Opie were told by a Birmingham schoolgirl: 'The way we tell our fortune is to keep our bus tickets and add up the numbers at the top, see how many times seven goes into the number, see how many you have over.' The remaining figure was then measured against the first of the rhymes above. The same traditions were found in Doncaster, Leicester, London, Oxford, Sheffield, Warwick and Hull, 'where children are said to have used this rhyme with tram tickets since about 1920'.[14]

The magpie's black and white plumage seems a perfect metaphor for its deeply ambiguous reputation.

Magpies are widely caught and killed by means of traps like this one.

The Opies also unearthed a version of the game in Coleraine Ireland, which involved a strikingly feminine version of the rhyme:

> One for sorrow, two for joy,
> Three for a kiss and four for a boy,
> Five for silver, six for gold, seven for a secret never to be told.
> Eight for a letter from over the sea,
> Nine for a lover as true as can be.[15]

One wonders if the projection of a female personality on to the bird, as in the name 'magpie', has any bearing on the tendency for the superstitions to resonate strongly among women and girls. 'My sister is very superstitious about magpies. If she sees a lone one she stands up, salutes and says "Aye-aye Cap'n, Aye-aye Cap'n, Aye-aye Cap'n." This is supposed to ward off sorrow and bad luck.'[16]

The same pattern is particularly evident in my own family. At the sight of a single bird, Jayne Cocker, my sister-in-law, announces: 'Hello Blackie, hello blackie, hello blackie.' Yet my two nieces, Hannah and Laura, have their own personalised responses. One says 'Good morning blackie, good morning sir', while her older sister, making a simultaneous salute, greets it with 'Good morning blackie, how's your wife?' Similar formulae are apparently found among their Derbyshire schoolfriends. As in most of the traditional rhymes, the sight of two magpies is taken as a reassuring sign, but my brother describes the collective wave of anxiety and then the simultaneous rattle of responses should a single bird happen to cross the family's path.[17]

Yet there is by no means a female monopoly on magpie rituals: 'A male colleague from Somerset says that if you see a magpie on its own you must hold on to your left collar with your right hand until you see a four-legged animal. This even applies nowadays with T-shirts when the neck is grasped where the collar would be.'[18] Another contributor recalls: 'Fifty years ago when I was a child I used to work on a farm in West Yorkshire and the brothers who owned it always said that if you see a magpie, say, "Good morning Mr Magpie", and I still do it as a habit.'[19]

The great Cheshire bird man, Arnold Boyd, diarist for the *Manchester Guardian* and author of the Collins New Naturalist volume, *A Country Parish*, 'never fail[ed] to raise his hat to a passing Magpie, explaining that this was an old Cheshire custom'.[20]

Aside from their willingness to feed on carrion, the characteristic that has earnt magpies most disapproval is their taking of other birds' eggs. Although the issue has recently resurfaced in the matter of falling songbird populations, modern opponents of the magpie draw upon the long-standing hostility of sporting interests. During the nineteenth century it was the gamekeeper's enemy-in-chief for its predation of young pheasants, partridges and grouse. By the end of the Victorian era the magpie population had probably slumped to its lowest levels and some authors even contemplated its extinction. According to the great Victorian ornithologist, Alfred Newton, this persecution reversed the rural spirit of an earlier age when the bird was 'the cherished neighbour of every farmer'.[21] Newton noted:

Since the persecution to which the Pie has been subjected in Great Britain, its habits have undoubtedly altered greatly in character. It is no longer the merry, saucy hanger-on of the homestead as it was to writers of former days, who were constantly alluding to its disposition, but is becoming the suspicious thief, shunning the gaze of man, and knowing that danger may lurk in every bush.[22]

Chaucer in particular provides evidence for Newton's theory of a radical shift in attitude, describing it as a 'joly', 'jolif' (merry) and 'peert' (saucy) bird. During the Middle Ages its chatter calls were put to good use, when magpies were housed with the poultry to give alarm at the approach of predators or human thieves.[23] The tradition of keeping them as pets is also long-established, the birds being popular for their vocal ability, which extends to a mastery of words and whole sentences, and for their intelligence and mischievous sense of fun:

Last spring a magpie fell out of its nest in my garden. It couldn't fly, its parents did not want to know, the local cats were showing interest so we hand-reared it. 'Minstrel', as my girlfriend named it, roosted with the chickens at night, and stayed with us for about four months, flying off for an hour or two, coming back to be fed. Sitting on my girlfriend's head, stealing anything shiny that took its fancy (bottle tops, spoons, tweezers) and hiding them around the garden, and every night he would sit on the perch with the chickens. He had character, was very funny, used to pluck the cockerel's tail feathers and my head. The cockerel would chase him round the garden until nearly caught, but Minstrel would always roost next to the cockerel, similar colours perhaps? He was a joy to watch and be with.[24]

Most studies of magpie diet indicate that the birds eat mainly vegetable material in winter and ground invertebrates during summer. It is largely in spring that the range of food widens to include the contents of other birds' nests. The sight of the larger, more aggressive corvid tearing open a small nest in the hedgerow, then devouring the helpless chicks has aroused deep passions among many garden owners, particularly when it is 'their' blackbirds or thrushes being eaten. Even the bird's sheer success and physical ability to brush aside competitors arouses opposition:

I spend a small fortune on wildbird seed and bucketfuls of peanuts but I simply hate magpies. I find them the bully of all bird life, their aggression making life a misery for the small birds. I don't doubt that they kill their share of sparrows, tits and robins, but they also wreak havoc among the twenty-odd pheasants that come each day to be fed at our garden. The magpies dive in and steal the bread from under their beaks.[25]

Such experiences have become all the more common because magpie populations have virtually quadrupled since the 1970s, to more than 900,000 pairs in Britain and Ireland, with the rate of increase being higher in suburban gardens and large cities than in rural areas. 'So much for one for sorrow, two for joy – I often wonder what eight or ten would be. Sometimes in winter I see 50–60 in one of our 200-year-old oaks, all of them chattering away like machine guns. I see far more magpies in London than in the countryside.'[26] These increases have coincided with significant declines in other birds, such as the song thrush and house sparrow, and some have presumed that the magpie is at least partly responsible:

The effects of predation by Magpies ... was quite evident at suburban Dollis Hill [London]. The first magpie arrived in 1969 and the first pair in 1973. The first nest was built in 1977. The level of predation rose rapidly and in the spring of 1979 magpies took all the first clutches and broods of all the blackbirds and song thrushes nesting within 200 metres of my house and 40 per cent of the replacements. The breeding population of blackbirds fell from 170 pairs in 1976 to 126 in 1979 and of song thrushes from 15 pairs in 1977 to 6 in 1980.[27]

Such views are aired almost every spring in the local and national press. An article in *Country Life* typifies the prejudicial tone: 'In a supposedly more enlightened age, fewer people shoot at the black and white brutes, so . . .

The magpie's reputation as a thief is little more than a myth.

every year there are more and more five-strong clutches of squalling young inhabiting the bunker-like nests in woods and grown-out hedges.'[28] Several local councils have threatened to implement a magpie cull and the issue has surfaced in the upper chamber of the Houses of Parliament. In May 1989 Lord Winstanley insisted on 'capital punishment for the thieving and murderous magpie', while Lord John-Mackie described it as the 'biggest possible killer of bird life'.[29]

Environmentalist and writer Kenny Taylor has argued that 'Such outpourings tell us very little about magpies, but a great deal about the darker side of human psychology. A scapegoat, once identified, can do no right in the eyes of many people.'[30] Professor Tim Birkhead has overseen a 15-year study of the magpie in the Rivelin valley, Sheffield, and his research largely bears out Taylor's assessment:

> We looked at breeding success and population status of eleven common songbird species, which we thought might be vulnerable to magpies. These were: Blackbird, Song Thrush, Mistle Thrush, Dunnock, Robin, Chaffinch, Greenfinch, Goldfinch, Skylark, Wren and Yellowhammer. The results are for birds in rural England, mainly on farmland and woodland, and were as follows (a) Nine of the eleven songbird species showed no change in nest mortality with increasing magpie density, and two showed significantly reduced nest mortality as magpies became more abundant! (b) The nest mortality of all songbird species was not related to magpie density. (c) Songbird populations actually did better (not worse), i.e. they increased more, or decreased less, in areas where magpie density was higher ... Overall, this analysis provides good evidence that, despite people's fears, magpies have had no detectable effect on songbird breeding success or population levels in rural habitats.[31]

A magpie habit that has compounded its notoriety is that of caching food. The retrieval of these stores depends upon the magpie's remarkably accurate memory. However young hand-reared magpies, without parents to show them the function of caching, will lay up normal food items and a wide range of inedible objects: 'spoons, silver paper, pens, screwed up bits of paper of various colours, pencils (taken from out a pocket)'.[32] It is this variation on the food-storing behaviour that accounts for the magpie's reputation for stealing, which was made famous in Rossini's opera, *La Gazza Ladra*, 'The Thieving Magpie'. (Incidentally, the Italian name, *gazza*, is where we derive the word 'gazette', a chattering gossip-filled rag.)

It appears some people took the bird's reputation seriously:

> When I was a child a magpie – presumably an escaped pet – flew repeatedly into my bedroom and my mother would not leave upstairs windows open in case it came in to steal her jewellery. I was under the impression as a child that all magpie nests would be brimming with stolen treasure, so when I found a magpie nest high in a poplar tree, I risked life and limb to climb up to the thin branches to see what I could find.[33]

More recently the myth was given a new lease of life through a police publicity drive against household burglary and car theft, featuring posters of a magpie with jewellery in its beak, and through the screening of a television commercial. 'The "Magpie" campaign was a Home Office initiative launched in 1985. The TV adverts featured a small flock of magpies seemingly breaking into a house through an open window. Once inside, the birds were shown crashing around in a fairly manic manner and generally appeared to be ransacking the property. The magpie was the obvious animal to use, but I'm afraid its reputation as a thief is rather undeserved.'[34] Eric

The nutcracker occurs in Britain as an occasional wanderer, when its normal winter diet of pine and spruce seeds fails completely on its northern Eurasian breeding grounds.

Simms records an interesting variation on the thief image: 'One day I was walking in Richmond Park when quite unexpectedly a magpie flew down from a tree and landed on my shoulder. In its bill was a small ball of silver paper which it offered to me. I took it and handed it back. This occurred several times until the bird lost interest and flew away. It had obviously been domesticated.'[35]

In a garden at Bebington, on the Wirral, the bird's standard role was turned completely on its head when a garden owner 'started finding coins around the bird bath'. The mystery donations were completely baffling until 'one day, I saw the magpie leaving money', which it continued to do each morning until a total of £1.70 had been deposited.[36]

However there are acts of theft of which magpies are indisputably guilty. In Chepstow, Gwent, throughout a particularly dry spell in July–August 1991, a magpie was observed on a housing-estate doorstep drinking the cream off a milk bottle, which it accessed by poking a double hole in the silver cap or ripping it off entirely. On one occasion it tackled four bottles in succession. The following summer similar behaviour was noted in Southampton and the nearby city district of Rownhams, Hampshire, and has since been widely observed across Britain. 'While living in rural Devon, I was for a while woken in the morning by the harsh rattling chuckles of a pair of magpies, to find they had plundered the doorstep milk bottles; knowing that the birds may well have been feeding earlier on dead rat or dog faeces, I decided to forgo the usual bowl of breakfast cereal.'[37] (Milk pecked by magpies and other corvids is thought to be a cause of human enteritis and to carry the risk of spreading a Salmonella-type organism, Campylobacter.[38])

A more ingenious case of theft involved eggs from cardboard cartons left by the milkman on the doorstep. This was first noted in 1975 at Banstead, Surrey, and described in a *Daily Mirror* article, which prompted a further report from Ecclesfield, South Yorkshire. 'There, the milkman's customers leave bowls to be placed over the egg-cartons to protect them from Magpies, but the birds sometimes overturn these. Eggs have been attacked even in the storeroom, where they are kept in cartons inside a wooden box; the Magpies entered through a broken window and reached the eggs through the gaps in the wooden box.'[39]

Spotted Nutcracker, *Nucifraga caryocatactes*. Looking rather like a huge starling, this spotty long-billed corvid has two races, the western nominate *caryocatactes* found in central and northern Europe, and the slender-billed form *macrorhynchos*, which occurs from the western slopes of the Urals east to Manchuria. Rather surprisingly it is this eastern form that occurs regularly in Britain.

It is essentially a woodland species and shares an extraordinarily close relationship with a number of seed- or nut-bearing trees, an interdependence that some authors consider an example of mutualism or symbiosis. During the snow-bound winters of the Siberian taiga, the eastern form relies almost entirely on the seeds of pine and spruce trees. The birds gather them during the autumn and store away as many 100,000 in numerous hidden larders. While this far exceeds each bird's individual requirements (about 27,000 seeds), a high percentage of the remainder are taken by rodents or the whereabouts are forgotten by their owners, thus helping to sow a healthy crop of new trees.

However if the seed harvest fails completely, nut-crackers are forced to perform irruptive migrations westwards into Europe – one author describing them rather forlornly as 'death-wanderings' – with important movements recorded in 1911, 1933, 1954, 1968 and 1985.[40] The last was the largest in Europe, but the 1968 invasion resulted in the biggest influx to Britain with 315 records, more than in all previous years combined. They were spread across 29 counties including Cornwall, Lancashire and Carmarthenshire, but the majority of birds (232) were shared between three east-coast counties – Kent, Norfolk and Suffolk.

In Russia nutcrackers experience very little human contact and when they arrive in Britain can show remarkable fearlessness. One Suffolk bird in 1922 was heard scratching at a bedroom window and when this was opened the nutcracker flew in and roosted on top of a cupboard.[41] In 1968 the birds were seen in a wide variety of situations including golf courses, churchyards and on large garden lawns.

In the absence of their usual diet, they turned to a variety of substitutes which mainly comprised fruit, berries and insects, but one bird was noted to chase, catch, dispatch and tear strips off a small rodent, while a nutcracker in Lerwick, Shetland – the only Scottish representative in the entire influx – was watched as it devoured three sparrows. This was matched by a Norfolk bird that decapitated 'a freshly dead House Sparrow, split open its skull, as though it were a nut, and [ate] the contents'. Many were attracted to garden bird-tables and happily took scraps of bread or fat, although the luckiest individual wound up living behind a Kent butcher's shop, where it thrived on a daily diet of mince from November 1968 to autumn 1969.[42]

Red-billed Chough, *Pyrrhocorax pyrrhocorax*. Even if this charismatic bird were the commonest in its family,

The 'Cornish' chough is proudly featured on the county crest on the Tamar Bridge.

it would probably still enjoy a reputation for beauty and for its dashing powers of flight. The intensely glossy plumage with bright-red feet and bill make it the most distinctive of the five black crows, while the long wings give it enormous aerial grace. The small size of the present population – there are just 1170 pairs in Britain and Ireland – simply adds the glamour of rarity to the chough's intrinsic appeal.

Almost three-quarters occur in Ireland, primarily in western coastal areas from County Donegal to Cork, and most of the British population has a similar partiality for Celtic shorelines, with concentrations in north/central Wales and the Inner Hebridean islands of Jura and Islay. Yet perhaps the most celebrated of all British choughs – the only birds found anywhere in England – are the handful in Cornwall.

At one time the species was known as the 'Cornish chough' because of its abundance there, although its nomenclature has long been a matter of controversy. A persistent modern error is the pronunciation of the second word as 'cough', instead of the more customary rendering to rhyme with 'rough'. And even this second version is not entirely free of dispute. The name was originally coined as an onomatopoeic re-creation of the call and for some people this sound accords more closely with 'chow'.

By far the most confusing aspect of the name is the fact that it was originally intended to mimic not this bird, but another corvid. 'Chough' was an alternative name for the jackdaw (see also page 409), and Lockwood explains how

Choughs are now largely confined to the coasts of western Ireland and Wales, the Isle of Man and a few islands in south-west Scotland.

it was gradually transferred from one species to the other: 'The Chough (*Pyrrhocorax pyrrhocorax*) was once abundant in Cornwall and writers, from Turner 1544 on, often gave it the name Cornish Chough which for them, of course was literally Cornish Jackdaw . . . This practice continued through . . . to authors of the early nineteenth cent[ury] . . . Meanwhile Bewick 1804 had dispensed with the epithet *Cornish* . . . and Yarell 1843 definitively established Chough, pure and simple, as the recognized equivalent of *Pyrrhocorax pyrrhocorax*.'[43]

The existence of several archaic versions with an identical structure – 'Cornish jack', 'Cornish daw' and 'Cornish kae' – clearly shows how the larger red-billed bird drew its identity from the commoner relative. An underlying association between the two is easy to understand. Both are of similar size and are regularly found together in wild coastal areas, while some of their calls are alike, although the chough's notes are louder, higher, more musical and with a percussive, at times, almost explosive quality.

They also share a reputation for aerial prowess, although the chough outstrips jackdaw both in terms of gracefulness and sheer eccentricity. The wings are broader with deeply fingered tips and they give it enormous control even in the strongest winds. Its move-

ments often have a leisurely appearance – a deep-winged action reminiscent at times of a butterfly – and choughs are also capable of dramatically fast swooping dives and twists. According to David Bannerman, these manoeuvres give 'the impression of . . . a gay and joyous bird'.[44] Choughs can also climb to enormous altitudes. Elsewhere in Europe and across the disjunct Asiatic range, the species is a bird of high mountains and flocks often appear as insect-sized specks soaring around the distant peaks. In 1921 Sandy Wollaston, medical officer and naturalist on the British Mount Everest expedition, recorded several birds visiting their camp at 20,000 feet (6060m).[45]

The chough's cultural associations are decidedly odd. In addition to an ambiguous connection with Arthurian legends – the king was said to have been turned into a raven or a chough – the species once had an intriguing reputation for starting fires. *Incendiaria avis* was an old Latin tag. One of the first to refer to this behaviour was William Camden in his *Britannia* of 1610: 'oftentimes it secretly conveieth fire sticks, setting their houses a fire, and as closely filcheth and hideth little pieces of money'.[46] The tradition survived until the eighteenth century, when Daniel Defoe saw choughs during his tour of Cornwall. For all the bird's subsequent regional popularity, it seems that Cornish people had no great affection for it. Defoe wrote:

> I could not find that it was affected for any good quality it had, nor is the flesh good to eat, for it feeds much on fish and carrion; it is counted little better than a kite, for it is of ravenous quality, and is very mischievous; it will steal and carry away any thing it finds about the house, that is not too heavy tho' not fit for its food; as knives, forks, spoons and linnen cloths, or whatever it can fly away with, sometimes they say it has stolen bits of firebrands, or lighted candles, and lodged them in the stacks of corn, and the thatch of barns and houses, and set them on fire; but this I only had by oral tradition.[47]

The myth may be explained partly by the ancient name used by Pliny – and now used in the scientific title – *Pyrrhocorax*; literally 'fire raven'. But the association is most likely to have arisen with those people who kept choughs as pets, a practice recorded as early as the sixteenth century. Even 300 years later the capturing of wild birds for pets was cited as a factor in the Cornish population decline. Tame crows of several species have a propensity to take and cache inanimate objects (the habit is most notorious in magpie; see page 404 for an explanation of its origins), particularly attractive shiny items and even possibly glowing embers or sticks. It is most likely that this atypical behaviour by domesticated choughs gave rise to the species' wider reputation, but there is no modern evidence to suggest that wild birds share the habit.

In Britain and Ireland, where choughs have always shown a bias for coastal areas, the distribution has shrunk dramatically over the centuries. The bird was once found extensively along Channel cliff areas as far east as Dover. In 1773 Gilbert White wrote that 'Cornish choughs abound, and breed on Beachy-head and on all the cliffs of the Sussex coast.'[48] They were also found along almost the entire Celtic fringe in Ireland, Wales and Scotland, and on the North Sea coast between Edinburgh and Northumberland. A steady decline began in the 1820s and accelerated in the second half of the century, most likely as a consequence of habitat loss, although the exact reasons have never been conclusively established. Yet at a certain point in the chough's misfortunes, the camp followers of many extinctions – the taxidermist, egg collector and trophy hunter – played their own dismal part. By the 1920s the only mainland English population was in Cornwall.

Unfortunately the chough found the West Country no more a sanctuary than any other English region. By 1880 there were prophecies of its disappearance even from Cornwall and, although the decline was agonisingly slow, nothing seemed to halt the process. The last successful nesting attempt occurred in 1947, while the final native bird, which survived to a ripe old age of at least 26 and outlived its mate by six years, was last seen on 17 June 1973. 'In 1945 I was holidaying at a farm near Port Isaac in north Cornwall. Knowing that I was keen on birds, the farmer took me out for a day to look for what he called "Cornish Chows". He hadn't seen one for years, but hoped we would find one. We didn't, and I remember the acute disappointment and my realisation that birds were unpredictable and could even vanish from places where they had once been common.'[49]

The bird's long association with the area had led to its inclusion in the crests of several Cornish families and in the county coat of arms, where it still perches above the tin miner and the fisherman. As if to underscore how much the bird stood for the other great traditions of Cornish life, its passing has been closely linked to the decline of these totems. Large numbers of pit ponies used in the tin mines had grazed the coastal areas, and the short turf had been perfect for a bird whose long red bill was designed to probe for grassland invertebrates. The eventual closure of the pits had knock-on effects for both ponies and choughs alike.

Yet the species has retained a symbolic importance, both in Cornwall's public life and at a deeply personal level: 'While visiting the picturesque St Enedoc's Church near Rock, Cornwall, where Sir John Betjeman is buried, I came across a relatively recent gravestone with an intricate carving of a chough upon it. It struck me how deeply the bird has taken root in local imagination, given that at the time the engraving was completed the species had probably not bred in Cornwall for many years.'[50]

Symbolism was no doubt one of the key factors in the Cornish conservation measures aimed at recreating coastal grassland suitable for the species. This long-term project was finally crowned with the return of up to seven birds in 2001. Just over 12 months later the county's ancient bird emblem resumed full legitimacy, when a pair nested and raised three Cornish choughs near Predannack Head on the Lizard.

Eurasian Jackdaw, *Corvus monedula*. VN: Jackie (Midlands); Caddow/Caddy (East Anglia); Chaw (Cornwall). Both in the air and on the ground there is an irrepressible jauntiness about jackdaw movements. It is the smallest of our crows and 'the most dovelike . . . in wingbeats as in the close trim plumage and rounded head and body'.[51] It is easily separated from other corvids by its ash-grey hood and the 'small malicious serpent-like grey eyes', as W. H. Hudson rather fancifully described them.[52] Yet perhaps the most useful distinguishing feature of this intensely sociable bird is its voice.

Jackdaws and rooks were once widely killed and outlawed for their depredation of cereal fields.

The full range of calls is complex, although the best known is a monosyllabic, almost dog-like yap, of which the first part of the name is descriptive. It is a contact note and when jackdaws are flying in unison the calls – 'spirited, rather light in timbre, crisp and clear-cut' – ricochet beautifully from one bird to another.[53] The same call is also particularly striking when jackdaws are in the company of rooks, because the two species make highly contrasting but somehow complementary sounds, the former bird's metallic notes seeming like sharp fragments embedded in the more continuous, deep, shovelling-gravel roar of the rooks.

Jackdaws make another loud, resonant alarm note, an almost rook-like grating caw, and Lockwood supposes that the bird's old name of 'daw' is onomatopoeic of this sound. The bird's calls also gave rise to an older alternative dating back to the fourteenth century and variously spelt 'chuff', 'choughe', 'chowghe', 'chough' and originally 'chogen'.[54] Unfortunately its incorporation into the modern name, red-billed chough, and its transferral from one species to another have led to a degree of confusion over which was intended in earlier literature (see the previous species).

A classic point of contention is in Shakespeare's *King Lear*, during Edgar's remarks to Gloucester on Dover cliffs (Act 4, Scene 6), as he tries to awaken in his blinded father a new purpose for living:

How fearful
And dizzy 'tis to cast one's eyes so low!
The crows and choughs that wing the midway air
Show scarce so gross as beetles.

The coastal cliff habitat fits either jackdaw or chough and the latter is likely to have occurred in Kent during the sixteenth century (in fact, this passage is sometimes cited as evidence), but judging from Shakespeare's other references to 'chough', this was not the species he intended. In *A Midsummer Night's Dream* (Act 3, Scene 2) Puck says:

When they him spy,
As wild geese that the creeping fowler eye,
Or russet-pated choughs, many in sort,
Rising and cawing at the gun's report,
Sever themselves, and madly sweep the sky . . .

The original meaning of 'russet' was a coarse home-spun cloth that could be reddish-brown, but also a neutral or grey colour. The grey-headed bird that associates with other corvids, that has cause to fear persecution and gives a caw-like alarm note, is without question the jackdaw (the red-billed chough's main diet of grassland invertebrates spared it from legal persecution).

The jackdaw was clearly intended in Henry VIII's anti-vermin statute of 1532, whose preamble read: 'For asmoche as innumerable nombre of Rookes Crowes and Choughes do daily brede and increase throughout this Realme, which Rookes Crowes and Choughes do yerely distroye devoure and consume a wonderfull and marvelous great quantitie of Corne and Greyne of all kyndes.' The act decreed that henceforth every parish with a population of more than 10 families was to maintain baited nets for these three pest species, or face a fine.[55] Fortunately jackdaws are less granivorous than rooks and are much less significant as predators of other birds' eggs than crows or magpies. As a consequence they have avoided the more intense campaigns waged against the other three. Today the jackdaw has a generally positive image and until recently was valued as an amusing pet:

> In Scalby near Scarborough there was a cottage where we used to buy fishing permits for a stretch of the beck. The bloke there had a tame jackdaw and when you knocked on the door it would hop up to your feet and I swear it would say, 'Door Jack, Jack door.' It caused us great mirth and the three of us who went fishing would always buy permits one at a time with the other two hiding around the corner.[56]

> I had a jackdaw when I was a schoolboy and used to sit quietly doing my homework in the evening with the bird on my shoulder. After a while Jackie would become bored and it would lean forward and face me with its beak only millimetres from my eye. Its game was to catch my eyelid as I blinked, which it did very successfully – in mid-blink – holding my lid for just a second before repeating the action. I was banished to my room by my distraught mother who did not want to witness the blinding of her strange child.[57]

The present and still-expanding population in Britain and Ireland stands at 600,000 pairs, more than one-tenth of the entire European total.[58] It flourishes particularly in the modern landscape, taking advantage of a whole spectrum of industrial and urban settings, such as rubbish tips, factory dumps, motorway service stations and the motorway verge itself, 'unperturbed by the traffic passing close to them'.[59] Derek Goodwin has noted that jackdaws can out-compete their larger relatives in these situations.

Jackdaws were once valued as amusing and talkative pets.

'Often while a Rook is still fearfully eyeing a piece of bread in some street or garden, a Jackdaw will dash down, seize it and bounce up and away.'[60]

Despite its opportunist flair it is surprisingly rare in London except in the suburban periphery. In 1999 the largest group recorded in the city's heartland was three in Regent's Park. After many years' residence in the capital, Max Nicholson could recall only a handful of personal sightings. With a nod towards the bird's former status as an omen of doom, he noted that one of these – possibly an escaped pet – was 'sat on the roof of No. 10 Downing Street uttering low hoarse chuckles while a Cabinet meeting was being held underneath during the economic crisis of October 1949'.[61]

In the nineteenth century jackdaws had bred regularly on many London landmarks, including St Michael's Church on Cornhill near the Bank of England, and Grosvenor Chapel on South Audley Street in Mayfair. When alterations were undertaken on the Baptist Chapel in Hampstead, the workmen removed two or three cartloads of sticks from the towers, where a colony had nested for many years.[62] Occasionally these are put to further use: 'I have some friends in Suffolk who "harvest" their jackdaw nests as kindling.'[63]

The jackdaw has a well-earnt reputation as the most ecclesiastical of birds. At one time this religiosity extended even to pagan beliefs. Gilbert White found jackdaws nesting on Stonehenge.[64] But it is essentially a hole-nesting species and has adapted equally well to hollow trees, old rabbit burrows or cavities in rock faces. It is one of the first species to occupy industrial quarry sites after operations have ceased and, sometimes, even as extraction is ongoing. There is a Jackdaw Quarry near Heysham, Lancashire. (Kaber in Cumbria, Caville in east Yorkshire and Lancashire's Cawood are three of several older jackdaw place names, which derive from a Middle English word for the bird, *Ca* or *Co*.[65])

Belfries, church towers, the rooftop statuary on cathedrals, ancient battlements, castle ramparts, city walls, bridge arches, dislodged slates in domestic roofs and chimney pots on terraced houses all provide highly acceptable substitute holes, while abandoned structures of any kind are another favourite. Occasionally the jackdaw colony adds substantially to a derelict building's character and atmosphere:

Some 70 years ago when I lived with my parents at Badgersclough, Higher Disley, our cottage stood near a ruined house which was reputed to be haunted. We knew differently. Jackdaws used to roost in the rafters and they overheard the talk of hikers and courting couples who took shelter there. It seems that these birds, well-concealed, imitated the visitors' chatter. Hence the 'haunted house'.[66]

Despite their wider reputation for guile and intelligence, jackdaws are well known for making heavy weather of the nest itself. Julian Huxley noted that they drop sticks into the cavity to make the foundations of the nest. 'Sometimes it happens that a nice-looking hole communicates with some bigger space below, and the sticks simply drop through. But once the birds have chosen a hole they may continue bringing and dropping in sticks for days and days until a really enormous pile accumulates in the hollow trunk below.'[67] Some nests have been of extraordinary dimensions. One in Oxenton church, Gloucestershire was 8 feet (2.4m) high and 'not much less in diameter at the base'.[68]

The bird is also capable of carrying material out of all proportion to the size of the nest hole. W. H. Hudson saw birds on Wells Cathedral in Somerset bearing sticks that were 7 feet (2.1m) long.[69] A bizarre departure from the norm was the jackdaw pair in Malmesbury, Wiltshire, that stole 67 6-inch (15-cm) lead flower labels and twisted them into their nest in a household chimney.[70]

Once the foundation platform has been assembled,

Like all of the crow family, jackdaws take advantage of many manmade opportunities.

jackdaws love to line it with all sorts of softer fur and feathers, sometimes plucking hair directly from the back of animals like deer, sheep and cows. They often repay the gift by searching the fleece for parasites, an exercise in which the livestock can show remarkable patience. In Pembrokeshire Max Nicholson noted that: 'The sheep remained absolutely impassive even when a jackdaw walked down between its eyes on to the tip of its nose, or clung on to its right ear with the splayed toes apparently cutting right in, or balanced with thrashing wings on the side of its face.'[71]

Rook, *Corvus frugilegus*. VN: Craa (Scotland). Similar in size and shape to carrion crow, the rook is separated by the looser fit of its plumage, especially on the upper legs where the feathers hang down rather like a pair of baggy shorts. The other classic feature is the prominent bare-skin patch of 'a whitish, dried bone colour' around the base of the adult rook's bill.[72] At any distance the bird simply looks all-black, but at close range the plumage is shot with a glorious oil-on-water mix of purples, mauve, bronze and blues. One effect I see routinely in rooks but not in other corvids is well described by Richard Jefferies: 'the rook will sometimes . . . reflect the sun's rays in such a manner that instead of looking black the bird appears clothed in shining light . . . as if the feathers were polished like a mirror'.[73]

Yet of all rook characteristics we have probably been most captivated by the intense sociability, which seems at times a mirror for our own and is starkly contrasted by the carrion crow's solitary or paired existence. Hence the Norfolk adage: 'When thass a rook, thass a crow/And when thass crows, thass rooks.'[74] Historically country people were not too concerned to separate the two

The rook's bone-coloured patch at the base of its bill is a good means of separating it from a carrion crow.

corvids and each has probably suffered a form of compound odium and persecution. A classic misidentification is the word 'scarecrow', which was never intended to guard cereal crops from a solitary bird, but from grain-devouring rook flocks.

There is a similar inaccuracy in the phrase 'as the crow flies'. For much of the year rooks travel to a roost site, which may be anything up to 27 miles (45km) from the daytime feeding areas. One at Hatton Castle in Aberdeenshire was at one time the country's largest, with as many as 65,000 birds. Since rooks are faster in flight than their close relative and since they complete the distance in noisy, conspicuous flocks, it is likely that 'as the crow flies' has its origins in these ritualised movements.

British poets, including Shakespeare ('the crow makes wing to th' rooky wood') and Tennyson ('the many-winter'd crow that leads the clanging rookery home'), have regularly responded to them and sometimes compounded the old rook/crow muddle. Few have written more accurately or memorably of these faithful dawn-and-dusk movements than John Clare in 'The Shepherd's Calendar':

> Whilst many a mingled swarthy crowd –
> Rook, crow, and jackdaw – noising loud,
> Fly to and fro to dreary fen,
> Dull winter's weary flight again;
> They flop on heavy wings away
> As soon as morning wakens grey,
> And, when the sun sets round and red,
> Return to naked woods to bed.

However much we visit the crow's sins on its cousin (or vice versa), rooks have given us far more scope for pleasure. This is partly bound up with the spectacle and symbolism of the rookery, which is as closely tied to our sense of spring as the sight of snowdrops, newborn lambs or, indeed, the sound of Easter bells.

Large rook roosts, like this one at Buckenham, Norfolk, are among the most spectacular and underrated spectacles in British ornithology.

'Caw' is invariably used to describe the calls of both birds, but rook and carrion crow have strikingly different vocalisations. Rook, derived from an Old English word *hroc*, is onomatopoeic in origin, but '*krah*' is a better transliteration of the principal note and is perfectly rendered in the Scottish vernacular name 'Craa'.[75] It captures something of the drawn-out nasal 'r' sound that

is so much a part of the rook's voice. Yet the species also has a wider repertoire – Edmund Selous claimed to identify 30 different notes – and in concert the deep sonorous calls have a euphonious quality that is hardly ever associated with the carrion crow's harder tones.[76]

The cacophony at the rookery is matched by the colony's atmosphere of commotion. While George

A rookery in full swing is as redolent of spring as crocuses in bloom or Easter bells.

Yeates' claim that he 'would not exchange a "seat" at a rookery for the best entertainment in London' sounds like special pleading for a favourite bird, it should at least suggest the excitement of a colony in full swing. His remark on the change in tempo triggered by the appearance of the young – like 'a London tube station at lunch-hour' – nicely conveys how the endless bustle parallels the rhythms in human crowds.[77]

There may also be a deeper level of symbiosis between humans and rooks. Derek Goodwin observes: 'The Rook is often thought of as one of the most characteristic birds of the British countryside. So it is, at least of the agricultural countryside; it is not usually found in extensive built-up areas nor in completely wild country as is its more versatile relative the Carrion Crow. It is, however, unlikely that there were any Rooks in Britain, or indeed in western Europe, before there were any farmers.'[78] Like the skylark and lapwing, the rook is directly dependent upon open habitats and has flourished in the wake of woodland clearance. In turn the birds have reflected back our ongoing triumph over the landscape and one wonders if this underlying affinity was at work when nineteenth-

century colonists took rooks with them to New Zealand (their transportation seems all the more exceptional, given the rook's old image as an agricultural pest).

Of all the birds in the farmland environment rooks form what is easily the most conspicuous bird community. They perform spectacular communal movements, with towering spiral flights above the colony that are known as 'crows' weddings' and are still taken as a weather prophecy. High manoeuvres mean fair conditions, low flights signify rain. The rooks' low-level chases have also given risen to more regional lore: 'In north Lincolnshire the farm workers used to say that the rooks were "footballing" when they saw these bundles of chasing birds.'[79]

The dusk assemblies at their roosts are even more unavoidable. Ian Francis describes a typical gathering at Alford in Aberdeenshire:

> On a cold winter's evening you can often wait a long time before the birds come in. They gather in nearby fields for one last feed where the hundreds upon hundreds can look like a seething black carpet on the stubbles. Then the leading birds decide it's time for roost and all hell breaks loose. They rise in one great mass and circle above the wood. It's like one of those childhood snowstorms, only in black; or like being in a planetarium where someone has speeded up the stars. The sky is filled with thousands of crows, calling excitedly and undertaking the most amazing aerobatics, pirouettes and loops. It is impossible to convey on film or photograph, while the wall of noise descends and overtakes your senses.
>
> Gradually the birds begin to drop into the wood, sometimes reappearing, only eventually to settle. Within five minutes 20,000 corvids are in, and all that remains is a few half-hearted caws and chacks as they bed down in the tree tops. Some very late flocks zoom in low and drop straight in, but the show is over and one of the most under-rated bird spectacles in Britain has finished for another night.[80]

The rookery itself is assembled long before leaf-burst and stands out so starkly in the winter canopy that it is impossible to overlook. Some nest sites are as ancient as they are conspicuous, with birds returning to build in the same area for decades and even centuries. Tim Melling suggests that the rookery is the most conspicuous nest site created by any British land bird, while its site-persistence is central to its frequency in place names:

> The rook has probably given its name to more places than any other British bird, including at least 14

villages. Even a fairly informal survey indicates a further 170 locations on British Ordnance Survey maps whose names begin with 'Rook'. Rookwoods, Rook's Nest and Rook Hill are all to be found, but there are 82 Rookery Farms, with several variations like Rookgrove Farm, Rook's Nest Farm and plain old Rook Farm. These are mainly in southern England with a remarkable concentration of 44 Rookery Farms in Suffolk (28) and Norfolk (16).

Given the widespread use of 'Craa' or 'Craw' as a Scottish alternative for the bird, it is hardly surprising to find 'Rook' localities petering out around Cheshire and 'Craw' places becoming more common. There are at least 80 in Britain with 55 north of Lancashire. The one exception is Crawley (literally 'crows' wood') and its derivatives, which are mainly in southern England. Then we find about 240 'Crow' places. These show a more even geographical spread with a small bias towards the south. They are also more ambiguous. For instance some like Crow Crags (1), Crow Rock (3), Crow Stones (4) imply the habitat of Carrion Crow or possibly Raven. Yet others such as the Crowhurst locations (12) – 'hurst', a wooded hill – most of the Crow Hill (25) and Crow Wood (12) sites have clear Rook associations.[81]

Rooks flourish best in areas of mixed farming and range from north-eastern Scotland to Cornwall and across Ireland, except for the western fringes of County Mayo and Galway. The present total in the British Isles is around 1,375,000 pairs, with areas of extensive pastureland supporting the highest populations. In the 1960s the Ythan valley in Aberdeenshire had densities unknown anywhere else in the world, with 71 pairs per square mile (2.6sq km).[82]

The typical English colony consists of fewer than 50 nests, although Celtic rookeries tend to be bigger, while those in Scotland are on average three times larger. Some are huge. In the second half of the nineteenth century there was a veritable metropolis at Rash Wood in County Tyrone with an estimated 10,000 nests.[83] Another impressive ancient site is in Crow Wood (once known locally as 'Craa Wid') at Hatton Castle, Aberdeenshire.[84] As recently as 1957 it included 6700 nests and, while it has declined to 2600 spread between 16 groups, it is still Britain's largest rookery and, in fact, our largest breeding colony of any land bird.[85]

There is clear regional variation in the choice of nest tree, with evergreens being most favoured in the windier parts of the country like Cornwall, Cumbria and Scotland, where they give the birds additional protection. Altogether 60 trees, more than one-third of them conifer

species, have been recorded, including occasional eccentrics such as box, blackthorn, elder and yew – and sometimes even on the ground.[86] In England, elm was long considered the classic rookery tree and even in 1975, long after Dutch elm disease ravaged the native population, it still accounted for more than a quarter of all English rook nests. Prior to the outbreak, elms supported four-fifths of all the Gloucestershire rookeries, while in the 1930s, on the Isle of Wight and in the Oxford area, the species held nine-tenths of rook nests.

Human structures are seldom used, but rooks particularly enjoy the settled conditions and the mature parkland trees associated with large estate houses. Hatton Castle is a prime example of an historical building matched by the ancient state of its rookery. Often the fate of its human settlement is projected on to the fortunes of the neighbouring birds:

> Between Helston and Penzance and very near the shore, Pengersick Castle has a long legend-ridden history. The rooks – which have survived elms dying with Dutch elm disease and trees falling in mighty gales, still form a large colony ...We in the village nearby are glad they are there, for the outstanding superstition of the castle is that if the rooks forsake the grounds, the castle will fall – and a part of our local heritage would be gone for ever.[87]

The bird's strongly collective lifestyle lends itself to interpretation according to human norms and there is a long tradition of anthropomorphic writing. A classic example occurs in Oliver Goldsmith's *A History of the Earth and Animated Nature*. During the period of nest construction rooks are well known to steal sticks from neighbours – a habit that helps explain 'rook' as a synonym for theft or trickery. However the idea of a property free-for-all in the rookery offended Goldsmith's legal sensitivities: 'But these thefts never go unpunished ... I have seen eight or ten rooks come upon such occasions, and, setting upon the new nest of the young [thieving] couple all at once, tear it in pieces in a moment.'[88]

There is a similar belief that rogue birds building away from the main body of the rookery have their nests destroyed as punishment for deviation from the collective norm.[89] As in much country lore there is an underlying ecological basis. Dominant rooks take the central locations in a rookery while younger, less experienced pairs are forced to the margins and these birds *per se* are susceptible to breeding failure and to having their nests later dismantled by neighbours.

Many of the retributive ideas converge in the older

and deeper legend of the rook 'parliament' or its Scottish equivalent, the 'craa's court'. A *Daily Telegraph* article from 2002 suggests that the myth still holds currency: 'Occasionally, a wayward or sick individual is condemned to death . . . In this bizarre avian trial, the entire population of the rookery takes to the sky . . . as a prelude to battering the victim to death.'[90]

Most eye-witness accounts date from the first half of the twentieth century:

> J. Anderson, a Norfolk journalist . . . was walking . . . from King's Lynn to Gayton when he saw some thousands of rooks gathered in a four-acre grass field . . . In the middle some thirty rooks formed a circle . . . At the centre of the circle stood five rooks which had 'an appearance of utter misery and dejection' . . . Then one of the five . . . suddenly perked up, completely lost its dejected appearance and flew quickly away unmolested. After another short interval the encircling birds suddenly made a combined attack on the four remaining in the middle, and in a few seconds had pecked them to death. Mr Anderson . . . felt sure that he witnessed a trial and execution of 'criminal' rooks, and assumes that the bird which flew away had been 'acquitted'.[91]

It is not always easy to account for the consistent elements in such observations: the 'court-like' circle of birds, the central protagonists and the collective violence against a 'victim'. However, corvid specialist Derek Goodwin once witnessed a scenario that may help explain some reports:

> The nearest thing I have seen to a 'parliament' was about 20–25 years ago near Lullingstone Park, at Eynstone, Kent. I heard a great clamour of rooks and saw a rough circle of 30–40 surrounding two that were fighting on grass. Although the watchers were in a circle they were not side by side in a ring, but continually moved about and every now and then would fly a little towards the couple. The excitement of the watchers greatly increased when the fighting intensified and I noticed at one point that when one combatant was struggling on its back and trying to get free, 2–3 of the circle flew right up to them. At the time I recall thinking that with only slight 'encouragement', several would attack the 'loser' in the fight and anyone coming on them at that point might well think they had seen verification of the old yarn about rooks holding court and punishing offenders.[92]

The rook's diet – and thus its impact upon ourselves – is probably Britain's oldest ornithological controversy. It is essentially an omnivorous bird but during the breeding

The artist Richard Sell drew a rook parliament he saw in the 1930s and writes: 'It was on a farm between Berkhamsted and Chesham on the Bucks/Herts border. I was struck by the symmetry. In the centre were two birds facing one another while there must have been thirty or more birds in the circle, close together facing inwards to the two protagonists.'

season the principal diet is grassland invertebrates. Rooks have also been quick to exploit modern opportunities, such as rubbish dumps, dustbins, picnic areas and roads or the slow lane of motorways for road casualties. Piggeries are now regular haunts, and in Wales the birds are disliked for their mass raids on feed put down for sheep.

However it is the taking of grain that has earnt the rook its worst reputation (the Welsh name *Ydfran* means 'corn crow') and given rise to that fine old totem of the British countryside, the scarecrow. Today the human figure is giving way to little more than a feed-sack on the end of a stick, but occasionally one sees dead rooks on poles, or their carcasses strewn on the ground or strung up on barbed-wire fences. 'During the 1960s in north Lincolnshire . . . one of my farm staff once encircled a plot of newly sewn wheat with jam-jars containing flowers of sulphur. Other farmers would take a shot bird and walk with it round and across the field plucking and scattering the feathers. When all that was left was a plucked carcass this would be dismembered and the bits thrown to the ground.'[93] Unfortunately none of these techniques is more effective than any other form of sympathetic magic and rooks frequently feed alongside them; they can even get used to the loud thump of a gas-gun.

Yet rook control is an ancient business. As early as 1424 legislation was enacted in Scotland, ordering landowners to prevent the birds nesting or the young fledging, on pain of confiscation of the rookery trees themselves.[94] The refinement of an existing statute under Elizabeth I organised bounty payments from parish wardens, at a rate of a penny for three adult rook heads (as well as crow, magpie and jackdaw) and a halfpenny for three young or three eggs.[95] Another standard method was for a landowner to employ bird scarers. Armed with sling and shot and something to make a loud noise, the youths were in great demand at critical moments in the corn season. An old Bedfordshire song gives some sense of their activities:

Away, birds, away!
I'll pick up a stone
And break your backbone
So, away, birds, away![96]

A Lancashire rhyme of the late nineteenth century ran: 'Crow, crow, get out of my sight/Or else I'll pull thi liver out at morn and neet.'[97]

The scarer's lot was one of low pay and semi-isolation and was probably reserved for the youngest and oldest members of the rural community. That image certainly squares with the character of Hugh, Charles Dickens' central villain in *Barnaby Rudge*. The illiterate hostler at the Maypole Inn is described as having 'had to mind cows, and frighten birds away . . . for a few pence to live on' during his orphaned childhood.[98] Yet the bird-scarer's arts continued for at least 2000 years and probably died out only in the early twentieth century:

There is a holly tree which grows in the parish of Ewarton on the Shotley peninsula in south-east Suffolk. It has quite a large girth for a holly, but what caught my attention was the graffiti carved into the trunk bark. The lettering has stretched and split (apparently with age) leading me to believe that the carving is genuine. The two panels read:

C. Mann	C. MANN
SHOTLEY	SHOTLEY
STREET	STREET
ROOK SCARER	SHEPHERD
	1911

I presume that C. Mann's job for at least part of the year was to scare rooks away from the young crops. There is another piece of carving on the other side of the tree which reads 'F. DOUBLE, ROOK SCARER'.[99]

However much people try to suppress rooks, there seems to be a parallel acceptance of their place in the British countryside. The old farmer's rhyme – 'One for the pigeon, one for the crow/Two to rot and one to grow' – suggests a more philosophical approach than was embodied in the draconian Tudor legislation. In fact it was probably a law honoured more in the breach than in

The scarecrow is a fine old totem of the British countryside.

strict observance. In the seventeenth century John Aubrey noted:

In the peaceful raigne of King James I. the Parliament made an Act for provision of Rooke-netts and catching Crows to be given in charge of Court-barons . . . but I never knew the execution of it. I have heard knowing countrymen affirme that Rooke-wormes, which the Crowes and Rookes doe devour at sowing time, do turne to chafers, which I think are our English locusts; and some yeares wee have such fearfull armies of them that they devour all manner of green things; and if the Crowes did not destroy these wormes, it would often times happen. Parliaments are not infallible, and some thinke they were out in this bill.'[100]

One thing that further softens attitudes towards rooks is their palatability. The birds were once widely eaten – they are still – and landowners looked upon rookeries if

George Clausen's 1896 painting powerfully evokes the lonely and desperate life of the Victorian bird scarer.

not as an economic resource, then certainly as a good source of protein. At one time they were also valued as a kind of medicine; Sir Thomas Browne recorded that many rooks were taken around Norwich for their livers, which were considered a remedy for rickets.[101] The total harvest could be substantial: a rookery in the lime trees at Hampton Court Palace yielded an annual total of 1200 birds.[102] The idea that farmers valued their rookeries finds confirmation in the figure of the rook poacher, whose methods were described in Richard Jefferies' *Wild Life in a Southern County*: '[They] go up the tree in the dead of night; and as the old rooks would make a tremendous noise and so attract attention, they carry a lantern with them, the light from which silences the birds . . . The time selected to rob a rookery is generally just before the date fixed for the shooting, because the young birds are of little use for cooking till ready to fly.[103]

Rook pie is one of those archly rustic dishes that has not yet quite vanished from the British board. The meat is bright red, 'rather like rabbit' in flavour, while the young birds, called 'branchers', are considered the most tender and palatable. 'We always held an annual rook-shoot on our Lincolnshire farm when the fledglings were made into rook-pies. I have prepared many birds for the kitchen. Skinning carcasses was very easy and the breasts and legs were readily separated from the unwanted portions. We used up to twelve birds in a dish and served with hard-boiled eggs they made a very acceptable meal.'[104]

Leicestershire and Gloucestershire still have a tradition both of organised rook shoots and of rook suppers:

Several pubs in the Badminton area take advantage of the May cull and have a Rook Pie Night. We've had one for seven years at the 'Fox and Hounds' in Acton Turville. The actual shoots take place around the second Tuesday of the month, but we host our events towards the end of May to ensure our supply of birds. Nowadays I'm getting up to 200 from as far away as Hampshire. We combine the event with morris dancing, but the centre-piece is my own rook-pie recipe, which involves marinading the rook breasts and mixing them with beef and chopped chipolattas, served in a sauce of port, red wine and sherry and topped with pastry. It's extremely popular, with as many as 100 people coming for the night.[105]

Carrion Crow, *Corvus (corone) corone*/**Hooded Crow**, *C. (c.) cornix*. VN: Hoodie (widespread); Corby/Corbie (Scotland). This is the plainest of the corvids, although hoodies often have a pleasing pinkish tone to the smoky-grey underparts and mantle. Each has recently been given specific status although they were long treated simply as different races of one bird and their cultural 'profiles' are virtually indistinguishable. On that basis they are considered together here.

Traditionally the hooded crow, the smarter-looking of the two, was seen as the Scottish and Irish counterpart of its all-black English sibling. This still holds true in

Ireland, where the carrion crow is a rare visitor, but the Scottish situation has become more complex. Both birds freely interbreed and produce fertile young and there has long been a zone of hybridisation where the two populations meet. The striking feature of this 'border' territory is its steady retreat towards northern Scotland. As long ago as the early nineteenth century the carrion crow was said to be ousting its twin from southern parts.[106] Today hoodies still hold their own on the west coast southwards to the Mull of Kintyre, but in the east carrion crows and hybrids are common as far north as Caithness and even Orkney.

The hoodie's northward retreat as a breeding species has coincided with its decline as a regular winter bird in eastern England. Now, sadly it is no more than an occasional visitor, while birds resembling pure-bred *C. c. cornix* are scarcer still. Yet at one time a large influx was routine every October and November as far as Kent and other southern counties, where it passed under a variety of names. Together with the more obvious 'winter', 'grey', 'grey-backed' and 'dun crow', it was known as the 'Danish' or 'Norway crow' (in Norfolk the first was corrupted to 'Denchman'), indicating the presumed countries of origin. 'In the 1950s my north Lincolnshire farm workers always used to refer to them simply as "Denmarks".'[107]

The most widely used alternative was 'Royston crow', named after the Hertfordshire town, to whose vicinity the birds were attracted by winter casualties among the large sheep flocks on the surrounding downs. 'Likewise the Hoodie was known to haunt the sheep-folds between Berkhamsted and Luton where it was also known as the Dunstable crow.'[108] Today the only reminders of this old tradition are a few stuffed hoodies in local pubs and the title for the local newspaper:

The Royston Crow has been covering the news for this small market town since 1855. The original Victorian publishers were clearly taken with the idea of the town's famous winter bird and enjoyed their rather punchy play on the verb 'to crow'. Today it sells 6300 copies and still has the distinctive image of the bird on its front page mast-head. Indeed, the logo comes from a photograph of a stuffed Hooded Crow on display in the town museum.[109]

Despite the variety of names used for them, both crows have long generated a single dominant response. They remain the most unloved of British species and have been severely persecuted for centuries. Typically in Cork, Ireland, the county's federation of gun clubs recorded a harvest of 22,300 hoodies during just two winters in the early 1980s.[110] Game interests routinely cull

The 150-year-old Royston Crow *newspaper goes back to an age when hooded crows were common on the sheep walks around the Hertfordshire town.*

them for their predation of grouse or pheasant chicks and eggs, which they are supremely adept at finding. A tale illustrative of both the crow's abilities and our regulation response to their powers is recounted by Derek Ratcliffe:

researchers on Red Grouse began marking nests they had found with canes placed a short distance away. Crows in the area learned what the canes signified and the marked nests were systematically predated. The Crows were not smart enough to know when the canes began to mark the location of poisoned egg-baits instead, but the human observers learned a lesson all the same.[111]

David Bannerman reported that 'upwards of 200 grouse eggs have been counted around one little pool and that on a moor under the care of a capable and zealous keeper'.[112] Few bird species sharing the crow's habitat and range are exempt from these egg-raiding forays. Seton Gordon once found a pile of 150 assorted seabird eggs 'on a small Hebridean island', while at Welney WWT reserve, Norfolk, the marsh warden John Kemp was inspired to population-control operations by the routine discovery of 'egg dumps' involving 40–60 wildfowl and wader eggs:

Larsen traps were first used in 1990 and an incredible 121 crows were caught. The surrounding population was so high that fresh birds (pairs) sometimes arrived within twenty minutes of a territorial pair being caught. As the weeks progressed the arrival time of new birds was much slower until a temporary 'crow-free' period was obtained. After 1990 numbers fell to 61 the following year and currently averages 48 crows a year. Predator control is certainly a significant factor in the increased number of waders breeding on the site.[113]

Hill farmers also detest crows for their harassment of pregnant or cast ewes and newborn lambs. If anything, crows have a worse reputation than ravens in the matter of pecking out sheep's eyes or tongues.[114]

However it is their long history of predating human

Although they prefer the middle crown of a tall tree, hooded crows will readily adapt to nesting on the ground.

flesh that is probably at the heart of our visceral antagonism towards crows (see page 424 for a fuller discussion). The raven once surpassed its lesser relative on the matter of dark symbolism, but its current rarity has led to a shift in attitudes. Yet the carrion crow and hoodie pay for their success in the teeth of bitter human opposition by retaining their scapegoat status.

In modern Britain and Ireland the crow is the classic symbol of evil and a portent of misfortune. Writing on the bird lore of Lancashire, Ken Spencer quoted a correspondent on the widespread fear of corvids: ' "When I lived in a community of quarry workers and drift-pit workers at Rakehead in Rossendale in the 1930s belief in the Doom Crow was very common. To see a single Rook or Crow in flight was very bad luck or an omen of disaster." '[115] A more recent contributor to *Birds Britannica* writes: 'I grew up in Radcliffe (now Greater Manchester). During my childhood in the 1940s if ever a crow appeared in the skies, which was quite rare in such an urban area, everyone would watch to see where it landed. It was firmly believed that if a crow landed on a house, it foretold a death in that household.'[116]

In television programmes and Hollywood films, crows are a stereotypical motif – often a silhouette image on a bare stump – to convey danger, death, murder, evil, even specifically the Devil. Famous examples include

Alfred Hitchcock's *The Birds*, in which the corvids share their terrorist role with gulls, and Disney's *Snow White*, where a pet crow contemplates the wicked witch as she brews her evil potion. It is interesting to note a creeping but inappropriate trend among the makers of British television drama to use the vocalisations of the American crow *Corvus brachyrhynchos* on these occasions, presumably because they sound even harder than the native bird. The popular TV series, *Six Feet Under*, featuring a family of undertakers, uses a corvid on a gravestone in its credits.

The crow's dark image extends to language. 'Crow' is a northern dialect word for dried snot and more widely for a bad-tempered old woman, while 'crow's-feet' is a term for wrinkles around the eyes. The converging creases resemble the outline of a bird's foot – which explains its usage in the names of various flowers – but one wonders if there is a submerged, darker association with the general decay of old age. The word is also entwined with one of the most depressing episodes in British imperial history. During the genocidal war against the indigenous inhabitants of Tasmania, the Aborigines were dehumanised as 'crows'; the colonists' euphemism, 'crow shoot', giving a sense of mere vermin control to their brutal activities.[117]

One ray of light in so much darkness is the fact that

The arch survivor – the carrion crow is as loathed and persecuted as it is common and widespread.

carrion crows and hoodies flourish despite their notoriety. They are the arch-survivors, and it is their qualities of intelligence and indomitability that Ted Hughes blended with the birds' bleaker associations in his dense, complex and brilliant cycle of poems, *Crow* (1970). Hughes' bird is a creature endowed with a primal life force ('Trembling featherless elbows in the nest's filth') and a salty, comedic delight in deception and disorder, rather like the coyote in many Native American legends or the Norse trickster god Loki. Hughes' crow is also a witness to the environmental destruction inflicted by our civilisation:

All that remained of it a brittle desert
Dazzling with the bones of earth's people

Where Crow walked and mused. (*A Disaster*)

A corvid is precisely the kind of bird to endure on our blasted planet, but the idea of its invulnerability is ancient. 'To pierce a crow's eye' was a Roman adage for something impossible.[118] Crows are among the most vigilant of all birds. Their contact calls as they leave the roost is one of the first sounds to signal the breaking dawn, yet they are one of the last diurnal birds to settle for the night.

The wild bird's triumph in a hostile world also relies on a fabulous ability to improvise. The principal diet of grassland invertebrates and vegetable matter is some-times supplemented with mammals as large as hare, or birds the size of lapwing and wood pigeon, which crows can take peregrine-like in mid-air. Hoodies have even been accused of taking cats.[119] By contrast, horse dung, sheep droppings, the rubber housings for car mirrors and wiper blades are all in the list of standbys.[120]

A classic example of opportunism was a crow feeding on a sheep corpse as it drifted down the River Severn; the observer watched this 'extraordinary spectacle' for five minutes, 'until both floating restaurant and customer disappeared from view'.[121] Crows also snatch fish clean out of the water, or wade to drive fry into the shallows, while in the Arctic they haul up fishing lines from ice holes and rob the bait. Hoodies routinely drop mussels and other shellfish down on to rocks in order to break them open, while an old Scottish name for empty sea-urchin shells was 'crow's cups' for the same reason.[122] Bread crusts too tough for sparrows or pigeons are easily tackled, the bird using a technique similar to this one: 'My grandson called and he had a box of french fries which he didn't want, so I put them on the bird table. Along came Mr Crow, took a french fry, flew over to the fountain and dunked it in the water, then ate it, this he repeated several times until he had had his fill.'[123]

The bird's survival skills are probably best appreciated by farmers and no doubt inspired one Welsh ironist in the naming of his property: 'Near to Abergavenny there is a smallholding on a hill called "Starve Crow".'[124]

Their breeding arrangements are similarly elastic. English birds prefer to build in the middle crown of a tall tree, but where these are absent, as in northernmost Scotland, hoodies regularly nest on the ground. Likewise the normal structure is a solid, durable stick-built affair, although a nest found once in Breconshire would have delighted the heart both of Ted Hughes and of his poetic creation. It incorporated many bleached pelvic bones of sheep which had been collected from 'numerous skeletons . . . grim relics of the bitter 1946–47 winter'.[125] A similar ossuary-like nest in Shetland was 3 feet (90cm) across and 1 foot (30cm) deep.[126]

Its industrial equivalent was found about 125 feet (38m) up on a floodlit gantry in railway sidings close to Nottingham station. The beautifully made structure consisted almost entirely of man-made materials including nylon box tape, cable twists, butterfly-shaped brick ties, barbed wire, copper lengths of various sizes and grades, baling twine, steel wire and wood chippings.[127]

While the measures adopted by crows in their breeding are flexible, the desire to reproduce is unyielding. Gamekeepers or farmers often pull down the nests or destroy the eggs and young in an effort to thwart them. Undaunted, crows have been known to lay three and

The huge bill and wedge-shaped tail are good features for identifying a raven.

He was brought to me after being handreared and the garden became his world. From the beginning he took immediate possession of everything in it. He could create in me such a variety of emotions – immense amusement at his many antics, utter melancholy whenever he went missing and screaming irritation whenever he decided to 'help' me with my various garden activities.

There can be few things more frustrating than to have one's pliers, nails, screwdriver etc. repeatedly removed and hidden. Even the claw hammer did not escape Foster's devoted attention. To give chase was fatal as this would inevitably turn the whole thing into a game. Foster had an exceedingly powerful beak. Even quite heavy and ungainly objects such as the garden watering can and wellington boots could be removed and later found in odd places. He became particularly adept at taking apart pegs on the clothes line, especially if they happened to be anchoring a load of wet washing!

He eventually went to a friend of mine, who had a large rambling garden with aviaries. It was ideally suited for Foster and for his eventual release into the wild. But one night a storm brought a large tree branch down on to his enclosure and in the morning he was gone. We knew there was nothing we could do except hope he had not been injured. For many months he stayed in my thoughts and then in the summer of the following year I had an excited phonecall. Foster had returned and brought his family with him. Foster, my crow – he was indeed a survivor.[129]

Northern Raven, *Corvus corax*. VN: Corbie (northern Scotland, Orkney, Shetland). In the nine-volume *Birds of the Western Palearctic* no sentence resonates more strongly than Max Nicholson's judgement on this species: 'So wide-ranging that concept of habitat is hardly applicable.'[130] It has a world range spanning almost the entire northern hemisphere from the Mesoamerican and Middle Eastern tropics to the Arctic tundra well beyond the 80° N meridian. Its altitudinal range is equally impressive. Ravens can survive in desert landscapes like Israel's Dead Sea region, 1200 feet (360m) below sea level, yet they are equally at home in high mountains. In 1921 ravens went to scavenge in the camp of the British Mount Everest expedition at 21,000 feet (6350m).[131]

The raven's adaptability extends to a remarkable catholicity in diet which, in one commentator's memorable phrase, 'ranges from a worm to a whale'.[132] At times it can make do with vegetable matter, although it is well

occasionally five consecutive clutches until they succeed.[128]

Some people have found the widespread condemnation of crows a perverse cue for sympathy, but perhaps we should leave the last word to that rare Briton who selects it as a favourite bird. Ellen Kershaw's tale of Foster – one is tempted to call it a parable – offers a perfect reprise of the crow's indomitable qualities:

Claire Guest's raven sculpture in ancient bog oak suggests the bird's innate brooding power.

able to catch and kill live prey, such as rabbits, rats, hedgehogs, moles and stoats. The list of birds covers a size gradient from ducks to pipits, and bird's eggs, occasionally as large as those of guillemot or buzzard, are another speciality. Ravens are also skilled at dispossessing other predators of their food, outwitting even great black-backed gulls (the one bird with a modern reputation as malignant as the raven's used to be). While one of the pair distracts the gull, its partner steals the prize.

Without question the raven's most favoured food item is carrion – hence the Welsh name *Cigfran*, 'meat, or butcher, crow' – and it is the bird's talent for locating and exploiting dead carcasses that lies at the heart of its long-standing relationship with humans. Our intimacy with ravens may well exceed that with any other bird, because in addition to them taking our dead livestock, they have taken human flesh with equal relish from the battlefield or gibbet. Even earlier, from the Mesolithic onwards, some communities exposed their dead on excarnation platforms where the body was picked clean by birds and animals, before the bones were disarticulated and placed in a special chamber. Exactly this kind of funerary site has recently been discovered at Longstone Edge, near Stoney Middleton in Derbyshire. Ravens have been resident in the Peak District for thousands of years (interrupted by an absence from 1863 to 1967) and it is impossible to create a mental image of these ceremonial grounds without also hearing the guttural calls of the great black birds.[133]

Raven gatherings at these most sacred places, and at a moment that was most spiritually charged for the relatives, converted the bird into a species like few others.

Both dreaded and cherished, admired and persecuted, the raven is, according to Peter Matthiessen, the 'great requiem bird of myth and legend'.[134] It is, or at least it *was*, among the most significant birds in western society. Yet even this understates its importance.

The bird's honorary place in Europe was merely a tributary part in a great system of mythologies that entwined the entire hemisphere. The result of all these ancient responses is an extraordinary sweep of reference, from the Gilgamesh epic of the ancient Babylonians to the Book of Genesis, and on through western literature to Edgar Allan Poe's haunting and melancholy classic, 'The Raven'. As imaginative symbol the bird functioned throughout this period as a metaphor for death and evil foreboding, but also for spiritual and even divine power.

We needed to explore the raven's momentous past, partly to give a context for the references to it in British literature (some of which are quoted below), but primarily to recognise how little of the bird's cultural baggage remains with us now. No one fears the raven's croak as an omen of doom (but please contact us if you do!). Modern life has drained the bird of its symbolic significance. Even as a predator of our livestock we view it as hardly more than an occasional nuisance. The bird's present scarcity – just 4300 pairs despite a steady recovery from persecution – has made it for some people a bird to be valued and enjoyed.[135]

Chief among British coraciphiles is Derek Ratcliffe, who has studied ravens for 60 years:

The raven caught my youthful attention as one of the grander birds of Lakeland, where I grew up. The bird's appeal was also in its relative scarcity, in living farthest from the haunts of humans, nesting in remote and difficult precipices, and laying its eggs while the fells were still in the grip of winter. It became a challenge to learn more of its ways, in the wild and beautiful country to which the bird belonged and added still more character.[136]

The largest of the crows, and indeed of all the passerines, looks completely black at any range but the plumage is glossed with purple, green and blue. The throat feathers are long and shaggy, forming a conspicuous 'dewlap', while the black bill is thick, pointed and shaped like a slender flint axe. The flight is powerful and majestic, but ravens often suggest that they derive pleasure from their aerial mastery, floating along hill crests or ridges where they hang on the wind, performing elegant twists and soaring manoeuvres. Often these are combined with a good deal of chasing and horseplay, all of which convey a spirit of recreation.

The best known of all their aerial repertoire is an ability to roll during display, when a bird draws its wings in and turns briefly on to its back, occasionally performing a complete revolution. Equally compelling evidence for the raven's sense of fun is the account of two birds sledging in the Welsh mountains:

> while fluttering during bathing movements, it rolled on to its side and then on to its back, and being on a slope, started sliding; after sliding 2.5–3m, it stopped, righted itself and, with typical loping gait, hopped back to its starting place and repeated the manoeuvre two or three times. Its mate, which had been watching from a short distance, came to the same spot, began snow-bathing and, as its partner, rolled on to its back and slid at about 3–5kph down the slope.[137]

The raven has a powerful voice, both in terms of the sound itself and in its ability to conjure bleak upland landscapes. The most common calls have an unmistakable deep throaty quality and in Shetland to speak with an uvular 'R' is known as 'to corbie'.[138] The note is typically described as a 'croak' although ravens have a wider vocabulary than this word suggests. In ancient Rome the state augurs, who considered it the most important bird of omen, differentiated 65 separate raven vocalisations and ascribed significance to each.[139] It is also renowned for its ability to mimic speech. Derrick Coyle, the present Raven Master at the Tower of London, writes: 'One of our six birds, Thor, will say things like "Good morning", "Hello" and "Come on then". Sometimes when I give him an item to eat and say, "That's for you", Thor will reply, "That's for me".'[140]

In Britain we now associate the hollow notes with Welsh hill country, the uplands of northern England, the Scottish and Irish highlands and the cliff coasts in all four countries. But the bird's present distribution is largely a human artefact. Historically ravens were found across the whole of the islands and were as familiar to inhabitants of large cities as they were to rural communities. Simon Holloway judges that at the beginning of the nineteenth century ravens nested in every British county.[141] The addition of the shotgun to its opponents' arsenal meant that for 100 years it was subjected to almost relentless slaughter. The last known records for the bird's breeding attempts in England mark the route of a long retreat to the north and west: London (1830), Oxfordshire (1834), Leicestershire (c. 1840), Northamptonshire (c. 1850) and Derbyshire (c. 1860).

The scale of the campaign against ravens is illustrated by parish records from places like Greystoke in Cumbria, where the wardens made bounty payments on

The totem bird features in the livery of the present Raven Master at the Tower of London.

966 birds in the 90-year period from 1752.[142] In its traditional highland stronghold the cull was even more systematic. In the county of Sutherland and the Caithness estates of Langwell and Sandside a total of 1962 ravens were killed in a seven-year period from 1819, while on the estate of the Duchess of Sutherland a bounty of two shillings each was paid for 936 ravens between 1831 and 1834.[143]

The downward pressures were increased by the attentions of taxidermists, egg collectors and those who took live nestlings for the pet trade. It seems a complete contradiction of the raven's evil reputation, but the birds make extremely friendly, entertaining companions. The poet John Clare had a pet raven, while Charles Dickens had two birds, which were the models for Grip in his novel *Barnaby Rudge*. In the early twentieth century they were still very popular, and among the dealers at Leadenhall Market the price was 'so high – ten or fifteen shillings each – that a brood is rarely reared in safety'.[144] An equivalent contemporary figure is about £30–43 a bird.

> Before the war we had a raven called Pauline which my father had obtained from a keeper on a grouse moor in Sutherland. Pauline was pinioned and could not fly but walked everywhere in the garden and lived in a wooden hut. Pauline was completely domesticated and dominated our two cairn terriers and would often sit beside them on a grass terrace which edged the house. She was not scared of them, but they were of her. She had a great sense of humour and often baited our dogs by pecking their tails.[145]

The unkindness of ravens at the Tower of London currently includes seven birds.

More recently ravens have started to recover some lost ground, particularly with the introduction of legal protection in 1981 under the Wildlife and Countryside Act. In Wales the decline of grouse shooting and a consequent reduction of gamekeeping have greatly benefited this much-maligned predator. Today central Wales holds the highest breeding densities of ravens in Europe, if not anywhere in the world.[146] Yet there are surprising gaps. Declines in Northumberland, parts of Galloway and the Scottish borders – much of it traditional raven country – has been attributed to the increase in afforestation, the

conversion of grazing areas to arable and more efficient sheep-rearing methods.

Raven distribution in the British uplands is closely correlated to areas of sheep farming. But the birds need a degree of 'untidiness' in husbandry practices, particularly in high country where the stock regularly falls victim to the climate or terrain. These carcasses are picked clean by ravens, while another important feeding opportunity arises at lambing time in the form of placental remains or stillborn and sickly lambs. The raven's breeding cycle is closely synchronised to the protein bonanza, with the result that it regularly lays eggs in late winter. Young birds have been found in the nest as early as the end of February and the adults usually have a full clutch by mid-March. Derek Ratcliffe also suggests that there 'is some evidence ... to confirm the egg collectors' view that in hard winters which produce much carrion mutton, Ravens tend to lay bigger clutches'.[147]

The bird's predation of lambs was long held as an excuse to kill ravens, although the case against them is not clear-cut. An early defender was the author of *Bird Life in Cornwall* (1948), Colonel R. B. Ryves, who claimed that he had never met anyone who had seen a raven actually kill either a lamb or ewe. His observations of two pairs feeding in lambing fields indicated that the birds fed on invertebrates if there was no carrion or placenta to eat. They would occasionally jump on a ewe's back and probe the fleece for parasites but the sheep, even with a lamb at heel, showed no distress or considered the birds a threat.[148]

Against this more benign image must be set eye-witness testimony of ravens killing young lambs and disabling sheep. The habit for which they have been most vilified, documented since the Old Testament, is pecking out their victim's eyes ('The eye that mocketh at his father, and despiseth to obey his mother, the ravens of the valley shall pick it out' [Proverbs 30:17]). The same practice is described to great emotional effect in the anonymous Scottish poem 'The Twa Corbies', when one of a raven pair says of the newly slain knight, 'Ye'll sit on his white hause-bane/And I'll pick out his bonny blue een'. Derek Ratcliffe notes that 'This damning behaviour is remarked upon time and time again ... in the testimony of hill shepherds.'[149] Gruesome and cruel though it seems to us, it has an ecological function. In dead animals the eyes are soft, nutritious and immediately available to the raven and, in attacking live animals at this vulnerable point, ravens render them blind so hastening their death.

Although one can completely understand the shepherd's visceral response on finding his charges mutilated in this fashion, scientific studies conducted in the 1960s and 1970s gave a clearer picture of the real impact of ravens and other corvids on sheep. An inquiry in 1963 gathered evidence from 214 Lakeland farms with a total ewe population of 82,000. These farms reported attacks on 16 adults, half of which were already sickly and either trapped in hedges or snowdrifts. Unless freed, these 'cast' animals, several of them suffering from staggers, die within a day even when unmolested by corvids. Of the 69 lambs predated, only 50 per cent were alive and half of these were already sickly. The loss of lambs because of corvid attacks was estimated at well under 0.5 per cent. A

1969 survey of farms in Radnorshire, Breconshire and Montgomery put predation levels at 0.01 per cent of 114,751 ewes and 0.6 per cent of 119,680 lambs. Studies in Argyllshire suggested that the 'normal' mortality rates among lambs, caused by a whole array of factors, was 18 per cent.[150]

Derek Ratcliffe writes: 'The reality is that hill shepherds as a whole have taken a pretty relaxed view of Ravens during the past few decades. The impression of general hostility from flock-masters, which the pre-1920 literature certainly gives, is far from the prevailing attitude ... Most of the shepherds that I have talked to were quite tolerant of Ravens and at most seemed to regard them as no more than a minor problem.'[151]

The ability of ravens to locate dead animals is legendary. They are well known to follow deer-stalkers and are said to be attracted by the sound of their guns. Seton Gordon records how the bird's love of the gralloch (the entrails) led to an interesting reversal of the traditional doom-laden associations: 'the raven is at the present day the emblem of good luck with stalkers, because it appears when a deer is killed, and to hear the raven's croak when setting out on a day's stalking fills the hunter's heart with joy'.[152]

Their dependence on carrion means that when the pickings are particularly rich, they can assemble in large flocks like vultures at a kill. Shetland has produced some of the most impressive records, with a stranding of five killer whales *Orca orcinus* at Weisdale Voe in about 1900 attracting 500 birds, many arriving from the outlying islands to join the feast.[153] Larger still was a flock of 800 birds feeding on cetacean carcasses at Uya Sound in 1864. Industrial society's equivalent of stranded whale blubber was the rubbish dump associated with Sullom Voe oil terminal. In 1968 it produced 'an unkindness' of 300.[154]

During the winter, non-breeding immatures can also form temporary night-time roosts, which are thought to act as information centres on the whereabouts of important food concentrations like a carcass. The assemblies seldom number more than a few dozen, although one of the largest ever recorded anywhere in the world is currently found at Newborough Forest in Anglesey. The gathering has been known since the late 1980s and has included as many as 1900 birds. These are believed to come from as far away as south Wales, Scotland and even Ireland, which is only an hour's flight away.

At least until Tudor times, ravens were highly valued for their refuse-disposal service, particularly in the waste-choked streets of British cities. The Venetian ambassador in London during the reign of Henry VII wrote: 'the raven may croak at his pleasure, for no one cares for the omen; there is even a penalty attached to destroying them, as they say that they keep the streets of the towns free from all filth'.[155] Provincial towns also had protective by-laws. In 1584 a German visitor to Berwick-upon-Tweed noted that 'There are many ravens in the town which it is forbidden to shoot, upon pain of a crown's payment, for they are considered to drive away bad air.'[156] In seventeenth-century Norwich, Sir Thomas Browne noted that the presence of so many ravens accounted for the absence of that other great refuse scavenger, the red kite (see page 115).[157] It was said that the London ravens involved in the city's clean-up services came complete with a distinctive livery. Digging in the refuse left their wings soiled with dirt, and the same birds could easily be picked out when feeding at rabbit warrens 20 miles (33km) from the capital.[158]

The species' connections with London are both ancient – probably dating back to its Roman origins – and multi-faceted, although today the most celebrated link is with the Tower of London. Derrick Coyle speculates that ravens probably nested on the White Tower soon after its construction was completed in 1098, although the tradition of keeping pinioned birds began only in the Victorian age, while the post of Raven Master dates from just 1968. Coyle writes:

> During World War Two the Tower ravens were reduced to just a single bird, Gripp. Now I look after an unkindness of seven: Hardey, Cedric, Gwylum, Munin II, Hugin II, Odin and Thor. It includes five males and two females although they are notoriously difficult to sex. In 1986 we had one called George who was retired off to Wales, where 'he' promptly laid an egg. After a name-change to Georgina, she eventually gave birth to Gwylum, who is one of our present contingent.
>
> I take out 1–2 of their secondary feathers to prevent them flying away and although they occasionally escape they seem fairly contented. We take enormous care of them and they often live to a ripe old age. Hardey, a Dorsetshire bird, is fairly special because he's now 25 and has recently had both his eyes done for cataracts. (Although we haven't yet had to go as far as the vet from London Zoo, who said that the strangest job he'd ever done was making a wooden leg for a Tower raven!) Even Hardey has a long way to go before he equals the record of James the Crow, a raven born in 1880 which died in 1924.[159]

There are more than 60 London roads and locations that include 'raven' in the name, although none is thought to bear a definite connection with the wild creature. However P. G. Moore notes that there are in excess of 400 other British place names, many of which imply the shadow of the large black bird:

> Most of the 'raven' place-names signify features in wild landscapes and hence are likely to have an ancient origin: Raven's Barrow (OE *beorg* 'hill, hillock or tumulus'), Raven Beck . . . Raven's Bowl, Ravenbourne . . . Raven Brow, Ravendean Burn, Ravenscliff(e), Raven's Cleugh (OE *cloh* 'a gorge or ravine with precipitous sides'), Ravens Clough, Ravencragg, Raven's Crag, Ravenscraig, Ravensdale . . . Ravensden (OE *denu* 'valley'), Ravengill Dod (OS *ghyl* 'ravine or valley'. Scots *dod* 'a rounded hill top'), Ravens Heugh (OS *heugh* 'headland'), Ravenshead, Ravenshill, Raven Howe (OS *haugr* 'a hill'), Raven Knowe (Scots *knowe* 'a knoll or peak'), Ravens Leach (OE *laec* 'stream'), Raven's Peak, Raven Currick Rigg (OS *rigg* 'a ridge'), Raven Rock, Ravenscar (OS *sker* 'a cliff or line of rocks'), Ravenstruther (Gaelic *struthair* 'little stream'; or OE *strod* 'a marsh'), Raven Stones Brow, Ravendale Top, Raven Tor (OE *torr* 'rocky peak') and Ravenswyke (OS *vik* 'creek').[160]

Perhaps the grandest of all raven landmarks is the RSPB reserve of Ramsey off St David's Head in Pembrokeshire, derived from the Norse *Hrafn's-ey*, meaning 'ravens' island'.

Many names undoubtedly hinge on the bird's enormous loyalty to a traditional site. Gilbert White gave a good example of a landmark near Selborne acquiring raven associations through the presence of an old nest. A fortuitous swelling in the trunk of a large old oak prevented local boys from climbing it and robbing the eggs, so that the birds had 'built on, nest upon nest, in perfect security' until the oak had become known as the 'Raven-tree'.[161]

Some nests become almost landmarks in their own right. Henry Stevenson recorded a nest at Geldeston in Suffolk, which was 'so high that in standing on the supporting branch [Mr Spalding] could barely see into it'.[162] Derek Ratcliffe recalls seeing a structure in the Tweedsmuir hills that was 10 feet (3m) high and reports on a Lakeland nest more than 6 feet (2m) high and 6 feet (2m) across its base. Yet ravens are not above adorning these fortresses with a little cosmetic decoration. Rope, string and wire appear in some structures, while a wartime nest in Cornwall, located near a military hospital, was lined with cotton-wool swabs.[163]

Starling family *Sturnidae*

Common Starling, *Sturnus vulgaris*. VN: Starnel (Midlands); Shepster, Sheppy, Shebster, Shep, Stinker, Shitlegs (northern England); Scootie, Stirling, Stirlin, Stirleen (Orkney and Shetland). Although sparrows and starlings hold neighbouring positions in the British taxonomic list they are not actually closely related. But the impression of some deeper affinity certainly strikes a chord in the public imagination, where they are forever yoked together – the two eave-nesting garden birds which take advantage of us with the same determination that we seem to show in taking them for granted.

The archetypal view of the bigger bird involves the male perched on a rooftop or television aerial, wings flicking intermittently and throat hackles raised to give it a slightly bearded appearance as it lets fly with 'a weird array of ecstatic noises that pass for a song'. The sheer familiarity and almost year-round delivery make the performance one of the most underrated of all our common bird songs. Bernard Tucker, the master of succinct ornithological description, captured it beautifully when he called it 'a lively rambling medley of throaty warbling, chirruping, clicking, and gurgling sounds interspersed with musical whistles and pervaded by a peculiar creaky quality'.[1] Recent studies have revealed that the structure of starling song becomes even more complex as its creator gets older and adds new motifs to his repertoire.[2]

An old Norfolk name for the bird, 'wheezer', nicely suggests the asthmatic breathy notes, while a low-pitched whistle in the song has been likened by one contributor to 'milk spurting from a cow's udder into a bucket'.[3] The starlings' capacity to evoke other sounds is legendary. They are great mimics, and owl hoots, buzzards mewing, golden oriole and quail song, goose, pheasant, curlew, lapwing and chicken notes are all beautifully incorporated. Some are so perfect they often have birdwatchers scanning the sky for the original, and starlings are by no means restricted to bird imitations. Cat, goat and frog soundalikes have all been documented. 'One bird perfectly imitated my mother's whistle used to call our mongrel dog. The poor animal spent most of the day responding to find nobody there.'[4]

Sexy wolf whistles (acquired 'from errand boys' according to one commentator)[5] and reproductions of modern trim-phones are commonly copied by town- and

Starling flocks in autumn include many of these motley juveniles with spotted bodies and grey-brown heads.

Starlings are one of the most common occupants of our domestic roof space.

By the nineteenth century the bird appears to have lost some of its pet appeal, and in his classic book, *London Labour and the London Poor*, Henry Mayhew suggested that its status as the poor man's parrot – 'taught to speak, and sometimes to swear' – was a thing of the past. Small numbers were, however, still for sale in the London streets of the 1870s and Mayhew described the dodge employed by vendors to suggest the bird's extreme docility. 'It is true starlings may be seen carried on sticks in the street as if the tamest of the tame, but they are "braced". Tapes are passed round their bodies, and so managed that the bird cannot escape . . . while his fetters are concealed by his feathers, the street-seller of course objecting to allow his birds to be handled.'[8]

Starlings were also once coached to reproduce melodies and tunes. Mozart kept one as a pet, whose song was said to have been incorporated by him into his Piano Concerto in G Major, K453. In fact, he acquired the bird six weeks *after* the first public performance of the work, and Jeffrey Boswall speculates that the bird had either been specially taught the song following its composition, or that Mozart's work was based on a common melody of the day which the bird had, by coincidence, also learnt.[9]

The British have never really developed the more widespread continental custom of eating the bird, although in the exigencies of wartime there was a letter in *The Times* describing 'rows of starlings at 9d each' on the shelves of one of the greatest London stores.[10] Its rarity as food may well hinge on our greater reserve in culinary matters. 'In 1988, after giving a lecture on starlings at a conference in the Camargue, tins of starling pâté stacked high at Marseilles airport tempted me to sample this French product. I still recall the flavour, for which a taste must only be acquired after many years of subjecting the palate to torture.'[11]

While its flavour may have small appeal, most people are willing to acknowledge, albeit sometimes grudgingly, the bird's physical beauty. It has different proportions to a blackbird, with a short tail, long fine bill (hence the lovely arch old Norfolk name, 'chimney snipe') and a low centre of gravity that imparts a waddling quality to the bird's walk. In autumn the adult's dark purplish body is covered with dense white or buff arrowhead-shaped spots, but these gradually wear away during the winter so that it appears to re-emerge in spring as a smarter, darker breeding bird sumptuously glossed with violet and emerald iridescence.

The young, by contrast, are plain sandy olive with a white or creamy chin, and look totally different – so much so that at one time they were occasionally considered a separate species, the solitary thrush.[12] Just as

city-dwelling birds. It is intriguing to recount a note published in 1952 of a starling that sounded so similar to a telephone bell that it had the author's wife running indoors to pick up the receiver. It was probably the first occasion that such mimicry was ever recorded.[6]

The starling's capacity to imitate humans has long been recognised. Pliny made the somewhat suspicious claim that in ancient Rome starlings had been taught to speak Latin and Greek and that they could repeat whole sentences.[7] Yet its status as a caged bird with the gift of speech is certainly recorded in British literature and features in Shakespeare's *Henry IV* (Part One, Act 1, Scene 3). When the king refuses to consider Hotspur's requests to have a ransom paid on his brother-in-law, Earl Mortimer, Hotspur declares:

Nay, I'll have a starling shall be taught to speak
Nothing but 'Mortimer', and give it him
To keep his anger still in motion.

Despite the starling's continued high numbers, its population has suffered a very troubling decline in recent years.

odd are the partly moulted immatures, which have aquired an adult's spotty body but retain the youngster's plain-looking head. One of the classic sights of autumn is a group of starlings, which run the full gamut of moulting variations, clambering busily through an elder bush already weighed down by their gorgeous bunches of fruit.

If a small group is itself a visual delight, then a large flock of starlings – memorably known as a 'murmuration' – is one of the truly great spectacles of the entire British avifauna. During summer, family parties amalgamate at dusk to assemble in a night-time roost, but as the year wears on the gatherings can involve enough birds, as one contributor noted, 'to blot out the sun as they fly past'.[13] Winter is the classic period for observing these congregations and many European birds arrive from as far away as Russia to boost the British seasonal total. Until the early twentieth century in parts of south-west England, west Wales and northern Scotland starlings were known only as winter visitors, often pushed into these milder areas by cold weather. In the

1950s a Welsh name in Cardiganshire was *Adern yr Eira*, 'snow bird', because locals 'regarded their arrival as a sign of impending snow'.[14]

In areas without suitable trees and bushes, starlings will roost on cliff-ledges, and they have also found a satisfactory substitute for this type of site in the steep-sided rock and brick 'ravines' of an inner-city street. For several decades they famously congregated near Trafalgar Square and on the north bank of the Thames between Westminster and the Tower of London. The area was first used at the end of the nineteenth century, but only started to attract major numbers between 1910 and 1920. It was initially believed that the unwonted hordes were invaders from the Continent, but the truth proved a little more prosaic. A young Max Nicholson undertook a novel form of bird study from the upper deck of open-topped London buses and traced the birds to their real roots in the capital's outer suburbs.[15]

At dusk they simply commuted to the bright lights of the inner city and in their heyday occupied a good cross-section of London's major cultural monuments, such as the British Museum, the Royal Opera House, St Paul's Cathedral, the Guildhall, the Foreign Office and Cabinet Office buildings, Marble Arch, St Pancras and Charing Cross stations. Eventually the flocks were sufficiently large and noisy for their bustling din to blot out the sound of traffic and to become, in turn, a natural spectacle to rival the man-made glories of the locality:[16]

> One of the joys of the city was the great swirls of starlings as each of us was heading for home: *me* on my way from the office in Covent Garden, via the tube at Leicester Square, not alone in pausing to look up and smile; *they* after a hard autumn's day in the surrounding areas, homing to the centre of the city. The way they formed huge shoals and then broke away and merged once more always took the breath away. After many fly-pasts and fragmentations they would land. Behind the neon signs, on the pinnacles of cupolas, in the London plane trees in Leicester Square itself, you could see them pushing and shoving, oblivious to the great view of film stars attending first nights. Even above the busiest of the day's traffic you could hear them gossiping, grumbling, celebrating the day. How I miss them. Not because I've moved out of London, but because they have been pushed out of their place. Are we really too tidy to live with one of nature's wonders?[17]

It would seem so. As well as appearing magically beautiful, starling murmurations are widely considered a problem. The nightly shower of droppings smells strongly – apparently carrying downwind for 500 yards (450m) in damp conditions – strong enough, in fact, to allow a fox to escape when the hounds got lost once among the miasmic stink of starling roost.[18] Chris Feare, Britain's leading authority on the bird, speaks with equal expertise on its odour: 'In the 1970s I undertook studies in a large roost in Norfolk, which involved many hours in the wood as the birds arrived and settled down for the night. My Barbour jacket retained the distinctive aroma of starling roost for over a year and visitors who came to meetings in my office would do so with wrinkled noses, but few dared ask for an explanation!'[19]

In London the gauntlet was finally thrown down to the starlings when the unthinkable happened:

> Their ultimate crime was landing in such flocks on the hands of Big Ben in 1949 that they stopped the clock! This, together with the noises and droppings, led to political concern with lengthy discussions in parliament. Perhaps the greatest accolade to the starling came about five years later when on 31 August 1954 an

The starling roost at Brighton's West Pier was the source of a natural spectacle every bit as beautiful as the town's architectural splendours.

entire *Goon Show* was devoted to their removal from London. Suggested techniques included rice puddings fired from catapults, a military 'Operation Cacopohony' (where the noises generated had no effect on the birds but led to partial evacuation of

London's human population!) and exploding bird lime. Sadly an error in the formulation of the last led to the destruction of St Martin-in the-Fields Church.[20]

The benches around Leicester Square had to be turned over to avoid the blizzard of white and the cost of clean-up operations eventually led to attempts to evict the starlings with a mixture of netting, bird-repelling chemicals on the ledges, and broadcasts of the bird's own alarm calls. The attempts all failed but the speakers that were used still survive in the trees around Leicester Square. However recent huge declines in starling numbers – they have fallen by 60 per cent over the last 25 years – have led to a sharp reduction in urban roosts, and the mixed-media display of swirling flocks and inner-city neon is now largely a thing of the past.

Other major urban roosts in Manchester, Liverpool, Belfast, Leeds, Newcastle, Edinburgh and Glasgow have

The starling's striking beauty is often overlooked.

also gone, but none of these ever achieved the scale of some rural sites. At Thorne Moors, for example, near Goole in south Yorkshire, they gathered in one of the largest flocks ever assembled by a land bird:

As afternoon darkened, successive waves arrived from the west and at their most numerous, the incoming birds were of locust proportions, forming a broad front, its limits seemingly defined more by visibility and fading light than by numbers. Straining through binoculars only expanded the horizon of birds. There was no purpose in attempting an estimate but to share the fading light – and the gathering chill – with that excitable, almost overwhelming, throng of birds was deeply memorable. Swathes of starlings dissolved as groups broke rank, their purposeful flight ending in coordinated gyrations before they plummeted downwards. As these birds disappeared into the blackness of woodland, the senses shifted and it was the clamour of the roost which became dominant. On 18 March

two observers estimated 1,438,000 and on 5 March 1972 a million was regarded as a realistic figure. Starlings are fickle birds and when they eventually vanished the interface between day and night at Thorne was never so animated, so frenetic, and certainly never so impressive.[21]

Another huge gathering occurred at Wenderton Wood, not far from Stodmarsh in Kent. Between the late 1950s and 1970s estimates ranged up to 1–2 million birds:

Flocks tended to alight in stubble, winter cereal fields or pastures before going into the wood, and moved across them, apparently feeding, like a rolling carpet with birds at the back leapfrogging those at the front. Periodically the whole lot would rise in noisy panic. Above the wood, as birds went into the roost, were the familar smoke-like clouds of starlings swirling back and forth and giving that distinctive crackling hiss of a big starling flock – far less peaceful than is suggested by 'murmuration'.[22]

When starlings leave their roost the following morning, the sound of their departure has been likened to a passing express train.[23]

The sheer weight of numbers can have baleful results. Densities of 500 birds a cubic yard (0.76cu m) weigh about 75 pounds (35kg) and can eventually flatten reedbeds (another common roost site) and break large branches in woodland settings, while the accumulating layers of guano can kill trees or bushes because of their acid content.[24] Moulds and other fungi also flourish and can add 'to the atmosphere of death and foulness'. At Wenderton Wood the quagmire was deep enough to maroon a Land-Rover almost up to its axle.[25] 'I used to visit in winter and there were, of course, no leaves on the trees, but it looked as though there would never be again. The whole wood, from twigs to floor, was thickly coated with starling guano, and the air pervaded with an almost choking ammoniacal fragrance. I remember thinking that some of the Somme woodlands must have looked like this after they were completely shattered.'[26]

Such scenes of devastation help give context to vernacular names like 'shitlegs' and the Orcadian 'scootie', which has much the same meaning (see also Arctic Skua, page 229). Yet the northern English version, 'stinker', has no direct link with the bird's guano; instead, it comes from the starling's willingness to nest in the stink-pipe in old outdoor privvies.[27] However derived, the scatological associations are part of a strongly negative element in the starling's persona. 'Its busy, boisterous and greedy behaviour led a friend of mine to describe it as the

Large starling roosts, like the one at Westhay, Somerset, can become popular public attractions.

"secondhand car salesman of the bird world".[28] There is a comparable distaste implicit in the following: 'I used to feed the birds in our Glaswegian garden and our name for starlings was "the Gorbal boys".'[29]

Our lack of sympathy is particularly evident now that the bird has joined the red list of severely declined species. While the plight of the song thrush, skylark and even house sparrow arouses our concern, the starling is still too numerous for many people. 'I have watched these birds closely. They are very aggressive, greedy and swamp our gardens in large flocks and are very noisy. We need a device that only allows the smaller birds to feed, i.e. sparrows, tits, robins, and stops the starlings. They are a major pest.'[30]

The bird's reputation for uncleanliness, cemented by its attachment to sewage works and rubbish dumps, almost inexorably feeds into darker allegations. These arise partly from the starling's propensity to forage among grazing animals (and also pasture-probing birds such as rooks, jackdaws and lapwings). The large suite of northern vernacular names ('shep', 'shepster', etc.) comes from the species' relationship with sheep and, while they

are valued for searching the fleece for ovine parasites, starlings are also widely accused of carrying disease. They may occasionally play some role in the transmission of a stomach virus affecting pigs, but the allegation involving the spread of foot-and-mouth disease, or Newcastle disease among poultry, is based on very little evidence.[31] Even so, some still like to consider the starling a 'plague upon the land'.[32]

Nowhere does the bird have a darker reputation than in parts of North America. One could make a case that its explosive spread across the continent is partly the fault of the Bard. In 1890 a crank called Eugene Schieffelin, a drug manufacturer and would-be thespian, decided to introduce all the birds mentioned in Shakespeare's works. The lines from *Henry IV* (quoted above) duly led to the release of 40 pairs of English starlings in Central Park, New York, with a similar batch the following year. No sooner had the genie swirled from the bottle than it started to expand and spread. Within 80 years it had a range from the Atlantic to the Pacific Oceans, north into Alaska and south to the subtropical Mexican state of Yucatan, where the increase is ongoing. Similar releases were successful in Australia (1862), New Zealand (late 1850s) and South Africa (1890s) but nowhere have starlings thrived so well as in North America, where the unwanted alien is now one of the commonest birds.[33]

Pest status followed hard on the starling's ineradicable tenure of that continent. As well as the usual claims of spreading disease and the fouling charges associated with roosts, starlings are disliked for their voracious depredations of fruit and grain crops, as well as feed put out for livestock and poultry. Control measures, costing millions of dollars, include poisoning, shooting, trapping, dynamiting and spraying them with detergents. In some instances as many as a million birds have been killed in one operation.[34] Jelly-like chemical deterrents (one entitled 'Roost No More') are smeared on window ledges, while a poison (DRC-1339: 3-chloro-4-methyl-benzenamine hydrochloride) is more memorably marketed as Starlicide. Despite all these efforts, the common starling maintains an American population of 500 million birds, one-third of the entire world total.[35]

How differently matters stand in the east. In communist times, the practically minded Russians encouraged common starlings – one of their traditional heralds of spring and a dear friend to the Soviet farmer – by the provision of 22.5 million nest boxes, all monitored by school children as part of their education.[36]

If anything the **Rosy Starling**, *Sturnus roseus*, is held in higher esteem. The name alone suggests the bird's physical beauty and positive standing. In Britain it is welcomed by birdwatchers as a strikingly handsome rarity in spring and autumn, but on its central Asian breeding grounds it is even more cherished. A major component of its diet is the insect family *Orthoptera*, which includes the grasshopper species that can develop into locusts. A breeding colony of 3000 birds has been estimated to harvest 2.5–3 ton(ne)s of grasshoppers a day.[37] Since classical times people from the region, including Christians and Muslims, have looked upon the rosy starling's appearance after the arrival of ravening swarms of insects as a form of almost divine deliverance. Waters taken from various sacred wells and springs throughout the bird's range, once they had been blessed by the appropriate religious authority and sprinkled on the locust-infested grounds, were said to conjure rosy-starling flocks with a magical irresistibility.[38]

Sparrow family *Passeridae*

House Sparrow, *Passer domesticus*. VN: Spadge/r, Spug, Spuggy, Sprog, Sparrer, Spadgick (widespread); Squidgie (Kent); Speug, Spyug, Sparrag, Sporrow (Orkney); Sparky, Spjugg, Sporra (Shetland). House sparrows are so much a part of our lives that even the most scientifically minded authors can hardly refrain from ascribing to them human characteristics: 'a sharp-eyed, quick-witted exploiter . . . relies at all seasons upon the advantages of operating in gangs' (Max Nicholson); 'In its demeanour the sparrow is everywhere recognised as a bold and often pugnacious bird' (David Bannerman); 'perky and bustling . . . Bold and impudent yet wary and suspicious' (Bernard Tucker); 'Behaviour variable; . . . tame around human habitation whose food sources cheekily utilized, but . . . shy and wary, when in farmland or wild country' (Ian Wallace).[1] The bird's seemingly contradictory manner is nicely choreographed to our own ambivalent responses, which have traditionally swung between wry affection and warm-hearted annoyance.

Although there are many vernacular names, it is striking how they are really only variations on a theme. Most derive from the Middle English *sparewe*; and behind that version, the Old English word, *sparwa*.[2] Much the same word has therefore served us for 1500 years and, as with another bold garden bird, the magpie (see page 400), there seems to be something in its simple disyllablic name that goes to the heart of its personality and makes alternatives unnecessary. They are all names tinged with a sense of emotion or humour, which is highly appropriate given that this is our most loyal avian companion. The modern Scouse vernacular – 'brown budgie' – is also intriguing because it implies a bird at one remove from a truly wild species; if not quite a household pet, then it seems at least partly domesticated.[3]

It is equally notable how often the bird enters our vocabulary as a way to describe aspects of ourselves. 'In and around Scarborough about 30 years ago skinny kids were often called spugsy.'[4] The surnames Sparrow and Spurling are thought to have arisen as nicknames for people with the bird's chirpy manner or small size.[5] But perhaps the best known of the pet names is the surviving cockney jargon for a male friend, 'my old cock sparrow'. It seems to combine the customary affection of a diminutive with an added hint of cheeky prowess that, if not quite sexual, is at least securely masculine in character.

Even the smallest chink in the roof tiles will give access to nesting house sparrows.

Sparrows were once synonymous with sex and lechery because of their obvious abundance and the highly public nature of their copulation. The association dates back to ancient Egypt, where the bird was the hieroglyph denoting libidinousness.[6] In the classical world the sparrow was sacred to Aphrodite and her Roman equivalent, Venus, while among Roman courtesans there was a tradition of keeping hand-raised male sparrows as playthings.[7] The poem 'To Lesbia's pet sparrow' by Catullus (84–c. 54 BC) alludes to the habit and is laced with sexual innuendo. There are also many comparable references in English literature, such as the sex-mad summoner in Chaucer's *Canterbury Tales*, who runs a thriving brothel and is said to be as 'lecherous as a sparwe'.[8] In Shakespeare's *Measure for Measure* (Act 3, Scene 2), the womanising Lucio complains of the Duke's deputy, Angelo, 'This ungenitur'd agent will unpeople the province with continency; sparrows must not build in his house-eaves because they are lecherous.'

In fact the sexual mores of the house sparrow are more intriguing – and far more like our own – than the simple old promiscuity charge would suggest. Denis Summers-Smith, one of the world's great experts on sparrows, whose studies date back 60 years, writes:

When I did my initial work in the 1940s and 1950s I recorded very few cases of birds with multiple partners and my evidence flatly contradicted the sparrow's old lechery tag. Yet it seems that recent DNA studies have unearthed a different picture. They indicate that 15 per cent of offspring are the result of copulations by both males and females with others' partners. However like ourselves, sparrows seem to conduct their 'illicit couplings' in private, hence my failure to record them. Ironically the copulation we see out in the open, and which was a main reason for the bird's old reputation, is between established couples. I was fascinated to learn recently of an unpublished government study of illegitimacy in a high-rise block of flats, which showed it to be running at much the same rate amongst the human occupants as in the sparrow colony where the DNA studies were conducted. In more ways than one the sexy image we've projected on to the sparrow says as much about us as it does about the bird.[9]

One aspect of the sparrow's breeding regime not open to dispute, and which has played an integral part in its spread across six continents, is its willingness to utilise

A vanished heyday for the London sparrow – these scenes from St James's Park may never be recreated.

every conceivable man-made opportunity. The Welsh name, *Aderyn y To*, 'roof bird', is perfectly apposite, given the sparrows' love for nesting under eaves, beneath roof slates, in water pipes, holes in masonry and almost any other access point. Another stock favourite is a hole in a street light, where the birds also benefit from the inbuilt heating system.[10] The most remarkable extremes involve sparrows found on the 80th floor of the Empire State Building in New York, and several records of them living down English coal mines. At Frinkley Colliery in south Yorkshire two or three birds survived for several years during the 1970s and bred 2000 feet (640m) beneath the surface of the earth, living largely on scraps provided by the miners.[11]

However a well-deserved second prize should go to the sparrows that nested 'in the coke oven ram machines at a steel works in south Wales, tolerating not only the continuous movement, but also the high temperature when the coke oven was "pushed"'.[12] The mobility of the nest seems not to be an issue troubling house sparrows, if Bishop Stanley can be believed. In 1857 he claimed that a pair built in the rigging of a coal vessel from Newcastle, which had put into Nairn in Scotland. After the vessel sailed, the sparrows accompanied the boat and were fed

by the crew on bread. The voyage lasted several days and, on returning to the Tyne, the nest with its four chicks was taken down and put into a crevice of a ruined house where the adults continued to brood.[13] Another elusive source, Richard Meinertzhagen (see Albatross, page 10), wrote of two house-sparrow pairs that similarly nested in the rigging of a house-boat on the Sudanese Nile. The birds apparently travelled with him during four days of consecutive journeys of up to 18 miles (30km), putting ashore to feed as the vessel proceeded.[14]

The nest itself is an untidy bundle of straw and feathers, although man-made materials are widely recorded, including string, paper, bits of cloth or plastic and cigarette butts, while Eric Simms records a nest made entirely out of cassette tape.[15] Sparrows also readily evict house martins and even sand martins from their own nests, a habit that has earnt them condemnation from a wide number of people, including otherwise sympathetic commentators like Gilbert White and the Norfolk ornithologist Henry Stevenson: '[it] annually excites my warmest indignation . . . I am often obliged to come to the rescue and shoot the intruders.'[16]

The sparrow's willingness to take over any suitable nest hole was once exploited by country people to secure a welcome source of protein. The earthenware sparrow pot was probably invented in the Low Countries (most likely in Delft, a city whose wealth depended on brewing and grain) and was brought over to England with Dutch engineers working on the Fens drainage. Such pots were hung around the farm walls, both to entice the birds out of the roof to prevent damage to the thatch and to enable the housewife to harvest the newly fledged young at her convenience. The pots offered an additional benefit in allowing farmers to control a well-known grain pest. Pots very similar to those used in Britain appear in Pieter Brueghel's painting 'Dulle Griet', suggesting that they were in operation by the 1560s. There is also an amusing metaphysical poem of 1640 by Thomas Randolph entitled 'To his well Timbred Mistresse' that includes the lines: 'Another story make from wast to chinne/With breasts like Pots to nest young Sparrowes in.' Judging from the urbane tone, Randolph clearly presumed sparrow pots were a well-known household item.[17] They remained commonly in use until at least the nineteenth century, and possibly later, particularly in Sussex and Kent.[18]

Sometimes it was not just the nestlings that were harvested.

In the spring before the war we used to go round the farm to all the sparrow nests we could find. These were often great big balls of straw mixed with feathers

House sparrows were long considered a major agricultural nuisance and were netted in their millions.

from the chicken run and old baler twine. These big clumps could have several nests in them and we might get 20–30 eggs from each. The farmer used to crack them one by one into a cup to make sure they weren't set and then put them in his milk can. He'd get as many as he could, then cook these up into an omelette. Sometimes we'd get a few blackbird or waterhen eggs and they'd all go in together just the same.[19]

Although the sparrow pot had the advantage of ease of access, it had none of the devastating efficiency of a net. Various kinds were used for sparrows and continued to serve their purpose until at least the Second World War. One device had a bag-shaped net on a long pole, which could be opened and closed with cords and rather resembled a huge version of the child's pond-dipping net. Another more efficient method was the true 'sparrow-net', some of which were 10 yards (9m) long and were laid around the stack yards. A mechanism used in northern England was called a 'guelder' and was shaped rather like a large snow-shoe, with numerous hair nooses attached to the crosshatched strings running from side to side. The whole thing was baited with grain and the sparrows entangled themselves in the nooses.[20]

Other methods combined profit with sporting entertainment. 'In the 1930s and '40s a good friend with a gang of chums would line up 6–8 feet from the stable eaves on a Norfolk farm and, when ready, one with a long stick ran quickly along the length of the eaves rattling the sparrows out. As they flew they described a downward curve to gain speed, straight into the racket swipe of the sharp-eyed kids.'[21] Birds were also frequently trapped in

their roost at night, when the catchers had the additional advantage of being able to startle them:

In the hard days before the Second World War what we used to do was walk with the farmworkers around the corn stacks before they were threshed. The sparrows used to roost in the sheltered ends of the stacks and we used to dazzle them with an old bike gas lamp or stable lamp and then, taking a long willow stick with a net on the end, we'd sweep it across the stacks and drag the birds to the ground. The farmworker used to break their necks between first and middle fingers and he'd slice the breast meat off with his pocket knife – a sliver about the size of your little finger. These were dropped into an old white enamel milk can with a blue rim and after about two hours, when we'd walked round all the stacks and barns, this would be full. The next night he'd invite us up to the farm for supper.[22]

Like sparrow pots and sparrow nets, sparrow pie (or pudding) had a long, distinguished tradition that probably stretched back more than 1000 years. The meat is dark and flavoursome, formerly endowed with powers of sexual arousal – a reflection of the old lechery association – and cheap. In *Troilus and Cressida* (Act 2, Scene 1) Shakespeare lists them at a penny for nine. Yet it was by no means a dish confined to the rustic cottage. A delicious-sounding Elizabethan recipe recommended either larks or sparrows prepared in mutton broth, flavoured with whole mace and pepper in claret, with marigold leaves, burberries, rosewater, verjuice, vinegar,

439

The house sparrow's personality seems a curious blend of cocky mischief and crafty distrust.

sugar and marrow or sweet butter.[23] Several contributors to *Birds Britannica* confirm that the memory of sparrow pudding is by no means lost: 'I had an old friend, a real Hertfordshire countryman, who would remove the lead shot from a .410 cartridge and replace it with sand, then scatter corn beneath the washing line. He'd stand a little way off and when sparrows came to eat the corn, a clap of the hands sent them up to the clothes line when he'd let fly lengthwise down the line. The birds were skinned, twelve to a pie, cooked and eaten whole.'[24]

For many centuries sparrows also provided a source of fresh meat for the falconer's birds, while in his *History of the Birds of Middlesex* William Glegg recalled how keepers at London Zoo used to net them to feed to the other animals.[25] This oblique comment on their former abundance casts a perverse light in the eco-friendly capital of today, where the humble sparrow is an increasing rarity. Yet until relatively recently the bird was widely considered a serious pest species and a stanza from 'The Farmer's Boy' (1800), by the Suffolk-born poet Robert Bloomfield, gives an indication of what was at stake:

Whilst thousands in a flock, for ever gay,

Loud chirping *sparrows* welcome on the day,
And from the mazes of the leafy thorn
Drop one by one upon the bending corn.

While today this would be a vision to gladden the heart of any modern ecologist working on the current declines of 60 per cent in rural areas, the main response in a less environmentally troubled age was a phenomenon known as the sparrow club. It drew on the pre-existing tradition of parish bounties paid by church wardens for the beaks of notable pest species, but in the nineteenth century it blossomed into a widespread local institution where the members' competitive instincts could be indulged in a context of civic responsibility. They held regular meetings and annual dinners when the year's top sparrow-killer could be honoured. Some clubs survive even today simply as recreational groups, but at the time they were thought to perform an important agricultural function:

I have a silver cup that stands on my sideboard. Just before the First World War on the Isle of Thanet the county council formed the Isle of Thanet Sparrow Society. A cup was presented annually to the person who killed the most sparrows and my grandfather, aided by my father, won it in 1911, 1912 and 1913 with a total of 4574 birds. He was then given the cup outright. My father always said that the numbers they got were only the tip of the iceberg because huge flocks survived for years.[26]

While the sparrow clubs were revived in the First World War and the BBC broadcast fresh government appeals for sparrow destruction during the Second World War, the species has eventually received legal protection. Today there are periodic reductions in cases of severe agricultural damage or potential health risk, particularly in the vicinity of grain silos where the birds may cause contamination, but the exceptions represent the lag-end of our anti-sparrow campaign, which was as long-lived as it was, at times, intense. A study of parish records in Bedfordshire, for example, indicated that in just one arable county, the parish bounties of the seventeenth and eighteenth centuries led to a harvest of several million birds and tens of thousands of eggs.[27] In turn they imply a national total running towards nine figures. Yet even these huge numbers seem only to have suppressed local populations without affecting the house sparrow's overall abundance, and in 1970 there were thought to be 25 million, making it our commonest breeding bird.[28]

Taking sparrows' lives and exploiting them have never represented the whole of our relationship, if only because the evidence is not all on one side. The birds also eat insects, some harmful to arable crops. Henry Saxby recorded how the Shetland potato harvest had once failed repeatedly because the locals would not recognise that the sparrows they suppressed also eliminated more serious pests.[29] Behind Saxby's precept is a much longer and deeper tradition of finding instruction in the life of the most familiar of our birds. The sparrow's very smallness and triviality have made it the classic contrast with its diametric opposite. 'Who sees with equal eye, as God of all,' wrote Alexander Pope in his *Essay on Man* (lines 87–90),

A hero perish, or a sparrow fall,
Atoms or systems into ruin hurled,
And now a bubble burst, and now a world.

In Shakespeare's *Hamlet* (Act 5, Scene 2), the prince remarks to Horatio 'there is special providence in the fall of a sparrow', while in the eighth century the Venerable Bede likened the human span on earth to the passage of a sparrow through the banqueting hall, in at one door and exiting instantly through another. All three writers drew

on an original moral lesson given by Christ (described in both Luke and Matthew), that if the fate of each sparrow did not escape God's notice, then how much more did he value humans.

The sense that profundity lies hidden in the most humble creature has found recent expression in the wellspring of concern for sparrow declines. In eastern England the fall is running as high as 90 per cent in 30 years, while London is worst affected, with three-quarters of its sparrows lost in just six years (1994–2000). *The Independent*, one of the catalysts for public concern and at the forefront of national media coverage, runs a dedicated 'Save the Sparrow' campaign and offers £5000 for the scientific paper that unravels the causes. So far the line-up of suspects includes cats as well as the customary avian scapegoats – magpie and sparrowhawk – unleaded petrol, increased use of garden pesticides and, more bizarrely, mobile phones (originally a Spanish theory reported, among other places, on the *Times of India* website and said to hinge on electromagnetic waves that interfere with the bird's capacity to reproduce or navigate). *Birds Britannica* contributors have suggested modern roofing methods that bar access to the breeding sparrows (now widely viewed as an important problem) and the lost tradition of shaking crumbs from the tablecloth.[30]

The decline has been raised in the House of Lords and in the Commons, while Prime Minister Tony Blair has spoken elsewhere on the issue. Denis Summers-Smith argues that the bird's plight has genuine implications for ourselves:

Much of the concern about the decline of the house sparrow is purely sentimental (and there is nothing wrong about that), but there is a more serious side. The UK government recognises wild birds as indicators of the 'quality of life'. What then does a 99 per cent decline in some of the urban centres in Britain tell us about the quality of life in our cities? Like the sparrow, most of us live in towns. We can fairly ask the questions: 'Is the house sparrow today's equivalent of the miner's canary? Is something nasty going on in our towns that might affect us all?'[31]

It was an American writer who expressed most succinctly another deeply positive element in our relationship with sparrows. Although he was speaking of a different species from our own bird, Henry Thoreau's remark in *Walden* loses none of its resonance: 'I once had a sparrow alight upon my shoulder for a moment when I was digging in a village garden, and I felt that I was more distinguished by that circumstance than I should have been by any epaulette I could have worn.'[32] The physical and emotional proximity of other species is a profoundly important part of human life and no species of bird is more proximate than the sparrow.

Feeding them in parks and our own private gardens is so deeply rooted in British society that it is hard to imagine a time when they were not actively encouraged. The vision of children or of an elderly person tending to the needs of wild birds is now embedded in our culture as an iconic expression of Christian giving, and behind all such images there probably looms the legend of St Francis. Feeding birds also suggests more pagan associations. In one of the most beautifully observed passages from his *Birds in London*, W. H. Hudson captured both the underlying sense of ritual and its quasi-religious motivation in his account of those coming down to feed sparrows in the Dell in Hyde Park:

> 'I call these my chickens, and I am obliged to come every day to feed them,' said a paralytic-looking, white-haired old man in the shabbiest clothes, one evening as I stood there; then, taking some fragments of stale bread from his pockets, he began feeding the sparrows, and while doing so he chuckled with delight, and looked round from time to time, to see if the others were enjoying the spectacle.
>
> To him succeeded two sedate-looking labourers, big, strong men, with tired, dusty faces, on their way home from work. Each produced from his coat-pocket a little store of fragments of bread and meat, saved from the midday meal, carefully wrapped up in a piece of newspaper. After bestowing their scraps on the little brown-coated crowd, one spoke: 'Come on, mate, they've had it all, and now let's see what the missus has got for our tea'; and home they trudged across the park, with hearts refreshed and lightened.[33]

Spanish Sparrow, *Passer hispaniolensis*. It occurs far more widely across Mediterranean latitudes into central Asia than the name implies and has been recorded six times in Britain. The last, a male, turned up in the tiny hamlet of Waterside, Cumbria, in July 1996 and remained with the local sparrow flock until December 1998. Despite the long residence of this handsome bird – far more striking than any male house sparrow – no hybrids were ever recorded.

Eurasian Tree Sparrow, *Passer montanus*. VN: Tree Dick, Tree Spug/gy (northern England). The smaller hole-nesting sparrow now predominantly found on English farmland and hedgerows is scarcer than its close relative and has never achieved the same level of household familiarity or cultural importance as the house

With its black-spotted cheeks and chestnut crown, the tree sparrow is a very handsome creature.

sparrow. Few people see it regularly today, particularly since it has undergone a massive 95 per cent reduction in the last 25 years, although our capacity to overlook the tree sparrow is long-standing. It was not even differentiated in England from *the* sparrow until 1720 and it was a Scottish naturalist, Sir Robert Sibbald, who first listed it separately in the seventeenth century.[34]

Possibly because it lives so completely in its relative's shadow, it is quietly championed by some people. There is a curious pleasure in sifting through sparrow flocks and finding the birds of daintier build and more distinguished colours, particularly the lovely copper-coloured crown and 'the triangular black mark which stands like an elaborate "muttonchop" upon its cheek'.[35]

Another attraction may be the tree sparrow's rather capricious distribution, which has excluded it at times from much of Scotland, the west country, western Wales and large parts of Ireland. The gaps have increased with the recent slump in numbers, although the current picture needs to be set in the context of major known fluctuations for more than 150 years. For the partisan the element of ecological mystery is one more ingredient to stir into the tree-sparrow pot.

Our ancestors clearly shared some sense of pleasure in the bird, given that they attempted to introduce it to a number of countries in the nineteenth century. The releases in New Zealand and Australia were unsuccessful, but there is a thriving if isolated colony of about 15,000 birds around the city of St Louis in Missouri, USA. This is in contrast to the near-global spread of house sparrows, which were released at much the same time. That bird's rapid colonisation may have been a factor in the tree sparrow's inability to take root, although the house sparrow is not universally dominant.

The tree sparrow has a massive Asiatic range and in countries like Nepal and China it has achieved the same population levels and lives in the same commensal manner as its more aggressive relative. It also suffers at times similar kinds of persecution. Most famous was China's 'sparrocide' of April 1958, which reads today like a biblical parable. During the Great Leap Forward, there was a Mao Zedong-inspired drive towards a complete eradication because of the tree sparrow's presumed effect on grain yields.

Three million people were duly mobilised in 'shock battalions' (with a fifth column of newly stuffed scarecrows) to wage continuous war on the birds. On the appointed day the tree sparrows were shot and trapped or simply harassed with gongs, drums and long poles until they fell from the sky with exhaustion. In their 'noble struggle against this public enemy' Chinese scientists had worked out that sparrows are worn out after two hours' flying. The whole campaign was spurred on by vans broadcasting messages of support, or bearing red-daubed slogans such as 'BRAVELY STRUGGLE FORWARD, ELIMINATE THE SPARROW PEST!'[36]

Unfortunately the fall-out from unravelling nature's delicate web of relationships was not a point well covered in Mao's *Little Red Book*. In the years following the campaign, grain yields plummeted and millions of people starved. The Chinese eventually realised that they had underestimated the fall of the sparrow and the birds were politically rehabilitated. Happily, they have since largely recovered their former numbers.[37]

Finch family *Fringillidae*

Chaffinch, *Fringilla coelebs*. VN: Chaff/ie, Spink (widespread, particularly in northern England), Pie Finch, Pay Linnet (Midlands), Pinkie. Richard Fitter nicely captured the chaffinch's catholic tastes when he wrote, 'I have seen it in Lincoln's Inn Fields in central London and in the northernmost birchwood on the mainland of Great Britain.'[1] Originally a woodland species, the chaffinch has completely adapted to all sorts of agricultural settings and continues to buck the downward trend of many farmland birds. It is also very much at home in town or village gardens, where the critical habitat component is trees, and recently oaks have been identified as particularly important, providing them with rich invertebrate populations to feed their young during the nestling stage.[2]

Wild chaffinches can become remarkably tamer especially in country car parks where they hunt for scraps, shuffling among the vehicles or across the picnic tables – the males a striking blend of salmon-pink underparts with blue-grey head and shawl. Its action suggests a rather perky bird and characterisations of it have often dwelt on the apparent air of cheerfulness. 'To parents . . . with a morose and sulky boy,' wrote one Victorian commentator, 'my advice is, buy him a chaffinch.' That much-altered adjective, 'gay', was frequently applied and at one time 'as gay as a chaffinch' was proverbial for a well-dressed or vivacious person ('As gay as a goldfinch' had much the same meaning).[3]

The bird's striking monosyllabic call, which has a bright and purposeful quality, is often transliterated as '*pink*' or '*spink*'. The second version is still used as an alternative name for the bird in parts of northern England. But it is the song that is central to the chaffinch's cheery persona. It is a simple three-second burst with two or three notes repeated several times, followed by a more rapid terminal flourish known as the cadence. One ornithologist likened the introductory notes to a cricketer's run-up to the wicket, with the cadence as the bowling action. He added that in early spring a chaffinch sometimes needs practice before managing to 'deliver the ball'.[4] In its prime, the bird repeats the phrase about six times a minute and up to 3000 times a day, which explains the occasional charge of monotony.

Chaffinches are well known for the many regional variations on the basic theme and there are several mnemonics to describe it. An old name for the species in

northern England is the 'Hebrew bird', 'Hebrew' being spelt out in the song. In Kent it was thought to be saying, 'If we wait another month, we shall have the Wheatear.'[5] And 'It was told me at Hurstbourne [Hampshire] that when the yellowhammer sings "A little bit of bread and no cheese", the chaffinch replies, "I haven't had a bit of bread and cheese this five year".'[6]

The old bird catchers had such a fine-tuned ear for the chaffinch's songs that they named different populations according to the particular structure of the final cadence, those from Essex being known as 'chuckwados', while Kent birds were called 'kiss-me-dears'.[7]

Interest in these hair-splitting differences arose from a cult long surrounding the chaffinch and its song, which was once, in its way, as significant as the literary traditions attaching to the nightingale. In the nineteenth century it was largely an activity among the urban working class and is now almost entirely lost to view. Yet its origins go back at least to the medieval period and in parts of mainland Europe, particularly Germany, chaffinch keeping was more akin to a fanatical obsession. It centred on competitions between owners to see whose bird could out-sing its opponent. The winner was the one adjudged to have delivered the greatest number of phrases in a set time, usually 15 minutes.

Singing matches were especially common in the poor districts of the East End and often took place in taverns accompanied by much ceremony, not to mention drinking and gambling.[8] The *Avicultural Magazine* of 1896 carried a first-hand account of a chaffinch contest between the 'Kingsland Roarer' and 'Shoreditch Bobby'. It is worth quoting at length if only for its wonderful evocation of the atmosphere in the Dickensian 'Cock and Bottle' at Shoreditch, and for the unscrupulous tactics of the chaffinch owners.

In the parlour all the gas-jets are lighted, but have some trouble to penetrate the fumes of tobacco, beer, etc. At last the contesting parties enter, each dressed in his Sunday best . . . The two markers take their places, and as the clock strikes the two cages are uncovered and hung up. The battlers look around for a moment, shake their plumage, whet their beaks and one may take a grain of seed, but before it is cracked he hears a familiar sound uttered by his opponent. Immediately he replies by a full strophe of his song, to which the other answers with fuller power. Before each marker is already a stroke of his chalk, and now the combat is

The chaffinch is one of our most numerous and widespread species.

fairly 'started'. The chalks are busily employed to mark each properly delivered strophe, and keep pace with each other for a time, until 'Bobby' takes it into his head to betake himself to the food trough.

Meanwhile the 'Roarer' continues steadily to pour out his heart, and gains considerably in chalk marks. 'Costermonger Joe' is getting very uneasy and cannot understand this 'trick' of his much-renowned bird. Never before did he think of food while in the presence of an opponent. In order to draw his bird's attention upon himself and from the food trough, he moves uneasily in his seat and ventures at last to cough aloud.

It must be understood, that while a match is proceeding no words of encouragement are allowed; no whistling or other means may be resorted to, to recall a truant to his duty . . . At last, Joe can stand it no longer; *accidentally* his beer glass gets knocked over and falls on the floor with much clatter. Bobby peers across the room to ascertain the cause of the unusual disturbance and catches sight of his master, and immediately resumes his battle-cry. The ruse has succeeded, although there is a tumbler to pay for.

The chalk marks on the tables are getting numerous. The Roarer has challenged without a fault for thirteen minutes and is forty points ahead of Bobby, but now he feels rather 'dry'. He stops working, takes a drink of water and – hops to the food box. But 'Kingsland Bill' does not give his bird time to lose ground by feeding like the other. In a moment he whips out the brightly-colored handkerchief the Roarer knows so well and pretends to wipe the perspiration from his anxious brow. His finch takes the hint, and gallops through the remaining two minutes of the appointed fifteen in grand style. Bobby also had tried hard to make up for the precious time he had lost so wantonly, but could not recover all of it. Although credited with 212 marks, the Roarer beat him by 28 strokes.[9]

After all the singing and dubious practice, Costermonger Joe and Kingsland Bill fall to mutual complaint, then almost to blows, while the judge (the landlord) deems the contest null and void and asks for a rematch at the Cock and Bottle for the same stakes the following week.

Good singing birds were extremely valuable and were said to change hands for 20–50 shillings apiece, a small fortune by Victorian standards.[10] (This was modest in comparison with the extravagant prices paid in the German district of Harz, where the expression 'This chaffinch is worth a cow' was sometimes literally true.[11]) The associated economics had a knock-on effect on some wild populations, with severe declines noted in parts of London and Kent because of over-trapping.

One of the few aspects to receive wider notice was the associated cruelty, and Thomas Hardy explored its moral implications in 'The Blinded Bird'. It was widely held that a finch sang sweeter and louder if deprived of its sight and the usual method was to drive hot needles into its eyes. The deep contrast between the brutality of the human action and the seeming forgiveness of nature, as expressed through the beauty of the finch's song, is the point of emotional leverage in Hardy's impassioned verse:

Who hath charity? This bird.
Who suffereth long and is kind,
Is not provoked, though blind
And alive ensepulchred?
Who hopeth, endureth all things?
Who thinketh no evil, but sings?
Who is divine? This bird.

Other finches such as linnet and goldfinch were also abused, but the cult surrounding chaffinches made them frequent victims. Many bird keepers themselves loathed the practice, although the bird's disability had the secondary effect of cementing its dependence upon the owner, who normally reciprocated with deep emotional attachment. W. H. Hudson recorded an East End fancier sobbing at the sight of his 'poor Chaffie' lying dead at the bottom of his cage.[12]

It is surprising that Hudson, one of the period's most effective advocates of bird protection, did not condemn chaffinch-keeping outright when he described the activities with customary insight in *Birds in London*:

I have met as many as a dozen men slouching about among the shrubberies [in Victoria Park], each with a small cage covered with a cotton handkerchief or rag, in quest of a wild bird for his favourite to challenge and sing against.

Yet Hudson's tone is one of sadness rather than anger, perhaps judging that the birds were one of the few private pleasures granted to the chaffinch fancier, 'who strikes one as nothing worse than a very quiet inoffensive person, down on his luck, as he goes softly about among the shrubberies'.[13]

Trapping finches was eventually outlawed in 1896 and the practice died out, since when the chaffinch has become the commonest of its family and among the most successful of all our birds, with a combined population of 7.5 million pairs.

The chaffinch's northern counterpart is the **Brambling**, *Fringilla montifringilla*, and J. A. Baker felt that there was a suggestion of its wider boreal landscape in the male's lovely mix of colours: 'His underparts are orange and white; glowing orange, like a sunset on silver scales of birch bark.'[14] The breeding range extends in a broad belt right across Eurasia, although small numbers have recently started to nest in Scotland, with a maximum of eight pairs in 1995.

Bramblings have a much longer history as winter visitors. Bewick called this bird the 'Mountain Finch' and noted that it made better eating than chaffinch, if rather bitter in taste, while almost three centuries earlier William Turner had referred to it as the 'bramlyng'.[15] Like the modern name, it suggests a connection with bramble but Lockwood argues that the real derivation is 'brandling', an old word for a young salmon or an animal of brindled pattern. This is certainly an excellent description of the non-breeding plumage, when the dark upperparts become frosted with a series of pale crescentic lines.

The tortoiseshell colours then provide perfect camouflage as bramblings feed in the dappled conditions of the

Bramblings are birds of the northern conifer forests and come to these islands only in winter.

woodland floor, where their main winter diet is beech-mast. In Britain and Ireland the crop of seeds varies greatly from year to year and this largely determines the numbers each winter. After a good harvest flocks of several hundreds, even thousands, can build up and in 1981 there was a concentration on Merseyside, involving an estimated 150,000 birds.

European Serin, *Serinus serinus*. This tiny finch, the only wild canary in mainland Europe, is a common bird of gardens, orchards and parkland. Many people first encounter it during holidays in the Mediterranean, where the loud jangling song is one of the classic background sounds in hotel gardens: 'resembling at times more the sound made by the [cicada] cricket than the song of a bird'; 'somewhat like splinters of glass being rubbed together'; 'song a long fast hissing jangle of twittering notes'.[16] It is often delivered from a telegraph wire or during a strange bat-like display flight, when the bird looks as if it is moving in slow motion.

In Britain and Ireland it is a regular spring and autumn migrant in small numbers, which increased as serins expanded their European range as far as the whole of the French and Belgian Channel coasts. The seemingly inevitable British invasion began in the 1960s and serins increased slowly to as many as seven pairs during the 1980s. But it proved a false dawn and during the 1990s they have returned consistently only to the Channel Islands, where there are 20 pairs on Jersey.

European Greenfinch, *Carduelis chloris*. VN: Greeny/Greenie, Green Linnet. 'Greenfynch' has been in use for this common and widespread species since about 1400, although it had other names, especially among the old bird men. The nineteenth-century ornithologist Hugh Macpherson described in his classic *History of Fowling* how thousands of linnets and green-finches were trapped each autumn by the London bird catchers: 'I have seen the shops in Seven Dials [near Covent Garden] so glutted with newly caught "Green-birds", that the dealers were thankful to sell them for a penny a piece.'[17]

Another vernacular name is 'green linnet' – a version just surviving today and used by John Clare in 'The Green Lane'. While Clare knew it as a bird of the wider countryside, the greenfinch has acquired much stronger associations with town gardens. They are most obvious when the males perform a fantastic butterfly display flight, the wingbeats exaggeratedly slow and deep, so that the bird can be briefly mistaken for a much larger species. The performance is accompanied by a liquid twittering song and often terminates in a drawn-out sneezing note. In spring both sounds have become part of the Sunday-morning soundtrack in British suburbia.

Greenfinches have adapted to what are often con-sidered the worst, most artificial aspects of the habitat, such as the cypress hedges that have sprung up with triffid-like aggression. They nest semi-colonially and several pairs are often close neighbours in a single border. They are also fiercely loyal to the birdtable, where they alternate with great and blue tits on the peanuts or the new specialised seed mixes. 'The RSPB has run the Big Garden Birdwatch since 1979 and the greenfinch has always featured in the top ten most common species. In the first year of the survey it was at number eight, but by 1993 it had moved up the chart to seven and last year (2003) it was at the number six slot. Over the whole period its abundance has virtually doubled with the average per garden rising from 1 to 1.9.'[18]

The strong attachment to human food sources was known as early as the 1920s, when Max Nicholson ran a ringing site in Oxford. Some greenfinches visited the trap so often for the pinhead oatmeal that they became 'a

The long pointed beak of the goldfinch is specially adapted for plucking the plumed seeds from thistle heads and other weeds.

nuisance, and they would often return, sometimes within a day or two, even if taken off and released six and nine miles away in various directions. One was retrapped twenty-nine times in seven weeks, and another thirteen times in one week.'[19]

European Goldfinch, *Carduelis carduelis*. VN: Goldy, Draw-Water (Norfolk); King Henry/Harry (East Anglia); King Harry Redcap, Seven-coloured Linnet, Petaldick (Midlands). With its black-and-red facial mask, white rump and brilliant bar of yellow across the black wings, the goldfinch is completely unmistakable. It is found across almost the whole of Britain and Ireland, where there are both resident and migratory populations, with large numbers moving south to Spain and France during winter.

They are particularly noticeable in early autumn, when post-breeding flocks gather on areas of wasteground, drawn by the white-flossed banks of seed-bearing weeds. In winter they also combine with other family members, like redpoll and siskin, to feed among alder and birch trees. However, the classic food plant is thistle (*Carduelis* derives from the Latin for thistle, *carduus*). The contrast between the dead, wizened plants

and the dazzling colour of the birds is particularly striking. So attracted were goldfinches to thistle seeds that the old Norfolk bird catchers 'stored thistle heads in brown paper in a dark cupboard and brought them out in the winter, when the King Harrys would flock to them and could be easily caught'.[20]

Several vernacular names have recently slipped into disuse. 'My paternal grandfather had a large garden and I remember him showing me the nest of what he called "tailor birds" deep in rose bushes round a trellis. When the birds appeared they turned out to be goldfinches and he explained that they were known as tailor birds because the white tips to the feathers (tertials and primaries) looked like stitches.'[21]

Other old names draw on its physical beauty. 'King Harry' (or 'King Harry redcap'), for instance, which survives – just – in Suffolk, was a reference to Henry VIII, a man as renowned as the bird for his dapper appearance. The more obvious and now possibly lost 'redcap' alluded to the satin-textured crimson on the forehead and is the title of John Clare's typically observant poem:

A charm of goldfinches is as pleasant to the ear as it is beautiful to the eye.

The redcap is a painted bird
and beautiful its feathers are;
In early spring its voice is heard
While searching thistles brown and bare;
It makes a nest of mosses grey
And lines it round with thistle-down;
Five small pale spotted eggs they lay
In places never far from town.

Many would probably agree with the correspondent who wrote, 'my favourite collective noun is a charm of goldfinches'.[22] Nothing seems more appropriate, although the word did not originally describe the appearance, since it derives from the Old English *c'irm* and meant the blended tinkling sounds produced by a small flock.[23]

Goldfinches were once the classic target for nineteenth-century trappers and even today the name for a trap that is still used by bird ringers (as well as continental bird catchers) is 'chardonerret', the French word for the species. However, keeping them in cages is a tradition stretching back a thousand years and probably longer, while the occasional prosecution of modern bird-fanciers proves that it continues still. Present trapping methods, like the smearing of perches with 'rodent glue', are horribly crude but the original time-honoured technique also involved a sticky gum called bird lime, made from boiled mistletoe berries.

Clap-nets in combination with trained 'call-birds' and decorated by a small flock of 'stales' – stuffed skins – was another highly successful formula, and Victorian writers offer us frequent glimpses of the scale of the harvest. In 1860 it was alleged that 132,000 were taken each year near Worthing, Sussex, while a figure of 3000 by a single trapper in Llandudno in north Wales suggests how wide-spread the activities were.[24] The most oft-repeated statistic comes from London. In the 1890s a retired catcher told Richard Bowdler Sharpe, the great keeper of birds at the British Museum, that in his youth he had caught twelve dozen goldfinches in a single morning on the wasteground where Paddington Station now stands.[25] By the start of the twentieth century the species had become virtually extinct in many areas, and in the 1890s the Society for the Protection of Birds (the predecessor of today's RSPB), saw the saving of the goldfinch as one of its first tasks. The present population of 275,000 pairs bears testimony to the impact of legal protection.

The sinister-looking beast in Bosch's painting The Garden of Earthly Delights *is an ironic commentary on the goldfinch's ancient Christian associations.*

In a sense the goldfinch was thrice cursed as a cagebird. As well as being beautiful it has an 'unfailingly pleasant' song, which seemed to one expert ear 'more expressive of the joy of living than of challenge to rivals'.[26] Another part of the appeal is its highly developed coordination of bill and feet, which it shares with siskin and redpoll. All three are able to hold potential food down with their toes or pull objects towards them for investigation, the full array of skills being evident when birds feed on thistle- or teasel-heads. Owners exploited the talents by forcing caged finches to take seed or water from tiny pails that could only be reached by manipulating threads, and it is this string-pulling dexterity that gave rise to an old Norfolk name for goldfinch, 'draw-water'.[27]

A final element in the bird's popularity had its roots in classical Europe. Goldfinches, like gold itself, were thought to have curative powers, and Dante describes young Italian children keeping the birds on hand-strings because of their supposed health-giving properties. The idea that goldfinches also bring good fortune has not quite vanished. 'I recently heard a story that if a swallow flies over an eligible girl, she'll marry a sailor; if a sparrow, she'll marry a poor man but be happy, but if a goldfinch she'll marry a millionaire.'[28]

The exact origin of the beliefs is obscure, but Pliny listed the goldfinch as a symbol of fertility and an old medieval Latin name for it was *lucina*. In turn Lucina was another name or aspect of the Roman deity Juno, goddess of light, childbirth and fertility. It is likely that the powers attaching to Juno/Lucina were subsequently bestowed on the Virgin, while the pagan bird symbol of fertility was similarly passed on to her Christian successor. A nineteenth-century slang term for the vagina, 'Goldfinch's nest', may possibly be a far earthier vestige of the lost fertility symbolism.[29]

The same pattern of association could also have led to Hieronymus Bosch's inclusion of a goldfinch in his famous triptych, 'The Garden of Earthly Delights'. Among the many scenes of bizarre and distorted sensuality, the Dutch artist painted a peculiarly menacing image of the otherwise benign finch. Yet its inclusion may also have been an ironic reference, instantly recognisable to his fifteenth-century audience. The goldfinch was the thistle bird, and the combination of thorns and red plumage led to its association with Christ and the Crucifixion.[30] It is this symbolism that may well explain the presence of goldfinches in more than 500 medieval and Renaissance paintings, many of them depicting Mary with the infant Jesus.[31]

Eurasian Siskin, *Carduelis spinus*. This is one of the most welcome visitors to our garden birdtables in winter for its bright colours and tit-like gymnastics. Siskins happily feed completely upside-down, 'hanging like little parrots' from the netted bags of peanuts or balls of fat.[32] They are one of the great success stories of the last 50 years, benefiting from changes both in the landscape and in our own behaviour.

It was traditionally a bird of the Old Caledonian pine forests of northern Scotland, a range shaped by a preference for the seeds from mature cone-bearing trees. The recent massive increase in conifer plantations has been a major factor in the bird's expansion. Siskins also particularly like the seeds of spruce and this is one of the commonest exotic conifers to be planted. While at the time of the 1968–72 bird atlas there were 815,000 acres (330,000ha) of plantation more than 25 years old, this total had doubled in less than 20 years.[33] Over a comparable period the bird's population has gone from fewer than 40,000 to 360,000 pairs. The increase has been particularly marked in western Ireland, southern Scotland, northern England and in a southern belt from Devon to East Anglia.

The only substantial gap is in the Midlands, and here siskins have become common visitors during winter, when the birds switch diet to birch and alder seeds. They regularly team up with roving parties of redpolls, to which the siskins add their dash of bright yellow and a high-energy liquid cacophony. The name 'siskin' is thought to be onomatopoeic of these random twitterings, and of German (and ultimately Czech) origin, probably indicating the main region from which caged siskins were obtained during the Middle Ages.

Chaucer certainly knew the species and it was long a favourite of the English drawing room, both for its song and its docility. Henry Stevenson knew of no other cage pets that 'so soon become tame and contented with their new existence'.[34] Even wild birds were occasionally so tame they could be caught with a noose at the end of a fishing rod or a rod tip daubed in bird lime.[35] Trapping for the cagebird trade may have suppressed the native siskin population but it also occasionally seeded new communities. Birds that started breeding in Surrey during the early nineteenth century were thought to have escaped from captivity.[36]

The other key element in the siskin's recent success

Siskins are now commonplace visitors at the nut dispenser, yet just fifty years ago this behaviour had never been recorded.

has been a change in behaviour – one of the most striking by any bird in the last half-century. Prior to the 1960s it was almost never seen in gardens, and one of the first siskins ever recorded to visit a birdtable was in March 1963 in Guildford, Surrey, no doubt driven by the intense cold of that notorious winter. During 1966 the habit suddenly popped up in Cambridgeshire and by 1971 fresh 'outbreaks' had been noted in 19 counties from Aberdeenshire to Devon and Kent. The behaviour has now spread across the whole country, driven partly by the siskin's roving habits and its use of communal roosts. It is thought that these act like an information clearing-house, from which previously garden-shy birds follow their well-nourished neighbours to the food bonanza.[37]

A caged cock linnet was once prized in the Victorian drawing room both for his beautiful colours and his sweet liquid song.

The other key revelation arising from the siskin's rise to garden favourite concerns our own behaviour, both modern and ancient. In the 1960s entrepreneurs spotted a growing market for convenient seed mixes and other products for wild garden birds, which has since given rise to a multi-million-pound industry. Behind that innovation was our own much older, very human pleasure in the company of winter birds.

Common Linnet, *Carduelis cannabina*. VN: Lintie, Lintoe, Lintick, Lintack, Rose Lintie, Lintoo (Orkney). With its warm chestnut-cinnamon upperparts and striking flashes of white in the wing and tail, this is one of the most easily recognised finches. In spring the male also acquires a 'cutaway flush of carmine on his breast and a touch of it on his forehead'.[38]

Its various names refer to the bird's presumed diet. Linnet – also once written 'linot', 'linard' or 'lennett' – derives from the French *linette*, indicating the bird's attachment to the seeds of flax *Linum usitatissimum*. The second element in the scientific name similarly refers to *Cannabis sativa*, from which hempseed – and now marijuana – is obtained. Hemp was another of the bird's supposedly favourite foods, although it may better reflect choices made by the old trappers and fanciers on their behalf, rather than by the birds themselves.

In the wild they eat a wide range of weed and thistle seeds and thrive in all kinds of scrubby country, heathland, even coastal patches of suaeda and buckthorn. However the classic association is with gorse and several old names – 'gorse thatcher', 'whin grey' and 'furze linnet' – celebrated the link.[39] The linnet and its favoured shrubs are inhabitants of an indeterminate kind of country often referred to as 'wasteground'. Even the name declares our indifference and helps explain why it has been lost between the farmer's quest for arable and the public preference (one is tempted to say obsession) for woodland. Shrinking habitat has caused the linnet's range to contract, while the population of 650,000 pairs is 50 per cent below the 1970s total.[40]

In many ways the recent slump has returned the bird to the circumstances of the nineteenth century, when it was severely affected by the Victorian passion for cagebirds. Linnets were particularly popular for their song, which is arguably the most beautiful of any British finch. It is sweet and liquid in tone, while its wonderfully rambling structure makes it almost an analogue of the bird's favourite habitat. Bewick noted that in captivity 'its manners are gentle, and its disposition docile; it easily adopts the song of other birds, when confined with them, and in some instances has been taught to pronounce words with great distinctness'. However he added that these rote-learnt vocalisations were 'a perversion of its talents'.[41]

W. H. Hudson also felt that there was an indivisible relationship between the bird, its natural habitat and the beauty of its song. Climbing up Brean Down in Somerset, Hudson came to 'a long strip of rock . . . crowned with furze and bramble and thorn':

high above appeared a swift-moving little cloud of linnets . . . when directly over me, the birds all came straight down, to drop like a shower of small stones into the great masses of ivy and furze and bramble. And no sooner had they settled, vanishing into that warm and windless greenery, than they simultaneously burst into such a concert of sweetest wild linnet music, that I . . . thought that never in all the years I had spent in the haunts of wild birds had I heard anything so . . . beautiful.[42]

Twite, *Carduelis flavirostris*. VN: Lintoe, Heather Lintie (Orkney); Lintie (Shetland). Small, dark and streaky, this is one of the duller finches except in spring, when the 'cocks have a rose-white patch above the tail and a touch of faded orange on the throat'.[43] Yet the twite's plainness has never discouraged affection or interest: 'an engaging bird';[44] 'a fascinating little finch'.[45] Its recent declines have also added poignancy to fond memories:

When I was a teenager in north-west Derbyshire one of the best bits of the weekly games lesson was the sight of a regular twite flock feeding on newly sown grass-seed in the goal mouth of the second-eleven football pitch. So began my relationship with these charming moorland finches that saw many a morning paper-round punctuated with small flocks flying towards the moor from their feeding grounds in upland meadows, or routine post-school visits to their favoured habitat in the football goal mouths. The fact that such a decline has taken place in just thirty years reminds me how easy it is for a common bird of adolescence to be consigned to memories and the history books.[46]

Part of the bird's appeal also lies in its status as the only European bird derived from the Tibetan fauna.[47] It is thought originally to have spread from the Tibetan plateau into central Europe, but after the Würm glaciation some birds followed the retreating ice edge into northern Europe, while the main stock contracted back into the uplands of central Asia. It is left with a highly disjunct range and, apart from the twite of northern Scandinavia, the nearest to the British birds – considered a separate race, *C. f. pipilans* – are those in eastern Turkey.

Twite, originally pronounced 'tweet', is an echo of the bird's strikingly nasal call, but *'chweek'* is a better transliteration. The wide range of alternative names, living and archaic, such as 'heather lintie', 'hill lintie', 'highland lintie', 'mountain linnet' and 'lintie', all suggest the physical similarities to its better-known sibling, but also their ecological separation. Twite occur in higher and harder environments, a preference that seems curiously mirrored in the bird's less sweet, more scratchy, nasal song.

They breed on high heather moorland, although in spring they descend to hay meadows for the seeds on which the young are fed almost exclusively. It is the loss of this latter habitat that is partly responsible for the recent declines. However, there are now supplementary feeding schemes in part of the core area. Linda Williams describes a project that she oversees near Burnley, as well as the personal attachment these birds have engendered:

A love affair with 'my' twite, as I now refer to them, started when I began feeding them on their preferred brand of seed in April 2002. It then amazed me to discover that not only did they have a favourite seed, but also a favourite vehicle – MINE! I went to feed them as normal one morning while a few birders were watching and they later described how the twite had followed me. It was only when I saw it for myself that I believed it – my birds were following their 'meat wagon'. I then took it one step further. I started calling 'Come on birds' while feeding (only when no one could see or hear me!). And not only do they recognise the vehicle but also my voice. During cold, wet winter months I lose sleep worrying about my twite but I needn't really, they are tough little birds.[48]

They are also remarkably tame. Seton Gordon recalled a brooding female that would eventually allow him to feel her eggs beneath her while she continued to brood.[49] Sometimes, their physical closeness is not quite so voluntary. W. D. Campbell, revered country diarist for the *Guardian*, recalled an occasion in Connemara when out of a fuchsia hedge a twite exploded, which he ringed after extracting it from 'the curly mop of my niece'.[50]

Lesser redpolls seem to spend a good deal of their lives suspended upside-down as they feed on birch and larch cones.

Lesser Redpoll, *Carduelis cabaret*. Weighing as little as ⅓ ounce (10gm), this is one of the smallest finches, and even large flocks can appear to melt away completely in the leafless tops of winter birch trees. Yet feeding parties will sometimes allow an observer to stand directly beneath them, when the lowest birds can be almost within touching distance. 'It is one of the prettiest sights that our whole calendar of bird life affords, to watch these tiny linnets at work in the delicate birch-boughs. They fear no human being . . . They almost outdo the titmice in the amazing variety of their postures. They prefer in a general way to be upside down and decidedly object to the commonplace attitudes of more solidly built birds.'[51]

At other times the same flock can be extremely flighty, suddenly rising in a tight, dancing mass and shattering in all directions should they sense a predator. Wherever they go the birds are permanently enveloped by a bubble of nasal, almost insect-like rattling calls. They are far less tuneful songsters than most of the other finches, but they were still widely kept as cagebirds, with many being imported from Belgium. In summer the brighter males develop rosy breasts and a blob of bright red on the forecrown, from which the name derives.

Their main diet is birch seeds, although alder, sallow, larch and spruce are also important, and it was the dramatic increase in these invasive scrub species, as well as the widespread planting of conifers, that helped to explain the parallel rise in redpoll numbers during the mid-twentieth century. The numbers then just as dramatically declined, when the young plantations reached maturity and became unsuitable for redpolls.

Should the crop of birch seeds fail during winter, British redpolls migrate to the Continent in large-scale irruptive movements. Similarly the larger redpoll species of northern boreal forests, the **Mealy Redpoll**, *C. flammea*, can occasionally arrive in Britain in good numbers (sometimes staying to breed) if a food shortage occurs in mainland Europe. The **Arctic Redpoll**, *C. hornemannii*, is no more than a rare vagrant from the circumpolar zone and has occurred in Britain about 800 times, mainly on the east coast from Shetland to Kent.

Common Crossbill, *Loxia curvirostra*. The repeated comparisons in British ornithology between parrots and these large heavy-bodied finches of conifer woodland are easy to understand. Along with the heavy bill, bright colours and remarkable tameness, crossbills have a parrot's technique for manoeuvring among the upper canopy using their beak and strong toes. They will sidle along a twig to a pine cone and silently extract the seeds with striking psittacine-like dexterity, when the best clue to their presence is the snowstorm of papery seed-wings or the occasional thump of an emptied cone as it hits the ground.

The features that have held our attention longest are those uniquely crossed mandibles. The scientific name, *Loxia* (derived from a Greek word *loxos*, meaning 'cross-wise') was coined by the sixteenth-century Swiss naturalist, Conrad Gesner, who is presumed to have derived it from an old Swiss-German word, *Krützvogel*, literally 'crossbird'.[52] The felicitious links between the name and the cross of Christ, coupled with the male's bright-red plumage, were cues for medieval bestiarists to entwine the bird in the legend of the Crucifixion. It was said to have deformed its mandibles in trying to remove the nails from Jesus' hands and feet, simultaneously smearing its feathers with his blood. From these spurious linkages flowed the crossbill's long reputation in central Europe as a bird of magico-medicinal power.[53]

Little of the religious mythology had a natural place in Britain, but it was a monastic chronicler who claimed the first national record. In 1251 Matthew Paris wrote: 'In the course of this year about the fruit-season there appeared, in the orchards chiefly, some remarkable birds which had never before been seen in England, somewhat

The crossbill's strange bill has evolved to extract seeds from pine cones.

larger than Larks, which ate the kernel of the fruit and nothing else, whereby the trees were fruitless, to the loss of many. The beaks of these birds were crossed . . .'[54]

He noted that the birds split the apples to remove the pips with their bills 'as if with pincers or a pocket-knife'.[55] The observations constituted not only the first species description, but also the first evidence for the irruptive pattern of their migration.

Crossbills are the most specialised of the finches, feeding almost entirely on seeds from mature conifers. When the crop fails in one area the birds are compelled to travel, sometimes huge distances, in search of new forests. Aside from the influx of 1251, crossbill invasions were noted in 1593, 1757 and 1791.[56] A major arrival in 1815 is thought to have been the background to the colonisation of the New Forest and East Anglian Breckland, which are still their main breeding areas in southern England.

Crossbills are in many ways the Galapagos finches of Europe, with different populations evolving slightly different bill shapes according to diet. The **Two-barred Crossbill**, *Loxia leucoptera*, has the smallest bill of all and is a specialist of larch and spruce in northern Europe,

from which it is no more than a rare wanderer to Britain and Ireland (more than 125 records). As its name implies, the common crossbill is the generalist of the group, occupying a middle ground in matters of diet. The massive increase in plantations, particularly of lodgepole pine and sitka spruce, has been central to its spread across Wales, south-west Scotland, Ireland and areas like the Kielder Forest in Northumberland.

The largest, with its bull-neck and massive bill, is the aptly named **Parrot Crossbill**, *Loxia ptyopsittacus*, whose impressive armoury enables it to extract seeds even from closed pine cones. Occasional irruptive movements from Russian and Scandinavian boreal forests account for about 500 records in Britain and Ireland. Some invasions have also resulted in sporadic breeding (Norfolk, 1984/5, 1990), with a recent small colony established in Abernethy Forest, on the slopes of Cairngorm.

One of the most intractable ornithological puzzles in Britain is the exact taxonomic status of the crossbill population found in northern Scotland. These are birds with bills just a little smaller than those of the parrot crossbill, they feed largely on pines and are permanently resident in the region's remaining fragments of Old

Caledonian forest. Initially they were recognised as a separate race, but were then upgraded in 1997 to become Britain's only endemic species, the **Scottish Crossbill**, *Loxia scotica*.[57]

Common Rosefinch, *Carpodacus erythrinus*. During its 150 year history in Britain, this finch has been known variously as the 'scarlet grosbeak', 'common grosbeak', 'rosefinch', 'scarlet rosefinch' and now 'common rose-finch'. There is a certain irony in these rose-tinted names, given that most of the autumn juveniles appearing in Britain (c. 2200 records) are duller than female house sparrows.

It now has a massive world range from 10° W to 140° E. Yet until 1900 the bird hardly bred further west than Russia. It has since expanded more rapidly than any species except the collared dove and in the last 30 years has consolidated a hold over much of Scandinavia with outposts in Austria, Germany, Switzerland, the Netherlands and France.[58] Its account as a British breeding bird opened in 1982, when a nest with four eggs was found in northern Scotland. Since then the total has fluctuated between none and 20 pairs. It has one of the briefest breeding seasons, with most birds returning to their little-known Asian winter grounds just two months after their arrival in late May.[59]

Common Bullfinch, *Pyrrhula pyrrhula*. VN: Bully (northern England). W. B. Lockwood feels that the explanation for the name, which in medieval times was shortened simply to 'bull', 'remains elusive'.[60] Yet one cannot help thinking that the bird's globular bill and neckless rotundity are the key. As in 'bulldog' or 'bull-frog', the name was intended to convey the creature's front-heavy – literally bull-headed – construction.

With its soft silky plumage, glossy black cap and rose-pink underparts, the male is one of the most beautiful visitors to our gardens. Partly for these attractions and partly for their gentleness of manner, bullfinches were long valued as ornamental cagebirds and were imported in large numbers from Germany. But they were also famed for their voice, which might seem strange, given that the main call is a soft and rather mournful two-note piping. Turner referred to the reputation in 1544: 'It is the readiest bird to learn, and imitates a pipe very closely with its voice.'[61]

The tradition, which survived for many centuries and flourished in the Victorian age, was to catch and train them through playing a special bird-flute or bird-organ in their presence, of which they were skilled mimics. For what was seen as their gullible compliance in the process, 'bullfinch' became a slang term for a fool or simpleton.[62]

Another standard teaching method was to whistle to them repeatedly until they copied the tune. In Thomas

Bullfinches were once widely persecuted for their habit of feeding on the buds of fruit trees.

Hardy's *Tess of the d'Urbervilles*, it is one of Tess' daily chores to whistle to bullfinches when she goes to work at the house of Mrs d'Urberville. Although Hardy describes how the birds are routinely let out of their cage and given the run of the mistress's bedroom, where they 'made little white spots on the furniture and upholstery', one senses that they are yet one more symbol for Tess' own tragic incarceration in the narrow-minded conservatism of Victorian society.[63]

The bird's capacity for rote-learning was occasionally used as a positive moral example. On 9 June 1740 Lord Chesterfield wrote to his eight-year-old son:

> I hope you have got the linnets and bullfinches you so much wanted, and I recommend the bullfinches to your imitation. Bullfinches, you must know, have no natural note of their own, and never sing, unless taught; but will learn tunes better than any other birds. This they do by attention and memory; and you may observe, that, while they are taught, they listen with great care, and never jump about and kick their heels. Now I really think it would be a great shame for you to be outdone by your own bullfinch.[64]

Trapping for the cagebird trade was an historical check on numbers in Britain, although far more significant

The hawfinch's powerful bill can crack open cherry stones and the knuckles of unsuspecting bird ringers.

losses were inflicted by commercial fruit growers. Until recently many thousands were killed every year because of their notorious reputation for eating flower buds from fruiting trees. Turner knew of the habit ('they feed most greedily on those earliest buds') and there was even an Elizabethan statute outlawing the 'bulfynche' with a bounty of a penny a head.[65] The birds also take the buds of wild native trees, such as hawthorn, blackthorn and sallow, while their main winter diet has been shown to consist largely of the seeds of dock, nettle, bramble, birch and, above all, ash. However when the crop of ash keys fail, they move into orchards and, with a capacity for eating 30 buds a minute, can cause great damage to gooseberries, cherries, pears, apples, plums and currants.

In their defence, environmentalists have pointed out that a commercial fruit tree can lose up to 50 per cent of its buds without the overall fruit harvest being affected. Also bullfinches show a strong predilection for only certain fruit strains. They are most attracted, for instance, to the Morello cherry and to Conference, Williams or Dr Jules varieties of pear; others like Hardy and Comice pears are often largely ignored.[66]

The value of culling is also of questionable value, as illustrated by a paper entitled 'A thousand Bullfinches'. Over a five-year period a total of 200 birds were culled per annum in a 10-acre (4-ha) Herefordshire garden, yet at the end the bullfinch population in the surrounding countryside was more or less identical.[67] Today it is illegal to kill or trap bullfinches (except under special licence) because of the recent disastrous downward trend in the British population. In 1999 and 2000 just a single licence was issued and only three birds were trapped.[68]

Hawfinch, *Coccothraustes coccothraustes*. The name of this large, subtly beautiful and increasingly scarce bird is slightly misleading, since hawthorn berries are by no means its main diet. The extraordinary scientific name, which acquires a third *coccothraustes* in the nominate race and is the longest for any of our birds, better describes its lifestyle. It derives from the Greek, *kokko* 'a kernel', and *thrauo*, 'I break in pieces' – a reference to the hawfinch's gift for cracking open seeds from a wide range of trees, including hornbeam, wych elm, beech, yew and holly. But the most impressive feat is an ability to break cherry stones (and, according to modern bird ringers and old bird catchers, to crack knuckles and draw blood).[69]

The bill is almost as broad as it is deep and has four horny bosses or pads inside the upper and lower palates, which hold the stone centrally and distribute stress evenly to the massive musculature on both sides of the head. It is this that gives the hawfinch its bull-neck and 'bulging parrot-like cheeks', but it also enables the bird to deliver a crushing pressure more than a thousand times greater than its own weight (1¾–2 ounces/50–60gm). (The equivalent force in a human would be more than 60 ton(ne)s.) Experiments in the 1950s demonstrated that to crack a cherry stone required a load of 60–95 pounds (27–43kg) and olive stones a 106–159-pound (48–72-kg) load.[70]

Until the middle of last century hawfinches were widely persecuted for their supposed depredations upon fruit. They also visit gardens to raid the lines of green peas, popping the pods open with their massive bill and leaving a characteristic V mark on the empty husk.[71] But the bird's rarity means that its impact is marginal. One commentator noted, 'Some people are fortunate . . . to have their cherries eaten by a hawfinch!'[72]

While the bird's physiological adaptations give it a curiously top-heavy appearance, it is undeniably handsome. The bill itself is 'gunmetal blue, with a high paint-like polish'.[73] A narrow grey shawl separates a tawny-cinnamon head from the dark burnt-chestnut mantle and buff-peach underparts, while all these warm tones are offset by a black bib and a broad white panel across the iridescent blue-black wings. There is a further gloss to the bird's subtle beauty, because it is normally only enjoyed after great effort or luck. Hawfinches are 'notoriously self-effacing' and in Britain are the most challenging songbird to observe well.[74]

Even more difficult to see is its nuptial display, but part of it was beautifully described by the bird's chief biographer, Guy Mountfort, after chance observations that first launched his 20-year fascination with the hawfinch:

> One magnificently marked bird . . . took three long, powerful hops towards her, stopping when about fifteen inches away. Then, with his neck and breast 'blown up' like a little pouter pigeon, he waddled towards her, with tiny, mincing steps, swivelling his body from side to side at each step and displaying his white shoulder patches. The female slowly crouched, with her feathers tightly sleeked and her head thrust forward, in an attenuated, serpentine attitude. The male hesitated, then made her a very deep obeisance, with his huge bill tucked right down between his legs. Rising again, he half extended his wings and, in a dramatic movement, swung half round, dragging the tips of the feather in a stiff semi-circle in front of her . . . It strongly recalled the stiff-winged display of the domestic turkey cock. At that moment the female lunged forward and snapped her bill at him, with an astonishing sound like a miniature pistol shot.[75]

Sometimes the birds crown these manoeuvres with a far more tender gesture – extending their almost telescopic necks and touching each other with bill tips in a display known as 'the kiss'.

Bunting family *Emberizidae*

Snow Bunting, *Plectrophenax nivalis*. VN: Snowflake (Orkney); Snaa Fool, Sna Fuhl (Shetland). This is the most northerly-breeding of any land bird on earth, nesting beyond the 80° meridian and in some places living in such intimacy with Inuit settlements that it resembles an Arctic version of the sparrow. In Britain it is chiefly a winter visitor with the highest numbers occurring in the north or along the east coast.

Snow buntings love to feed on short, open vegetation, often among sand-dunes or even out on the exposed beach, where they follow the wrackline in search of tide-drifted seed. Flocks routinely move in a characteristic formation, with the hindmost contingent leap-frogging the front birds to create a constantly rolling 'blizzard of white wings and tail markings'.[1] This glorious sight, which is enhanced by their enormous individual variation and is usually accompanied by a soft, conversational rippling trill, instantly explains the old names – 'snow fleck' or 'snow flake'.

In any winter there are about 10,000–15,000 in Britain and Ireland, although judging from descriptions of immense flocks seen in the nineteenth century this may represent a decline. The Shetland naturalist Henry Saxby recounted an occasion when a snow-bunting flock completely covered several acres of ground:

> So unwilling were they to rise that I could have reached many of them with my stick; and as I advanced the sight became perfectly confusing, the birds fluttering up as I approached, and immediately settling in front, behind, and upon either side . . . It seemed as though I were literally wading through them, the continual shimmering of white producing an effect altogether indescribable.[2]

Until the early twentieth century in some parts of their winter range, snow buntings were looked upon as a northern counterpart to that better-known Mediterranean dainty, the ortolan bunting (see page 463). Saxby thought them 'a perfect luxury for the table', while Banffshire farmers judged the boiled or roasted flesh 'simply delicious'. The flock's density and confiding manner enabled strict economy of ammunition with as many as 118 being downed by a single shot. In Inverness-shire such a bonanza was sometimes treated as more commonplace fare, when they were stewed up and fed to the gun dogs. On Fair Isle 'the islanders used to snare

When snow bunting flocks take flight they produce a delightful mix of flashing white wings and soft rippling calls.

snow buntings for food with horse-hair nooses attached to a "Sna Fuhl Brod" (board)'.[3] 'Fuhl' or 'fool', incidentally, does not refer to the bird's lack of intelligence at being caught; it simply meant 'fowl'.

Snow buntings are part of an elite group of truly Arctic species that finds suitable breeding habitat among Scotland's most elevated and austere upland landscapes, such as the Cairngorms or parts of the western Highlands. A tiny population was first found in the late nineteenth century and numbered no more than a couple of dozen birds, although more recently there appears to have been a genuine expansion to 70–100 pairs in good years.[4] Much of what we know about this isolated group, the most southerly in the species' range, has come from the work of the redoubtable bird dynasty, the Nethersole-Thompsons.

Desmond and Maimie watched snow buntings in the Cairngorms for several decades, often camping at high altitude for weeks at a stretch. Their son Brock was born in 1935, the second year of the studies, when his mother used to put him in a game bag, 'and hump him to camp on the tops along with our stores and gear'.[5] Part of the attraction of snow buntings, aside from their remoteness and extreme rarity, was the challenge of tracking one to

its nest, which is often concealed in an isolated corrie or boulder field. One extraordinary example located by Brock Nethersole-Thompson incorporated into its structure some red-deer fibres, a little sheep's wool, mountain-hare fur, several dotterel feathers, a few feathers thought to come from a golden eagle and 567 off a ptarmigan – a high percentage of the fauna sharing the bird's barren domain.[6]

In the Arctic they will occupy any form of natural cavity but also adapt to the interior of buildings, under roofs, in nest boxes, among domestic waste or rubble, in abandoned tin cans or boxes, inside old cairns or graves and, in one instance, the body cavity of a dead Inuit child.[7]

Lapland Bunting (Longspur), *Calcarius lapponicus*. VN: Lap bunt (birders). One of the commonest passerines in the Arctic tundra, it has a continuous range around the territories that crown the northern hemisphere. In autumn about 200–500 birds arrive here mainly on the Irish north and the British east coasts, where they are easily overlooked as they scuttle almost rodent-like among tall grass or saltmarsh vegetation.

In winter Lap bunts (the name 'longspur', referring to the elongated hindclaw, is used in North America but has

Flocks of yellowhammers like this one have become scarce with the loss of winter stubbles from our countryside.

not yet taken hold here) are plump, rather featureless, streaky birds. However, the spring male, with his chestnut nape patch and bold black-and-white head pattern, is very handsome. In the late 1970s a small population began to breed in northern Scotland, with 11 confirmed breeding pairs in 1979. Sadly it proved a short-lived colonisation.

Yellowhammer, *Emberiza citrinella*. VN: Yellow Bunting (northern England); Yellow Yorlin (Northern Ireland). Apart from 'cuckoo', 'a-little-bit-of-bread-and-no-cheese' is probably the best-known mnemonic for a British bird song. It is actually a few syllables short of the usual full phrase, but 'cheese' is a perfect description of the drawn-out terminal note. Coleridge once wrote (bad verse) in disparaging terms of this unforgettable ditty:

The spruce and limber yellowhammer
In the dawn of spring and sultry summer,
In hedge or tree the hours beguiling
With notes as of one who brass is filing.

What the yellowhammer's performance may lack in quality or variety is more than compensated for by sheer stamina. It is one of only two or three species that continue right through until late summer and the insinuating power of that song could well serve as a case study among modern advertising agencies on the merits of a simple, persistent message. We do not so much listen to yellowhammer, as hear it subconsciously, and by sheer repetition it triumphs over us to create an impression far greater than louder or more beautiful bird sounds.

The hypnotic song of the yellowhammer has a Proustian effect on me, recalling the dusty silence of August lanes in the late 1950s, when the harvest fields on the Norfolk coast were still full of flowers, and the telephone wires would utter harp-like harmonies at the touch of the onshore breeze. These would be the only sounds in a vast, slumbering landscape and intensify the mood of solitude, stillness and anticipation. I can only recapture that August voice, that listening stillness, in the lines of William Allingham:

Little cow-boy what have you heard
Up on the lonely rath's green mound?
Only the plaintive yellow bird

The intricate pattern of squiggles on yellowhammer eggs lay behind the bird's old country name, the 'scribble lark'.

Sighing in sultry fields around –
Chary, chary, chary chee –
Only the grasshopper and the bee.
(from the *Fairy Shoemaker, A Hundred Poems for Children*, 1927)[8]

To David Bannerman the bird evoked a very different but equally powerful sense of place: 'The yellow hammer's song brings to mind so forcibly the hot summer days on that bare Cornish coast, the endless gorse and bracken, the granite boulders ringed around the mine shafts ... the bracken-clad slopes of the cliffs dropping to the sea, and the incomparable coast scenery with the Atlantic far below.'[9] Colin Harrison unearthed a similar Celtic resonance: 'I once heard a male Yellowhammer, temporarily incarcerated in a tiny show cage at a winter bird show, raise its head and give a quieter version of the song and its owner, a Welsh miner, said dreamily "Man! can't you just smell the gorse?"'[10]

Its modern Welsh name is *Melyn yr Eithin*, 'yellow bird of the gorse', and while gorse scrub is a favoured habitat in parts of south-west England, Wales and Scotland, it is also a bird of the arable landscape in the eastern half of the country.[11] Sadly changes in farm practice and loss of habitat are now having the same effect on yellowhammers as they have already had on other granivorous passerines of our agricultural environment (see Corn Bunting, page 466). In Chris Mead's words, the bird is in 'Dire straits' and while the last census returned a population in Britain and Ireland of 1.5 million pairs, these are now 'dropping like a stone'.[12]

People sometimes ponder on the rather odd-sounding name. It is thought to derive from an original Old English name, *amer*, and to come from the same linguistic root as the current German for bunting, *Ammer*. It was sometimes further shortened simply to 'ham' and this version can be found near Dorchester, Dorset, in Yellowham Wood and Yellowham Hill, where, happily, the eponymous bird is still a common species in the surrounding countryside.[13]

'Yorlin', a name once used in Scotland (in Northern Ireland still), is in the title of a Robbie Burns poem ('The Yellow yellow yorlin'), in which it has a less than subtle double meaning:

'O no young man,' says she, 'you're a stranger to me
'An' I am anither man's darlin,
'Wha has baith sheep an' cows, that's feedin' in the hows,
'An' a cock for my yellow yellow yorlin'.'

'But, if I lay you down upon the dewy ground,
'You wad nae be the waur ae farthing;
'An' that happy, happy man, he never cou'd ken
'That I play'd wi' your yellow yellow yorlin'.'

Quite why a yellowhammer was chosen for this part of the female anatomy is not easy to understand. But 'goldfinch's nest' once meant much the same and perhaps one strikingly yellow bird was as good as another for Burns.[14]

Another strange bit of symbolism was the yellowhammer's association with evil. A drop of the Devil's blood was said to be on its tongue and its beautifully marked eggs (whence the old name 'scribble lark') were thought to carry an arcane, possibly demonic, message. Fortunately the tradition has expired although we perhaps just caught its dying echo: 'When I was seven, 79 years ago on my grandfather's farm in County Tyrone I was standing at the entrance to a old hay shed with my uncle when a yellowhammer flew in and landed on a rafter at the far end. My uncle picked up either a stone or potato, said something about a yellow devil, threw the missile and struck and killed the bird.'[15]

Cirl buntings are now confined to a small area of south Devon.

With its black head stripes and olive-green breast band, the male **Cirl Bunting**, *Emberiza cirlus*, is like a strikingly patterned yellowhammer. Both have similar rattling songs, although the cirl bunting's delivery is faster and often thought reminiscent of lesser whitethroat song. It also lacks the final wheeze – the 'cheese' note – of its sibling's more famous phrase.

There is a curious symmetry to its 200-year history in Britain. It was first discovered at Kingsbridge, Devon, in 1800 by Lord Montagu, the absence of earlier records presumed to indicate that it was a relatively recent colonist. Thereafter it seemed to achieve a rapid expansion across southern England. By the second half of the nineteenth century cirl buntings bred in London suburbs such as Wembley Park and Wimbledon Common, while in parts of the Kent chalk downs it was said to replace the yellowhammer as the most numerous bunting.[16]

It was equally common in Hampshire, where W. H. Hudson referred to it as 'the village bunting'.[17] It was also discovered to breed widely in the Midlands. Perhaps the most unusual of these finds was the second breeding record for Herefordshire. In 1884 a carter happened to crack his whip while trundling down a track near Wormbridge and accidentally flicked a hen bird out of the hedge, where her nest and eggs were then located.[18]

The British range reached its limit by about the 1930s, with an isolated population on the north Wales coast representing its furthest extent. The striking advance then just as dramatically started to reverse and, county by county, cirl buntings disappeared until by 1989 there were just 118 pairs, most of them in the area where Montagu first found the species – near Kingsbridge in south Devon.

Max Nicholson once suggested that 'A map of the Roman Empire would give a tolerable idea of the distribution of the cirl bunting'[19] (ignoring, no doubt deliberately, British colonists' successful introduction of the species between 1871 and 1880 to New Zealand where it still flourishes).[20] Given that the British birds are at the northernmost limit of the species' world range and that their retreat had been towards one of the warmest parts of the country, many people proposed climate change as the cause of decline. In fact changes in farm practices, particularly the increased use of pesticides and the loss of winter stubbles resulting from autumn-sown cereals, have proved to be the main problems. These are now being addressed in an RSPB/English Nature recovery project that works with Devon farmers to restore the habitats needed by the county's highest-profile bird.

The success has been dramatic. There are now more than 570 pairs, almost all in Devon, where they have acquired celebrity status in parts of the core area. During the millennium celebrations the village of Bishopsteignton titled itself 'The Home of the Cirl Bunting' and sold mugs illustrating its totem species. At nearby Stoke-inteignhead it has been incorporated into the school emblem, while the school team has a football strip with a cirl bunting featured in the logo.[21]

Ortolan Bunting, *Emberiza hortulana*. Despite the horticultural associations implied by both its English and scientific names, this is not a garden bird at all. Ortolans inhabit scrubby subalpine slopes across large parts of Eurasia and appear in this country merely as a widespread but very scarce spring and autumn migrant.

Their greater claim to fame is as a culinary delicacy. From the time of ancient Rome ortolans were trapped in huge numbers throughout the Mediterranean region and then artificially fattened in special establishments. A belief that they only fed first thing in the morning led them to be kept in semi-darkness. The appearance of the keeper with his bags of millet or oats and his lantern every two hours was meant to simulate the breaking dawn and trick them into feeding day and night.[22] Such methods can cause a bird sometimes to quadruple in weight to 3–4 ounces (84–112gm) and become, in David Bannerman's words, 'little more than a ball of fat'.[23]

Large numbers of ortolans were once imported into Victorian Britain, where they were the exclusive preserve of the super-rich. Quite how expensive is beautifully, if incidentally, conveyed in Oscar Wilde's *De Profundis*. As he suffered the privations of Reading gaol, the broken playwright poured out to Bosie (Lord Alfred Douglas) his sense of bitter grievance at their earlier extravagance: 'I have still got to pay my debts. The Savoy dinners – the clear turtle soup, the luscious ortolans wrapped in their crinkled Sicilian vine-leaves, the heavy amber-coloured, indeed amber-scented champagne – Dagonet 1880, I think, was your favourite wine? – all have still to be paid for.'[24]

In his poem 'The Glutton', Thomas Warton included lines that give a comparable sense of the ortolan's exorbitant price and high cachet:

Fat, pamper'd Porus, eating for Renown,
In soups and Sauces melts his Manors down;
Regardless of his Heirs with Mortgag'd Lands,
Buys hetacombs of Fish, and Ortolans;[25]

The ortolan has a culinary reputation that dates back to ancient Rome.

The catching and eating of them is now illegal but still continues in continental Europe surrounded by near-Masonic secrecy and retaining much of its Epicurean ritual. The traditional method of killing them, for instance, is to drown them in cognac. In his book *The Red Canary* Tim Birkhead recounts the words of one recent French novitiate on her induction into these ancient rites: 'I was told very firmly to put the whole, very hot bird in my mouth and then to press it up against the roof of my mouth with my tongue, rather than biting it. This makes the juice and the fat explode into your mouth, which I have to say is the best bit of the whole experience, since all you are left with after that is a mouthful of fine bones.'[26]

Before dying of cancer, François Mitterrand is said to have indulged in a final tour of earthly pleasures including an illicit banquet, where the former French President was seated, head draped and concealed by a large napkin, as he drank down the celestial vapours from his dish of ortolans.[27]

Reed Bunting, *Emberiza schoeniclus*. Although it has suffered severe declines in the last two decades, the striking sight of a black-headed male sitting on a prominent song perch, such as a bush top or reed stem, is still a classic scene of British and Irish wetlands in spring. Although 'song perch' is possibly stretching a point. The four- or five-note ditty – 'I've heard it rendered as "Here comes the bride"' – is unmusical, monotonous and among the least noteworthy performances by any of our songbirds.[28]

It was once exclusively a species of wet meadows, rushy pastures, reedbeds and rank vegetation surrounding freshwater bodies of almost any size. The earliest

The black-capped male of the reed bunting is one of the most striking songbirds of British and Irish wetlands.

stirrings of a change in behaviour were noted in the 1930s, when reed bunts started to encroach upon farm-land and new habitats like young conifer plantations. Now they are found widely in a range of settings well away from water. They have developed a parallel

willingness to visit garden birdtables, partly because of their susceptibility to snow-bound winters and partly because of the loss of weed-seeds inflicted by modern herbicides. They are known to take bread left by fishermen, and Derek Goodwin wonders whether they learnt to eat it after acquiring the habit during their garden visits, or vice versa.[29]

Corn Bunting, *Miliaria calandra*. VN: Corn Blob

Lockwood tells us has been found in documents dated 1275.[31]

The word captures equally well the bird's fat, rather untidy appearance, especially when the male puffs out his chest as he sings his unmistakable key-jangling phrase. There has long been a tradition of almost moral reproach mingled, it should be said, with sincere affection for this quintessentially streaky brown species. Its sheer dullness may be one factor in this: 'Father always called them "clod birds".'[32]

Part of it may also derive from the promiscuity of the cock, which can mate and breed with up to 18 females (six simultaneously) over the course of a summer.[33] Obesity and laziness are other routine charges: 'That fat and unkempt country bumpkin of the mosslands';[34] 'a pale brown streaky bird, lumpy and lazy';[35] 'stout of beak, indelicate of figure, drab of colour, undoubtedly boorish in manners, and with as little musical ability as a cricket';[36] '[they] drone forth their monotonous dirge with almost irritating persistency'.[37]

Foremost among its amused critics was Lord Grey of Fallodon in *The Charm of Birds*, where he called it 'the carthorse' of the buntings. Grey linked his censure to a wider condemnation of barbed wire, which had recently spread its lethal net across the countryside.[38] 'I can even imagine,' wrote the Liberal politician in feigned horror, 'that corn-buntings *like* barbed wire.' They also seem to like telegraph poles and their lines, fence posts, gates, hedges – in fact, almost anything in an arable setting that offers them an elevated perch.

The species' relationship to human agriculture goes far deeper than simply a matter of songposts. It is a bird of open grassland habitats and its colonisation of these islands is a direct consequence of woodland clearance by Neolithic and Bronze Age farmers. It has thrived particularly in association with cereal production and was once found across almost the whole of Britain and Ireland, as well as Shetland, Orkney and the Hebrides. Yet the range was never continuous and the bird's precise requirements were little understood until the late twentieth century. Max Nicholson once used a 'leisurely summer journey from London to Scotland' to keep 'a close eye on the corn-bunting patchwork'. While it may have been a rather unstructured transect, Nicholson's observations offer a sharp insight into the bird's capricious range:

The first to be met going north were straddling the Bedfordshire–Cambridgeshire–Huntingdon border between Potton and Eltisley and from there on they were pretty well continuous across the Isle of Ely, over the fens into Lincolnshire through Boston and up the coast to about Saltfleet. From there on I saw none

(Yorkshire); Common Bunting, Skitter-broltie (Orkney). This is the original 'bunting'. The name was in use by about 1300 and the fact that the Hertfordshire town, Buntingford (literally, a ford haunted by buntings), was known as such by 1185 indicates an even longer history.[30] Initially it described a plump or thickset person, a meaning still present in the nursery rhyme, 'Bye, Baby Bunting' and in the (rather irreverent) surname, which

Before the recent huge decline in population, the corn bunting was one of the classic birds of open farmland.

along the Humber to Goole, and only one down the Yorkshire side until Hull. They reappeared strongly about Hedon and were very common from there to Spurn Point and on up the Yorkshire coast to Scarborough, as many as seven being seen along a mile of road at one point. Turning inland I found no more south of the Tees, and in Durham only one near Hartlepool, but up the Northumberland coast they were frequent from near Alnmouth past Bamburgh to Beal opposite Holy Island.[39]

Paul Donald, one of those who recently pinpointed the corn bunting's ecological requirements, adds detail to Nicholson's original picture:

The patch of country between Potton (where I now live) and Eltisley still has corn buntings. One of the paradoxes of this species is that although numbers have undoubtedly declined because of agricultural intensification, it still survives in greatest numbers in the tractor-battered Fens. I suspect that some of Nicholson's patchiness is due to soil type, there is some evidence that heavy clay soils are less preferred to free-draining ones.[40]

Corn buntings also seem particularly susceptible to the switch from spring- to autumn-sown cereals and the earlier harvest associated with silage as opposed to hay. The grubbing out of 105,000 miles (175,000km) of hedgerow between 1947 and 1985, and the absence of winter stubbles, have also robbed it of favoured feeding habitats and it is now in a decline as steep as those suffered by two other old fixtures of British farmland, the corn crake and grey partridge. In its own unassuming way the corn bunting is as much the miner's canary of our agricultural environment as these other more celebrated species.

The combined changes have ripped through the corn bunting's original mosaic. In the last 70 years it has gone almost completely from Ireland, Wales, south-west England, much of western Scotland and the Hebrides. In Shetland it was once one of the commonest songbirds, yet it has now totally disappeared and its going indicates how extinction impacts not just upon the local ecology, but upon culture and language. In Shetland it was known by a rich array of names: 'docken sparrow', 'docken fool', 'docken laverock', 'trussy laverock', 'shurl', 'titheree', 'cornbill', 'corn-tief' and 'song thrush'.[41]

Each of these embodied finely nuanced observations or, in the last instance, a quirky and equally fascinating error. But all of them will presumably be lost from Shetland vernacular in the very near future. Sadly the same is likely to happen in Orkney, which now has the most northerly corn buntings in the world. The minuscule population is still known by the wonderfully graphic name of 'skitter-broltie' – one who shits on the braithes, the cross-ropes over a corn stack.[42]

APPENDICES

APPENDIX 1:

Species on the British list, but not treated in the text

White-faced Storm-petrel *Pelagodroma marina*
Madeiran Storm-petrel *Oceanodroma castro*
Double-crested Cormorant *Phalacrocorax auritus*
Magnificent Frigatebird *Fregata magnificens*
Greater Flamingo *Phoenicopterus ruber*
Ruddy Shelduck *Tadorna ferruginea*
Falcated Duck *Anas falcata*
American Black Duck *Anas rubripes*
Marbled Duck *Marmaronetta angustirostris*
Redhead *Aythya americana*
Harlequin Duck *Histrionicus histrionicus*
Bufflehead *Bucephala albeola*
Barrow's Goldeneye *Bucephala islandica*
Hooded Merganser *Lophodytes cucullatus*
Egyptian Vulture *Neophron percnopterus*
Pallid Harrier *Circus macrourus*
Greater Spotted Eagle *Aquila clanga*
Short-toed Eagle *Circaetus gallicus*
Booted Eagle *Hieraaetus pennatus*
American Kestrel *Falco sparverius*
Eleonora's Falcon *Falco eleonorae*
Sora *Porzana carolina*
Allen's Gallinule *Porphyrula alleni*
American Purple Gallinule *Porphyrula martinica*
American Coot *Fulica americana*
Sandhill Crane *Grus canadensis*
Little Bustard *Tetrax tetrax*
Collared Pratincole *Glareola pratincola*
Oriental Pratincole *Glareola maldivarum*
Black-winged Pratincole *Glareola nordmanni*
Semipalmated Plover *Charadrius semipalmatus*
Killdeer *Charadrius vociferus*
Caspian Plover *Charadrius asiaticus*
American Golden Plover *Pluvialis dominica*
Pacific Golden Plover *Pluvialis fulva*
Sociable Plover *Vanellus gregarius*
White-tailed Plover *Vanellus leucurus*
Great Knot *Calidris tenuirostris*
Red-necked Stint *Calidris ruficollis*
Long-toed Stint *Calidris subminuta*
Least Sandpiper *Calidris minutilla*
White-rumped Sandpiper *Calidris fuscicollis*
Baird's Sandpiper *Calidris bairdii*
Pectoral Sandpiper *Calidris melanotos*
Sharp-tailed Sandpiper *Calidris acuminata*

Broad-billed Sandpiper *Limicola falcinellus*
Stilt Sandpiper *Micropalama himantopus*
Buff-breasted Sandpiper *Tryngites subruficollis*
Wilson's Snipe *Gallinago wilsonia*
Great Snipe *Gallinago media*
Short-billed Dowitcher *Limnodromus griseus*
Long-billed Dowitcher *Limnodromus scolopaceus*
Hudsonian Godwit *Limosa haemastica*
Little Curlew *Numenius minutus*
Upland Sandpiper *Bartramia longicauda*
Greater Yellowlegs *Tringa melanoleuca*
Lesser Yellowlegs *Tringa flavipes*
Solitary Sandpiper *Tringa solitaria*
Terek Sandpiper *Tringa cinereus*
Spotted Sandpiper *Tringa macularia*
Grey-tailed Tattler *Heteroscelus brevipes*
Wilson's Phalarope *Phalaropus tricolor*
South Polar Skua *Catharacta maccormicki*
Pallas's (Great Black-headed) Gull *Larus ichthyaetus*
Laughing Gull *Larus atricilla*
Franklin's Gull *Larus pipixcan*
Sabine's Gull *Larus sabini*
Bonaparte's Gull *Larus philadelphia*
Slender-billed Gull *Larus genei*
Audouin's Gull *Larus audouinii*
Yellow-legged Gull *Larus michahellis*
Caspian Gull *Larus cachinnans*
Gull-billed Tern *Sterna nilotica*
Caspian Tern *Sterna caspia*
Royal Tern *Sterna maxima*
Elegant Tern *Sterna elegans*
Aleutian Tern *Sterna aleutica*
Forster's Tern *Sterna forsteri*
Bridled Tern *Sterna anaethetus*
Brünnich's Guillemot *Uria lomvia*
Oriental (Rufous) Turtle Dove *Streptopelia orientalis*
Mourning Dove *Zenaida macroura*
Northern Hawk Owl *Surnia ulula*
Eurasian Scops Owl *Otus scops*
Tengmalm's Owl *Aegolius funereus*
Red-necked Nightjar *Caprimulgus ruficollis*
Common Nighthawk *Chordeiles minor*
Chimney Swift *Chaetura pelagica*
White-throated Needletail *Hirundapus caudacutus*
Pallid Swift *Apus pallidus*

Pacific Swift *Apus pacificus*
Alpine Swift *Apus melba*
White-rumped Swift *Apus caffer*
Little Swift *Apus affinis*
Belted Kingfisher *Ceryle alycon*
Blue-cheeked Bee-eater *Merops superciliosus*
Yellow-bellied Sapsucker *Sphyrapicus varius*
Eastern Phoebe *Sayornis phoebe*
Calandra Lark *Melanocorypha calandra*
Bimaculated Lark *Melanocorypha bimaculata*
White-winged Lark *Melanocorypha leucoptera*
Black Lark *Melanocorypha yeltoniensis*
Short-toed Lark *Calandrella brachydactyla*
Lesser Short-toed Lark *Calandrella rufescens*
Crested Lark *Galerida cristata*
Tree Swallow *Tachycineta bicolor*
Eurasian Crag Martin *Hirundo rupestris*
Red-rumped Swallow *Hirundo daurica*
Cliff Swallow *Hirundo pyrrhonota*
Richard's Pipit *Anthus novaeseelandiae*
Blyth's Pipit, *Anthus godlewskii*
Olive-backed Pipit *Anthus hodgsoni*
Pechora Pipit *Anthus gustavi*
Red-throated Pipit *Anthus cervinus*
Buff-bellied Pipit *Anthus rubescens*
Citrine Wagtail *Motacilla citreola*
Cedar Waxwing *Bombycilla cedrorum*
Northern Mockingbird *Mimus polyglottos*
Brown Thrasher *Toxostoma rufum*
Alpine Accentor *Prunella collaris*
Rufous-tailed Scrub Robin *Cercotrichas galactotes*
Thrush Nightingale *Luscinia luscinia*
Siberian Rubythroat *Luscinia calliope*
Siberian Blue Robin *Luscinia cyane*
Red-flanked Bluetail, *Tarsiger cyanurus*
White-throated Robin *Irania gutturalis*
Moussier's Redstart *Phoenicurus moussieri*
Black-eared Wheatear *Oenanthe hispanica*
Desert Wheatear *Oenanthe deserti*
White-tailed Wheatear *Oenanthe leucopyga*
Black Wheatear *Oenanthe leucura*
Rufous-tailed Rock Thrush *Monticola saxatilis*
Blue Rock Thrush *Monticola solitarius*
Varied Thrush *Zoothera naevia*
Wood Thrush *Hylocichla mustelina*
Hermit Thrush *Catharus guttatus*
Swainson's Thrush *Catharus ustulatus*
Grey-cheeked Thrush *Catharus minimus*
Veery *Catharus fuscescens*
Eyebrowed Thrush *Turdus obscurus*
Dusky Thrush *Turdus naumanni*
Dark-throated Thrush *Turdus ruficollis*

Moustached Warbler *Acrocephalus melanopogon*
Aquatic Warbler *Acrocephalus paludicola*
Thick-billed Warbler *Acrocephalus aedon*
Olivaceous Warbler *Hippolais pallida*
Booted Warbler *Hippolais caligata*
Marmora's Warbler *Sylvia sarda*
Spectacled Warbler *Sylvia conspicillata*
Subalpine Warbler *Sylvia cantillans*
Sardinian Warbler *Sylvia melanocephala*
Rüppell's Warbler *Sylvia rueppelli*
Desert Warbler *Sylvia nana*
Orphean Warbler *Sylvia hortensis*
Barred Warbler *Sylvia nisoria*
Greenish Warbler *Phylloscopus trochiloides*
Arctic Warbler *Phylloscopus borealis*
Hume's Leaf Warbler *Phylloscopus humei*
Radde's Warbler *Phylloscopus schwarzi*
Dusky Warbler *Phylloscopus fuscatus*
Western Bonelli's Warbler *Phylloscopus bonelli*
Eastern Bonelli's Warbler *Phylloscopus orientalis*
Iberian Chiffchaff *Phylloscopus brehmii*
Asiatic Brown Flycatcher, *Muscicapa latirostris*
Mugimaki Flycatcher, *Ficedula mugimaki*
Collared Flycatcher *Ficedula albicollis*
Red-breasted Flycatcher *Ficedula parva*
Red-breasted Nuthatch *Sitta canadensis*
Short-toed Treecreeper *Certhia brachydactyla*
Brown Shrike *Lanius cristatus*
Isabelline Shrike *Lanius isabellinus*
Long-tailed Shrike *Lanius schach*
Lesser Grey Shrike *Lanius minor*
Southern Grey Shrike *Lanius meridionalis*
Woodchat Shrike *Lanius senator*
Daurian Starling *Sturnus sturninus*
Rock Sparrow *Petronia petronia*
White-winged Snowfinch *Montifringilla nivalis*
Yellow-throated Vireo *Vireo flavifrons*
Philadelphia Vireo *Vireo philadelphicus*
Red-eyed Vireo *Vireo olivaceus*
Trumpeter Finch *Rhodopechys githaginea*
Pine Grosbeak *Pinicola enucleator*
Evening Grosbeak *Hesperiphona vespertina*
Black-and-white Warbler *Mniotilta varia*
Golden-winged Warbler *Vermivora chrysoptera*
Tennessee Warbler *Vermivora peregrina*
Northern Parula *Parula americana*
Yellow Warbler *Dendroica petechia*
Chestnut-sided Warbler *Dendroica pensylvanica*
Blackburnian Warbler *Dendroica fusca*
Cape May Warbler *Dendroica tigrina*
Magnolia Warbler *Dendroica magnolia*
Yellow-rumped Warbler, *Dendroica coronata*

Palm Warbler, *Dendroica palmarum*
Blackpoll Warbler *Dendroica striata*
Bay-breasted Warbler *Dendroica castanea*
American Redstart *Setophaga ruticilla*
Ovenbird *Seiurus aurocapillus*
Northern Waterthrush *Seiurus noveboracensis*
Common Yellowthroat *Geothlypis trichas*
Hooded Warbler *Wilsonia citrina*
Wilson's Warbler *Wilsonia pusilla*
Summer Tanager *Piranga rubra*
Scarlet Tanager *Piranga olivacea*
Eastern Towhee *Pipilo erythrophthalmus*
Lark Sparrow *Chondestes grammacus*
Savannah Sparrow *Passerculus sandwichensis*
Fox Sparrow *Passerella iliaca*
Song Sparrow *Melospiza melodia*
White-crowned Sparrow *Zonotrichia leucophrys*
White-throated Sparrow *Zonotrichia albicollis*

Dark-eyed Junco *Junco hyemalis*
Black-faced Bunting *Emberiza spodocephala*
Pine Bunting, *Emberiza leucocephalos*
Rock Bunting *Emberiza cia*
Cretzschmar's Bunting *Emberiza caesia*
Yellow-browed Bunting *Emberiza chrysophrys*
Rustic Bunting *Emberiza rustica*
Little Bunting *Emberiza pusilla*
Yellow-breasted Bunting *Emberiza aureola*
Pallas's Bunting *Emberiza pallasi*
Red-headed Bunting *Emberiza bruniceps*
Black-headed Bunting *Emberiza melanocephala*
Rose-breasted Grosbeak *Pheucticus ludovicianus*
Indigo Bunting *Passerina cyanea*
Bobolink *Dolichonyx oryzivorus*
Brown-headed Cowbird *Molothrus ater*
Baltimore Oriole *Icterus galbula*

APPENDIX 2:
Biographical details

This gallery of snapshots is intended as background information on some of the voices and names that are encountered most frequently in the text.

David Bannerman (1886–1979): one of the most prolific ornithologists of the twentieth century, producing the eight-volume *The Birds of Tropical West Africa* and four other major works on island avifaunas. His 12-volume *Birds of the British Isles* was an extraordinary one-man achievement and is still a fabulous treasure-trove of anecdote and historical detail.

Thomas Bewick (1753–1828): his wood engravings are some of the best early images of birds, while his *History of British Birds* was one of the catalysts for the nineteenth-century explosion of interest in natural history.

Sir Thomas Browne (1605–82): English polymath and pioneer of natural history, who wrote about the birds of East Anglia and enjoyed exploding long-held myths about natural history.

Abel Chapman (1851–1929): author, sportsman and one of Britain's earliest 'repentant butchers', he was a renowned hunter of European and African birds and mammals, who later took to the nascent cause of con-servation. At one time he was a joint-lessee of Andalusia's Coto de Doñana, now the premier wildlife national park in Spain. He also wrote an influential book on his home area, *Bird-Life of the Borders*.

Eric Ennion (1900–81): One of the great originals of wildlife art in the twentieth century and while not as well known as contemporaries like Peter Scott, Ennion will probably leave a greater artistic legacy through his influence on younger generations. His gift was for capturing the intensity and living essence of birds, rather than some idealised painter's image. His writing in a string of books, including *The British Bird* and *The Lapwing*, demonstrated the same concern for immediacy and detailed observation.

James Fisher (1912–70): when he died in a car crash at just 58, the naturalist community lost one of its most gifted and imaginative figures. Fisher brought a Renaissance breadth to his preoccupation with birds and seemed to have an equally deep understanding of all aspects of the subject, from bird poetry to the avian fossil record. He was a senior editor at Collins and a key populariser of natural history through numerous BBC broadcasts and bird books.

Richard Fitter: one of the great perennials of British wildlife, he published his first writings on nature in the 1920s and has issued his latest British flora in the twenty-first century. He has also published numerous books on birds.

Derek Goodwin: scientific officer at the British Museum (Natural History) during his professional life and in his spare time one of the most acutely observant students of bird behaviour of our time, he has published a mountain of papers and a number of key bird books, including *Crows of the World* and *Pigeons and Doves of the World*. Immensely well read and largely self-taught, he is probably the only (non-German) ornithologist in the world who can – and regularly does – quote Goethe's poetry in its original form.

Lord Grey of Fallodon (1862–1933): Edward Grey was a Liberal statesman with a passion for wildlife, especially birds. His *The Charm of Birds*, still in print after 80 years, is full of original insights into the impact of birds on their human neighbours, especially the power of bird song.

William Henry Hudson (1841–1922): one of the most prominent and eloquent voices in early bird conservation. He was a prolific author, most notably on his Argentinian childhood (*Far Away and Long Ago*). His writings on British birds are rather out of favour for the occasionally fey tone, but books such as *Birds and Man* are full of wonderfully fresh insights and appear deeply modern in their approach almost a century after they were first published.

Julian Huxley (1887–1975): grandson of Charles Darwin's champion, Thomas Huxley, and elder brother of the author, Aldous Huxley. He was a biologist, professor of zoology at King's College London, and a pioneer student of the evolution of animal behaviour, known as ethology. Many of his early studies focused on waterbirds.

Janet Kear, OBE (1933–2004): Britain's senior authority on wildfowl, she wrote numerous books and papers on these charismatic birds, especially their long and complex relationship with humans. She also held most of the senior offices in British ornithology, including editor of *Ibis* and presidency of the BOU. She worked for many years for the Wildfowl & Wetlands Trust and was often given jobs men could not do, such as hand-rearing ducklings or talking to irate Scottish farmers about goose-damage to crops. Unlike her male colleagues, she was never turned away; more often she was plied with glasses of single malt.

David Lack (1910–73): a near-contemporary of W. H.

Auden at Gresham's School in Norfolk, he went on to become one of the foremost ornithologists of the twentieth century and a pioneer of ecology and behavioural studies. He was a theoretician, but with a common touch in print, as shown by his two popular ground-breaking books, *The Life of the Robin* and *Swifts in a Tower*. In life he was a rather intense, unclubbable man who held few official positions and listed his recreations in *Who's Who* as 'home help'.

Ronald Lockley (1903–2000): a prolific author on birds and a conservationist. For 21 years he lived on the islands of Skokholm where he pursued pioneer studies of seabirds and of migration. He wrote nearly 60 books on very diverse wildlife themes, one of which was *The Private Life of the Rabbit* (1964), the inspiration for Richard Adams' bestseller *Watership Down*.

Martin Martin (1660s–1719): Scottish traveller, author and naturalist who wrote two early portraits of Hebridean life, *A Description of the Western Islands of Scotland* (c. 1695) and *A Voyage to St Kilda* (1698). They are full of detailed and accurate observations of these once-remote Atlantic islands and their Gaelic-speaking inhabitants.

Chris Mead (1940–2003): spent his entire working life with the BTO, writing numerous papers and books, ringing 400,000 birds and serving latterly as one of the great communicators about British birds and conservation.

Richard Meinertzhagen (1878–1967): a soldier, big-game hunter, intelligence officer and explorer, who was considered one of the great originals of British natural history until it was demonstrated that he was also a fantasist on a grand scale. Despite his recent notoriety he remains a fascinating observer and writer on birds with a distinctive, forthright, often humorous style. 'I should dearly love to unleash six female goshawk in Trafalgar Square and witness the reaction of that mob of tuberculous pigeon.'

Reg Moreau (1897–1970): a colonial agronomist, great scholar of African birds, editor for the BOU and author of a score of papers as well as several books. He checked the proofs of his final work, a major study of bird migration, as he lay dying in Hereford General hospital; his hope that it would prove 'no bum swansong' was amply fulfilled.

Ron Murton (1932–78): academic and prolific author on bird ecology, focusing on 'problem' species such as those involved in air strikes. He was author of a monograph,

The Wood Pigeon, and during observations of their migration was aboard the South Goodwin Lightship, which subsequently broke free of its moorings and sank; he was the only survivor.

Desmond Nethersole-Thompson (1908–89): a fiery local socialist politician who was also one of the most colourful birders of his age. He was recently adjudged to have spent more time watching birds in the field than any of his contemporaries. A sequence of monographs on Greenshank, Snow Bunting and Dotterel are among the most sought-after bird books of the century and all demonstrate his great literary 'feel' for nature. He became controversial for his early days as an egg collector and was shabbily mistreated by those who dwelt on his past and overlooked his massive contribution to the study of birds.

Alfred Newton (1829–1907): professor of zoology at Cambridge and one of the first major organisers of British ornithology. He co-founded the British Ornithologists' Union in 1859 and wrote the first *Dictionary of Birds*, a wonderful synthesis of all that was known about birds; its successor is still in print today.

Edward Max Nicholson (1904–2003): the godfather of British environmentalism, if such a figure could be said to exist, would be this remarkable, multi-talented man. In his long life he helped to define our approach to wildlife and to birds in particular, publishing his first bird book in 1926; yet he was also an editor of the nine-volume *Birds of the Western Palearctic* from its inception in the 1960s until its completion in 1994. He was the founding director-general of the Nature Conservancy, was instrumental in the creation of a sheaf of environmental organisations, including the BTO (1933), editor of *British Birds* (1951–60) and president of the RSPB (1980–8). In his busy working life he was a senior civil servant – he was in Churchill's team at Yalta, where the latter met Stalin and Roosevelt in 1944 – of rather rebellious bent and wrote a damning study of administrative incompetence entitled *The System*. Probably as a consequence he was among the most deserving of Britons not to be properly honoured.

Thomas Pennant (1726–97): Welsh author and naturalist, who was a correspondent of Gilbert White and Carl Linnaeus. His four-volume *British Zoology* was a catalyst for the growing interest in natural history, although Pennant was not always the most reliable authority on his subject (see page 52). Some of his books of travel were written about countries he had never even visited.

John Ray (1627–1705): vies with William Turner (see below) for the title of the father of British ornithology. His name is forever yoked with that of Francis Willughby (1635–72) for his editorship of the latter's seminal book, *The Ornithology of Francis Willughby*. Most of it was probably written by Ray and published after Willughby's early death.

Eric Simms, DFC: must have been the only member of 626 Squadron to be distracted by visible migration while flying Lancaster bombers over wartime Europe. In later life this distinguished naturalist worked in the BBC's wildlife sound-recording unit and as a senior BBC producer. He started the *Countryside* programme in 1952 and broadcast in every one until it ceased in 1990. His 20 books include four titles in the famous New Naturalist series, a feat achieved by no other wildlife author.

Bernard Tucker (1901–50): a widely travelled naturalist and one of the most fastidious intellects of twentieth-century ornithology. He was an editor of the journal *British Birds* and one of the principal authors of the *Handbook*, where his economical, precise style had a huge impact on subsequent bird literature. Even as he lay dying in a hospital bed of a painful debilitating illness, he could be found surrounded by the galley proofs of *British Birds*, 'each misprint . . . corrected, every missing comma inserted.'

William Turner (c. 1500–68): author of one of the earliest books on birds, in 1544. Largely a commentary on the natural-history writings of Aristotle and Pliny, the book also incorporated Turner's own original observations of British birds, which included some of the first accurate details on the subject.

D. I. M. (Ian) Wallace: editor, author, artist and public speaker, whose four initials are among the most reproduced letters in British ornithological writing. Scottish by birth and in choice of dress, he is one of the most colourful, inspiring and multi-talented advocates of birds in modern times. He has written several books and was one of the main editors of *Birds of the Western Palearctic*.

John Walpole-Bond (1878–1958): a descendant of Horace Walpole, 'Jack' or 'Jock' Walpole-Bond had a lifelong fascination with bird breeding behaviour and was one of the few egg collectors to put his massive experience to good use, particularly in his *magnum opus*, *A History of Sussex Birds*. A man of private means, he was noted for his tramp-like appearance and boasted of twice being offered the price of his bus fare by kind old ladies. His prose was famously convoluted: 'During Armageddon and just after, the Kestrel, owing to a slackening of slaughter, and nothing else, became for a bird of prey positively prosperous in the county.'

Gilbert White (1720–93): the patron saint of amateur field naturalists, he exemplified the naturalist cleric and, through his minutely detailed observations of his Dorset parish, helped inspire wide interest in the environment. *The Natural History of Selborne* is still one of the most reproduced and enduring works in the English language.

Harry Witherby (1873–1943): publisher, author and key mover and shaker of modern ornithology. His company published most of the important bird books of the early twentieth century. He also founded and published the journal *British Birds*, was the main editor of the seminal five-volume *Handbook of British Birds*, and was a pioneer student of migration through the trapping and ringing of birds.

William Yarrell (1784–1853): a founder of the Zoological Society and author of the three-volume *History of British Birds*, which was enormously influential and popular; it went through several editions and remained in print for much of the nineteenth century.

APPENDIX 3:

Birds in public houses

by Steve Shaw

Over a period of 20 years Steve Shaw has built up a comprehensive list of well in excess of 3000 public houses (inns, taverns and hotels), both extant and historical, whose names include reference to birds. The following list includes the full range of bird-related names for pubs. Those that have bird names but refer to something else are marked * (e.g. the LITTLE OWL depicts a racehorse on its sign). Those that are known only from historical research and possibly (or probably) no longer exist and for which there is no current address, are marked #. The bracketed numbers indicate the number of pubs with the same name. The author would be pleased to hear of any suggested amendments or additions and may be contacted by email at: Steveshaw@ornsoc.freeserve.co.uk

ALBATROSS	Earleswood, Redhill, Surrey (2)
AVIARY	Trent Bridge, Nottingham
BARN OWL	Elmton, Derbyshire (7)
OLD BARN OWL	Isle Brewers, Somerset
BIRD	Birtley, Sunderland (2)
BIRDS	Spalding, Lincolnshire
BIRD & BABBY	#
BIRD & BANTLING	#
BIRD & BUSH	Bushmead, Luton (2)
BIRDS & BEES	Stirling
BIRD CAGE	Thame, Oxfordshire (2)
BIRD in the Barley	Messingham, Lincolnshire
BIRD in the Bush	Littletown, Durham (3)
BIRD in Hand	Eckington, Derbyshire (115)
BIRD in View	Kingswood, Bristol
BIRD's Nest	Twickenham, Richmond-upon-Thames (2)
Dutch BIRDS	Failsworth, Oldham
T BIRD	Waltham Forest, London
BITTERN	Southampton
BLACKBIRD	Blackbird Road, Leicester (8)
BLACKBIRDS	Flitwick, Bedfordshire (3)
Bush BLACKBIRD & THRUSH	East Peckham, Kent
Three BLACKBIRDS	Flamstead, Hertfordshire (5)
White BLACKBIRD	Loudwater, Buckinghamshire
Ham & BLACKBIRD	Farnborough, Hampshire
BLACKCAP*	Camden, London
BLUE TIT	Boughton, Nottinghamshire
BULLFINCH	Belper, Derbyshire (4)
BUSTARD	South Rauceby, Lincolnshire (2)
CANARY & LINNET	Little Fransham, Norfolk
CHOUGH	Chard, Somerset (2)

CHOUGH's Nest	Lynton, Devon
CORNISH CHOUGH	Porth, Newquay, Cornwall
Three CHOUGHs	Blandford Forum, Dorset (2)
COB & PEN	Fareham, Hampshire
COCK & BLACKBIRDS	Bulmer, Sudbury, Suffolk
COCK & MAGPIE	Chesterfield, Derbyshire (6)
COCK & MAGPIES	Smethwick, Birmingham
COCK & PHEASANT	Bollington Cross, Cheshire
COCK & PYE	Ipswich, Suffolk
COCK & PYNOT	Chesterfield, Derbyshire
COCK & SWAN	Wakefield
COCK ROBIN	Swindon
Black COCK	Blyth Bridge, Staffordshire (9)
COLLARED DOVE	West End, Southampton
COOT	Horsham, West Sussex
Twa CORBIES	Cumbernault, North Lanarkshire
CORMORANT	Portchester, Hampshire
CRANE	Pitsea, Essex (4)
Golden CRANE	Cranham, Havering
Three CRANES	Sheffield (5)
Fox & CRANE	#
CRAW's Nest	Anstruther, Fife (2)
Three CRAWS	Montrose, Angus
CARRION CROW	Tenbury Wells, Herefordshire (2)
CROW & Gate	Crowborough, Kent
CROW in the Oak	Coventry
CROW Park	Keswick, Cumbria
CROWpie	Rugby, Warwickshire
CROW's Nest	Horndean, Hampshire (24)
Old CROW	Newton-le-Willows, St Helens
Split CROW	#
Three CROWS	#

Whale & CROW	#
CUCKOO	Orrell Park, Liverpool (8)
CUCKOO Bush	Gotham, Nottinghamshire
CUCKOO Oak	Madeley, Shropshire
CUCKOO Wharf	Worksop, Nottinghamshire
CUCKOO's Nest	Gawcott, Buckinghamshire
Bell & CUCKOO	Walsall
CURLEW	Havant, Hampshire
CYGNET	York (5)
CYGNETs	Hook-a-gate, Shropshire
Three DAWs	Gravesend, Kent
DOTTEREL	Reighton, North Yorkshire
DOVE	Barnsley (20)
DOVEs	Edinburgh
Old DOVE	Derby
DOVE & Olive Branch	Trafford (2)
DOVE & Rainbow	Hartshead, Sheffield
DOVEcot	Roby, Knowsley
DOVEcote	Laxton, Nottinghamshire (9)
DOVEtail	City of Westminster, London
Crown & DOVE	Bristol
Rainbow & DOVE	Leicester (2)
Sun & DOVEs	Camberwell, Southwark
Two DOVEs	Canterbury, Kent (2)
DRAKES	Bransholme, East Riding of Yorkshire (3)
DUCK	Newney Green, Essex (14)
DUCK & Acid Drop	#
DUCK & DRAKE	Leeds (2)
DUCK & DRAKES	Kensington & Chelsea, London
DUCK & Firkin	Bolton
DUCK & Iron	Brierly Hill, Dudley
DUCK & Kangaroo	Sunderland
DUCK & PHEASANT	Cheltenham, Gloucestershire
DUCKs Don't Float	Evesham, Worcestershire
DUCK in the Pond	Harrow Weald, Brent, London
DUCK Pond	Redditch, Worcestershire
Black DUCK	Malmesbury, Wiltshire (2)
Black Dog & DUCK	Bury, East Sussex
City DUCK	Milton Keynes
Dirty DUCK	Stratford-upon-Avon, Warwickshire
Dog & DUCK	Shardlow, Derbyshire (32)
Drookit DUCK	Falkirk
Drouthy DUCK	Conon Bridge, Highland
Drunken DUCK	Hawkshead, Cumbria
Fish & DUCK	Little Thetford, Cambridgeshire
Flying DUCK	Rillington, North Yorkshire
Fox & DUCK	Tinsley, Sheffield (6)
Juicy DUCK	Bishop's Stortford, Hertfordshire
Mucky DUCK	Sheffield (4)
Quaggy DUCK	Lewisham
Royal Dog & DUCK	Flamborough, East Riding of Yorkshire
Strawberry DUCK	Entwistle, Lancashire (2)
Whistling DUCK	Weston-super-Mare, North Somerset
Wild DUCK	Alton, Staffordshire (5)
DUCK's Nest	Douglas, Isle of Man
Ugly DUCKLING	Haywards Heath, East Sussex (2)
EAGLE	Anlaby, East Riding of Yorkshire (129)
EAGLEs	Welshpool, Powys (16)
EAGLE & Ball	Birmingham
EAGLE & Chicks	#
EAGLE & Child	Billinge, St Helens (26)
EAGLE & Crown	Upton, Wirral
EAGLE & HAWK	Leigh, Wigan
EAGLE & Hind	Chelmsford, Essex
EAGLE & Serpent	Kinlet, Shropshire
EAGLE & Snake	Burslem, Staffordshire
EAGLE & Spur	Cookley, Worcestershire
EAGLE & Sun	Droitwich, Worcestershire
EAGLE Brewery Tap	Ryde, Isle of Wight
EAGLEbush	Melincrythan, Neath & Port Talbot
EAGLE House	Launceston, Cornwall
EAGLE Tap	Kingston-upon-Thames, London
EAGLE's Foot	Lancashire
EAGLE's Head	Satterthwaite, Cumbria (2)
EAGLE's Nest	Kidderminster, Worcestershire

Black EAGLE	Burton-on-Trent, Staffordshire (4)
Glen EAGLE	Harpenden, Hertfordshire
Grey EAGLE	#
Halfmoon & Spread EAGLE	Micheldever, Hampshire
Mountain EAGLE	Mountain, Bradford
New EAGLE	Leeds
Old EAGLE	Camden, London (2)
Old EAGLEs	Whitchurch, Cheshire
Spread EAGLE	Belper, Derbyshire (101)
Star & EAGLE	Goudhurst, Kent
Two EAGLEs	Lambeth, London
White EAGLE	Rhoscelyn, Anglesey (3)
EAGLET	Hackney, London
FALCON	Chester (102)
FALCON & Fetterlock	#
FALCON & Firkin	Hackney, London
FALCON & Horseshoe	#
FALCON Bearer	Knutsford, Cheshire
FALCONdale	Lampeter, Powys
FALCONer	Daventry, Northamptonshire (2)
FALCONer's Rest	Middleton, Leeds
FALCON on the Hoop	#
FALCON's Nest	Port Erin, Isle of Man (2)
Castle & FALCON	Derby (2)
Crown & FALCON	Puckeridge, Hertfordshire
Horse & FALCON	#
Talbot & FALCON	Wakefield
Old FALCON	Driffield, East Riding of Yorkshire (3)
FINCH's*	Hambledon, Rutland
FIREBIRD	Edgbaston, Birmingham
FIRECREST	Wendover, Buckinghamshire
FLAMINGO	Worksop, Nottinghamshire (3)
FLAMINGO Land	Malton, North Yorkshire
FOWL & Firkin	Coventry
FULMAR & Firkin	City of Westminster, London
GAMEBIRD	Rainford, Lancashire (5)
GAMECOCK	Harworth, Doncaster (14)
GANDER	Cheam, Croydon, London
GANDER on the Green	Lansdown, Gloucestershire
GANNET	Bideford, Devon
Gaggle of GEESE	Buckland Newton, Dorset
The GEESE Have Gone Over the Water	Brighton
GOLDEN EAGLE	Derby (25)
GOLDEN PHEASANT	Plumley, Cheshire (7)
GOLDEN PLOVER	Waterthorpe, Sheffield
GOOSE	Illingworth, Calderdale (4)
GOOSE & Cabbage	Plymouth
GOOSE & Cuckoo	Llanover, Monmouthshire
GOOSE & Firkin	Southwark, London
GOOSE & GANDER	South Molton, Devon
GOOSE & Granite	Kingsheath, Birmingham (2)
GOOSE & Gridiron	City of London
GOOSE Fair	Bulwell, Nottingham
GOOSE on the Square	Nottingham
Fox & GOOSE	Washwood Heath, Birmingham (20)
Flying GOOSE	Fleet, Hampshire
Gade & GOOSE	Hemel Hempstead, Hertfordshire
Gaping GOOSE	Garforth, Leeds
Grey GOOSE	Gedling, Nottinghamshire (2)
Marsh GOOSE	Moreton-in-Marsh, Gloucestershire
Old GOOSE	Bedworth, Warwickshire
Paddy's GOOSE	Combeinteignhead, Devon (2)
Sitting GOOSE	Lower Bartle, Lancashire
Wild GOOSE	Redditch, Warwickshire (3)
GOSHAWK	Mouldsworth, Cheshire
GREBE	Stalham, Norfolk (2)
GROUSE	Haworth, Bradford (8)
GROUSE & Claret*	Rowsley, Derbyshire (3)
GROUSE & Firkin	Lambeth, London
GROUSE & Trout	Farr, Highland
GROUSE's Nest	Tomintoul, Highland
GULL	Upper Burnmouth, Scottish Borders (3)
HALCYON	Winchester, Hampshire

HARRIER	Brampton, Cambridgeshire (7)
HARRIERS*	Birmingham
MARSH HARRIER	Stamford, Lincolnshire (2)
Merry HARRIERS*	Forches Corner, Somerset (4)
HAWK	Hawksley Hall Estate, Wigan (3)
New/Old HAWK	Byker, Newcastle
White HAWK	Brighton
HAWK & Buck	#
HAWK & Buckle	Denbigh (3)
HAWK & DOVE	Waterthorpe, Sheffield
HAWK & DUCK	#
HAWK & HARRIER	Dunsfold, Surrey
HAWK & PARTRIDGE	Bloxham, Oxfordshire
HAYCHATTER	Bradfield Dale, Sheffield
HEATHCOCK	Llandaff, Cardiff
Grey HEN	South Shields, South Tyneside
Red HEN	Cradeley Heath, Worcestershire
Tappit HEN	Aberdeen
Travelling HEN	Ross-on-Wye, Herefordshire
HERON	Havant, Hampshire (7)
HERONgate	Brentwood, Essex
Pike & HERON	Brinsworth, Rotherham
Potter's HERON	Ampfield, Hampshire
HIRONDELLES	#
HOPOPS	Bideford, Devon
JACKDAW	Tadcaster, North Yorkshire (2)
JACKDAW & ROOK	Lambeth, London
JAYS	Camden, London
Three JAYS	Jaywick, Essex (2)
KESTREL	Hatton, Derbyshire (5)
KINGFISHER	Derby (30)
KINGFISHER's Catch	Bishop's Lydeard, Somerset
KITE	Oxford
KITE's Nest	Stretton Sugwas, Herefordshire
KITTIWAKE	Whitley Bay, North Tyneside
KITTYWAKE	Hayling Island, Hampshire
LARK	Lincoln (2)
LARK's Nest	Nuthall, Nottingham
Lamb & LARK	Kingswood, Bristol (3)
LITTLE Lark	Studley, Warwickshire
LINNET	Great Hinton, Wiltshire
Red LINNET	Barton-on-Sea, Hampshire
LINNET & LARK	Kingston-upon-Hull
Railway & LINNET	Middleton Junction, Bury
LITTLE OWL*	Cheltenham, Gloucestershire
MAGPIE	Greenhill, Sheffield (23)
MAGPIES	Trent Bridge, Nottinghamshire (2)
MAGPIE's Nest	Bromley Common, Bromley
MAGPIE & Crown	Brentford, Kensington & Chelsea, London
MAGPIE & Stump	Lambeth, London (5)
Bull & MAGPIE	Boston, Lincolnshire
Gun & MAGPIE	Enfield, Essex
Horseshoe & MAGPIE	City of London
Rising Sun & MAGPIE	Barnstaple, Devon
Three MAGPIES	Brinsworth, Rotherham (2)
MALLARD	Felling, Gateshead (16)
MARTIN	Burscough, Lancashire
MARTIN's Arms	Colston Bassett, Nottinghamshire
MARTIN's Nest	Elland, Calderdale (2)
MARTLET	Langford Budville, Somerset (2)
Golden MARTLET	Hellingly, Hailsham, East Sussex
MERLIN	Crewe, Cheshire (10)
MOORCOCK	Littleborough, Rochdale (11)
Bonny MOORHEN	Stanhope, Durham
Three MOORHENS	Hitchin, Hertfordshire
NIGHTINGALE	Derby (5)
NIGHTJAR	Basingstoke, Hampshire (2)
NIGHT JAR	Worle, Somerset
OSPREY	Shoeburyness, Essex (4)
Grand OSPREY	Lytham St Anne's, Lancashire
Royal OSPREY	Ashby-de-la-Zouch, Leicestershire
OWL	Neepsend, Sheffield (9)
Blinking OWL	Tuffley, Gloucestershire (4)
Green OWL	Camber, East Sussex
Oadby OWL	Oadby, Leicestershire
Three OWLS	Kirkburton, Wakefield
Winking OWL	Aviemore, Highland
Wise OWL	Huddersfield, Kirklees
OWL & Crescent	Calshot, Southampton
OWL & Pussycat	Leicester (6)
OWL & Tod	#
OWL in the Ivy Bush	St Helens
OWL's Nest	St Helens (2)
OYSTERCATCHER	Portmahomack, Highland (3)
PARAKEET	Kilmarnock, East Ayrshire
PARROT & MAGPIE	Shinfield, Wokingham
PARTRIDGE	Partridge Green, West Sussex (6)
Dog & PARTRIDGE	Attercliffe, Sheffield (71)
Old Dog & PARTRIDGE	Nottingham
Original Dog & PARTRIDGE	Nottingham
Pear & PARTRIDGE	Perton, Staffordshire
PEACOCK & MAGPIE	#
PEEWIT	Astwick, Bedfordshire
PELICAN	Stroud, Gloucestershire (26)
Fox & PELICAN	Hindhead, Surrey
Ship & PELICAN	Heavitree, Devon
Three PELICANS	Lewes, East Sussex
PEN & COB	Huddersfield, Kirklees
PHEASANT	Carbrook, Sheffield (105)
PHEASANT & Firkin	City of London
PHEASANT Plucker	Atherton, Wigan (3)
Bear & PHEASANT	Stafford, Staffordshire
Brace of PHEASANTS	Plush, Dorset
Charlecote PHEASANT	Charlecote, Warwickshire
Dog & PHEASANT	Ashton-under-Lyne, Tameside (11)
Fox & PHEASANT	Bradford (5)
Lion & PHEASANT	Shrewsbury, Shropshire
Moor & PHEASANT	Dalton, North Yorkshire
Old PHEASANT	Worcester, Worcestershire (3)
Pleasant PHEASANT	Croydon, London
Stag & PHEASANT	Mansfield, Nottinghamshire (11)
White PHEASANT	Fordham, Cambridgeshire
Wild PHEASANT	Llangollen, Denbighshire
Three PHEASANTS & Sceptre	#
PIDGEON	Spalding, Lincolnshire
PIED WAGTAIL	Tower Hamlets, London
PIGEON Box	Priorslee, Telford, Shropshire
PIGEON Pair	Kingswood, Reigate, Surrey
PIGEON Pie	Sherburn, North Yorkshire
Blue PIGEONS	Worth, Sandwich, Kent
Naughty PIGEON	Treharres, Newquay, Cornwall
Old Three PIGEONS	Nesscliffe, Shropshire
Three PIGEONS	Halstead, Essex (20) (This is believed to be Charles Dickens' THREE MAGPIES in *Our Mutual Friend*.)
Three PIGEONS & Sceptre	#
Wheatsheaf & PIGEON	Staines, Surrey
Sociable PLOVER	Cosham, Hampshire
POPINJAY	Rosebank, South Lanarkshire
PUFFIN	Weston-super-Mare, Somerset
PUFF-INN	St Kilda, Western Isles
PYEWIPE	Lincoln, Lincolnshire
QUAIL	Wandsworth, London
QUESLETT	Streetly, Birmingham
RAVEN	Brinklow, Warwickshire (43)
RAVEN & Bell	Newport
RAVENsbourne	Catford, Croydon, London
RAVENsdale	Mansfield, Nottinghamshire
Black RAVEN	City of London
Crown & RAVEN	Bridgnorth, Shropshire
Three RAVENS	Tilmanstone, Kent
White RAVEN	#
RED GROUSE	Stocksbridge, Sheffield (2)
REDSTART	Banning, Kent
REDWING*	Lumpstone, Devon
RHIWDERIN	Rhewderin, Powys
ROBIN	Mickleover, Derby (2)

ROBINS*	Bristol
ROBIN's Nest	Liverton, Edinburgh
ROBINswood	Matson, Gloucester
Black ROBIN*	Kingston, Kent
Cock ROBIN	Sale, Trafford
Rock ROBIN	Wadhurst, East Sussex
Round ROBIN*	Sunderland
ROOK	Halifax, Calderdale (2)
ROOKERY	Ettiley Heath, Cheshire (2)
ROOKERY Hall	Worleston, Cheshire
RUDDY DUCK	Peakirk, Cambridgeshire (2)
SANDMARTIN	Castleford, Wakefield (2)
SANDPIPER	Ripley, Derbyshire (14)
SEABIRDS	Flamborough, East Riding of Yorkshire (2)
SEAGULL	Portchester, Hampshire (13)
SEAHAWK	Moss Side, Manchester
SHELDRAKE	Jaywick, Clacton, Essex
SKYLARK	Croydon, London (4)
SNIPE	Dukinfield, Tameside (2)
Dog & SNIPE	#
SNOW GOOSE	Inverness, Highland (2)
SPARROW	Letcombe Regis, Oxfordshire (3)
SPARROWs	City of Westminster, London
SPARROW's Nest	Lowestoft, Suffolk
SPARROW's Wharfe	Leeds
SPARROWHAWK	Burnley, Lancashire (2)
Old SPARROWHAWK	Fence Nelson, Lancashire
SPINK's Nest	Huddersfield, Kirklees
STARLING	Pinner, Harrow, London
STOCKDOVE	Romiley, Stockport
STORK	Burnley, Lancashire (9)
STORK at Rest	Gravesend, Kent
STORK's Head	Leicester
STORK's Nest	#
Fox & STORK	Bolton
STORMY PETREL	Market Drayton, Shropshire
SWALLOW	Andover, Hampshire (13)
SWALLOWnest	Swallownest, Sheffield
SWALLOWS	Worksop, Nottinghamshire (2)
St John's SWALLOW	Solihull
Three SWALLOWs	Cley, Norfolk
SWAN	Long Melford, Suffolk (362)
SWANN	Westerfield, Suffolk (3)
SWAN & Antelope	#
SWAN & Bottle	Ealing, London
SWAN & Brewers	Wendover, Buckinghamshire
SWAN & Castle	Quainton, Buckinghamshire
SWAN & Cemetery	Bolton
SWAN & Chequers	Sandbach, Cheshire
SWAN & Chough	#
SWAN & Cues	Walsall
SWAN & CYGNET	Swanland, Kingston-upon-Hull
SWAN & CYGNETs	South Laggan, Highland
SWAN & Three CYGNETs	Durham
SWAN & FALCON	Hereford
SWAN & Grapes	Gamlingay, Cambridgeshire
SWAN & Harlequin	Faversham, Kent
SWAN & Harp	#
SWAN & Helmet	Northampton
SWAN & Hoop	#
SWAN & Lambe	Hackney, London
SWAN & Maidenhead	#
SWAN & Mitre	Bromley, Kent (2)
SWAN & Pyramids	Brent, London
SWAN & Railway	Radcliffe, Manchester (2)
SWAN & Rushes	Leicester
SWAN & Salmon	Alfreton, Derbyshire
SWAN & Sugarloaf	Lambeth, London (2)
SWAN & Talbot	Wetherby, Leeds
SWAN & White Hart	#
SWAN at Forton	Forton, Staffordshire

SWAN at Nibley	Nibley, South Gloucestershire
SWAN at Nordley	Nordley, Shropshire
SWAN at Salford	Salford, Bedfordshire
SWAN at Sherburn	Sherburn-in-Elmet, North Riding of Yorkshire
SWAN at Yardley	Yardley, Birmingham
SWAN Bank	Bilston, Wolverhampton
SWAN Diplomat	Streatley, West Berkshire
SWAN Garden	Wolverhampton
SWANholme	Lincoln
SWAN House	Wilmcote, Warwickshire
SWAN in the Rushes	Loughborough, Leicestershire
SWAN Lake	Jameston, Pembrokeshire
SWAN Revived	Higham Ferrers, Northamptonshire (2)
SWAN's Nest	Stratford-upon-Avon, Warwickshire (2)
SWAN with Three CYGNETs	Durham
SWAN with Two Necks	Todmorden, Calderdale (11)
SWAN with Two Nicks	Little Bollington, Cheshire (2)
SWANswell	Coventry
Bear & SWAN	Chew Magna, Bath
Bedford SWAN	Bedford
Bible & SWAN	#
Black SWAN	Ashover, Derbyshire (113)
Old Black Swan	Bedale, North Riding of Yorkshire
Bull & SWAN	Stamford, Lincolnshire (2)
Four SWANs	Sudbury, Suffolk (2)
Golden SWAN	Wilcot, Wiltshire
Green SWAN	Clacton-on-Sea, Essex
Henny SWAN	Henny Street, Essex
Lamport SWAN	Lamport, Northamptonshire
Lion & SWAN	Crewe, Cheshire (2)
Lyre & SWAN	#
New SWAN	Atherstone, Warwickshire (3)
Old SWAN	Worthington, Leicestershire (20)
Old SWAN & Mill	Minster Lovell, Oxfordshire
Old SWAN Uppers	Bourne End, Bedfordshire
Olde SWAN	Bletchley, Buckinghamshire (3)
Original SWAN	Cowley, Oxfordshire
Railway SWAN	Bedford (2)
Royal SWAN	Huddersfield, Kirklees (2)
Severn SWAN	Worcester
Three SWANS	Selby, North Riding of Yorkshire (4)
Three SWANs & Pea	Walsall
Top SWAN	Gateshead
Two-necked SWAN	Great Yarmouth, Norfolk
White SWAN	Ockbrook, Derbyshire (162)
White SWAN & CUCKOO	Tower Hamlets, London
Old White SWAN	York
Olde Whyte SWANNE	Louth, Lincolnshire (4)
SWIFTs	Bootle, Liverpool
TERN	Yate, South Gloucestershire (2)
THROSTLE's Nest	Congleton, Cheshire (4)
THRUSH	Bury
TURNSTONE	Hopton, Suffolk
Culture VULTURE	High Wycombe, Buckinghamshire (2)
VULTURE's Perch	Camden, London
George & VULTURE	Camden, London (2)
WOODCOCK	Ashton-under-Lyne, Tameside (10)
WOODCOCKS	Lincoln
Two WOODCOCKS	Croydon, London
WOODLARK	Derby (2)
WOODPECKER	Newbury, West Berkshire (11)
Crown & WOODPECKER	#
WOODPIGEON	Witley, Surrey (2)
WRENs*	Leeds
WREN's Nest	Kidderminster, Worcestershire (2)
Jenny WREN	Susworth, Lincolnshire (3)
YELLOW WAGTAIL	Yeovil, Somerset
YUTICK's Nest	Blackburn

APPENDIX 4:

Welsh names of birds

by Daniel Jenkins-Jones and Jonathan Elphick

COMMON NAME	WELSH NAME	TRANSLATION
Red-throated Diver	*Trochydd Gyddfgoch*	Red-throated Diver
Black-throated Diver	*Trochydd Gyddfddu*	Black-throated Diver
Great Northern Diver	*Trochydd Mawr*	Great Diver
Little Grebe	*Gwyach Fach*	Little Grebe
Great Crested Grebe	*Gwyach Fawr Gopog*	Great Crested Grebe
	Dowciar	Diving Hen
Red-necked Grebe	*Gwyach Yddfgoch*	Red-necked Grebe
Slavonian Grebe	*Gwyach Gorniog*	Horned Grebe
Black-necked Grebe	*Gwyach Yddfddu*	Black-necked Grebe
(Northern) Fulmar	*Aderyn-drycin y Graig*	Rock Storm Bird
	Gwylan y Graig	Rock Gull
Manx Shearwater	*Aderyn-drycin Manaw*	Manx Storm Bird
(European) Storm-petrel	*Pedryn Drycin*	Storm Petrel
Leach's Storm-petrel	*Pedryn Gynffon-fforchog*	Fork-tailed Petrel
(Northern) Gannet	*Hugan*	Sea-fowl? (literal translation 'Cloak'); or perhaps from Hucanwydd, Gull Goose
	Mulfran Wen	White Cormorant
(Great) Cormorant	*Mulfran*	Bashful Crow
	Bilidowcar	Billy the Diver
(European) Shag	*Mulfran Werdd*	Green Cormorant
	Mulfran Fach	Little Cormorant
(Great) Bittern	*Aderyn y Bwn*	Booming Bird
Grey Heron	*Crëyr Glas*	Blue Heron
	Crychydd (south Wales)	Screamer? Rippling, Quavering or Curly Crest?
(Eurasian) Spoonbill	*Llwybig*	Spoonbill
Mute Swan	*Alarch Dôf*	Tame Swan
	Alarch Mud	Mute Swan
Bewick's Swan (Tundra Swan)	*Alarch Bewick*	Bewick's Swan
Whooper Swan	*Alarch y Gogledd*	Northern Swan
Bean Goose	*Gŵydd y Llafur*	Corn Goose
Pink-footed Goose	*Gŵydd Droedbinc*	Pink-footed Goose
(Greater) White-fronted Goose	*Gŵydd Dalcen-wen*	White-foreheaded Goose
Greylag Goose	*Gŵydd Wyllt*	Wild Goose
Canada Goose	*Gŵydd Canada*	Canada Goose
Barnacle Goose	*Gŵydd Wyran*	Barnacle Goose
	Gŵydd y Môr	Sea Goose
Brent Goose	*Gŵydd Ddu*	Black Goose
(Common) Shelduck	*Hwyaden yr Eithin*	Gorse Duck
(Eurasian) Wigeon	*Chwiwell*	Whirling Sound; or onomatopoeic
Gadwall	*Hwyaden Lwyd*	Grey Duck

COMMON NAME	WELSH NAME	TRANSLATION
Gadwall	*Cors-hwyaden Lwyd*	Grey Marsh Duck
(Eurasian) Teal	*Corhwyaden*	Little Duck
Mallard	*Hwyaden Wyllt*	Wild Duck
(Northern) Pintail	*Hwyaden Lostfain*	Slender-tailed Duck
Garganey	*Hwyaden Addfain*	Slender Duck
(Northern) Shoveler	*Hwyaden Lydanbig*	Broad-billed Duck
(Common) Pochard	*Hwyaden Bengoch*	Red-headed Duck
Tufted Duck	*Hwyaden Gopog*	Tufted Duck
(Greater) Scaup	*Hwyaden Benddu*	Black-headed Duck
	Hwyaden Lygad Arian	Silver-eyed Duck
Common Eider	*Hwyaden Fwythblu*	Puffed-up-feathered Duck, or Smooth and Puffed-up Duck
Long-tailed Duck	*Hwyaden Gynffon-hir*	Long-tailed Duck
	Hwyaden Gynffon-wennol	Swallow-tailed Duck
Common Scoter (Black Scoter)	*Môr-hwyaden Ddu*	Black Sea-duck
Velvet Scoter	*Môr-hwyaden y Gogledd*	Northern Sea-duck
(Common) Goldeneye	*Hwyaden Lygad Aur*	Golden-eyed Duck
Smew	*Lleian Wen*	White Nun
Red-breasted Merganser	*Hwyaden Frongoch*	Red-breasted Duck
Goosander	*Hwyaden Ddanheddog*	Toothed Duck
	Hwyadwydd Gyffredin	Common Goose-duck
(European) Honey Buzzard	*Bod y Mêl*	Honey Buzzard
Red Kite	*Barcud*	Kite
White-tailed Eagle	*Eryr y Môr*	Sea Eagle
Marsh Harrier	*Bod y Gwerni*	Marsh Harrier
	Hebog y Gors	Marsh Hawk
Hen Harrier	*Bod Tinwen*	White-bottomed Buzzard
Montagu's Harrier	*Bod Montagu*	Montagu's Buzzard
(Northern) Goshawk	*Gwalch Marth*	Wonder Hawk or Fear Hawk
(Eurasian) Sparrowhawk	*Gwalch Glas*	Blue Hawk
	Corwalch	Little Hawk
(Common) Buzzard	*Bwncath* (south Wales)	Buzzard
	Boda	Buzzard
Rough-legged Buzzard	*Bod Bacsiog*	Hairy-legged Buzzard
Golden Eagle	*Eryr Euraid*	Golden Eagle
Osprey	*Gwalch y Pysgod*	Fish Hawk
(Common) Kestrel	*Cudyll Coch*	Red Falcon
Merlin	*Cudyll Bach*	Little Kestrel
Hobby	*Hebog yr Ehedydd*	Lark Hawk
Peregrine Falcon	*Hebog Tramor*	Overseas Hawk or Travelling Hawk
Red Grouse (Willow Ptarmigan)	*Grugiar*	Heather Hen
Black Grouse	*Grugiar Ddu*	Black Heather Hen
Red-legged Partridge	*Petrisen Goesgoch*	Red-legged Partridge
Grey Partridge	*Petrisen*	Partridge
(Common) Quail	*Sofliar*	Stubble Hen
	Cwâl (south-west Wales)	corruption of 'Quail'
(Common) Pheasant	*Ffesant*	corruption of 'Pheasant'
Water Rail	*Rhegen y Dŵr*	Water Crake
Spotted Crake	*Rhegen Fraith*	Spotted Crake
Corncrake (Corn Crake)	*Rhegen y Ŷd*	Corn Crake

COMMON NAME	WELSH NAME	TRANSLATION
Corncrake (Corn Crake)	*Rygar-rug*	corruption of Rhegyn-Rug, Rye Crake
(Common) Moorhen	*Iâr Ddŵr*	Water Hen
(Common) Coot	*Cwtiar*	Short Hen
Common Crane	*Garan*	Crane (also used for a boy's name, as in Garan Evans, rugby player)
(Eurasian) Oystercatcher	*Pioden y Môr*	Sea Magpie
(Pied) Avocet	*Cambig*	Bent Bill
Little Ringed Plover (Little Plover)	*Cwtiad Torchog Bach*	Little Collared Plover
Ringed Plover	*Cwtiad Torchog*	Collared Plover
(Eurasian) Dotterel	*Hutan y Mynydd*	Mountain Fool
(European) Golden Plover	*Cwtiad Aur*	Golden Plover
Grey Plover	*Cwtiad Llwyd*	Grey Plover
(Northern) Lapwing	*Cornchwiglen*	(Bird with a) Sharp, horn-like call; possibly also onomatopoeic
	Hen Het (north Wales)	Old Hat
(Red) Knot	*Pibydd yr Aber*	Estuary Piper
Sanderling	*Pibydd y Tywod*	Sand Piper
Little Stint	*Pibydd Bach*	Little Piper
Curlew Sandpiper	*Pibydd Cambig*	Bent-billed Piper
Purple Sandpiper	*Pibydd Du*	Black Piper
Dunlin	*Pibydd y Mawn*	Peat Piper
Ruff	*Pibydd Torchog*	Collared Piper
	Paffiwr	Boxer
Jack Snipe	*Gïach Bach*	Little Snipe
(Common) Snipe	*Gïach*	Snipe; onomatopoeic
(Eurasian) Woodcock	*Cyffylog*	Bird of the Tree Trunk
Black-tailed Godwit	*Rhostog Gynffonddu*	Black-tailed Fen Bird
Bar-tailed Godwit	*Rhostog Gynffonfrith*	Speckled-tailed Fen Bird
Whimbrel	*Coegylfinir*	Sham Curlew
(Eurasian) Curlew	*Gylfinir*	corruption of Gylfinhir, Long Bill
Spotted Redshank	*Pibydd Coesgoch Mannog*	Upright or Tall Redshank
(Common) Redshank	*Pibydd Coesgoch*	Red-legged Piper
(Common) Greenshank	*Pibydd Coeswerdd*	Green-legged Piper
Green Sandpiper	*Pibydd Gwyrdd*	Green Piper
Wood Sandpiper	*Pibydd y Graean*	Gravel Piper
Common Sandpiper	*Pibydd y Dorlan*	Riverbank Piper
(Ruddy) Turnstone	*Cwtiad y Traeth*	Beach Plover
Pomarine Skua	*Sgiwen Frech*	Spotted Skua
Arctic Skua	*Sgiwen y Gogledd*	Northern Skua
Long-tailed Skua	*Sgiwen Lostfain*	Slender-tailed Skua
Great Skua	*Sgiwen Fawr*	Great Skua
Little Gull	*Gwylan Fechan*	Little Gull
Sabine's Gull	*Gwylan Sabine*	Sabine's Gull
Black-headed Gull	*Gwylan Benddu*	Black-headed Gull
Common Gull (Mew Gull)	*Gwylan y Gweunydd*	Moor Gull
Lesser Black-backed Gull	*Gwylan Gefnddu Leiaf*	Lesser Black-backed Gull
Herring Gull	*Gwylan y Penwaig*	Herring Gull
Iceland Gull	*Gwylan yr Arctig*	Arctic Gull
Glaucous Gull	*Gwylan y Gogledd*	Northern Gull
Great Black-backed Gull	*Gwylan Gefnddu Fwyaf*	Great Black-backed Gull

COMMON NAME	WELSH NAME	TRANSLATION
(Black-legged) Kittiwake	*Gwylan Goesddu*	Black-legged Gull
	Gwylan Gernyw	Cornish Gull
	Gwylan Dribys	Three-toed Gull
Sandwich Tern	*Morwennol Bigddu*	Black-billed Sea-swallow
Roseate Tern	*Morwennol Wridog*	Rosy Sea-swallow
Common Tern	*Morwennol Gyffredin*	Common Sea-swallow
Arctic Tern	*Morwennol y Gogledd*	Northern Sea-swallow
Little Tern	*Morwennol Fechan*	Little Sea-swallow
Black Tern	*Corswennol Ddu*	Black Marsh-swallow
(Common) Guillemot	*Gwylog*	Guillemot; possibly 'one that whirls about'
Razorbill	*Llurs*	no literal translation; possibly onomatopoeic
Black Guillemot	*Gwylog Ddu*	Black Guillemot
Little Auk	*Carfil Bach*	Little Auk
	Gwalch y Penwaig	Herring Hawk
(Atlantic) Puffin	*Pâl*	no literal translation
	Cywion Esgob	Bishop's Chicks
Rock Dove (Rock Pigeon)	*Colomen y Graig*	Rock Dove
Feral Pigeon	*Colomen Ddôf*	Tame Dove
Stock Dove (Stock Pigeon)	*Colomen Wyllt*	Wild Dove
Woodpigeon (Wood Pigeon)	*Ysguthan*	no literal translation
(Eurasian) Collared Dove	*Turtur Dorchog*	Collared Turtle Dove
(European) Turtle Dove	*Turtur*	onomatopoeic
(Common) Cuckoo	*Cog*	although one-syllabled, possibly onomatopoeic, related to Irish *cuach* and Old Norse *gaukr*, representing the two-note call
Barn Owl	*Tylluan Wen*	White Owl
Little Owl	*Tylluan Fach*	Little Owl
Tawny Owl	*Tylluan Frech*	Speckled Owl
Long-eared Owl	*Tylluan Gorniog*	Horned Owl
Short-eared Owl	*Tylluan Glustiog*	Eared Owl
(European) Nightjar	*Troellwr*	Spinner
(Common) Swift	*Gwennol Ddu*	Black Swallow
(Common) Kingfisher	*Glas y Dorlan*	Blue Riverbank (Bird)
Hoopoe	*Copog*	Crested (Bird)
Wryneck	*Pengam*	Crooked Head
Green Woodpecker	*Cnocell Werdd*	Green Knocker
Great Spotted Woodpecker	*Cnocell Fraith Fwyaf*	Great Spotted Knocker
Lesser Spotted Woodpecker	*Cnocell Fraith Leiaf*	Lesser Spotted Knocker
Woodlark (Wood Lark)	*Ehedydd y Coed*	Wood Lark
Skylark (Sky Lark)	*Ehedydd*	Lark (*Ehedydd* is literally 'Flier')
Shore Lark (Horned Lark)	*Ehedydd y Traeth*	Beach Lark
Sand Martin	*Gwennol y Glennydd*	Bank Swallow
(Barn) Swallow	*Gwennol*	Swallow
House Martin	*Gwennol y Bondo*	Eaves Swallow
Tree Pipit	*Corhedydd y Coed*	Little Tree Lark
Meadow Pipit	*Corhedydd y Waun*	Little Meadow Lark
Rock Pipit	*Corhedydd y Graig*	Little Rock Lark
Water Pipit	*Corhedydd y Dŵr*	Little Water Lark

COMMON NAME	WELSH NAME	TRANSLATION
Yellow Wagtail	*Siglen Felen*	Yellow Wagger
Grey Wagtail	*Siglen Lwyd*	Grey Wagger
Pied Wagtail (Pied/White Wagtail)	*Siglen Fraith*	Pied Wagger
(Bohemian) Waxwing	*Cynffon Sidan*	Silk Tail
(White-throated) Dipper	*Bronwen y Dŵr*	White-breasted Water (Bird)
(Winter) Wren	*Dryw*	Wren
Dunnock (Hedge Accentor)	*Llwyd y Gwrych*	Grey Hedge (Bird)
(European) Robin	*Robin Goch*	Red Robin
(Common) Nightingale	*Eos*	no literal translation
Black Redstart	*Tingoch Du*	Black Red-tail
(Common) Redstart	*Tingoch*	Red-tail
Whinchat	*Crec yr Eithin*	Gorse Chat; *Crec* is onomatopoeic
Stonechat	*Clochdar y Cerrig*	Stone Clucker
(Northern) Wheatear	*Tinwen y Garn*	White-rumped Cairn (Bird)
Ring Ouzel	*Mwyalchen y Mynydd*	Mountain Blackbird
Blackbird	*Aderyn Du*	Black Bird
	Mwyalchen	no literal translation
Fieldfare	*Socan Eira*	possibly Little Snow Gaiters or Snow Lover
Song Thrush	*Bronfraith*	Speckled Breast
Redwing	*Coch dan Aden*	Red Underwing
Mistle Thrush	*Brych y Coed*	Spotted Wood (Bird)
Cetti's Warbler	*Telor Cetti*	Cetti's Warbler
(Common) Grasshopper Warbler	*Troellwr Bach*	Little Spinner
Sedge Warbler	*Telor yr Hesg*	Sedge Warbler
(Eurasian) Reed Warbler	*Telor y Cyrs*	Bog Warbler
Marsh Warbler	*Telor y Gwerni*	Marsh Warbler
Dartford Warbler	*Telor Dartford*	Dartford Warbler
Lesser Whitethroat	*Llwydfron Fach*	Little Grey-breasted (Bird)
(Common) Whitethroat	*Llwydfron*	Grey-breasted (Bird)
Garden Warbler	*Telor yr Ardd*	Garden Warbler
Blackcap	*Telor Penddu*	Black-headed Warbler
Wood Warbler	*Telor y Coed*	Wood Warbler
(Common) Chiffchaff	*Siff-saff*	onomatopoeic
Willow Warbler	*Telor yr Helyg*	Willow Warbler
Goldcrest	*Dryw Eurben*	Golden-headed Wren
Firecrest	*Dryw Penfflamgoch*	Flame-red-headed Wren
Spotted Flycatcher	*Gwybedog Mannog*	Upright or Tall Flycatcher
Red-breasted Flycatcher	*Gwybedog Brongoch*	Red-breasted Flycatcher
Pied Flycatcher	*Gwybedog Brith*	Pied Flycatcher
Bearded Tit	*Titw Barfog*	Bearded Tit
Long-tailed Tit	*Titw Gynffon-hir*	Long-tailed Tit
Marsh Tit	*Titw'r Wern*	Marsh Tit
Willow Tit	*Titw'r Helyg*	Willow Tit
Coal Tit	*Titw Penddu*	Black-headed Tit
	Llygoden y Derw	Oak Mouse
Blue Tit	*Titw Tomos Las*	Blue Tom Tit
	Glas Bach y Wal	Little Blue Wall (Bird)
	Gwas y Dryw	Wren's Servant
Great Tit	*Titw Mawr*	Great Tit
(Wood) Nuthatch	*Delor y Cnau*	Nut Warbler

COMMON NAME	WELSH NAME	TRANSLATION
(Eurasian) Treecreeper	*Dringwr Bach*	Little Climber
	Aderyn Penbawd	Thumb-tip Bird (possibly from its small size, as in Tom Thumb)
(Eurasian) Golden Oriole	*Euryn*	Gold Jewel
Red-backed Shrike	*Cigydd Cefngoch*	Red-backed Butcher
Great Grey Shrike	*Cigydd Mawr*	Great Butcher
(Eurasian) Jay	*Ysgrech y Coed*	Wood Screamer
(Black-billed) Magpie	*Pioden*	Magpie
(Red-billed) Chough	*Brân Goesgoch*	Red-legged Crow
(Eurasian) Jackdaw	*Jac-y-do*	onomatopoeic
Rook	*Ydfran*	Corn Crow
Carrion Crow	*Brân Dyddyn*	Small-farm Crow
Hooded Crow	*Brân Lwyd*	Grey Crow
(Common) Raven	*Cigfran*	Meat Crow
(Common) Starling	*Drudwy*	Precious Egg? Chatterer?
	Drudwen	Brave Bird?
House Sparrow	*Aderyn y Tô*	Roof Bird
(Eurasian) Tree Sparrow	*Golfan y Mynydd*	Mountain Sparrow
Chaffinch	*Ji-binc*	onomatopoeic
Brambling	*Pinc y Mynydd*	Mountain 'Pinc' (*Pinc* is an archaic onomatopoeic name for Chaffinch)
(European) Greenfinch	*Llinos Werdd*	Green Linnet
(European) Goldfinch	*Nico*	no literal translation
(European) Siskin	*Pila Gwyrdd*	Green Garment
(Common) Linnet	*Llinos*	Linnet (Llinos is also a very common girl's name in Wales)
Twite	*Llinos y Mynydd*	Mountain Linnet
Lesser Redpoll	*Llinos Bengoch*	Red-headed Linnet
Common Crossbill	*Gylfin Groes*	Crossbill
	Croesbig	Crossbill
(Common) Bullfinch	*Coch y Berllan*	Red Orchard (Bird)
Hawfinch	*Gylfinbraff*	Stout Bill
Lapland Bunting (Lapland Longspur)	*Bras y Gogledd*	Fat Northern (Bird)
Snow Bunting	*Bras yr Eira*	Fat Snow (Bird)
Yellowhammer	*Bras Melyn*	Fat Yellow (Bird)
Cirl Bunting	*Bras Ffrainc*	Fat French (Bird)
Ortolan Bunting	*Bras y Gerddi*	Fat Garden (Bird)
Reed Bunting	*Bras y Cyrs*	Fat Reed (Bird)
Corn Bunting	*Bras yr Ŷd*	Fat Corn (Bird)

Select bibliography

All the books are published in London unless otherwise stated.

Addison, J. and Hillhouse, C., *Treasury of Bird Lore*, André Deutsch, 1998.

Allen, Brigid, *Food: An Oxford Anthology*, Oxford University Press, Oxford, 1994.

Anon., *The Book of Home Pets*, S. O. Beeton, 1861.

Apperson, G. L. (ed.), *The Wordsworth Dictionary of Proverbs*, Wordsworth, Ware, 1993.

Aristophanes, *The Birds*, translated by K. McLeish, Methuen, 1993.

Armstrong, Edward, *The Wren*, Collins, 1955.

——, *The Folklore of Birds: An Enquiry into the Origin and Distribution of some Magico-Religious Traditions*, Collins, 1958.

Aubrey, John, *Remaines of Gentilisme and Judaisme*, edited by John Buchanan-Brown, Centaur, Fontwell, 1972.

Axell, Herbert, *Of Birds and Men*, The Book Guild, Lewes, 1992.

Baker, J. A., *The Peregrine*, Penguin, Harmondsworth, 1976.

Bannerman, David, *Birds of the British Isles Vols 1–12*, Oliver & Boyd, Edinburgh, 1953–63.

Barber, Richard (ed.), *British Myths and Legends*, Folio, 1998.

Barber, Theodore X., *The Human Nature of Birds*, Bookman, Melbourne, 1993.

Baxter, Evelyn, and Rintoul, Leonora, *The Birds of Scotland Vol. 1*, Oliver & Boyd, Edinburgh, 1953.

Beebe, William, *A Monograph of the Pheasants*, 4 vols, Dover, 1990.

Beeton, Isabella, *Household Management*, Ward Locke, 1901.

Bewick, Thomas, *Selections from A History of British Birds*, Paddington Press, 1976.

Birkhead, Mike and Perrins, Christopher, *The Mute Swan*, Croom Helm, Beckenham, 1986.

Birkhead, Tim, *The Magpies*, Poyser, Calton, 1991.

——, *The Red Canary*, Weidenfeld & Nicolson, 2003.

Bishop, Billy, *Cley Marsh and its Birds*, Bydell Press, Woodbridge, 1983.

Boag, David, *The Kingfisher*, Blandford, 1988.

Bosworth Smith, R., *Bird Life and Bird Lore*, John Murray, 1905.

Bromhall, Derek, *Devil Birds*, Hutchinson, 1980.

Brown, Leslie, *British Birds of Prey*, Collins, 1979.

Brown, P. E. and Davies, M. G., *Reed-Warblers*, Foy, East Moseley, 1949.

Brown, Philip, *Birds of Prey*, André Deutsch, 1964.

——, and Waterston, George, *The Return of the Osprey*, Collins, 1962.

Brown, W. J. *The Gods Had Wings*, Constable, 1936.

Browne, Sir Thomas, *The Works of Sir Thomas Browne, Vulgar Errors*, Vol. 1, Henry Bohn, 1852.

——, *Notes and Letters on the Natural History of Norfolk*, Jarrolds, 1902.

——The Works of Sir Thomas Browne, Vulgar Errors, Vol. 1, Henry Bohn, 1852.

Buxton, John, *The Redstart*, Collins, 1950.

Byers, Clive, Olsson, Urban and Curson, John, *Buntings and Sparrows*, Pica Press, Mountfield, 1995.

Byrkjedal, Ingvar and Thompson, D. B. A., *Tundra Plovers*, Poyser, 1998.

Cade, Tom, *The Falcons of the World*, Comstock/Cornell University Press, New York, 1982.

Chance, Edgar, *The Cuckoo's Secret*, Sidgwick & Jackson, 1922.

——, *The Truth About the Cuckoo*, Country Life, 1940.

Chapman, Abel, *Bird-Life of the Borders*, Gurney and Jackson, 1907.

Chapman, Anthony, *The Hobby*, Arlequin, Chelmsford, 1999.

Clement, Peter, Harris, Alan and Davis, John, *Finches and Sparrows*, Helm, 1993.

Conder, Peter, *The Wheatear*, Christopher Helm, Bromley, 1989.

Cook, A. B., *Zeus: A Study in Ancient Religion Vols 1–3*. Cambridge University Press, Cambridge, 1914–40.

Coombs, Franklin, *The Crows: A Study of the Corvids of Europe*, Batsford, 1978.

Cramp, S., Simmons, K. and Perrins, C., *Handbook of the Birds of Europe, the Middle East and North Africa* Vols 1–9, Oxford University Press, Oxford, 1977–95.

Cunningham, Peter (ed.), *The Works of Oliver Goldsmith* Vol. 4, John Murray, 1878.

Davies, N. B., *Cuckoos, Cowbirds and Other Cheats*, Poyser, 2000.

de Gubernatis, Angelo, *Zoological Mythology* Vol. 2, Trubner, 1872.

de Kay, Charles, *Bird Gods of Ancient Europe*, Harry Allenson, 1898.

Diamond, A. W. and Filion, F. L., *The Value of Birds*, International Council for Bird Preservation, Cambridge, 1987.

Dixon, Charles, *Lost and Vanishing Birds*, John Macqueen, 1898.

Donald, Paul, *The Skylark*, Poyser, 2004.

Douglas, Norman, *Birds and Beasts of the Greek Anthology*, Minerva, 1974.

Ehrlich, Paul R., Dobkin, David S. and Wheye, Daryl, *The Birdwatcher's Handbook*, Oxford University Press, Oxford, 1994.

Ekwall, Eilert, *The Oxford Dictionary of English Place-Names*, Oxford University Press, Oxford, 1960.

Elphick, Jonathan, *A Guide Book to British Birds*, BBC, 1997.

Ennion, Eric, *The British Bird*, Oxford University Press, Oxford, 1943.

——, *The Lapwing*, Methuen, 1949.

——, *The Living Birds of Eric Ennion*, Gollancz, 1982.

Feare, Chris, *The Starling*, Oxford University Press, Oxford, 1984.

——, *The Starling*, Shire Books, Aylesbury, 1985.

Ferguson-Lees, James and Christie, David, *Raptors of the World*, Helm, 2001.

Fisher, James, *The Fulmar*, Collins, 1952.

——, *The Shell Bird Book*, Ebury Press and Michael Joseph, 1966.

—— and Lockley, Ronald, *Sea-Birds*, Collins, 1954.

Fitter, Richard, *London's Natural History*, Collins, 1945.

——, *London's Birds*, Collins, 1949.

Flegg, Jim (ed.), *A Notebook of Birds 1907–1980*, Macmillan, 1981.

——, *The Puffin*, Shire Books, Aylesbury, 1985.

Frazer, James, *The Golden Bough*, Wordsworth, Ware, 1993.

Frohawk, F. W., *British Birds with their Nest and Eggs*, Vols 2 & 3, Brumby and Clarke, 1896–8.

Fuller, Errol, *Extinct Birds*, Viking/Rainbird, 1987.

——, *The Great Auk*, self-published, Southborough, 1999.

Furness, Robert, *The Skuas*, Poyser, Calton, 1987.

Gaskell, Jeremy, *Who Killed the Greak Auk?*, Oxford University Press, Oxford, 2000.

Gaston, Anthony and Jones, Ian, *The Auks*, Oxford University Press, Oxford, 1998.

Gibbons, David, Reid, James and Chapman, Robert, *The New Atlas of Breeding Birds in Britain and Ireland: 1988–1991*, Poyser, 1993.

Gibson-Hill, C. A., *British Sea Birds*, Witherby, 1947.

Glegg, William, *A History of the Birds of Middlesex*, Witherby, 1935.

Goodwin, Derek, *Crows of the World*, British Museum (Natural History), 1976

——, *Birds of Man's World*, British Museum (Natural History), 1978.

——, *Pigeons and Doves of the World*, British Museum (Natural History), 1983.

Gordon, R. K., (ed.), *Anglo-Saxon Poetry*, Dent, 1934.

Gordon, Seton, *Days with the Golden Eagle*, Williams and Norgate, 1927.

——, *The Golden Eagle*, Collins, 1958.

Gosler, Andrew, *The Great Tit*, Hamlyn, 1993.

Gotch, A. F., *Latin Names Explained*, Cassell, 1995.

Graves, Robert, *The White Goddess*, Faber & Faber, 1948.

Gray, Phil, *The Washlanders*, Terence Dalton, Lavenham, 1990.

Green, Jonathon, *Slang Down the Ages*, Kyle Cathie, 1993.

——, *The Cassell Dictionary of Slang*, Cassell, 1998.

Greenoak, Francesca, *British Birds: Their Folklore, Names and Literature*, Helm, 1997.

Grey, Edward, *The Charm of Birds*, Hodder & Stoughton, 1927.

Gurney, J. H., *Early Annals of Ornithology*, Paul Minet, Chicheley, 1972.

Hagemeijer, W. J. M. and Blair, M., *The EBCC Atlas of European Breeding Birds*, Poyser, 1997.

Halle, Louis, *The Storm Petrel and the Owl of Athena*, Princeton University Press, Princeton, NJ, 1970.

Hancock, James and Elliott, Hugh, *The Herons of the World*, London Editions, 1978.

Hanks, Patrick and Hodges, Flavia, *A Dictionary of Surnames*, Oxford University Press, Oxford, 1990.

Hansell, Peter and Jean, *Dovecotes*, Shire, Princes Risborough, 2001.

Hare, C. E., *Bird Lore*, Country Life, 1952.

Harrap, Simon and Quinn, David, *Tits, Nuthatches and Treecreepers*, Helm, 1996.

Harris, R., *Picus Who Is Also Zeus*, Cambridge University Press, Cambridge, 1916.

Harrison, Colin, *The History of the Birds of Britain*, Collins, 1988.

Harrison, T. P., *They Tell of Birds*, Greenwood Press, Westport, CT, 1956.

Hart-Davis, Duff, *Fauna Britannica*, Weidenfeld & Nicolson, 2002.

Harting, J., *The Birds of Shakespeare*, John Van Voorst, 1871.

Hedges, John, *Tomb of the Eagles: A Window on Stone Age Tribal Britain*, John Murray, 1984.

Heinrich, Bernd, *Ravens in Winter*, Barrie & Jenkins, 1990.

Holloway, Simon, *The Historical Atlas of Breeding Birds in Britain and Ireland 1875–1900*, Poyser, 1996.

Hope, Annette, *Londoners' Larder: English Cuisine from Chaucer to the Present*, Mainstream, 1990.

Howard, Henry Eliot, *The British Warblers*, Vol. 1–2, R. H. Porter, 1907–14.

Hudson, W. H., *Birds in London*, Longmans Green, 1898.

——, *Birds and Man*, Duckworth, 1924.

——, *Adventures Among Birds*, Dent, 1951.

——, *Nature in Downland*, Dent, 1951.

Hull, Robin, *Scottish Birds: Culture and Tradition*, Mercat Press, Edinburgh, 2001.

Hulme, F. E., *Natural History Lore and Legend*, Bernard Quaritch, 1895.

Hume, Rob, *The Common Tern*, Hamlyn, 1993.

—— and Pearson, Bruce, *Seabirds*, Hamlyn, 1993.

Hutchinson, Clive, *Birds in Ireland*, Poyser, Calton, 1989.

Hutton, Ronald, *Stations of the Sun: A History of the Ritual Year in Britain*, Oxford University Press, Oxford, 1996.

Ingersoll, Ernest, *Birds in Legend, Fable and Folklore*, Longmans Green, 1923.

Johnsgard, Paul, *The Grouse of the World*, University of Nebraska Press, Lincoln, NE, 1983.

——, *The Avian Brood Parasites*, Oxford University Press, Oxford, 1997.

Jones, P. E., *The Worshipful Company of Poulterers of the City of London: A Short History*, Oxford University Press, Oxford, 1965.

Jubes, Gertrude, *Dictionary of Mythology, Folklore and Symbols*, The Scarecrow Press, New York, 1961.

Kear, Janet, *Man and Wildfowl*, Poyser, 1990.

Kirke-Swann, H., *A Dictionary of English and Folk-Names of British Birds*, E. P. Publishing, Wakefield, 1977.

Lack, David, *Robin Redbreast*, Clarendon Press, Oxford, 1950.

——, *Swifts in a Tower*, Methuen, 1956.

——, *The Life of the Robin*, Witherby, 1976.

Lack, Peter, *The Atlas of Wintering Birds in Britain and Ireland*, Poyser, Calton, 1986.

Lambert, Robert (ed.), *Species History in Scotland*, Scottish Cultural Press, Edinburgh, 1998.

Lawrence, Elizabeth, *Hunting the Wren: Transformation of Bird to Symbol*, University of Tennessee Press, Knoxville, TN, 1997.

Lever, Christopher, *The Naturalized Animals of the British Isles*, Paladin, 1979.

——, *Naturalized Birds of the World*, Longman, Harlow, 1987.

Linsell, Stewart, *Hickling Broad and its Wildlife*, Terence Dalton, Lavenham, 1990.

Lockley, R. M., *Shearwaters*, Dent, 1942.

——, *Flight of the Storm Petrel*, David & Charles, Newton Abbot, 1983.

Lockwood, W. B., *The Oxford Dictionary of British Bird Names*, Oxford University Press, Oxford, 1993.

Love, John, *The return of the Sea Eagle*, Cambridge University Press, Cambridge, 1983.

——, *Eagles*, Whittet Books, 1989.

Lovegrove, Roger, Williams, Graham and Williams, Iolo, *Birds in Wales*, Poyser, 1994.

Lowe, Frank, *The Heron*, Collins, 1954.

Loyd, Lewis R. W., *Bird Facts and Fallacies*, Hutchinson, undated.

Lutwack, L., *Birds in Literature*, University of Florida Press, Gainesville, FL, 1994.

Mabey, Richard, *Whistling in the Dark: In Pursuit of the Nightingale*, Sinclair-Stevenson, 1993.

——, *Flora Britannica*, Chatto & Windus, 1996.

Macgillivray, William, *A History of British Birds, Indigenous and Migratory*, Scott, Webster and Geary, 1837.

McKelvie, Colin, *A Future for Game?*, George Allen & Unwin, 1985.

Macpherson, H. A., *A History of Fowling*, David Douglas, Edinburgh, 1897.

Madge, Steve and Burn, Hilary, *Wildfowl*, Christopher Helm, 1988.

—— and McGowan, Phil, *Pheasants, Partridges and Grouse*, Christopher Helm, 2002.

Marples, George and Anne, *Sea Terns*, Country Life, 1934.

Martin, Brian, *Sporting Birds of the British Isles*, David & Charles, Newton Abbot, 1984.

——, *The Glorious Grouse: A Natural and Unnatural History*, David & Charles, Newton Abbot, 1990.

——, *Wildfowl of the British Isles and North-West Europe*, David & Charles, Newton Abbot, 1993.

Martin, Martin, *A Description of the Western Islands of Scotland*, (with *A Voyage to St Kilda*), Birlinn, Edinburgh, 1999.

Mason, C. F., *The Blackcap*, Hamlyn, 1995.

Mayhew, Henry, *London Labour and the London Poor* Vols 1–4, Charles Griffin, 1861–2.

Mead, Chris, *Robins*, Whittet, 1984.

——, *Owls*, Whittet, 1987.

——, *The State of the Nation's Birds*, Whittet, Stowmarket, 2000.

Mearns, Barbara and Richard, *Biographies for Birdwatchers*, Academic Press, 1988.

Meinertzhagen, Richard, *Pirates and Predators*, Oliver & Boyd, 1959.

Morus, R. L., *Animals, Men and Myths*, Gollancz, 1953.

Moss, Stephen, *Birds and Weather*, Hamlyn, 1995.

Mountfort, Guy, *The Hawfinch*, Collins, 1957.

Murton, R. K., *The Wood Pigeon*, Collins, 1965.

——, *Man and Birds*, Collins, 1971.

Nelson, Bryan, *The Gannet*, Poyser, Berkhamsted, 1978.

Nethersole-Thompson, Desmond, *The Greenshank*, Collins, 1951.

——, *The Snow Bunting*, Oliver & Boyd, 1966.

——, *The Dotterel*, Collins, 1973.

——, *Pine Crossbills*, Poyser, Berkhamsted, 1976.

—— and Maimie, *Greenshanks*, Poyser, Calton, 1979.

——, *Waders: their Breeding, Haunts and Watchers*, Poyser, Calton, 1986.

Nethersole-Thompson, Desmond and Watson, Adam, *The Cairngorms*, Collins, 1974.

Newton, Ian, *Finches*, Collins, 1985.

——, *The Sparrowhawk*, Poyser, Calton, 1986.

Nicholson, E. M., *Birds and Men*, Collins, 1951.

Norman, David, *The Fieldfare*, Hamlyn, 1994.

Ogilvie, M. and Pearson, B., *Wildfowl*, Hamlyn, 1994.

Palin, Steve, *A Dissimulation of Birds*, Minerva, 1998.

Palmer, Phil, *First for Britain and Ireland*, Arlequin Press, Chelmsford, 2000.

Parmelee, Alice, *All the Birds of the Bible: Their Stories, Identification and Meaning*, Lutterworth Press, 1959.

Percy, Lord William, *Three Studies in Bird Character: Bitterns, Herons and Water Rails*, Country Life Press, 1951.

Perrins, Chris, *British Tits*, Collins, 1979.

Perry, Kenneth, *The Irish Dipper*, privately published, 1986.

Pliny, *Natural History*, Books 8–11, translated by H. Rackham, Harvard University Press, Cambridge, MA, 1997.

Pollard, John, *Birds in Greek Life and Myth*, Thames & Hudson, 1977.

Poole, Alan, *Ospreys: A Natural and Unnatural History*, Cambridge University Press, Cambridge, 1989.

Rackham, Oliver, *The History of the British Countryside*, Dent, 1986.

Rankin, Niall, *Haunts of British Divers*, Collins, 1947.

Ratcliffe, Derek, *The Peregrine Falcon*, Poyser, Calton, 1980.

——, *Bird life of mountain and upland*, Cambridge University Press, Cambridge, 1990.

——, *The Raven*, Poyser, 1997.

Read, Mike, King, Martin and Allsop, Jake, *The Robin*, Blandford, 1992.

—— and Allsop, Jake, *The Barn Owl*, Blandford, 1994.

Richmond, Kenneth, *British Birds of Prey*, Lutterworth, 1959.

Ritchie, James, *The Influence of Man on Animal Life in Scotland*, Cambridge University Press, Cambridge, 1920.

Robertson, Peter, *A Natural History of the Pheasant*, Swan-hill Press, Shrewsbury, 1997.

Rowland, Beryl, *Birds with Human Souls: A Guide to Bird Symbolism*, University of Tennessee Press, Knoxville, TN, 1978.

Savage, Christopher, *The Mandarin Duck*, Adam and Charles Black, 1952.

Scott, Peter, *The Eye of the Wind*, Brockhampton, Leicester, 1968.

——, *The Swans*, Michael Joseph, 1972.

Sharrock, J. T. R., *The Atlas of Breeding Birds in Britain and Ireland*, Royser, Calton, 1976.

Shawyer, Colin, *The Barn Owl*, Arlequin, Chelmsford, 1998.

Simms, Eric, *The Public Life of the Street Pigeon*, Hutchinson, 1979.

——, *British Warblers*, Collins, 1985.

——, *British Larks, Pipits and Wagtails*, Collins, 1992.

Skutch, Alexander, *The Life of the Pigeon*, Cornell University Press, Ithaca, NY, 1991.

Smout, T. C., and Lambert, R. A., (eds), *Rothiemurchus: Nature and People on a Highland Estate 1500–2000*, Scottish Cultural Press, Dalkeith, 1999.

Snow, David, *A Study of Blackbirds*, British Museum (Natural History), 1988.

—— (ed.), *Birds, Discovery and Conservation*, Helm, Robertsbridge, 1992.

Spencer, Ken, The Lapwing in Britain, Brown, 1953.

Stevenson, Henry, *The Birds of Norfolk*, Vols 1–3, John Van Voorst and Gurney & Jackson, London, 1866–90.

Summers-Smith, J. Denis, *The House Sparrow*, Collins, 1963.

——, *The Sparrows*, Poyser, Calton, 1988.

Swainson, C., *The Folklore and Provincial Names of British Birds*, Llanerch Publishers, Felinfach, 1997.

Tapper, Stephen, *A Question of Balance, Game animals and their role in the British countryside*, Game Conservancy Trust, Fordingbridge, 1999.

Taylor, Barry and van Perlo, Ber, *Rails*, Pica Press, Mountfield, 1998.

Taylor, Kenny, *Puffins*, Whittet, 1993.

Taylor, Moss, Seago, Michael, Allard, Peter and Dorling, Don, *The Birds of Norfolk*, Pica Press, Mountfield, 1999.

Theophrastus, *Enquiry Into Plants and Minor Works on Odours and Weather Signs*, translated by Sir Arthur Hort, Heinemann, 1916.

Thomas, Keith, *Religion and the Decline of Magic*, Weidenfeld & Nicolson, 1997.

Ticehurst, Norman, *The Mute Swan in England*, Cleaver-Hulme, 1957.

Tickell, W. L. N., *Albatrosses*, Pica Press, Mountfield, 2000.

Tinbergen, Niko, *The Herring Gull's World*, Collins, 1953.

Tomkies, Mike, *Golden Eagle Years*, Heinemann, 1982.

Treleaven, R. B., *Peregrine*, Headland, Penzance, 1977.

Trodd, P. and Kramer, D., *The Birds of Bedfordshire*, Castlemead, Ware, 1991.

Tubbs, Colin, *The Buzzard*, David & Charles, Newton Abbott, 1974.

Tucker, Graham and Heath, Melanie, *Birds in Europe*, BirdLife International, Cambridge, 1994.

Turnbull, A. L., *Bird Music*, Faber & Faber, 1943.

Turner, Angela, *The Swallow*, Hamlyn, 1994.

Turner, William, *Turner on Birds*, Cambridge University Press, Cambridge, 1903.

Tyler, Stephanie and Ormerod, Steve, *The Dippers*, Poyser, 1994.

Vaughan, Richard, *Plovers*, Terence Dalton, Lavenham, 1980.

Vesey-Fitzgerald, Brian, *British Game*, Collins, 1946.

Village, Andrew, *The Kestrel*, Poyser, 1990.

——, *Falcons*, Whittett, 1992.

Vincent, J., *A Season of Birds*, Weidenfeld & Nicolson, 1980.

Walpole-Bond, John, *A History of Sussex Birds*, Vols 1–3, Witherby, 1938.

Watson, Donald, *The Hen Harrier*, Poyser, Berkhamsted, 1977.

Weinstein, K., *The Owl in Art, Mythology and Legend*, Grange, 1985.

Wentworth Thompson, D., *A Glossary of Greek Birds*, Clarendon Press, Oxford, 1895.

White, Gilbert, *The Natural History of Selborne*, edited by R. Kearton, Arrowsmith, 1924.

Williamson, Kenneth, *The Atlantic Islands*, Routledge & Kegan Paul, 1948.

Wilson, C. A., *Food and Drink in Britain from the Stone Age to Recent Times*, Constable, 1991.

Witherby, H. F., Jourdain, F. C. R., Ticehurst, Norman, and Tucker, Bernard, *The Handbook of British Birds*, Vols 1–5, Witherby, London, 1938–40.

Wood, C. A., and Fyfe, Marjorie (ed.), *Art of Falconry of Frederick II of Hohenstaufen*, Stanford University Press, Stanford, CT, 1969.

Wyllie, Ian, *The Cuckoo*, Batsford, 1981.

Yapp, Brunsdon, *Birds in Medieval Manuscripts*, British Library, 1980.

Yapp, W.B., *Birds and Woods*, Oxford University Press, 1962.

Yarrell, William, *A History of British Birds*, Vols 1–3, John Van Voorst, 1845.

Yeates, G. K., *The Life of the Rook*, Philip Alan, 1934.

Notes

Abbreviations

Where the full reference is included in the Select bibliography, only the author, title and page number(s) are listed below. When a title is not listed, the bibliographic details are given in full below. Several books and journals have been extensively used and are abbreviated to the following:

Bannerman – *Birds of the British Isles* (twelve volumes). Bannerman, 3:45 means volume three, page 45.
BB – *British Birds*
BS – *Bird Study*
Bull BOC – Bulletin of the British Ornithologists' Club
BWP – Birds of the Western Palearctic, S. Cramp et al. This is the more familiar title for the nine-volume *Handbook of the Birds of Europe, the Middle East and North Africa*. *BWP* 1:48 means volume one, page 48.
European Atlas – W. J. M. Hagemeijer and M. Blair, *The EBCC Atlas of European Breeding Birds*
Handbook – Harry Witherby et al., *The Handbook of British Birds* (five volumes)
HBW – Handbook of the Birds of the World
Historical Atlas – Simon Holloway, *The Historical Atlas of Breeding Birds in Britain and Ireland 1875–1900*
Lockwood – W. B. Lockwood, *The Oxford Dictionary of British Bird Names*
Migration Atlas – Chris Wernham et al., *The Migration Atlas: Movements of the Birds of Britain and Ireland*, Poyser, 2002
New Atlas – D. W. Gibbons, J. B. Reid and R. A. Chapman, *The New Atlas of Breeding Birds in Britain and Ireland: 1988–1991*
The Atlas – J. T. R. Sharrock, *The Atlas of Breeding Birds in Britain and Ireland*
Winter Atlas – Peter Lack, *The Atlas of Wintering Birds in Britain and Ireland*

Divers, *Gaviidae*

1   Chris Mead, *The State of the Nation's Birds*, page 122.
2   Colin Bibby, Peter Robinson and Emma Bland, *RSPB Conservation Review*, 4:22–6.
3   *BWP* 1:48.
4   *Handbook* 4:125.
5   *Handbook* 4:120.
6   *BWP* 1:59.
7   Eric Meek, Kirkwall, Orkney; Paul Harvey, Lerwick, Shetland.
8   Eric Meek with the assistance of Mary Bichan, Peter Leith, Sandy Scarth (Orkney mainland), Mike Cockram, Geordie Hewison, Ernest Miller (Eday), Terry Thomson, Jack Rendall (Hoy), Alec Harcus (Stronsay), Neil Rendall (Papa Westray), Sheila and Kenny Garson, Kenny Meason, Robert Wallace (Shapinsay), Herbert Mackenzie (South Ronaldsay), Alan Bews, Sam Harcus (Westray); Margaret Flaws (Wyre).

Hereafter listed as Eric Meek et al., Kirkwall, Orkney.
9   Edward Armstrong, *The Folklore of Birds*, pages 62–70.
10   Martin Martin, *A Description of the Western Islands of Scotland* (with *A Voyage to St Kilda*), page 53.
11   *Handbook* 4:113.
12   Seton Gordon, *The Immortal Isles*, Williams & Norgate, 1936, page 45.
13   A. F. Gotch, *Latin Names Explained*, page 186.

Grebes, *Podicipedidae*

1   D. D. Harber et al., *BB* 59:282–3.
2   F. R. Smith et al., *BB* 62:460.
3   Eric Ennion, *The Living Birds of Eric Ennion*, page 12.
4   Brian Tollitt, Manchester; Eric Meek et al., Kirkwall, Orkney.
5   Moss Taylor, Michael Seago, Peter Allard and Don Dorling, *The Birds of Norfolk*, page 100.
6   Brian Tollitt, Manchester.
7   Richard Barton, South Molton, Devon.
8   Henry Stevenson, *The Birds of Norfolk*, Vol. 3, pages 233–5.
9   T. H. Harrisson and P. A. D. Hollom, *BB* 26:106.
10   An error crept into the ornithological literature over the precise date of the first collection of great crested grebes for the 'fur' trade. A number of recent works (N. Rankin's *The Haunts of British Divers*, R. K. Murton's *Man and Birds*, and Tim Sharrock's *The Atlas of Breeding Birds in Britain and Ireland*) give 1857 as the starting date for the slaughter. All of them were presumably following T. H. Harrisson's and Phil Hollom's 'Great Crested Grebe Enquiry, 1931', *British Birds*, Vol. 26. The authors of the paper suggested that the commercial possibilities of British grebe fur were first realised in a letter to *The Zoologist* in July 1857 by Robert Strangeways. In fact the man's name was Richard Strangwayes and his letter was published in 1851. Thus, the wholesale reduction of the UK's great crested grebe population, which reached its nadir of under 50 pairs by 1860, took place over a period of nine years, not the three that is regularly asserted. See *The Zoologist*, Vol. 9, 1851, page 3209.
11   T. H. Harrisson and P. A. D. Hollom, *BB* 26:109–10.
12   T. H. Harrisson and P. A. D. Hollom, *BB* 26:62–5.
13   T. H. Harrisson and P. A. D. Hollom, *BB* 26:190.
14   Malcolm Falkus and John Gillingham (eds), *Historical Atlas of Britain*, Kingfisher, 1989, pages 210–11.
15   John Pugh, Frettenham, Norfolk.
16   Richard Chandler, *BB* 74:55–81.
17   Eric Ennion, *The Living Birds of Eric Ennion*, page 13.

18   George Humphreys, *Irish Birds*, 1:171–87.
19   C. V. Stoney and G. R. Humphreys, *BB* 24:173.

Albatrosses, *Diomedeidae*

1   W. L. N. Tickell, *Albatrosses*, page 358.
2   Eric Hosking and Bryan Sage, *Antarctic Wildlife*, Croom Helm, 1982, page 94.
3   James Fisher and Ronald Lockley, *Seabirds*, page 28.
4   Pat Morris, *The Linnean*, Vol. 17, no. 1, pages 15–16.
5   George Waterston, *BB* 61:23.
6   James Macdonald, *BB* 46:110–11.
7   George Waterston, *BB* 61:23.
8   Mike Pennington, Unst, Shetland.
9   Mike Rogers et al., *BB* 84:452.
10   George Waterston, *BB* 61:24.

Fulmars, Petrels and Shearwaters, *Procellariidae*

1   James Fisher, *The Fulmar*, page 468.
2   James Fisher, *The Fulmar*, page 239.
3   Moss Taylor, Michael Seago, Peter Allard and Don Dorling, *The Birds of Norfolk*, page 106.
4   Jonathan Elphick, London.
5   Eric Simms, South Witham, Lincolnshire.
6   Martin Martin, *A Description of the Western Islands of Scotland* (with *A Voyage to St Kilda*), page 172.
7   Martin Martin, *A Description of the Western Islands of Scotland* (with *A Voyage to St Kilda*), page 262.
8   James Fisher, *The Fulmar*, page 142.
9   Martin Martin, *A Description of the Western Islands of Scotland* (with *A Voyage to St Kilda*), page 256.
10   James Fisher, *The Fulmar*, page 137.
11   James Fisher, *The Fulmar*, page 142.
12   James Fisher, *The Fulmar*, pages 488–9.
13   Martin Martin, *A Description of the Western Islands of Scotland* (with *A Voyage to St Kilda*), pages 255–6.
14   James Fisher, *The Fulmar*, page 144.
15   *BWP* 1:123.
16   Cliff Waller, Blythburgh, Suffolk.
17   James Fisher, *The Fulmar*, pages 390–1.
18   Cliff Waller, Blythburgh, Suffolk.
19   John Love, *Eagles*, page 93.
20   James Fisher, *The Fulmar*, page 410.
21   James Fisher, *The Fulmar*, pages 418–19.
22   Bernard Zonfrillo, *BB* 78:350–1.
23   Alfred Newton, *The Zoologist*, 1852, pages 3691–8.
24   Barbara and Richard Mearns, *Biographies for Birdwatchers*, page 102.
25   *BWP* 1:134.
26   Richard Meinertzhagen, *Diaries*, Vol. 24, page 124.
27   Francis Roux and Christian Jouanin, *BB* 61:164–5.
28   Francis Roux and Christian Jouanin, *BB* 61:168.
29   R. G. Newell, *BB* 61:145–59.

30 *Handbook* 4:60–1.
31 David Saunders, Pembroke Dock, Pembrokeshire.
32 Ronald Lockley, *Shearwaters*, page 20.
33 David Saunders, Pembroke Dock, Pembrokeshire.
34 Ken Williamson, BS 20:310–11.
35 Sir John Sinclair (ed.), *The Old Statistical Account of Scotland*, Vol. 19. Orkney & Shetland, Walls & Flota, 1791–9, pages 352–4.
36 Hugh Macpherson, *A History of Fowling*, pages 476–7.
37 Hugh Macpherson, *A History of Fowling*, page 476.
38 Mike Pennington, Unst, Shetland.
39 Ronald Lockley, *Shearwaters*, page 147.
40 Max Nicholson, *BB* 46, supplement, page 3.
41 P. C. James, *BB* 79:28–33.

Storm-petrels, *Hydrobatidae*
1 *Handbook* 4:35.
2 Pete Davis, *BB* 50:89.
3 Pete Davis, *BB* 50:95.
4 Lockwood, page 115.
5 Lockwood, page 105.
6 Andy Stevenson, Bornish, South Uist.
7 Eric Simms, South Witham, Lincolnshire.
8 Charles Dixon, *British Seabirds*, Bliss, Sands and Foster, 1896, page 249.
9 *Handbook* 4:29–30.
10 Ronald Lockley, *Flight of the Storm Petrel*, page 111.
11 Stephen Moss, *Birds and Weather*, page 88.
12 Brett Westwood, Bristol.
13 Hugh Boyd, *BB* 47:137–63.
14 Mark Cubitt, *BB* 88:346.

Gannets, *Sulidae*
1 Lockwood, pages 143–4.
2 Dennis Claridge, Guisborough, Cleveland.
3 Bryan Nelson, *The Gannet*, page 222.
4 Ken Williamson, *BB* 41:26.
5 D. A. Butterworth, Morecambe, Lancashire.
6 R. F. Snook, *BB* 70:35.
7 Martin Martin, *A Description of the Western Islands of Scotland* (with *A Voyage to St Kilda*), page 172.
8 Colin Beckett, Eskbank, Midlothian.
9 Michael Thomas, Craigmore, Isle of Bute.
10 James Fisher, *The Shell Bird Book*, page 43.
11 Bryan Nelson, *The Gannet*, page 284.
12 Paul Harvey, Lerwick, Shetland.
13 Bryan Nelson, *The Gannet*, page 280.
14 Daniel Defoe, *A Tour Through the Whole Island of Great Britain*, Vol. 1, Dent, 1962, page 293.
15 Bryan Nelson, *The Gannet*, page 281.
16 James Ritchie, *The Influence of Man on Animal Life in Scotland*, page 147.
17 James Fisher and Ronald Lockley, *Seabirds*, page 94.
18 Eleanor Houston, *The Herald*, 15 September 2001, page 14.

Cormorants, *Phalacrocoracidae*
1 Alison Hunkin, Par, Cornwall.
2 Timothy Hallchurch, *BB* 94:145.

3 R. M. R. James and Rod Key, *BB* 94:436.
4 For an insight into attitudes among anglers during the late 1990s, see *Angling Times*, 4 December 1996; 25 December 1996 (an issue full of unchristian sentiments towards cormorants, despite the date); 8 January 1997; 22 January 1997; 12 August 1998.
5 Mike Marquiss and David Carss, *BTO News* 97:6–7.
6 Beryl Rowland, *Birds with Human Souls*, page 30.
7 Lord David Stuart, *BB* 41:194.
8 James McCallum, Wighton, Norfolk.
9 Frank Fraser Darling, *Island Years*, Bell, 1944, pages 120–1.
10 *New Atlas*, page 44.
11 Rob Hume, *Seabirds*, page 100.
12 Frank Fraser Darling, *Island Years*, Bell, 1944, page 124.
13 N. F. Ticehurst, *BB* 1:309–11.
14 *Historical Atlas*, page 60.
15 Thomas Bewick, *Selections from A History of British Birds*, page 325.
16 Paul Trodd and Dave Kramer, *The Birds of Bedfordshire*, page 42.
17 Mike Pennington, Unst, Shetland.

Pelicans, *Pelecanidae*
1 Sir Thomas Browne, *Notes and Letters on the Natural History of Norfolk*, page 16.
2 Tim Sharrock and James Ferguson-Lees, *BB* 61:47, 96.

Bitterns and Herons, *Ardeidae*
1 Gillian Gilbert, Sandy, Bedfordshire.
2 Claire Voisin, *The Herons of Europe*, Poyser, 1991, page 63.
3 Tim Melling, Shepley, Yorkshire.
4 Gwen Davies (ed.), *The Bird Notes Bedside Book*, no date, page 116.
5 In the House of Commons there have been four references to bitterns between 1996 and 2000. One of these was the maiden speech of the new Labour MP for Morecambe and Lunesdale, Geraldine Smith. In her eulogy to the constituency, she noted that 'It holds more than a quarter of the entire British breeding population of the bittern, one of our rarest and most threatened birds. On a clear day, the superb backdrop of the Lake District makes Morecambe bay one of the most picturesque areas in the world for bird watching.' Hansard, 10 July 1997: Column 1117.
6 The occurrence of the bittern in the Old Testament has become a matter of conjecture. It relies on three passages – Isaiah 14:23, Isaiah 34:11, and Zephaniah 2:14 – which deal respectively with the Lord's desecration of Babylon, Edom and Nineveh. In the Authorised Version the three passages are respectively:

I will also make it a possession for the bittern, and pools of water: and I will sweep it with the besom of destruction, saith the Lord of Hosts.

But the cormorant and the bittern shall possess it; the owl also and the raven shall dwell in it.

the bittern shall lodge in the upper lintels of it; their voice shall sing in the windows; desolation shall be in the thresholds.

However, in *The New English Bible* (1970) the bitterns are replaced in the three passages with bustards. This also alters the kind of desecration which the Lord of Hosts intended to visit on these cities, since bustards are desert-dwelling species. The occurrence of bitterns in the three places would imply God's more routine punishment with flood.
7 William Percy, *Three Studies in Bird Character*, pages 36–7.
8 P. E. Jones, *The Worshipful Company of Poulterers of the City of London*, pages 112–13.
9 Beryl Rowland, *Birds with Human Souls*, page 9.
10 Brigid Allen (ed.), *Food: An Oxford Anthology*, pages 273–7.
11 J. H. Gurney, *Early Annals of Ornithology*, page 87.
12 J. H. Gurney, *Early Annals of Ornithology*, page 69.
13 Sir Thomas Browne, *Notes and Letters on the Natural History of Norfolk*, page 6.
14 William Turner, *Turner on Birds*, page 41.
15 William Percy, *Three Studies in Bird Character*, page 19.
16 Thomas Bewick, *Selections from A History of British Birds*, page 201.
17 Gillian Gilbert, Sandy, Bedfordshire.
18 Moss Taylor, Michael Seago, Peter Allard and Don Dorling, *The Birds of Norfolk*, page 119.
19 Edward Armstrong, *The Folklore of Birds*, page 222.
20 Evelyn Baxter and Leonora Rintoul, *The Birds of Scotland*, Vol. 1, page 351.
21 Peter Cunningham, *The Works of Oliver Goldsmith*, Vol. 4, page 222.
22 Geoffrey Chaucer, *Wife of Bath's Tale*, Dent, 1978, lines 972–3.
23 Daniel Defoe, *A Tour Through the Whole Island of Great Britain*, Vol. 2, Dent, 1962, page 95.
24 Francesca Greenoak, *British Birds*, page 26.
25 Emma Turner, *BB* 5:91–3.
26 Billy Bishop, *Cley Marsh and its Birds*, page 49.
27 Geoff Welch, *Butterbump*, No. 3, 1998.
28 Ronald Lockley, *BB* 40:184.
29 Andrew Allport and David Carroll, *BB* 82:442–6.
30 Christopher Lever, *The Naturalized Animals of the British Isles*, page 251.
31 Christopher Lever, *The Naturalized Animals of the British Isles*, pages 255–6.
32 Malcolm Ogilvie et al., *BB* 92:177–8.
33 Robert Hudson, *BB* 65:424.
34 Mike Rogers et al., *BB* 76:480.
35 James Hancock and Hugh Elliot, *The Herons of the World*, page 174.
36 Derek Goodwin, *Birds of Man's World*, pages 42–3.
37 Derek Goodwin, *Birds of Man's World*, pages 43–4.
38 Jacques Franchimont, *BB* 86:17 and 90:385.
39 *Handbook* 3:144.

40 Leigh Lock and Kevin Cook, *BB* 91:273–80.
41 Anon., *BB* 4:60.
42 Paul Ehrlich, David Dobkin and Daryl Wheye, *The Birdwatcher's Handbook*, page 23.
43 Salim Ali and Dillon Ripley, *Handbook of the Birds of India and Pakistan*, compact edition, Oxford University Press, Oxford, 1983, page 19.
44 *HBW* 1:395–9; also James Hancock and Hugh Elliot, *The Herons of the World*, pages 34–5.
45 James Hancock and Hugh Elliott, *The Herons of the World*, page 35.
46 Frank Gribble, *BTO News* 241:4.
47 Evelyn Baxter and Leonora Rintoul, *The Birds of Scotland*, Vol. 1, page 343.
48 J. H. Gurney, *Early Annals of Ornithology*, page 235.
49 John Walpole-Bond, *A History of Sussex Birds*, Vol. 2, page 325; Sussex Ornithological Society, *Birds of Sussex*, page 125.
50 Alan Parker, Northwood Hills, Kent.
51 Frank Lowe, *The Heron*, page 150.
52 Brian Vesey-Fitzgerald, *British Game*, page 163; W. H. Hudson, *The Book of a Naturalist*, Hodder & Stoughton, 1919, page 91.
53 J. H. Gurney, *Early Annals of Ornithology*, page 116.
54 Frank Lowe, *The Heron*, page 148.
55 Max Nicholson, *BB* 22:335.
56 Frank Lowe, *The Heron*, page 143.
57 Frank Lowe, *The Heron*, page 59; R. V. A. Marshall, *BB* 54:202.
58 P. Amies, *BB* 83:425.
59 Frank Lowe, *The Heron*, page 63; H. M. Dobinson and A. J. Richards, *BB* 57:397.
60 Frank Lowe, *The Heron*, pages 54–5.
61 Frank Lowe, *The Heron*, page 51; Alan Parker, Northwood Hills, Kent.
62 Frank Lowe, *The Heron*, page 55.
63 Frank Lowe, *The Heron*, page 56; R. E. Batty and L. Forbes, *BB* 90:112; also Keith Bowey, *BB* 90:112–13.
64 Colin Jones, Haveringland, Norfolk.
65 Frank Lowe, *The Heron*, page 137.
66 Frank Lowe, *The Heron*, pages 136–7.
67 Reuben Singleton, Peebles, Borders.
68 Max Nicholson, *BB* 22:340.
69 Reuben Singleton, Peebles, Borders.
70 Keith Vinicombe and Dave Cottridge, *Rare Birds in Britain and Ireland*, HarperCollins, 1996, page 34.

Storks, *Ciconiidae*
1 Pete Allard, 'White Storks in Norfolk', *Norfolk Bird and Mammal Report 1967*, pages 163–4.
2 J. B. Bottomley, *BB* 65:3–5.
3 Henning Skov, *BB* 65:304.

Ibises and Spoonbills, *Threskiornithidae*
1 John Cantelo, Canterbury, Kent.
2 William Glegg, *The Birds of Middlesex*, page 108.
3 J. H. Gurney, *Early Annals of Ornithology*, page 132.
4 J. H. Gurney, *Early Annals of Ornithology*, page 181.
5 Sir Thomas Browne, *Notes and Letters on the Natural History of Norfolk*, page 10.

6 J. H. Gurney, *Early Annals of Ornithology*, pages 177–8.

Swans, Geese and Ducks, *Anatidae*
1 Norman Ticehurst, *The Mute Swan in England*, page 3.
2 Mike Birkhead and Chris Perrins, *The Mute Swan*, page 20.
3 Norman Ticehurst, *The Mute Swan in England*, pages 80–94.
4 Norman Ticehurst, *The Mute Swan in England*, pages 15–16.
5 Annette Hope, *Londoners' Larder*, page 21.
6 Janet Kear, *Man and Wildfowl*, page 167.
7 James Chambers, London; Bryan Nelson, *The Gannet*, page 280.
8 Peter Scott, *The Swans*, page 173.
9 Chris Perrins, Oxford, Oxfordshire.
10 James Chambers, London.
11 Peter Scott, *The Swans*, page 4.
12 Janet Kear, Umberleigh, Devon.
13 Mike Birkhead and Chris Perrins, *The Mute Swan*, pages 78–9.
14 J. H. Gurney, *Early Annals of Ornithology*, page 82.
15 Richard Archer, Exeter, Devon.
16 Martin Thoday, Clare, Suffolk.
17 Chris Perrins, Oxford, Oxfordshire.
18 Leslie Dunkling and Gordon Wright, *Pub Names of Britain*, Dent, 1994, pages 256–7.
19 Jacob Larwood and John Hotten, *English Inn Signs*, Chatto & Windus, 1985, pages 138–40.
20 Peter Scott, *The Swans*, pages 129–30.
21 Mike Birkhead and Chris Perrins, *The Mute Swan*, pages 137–8.
22 Chris Perrins, Oxford, Oxfordshire.
23 Janet Kear, *Man and Wildfowl*, pages 212–13.
24 Marianna Partasides, *The Haringey Advertiser*, 14 May 2003.
25 Anon., *BB* 58:513.
26 John Cooper, email contribution.
27 Ken Spencer, 'Wild Birds in Lancashire Folk-lore', *Journal of the Lancashire Dialect Society*, No. 15, 1966, page 3.
28 Christine Muir, North Ronaldsay, Orkney.
29 James Irvine-Robertson (ed.), *Random Shots: An Anthology from the First 50 Years of the Shooting Times*, Pelham Books, 1990, page 256.
30 *Handbook* 2:169.
31 Tim Melling, Shepley, Yorkshire.
32 Peter Scott, *The Swans*, page 12.
33 Janet Kear, *Man and Wildfowl*, pages 128–9.
34 Moss Taylor, Michael Seago, Peter Allard and Don Dorling, *The Birds of Norfolk*, page 137.
35 Peter Scott, *The Swans*, page 10.
36 Robin Hull, *Scottish Birds*, page 106.
37 Janet Kear, Umberleigh, Devon.
38 Carl Mitchell, Welney, Norfolk.
39 Janet Kear, *Man and Wildfowl*, page 196.
40 Mariko Parslow-Otsu, *BB* 84:161–70; Mariko Parslow-Otsu, *Norfolk Bird and Mammal Report 1991*, pages 273–6.
41 Malcolm Ogilvie and Bruce Pearson, *Wildfowl*, pages 46–7.
42 Malcolm Ogilvie and Bruce Pearson, *Wildfowl*, page 45.

43 W. H. Hudson, *Adventures Among Birds*, page 27.
44 Ian Francis, Alford, Aberdeenshire.
45 Edward Cross, *Norfolk Bird and Mammal Report 1993*, pages 115–18.
46 Eric Simms, South Witham, Lincolnshire.
47 Carl Mitchell, *Norfolk Bird and Mammal Report 1993*, pages 616–20.
48 Moss Taylor, Michael Seago, Peter Allard and Don Dorling, *The Birds of Norfolk*, page 147.
49 Peter Scott and Christopher Dalgety, *Bull BOC* 68:109–21.
50 Peter Scott, *The Eye of the Wind*, page 179.
51 Ian Wallace, *BWP* 1:410.
52 Peter Scott, *The Eye of the Wind*, pages 180–1.
53 Janet Kear, *Man and Wildfowl*, page 141.
54 Lockwood, page 74.
55 Edward Armstrong, *The Folklore of Birds*, pages 25–47.
56 Jonathon Green, *Slang Down the Ages*, pages 58, 210.
57 Edward Armstrong, *The Folklore of Birds*, pages 25–47.
58 Janet Kear, *Man and Wildfowl*, page 25.
59 Beryl Rowland, *Birds with Human Souls*, page 69.
60 G. L. Apperson, *The Wordsworth Dictionary of Proverbs*, Wordsworth, Ware, 1993, page 267.
61 Janet Kear, *Man and Wildfowl*, page 48.
62 Janet Kear, *Man and Wildfowl*, page 49.
63 Elspeth Huxley, *Peter Scott*, Faber, 1993, page 100.
64 Elspeth Huxley, *Peter Scott*, Faber, 1993, page 155.
65 Janet Kear, *Man and Wildfowl*, page 247.
66 Steve Madge and Hilary Burn, *Wildfowl*, page 146.
67 Derek Goodwin, Petts Wood, Kent.
68 George Watola et al., 'Problems and management of naturalised introduced Canada geese *Branta Canadensis* in Britain', in J. S. Holmes and J. R. Simons (eds), *The Introduction and Naturalisation of Birds*, London, HMSO, 1996.
69 Chris Feare et al., 'Canada geese (*Branta Canadensis*) droppings as a potential source of pathogenic bacteria', *Journal for the Royal Society for the Promotion of Health*, 1999, 119 (3), 46–155.
70 Graham Austin, *BTO News*, 237:8–9.
71 Edward Armstrong, *The Folklore of Birds*, page 226.
72 Bethan Mair, Pontardulais, Swansea.
73 Edward Armstrong, *The Folklore of Birds*, page 225.
74 Edward Armstrong, *The Folklore of Birds*, page 229.
75 C. A. Wood and M. Fyfe (eds), *Art of Falconry of Frederick II of Hohenstaufen*, pages 51–2.
76 Edward Armstrong, *The Folklore of Birds*, page 225.
77 Eric Simms, South Witham, Lincolnshire.
78 William Yarrell, *A History of British Birds*, Vol. 3, page 166.
79 William Yarrell, *A History of British Birds*, Vol. 3, page 166.
80 Abel Chapman, *Bird-Life of the*

Borders, page 326; William Yarrell, *A History of British Birds*, Vol. 3, page 166; Billy Bishop, *Cley Marsh*, page 26.

81 James McCallum, Wighton, Norfolk.

82 *Migration Atlas*, page 175.

83 Mike Daw, Slimbridge, Gloucestershire; http://www.wwt.org.uk/brent.

84 Bryan Sage, *The Ecology of the Egyptian Goose at Holkham Park, Norfolk*, Norfolk and Norwich Naturalists' Society, No. 8.

85 Christopher Lever, *The Naturalized Animals of the British Isles*, pages 278–81.

86 Moss Taylor, Michael Seago, Peter Allard and Don Dorling, *The Birds of Norfolk*, page 158.

87 Fish-hawk, *Studies of British Birds*, Duckworth, 1937, page 93.

88 Brian Vesey-Fitzgerald, *British Game*, page 101.

89 Robert Pinchen, *Sea Swallows*, Green, Lowestoft, 1935, page 37.

90 Ken Spencer, 'Wild Birds in Lancashire Folk-lore', *Journal of the Lancashire Dialect Society*, No. 15, 1966, pages 2–15.

91 Henry Boase, *BB* 58:175–9.

92 Friedrich Goethe, *BB* 54:147.

93 Friedrich Goethe, *BB* 54:106–15.

94 Derek Goodwin, *Birds of Man's World*, page 133.

95 Christopher Lever, *The Naturalized Animals of the British Isles*, page 289.

96 Christopher Savage, *The Mandarin Duck*, page 69.

97 Christopher Lever, *The Naturalized Animals of the British Isles*, page 296.

98 Christopher Savage, *The Mandarin Duck*, page 69.

99 Elizabeth Godwin, Great Witley, Worcestershire.

100 Phil Gray, *The Washlanders*, page 6.

101 John Humphreys, Bottisham, Cambridgeshire.

102 Eric Hardy, *The Bird Lover's Week-end Book*, Seeley Service, 1959, pages 155–6.

103 Eric Ennion, *The Living Birds of Eric Ennion*, page 23.

104 Lockwood, page 66.

105 Eric Ennion, *The Living Birds of Eric Ennion*, page 24.

106 Fish-hawk, *Studies of British Birds*, Duckworth, 1937, page 91.

107 Patrick Harrison and Kate Ferrol, Laure-Minervois, France.

108 Brian Vesey-Fitzgerald, *British Game*, page 107.

109 Brian Vesey-Fitzgerald, *British Game*, page 108.

110 *Handbook* 3:232.

111 E. H. Gillam, *BB* 54:357–9; J. M. Stainton, *BB* 56:339.

112 Eric Simms, South Witham, Lincolnshire.

113 Noel Corral, North Luffenham, Rutland.

114 Eric Simms, South Witham, Lincolnshire.

115 Isabella Beeton, *Household Management*, page 451.

116 Edward Grey, *The Charm of Birds*, page 214.

117 Hugh Macpherson, *A History of Fowling*, pages 252–3.

118 Janet Kear, *Man and Wildfowl*, page 80.

119 James Ritchie, *The Influence of Man on Animal Life in Scotland*, page 139.

120 Thomas Southwell, *Transactions of the Norfolk and Norwich Naturalists' Society*, 2:538–55.

121 Janet Kear, *Man and Wildfowl*, page 88.

122 Janet Kear, *Man and Wildfowl*, pages 109–10.

123 A. D. Fox and E. R. Meek, *BB* 86:152.

124 P. J. Sellar, *BWP* 1:535; Killian Mullarney et al., *Collins Bird Guide*, page 52.

125 Fish-hawk, *Studies of British Birds*, Duckworth, 1937, page 92.

126. J. H. Gurney, *Early Annals of Ornithology*, page 179.

127 Brian Vesey-Fitzgerald, *British Game*, page 115.

128 Eric Fuller, *Extinct Birds*, page 53.

129 Eric Simms, South Witham, Lincolnshire.

130 Eric Ennion, *The Living Birds of Eric Ennion*, page 24.

131 Hugh Macpherson, *A History of Fowling*, pages 288–9.

132 *Winter Atlas*, page 104.

133 Janet Kear, *Man and Wildfowl*, page 124.

134 Robin Hull, *Scottish Birds*, page 120.

135 Roy Frost, Chesterfield, Derbyshire.

136 Fish-hawk, *Studies of British Birds*, Duckworth, 1937, page 93.

137 James Adams, St Combs, Grampian.

138 Hugh Macpherson, *A History of Fowling*, page 293.

139 *Winter Atlas*, page 112.

140 L. H. Campbell, 'The Impact of Changes in Sewage Treatment on Seaducks Wintering in the Firth of Forth, Scotland', *Biological Conservation* 8: 173–80.

141 Gavin Maxwell, *Raven Seek Thy Brother*, Longmans Green, 1968, page 105.

142 Brian Martin, *Wildfowl of the British Isles and North-West Europe*, page 130.

143 Mike Rogers et al., *BB* 78:539.

144 Gavin Maxwell, *Raven Seek Thy Brother*, Longmans Green, 1968, pages 105–6.

145 *BWP* 1:595.

146 *Handbook* 3:338–42.

147 Janet Kear, *Man and Wildfowl*, page 172.

148 Janet Kear, *Man and Wildfowl*, page 173.

149 James Fisher, *The Shell Bird Book*, page 49.

150 John Day, Newcastle-upon-Tyne.

151 Janet Kear, Umberleigh, Devon.

152 John Day, Newcastle-upon-Tyne.

153 Janet Kear, *Man and Wildfowl*, page 203.

154 Brian Vesey-Fitzgerald, *British Game*, page 124.

155 Richard Perry, *A Naturalist on Lindisfarne*, Lindsay Drummond, 1946, page 161.

156 Paul Harvey, Lerwick, Shetland.

157 Brian Vesey-Fitzgerald, *British Game*, page 127.

158 Lockwood, page 134.

159 Malcolm Ogilvie and Stuart Winter (eds), *Best Days with British Birds*, British Birds, 1986, page 46.

160 Thomas Bewick, *Selections from A History of British Birds*, page 304.

161 Brian Vesey-Fitzgerald, *British Game*, page 129.

162 Malcolm Ogilvie and Bruce Pearson, *Wildfowl*, page 102.

163 Thomas Bewick, *Selections from A History of British Birds*, page 279.

164 Richard Chandler, *BB* 77:479–81.

165 Mike Armitage, *BTO News*, 225:2–3.

166 Janet Kear, *Man and Wildfowl*, page 203.

167 Eric Meek and Brian Little, *BB* 70:229–37.

168 Julian Hughes, Sandy, Bedfordshire.

169 Mick Marquiss and David Carss, *BTO News* 210/211:6–7.

170 Christopher Lever, *The Naturalized Animals of the British Isles*, pages 307–8.

171 *BWP* 1:691.

172 Robert Hudson, *BB* 69:132–43.

173 Alan Richards, Studley, Warwickshire.

174 Fred and Pauline Lormor, Peakirk, Lincolnshire.

175 Baz Hughes, Slimbridge, Gloucestershire.

176 David James, Hinton, Birmingham, *Birdwatching*, June 1999.

177 Mrs V. C. Lander, Mansfield, Nottinghamshire, *Birdwatching*, May 1999.

178 Chris Anson, Norwich, *Birdwatching*, May 1999.

179 Steven Gregory, *BB* 90:150–1.

180 John Birkett, Sanderstead, Surrey, *Birdwatching*, November 1999.

181 Nathan Roche, email contribution, *Birdwatching*, May 1999.

182 Bernard Zonfrillo, *BB* 93:395–6.

183 Steve Kirk, Bessacarr, Yorkshire, *Birdwatching*, May 1999.

184 Paul Raymer, Swanage, Dorset, *Birdwatching*, June 1999.

185 Bernard Zonfrillo, *BB* 93:395–6.

186 Eric Clare, Derbyshire, *Birdwatching*, March 2002.

Birds of Prey, *Accipitriformes*

1 Leslie Brown, *British Birds of Prey*, page 66.

2 Gilbert White, *The Natural History of Selborne*, page 101.

3 Leslie Brown, *British Birds of Prey*, page 67.

4 Richard Meinertzhagen, *Pirates and Predators*, page 83.

5 S. J. Roberts, J. M. S. Lewis and I. T. Williams, *BB* 92:326–45.

6 Peter Fraser and Mike Rogers, *BB* 95:610–11; Mark Roberts, Tranmere, Cheshire.

7 Ian Carter, Peterborough.

8 Anon., *Birds*, Autumn 2000, page 13.

9 Abel Chapman, *Bird-Life of the Borders*, page 233.

10 Kenneth Richmond, *British Birds of Prey*, page 154.

11 Francesca Greenoak, *British Birds*, page 56.

12 J. H. Gurney, *Early Annals of Ornithology*, pages 82, 154.

13 Richard Fitter, *London's Natural History*, page 51.

14 Abraham Cutajar, Grantham, Lincolnshire.

15 Richard Meinertzhagen, *Pirates and Predators*, page 177.

16 Ken Spencer, Burnley, Lancashire.

17 Lockwood, pages 122–3.

18 Ian Carter, Peterborough.

19　Ian Carter, *The Red Kite*, Arlequin Press, Chelmsford, 2001, pages 123–34.

20　Richard Sheppard, email contribution.

21　Paul Fennell, email contribution.

22　George Lodge, *Memoirs of an Artist Naturalist*, Gurney & Jackson, Edinburgh, 1946, page 34.

23　David Lack, *The Life of the Robin*, page 176.

24　Eric Simms, South Witham, Lincolnshire; Ian Carter, Peterborough; Richard Fitter, *London's Birds*, page 101.

25　Ian Carter, Peterborough.

26　Seton Gordon, *Highland Summer*, Cassell, 1971, page 56.

27　Eric Simms, South Witham, Lincolnshire.

28　Chris Rollie, St John's Town of Dalry, Dumfries and Galloway.

29　Desmond Nethersole-Thompson, *The Greenshank*, page 29.

30　Norman Ticehurst, *BB* 14:34–7.

31　Ian Carter, Peterborough.

32　Ian Carter, Peterborough.

33　Henry Stevenson, *The Birds of Norfolk*, Vol. 1, page 4.

34　John Love, *The return of the Sea Eagle*, page 104.

35　Henry Stevenson, *The Birds of Norfolk*, Vol. 1, page 4.

36　William Yarrell, *A History of British Birds*, Vol. 1, pages 21–2.

37　Margaret Gelling, 'Anglo-Saxon Eagles', pages 173–81, in *Leeds Studies in English*, (eds Thorlac Turville-Petre and Margaret Gelling), University of Leeds, 1987.

38　John Love, *The return of the Sea Eagle*, page 101.

39　James Ritchie, *The Influence of Man on Animal Life in Scotland*, page 130.

40　Richard Meinertzhagen, *Pirates and Predators*, page 121.

41　Hugh Macpherson, *A History of Fowling*, page 183.

42　Pliny, *Natural History*, Books 8–11, page 303.

43　John Love, *Eagles*, pages 47–8.

44　R. K. Gordon, *Anglo-Saxon Poetry*, page 360.

45　John Hedges, *Tomb of the Eagles*, pages 147, 175.

46　Martin Martin, *A Description of the Western Islands of Scotland*, page 179.

47　Bobby Tulloch, *Scots Magazine*, June 1978, pages 260–4.

48　Charles Swainson, *The Folklore of British Birds*, page 135.

49　Stewart Linsell, *Hickling Broad and its Wildlife*, page 102.

50　John Walpole-Bond, *A History of Sussex Birds*, Vol. 2, page 288.

51　William Turner, *Turner on Birds*, page 19.

52　Mike Everett, *Birdwatch*, August 2002.

53　Kenneth Richmond, *British Birds of Prey*, page 19.

54　Donald Watson, *The Hen Harrier*, page 60.

55　Chris Mead, *The State of the Nation's Birds*, page 153.

56　Kenneth Richmond, *Wild Venture*, Geoffrey Bles, 1958, page 36.

57　Duncan Orr-Ewing, Edinburgh.

58　Lockwood, page 71.

59　J. H. Gurney, *Early Annals of Ornithology*, page 32.

60　Malcolm Ogilvie et al., *BB* 96:495.

61　Pier Lorenzo Florio, *BBC Wildlife*, July 1998, page 96.

62　Kenneth Richmond, *British Birds of Prey*, pages 142–3.

63　Leslie Brown, *British Birds of Prey*, page 139.

64　*BWP* 2:161.

65　Dennis Claridge, Guisborough, Cleveland.

66　F. W. Frohawk, *British Birds with their Nest and Eggs*, Vol. 2, page 66.

67　Robert Dunsford, Swinton, Manchester.

68　Robert Dunsford, Swinton, Manchester.

69　Richard Meinertzhagen, *Pirates and Predators*, page 90.

70　Chas Baxter, Bletchley, Buckinghamshire.

71　Tim Melling, Shepley, Yorkshire.

72　Kenneth Richmond, *British Birds of Prey*, page 97.

73　Kenneth Richmond, *British Birds of Prey*, page 92.

74　William Yarrell, *A History of British Birds*, Vol. 1, pages 83–4.

75　Brewer's *Dictionary of Phrase and Fable*, page 176.

76　Reuben Singleton, Peebles, The Borders.

77　N. W. Moore, *BB* 50:190.

78　Colin Tubbs, *The Buzzard*, page 79.

79　Chris Rollie, St John's Town of Dalry, Dumfries and Galloway.

80　John Walpole-Bond, *A History of Sussex Birds*, Vol. 2, page 282.

81　Kenneth Richmond, *British Birds of Prey*, page 97.

82　Clive Fairweather, Harbertonford, Devon.

83　Peter Fraser and Mike Rogers, *BB* 96:632.

84　Philip Brown, *Birds of Prey*, page 21.

85　Josephine Addison, *Treasury of Bird Lore*, page 32.

86　W. J. Brown, *The Gods Had Wings*, pages 64–9; Ernest Ingersoll, *Birds in Legend, Fable and Folklore*, pages 28–34.

87　Phil Palmer, *First for Britain and Ireland*, page 81.

88　Roy Dennis, Nethybridge, Inverness-shire.

89　James Ferguson-Lees, *BB* 61:465; G. S. Cowles, *BB* 62:542–3.

90　Philip Brown and George Waterston, *The Return of the Osprey*, pages 77–8.

91　James Harting, *The Birds of Shakespeare*, page 262.

92　R. Wildman, Bournemouth, Dorset.

93　Philip Brown and George Waterston, *The Return of the Osprey*, pages 91–2.

94　Roy Dennis, Nethybridge, Inverness-shire.

95　Philip Brown and George Waterston, *The Return of the Osprey*, pages 46–7.

96　Mike Everett, Hemingford Grey, Cambridgeshire.

97　Mike Everett, Hemingford Grey, Cambridgeshire.

98　Roy Dennis, Nethybridge, Inverness-shire.

99　Roy Dennis, Nethybridge, Inverness-shire.

100　Peter Strangeman, Waterlooville, Hampshire.

101　Anon., *Birdwatch*, September 2000, page 20.

102　Richard Fitter, *London's Birds*, Collins, 1949, page 29.

103　Eric Simms, South Witham, Lincolnshire.

104　J. Hewlett, *Breeding Birds of the London Area*, London Natural History Society, 2002, page 62.

105　Moss Taylor, Michael Seago, Peter Allard and Don Dorling, *The Birds of Norfolk*, page 334.

106　Tim Melling, Shepley, Yorkshire.

107　Wing-Commander David Scrimgeour, *Bird Life*, January 1966, page 11.

108　*Handbook* 3:26.

109　Andrew Village, *The Kestrel*, pages 66–7.

110　Lockwood, page 90.

111　David Skidmore, Wolverhampton.

112　Lockwood, page 147.

113　Lockwood, page 168.

114　*BWP* 2:316.

115　Tom Cade, *The Falcons of the World*, pages 112–16; Kenneth Richmond, *British Birds of Prey*, page 84.

116　Tom Cade, *The Falcons of the World*, pages 112–16.

117　Chris Mead, *The State of the Nation's Birds*, pages 158–9.

118　Peter Upton, email contribution.

119　John Walpole-Bond, *A History of Sussex Birds*, Vol. 2, page 262.

120　Francesca Greenoak, *British Birds*, pages 66–7.

121　J. H. Gurney, *Early Annals of Ornithology*, page 137.

122　Anthony Chapman, *The Hobby*, page 72.

123　Anthony Chapman, *The Hobby*, page 136.

124　T. G. Walker, *BB* 44:134–5.

125　Graham Etherington, Norwich.

126　J. H. Gurney, *Early Annals of Ornithology*, page 23.

127　Richard Vaughan, *In search of Arctic birds*, Poyser, Calton, 1992, pages 80–97.

128　Jonathan Hooton, *The Glaven Ports*, Blakeney History Group, 1996, page 69.

129　Richard Vaughan, *In search of Arctic birds*, Poyser, Calton, 1992, pages 80–97.

130　Kenneth Richmond, *British Birds of Prey*, page 12.

131　Kenneth Richmond, *British Birds of Prey*, page 50.

132　Philip Brown, *Birds of Prey*, page 5.

133　Andrew Village, *Falcons*, pages 62–3.

134　R. B. Treleaven, *Peregrine*, page 14.

135　Andrew Village, *Falcons*, page 53.

136　Derek Ratcliffe, *The Peregrine*, page 127.

137　Philip Brown, *Birds of Prey*, page 51.

138　Roger Lovegrove et al., *Birds in Wales*, page 128.

139　Kenneth Richmond, *British Birds of Prey*, pages 1–15; Emma Ford, *Falconry*, Shire, Princes Risborough, 1984, page 4.

140　James Ritchie, *The Influence of Man on Animal Life in Scotland*, pages 200–2.

141　Roger Lovegrove et al., *Birds in Wales*, page 129.

142　Gilbert White, *The Natural History of Selborne*, page 39.

143　Derek Ratcliffe, *The Peregrine*, page 39.

144　Eric Simms, *The Public Life of the Street Pigeon*, page 49.

145 Andrew Village, *Falcons*, page 125.
146 Derek Ratcliffe, *The Peregrine*, page 305.
147 Derek Ratcliffe, *The Peregrine*, pages 303–32; Derek Ratcliffe, *In Search of Nature*, Peregrine, Leeds, 2000, pages 213–25.
148 Max Nicholson, *The Environmental Revolution*, Pelican, 1972, page 256.
149 J. A. Baker, *The Peregrine*, page 88.
150 Humphrey Crick, Alex Bank and Rachel Coombes, *BTO News* 248:8–9.
151 Andrew Dixon, Colin Richards, Andrew Lawrence and Mike Thomas, 'Peregrine (*Falco peregrinus*) Predation on Racing Pigeons (*Columba livia*) in Wales', in *Birds of Prey in a Changing Environment*, (eds) D. B. A. Thompson, S. M. Redpath, A. H. Fielding, M. Marquiss and C. A. Galbraith, The Stationery Office, Edinburgh, 2003.
152 Derek Ratcliffe, Girton, Cambridgeshire.

Grouse, *Tetraonidae*

1 W. H. Hudson, *Adventures Among Birds*, page 129.
2 Desmond Nethersole-Thompson and Adam Watson, *The Cairngorms*, page 111.
3 Brian Vesey-Fitzgerald, *British Game*, page 13.
4 Henry Douglas-Home, *The Birdman*, Collins, 1977, page 74.
5 Tim Melling, Shepley, Yorkshire.
6 Henry Douglas-Home, *The Birdman*, Collins, 1977, page 73.
7 Brian Vesey-Fitzgerald, *British Game*, page 20.
8 A. H. R. Wilson, *BB* 16:328–9.
9 R. W. Chapman (ed.), *Johnson's Journey to the Western Islands and Boswell's Journal of a Tour to the Hebrides with Samuel Johnson*, Oxford University Press, Oxford, 1951, pages 49, 187.
10 Stephanie Coghlan, Almondbury, West Yorkshire.
11 Brian Martin, *The Glorious Grouse*, page 27.
12 Henry Douglas-Home, *The Birdman*, Collins, 1977, page 70.
13 Brian Martin, *The Glorious Grouse*, page 71.
14 Robin Hull, *Scottish Birds*, page 76.
15 Robin Hull, *Scottish Birds*, page 59.
16 Brian Martin, *The Glorious Grouse*, page 49.
17 Brian Martin, *The Glorious Grouse*, page 50.
18 Brian Martin, *The Glorious Grouse*, pages 63–5.
19 Robin Hull, *Scottish Birds*, pages 72–3.
20 Robin Hull, *Scottish Birds*, page 72.
21 Brian Martin, *The Glorious Grouse*, page 71.
22 Brian Martin, *The Glorious Grouse*, page 76.
23 Robin Hull, *Scottish Birds*, page 6.
24 W. H. Pearsall, *Mountains and Moorlands*, Collins, 1950, page 53.
25 James Ritchie, *The Influence of Man on Animal Life in Scotland*, page 136.
26 Lord Lilford, *Birds of the British Isles*, Vol. 4, 1891, unpaginated.
27 Tim Melling, Shepley, Yorkshire.

28 *Handbook* 5:229.
29 Brian Martin, *Sporting Birds of Britain and Ireland*, page 53.
30 Adam Watson, *BB* 65:25.
31 Desmond Nethersole-Thompson and Adam Watson, *The Cairngorms*, page 150.
32 Francesca Greenoak, *British Birds*, page 71.
33 Seton Gordon, BBC Archive number 33588. 'A field' broadcast 1 March 1971; Seton Gordon, *The Charm of the Hills*, Cassells, 1930, page 42.
34 *Handbook* 5:229.
35 Seton Gordon, *The Charm of the Hills*, Cassells, 1930, page 184.
36 Adam Watson, *BB* 65:15.
37 Desmond Nethersole-Thompson and Adam Watson, *The Cairngorms*, page 152.
38 R. Moss, *BB* 73:440–7.
39 Tim Melling, Shepley, Yorkshire.
40 Chris Mead, *The State of the Nation's Birds*, page 162.
41 Isabella Beeton, *Household Management*, page 513.
42 Isabella Beeton, *Household Management*, page 512.
43 Chris Mead, *The State of the Nation's Birds*, page 162.
44 Brian Gregory, Monmouth, Monmouthshire.
45 Tim Melling, Shepley, Yorkshire.
46 Jim and Joy Farms, email contribution. The 'Moorcock' pubs with Black Grouse on the sign include: Bleasdale, Waddington, Blacko, in Lancashire; Eggleston, Peterlee, Stanhope, County Durham; Garsdale, Cumbria; and Macclesfield, Cheshire. Other Moorcocks with unknown pub signs include Wainstalls, West Yorkshire; Ravenstonedale, Cumbria; Waskerley, County Durham; and Scarborough, North Yorkshire. The 'Moorcock' inn at Littleborough, Greater Manchester, previously featured a red grouse on the sign and the landlord still keeps a stuffed specimen behind the bar, while a 'Moorcock' at Norland, West Yorkshire, has a sign featuring red grouse. An old pub, now closed, at Oakenclough, three miles north-east of Garstang, Lancashire, also featured red grouse on its sign.
47 Dougal Andrew, *BB* 51:189–92.
48 R. Moss, *BB* 73:440–7; Christopher Lever, *The Naturalized Animals of the British Isles*, pages 315–16.
49 *Handbook* 5:210–11.
50 Dougal Andrew, *BB* 51:189–92.
51 Graeme Cresswell, Norwich, Norfolk.
52 James Ferguson-Lees, *BB* 56:19–22.
53 Gordon Hamlett, Longthorpe, Cambridgeshire.
54 Graeme Cresswell, Norwich, Norfolk.
55 Robin Hull, *Scottish Birds*, page 149.
56 Desmond Nethersole-Thompson and Adam Watson, *The Cairngorms*, page 88.
57 Christopher Lever, *The Naturalized Animals of the British Isles*, page 320.
58 James Ritchie, *The Influence of Man on Animal Life in Scotland*, page 273.

Partridges, Quails and Pheasants, *Phasianidae*

1 Max Nicholson, *Birds and Men*, page 93.
2 Christopher Lever, *The Naturalized Animals of the British Isles*, page 364.
3 F. M. Ogilvie, *Field Observations on British Birds*, Selwyn and Blount, 1920, page 55.
4 *Handbook* 5:247.
5 Derek Goodwin, *Ibis* 95:581–614.
6 Iona and Peter Opie (eds), *The Oxford Dictionary of Nursery Rhymes*, Oxford University Press, Oxford, 1985, pages 122–3.
7 Bryan Sage, *BB* 47:398–9; C. Alderson-Smith, *BB* 72:78.
8 Max Nicholson, *Birds and Men*, page 87.
9 Peter Thompson, Fordingbridge, Hampshire.
10 Malcolm Brockless, Royston, Hertfordshire.
11 Tony Hare, London.
12 Malcolm Brockless, Royston, Hertfordshire.
13 Peter Thompson, Fordingbridge, Hampshire.
14 Max Nicholson, *Birds and Men*, page 95.
15 Reg Moreau, *BB* 44:257–76.
16 Paul Tout, Duino, Italy.
17 Reg Moreau, *BB* 44:257–76.
18 John Cantelo, Canterbury, Kent.
19 Gilbert White, *The Natural History of Selborne*, page 46.
20 Pliny, *Natural History*, Books 8–11, page 335.
21 Reg Moreau, *BB* 44:257–76.
22 Brian Vesey-Fitzgerald, *British Game*, page 73.
23 *BB* 70:266.
24 Oliver Rackham, *The History of the British Countryside*, page 50.
25 Peter Robertson, *A Natural History of the Pheasant*, page 124.
26 Robin Hull, Strathtay, Perthshire.
27 Peter Addison, Riby, Lincolnshire.
28 Oliver Rackham, *The History of the British Countryside*, pages 51, 93.
29 Oliver Rackham, *The History of the British Countryside*, page 51.
30 Oliver Rackham, *The History of the British Countryside*, page 93.
31 W. H. Hudson, *Adventures Among Birds*, page 87.
32 Peter Robertson, *A Natural History of the Pheasant*, page 124.
33 Peter Robertson, *A Natural History of the Pheasant*, page 129.
34 Brian Vesey-Fitzgerald, *British Game*, page 52.
35 Alistair Crowle, Peterborough, Cambridgeshire.
36 Alistair Crowle, Peterborough, Cambridgeshire.
37 Ian Wallace, Anslow, Staffordshire.
38 Peter Robertson, *A Natural History of the Pheasant*, page 26.
39 Ted Pearman, transcribed by Faith Davis, Roydon, Essex.
40 Eric Ennion, *The British Bird*, page 23.
41 Henry Douglas-Home, *The Birdman*, Collins, 1977, page 80.
42 Brian Vesey-Fitzgerald, *British Game*, page 52.
43 Derek Goodwin, *Ibis* 90:280–4.
44 Stephen Browne, Mark Rehfisch and

45 Dawn Balmer, *BTO News* 210/211:13.
45 Dawn Balmer, Thetford, Norfolk.
46 William Beebe, *A Monograph of the Pheasants*, Vol. 4, page 29.
47 William Beebe, *A Monograph of the Pheasants*, Vol. 4, page 31.
48 Paul Trodd, Dunstable, Bedfordshire.
49 Paul Trodd, Dunstable, Bedfordshire.
50 William Beebe, *A Monograph of the Pheasants*, Vol. 4, page 29.

Rails, Crakes and Coots, *Rallidae*
1 *Winter Atlas*, page 172.
2 Reuben Singleton, Peebles, Borders.
3 J. Cassidy, *BB* 41:191.
4 John Wilson, Leighton Moss, Lancashire.
5 Thomas Bewick, *Selections from A History of British Birds*, page 253.
6 *New Atlas*, page 146.
7 Abel Chapman, *Bird-Life of the Borders*, page 137.
8 *BWP* 2:542.
9 Eric Ennion, *The British Bird*, page 137.
10 *Handbook* 4:194.
11 *BWP* 2:532.
12 Herbert Axell, *BB* 55:132–3; Alfred Blundell, *BB* 55:165.
13 John Wilson, Leighton Moss, Lancashire.
14 Chris Murphy, *BB* 69:369.
15 P. F. Holmes *BB* 42:364–5.
16 *European Atlas*, page 225.
17 D. M. Norman, *BB* 78:306.
18 Ian Dawson and Keith Allsopp, *BB* 78:257.
19 Mike Rogers et al., *BB* 83:459.
20 Max Nicholson, *Birds and Men*, page 85.
21 Audrey Keville, Whitley Bay, Tyne and Wear.
22 Colin Harrison, *The History of the Birds of Britain*, page 98.
23 Alistair Crowle, Peterborough, Cambridgeshire.
24 C. A. Norris, *BB* 40:240.
25 Tim Melling, Shepley, Yorkshire.
26 *Handbook* 5:175.
27 Robin Hull, *Scottish Birds*, page 157.
28 David Broome, Wigan, Lancashire.
29 C. A. Norris, *BB* 40:231–4.
30 C. A. Norris, *BB* 40:237.
31 Barry Taylor and Ber van Perlo, *Rails*, page 323.
32 Eric Ennion, *The British Bird*, page 139.
33 David Smallbridge, *BB* 77:155.
34 R. J. Salmon, *BB* 57:364.
35 Gordon Gent, Harleston, Norfolk.
36 Garth Waite, Falmouth, Cornwall.
37 Garth Waite, Falmouth, Cornwall.
38 Ron Freethy, *BB* 73:35.
39 A. F. Hawkins, *BB* 63:33–4.
40 Richard Fitter, *London's Birds*, pages 168–9.
41 Judy Relton, *BB* 65:248–56.
42 *New Atlas*, page 152.
43 J. H. Gurney, *Early Annals of Ornithology*, page 142.
44 Brian Martin, *Sporting Birds of Britain and Ireland*, page 185.
45 Gordon Gent, Harleston, Norfolk.
46 Jonathan Elphick, London.
47 Lockwood, page 143.
48 *BWP* 2:599.
49 John Wilson, Leighton Moss, Lancashire.

50 Adam Rowlands, Titchwell, Norfolk.
51 Brian Vesey-Fitzgerald, *British Game*, page 175.
52 Richard Lubbock, *The Fauna of Norfolk*, 1879, page 132.
53 Moss Taylor, Michael Seago, Peter Allard and Don Dorling, *The Birds of Norfolk*, page 228.
54 Jim Vincent, *A Season of Birds*, pages 22–3.

Cranes, *Gruidae*
1 Thomas Southwell, *Transactions of the Norfolk and Norwich Naturalists' Society*, 7:160–70.
2 J. H. Gurney, *Early Annals of Ornithology*, page 49.
3 Anne Wilson, *Food and Drink in Britain*, page 115; Thomas Southwell, *Transactions of the Norfolk and Norwich Naturalists' Society* 7:160–70.
4 J. H. Gurney, *Early Annals of Ornithology*, page 165.
5 J. H. Gurney, *Early Annals of Ornithology*, page 171.
6 Thomas Southwell, *Transactions of the Norfolk and Norwich Naturalists' Society* 7:165.
7 Simon Boisseau and Derek Yalden, *Ibis* 140:482–500.
8 James Fletcher, Northampton.
9 Eilert Ekwall, *The Oxford Dictionary of English Place-Names*, pages 122, 128, 479.
10 Paul Donald, Sandy, Bedfordshire.
11 Alan Gibson, London.

Bustards, *Otididae*
1 Herbert Axell, *BB* 57:247–8.
2 Ron Johns, Salthouse, Norfolk.
3 *Handbook* 4:437.
4 John Pollard, *Birds in Greek Life and Myth*, page 85.
5 Hugh Macpherson, *A History of Fowling*, page 435; *BWP* 2:659; Henry Stevenson, *The Birds of Norfolk*, Vol. 2, page 25.
6 Hugh Macpherson, *A History of Fowling*, page 435.
7 Henry Stevenson, *The Birds of Norfolk*, Vol. 2, page 18.
8 Henry Stevenson, *The Birds of Norfolk*, Vol. 2, page 5.
9 David Waters, Salisbury, Wiltshire.
10 David Waters, Salisbury, Wiltshire.

Waders, *Charadriiformes*
1 W. G. Hales, *Waders*, Collins, 1980, page 16.
2 Colin Harrison, *The History of the Birds of Britain*, page 123.
3 Paul Harvey, Lerwick, Shetland.
4 Robert Pinchen, *Sea Swallows*, Green, Lowestoft, 1935, page 224.
5 *BTO News* 243:25.
6 Eric Ennion, *The British Bird*, page 157.
7 Eric Simms, South Witham, Lincolnshire.
8 Phil Atkinson, *BTO News* 229:8–9.
9 Steve Rowland, Titchwell, Norfolk.
10 Steve Rowland, Titchwell, Norfolk.
11 Henry Stevenson, *The Birds of Norfolk*, Vol. 2, page 240.
12 Chris Mead, *The State of the Nation's Birds*, page 173.

13 Philip Brown and George Waterston, *The Return of the Osprey*, pages 164–5.
14 J. K. Stanford, *Bledgrave Hall*, Faber, 1950, pages 72–3.
15 Reg Partridge, *Bird Notes* 30:179.
16 J. K. Stanford, *Bledgrave Hall*, Faber, 1950, page 74.
17 Steve Gantlett, Cley-next-the-Sea, Norfolk.
18 *BWP* 3:67; Desmond and Maimie Nethersole-Thompson, *Waders*, page 53.
19 James Frazer, *The Golden Bough*, page 16.
20 Eric Simms, South Witham, Lincolnshire.
21 Desmond and Maimie Nethersole-Thompson, *Waders*, page 48.
22 *HBW* 1:352.
23 Rob Lucking, Norwich, Norfolk.
24 Rob Lucking, Norwich, Norfolk.
25 Thomas Hardy, *The Return of the Native*, Macmillan, 1974, pages 113 and 431.
26 Pete Allard, *Norfolk Bird and Mammal Report*, 1969, pages 12–13.
27 Desmond and Maimie Nethersole-Thompson, *Waders*, page 318.
28 Kenneth Allsop, *Adventure Lit Their Star*, Penguin, Harmondsworth, 1972, page 13.
29 E. R. Parrinder, *BB* 53:545–53; E. R. and E. D. Parrinder, *BB* 62:219–23; E. R. and E. D. Parrinder, *BB* 68:359–68.
30 Colin Harrison, *The History of the Birds of Britain*, page 103.
31 *Historical Atlas*, pages 172–3.
32 Desmond and Maimie Nethersole-Thompson, *Waders*, page 293.
33 Robin Hull, *Scottish Birds*, page 163.
34 Lockwood, page 54.
35 Charles Swainson, *The Folklore and Provincial Names of British Birds*, page 183.
36 Richard Vaughan, *Plovers*, page 17.
37 Richard Vaughan, *Plovers*, page 90.
38 Eric Simms, South Witham, Lincolnshire.
39 Andrew Wilson and Russell Slack, *Rare and Scarce Birds in Yorkshire*, 1996, privately published, page 149.
40 David Green, Linton, Cambridgeshire.
41 Bryan Sage, *A History of the Birds of Hertfordshire*, Barrie and Rockliff, 1959, pages 93–4.
42 Kate White, London.
43 Brian Vesey-Fitzgerald, *British Game*, page 164.
44 Charles Swainson, *The Folklore and Provincial Names of British Birds*, pages 180–1; Edward Armstrong, *The Folklore of Birds*, page 217.
45 Ingvar Byrkjedal and D. B. A. Thompson, *Tundra Plovers*, page xx.
46 Francesca Greenoak, *British Birds*, page 87.
47 Lockwood, page 93.
48 Garth and Vicky Waite, Falmouth, Cornwall.
49 Mary Muir, Claxton, Norfolk.
50 Dennis Sim, Glasgow.
51 Desmond and Maimie Nethersole-Thompson, *Waders*, page 85.
52 Graham Harvey, *The Forgiveness of Nature*, Jonathan Cape, 2001, pages 1–19.

53 Richard Vaughan, *Plovers*, page 11.
54 Beryl Rowland, *Birds with Human Souls*, page 96.
55 Thomas Bewick, *Selections from A History of British Birds*, page 227.
56 J. W. Hartley, Swansea.
57 Martin George, *Birds in Norfolk and the Law, Past and Present*, Norfolk and Norwich Naturalists' Society, 2001, page 12; Robin Hull, *Scottish Birds*, page 62.
58 Richard Vaughan, *Plovers*, page 127.
59 Colin Straker, Skipton, North Yorkshire.
60 Chris Gomersall, Potton, Bedfordshire.
61 Isabella Beeton, *Household Management*, page 524.
62 Billy Bishop, *Cley Marsh and its Birds*, pages 11–13.
63 Phil Gray, *The Washlanders*, pages 4–5.
64 Phil Gray, *The Washlanders*, page 20.
65 Elspeth Huxley, *Peter Scott*, Faber, 1993, page 88.
66 Ken Spencer, *The Lapwing in Britain*, page 126.
67 N. Calbrade, C. A. Entwistle, A. J. Smith and K. G. Spencer, *BB* 94:35–8.
68 Ray Easterbrook, Mortehoe, Devon.
69 Ken Spencer, *The Lapwing in Britain*, page 88.
70 Moss Taylor, Michael Seago, Peter Allard and Don Dorling, *The Birds of Norfolk*, page 254.
71 Brian Vesey-Fitzgerald, *British Game*, page 165.
72 Billy Bishop, *Cley Marsh and its Birds*, page 26.
73 Eric Simms, South Witham, Lincolnshire.
74 A. H. Daukes, *BB* 47:131–2.
75 Mark Shorten, Cork, County Cork.
76 Desmond and Maimie Nethersole-Thompson, *Waders*, pages 252–61.
77 *Winter Atlas*, page 196.
78 Thomas Bewick, *Selections from A History of British Birds*, page 38.
79 Abel Chapman, *Bird-Life of the Borders*, page 78.
80 David Stroud, T. M. Reed, M. W. Pienkowski and R. A. Lindsay, *Birds, Bogs and Forestry, The Peatlands of Caithness and Sutherland*, Nature Conservancy Council, 1987, pages 79–90.
81 Abel Chapman, *Bird-Life of the Borders*, page 77.
82 *The Atlas*, page 194.
83 Clifford Oakes, *BB* 41:226–8.
84 Derek Ratcliffe, *Bird life of mountain and upland*, page 112.
85 Ingvar Byrkjedal and D. B. A. Thompson, *Tundra Plovers*, pages 274–5.
86 Eric Ennion, *The British Bird*, pages 24–5.
87 Lockwood, page 128.
88 J. H. Gurney, *Early Annals of Ornithology*, page 87.
89 Hugh Macpherson, *A History of Fowling*, page 461.
90 J. H. Gurney, *Early Annals of Ornithology*, page 230.
91 Hugh Macpherson, *A History of Fowling*, page 462.
92 P. E. Jones, *The Worshipful Company of Poulterers of the City of London*, page 142.

93 James Ritchie, *The Influence of Man on Animal Life in Scotland*, page 371.
94 *Handbook* 4:198.
95 Phyllis Barclay Smith, *Bull BOC* 100:15–22.
96 David Snow, *Birds, Discovery and Conservation*, page 62.
97 Brian Vesey-Fitzgerald, *British Game*, page 141.
98 Brian Vesey-Fitzgerald, *British Game*, pages 157–8.
99 Paul Trodd, Dunstable, Bedfordshire.
100 John Fox, Ulverston, Cumbria.
101 Robin Hull, Strathtay, Perthshire.
102 W. B. Alexander, *Ibis* 87:512; 88:159–79, 271–86, 427–44; 89:1–28.
103 Brian Vesey-Fitzgerald, *British Game*, page 158.
104 Patrick Hanks and Flavia Hodges, *A Dictionary of Surnames*, page 582.
105 Eilert Ekwall, *The Oxford Dictionary of English Place-Names*, pages 111, 115.
106 Ken Spencer, Burnley, Lancashire.
107 Hugh Macpherson, *A History of Fowling*, pages 449–54.
108 Gilbert White, *The Natural History of Selborne*, page 114.
109 Isabella Beeton, *Household Management*, page 537.
110 Jeremy Holloway, Wotton, Surrey.
111 Colin Woolf, Betws-y-Coed, Conway.
112 Colin Woolf, Betws-y-Coed, Conway.
113 Andrew Hoodless, Fordingbridge, Hampshire.
114 Colin and Joanne Woolf, Betws-y-Coed, Conway.
115 H. M. Dobinson and A. J. Richards, *BB* 57:373–434.
116 Derek Toomer, Santon Downham, Suffolk.
117 Peter Davys, Hailsham, East Sussex.
118 *Handbook* 4:186.
119 Philip Brown and George Waterston, *The Return of the Osprey*, page 203.
120 Richard Richardson, 'The Godwits of Cley', *Norfolk Birds and Mammal Report 1969*, pages 9–10; Malcolm Ogilvie et al., *BB* 96:504–5.
121 C. T. Onions (ed.), *Shorter Oxford English Dictionary*, Vol. 2, Oxford, 1973, page 867.
122 Charles Swainson, *The Folklore and Provincial Names of British Birds*, page 199.
123 *Handbook* 4:156.
124 *HBW* 3:483.
125 Eric Meek, *BB* 95:299.
126 Arnold Illingworth, Knaresborough, North Yorkshire.
127 *European Atlas*, page 301.
128 Edward Grey, *The Charm of Birds*, page 170.
129 Desmond and Maimie Nethersole-Thompson, *Waders*, page 127.
130 *Anglo Saxon Poetry*, selected and translated by R. K. Gordon, Dent, 1926, page 84.
131 James Fisher, *The Shell Book of Birds*, pages 43–5.
132 G. L. Apperson, *The Wordsworth Dictionary of Proverbs*, Wordsworth, Ware, 1993, pages 129–30.
133 Arnold Illingworth, Knaresborough, North Yorkshire.
134 Brian Vesey-Fitzgerald, *British Game*, page 163.

135 James McCallum, Wighton, Norfolk.
136 Brian Vesey-Fitzgerald, *British Game*, page 165.
137 J. H. Taverner, *BB* 54:403–4 and 75:333–4.
138 Desmond and Maimie Nethersole-Thompson, *Waders*, page 230.
139 W. G. Hale, *BB* 48:455.
140 Peter Marren, *The New Naturalists*, HarperCollins, 1995, page 194.
141 Desmond Nethersole-Thompson, *The Greenshank*, Collins, page 76.
142 Eric Ennion, *The British Bird*, page 156.
143 A. R. Collins and R. D. Thomas, *BB* 77:567.
144 Bernard King, *BB* 57:250 and *BB* 75:88.
145 Frank King, *BB* 75:424.
146 S. D. MacDonald and David Parmelee, *BB* 55:241–4; Robert Gill, Jr, *BB* 79:402–3.
147 Colin Selway and Mike Kendall, *BB* 58:438; A. J. Mercer, *BB* 59:307.
148 Desmond and Maimie Nethersole-Thompson, *Waders*, page 221.
149 Mike Everett, Hemingford Grey, Cambridgeshire.
150 *BWP* 3:643.

Skuas, *Stercorariidae*
1 Lockwood, page 120.
2 Rob Hume, *Seabirds*, page 79.
3 Rob Furness, *The Skuas*, page 162.
4 Dennis Claridge, Guisborough, Cleveland.
5 Lockwood, page 135.
6 Eric Simms, South Witham, Lincolnshire.
7 Paul Harvey, Lerwick, Shetland.
8 Rob Furness, *The Skuas*, page 273.
9 Rob Furness, *The Skuas*, pages 273–4.
10 Rob Furness, *The Skuas*, page 118.
11 Lockwood, page 33; Paul Harvey, Lerwick, Shetland; Francesca Greenoak, *British Birds*, page 151.
12 Rob Hume, *Seabirds*, page 82; Colin Harrison, *The History of the Birds of Britain*, page 128.
13 Rob Furness, *The Skuas*, page 55.
14 Rob Furness, *The Skuas*, page 153.
15 Wendy Dickson and Bob Scott, *BB* 90:530.

Gulls, *Laridae*
1 Rob Hume, *Seabirds*, page 57.
2 http://www.dumaurier.org/birds.html.
3 http://news.bbc.co.uk/1/hi/uk/1459804.stm.
4 John Cooper, email contribution.
5 Eric Simms, *A Natural History of British Birds*, Dent, 1983, page 205.
6 Rob Hume, Sandy, Bedfordshire.
7 Tony Hare, London.
8 G. E. Took, *BB* 48:88–9.
9 http://news.bbc.co.uk/1/hi/uk/1459804.stm.
10 James Owen, *National Geographic News*, 7 January 2003; Stewart Payne, *Daily Telegraph*, 7 July 2001.
11 Gordon Hamlett, Longthorpe, Cambridgeshire.
12 Derek Goodwin, *Birds of Man's World*, page 95.
13 Rob Hume, Sandy, Bedfordshire.
14 James McCallum, Wighton, Norfolk.

15 Phil Palmer, *First for Britain and Ireland 1600–1999*, pages 127–8.
16 Dave Britton, *Yorkshire Birding* 11:143–4.
17 Richard Fitter, *London's Natural History*, page 177.
18 W. H. Hudson, *Birds in London*, 1898, Longmans Green, page 146.
19 W. H. Mullens, *BB* 2:222.
20 J. H. Gurney, *Early Annals of Ornithology*, page 189.
21 *Historical Atlas*, page 206.
22 J. H. Gurney, *Early Annals of Ornithology*, page 185.
23 Eric Simms, *A Natural History of British Birds*, Dent, 1983, page 208.
24 Annette Hope, *Londoners' Larder*, page 150.
25 Ron Murton, *Man and Birds*, page 161.
26 Chris Kehoe, Moreton, Cheshire.
27 Chris Mead, *The State of the Nation's Birds*, page 189.
28 *New Atlas*, page 207.
29 Cliff Waller, Blythburgh, Suffolk.
30 Stanley Cramp, *BB* 64:476–83.
31 *Winter Atlas*, page 238.
32 Mary Muir, Claxton, Norfolk.
33 Niko Tinbergen, *The Herring Gull's World*, pages 7–8.
34 Max Nicholson, *Birds and Men*, page 17; *BBC Wildlife*, February 1990, page 112.
35 J. M. Harrop, *BB* 50:352.
36 Nick Edwards, Cowes, Isle of Wight.
37 Chris Mead, *The State of the Nation's Birds*, page 190.
38 Ray Easterbrook, Mortehoe, Devon.
39 Cheryl Margiotta, *Press and Journal*, 24 April 1995.
40 Sue Raven, Sharnbrook, Bedfordshire.
41 Robin Young, *The Times*, 8 June 1998.
42 John Coulson, *New Scientist*, 17 August 1978.
43 Marcello Mega, *The Scotsman*, 14 June 1998.
44 Rob Hume, Sandy, Bedfordshire.
45 Nicol Hopkins and M. F. M. Meiklejohn, *BB* 46:112–13.
46 Chris Murphy, Belfast, Northern Ireland.
47 Tim Melling, Shepley, Yorkshire.
48 Moss Taylor, Michael Seago, Peter Allard and Don Dorling, *The Birds of Norfolk*, page 318.
49 C. A. Gibson-Hill, *British Sea Birds*, Witherby, 1947, page 69.
50 Rob Hume, *Seabirds*, page 58.
51 Francesca Greenoak, *British Birds*, page 154.
52 *Historical Atlas*, page 214.
53 Max Nicholson, *Birds and Men*, page 17.
54 Barbara and Richard Mearns, *Biographies for Birdwatchers*, page 307.
55 James Fisher and Ronald Lockley, *Seabirds*, page 235.
56 Bryan Sage, *The Arctic and its Wildlife*, Croom Helm, 1986, page 114.
57 Adrian Pitches, Tynemouth, Tyne and Wear.
58 Wendy Jones, Haveringland, Norfolk.
59 John Mather, *The Birds of Yorkshire*, Croom Helm, 1986, pages 347–9.
60 Martin George, *Birds in Norfolk and the Law, Past and Present*, Norfolk and Norwich Naturalists' Society, 2001, page 12.

61 John Mather, *The Birds of Yorkshire*, Croom Helm, 1986, page 347; J. C. Coulson, *BS* 10:158.

Terns, *Sternidae*
1 George and Anne Marples, *Sea Terns*, page 217.
2 Rob Hume, *The Common Tern*, pages 75, 68.
3 Colin Harrison, *The History of the Birds of Britain*, page 139.
4 George and Anne Marples, *Sea Terns*, page 7.
5 James Fisher and Ronald Lockley, *Seabirds*, page 253.
6 Rob Hume, *Seabirds*, page 87.
7 Mark Avery and Adrian del Nevo, *RSPB Conservation Review* 5:54–9; Hugh Macpherson, *A History of Fowling*, page 470.
8 Chris Mead, *The State of the Nation's Birds*, page 193; Malcolm Ogilvie et al., *BB* 93:570.
9 Rob Hume, *The Common Tern*, page 35.
10 Giles Dunmore (ed.), *Norfolk Bird and Mammal Report 2001*, page 194.
11 George and Anne Marples, *Sea Terns*, page 8.
12 James Fisher and Ronald Lockley, *Seabirds*, page 141.
13 *New Atlas*, page 220.
14 Chris Mead, *The State of the Nation's Birds*, page 194.
15 *New Atlas*, page 221.
16 Rob Furness, *BS* 35:199–202.
17 George and Anne Marples, *Sea Terns*, page 160.
18 Adrian Pitches, Tynemouth, Tyne and Wear.
19 *BWP* 4:115–16.
20 Rob Hume, *Seabirds*, page 125.
21 Garth Waite, Falmouth, Cornwall.
22 Herbert Axell, *Of Birds and Men*, page 39.
23 C. A. Gibson-Hill, *British Sea Birds*, Witherby, 1947, page 66.
24 Moss Taylor, Michael Seago, Peter Allard and Don Dorling, *The Birds of Norfolk*, pages 332–4.
25 F. Gotch, *Latin Names Explained*, page 274.
26 *Historical Atlas*, page 228.
27 Robin Hull, *Scottish Birds*, page 62.
28 Eric Ennion, *The Living Birds of Eric Ennion*, page 34.

Auks, *Alcidae*
1 Tim Birkhead, Sheffield, South Yorkshire.
2 *New Atlas*, page 224.
3 *The Atlas*, page 232.
4 *Handbook* 5:154.
5 James Fisher and Ronald Lockley, *Seabirds*, page 62.
6 Julian Huxley, *Birdwatching and Bird Behaviour*, Dennis Dobson, 1949, page 10.
7 Lockwood, page 75.
8 Anthony Gaston and Ian Jones, *The Auks*, page 16.
9 Martin Martin, *A Description of the Western Islands of Scotland* (with *A Voyage to St Kilda*), page 241.
10 James Fisher and Ronald Lockley, *Seabirds*, page 95.

11 *Historical Atlas*, page 230.
12 Jeremy Gaiskell, *Who Killed the Great Auk?*, page 172.
13 Chris Mead, *The State of the Nation's Birds*, pages 71–2.
14 Anthony Gaston and Ian Jones, *The Auks*, page 140.
15 Gwen Davies (ed.), *Bird Notes Bedside Book*, RSPB, Sandy, 1962, page 89.
16 *HBW* 7:30.
17 Jeremy Gaiskell, *Who Killed the Great Auk?*, page 8.
18 Jeremy Gaiskell, *Who Killed the Great Auk?*, page 14.
19 Rob Lambert (ed.), *Species History in Scotland*, page 21.
20 James Fisher and Ronald Lockley, *Seabirds*, page 69.
21 Anton Gill and Alex West, *Extinct*, Channel Four Books, 2001, page 201.
22 Rob Lambert (ed.), *Species History in Scotland*, pages 24–5.
23 Errol Fuller, *Extinct Birds*, page 98.
24 Rob Lambert (ed.), *Species History in Scotland*, pages 32–3.
25 Ken Williamson, *The Atlantic Islands*, page 125.
26 Paul Harvey, Lerwick, Shetland.
27 Paul Harvey, Lerwick, Shetland.
28 *The Atlas*, page 234.
29 C. A. Gibson-Hill, *British Sea Birds*, Witherby, 1947, page 116.
30 P. P. Bateson, *BB* 54:272–7; Richard Vaughan, *In search of Arctic birds*, Poyser, Calton, 1992, page 27.
31 Barry Nightingale and Keith Allsop, *BB* 89:583–4.
32 Eric Simms, South Witham, Lincolnshire.
33 C. A. Gibson-Hill, *British Sea Birds*, Witherby, 1947, page 141.
34 Colin Harrison, *The History of the Birds of Britain*, page 143.
35 P. P. Bateson, *BB* 54:272–7.
36 Rob Hume, *Seabirds*, page 73.
37 Richard Meinertzhagen, *Ibis*, 101:49.
38 Colin Harrison, *The History of the Birds of Britain*, page 142.
39 Kenny Taylor, *Puffins*, page 108.
40 J. H. Gurney, *Early Annals of Ornithology*, page 220.
41 Colin Jones, Haveringland, Norfolk.
42 C. A. Gibson-Hill, *British Sea Birds*, Witherby, 1947, page 121.
43 James Fisher and Ronald Lockley, *Seabirds*, pages 97–8.
44 Jim Flegg, *The Puffin*, page 21.
45 James Fisher and Ronald Lockley, *Seabirds*, pages 95–7.
46 Kenny Taylor, *Puffins*, page 56.
47 Kenny Taylor, *Puffins*, page 30.
48 Kenny Taylor, *Puffins*, page 32.
49 *BWP* 4:235.

Sandgrouse, *Pteroclididae*
1 Bannerman, 8:390.
2 Moss Taylor, Michael Seago, Peter Allard and Don Dorling, *The Birds of Norfolk*, page 343.

Pigeons and Doves, *Columbidae*
1 John Tully, *BTO News* 214:10.
2 Alexander Skutch, *The Life of the Pigeon*, page xi.
3 Paul Harvey, Lerwick, Shetland.

4   Robin Hull, *Scottish Birds*, page 198.
5   Derek Goodwin, *Pigeons and Doves of the World*, pages 57–8.
6   Peter and Jean Hansell, *Dovecotes*, page 10.
7   Nick Richardson, Cambridge.
8   Isabella Beeton, *Household Management*, page 483.
9   Brigid Allen, *Food: An Oxford Anthology*, pages 273–4.
10   Beryl Rowland, *Birds with Human Souls*, page 43.
11   Beryl Rowland, *Birds with Human Souls*, page 43.
12   Beryl Rowland, *Birds with Human Souls*, page 41.
13   Richard Fitter, *London's Natural History*, page 199.
14   Richard Fitter, *London's Natural History*, page 119; Derek Goodwin, *Pigeons and Doves of the World*, page 59.
15   Derek Goodwin, *Pigeons and Doves of the World*, page 61; Derek Goodwin, *BB* 53:202.
16   Peter Goodman, Plymouth, Devon.
17   Eric Simms, *The Public Life of the Street Pigeon*, page 14.
18   John Tully, *BTO News* 214:10.
19   Andy Coghlan, *New Scientist*, 1 December 1990.
20   Eric Simms, *The Public Life of the Street Pigeon*, page 134.
21   Eric Simms, *The Public Life of the Street Pigeon*, page 49.
22   Ron Murton, *Man and Birds*, page 15.
23   http://news.bbc.co.uk/1/hi/uk/1125708.stm.
24   Eric Simms, *The Public Life of the Street Pigeon*, page 59.
25   Ken Eardley, Stoke-on-Trent, Staffordshire.
26   *Historical Atlas*, page 242.
27   Mark Cocker, *Guardian*, 4 November 1997.
28   Killian Mullarney, Lars Svensson, *Collins Bird Guide*, page 200; W. H. Hudson, *Birds and Man*, page 89.
29   Derek Goodwin, *Pigeons and Doves of the World*, page 69.
30   Bannerman, 8:342–3.
31   David Butt and Anthony Vine, *BB* 41:89; Derek Goodwin and W. G. Teagle, *BB* 40:283.
32   Bannerman, 8:347.
33   Ursula Grigg, *BB* 43:11–12.
34   R. F. Dickens, *BB* 46:412–13.
35   Derek Goodwin, *Pigeons and Doves of the World*, page 69.
36   Bannerman, 8:328.
37   Brett Westwood, Bristol.
38   Tim Melling, Shepley, Yorkshire.
39   Barry Howes, Reading, Berkshire.
40   *Handbook* 4:132.
41   Gilbert White, *The Natural History of Selborne*, pages 103–4.
42   Ron Murton, *The Wood Pigeon*, page 168.
43   Bannerman, 8:327.
44   Ron Murton, *Man and Birds*, page 34.
45   Brian Vesey-Fitzgerald, *British Game*, page 177.
46   Ralph Crown, Ingoldisthorpe, Norfolk.
47   Gordon Gent, Harleston, Norfolk.
48   R. Whiteland, Bungay, Suffolk.

49   *Historical Atlas*, page 244.
50   H. M. Dobinson and A. J. Richards, *BB* 57:373–434.
51   John Ash, *BB* 57:226.
52   Derek Goodwin, *Pigeons and Doves of the World*, page 72.
53   Derek Goodwin, *Pigeons and Doves of the World*, page 141.
54   Audley Gosling, *BB* 78:238–9.
55   Derek Goodwin, Petts Wood, Kent.
56   Bannerman, 8:329.
57   Steven Gresham, Pateley Bridge, North Yorkshire.
58   Chris Kightley, Northrepps, Norfolk.
59   W. H. Hudson, *Birds and Man*, page 87.
60   Bethan Mair, Pontardulais, Swansea.
61   W. H. Hudson, *Birds and Man*, page 90.
62   Thomas Caldwell (ed.), *The Golden Book of Modern English Verse*, Dent, 1941, pages 132–3.
63   Derek Goodwin, Petts Wood, Kent.
64   Rev. O. C. Leigh-Williams, Basildon, Essex.
65   Mark Easton, Sandy, Bedfordshire.
66   Bannerman, 8:347.
67   Colin Harrison, *The History of the Birds of Britain*, page 147.
68   Chris Kightley, Northrepps, Norfolk.
69   *BWP* 4:341.
70   James Fisher, *BB* 46:151.
71   *New Atlas*, page 238.
72   Richard Richardson, Michael Seago and A. C. Church, *BB* 50:239–46.
73   *New Atlas*, pages 238–9.
74   Stephen Cousins, Ulverston, Cumbria.
75   Betty Jenkins, Brighton, East Sussex.
76   Sonja Gaffer, Norwich, Norfolk.
77   Bannerman, 8:368.
78   R. Bosworth Smith, *Bird Life and Bird Lore*, page 412.
79   Edward Grey, *The Charm of Birds*, page 91.
80   Bannerman, 8:368–9.
81   Angela Bate, Tamworth, Staffordshire.
82   *BWP* 4:356.
83   *New Atlas*, page 240.
84   Bannerman, 8:372.

Parrots, *Psittacidae*

1   Chris Butler, *BB* 95:345–8.
2   Salim Ali and Dillon Ripley, *Handbook of the Birds of India and Pakistan*, compact edition, Oxford University Press, Oxford, 1983, page 222.
3   Dave Harris, Walton-on-Thames, Surrey.

Cuckoos, *Cuculidae*

1   Rev. C. A. Johns (ed. W. B. Alexander), *British Birds in Their Haunts*, Routledge & Kegan Paul, 1948, pages 138–42.
2   Angela Bate, Tamworth, Staffordshire.
3   Ian Wyllie, *The Cuckoo*, page 55.
4   John Buchan-Hepburn, *BB* 48:512.
5   Bannerman, 4:137.
6   J. D. Harcourt Roberts, *BB* 48:512.
7   Kenneth Gregory, *The First Cuckoo*, George Allen & Unwin, 1976, pages 87–8.
8   Kenneth Gregory, *The Second Cuckoo*, George Allen & Unwin, 1983, page 112.
9   Kenneth Gregory, *The Third Cuckoo*, George Allen & Unwin, 1983, page 13.
10   Ian Wyllie, *The Cuckoo*, page 83.
11   Bannerman, 4:127.

12   Miriam Rothschild and Theresa Clay, *Fleas, Flukes and Cuckoos*, Collins, 1953, page 256.
13   Cherry Saville, Kenilworth, Warwickshire.
14   Clive Fairweather, Harbertonford, Devon.
15   Marjorie Campion, Murton, Cumbria.
16   E. L. McAdam, Jr, and George Milne, *Johnson's Dictionary: A Modern Selection*, Gollancz, 1963, page 141.
17   Pliny, *Natural History*, Books 8–11, page 309.
18   Thomas Harrison, *They Tell of Birds*, page 144.
19   Gilbert White, *The Natural History of Selborne*, page 115.
20   Frances Pitt, 'The Scandalous Cuckoo' in Richard Harman (ed.), *Countryside Mood*, Blandford, 1943, pages 104–5.
21   David Snow, *Birds, Discovery and Conservation*, page 84.
22   *Bull BOC*, 100 (1):4–43.
23   David Snow, *Birds, Discovery and Conservation*, page 83.
24   Edgar Chance, *The Truth about the Cuckoo*, page 147.
25   N. B. Davies, *Cuckoos, Cowbirds and Other Cheats*, pages 26–8.
26   Chris Mead, *The State of the Nation's Birds*, page 204.
27   Miriam Rothschild and Theresa Clay, *Fleas, Flukes and Cuckoos*, Collins, 1953, pages 256–7.
28   Cherry Saville, Kenilworth, Warwickshire.
29   Ken Spencer, 'Wild Birds in Lancashire Folk-lore', *Journal of the Lancashire Dialect Society*, No. 15, 1966, page 5.
30   Edward Armstrong, *The Folklore of Birds*, page 208.
31   David Finnis, Marsden, West Yorkshire.
32   Ken Spencer, 'Wild Birds in Lancashire Folk-lore', *Journal of the Lancashire Dialect Society*, No. 15, 1966, page 5.
33   Ian Wyllie, *The Cuckoo*, page 79.
34   N. B. Davies, *Cuckoos, Cowbirds and Other Cheats*, page 104.

Owls, *Strigiformes*

1   Clive Fairweather, Harbertonford, Devon.
2   David Holland, Corby, Northamptonshire.
3   R. Bosworth Smith, *Bird Life and Bird Lore*, pages 22–3.
4   C. T. Onions (ed.), *Shorter Oxford English Dictionary*, Vol. 2, Oxford, 1973, page 1487.
5   *The Atlas*, page 250.
6   Max Nicholson, *Birds and Men*, page 72.
7   Bannerman, 4:247.
8   John Pollard, Red Wharf Bay, Anglesey.
9   Gilbert White, *The Natural History of Selborne*, page 137.
10   W. H. Hudson, *Nature in Downland*, page 175.
11   Rev. C. A. Johns (ed. W. B. Alexander), *British Birds in Their Haunts*, Routledge & Kegan Paul, 1948, page 143.
12   C. M. Gentry, Horsham, Sussex.
13   Tim Melling, Shepley, Yorkshire.
14   Peter Walton, *The Cheerfulness of Sparrows*, Shoestring Press, Nottingham, 1998.

15 Derek Goodwin, Petts Wood, Kent.
16 Richard Vaughan, *In search of Arctic birds*, Poyser, Calton, 1992, page 27.
17 Paul Harvey, Lerwick, Shetland.
18 Bannerman, 4:163.
19 Martin Robinson and Dustin Becker, *BB* 79:228–42.
20 John Cantelo, *BB* 79:253.
21 Mike Rogers et al., *BB* 83:470.
22 Robert Spencer et al., *BB* 82:496.
23 Malcolm Ogilvie et al., *BB* 87:385.
24 *BWP* 5:517.
25 John Walpole-Bond, *A History of Sussex Birds*, Vol. 1, page 200.
26 F. M. Ogilvie, *Field Observations on British Birds*, Selwyn and Blount, 1920, pages 221–2.
27 Alice Hibbert-Ware, *BB* 31:162–87; 205–29; 249–64.
28 *Historical Atlas*, page 252.
29 Max Nicholson, *Birds and Men*, page 68.
30 Alice Hibbert-Ware, *BB* 31:162–3.
31 Anne Waddingham, Tonbridge, Kent.
32 Enid Goodwin, Knaresborough, Yorkshire.
33 Edward Armstrong, *The Folklore of Birds*, page 114.
34 R. Bosworth Smith, *Bird Life and Bird Lore*, pages 70–1.
35 A. M. Macfarlane, *BB* 70:348.
36 W. H. Hudson, *Birds and Man*, page 175.
37 Charles Waterton, *Essays on Natural History*, Frederick Warne, 1870, page 124; Paul Green, *BTO News* 196:24.
38 Simon Barnes, Sherborne, Dorset.
39 John Smith, Flore, Northamptonshire.
40 Richard Spirett, *BB* 77:24.
41 *BWP* 4:529.
42 T. F. F. Nixon, Pampisford, Cambridgeshire.
43 Clive Fairweather, Harbertonford, Devon.
44 Bannerman, 4:244.
45 Eric Hosking, *An Eye for a Bird*, Hutchinson, 1970, pages 18–21.
46 Eric Hosking and Jim Flegg, *Eric Hosking's Owls*, Pelham, 1982, page 19.
47 *Handbook* 2:328.
48 Bannerman, 4:226.
49 G. H. Brooks, *BB* 79:404.
50 Ron Murton, *Man and Birds*, page 53.
51 Bannerman, 4:223.
52 Robert Dunsford, Swinton, Manchester.

Nightjars, *Caprimulgidae*
1 John Walpole-Bond, *A History of Sussex Birds*, Vol. 1, page 156.
2 Walter Johnson (ed.), *Journals of Gilbert White*, Routledge & Kegan Paul, 1982, page 318.
3 H. Kirke-Swann, *A Dictionary of English and Folk-Names of British Birds*, pages 199, 233.
4 Phil Palmer, *First for Britain and Ireland*, page 152.
5 William Turner, *Turner on Birds*, pages 48–51.
6 John Clare, *Bird Poems*, Folio, 1980, page 17.
7 Derek Toomer, Santon Downham, Suffolk.
8 Michael Clegg, *BB* 78:198.
9 John Walpole-Bond, *A History of Sussex Birds*, Vol. 1, page 161.

10 Richard Meinertzhagen, *Middle East Diary 1917–1956*, Cresset Press, 1959, page 39.
11 Roy Frost, Chesterfield, Derbyshire; J. Whitaker, *Notes on the Birds of Nottinghamshire*, Walter Black, Nottingham, 1907, pages 141–2.
12 Carla Madeley, Mansfield, Nottinghamshire.

Swifts, *Apodidae*
1 Jane Waites, Lostwithiel, Cornwall; Muriel Fitt, Potters Bar, Hertfordshire.
2 Diane Myatt, Amberley, Gloucestershire.
3 L. Nixon, Pampisford, Cambridge.
4 Sonja Gaffer, Norwich.
5 Max Nicholson, *Birds and Men*, page 10.
6 William Yarrell, *A History of British Birds*, Vol. 2, page 261.
7 David Lack, *BB* 45:186–215; Chris Perrins, Oxford.
8 *BWP* 4:680; *HBW* 5:395.
9 Anon., *British Wildlife*, February 2003, page 205.
10 Norman Elkins, *Weather and Bird Behaviour*, Poyser, Calton, 1988, pages 67–72.
11 Max Nicholson, *Birds and Men*, page 216.
12 David Lack, *Swifts in a Tower*, page 35.
13 Tim and Shelagh Crafer, Stiffkey, Norfolk.
14 Charles Swainson, *The Folklore and Provincial Names of British Birds*, page 96.
15 Tim Melling, Shepley, Yorkshire.
16 Diane Myatt, Amberley, Gloucestershire.
17 Diane Myatt, Amberley, Gloucestershire.
18 Miriam Rothschild and Theresa Clay, *Fleas, Flukes and Cuckoos*, Collins, 1953, page 212.
19 Ann Lewis, Norwich.

Kingfishers, *Alcedinidae*
1 Charlie Hamilton James, email contribution.
2 David Boag, *The Kingfisher*, page 9.
3 W. H. Hudson, *Birds and Man*, page 12.
4 David Boag, *The Kingfisher*, page 11.
5 William Yarrell, *A History of British Birds*, Vol. 2, page 228.

Bee-eaters, *Meropidae*
1 Bernard Tucker, *BB* 41:18.
2 David Saunders, *Rare Birds of the British Isles*, Patrick Stephens, Sparkford, 1991, page 130.
3 Tim Melling, Shepley, Yorkshire.
4 Rob Sawyer, email contribution.

Hoopoes, *Upupidae*
1 Leo Batten, Colin Bibby, P. Clement, G. Elliott and R. Porter, *Red Data Birds in Britain*, Poyser, 1990, page 232.
2 Norman Ticehurst, *A History of the Birds of Kent*, Witherby, 1909, page 241.
3 Richard Mabey, Roydon, Norfolk.
4 *HBW* 6:321.
5 Bannerman, 4:57.

Woodpeckers, *Picidae*
1 William Yarrell, *A History of British*

Birds, Vol. 2, page 159; Norman Ticehurst, *A History of the Birds of Kent*, Witherby, 1909, page 230.
2 D'Arcy Wentworth Thompson, *A Glossary of Greek Birds*, page 71.
3 A. B. Cook, *Zeus: A Study in Ancient Religion*, Vol. 1, 1914, page 253; Robert Graves, *Greek Myths*, Folio, 1996, page 182.
4 Bannerman, 4:124.
5 Derek Moore, Salem, Carmarthenshire.
6 Derek Moore, Salem, Carmarthenshire.
7 Charles Swainson, *The Folk Lore and Provincial Names of British Birds*, pages 99–100.
8 William Yarrell, *A History of British Birds*, Vol. 2, page 142.
9 Edward Armstrong, *The Folklore of Birds*, pages 92–110; R. Harris, *Picus Who Is Also Zeus*, page 1.
10 *BWP* 4:867; Norman Pullen, *BB* 37:175.
11 Eric Simms, *A Natural History of British Birds*, Dent, 1983, page 94.
12 R. P. Parkhurst, *BB* 40:312; *HBW* 4:351.
13 Peter Roberts, *BB* 47:62.
14 Nick Richardson, Cambridge.
15 C. J. Pring, *BB* 23:129–31.
16 *Historical Atlas*, page 274.

Larks, *Alaudidae*
1 Derek Moore, Salem, Carmarthenshire.
2 Jeremy Mynott, Cambridge.
3 Chris Rollie, St John's Town of Dalry, Dumfries and Galloway.
4 W. H. Hudson, *Birds and Man*, pages 126–7.
5 *BWP* 5:182.
6 Robin Hull, *Scottish Birds*, page 219.
7 William Yarrell, *A History of British Birds*, Vol. 1, page 447.
8 Hugh Macpherson, *A History of Fowling*, page 56.
9 Isabella Beeton, *Household Management*, page 479.
10 Annette Hope, *English Cuisine from Chaucer to the Present*, page 134.
11 *Historical Atlas*, page 278.
12 Paul Trodd and Dave Kramer, *The Birds of Bedfordshire*, page 213.
13 Paul Donald, *The Skylark*, page 217.
14 *Historical Atlas*, page 278.
15 Paul Donald, *The Skylark*, page 218.
16 Paul Donald, Sandy, Bedfordshire.
17 Francesca Greenoak, *British Birds*, page 139.
18 Jonathan Elphick, London.
19 Clive Fairweather, Harbertonford, Devon.
20 Max Nicholson, *Birds and Men*, page 54.
21 Oliver Rackham, *Trees and Woodland in the British Landscape*, Phoenix, 1990, page 35.

Swallows and Martins, *Hirundinidae*
1 *BWP* 5:245.
2 P. L. Williams, *BB* 60:167–8.
3 Charles Waterton, *Essays on Natural History*, Frederick Warne, 1870, page 125.
4 Nicola Penford, *Birds*, Autumn 2000, pages 25–6.
5 Geoff Welch, Minsmere, Suffolk.
6 Chris Mead and G. R. M. Pepler, *BB* 68:89–99.
7 Gilbert White, *The Natural History of Selborne*, page 37.

8   Christine Muir, North Ronaldsay, Orkney.
9   Max Nicholson, *Birds and Men*, page 210.
10 Roy Frost, *BB* 64:279–80; Alan Green and Bernard King, *BB* 74:442–3; V. R. Tucker, *BB* 77:210.
11 William Yarrell, *A History of British Birds*, Vol. 2, pages 239–40.
12 Angela Turner, *The Swallow*, page 73.
13 Charles Swainson, *The Folk Lore and Provincial Names of British Birds*, page 53.
14 Ken Spencer, 'Wild Birds in Lancashire Folk-lore', *Journal of the Lancashire Dialect Society*, No. 15, 1966, page 7.
15 Angela Turner, *The Swallow*, page 80.
16 Christine Muir, North Ronaldsay, Orkney.
17 Christine Muir, North Ronaldsay, Orkney.
18 Geoffrey and Judy Grimes, West Malling, Kent.
19 Max Nicholson, *Birds and Men*, page 206.
20 Anne Cocker, Buxton, Derbyshire.
21 Richard Mabey, Roydon, Norfolk.
22 Anne Cocker, Buxton, Derbyshire.
23 Lockwood, page 101.
24 Gilbert White, *The Natural History of Selborne*, page 140.
25 William Yarrell, *A History of British Birds*, Vol. 2, page 248.
26 Eric Simms, South Witham, Lincolnshire.
27 Garth Waite, Falmouth, Cornwall.
28 *BWP* 5:292; *Migration Atlas*, pages 465–7.

Pipits and Wagtails, *Motacillidae*
1   Eric Simms, *British Larks, Pipits and Wagtails*, page 120.
2   Edward Grey, *The Charm of Birds*, page 57.
3   James Fisher, 'The Birds of John Clare' in *The First Fifty Years*, Kettering and District Naturalists' Society, Kettering, 1955, page 62.
4   William Yarrell, *The History of British Birds*, Vol. 1, page 424.
5   E. M. Nicholson and I. J. Ferguson-Lees, *BB* 55:299–345.
6   David Skidmore, Wolverhampton, West Midlands.
7   *Winter Atlas*, page 294.
8   Eric Simms, *British Larks, Pipits and Wagtails*, page 135.
9   Edward Grey, *The Charm of Birds*, page 37.
10 Bannerman, 2:74.
11 Eric Simms, *British Larks, Pipits and Wagtails*, page 151.
12 *The Atlas*, page 394.
13 Colin Harrison, *The History of the Birds of Britain*, page 199.
14 *BWP* 5:415.
15 William Yarrell, *The History of British Birds*, Vol. 1, page 397.
16 Lockwood, page 162.
17 Eric Simms, *British Larks, Pipits and Wagtails*, page 233.
18 Diana Mackey, Emsworth, Hampshire.
19 Don Potts, *Natural World*, Spring 2002, page 50.
20 Derek Moore, Salem, Carmarthenshire.

21 Bannerman, 2:137.
22 Eric Simms, *British Larks, Pipits and Wagtails*, page 245.
23 Richard Mabey, Roydon, Norfolk; Richard Chandler, *BB* 72:299–313.
24 Richard Chandler, Oundle, Northamptonshire.

Waxwings, *Bombycillidae*
1   Richard Vaughan, *In search of Arctic birds*, Poyser, Calton, 1992, page 132.
2   Gilbert White, *The Natural History of Selborne*, page 43.
3   *Migration Atlas*, pages 487–9.
4   Dick Bagnall-Oakley, *BB* 54:39–40.
5   John Gibb, *BB* 41:8; John and Christina Gibb, *BB* 44:160.

Dippers, *Cinclidae*
1   Charles Swainson, *The Folk Lore and Provincial Names of British Birds*, page 30; Lockwood, page 53; Kenneth Perry, *The Irish Dipper*, page 12.
2   *Handbook* 2:222.
3   Kenneth Perry, *The Irish Dipper*, pages 57–80.
4   James Adler, *BB* 56:73–6.
5   Kenneth Perry, *The Irish Dipper*, page 73.

Wrens, *Troglodytidae*
1   Max Nicholson, *Birds and Men*, page 162.
2   Bannerman, 3:349.
3   Bannerman, 3:348.
4   Lockwood, page 171.
5   Rita Clark, Woodingdean, East Sussex.
6   William Turner, *Turner on Birds*, page 155.
7   A. E. Armstrong, *The Wren*, pages 139–40.
8   Dick Jeeves, *Birds*, Autumn 1999, page 17; A. E. Armstrong, *The Wren*, pages 27, 136; Richard Meinertzhagen, *Pirates and Predators*, page 173.
9   A. E. Armstrong, *The Wren*, page 134.
10 Max Nicholson, *Birds and Men*, page 160.
11 Jeremy Mynott, Cambridge.
12 www.mustrad.org.uk/articles /drama.htm#wren www.dingle-peninsula.ie/ wren.html.
13 Elizabeth Lawrence, *Hunting the Wren*, page 107.
14 Ronald Hutton, *Stations of the Sun*, page 97.
15 *The Atlas*, page 324.
16 Max Nicholson, *Birds and Men*, page 162.
17 Vera Haynes, *BB* 73:104–5.
18 Winifred Flower, *BB* 62:157–8.

Accentors, *Prunellidae*
1   H. Kirke-Swann, *A Dictionary of English and Folk-Names of British Birds*, page 219.
2   *New Atlas*, page 296.
3   N. B. Davies, *BB* 80:604–24; *BWP* 5:553–5.
4   N. B. Davies, *BB* 80:604–24.
5   Edward Grey, *The Charm of Birds*, page 26.
6   Derek Goodwin, *Birds of Man's World*, page 120.
7   Lockwood, page 56.

Thrushes and Chats, *Turdidae*
1   Helen Grant, Glasgow.
2   David Lack, *Robin Redbreast*, pages 1–2.
3   Lockwood, page 132.
4   Cliff Waller, Blythburgh, Suffolk.
5   David Lack, *Robin Redbreast*, pages 107–9; Chris Mead, *Robins*, pages 74–6; also Eric Simms, South Witham, Lincolnshire.
6   David Lack, *Robin Redbreast*, pages 61–2.
7   David Lack, *Robin Redbreast*, page 1.
8   David Lack, *Robin Redbreast*, page 135.
9   David Lack, *Robin Redbreast*, pages 135–6.
10 Enid Goodwin, Knaresborough, North Yorkshire.
11 H. Kirke-Swann, *A Dictionary of English and Folk-Names of British Birds*, page 199.
12 Peter James, email contribution.
13 *The Midday Programme*, BBC Radio Norfolk, 2 June 2003.
14 Ken Spencer, 'Wild Birds in Lancashire Folk-lore', *Journal of the Lancashire Dialect Society*, No. 15, 1966, page 12.
15 Megan Dauksta, Builth Wells, Powys.
16 Adam Gretton, Hadleigh, Suffolk.
17 Maureen Larkin, Loddon, Norfolk.
18 David Lack, *Robin Redbreast*, pages 58–60.
19 Charles Swainson, *The Folk Lore and Provincial Names of British Birds*, page 18.
20 The Rev. Canon W. H. Barnard, Congresbury, Bristol.
21 Chris Mead, *Robins*, page 38.
22 Robert Halliday, *Country Life*, 7 December 2000.
23 Max Nicholson, *Birds and Men*, page 151.
24 David Lack, *Robin Redbreast*, page 73.
25 Frank Giddins, Littleborough, Lancashire.
26 Ronald Hutton, *Stations of the Sun*, pages 115–16.
27 W. J. Brown, *The Gods Had Wings*, page 172.
28 *Historical Atlas*, page 306.
29 Richard Mabey, *Whistling in the Dark*, page 13.
30 Josephine Addison, *Treasury of Bird Lore*, page 75.
31 William Glegg, *A History of the Birds of Middlesex*, page 83.
32 William Glegg, *A History of the Birds of Middlesex*, page 83.
33 Richard Fitter, *London's Birds*, page 134.
34 Bannerman, 3:296.
35 *BWP* 5:634.
36 Edward Thomas, *The South Country*, page 51.
37 Richard Mabey, *Whistling in the Dark*, pages 25–6.
38 Richard Mabey, *Whistling in the Dark*, page 14.
39 Richard Mabey, *Whistling in the Dark*, page 12.
40 Edward Grey, *The Charm of Birds*, page 65.
41 Louis Halle, *The Storm Petrel and the Owl of Athena*, page 154.
42 Richard Mabey, *Whistling in the Dark*, page 102.

43 Martin Limbert and Peter Roworth, 'White-spotted Bluethroats Nesting and Summering in Yorkshire', *Bird News* 4:22–7.

44 Richard Fitter, *London's Natural History*, pages 121–6; David Glue, *Birdwatch*, November 1994, pages 5–7.

45 Eric Simms, South Witham, Lincolnshire.

46 David Glue, Tring, Hertfordshire.

47 Cliff Waller, Blythburgh, Suffolk; Mathew Frith and Dusty Gedge, 'The Black Redstart in urban Britain – a conservation conundrum?', *British Wildlife*, August 2000, pages 381–8.

48 B. S. Meadows, 'Breeding distribution and feeding ecology of the Black Redstart in London', *London Bird Report*, No. 34, 1969, pages 72–9.

49 Mathew Frith and Dusty Gedge, 'The Black Redstart in urban Britain – a conservation conundrum?', *British Wildlife*, August 2000, pages 381–8.

50 Michael Adams, Marchwood, Hampshire.

51 John Buxton, *The Redstart*, page 3.

52 Peter Davis, *BB* 59:353–76.

53 Stephen Moss, *Birds and Weather*, page 41.

54 Peter Davis, *BB* 59:353–76.

55 Gilbert White, *The Natural History of Selborne*, pages 92, 99.

56 Lockwood, pages 64–5.

57 Roger Lovegrove et al., *Birds in Wales*, pages 266–7.

58 Charles Swainson, *The Folklore and Provincial Names of British Birds*, page 12.

59 *Handbook* 2:173.

60 Peter Conder, *The Wheatear*, pages 304–5.

61 Peter Conder, *The Wheatear*, page 5.

62 Eric Simms, South Witham, Lincolnshire.

63 Bert Axell, *Of Birds and Men*, page 86.

64 Daniel Defoe, *A Tour Through the Whole Island of Great Britain*, Vol. 2, Dent, 1962, page 222.

65 William Borrer, *The Birds of Sussex*, R. H. Porter, London, page 60.

66 W. H. Hudson, *Nature in Downland*, page 127.

67 W. H. Hudson, *Nature in Downland*, pages 130–1.

68 Moss Taylor, Sheringham, Norfolk.

69 Abel Chapman, *Bird-Life of the Borders*, page 76.

70 Gilbert White, *The Natural History of Selborne*, page 43.

71 Gilbert White, *The Natural History of Selborne*, page 68.

72 Alex Dunn, Colchester, Essex.

73 Eric Simms, South Witham, Lincolnshire.

74 Marscha Schlee, *BB* 77:74–5; Bruce and Mary Campbell, *The Countryman Bird Book*, David & Charles, Newton Abbot, 1974, pages 23–5.

75 Donald Wilson, Kibworth Beauchamp, Leicestershire.

76 Ken Briggs, *BB* 77:424.

77 Betty Jenkins, Brighton, East Sussex.

78 Roma Davies, Swanley, Kent.

79 M. L. Buckland, Wootton Bassett, Wiltshire.

80 Susan Stoneham, Truro, Cornwall.

81 Barry Howes, Reading, Berkshire.

82 Bruce and Mary Campbell, *The Countryman Bird Book*, David & Charles, Newton Abbot, 1974, page 24.

83 Eric Simms, South Witham, Lincolnshire.

84 Betty Jenkins, Brighton, East Sussex.

85 M. L. Buckland, Wootton Bassett, Wiltshire.

86 Y. Wakelin, Brentwood, Essex.

87 Roma Davies, Swanley, Kent.

88 *The New Atlas*, page 314.

89 *The New Atlas*, page 314.

90 Peter Wootton, Gloucester.

91 Eric Simms, South Witham, Lincolnshire.

92 *Handbook* 2:137.

93 A. F. C. Hillstead, *The Blackbird*, Faber & Faber, 1945, page 6.

94 W. H. Hudson, *Adventures Among Birds*, page 187.

95 W. H. Hudson, *Adventures Among Birds*, page 186.

96 Max Nicholson, *Birds and Men*, page 145.

97 *Handbook* 2:137.

98 Faith Davis, Roydon, Essex.

99 *The Midday Programme*, BBC Radio Norfolk, 2 June 2003.

100 Ralph Crown, Ingoldisthorpe, Norfolk.

101 Sue Jenkins, Dersingham, Norfolk.

102 Josephine Addison and Cherry Hillhouse, *Treasury of Bird Lore*, pages 8–9; *The Times*, Robin Young, 29 November 1997.

103 Jennifer Hucklenbunch, Wigton, Cumbria.

104 A. Timbrell, Quinton, Birmingham.

105 David Norman, *The Fieldfare*, page 10.

106 Eric Ennion, *The British Bird*, page 52.

107 J. E. Kelsall and P. W. Munn, *The Birds of Hampshire*, pages 4–5.

108 Robert Dunsford, Swinton, Manchester.

109 Edward Grey, *The Charm of Birds*, page 18.

110 Francesca Greenoak, *British Birds*, page 164.

111 Bruce and Mary Campbell, *The Countryman Bird Book*, David & Charles, Newton Abbot, 1974, page 153.

112 Susan Eckholdt, Bridgham, Norfolk.

113 Patrick Hanks and Flavia Hodges, *A Dictionary of Surnames*, page 532.

114 Derek Latham, Smethwick, West Midlands.

115 Tim Melling, Shepley, Yorkshire.

116 Homer, *Odyssey*, Penguin, 1976, page 340.

117 Rob Hume, *A Birdwatcher's Miscellany*, Blandford, Poole, 1984, page 19.

118 Robin Hull, West Carnliath, Perthshire.

119 John Fowles, *The Journals*, Vol. 1, Jonathan Cape, 2003, pages 66–7.

120 Valerie Thom, *Birds in Scotland*, Poyser, Calton, 1986, page 284.

121 Eric Simms, South Witham, Lincolnshire.

122 H. M. Dobinson and A. J. Richards, *BB* 57:373–434.

123 A. F. C. Hillstead, *The Blackbird*, Faber & Faber, 1945, page 20.

124 Christine Croton, Stroud, Gloucestershire.

125 Frank Stanford, Williton, Somerset.

126 *BWP* 5:1018–19.

127 J. E. Kelsall and P. W. Munn, *The Birds of Hampshire*, page 2.

Warblers, *Sylviidae*

1 Eric Simms, *British Warblers*, pages 156–8.

2 C. Suffern, *BB* 58:517.

3 Eric Simms, *British Warblers*, page 158.

4 Eric Simms, *British Warblers*, page 156.

5 Michael Bright, *Animal Language*, BBC, 1984, page 82.

6 Malcolm Ogilvie et al., *BB* 95:575.

7 Deryk Shaw, Fair Isle, Shetland.

8 Alan Bull, Fair Isle, Shetland.

9 Tim Loseby, West Malling, Kent.

10 David Tipling, Kemsing, Kent.

11 Alan Bull, Fair Isle, Shetland.

12 Deryk Shaw, Fair Isle, Shetland.

13 Henry Howard, *The British Warblers*, 'Grasshopper Warbler', page 14.

14 Gilbert White, *The Natural History of Selborne*, pages 51–2.

15 Rev. C. A. Johns (ed. W. B. Alexander), *British Birds in their Haunts*, Routledge & Kegan Paul, 1948, pages 216–17.

16 Eric Simms, *British Warblers*, page 139.

17 Peter Goodman, Plymouth, Cornwall.

18 Eric Simms, *British Warblers*, page 151.

19 *BWP* 6:84.

20 Peter Davies, *BB* 87:91.

21 J. F. Burton and E. H. D. Johnson, *BB* 77:87–104.

22 Eric Simms, *BB* 77:115.

23 Barbara and Richard Mearns, *Biographies for Birdwatchers*, page 333.

24 Henry Stevenson, *The Birds of Norfolk*, Vol. 1, page 112.

25 *Historical Atlas*, page 440.

26 *Handbook* 2:46.

27 Eric Simms, *British Warblers*, pages 190–1; Michael Bright, *Animal Language*, BBC, 1984, pages 84–5.

28 Eric Simms, *British Warblers*, page 224.

29 W. H. Hudson, *Adventures Among Birds*, page 204.

30 Françoise Dowsett-Lemaire, *Ibis* 121:453–68.

31 *The Atlas*, page 364.

32 *Guardian Weekly*, 11 July 1999.

33 John Walpole-Bond, *A History of Sussex Birds*, Vol. 2, page 12.

34 Stuart Winter, Luton, Bedfordshire.

35 Françoise Dowsett-Lemaire, *Gerfaut* 69:475–502; Françoise Dowsett-Lemaire, Sumène, France.

36 Simon Busuttil, Dungeness, Kent.

37 Richard Richardson and Richard Fitter, *The Pocket Guide to British Birds*, Collins, 1952, page 90.

38 Ian Wallace, Anslow, Staffordshire.

39 Eric Simms, *British Warblers*, page 102.

40 W. H. Hudson, *Birds and Man*, pages 222–48.

41 Colin Tubbs, *BB* 56:41.

42 Bruce Campbell, *BB* 68:38.

43 *Winter Atlas*, page 330.

44 Eric Simms, *British Warblers*, page 111.

45 *Handbook* 2:84.

46 Eric Hardy, *Bird Lover's Weekend Book*, Seeley Service, 1959, page 31.

47 Jonathan Elphick, *A Guide Book to British Birds*, page 264.

48 Clive Hopcroft, Gauteng, South Africa.

49 *The Atlas*, page 372.

50 Derek Winstanley, Robert Spencer and Kenneth Williamson, *BS* 21:1–14.
51 Ian Wallace, *BB* 57:283.
52 Thomas Bewick, *A History of British Birds*, Vol. 1, page 222.
53 Jonathan Elphick, London.
54 Robin Hull, West Carnliath, Perthshire.
55 Tim Melling, Shepley, Yorkshire.
56 Keith Betton, Farnham, Surrey.
57 Eric Simms, *British Warblers*, page 57.
58 Edward Grey, *The Charm of Birds*, page 51.
59 James McCallum, Wighton, Norfolk.
60 Henry Howard, *The British Warblers*, 'Blackcap', page 6.
61 Henry Howard, *The British Warblers*, 'Blackcap', pages 16–17.
62 Gilbert White, *The Natural History of Selborne*, page 96.
63 Jonathan Elphick, London.
64 Garth Waite, Falmouth, Cornwall.
65 *Winter Atlas*, page 332.
66 Graham Elliot, Sandy, Bedfordshire.
67 C. F. Mason, *The Blackcap*, page 52.
68 David Tipling, Kemsing, Kent; Adam Gretton, Hadleigh, Suffolk.
69 David Tipling, Kemsing, Kent.
70 Steve Rowland, Titchwell, Norfolk.
71 John Cantelo, Canterbury, Kent.
72 Bannerman, 3:38–9.
73 Edward Grey, *The Charm of Birds*, page 47.
74 W. H. Hudson, *Birds and Man*, page 105.
75 A. L. Turnbull, *Bird Music*, page 73.
76 Edward Grey, *The Charm of Birds*, page 48.
77 Killian Mullarney and Lars Svensson et al., *Bird Guide*, page 304.
78 Eric Simms, *British Warblers*, page 318.
79 Eric Simms, *British Warblers*, page 318
80 W. H. Hudson, *Birds and Man*, page 115.
81 Henry Howard, *The British Warblers*, 'Chiffchaff', page 7.
82 *Winter Atlas*, page 334.
83 Edward Grey, *The Charm of Birds*, page 42.
84 *The Atlas*, page 386.
85 A. F. Gotch, *Latin Names Explained*, pages 399–400.
86 Charles Swainson, *The Folklore and Provincial Names of British Birds*, pages 25–6.
87 John Ray, *The Ornithology of Francis Willughby*, Book II, pages 216–17.
88 Henry Howard, *The British Warblers*, 'Willow Warbler', page 28.
89 A. L. Turnbull, *Bird Music*, page 54.
90 Edward Grey, *The Charm of Birds*, page 46.
91 Eric Simms, *British Warblers*, page 360.
92 Rev. C. A. Johns (ed. W. B. Alexander), *British Birds in Their Haunts*, Routledge & Kegan Paul, 1948, page 229.
93 Ian Wallace, *Birdwatching*, September 1997.
94 A. L. Turnbull, *Bird Music*, page 60.
95 Gilbert White, *The Natural History of Selborne*, page 53; Jonathan Elphick, London.
96 Jonathan Elphick, *A Guide Book to British Birds*, page 272.
97 *The Atlas*, page 384.
98 Bannerman, 2:287.
99 Bannerman, 2:289.
100 *Winter Atlas*, page 338.
101 Paul Trodd, Dunstable, Bedfordshire.

Flycatchers, *Muscicapidae*
1 Edward Grey, *The Charm of Birds*, page 69.
2 *The Atlas*, page 388.
3 Gilbert White, *The Natural History of Selborne*, page 135.
4 Garth Waite, Falmouth, Cornwall.
5 Joan Maybury, Hartlebury, Worcestershire.
6 Roger Lovegrove et al., *Birds in Wales*, page 300; Chris Mead, *The State of the Nation's Birds*, page 246.

Babblers, *Timaliidae*
1 Colin Harrison, *The History of the Birds of Britain*, page 175.
2 John Wilson, Leighton Moss, Lancashire.
3 William Yarrell, *A History of British Birds*, Vol. 1, page 382.
4 John Wilson, Leighton Moss, Lancashire.

Long-tailed Tits, *Aegithalidae*
1 Colin Harrison, *The History of the Birds of Britain*, page 172.
2 Simon Harrap and David Quinn, *Tits, Nuthatches and Treecreepers*, page 422.
3 Jennifer Hindle, West Dulwich, London.
4 Roy Frost, *BB* 66:496.
5 Leonard New, Stone, Staffordshire.

Tits, *Paridae*
1 William Yarrell, *A History of British Birds*, Vol. 1, page 373.
2 Chris Mead, *The State of the Nation's Birds*, page 248.
3 Desmond Nethersole-Thompson and Adam Watson, *The Cairngorms*, page 93.
4 Lockwood, page 156.
5 Jonathon Green, *Slang Down the Ages*, page 25.
6 Andrew Cannon, Norwich, Norfolk.
7 William Yarrell, *A History of British Birds*, Vol. 1, page 363.
8 Christian Garth, *Down the Long Wind*, page 109.
9 John Ash, *BB* 44:184.
10 James Fisher and R. A. Hinde, *BB* 42:347–57; 44:393–6.
11 Pamela Grant-Wood, Edinburgh.
12 Tim Melling, Shepley, Yorkshire.
13 Carlos Martinez del Rio, *BB* 86:321–2.
14 Ian Dawson, Sandy, Bedfordshire.
15 Emma Turner, *Every Garden a Bird Sanctuary*, Witherby, 1935, page 155.
16 Yvonne Penfold, Pitchcombe, Gloucestershire.
17 Pamela Ralph, West Hoathly, West Sussex.
18 Pam Reekie, Norwich, Norfolk.
19 Andy Gosler, *The Great Tit*, page 11.
20 Keith Betton, Farnham, Surrey.
21 Tim Melling, Shepley, Yorkshire.
22 Andy Gosler, *The Great Tit*, page 68.
23 Andrew Cannon, *Garden Birdwatch Handbook*, BTO, 1998, pages 48–9.
24 Derek Moore, Salem, Carmarthenshire.
25 Chris Gomersall, Sandy, Bedfordshire.

Nuthatches, *Sittidae*
1 Lockwood, page 109.
2 *BWP* 7:307.
3 Chris Mead, *The State of the Nation's Birds*, page 252.
4 Emma Turner, *Every Garden a Bird Sanctuary*, Witherby, 1935, page 73.
5 Bannerman, 2:167.
6 H. and V. Anslow, Woodford Green, Essex.
7 Derek Moore, Salem, Carmarthenshire.

Wallcreepers, *Tichodromadidae*
1 Simon Harrap and David Quinn, *Tits, Nuthatches and Treecreepers*, page 173.
2 Bannerman, 2:164.
3 Timothy Gibson, Nottingham.

Treecreepers, *Certhiidae*
1 Edward Grey, *The Charm of Birds*, pages 26–7.
2 *The Atlas*, page 322.
3 *Winter Atlas*, page 358.
4 Jonathan Hildred, Rugeley, Staffordshire.

Penduline Tits, *Remizidae*
1 John Hollyer, Worth, Kent; Theodore Barber, *The Human Nature of Birds*, page 55.

Orioles, *Oriolidae*
1 J. F. Burton, *Birds and Climate Change*, Christopher Helm, 1995, page 227.
2 Charles Swainson, *The Folklore and Provincial Names of British Birds*, page 100.
3 Lockwood, pages 170–1.
4 Laurel Tucker, in *Best Days with British Birds*, (eds Malcolm Ogilvie and Stuart Winter), *British Birds*, 1986, pages 112–13.
5 Paul Mason, Haddenham, Cambridgeshire.

Shrikes, *Laniidae*
1 Thomas Bewick, *Selections from A History of British Birds*, page 78.
2 F. Gotch, *Latin Names Explained*, page 378.
3 Geoffrey Beven and M. D. England, *BB* 62:192–9.
4 Henry Stevenson, *The Birds of Norfolk*, Vol. 1, page 63.
5 *Handbook* 1:294.
6 Herbert Axell, *Of Birds and Men*, page 155.
7 M. J. Dawson (ed.), *H. J. K. Burne*, Oriel Stringer, Brighton, 1985.
8 Mark Avery and R. Leslie, *Birds and Forestry*, Poyser, 1990, page 197.
9 *New Atlas*, page 382.
10 William Turner, *Turner on Birds*, page 119.
11 *Winter Atlas*, page 360; Graham Tucker and Melanie Heath, *Birds in Europe*, pages 414–15.

Jays and Crows, *Corvidae*
1 W. H. Hudson, *Birds and Man*, page 100.
2 Peter Thomsett, Claxton, Norfolk.
3 Derek Goodwin, Petts Wood, Kent.
4 *Historical Atlas*, page 376.
5 W. H. Hudson, *Birds and Man*, page 100.

6 M. R. Chettleburgh, *BB* 65:359–64.
7 A. W. G. John and J. Roskell, *BB* 78:611–37.
8 Lockwood, page 99.
9 Derek Stokoe, Stockport, Cheshire.
10 Lockwood, page 117.
11 Paul Cavill, Nottingham; Tim Melling, Shepley, Yorkshire.
12 Claire Lowe, Chelmsford, Essex.
13 A. Timbrell, Quinton, Birmingham.
14 Iona and Peter Opie, *The Lore and Language of Schoolchildren*, Oxford University Press, 1987, page 333.
15 Iona and Peter Opie, *The Lore and Language of Schoolchildren*, Oxford University Press, 1987, pages 333–4.
16 Enid Goodwin, Knaresborough, North Yorkshire.
17 Andy, Jayne, Hannah and Laura Cocker, Buxton, Derbyshire.
18 John Cooper, email contribution.
19 Dave Sykes, Claxton, Norfolk.
20 Max Nicholson, James Ferguson-Lees and Phil Hollom, *BB* 52:418.
21 Tim Birkhead, *The Magpies*, page 217.
22 Tim Birkhead, *The Magpies*, page 221.
23 J. H. Gurney, *Early Annals of Ornithology*, page 65.
24 Jim Spellman, Gillingham, Kent.
25 Peter Cocker, Buxton, Derbyshire.
26 Georgina Malcolm, London.
27 Eric Simms, South Witham, Lincolnshire.
28 Kenny Taylor, *BBC Wildlife*, February 1990.
29 Tim Birkhead, *The Magpies*, page 221.
30 Kenny Taylor, *BBC Wildlife*, February 1990.
31 Tim Birkhead, *The Magpies*, page 230.
32 Keith Clarkson, Sheffield, Yorkshire.
33 Tim Melling, Shepley, Yorkshire.
34 Keith Clarkson, Sheffield, Yorkshire.
35 Eric Simms, South Witham, Lincolnshire.
36 Nilufer Atik, *Liverpool Echo*, 2 August 2000.
37 Jonathan Elphick, London.
38 J. D. Rae Vernon, *BB* 86:315; A. M. Snook, *BB* 89:143.
39 Chris Mead, *BB* 70:168.
40 J. N. Hollyer, *BB* 63:353–73.
41 W. Payn, *Birds of Suffolk*, Ancient House, Ipswich, 1978, pages 224–5.
42 J. N. Hollyer, *BB* 63:353–73.
43 Lockwood, page 42.
44 Bannerman, 1:55.
45 Bannerman, 1:57.
46 Charles Swainson, *The Folklore and Provincial Names of British Birds*, pages 74–5.
47 Daniel Defoe, *A Tour Through the Whole Island of Great Britain*, Vol. 1, Dent, 1962, pages 246–7.
48 Gilbert White, *The Natural History of Selborne*, page 91.
49 Martin Woodcock, Wiveton, Norfolk.
50 Tim Melling, Shepley, Yorkshire.
51 Max Nicholson, *Birds and Men*, pages 176–7.
52 W. H. Hudson, *Birds and Man*, page 91.
53 Max Nicholson, *Birds and Men*, pages 178–9.
54 Lockwood, page 42.
55 Martin George, *Birds in Norfolk and the Law, Past and Present*, Norfolk and Norwich Naturalists' Society, 2001, pages 4–5.
56 John Cooper, email contribution.
57 Clive Hopcroft, Gauteng, South Africa.
58 Chris Mead, *The State of the Nation's Birds*, pages 257–8.
59 Derek Goodwin, *Birds of Man's World*, page 22.
60 Derek Goodwin, *Birds of Man's World*, pages 164–5.
61 Max Nicholson, *Birds and Men*, page 170.
62 William Glegg, *A History of the Birds of Middlesex*, page 12.
63 Richard Mabey, Roydon, Norfolk.
64 Gilbert White, *The Natural History of Selborne*, page 63.
65 Eilert Ekwall, *The Oxford Dictionary of English Place-Names*, pages 92, 269.
66 Mark Bloomfield, Alsager, Cheshire.
67 Julian Huxley, *Bird Watching and Bird Behaviour*, Dobson, 1949, page 87.
68 Max Nicholson, *Birds and Men*, page 179.
69 W. H. Hudson, *Birds and Man*, page 63.
70 E. J. M. Buxton, *BB* 54:404.
71 Max Nicholson, *Birds and Men*, page 177.
72 Max Nicholson, *Birds and Men*, page 48.
73 Richard Jefferies, *Wild Life in a Southern County*, Thomas Nelson, page 273.
74 Tony Hare, London.
75 Lockwood, page 131.
76 Edmund Selous, *Bird Watching*, Dent, 1901, pages 298–300.
77 George Yeates, *The Life of the Rook*, pages 20, 54.
78 Derek Goodwin, *Birds of Man's World*, page 9.
79 Garth Waite, Falmouth, Cornwall.
80 Ian Francis, Alford, Aberdeenshire.
81 Tim Melling, Shepley, Yorkshire.
82 Ron Murton, *Man and Birds*, page 140.
83 *Historical Atlas*, page 384.
84 Adam Watson, Aberdeen.
85 *BWP* 8:260.
86 Evelyn Baxter and Leonora Rintoul, *The Birds of Scotland*, Vol. 1, page 15; Bryan Sage and J. D. R. Vernon, *BS* 26:64–86.
87 B. M. Grover, Praa Sands, Cornwall.
88 Oliver Goldsmith, *A History of the Earth and Animated Nature*, Vol. 2, 1774, page 96.
89 Ken Spencer, *Bird Notes* 24:160.
90 Adrian Sangar, *Daily Telegraph*, 18 May 2002.
91 Roy Palmer, Dymock, Gloucestershire; Richard Fitter, *The Countryman*, 1952, 46:333–7.
92 Derek Goodwin, Petts Wood, Kent.
93 Garth Waite, Falmouth, Cornwall.
94 J. H. Gurney, *Early Annals of Ornithology*, page 81.
95 J. E. Harting, *The Zoologist*, 1894, 18:47–53.
96 Paul Trodd and D. Kramer, *The Birds of Bedfordshire*, Castlemead, Ware, 1991, page 278.
97 Ken Spencer, 'Wild Birds in Lancashire Folk-lore', *Journal of the Lancashire Dialect Society*, No. 15, 1966, page 8.
98 Charles Dickens, *Barnaby Rudge*, page 78.
99 Neil Lister, Ipswich, Suffolk.
100 J. E. Harting, *The Zoologist*, 1894, 18:47.
101 Sir Thomas Browne, *Notes and Letters on the Natural History of Norfolk*, page 27.
102 Evelyn Baxter and Leonora Rintoul, *The Birds of Scotland*, Vol. 1, page 10; William Glegg, *A History of the Birds of Middlesex*, page 6.
103 Richard Jefferies, *Wild Life in a Southern County*, Thomas Nelson, page 272.
104 Garth Waite, Falmouth, Cornwall.
105 (Mad Chico) Ivo Ceccarelli, Fox and Hounds, Acton Turville, Gloucestershire.
106 Evelyn Baxter and Leonora Rintoul, *The Birds of Scotland*, Vol. 1, page 8.
107 Garth Waite, Falmouth, Cornwall.
108 Paul Trodd, Dunstable, Bedfordshire.
109 Stuart Winter, Luton, Bedfordshire.
110 Clive Hutchinson, *Birds in Ireland*, page 189.
111 Derek Ratcliffe, *The Raven*, pages 251–2.
112 Bannerman, 1:14.
113 Seton Gordon, *Wild Birds in Britain*, Batsford, 1949, page 53; John Kemp, Welney, Norfolk.
114 Derek Ratcliffe, Girton, Cambridgeshire.
115 Ken Spencer, 'Wild Birds in Lancashire Folk-lore', *Journal of the Lancashire Dialect Society*, No. 15, 1966, page 8.
116 Beryl Melling, Bolton, Lancashire.
117 David Davies, *The Last of the Tasmanians*, Frederick Muller, 1973, page 64.
118 W. J. Brown, *The Gods Had Wings*, page 274.
119 Bannerman, 1:22.
120 Mike Rogers, *BB* 77:120.
121 Jeremy Powne, *BB* 77:120.
122 Evelyn Baxter and Leonora Rintoul, *The Birds of Scotland*, Vol. 1, page 6.
123 H. Fasey, Tunbridge Wells, Kent.
124 Pamela Pugh, Newcastle, Monmouthshire.
125 Hubert Pounds, *BB* 48:185.
126 Bannerman, 1:23.
127 Malc Fentem, Chaddersden, Derbyshire.
128 Derek Ratcliffe, *Bird life of mountain and upland*, page 65; Bannerman, 1:24.
129 Ellen Kershaw, Newport, South Wales.
130 *BWP* 8:207.
131 Bannerman, 1:2.
132 R. Bosworth Smith, *Bird Life and Bird Lore*, page 93.
133 Peter Reeves, *The Excavation of Two Barrows at Longstone Edge in the Peak District, Derbyshire*, English Heritage Report, 1996.
134 Bernd Heinrich, *Ravens in Winter*, dustjacket blurb.
135 Derek Ratcliffe, *The Raven*, page 74.
136 Derek Ratcliffe, Girton, Cambridgeshire.
137 A. T. Moffett, *BB* 77:321–2.
138 Paul Harvey, Lerwick, Shetland.
139 Edward Armstrong, *The Folklore of Birds*, page 152.
140 Derrick Coyle, London.
141 *Historical Atlas*, page 390.
142 Hugh Macpherson, *A History of Fowling*, page 4.

143 James Ritchie, *The Influence of Man on Animal Life in Scotland*, page 136; Desmond Nethersole-Thompson, *The Greenshank*, page 29.
144 R. Bosworth Smith, *Bird Life and Bird Lore*, page 86.
145 A. R. Reid, Sevenoaks, Kent.
146 Bernd Heinrich, *Ravens in Winter*, page 154.
147 Derek Ratcliffe, *Bird life of mountain and upland*, page 52.
148 Derek Ratcliffe, *The Raven*, page 83.
149 Derek Ratcliffe, *The Raven*, page 85.
150 Ron Murton, *Man and Birds*, pages 79–80.
151 Derek Ratcliffe, *The Raven*, page 84.
152 Seton Gordon, *The Immortal Isles*, Williams & Norgate, 1936, page 21.
153 James Ritchie, *The Influence of Man on Animal Life in Scotland*, page 226.
154 Derek Ratcliffe, *The Raven*, pages 77, 264.
155 J. H. Gurney, *Early Annals of Ornithology*, page 82.
156 James Ritchie, *The Influence of Man on Animal Life in Scotland*, page 225.
157 Sir Thomas Browne, *Notes and Letters on the Natural History of Norfolk*, page 27.
158 William Glegg, *A History of the Birds of Middlesex*, pages 1–2.
159 Derrick Coyle, London.
160 P. G. Moore, *Journal of Biogeography*, 29:39–54.
161 Gilbert White, *The Natural History of Selborne*, pages 20–1.
162 Henry Stevenson, *The Birds of Norfolk*, Vol. 1, page 257.
163 B. H. Ryves, *Birdlife in Cornwall*, Collins, 1948, page 70.

Starlings, *Sturnidae*
1 Colin Harrison, *The History of the Birds of Britain*, page 200; *Handbook* 1:41.
2 Chris Feare, *BB* 89:549–68.
3 John Snape, Erpingham, Norfolk.
4 Derek Moore, Salem, Carmarthenshire.
5 F. H. Lancun, *Wild Birds and the Law*, Ministry of Agriculture and Fisheries Bulletin No. 140, HMSO, 1948.
6 S. H. Chalke, *BB* 55:365.
7 Pliny, *Natural History*, Books 8–11, page 369.
8 Henry Mayhew, *London Labour and London Poor*, Vol. 2, page 72.
9 Jeffrey Boswall, 'The Language of Birds', *Proceedings of the Royal Institution of Great Britain* 55:249–303.
10 A. Simon, *A Concise Encyclopedia of Gastronomy*, The Wine and Food Society, 1944, page 67.
11 Chris Feare, Haslemere, Surrey.
12 William Yarrell, *A History of British Birds*, Vol. 2, page 46.
13 John Cooper, email contribution.
14 J. L. Davies, *BB* 42:369–75.
15 Max Nicholson, *Birds and Men*, pages 179–188.
16 Richard Fitter, *London's Natural History*, page 129.
17 Sue Clifford, Shaftesbury, Dorset.
18 B. J. Marples, 'The Winter Starling Roosts of Great Britain 1932–1933', *Journal of Animal Ecology* 3:187–203.
19 Chris Feare, Haslemere, Surrey.
20 Chris Feare, Haslemere, Surrey.
21 Martin Limbert, Doncaster, Yorkshire.
22 Andrew Henderson, Garthorpe, Lincolnshire.
23 Chris Feare, Haslemere, Surrey.
24 Chris Feare, *The Starling*, Shire, page 19.
25 Ron Murton, *Man and Birds*, page 278.
26 Andrew Henderson, Garthorpe, Lincolnshire.
27 David Hargraves, Darlington, County Durham.
28 Chris Feare, Haslemere, Surrey.
29 Barry Howes, Reading, Berkshire.
30 C. Lloyd, Welling, Kent.
31 Chris Feare, *The Starling*, Shire, page 21.
32 Tony Hare, London.
33 Christopher Lever, *Naturalized Birds of the World*, pages 479–89.
34 Chris Feare, *The Starling*, Shire, page 23.
35 Chris Feare, *The Starling*, page 3; Christopher Lever, *Naturalized Birds of the World*, pages 483–4.
36 Chris Feare, *The Starling*, page 279.
37 *BWP* 8:273.
38 Bannerman, 1:75.

Sparrows, *Passeridae*
1 Max Nicholson, *Birds and Men*, page 189; Bannerman, 1:342–3; *Handbook* 1:157; *BWP* 8:291.
2 Lockwood, page 144.
3 Austin Watson, Rotherham, Yorkshire.
4 John Cooper, email contribution.
5 Patrick Hanks and Flavia Hodges, *A Dictionary of Surnames*, page 503.
6 Beryl Rowland, *Birds with Human Souls*, page 158.
7 Leonard Lutwack, *Birds in Literature*, page 193.
8 Geoffrey Chaucer, *Canterbury Tales*, The Prologue, Dent, 1978, line 626.
9 Denis Summers-Smith, Guisborough, Cleveland.
10 Denis Summers-Smith, *The Sparrows*, page 144.
11 Denis Summers-Smith, *The Sparrows*, page 138; Denis Summers-Smith, *BB* 73:325–7.
12 Denis Summers-Smith, *The Sparrows*, page 145.
13 Robin Hull, *Scottish Birds*, pages 269–70.
14 Richard Meinertzhagen, *Ibis*, 91:470.
15 Eric Simms, South Witham, Lincolnshire.
16 Henry Stevenson, *The Birds of Norfolk*, Vol. 1, page 212.
17 W. Meise, *BB* 46:36; E. J. M. Buxton, *BB* 46:272; Collingwood Ingram, *BB* 46:352; M. F. M. Meiklejohn, *BB* 47:95–6.
18 Denis Summers-Smith, Guisborough, Cleveland.
19 Ralph Crown, Ingoldisthorpe, Norfolk.
20 Hugh Macpherson, *A History of Fowling*, pages 36–45.
21 Pat Anderson, Stanwick St John, North Yorkshire.
22 Ralph Crown, Ingoldisthorpe, Norfolk.
23 Anne Wilson, *Food and Drink in Britain*, page 133.
24 Peter Thomsett, Claxton, Norfolk.
25 William Glegg, *A History of the Birds of Middlesex*, page 37.
26 E. G. Witherden, Freckenham, Suffolk.
27 Paul Trodd and Dave Kramer, *The Birds of Bedfordshire*, pages 286–7.
28 Denis Summers-Smith, Guisborough, Cleveland.
29 Bannerman, 1:342.
30 Margaret Mills, Pattiesmuir, Fife; Dave Kitson, email contribution.
31 Denis Summers-Smith, Guisborough, Cleveland.
32 Henry Thoreau, *Walden*, Penguin, 1986, page 323.
33 W. H. Hudson, *Birds in London*, pages 15–16.
34 Denis Summers-Smith, Guisborough, Cleveland.
35 Ronald Lockley, *Birds of the Green Belt*, Witherby, 1936, page 142.
36 Han Suyin, 'The sparrow shall fall', *New Yorker*, 10 October 1959, pages 43–50.
37 Denis Summers-Smith, *The Sparrows*, page 244.

Finches, *Fringillidae*
1 Richard Fitter, *Birds of Town and Village*, Collins, 1953, page 12.
2 *BTO News* 236:16–17.
3 Anon., *The Book of Home Pets*, page 261; G. L. Apperson, *The Wordsworth Dictionary of Proverbs*, Wordsworth, Ware, 1993, page 243.
4 Edward Grey, *The Charm of Birds*, pages 28–9.
5 F. W. Frohawk, *British Birds with their Nest and Eggs*, Vol. 2, page 94.
6 Rev. J. E. Kelsall and P. W. Munn, *The Birds of Hampshire and the Isle of Wight*, Witherby, 1905, page 64.
7 F. W. Frohawk, *British Birds with their Nest and Eggs*, Vol. 2, page 94.
8 Anon., *The Book of Home Pets*, pages 269–72.
9 Albert Rettich, *Avicultural Magazine*, 1896, 2:114–17.
10 F. W. Frohawk, *British Birds with their Nest and Eggs*, Vol. 2, page 92.
11 Charles Swainson, *The Folklore and Provincial Names of British Birds*, page 63.
12 W. H. Hudson, *Adventures Among Birds*, page 220.
13 W. H. Hudson, *Birds in London*, page 198.
14 J. A. Baker, *The Peregrine*, Collins, 1976, page 92.
15 Robin Hull, *Scottish Birds*, page 261; William Turner, *Turner on Birds*, page 73.
16 Bannerman, 1:163; *BWP* 8:515; Jonathan Elphick, *Birds*, page 303.
17 Hugh Macpherson, *A History of Fowling*, page 50.
18 Richard Bashford, Sandy, Bedfordshire.
19 Max Nicholson, *Birds and Men*, page 118.
20 James McCallum, Wighton, Norfolk.
21 Brett Westwood, Bristol.
22 Alison Chandler, Johnshaven, Aberdeenshire.
23 Steve Palin, *A Dissimulation of Birds*, no page nos.
24 Ian Newton, *Finches*, page 36; Roger Lovegrove et al., *Birds in Wales*, page 332.
25 William Glegg, *A History of the Birds of Middlesex*, page 26.

26 Max Nicholson, *Birds and Men*, page 122.
27 Ian Newton, *Finches*, page 112.
28 Adam Gretton, Hadleigh, Suffolk.
29 Jonathon Green, *Slang Down the Ages*, page 38.
30 Tim Birkhead, Sheffield, Yorkshire.
31 Beryl Rowland, *Birds with Human Souls*, pages 64–6.
32 Charles Swainson, *The Folklore and Provincial Names of British Birds*, page 59.
33 *New Atlas*, page 414.
34 Henry Stevenson, *The Birds of Norfolk*, Vol. 1, page 225.
35 W. Borrer, *Birds of Sussex*, R. H. Porter, 1891, page 132.
36 *Historical Atlas*, page 404.
37 Robert Spender and Geoffrey Gush, *BB* 56:91–8.
38 Eric Ennion, *The British Bird*, page 11.
39 Charles Swainson, *The Folklore and Provincial Names of British Birds*, page 65.
40 *The Atlas*, page 418.
41 Thomas Bewick, *Selections from A History of British Birds*, page 119.
42 W. H. Hudson, *Birds and Man*, page 189.
43 Eric Ennion, *The British Bird*, page 92.
44 Eric Simms, South Witham, Lincolnshire.
45 *New Atlas*, page 418.
46 Mark Beevers, Bolsover, Derbyshire.
47 *The Atlas*, page 420.
48 Linda Williams, Burnley, Lancashire.
49 Seton Gordon, *Hebridean Memories*, Neil Wilson, Glasgow, 1995, page 1698.
50 W. D. Campbell, *BTO Ringing Journal*
51 Bannerman, 1:134.
52 Lockwood, page 49.
53 Charles Swainson, *The Folklore and Provincial Names of British Birds*, pages 67–8.
54 J. H. Gurney, *Early Annals of Ornithology*, page 59.
55 James Fisher, *The Shell Bird Book*, page 180.
56 Bruce Campbell, *Crossbills*, HMSO, 1973, page 10.
57 Ron Summers and Stuart Pierney, *BB* 96:100–11.

58 Ian Wallace, *BB* 92:445–71.
59 *European Atlas*, pages 732–3.
60 Lockwood, page 36.
61 William Turner, *Turner on Birds*, page 161.
62 Jonathon Green, *The Cassell Dictionary of Slang*, Cassell, 1998, page 165.
63 Thomas Hardy, *Tess of the d'Urbervilles*, Macmillan, 1974, pages 92–3.
64 Lord Chesterfield, *Letters to His Son*, Dent, 1938, page 6; sent by Clive Fairweather, Harbertonford, Devon.
65 William Turner, *Turner on Birds*, page 161.
66 Ian Newton, *Finches*, page 117.
67 *New Atlas*, page 426.
68 Julian Hughes, Sandy, Bedfordshire.
69 Bob Pearson, *The Birds of East and West Horsley*, Willowend, East Horsley, 1994, pages 50–1.
70 Guy Mountfort, *The Hawfinch*, pages 7–12.
71 Guy Mountfort, *The Hawfinch*, page 100.
72 Ron Murton, *Man and Birds*, page 226.
73 Guy Mountfort, *The Hawfinch*, page 12.
74 *Winter Atlas*, page 406.
75 Guy Mountfort, *The Hawfinch*, page x.

Buntings, *Emberizidae*
1 *Winter Atlas*, page 410.
2 Bannerman, 1:328.
3 Desmond Nethersole-Thompson, *The Snow Bunting*, pages 168–9.
4 Chris Mead, *The State of the Nation's Birds*, page 271.
5 Desmond Nethersole-Thompson, *The Snow Bunting*, page vii.
6 Desmond Nethersole-Thompson, *The Snow Bunting*, pages 74–5.
7 Desmond Nethersole-Thompson, *The Snow Bunting*, page 76.
8 Clive Fairweather, Harbertonford, Devon.
9 Bannerman, 1:248.
10 Colin Harrison, *The History of the Birds of Britain*, page 218.
11 Daniel Jenkins-Jones, Swansea.
12 Chris Mead, *The State of the Nation's Birds*, page 272.

13 Tim Melling, Shepley, Yorkshire; Tom Brereton, Bothenhampton, Dorset.
14 Jonathon Green, *The Cassell Dictionary of Slang*, Cassell, 1998, page 511.
15 H. W. Gallagher, Comber, County Down.
16 Bannerman, 1:266.
17 Leigh Lock, Elaine Harrison and Paul St Pierre, 'Saving the cirl bunting', *Birds*, Spring 1996.
18 Clive Jones, email contribution.
19 Max Nicholson, *Birds and Men*, page 127.
20 Clive Byers, Urban Olsson and John Curson, *Buntings and Sparrows*, page 119.
21 Cath Jeffs, Exeter, Devon.
22 Beryl Rowland, *Birds with Human Souls*, page 15.
23 Bannerman, 1:280.
24 Oscar Wilde, *Complete Works of Oscar Wilde*, Collins, 1966, page 952.
25 Brigid Allen (ed.), *Food: An Oxford Anthology*, page 297.
26 Tim Birkhead, *The Red Canary*, page 15.
27 Tim Birkhead, Sheffield, Yorkshire.
28 Ian Johnson, Binham, Norfolk.
29 Derek Goodwin, *Birds of Man's World*, pages 166–7.
30 Lockwood, page 37; Eilert Ekwall, *The Oxford Dictionary of English Place-Names*, page 74.
31 Lockwood, page 37.
32 Derek Moore, Salem, Carmarthenshire.
33 *BWP* 9:329.
34 Eric Hardy, *The Bird Lover's Week-end Book*, Seeley Service, 1959, page 38.
35 Eric Ennion, *The British Bird*, page 22.
36 George Yeates, *Bird Haunts in Southern England*, 1947, page 84.
37 Abel Chapman, *Bird-Life of the Borders*, page 101.
38 Edward Grey, *The Charm of Birds*, pages 86–7.
39 Max Nicholson, *Birds and Men*, page 50.
40 Paul Donald, Sandy, Bedfordshire.
41 Paul Harvey, Lerwick, Shetland.
42 Charles Swainson, *The Folklore and Provincial Names of British Birds*, page 69.

Acknowledgements

Birds Britannica could never have reflected so many modern responses to birds by relying exclusively on ornithological literature. Although the words of many hundreds of people who have written about the subject in the past have been quoted, I have also been able to include a wonderful chorus of more than 600 contemporary voices, each contributing specifically to the project. Quite simply there would have been no book without them. I acknowledge my huge debt to the following (an asterisk after the name indicates those whose contributions deserve special thanks):

Michael Adams, Josephine and Peter Addison, Carry Akroyd, Keith Alexander, Vic Allen, George Anderson, Pat Anderson, Ian Andrews, Grant Annal, H. and V. Anslow, Chris Anson, Diana Arundale, Andrew Ashcroft, Richard Aspinall, Norman Aspinwall, Phil Atkinson, Robert Atkinson, Ian Bainbridge, Dawn Balmer, R. Bamford, Margaret Banthorpe, The Rev. Canon William H. Barnard, Simon Barnes, Joe Barr, Sylvia Barron, John Bartley, Richard Barton, Richard Bashford, Angela Bate, Sheila Bates, Chas Baxter, Mollie Bayfield, Stephen Beaton, Janet Beaumont-Nesbitt, Colin Beckett, Anthony Beese, Mark Beevers, Graham Bell, John Belsey, Audrey Berry, Sally Bett, Keith Betton, Stewart Betts, Alan Bews, Mary Bichan, Marion Biggs, David Bingham, C. Bird, John Birch, John Birkett, Tony Black, Helen Blakemore, Linda Blenkinship, Andrew Bloomfield, Mark Bloomfield, David Boag, Dr Andrew Boardman, Peter Bolton, J. J. Boswell, Douglas Botting, Tom Brereton, G. J. Bristow, Malcolm Brockless, David Broome, John Brydson, M. L. Buckland, Christine Buckley, Mick Buckley, Alan Bull, Richard Burfoot, Simon Busuttil, Margaret Butcher, Jennifer Butt, Colin Butters, Dennis Butterworth, Lord Buxton, Marjorie Campion, Andrew Cannon, Glenn Carter, Ian Carter*, Nick Carter, Paul Carter, Paul Cavill, James Chambers, Alison Chandler, Nicola Chester, Diana Chrzaszcz, Patrick Claffey, Dennis Claridge*, Rita Clark, John Clarke, Keith Clarkson, Tim Cleeves, Kevin Clements, Sue Clifford, Anne and Peter Cocker, Jayne, Hannah and Laura Cocker, Mike Cockram, Stephanie Coghlan, Bruce Coleman, Ray Collier, Rob Collis, Robert Congdon, Clive Coombes, John Cooper, Stephen Cousins, Jane Cox, Peter Cox (editor, John Clare Society Newsletter), James Cracknell, Shelagh and Tim Crafer, Graeme Cresswell, John Crompton, Christine Croton, Ralph Crown, Gill Crum, Steve Cummings, Abraham Cutajar, Mary Daniels, Megan Dauksta, Jim Davies, Michael Davies, Nick Davies, Rona Davies, Faith Davis, Peter Davys, Mike Daw, Ian Dawson*, John Day, Tim Dee, Emily Dening, Bernard Dennis, Roy Dennis*, John Dickinson, Tony Dickinson, Wendy Dickson, Antony Disley, Austen Dobbs, Janet Dolby, Paul Donald*, Françoise Dowsett-Lamaire, Mike Duckham, P. Dudley, Megan Dauksta, Robert Dunford, Magda Dunlop, Alex Dunn, Chris Durdin, Ken Eardley, Ray Easterbrook, Mark Eaton, Jane Eccles, Susan Eckholdt, Laura and Danielle Eddy, Ben Edwards, J. E. Edwards, Nick Edwards, Graham Elliott, Graham Etherington, Mike Everett, Richard Farmer, Joy and Jim Farms, Doreen Farrier, H. Fasey, Dr Chris Feare*, Malc Fentem, Kate Ferrol, Clemency Fisher, Muriel Fitt, Margaret Flaws, James Fletcher, Marion Fletcher, Ian Forsyth, Kieran Foster, John Fox, Ian Francis*, Dan Franklin, Hans Fried, Roy Frost, Sonja Gaffer, Steve Gaites, H. W. Gallagher, Peter Gann, Steve Gantlett, Margaret Gardiner, Sheila and Kenny Garson, Gordon Gent, C. M. Gentry, Alan Gibson, Mike Gibson, Timothy Gibson, Lynn Giddings*, Frank Giddins, Gillian Gilbert*, Ted Gilbert, Beatrice Gillam, David Glue, Joan and Cliff Goddard, Martin Godfrey, Elizabeth Godwin, John Goldsmith, Peter Goodman, Enid Goodwin, Jason Goodwin, Helen Grant, Pamela Grant-Wood, B. Gray, David Green, Rolfe Green, Brian Gregory, Steve Gregory, Steven Gresham, Adam Gretton, Larry Griffin, Judy and the late Geoffrey Grimes, Simon Grove, B. M. Grover, Charlie Hamilton James, Beryl Hamlett, Gordon Hamlett, Arthur Harcourt, Alec Harcus, Sam Harcus, Tony Hare, David Hargrave, Dave Harris, John Harris, Steve Harris, Gwyn Harrison, Liane Harrison, Patrick Harrison, J. W. Hartley, Leonard G. Harvey, Anne Hawkes, Tony and Josie Haywood, Andrew Heaton, Andrew Henderson, J. E. Hennessey, Jean Heseltine, Geordie Hewison, Julie Hewitt, Jonathan Hildred, Tim Hill, Jennifer Hindell, Ruth Hitchcock, Ray Hobbs, Tim Hodge, Andy Hoodless, David Holland, Jeremy Holloway, John Hollyer, Cordelia Holman, Anne Holt, Clive Hopcroft*, F. Horner, Barry Howes, Jennifer Hucklenbunch, Baz Hughes, Doreen Hughes, John Hughes, Julian Hughes*, The Rev. Clephane Hume, Rob Hume, John Humphreys, Sean Humphreys, Alison Hunkin, Gil Hutchings, Arnold

Illingworth*, Tony Irwin*, A. D. Jack, David James, Peter James, Conor Jameson, Cath Jeffs, Betty Jenkins, Sue Jenkins, W. G. Jennings, Ron Johns, Ian Johnson, Clive Jones, Colin and Wendy Jones, Norman Jones, Rosy Jones, Chris Jordan, Janet Kear*, Chris Kehoe, Mavis Kelly, John Kemp, Ellen Kershaw, Audrey Keville, Rod Key, Ros Kidman-Cox, Chris Kightley, Angela King, Robin King, Steve Kirk, David and Peter Kitson, Alan Knox, Rosemaire Kuechel, Lorie Lain-Rogers, V. C. Lander, Maureen Larkin, Joyce Larner, Derek Latham, Tom and Annette Ledger, The Rev. O. C. Leigh-Williams, Peter Leith, Ann Lewis, Martin Limbert, Neil Lister, C. Lloyd, Fred and Pauline Lormor, Tim Loseby, John Love, Claire Lowe, Mary Lowes, Mr and Mrs B. Lucas, Jill Lucas, Rob Lucking*, Andy Mabbett, Andy McCallum, James McCallum*, T. A. McCullen, Peter McDermot, Phillip McGough, Niall MacInerney, Herbert Mackenzie, Andrew McKeon, Diana Mackey, Colin McLeod, Di McMahon, Adam McNaughtan, Duncan McNiven, Elaine McQuade, Carla Madeley, Bethan Mair, Georgina Malcolm, Moira Mannion, Tony Marr, John Marriott, Eric Marshall, Tony Marshall, Patricia Mascall, Nick Mason, Paul Mason, Georgina Matthews, Joan Maybury, Peter Mayhew, Nick Mays, the late Chris Mead, Kenny Meason, Beryl Melling, Ernest Miller, Ruth Miller, Margaret Mills, Paul Mills, Carl Mitchell, Heather Monkhouse, Briain Morell, Derek Moore, Huw Morgan, Joan Morton, Stephen Moss, Peter Moyse, Christine and Tommy Muir, Mary Muir, Chris Murphy, Jeremy Mynott, J. R. Neighbour, Leonard New, Cedric Nickerson, L. Nixon, T. F. F. Nixon, David Nobbs, Kenneth Noble, Elizabeth O'Brien, Duncan Orr-Ewing, Ken Osborne, Steve Palin, Phil Palmer, Roy Palmer, Alan Parker, Ruth Partington, Howard Pate, Frank Pattinson, David Peart, Yvonne Penfold, Chris Perrins*, Alan Perry, M. E. Pewsey, Ben Phalan, Jean Philpott, Sarah Picton, Adrian Pitches, John Pollard, Joyce Pringle, Robert Prys-Jones, Pamela Pugh, Keith Pullman, Bill and Rowena Quantrill, Dr Philip Radford, Rosalind Radonicich, Eva Rainbow-Hills, Pauline Ralph, Derek Ratcliffe*, Sue Raven, C. P. Rawcliffe, Paul Raymer, Madeline Reader, Nigel Redman, Pam Reekie, A. R. Reid, Jack Rendall, Neil Rendall, John Rennie, Alan Richards, Gwendolen Richards, Nick Richardson, Roger Riddingon, Elizabeth Ringe, Mark Roberts, Peter Robinson, M. Robson, John Paul Roby, Nathan Roche, Chris Rollie, Adam Rowlands, Richard Rowlatt, Christine Ruskin, Malcolm Ryan, Bryan Sage, David Salmon, David Saunders*, Cherry Saville, Robert Sawyer, Sandy Scarth, Daphne Schiller, Wendy Schmitt, Pauline Schofield, Paul Scholey, Calum Scott, Richard Scott, Derek Seddon, G. G. Searles, Richard Sell, Deryk Shaw, George Sheridan, Mark Shorten, Dennis Sim, Reuben Singleton, David Skidmore, Andrew Smith, Angus Smith, Graham Smith, John M. Smith, Judith Smith, M. Smith, John Snape, Steve Snelling, Jim Spellman, Jenifer Spencer, Gordon Staff, Frank Stanford, Anne Stenson, Geoffrey and Elizabeth Stevens, Andrew Stevenson, D. C. Stock, Derek Stokoe, Susan Stoneham, Colin Straker, Peter Strangeman, Denis Summers-Smith*, Les Street, David Swithenbank, Dave Sykes, Barbara Talmage, Stephen Tapper, B. A. Taylor, Brian Taylor, Moss Taylor, Sandra Taylor, Val Taylor, Martin Thoday, Michael Thomas, OBE, Des Thompson, J. Thompson, Peter Thompson, Peter Thomsett, Terry Thomson, Alan Tilmouth, A. Timbrell, David Tipling, Adrian Tissier, Brian Tollitt, Derek Toomer, Paul Tout, Morwen Tregudda, Bob Trutzenbach, Fred Tuck, Daniel Turner, Miss Turner, Mick Turton, Will Tyler, Brian Unwin, Peter Upton, W. B. Waddingham, Dr Sarah J. Wager, Garth and Vicky Waite*, Jane Waites, Y. Wakelin, Robert Walker, Robert Wallace, Cliff Waller, Peter Walton, Vivien Wareing, Jill Warwick, David Waters, G. M. Watkins, Adam Watson, Austin Watson, Giles Watson, Geoff Welch, Paul Westley, Brett Westwood, Peter Whitcomb, Kate White, R. A. Whiteland, R. Wildman, Philip Willey, Linda Williams, Matthew Williams, Jack Willmott, Donald Wilson, John Wilson, Beryl Wintle, E. G. Witherden, Martin and Barbara Woodcock*, M. Wood-Weatherill, Colin and Joanne Woolf, Peter Wootton, Malcolm Wright, Derek Yalden, William Young, Albert Zijlstra; in addition we wish to give sincere thanks for the following quoted material: *The Peregrine*, J. A. Baker (Collins); *Magpies*, Tim Birkhead (Poyser); *The Journals*, Vol. 1, John Fowles (Jonathan Cape); 'A Disaster', 'Curlews', 'Lineage', 'Swifts', 'The Hawk in the Rain', 'Thrushes', Ted Hughes (Faber); *Naturalized Animals of the British Isles*, Sir Christopher Lever (Hutchinson); *Whistling in the Dark*, Richard Mabey (Sinclair Stevenson); *Raven Seek Thy Brother*, Gavin Maxwell (Longmans Green); *The Gannet*, Bryan Nelson (Poyser); *The History of the Countryside*, Oliver Rackham (Dent); *The Eye of the Wind*, Sir Peter Scott (Hodder and Stoughton); *The Puffin*, Kenny Taylor (Whittet).

There would have been no public contributions without people first hearing of the project in a wide range of publicising articles or radio features. I would like to thank all those who helped to get the message out, in particular Andrew Bloomfield, Andrew Branson (*British Wildlife*), John Burton, Angus Clarke and Jane Wheatley (*The Times*), Sue Clifford and Angela King (Common Ground), Steve Dudley (British Ornithologists' Union), Paul Evans, Angie Eyles and John Mills (BBC Radio

Norfolk), Francis Farrow, Steve Gantlett (*Birding World*), Ros Kidman Cox (*BBC Wildlife*), Chris Kightley, Tim Norman, Joanna Pinnock, Tony Pollock, Alex Reece (*Country Living*), Roger Riddington (*British Birds*), Tim Sharrock, Steve Snelling (*Eastern Daily Press*), Nicki Straughan, Derek Toomer (British Trust for Ornithology), Brian Unwin, John Vidal (*Guardian*), Gary Wilkinson and Stuart Winter (*Daily Star*). In this category, my foremost debt is to Rob Hume, editor of the RSPB's *Birds* magazine; as well as sending in a beautiful contribution to the book, Rob carried a sequence of features in *Birds* throughout 2003, which probably led to more submissions than any other single source.

There is a small number of people who played other vital roles, many of them throughout the project. Some, such as John Costello, Alistair Crowle, Clive Fairweather, Derek Gifford, Paul Harvey (Shetland), Robin Hull, Rob Lambert, Eric Meek (Orkney), Mike Pennington, Steve Rowland, Eric Simms, Ken Spencer, Paul Trodd, Ian Wallace and Stuart Winter, submitted a mass of valuable material, sometimes including books. Very often they backed up this generosity by dealing patiently with a stream of queries or additional requests or by engaging in lengthy discussions. Robin Hull's contribution was particularly important. He has assembled what is probably the largest personal archive on the role of birds in culture and folklore. He placed much of this at my disposal throughout the writing of the book and I am deeply grateful for his kindness.

Steve Rowland played a critical role in enabling me to air a whole range of themes in birdwatchers' email discussion groups, which led to much valuable material. Professor Tim Birkhead and Derek Goodwin were regularly engaged in fruitful discussions and speculation. They also read and commented upon several species accounts and suggested many avenues of further research. Daniel Jenkins-Jones (with Jonathan Elphick) and Steve Shaw kindly prepared two of the appendices, which appear under their respective names. We are honoured to include them in the book.

Lastly in the realm of public contributions, I come to Tim Melling. I can perhaps best indicate the nature and volume of his input by noting that he is the only person for whom I maintained an individual email in-tray. He has been in contact monthly, often weekly and even daily since the launch of *Birds Britannica* and has helped on such a large range of ideas, discussions and investigations that at times I looked upon him almost as a co-author. For giving so freely of his time and his encyclopaedic knowledge of birds, I offer him heartfelt thanks.

Now I come to the book's inner circle. Jonathan Elphick and Chris Gomersall have acted as researcher and picture editor respectively, with enormous expertise and wisdom. However this does not begin to describe their huge contributions as hosts, sounding boards, guinea pigs, brainstormers, discussion group, critics, adjudicators, sympathetic ears and simply as friends. They have been a wonderful source of support, inspiration and companionship over the last four years. Penelope Hoare and her assistants at Chatto & Windus, first Roger Cazelet, then Stuart Williams and finally Poppy Hampson, have given huge personal and professional support throughout a long and complicated project. My agent, Gill Coleridge, and her assistant, Lucy Luck, are models of professionalism. They have done a brilliant job unravelling the many knots and smoothing out the many creases that any publication involves. In the final stages, Mandy Greenfield (copy editor), Peter Ward (designer) and Helen Smith (indexer) each contributed hugely to the finished work.

And finally, I come to my wife Mary and our two girls, Rachael and Miriam. Quite simply I owe them everything, for allowing me to work uninterruptedly when things went well, and for reminding me how little it mattered when they didn't.

Mark Cocker,
Norfolk
2005

Picture credits

We would like to thank the following for the use of the pictures listed below according to page number.
Every effort has been made to trace the holders of copyright in text and illustrations. Should there be inadvertent
omissions or errors, the publishers will be pleased to correct them in a future edition.

General Index

Index of Places